# THE POST-COLONIAL STUDIES READER

One of the most exciting features of English literatures today is the explosion of post-colonial literatures, those literatures written in English in formerly colonised societies. This field has given rise to a great range of theoretical ideas, concepts, problems and debates, and these have been addressed in a great range of articles, essays, talks and books published or written from every continent. This book brings together a selection of these theoretical issues in a way that indicates and celebrates the immense diversity of post-colonial theory. As such it will be an indispensable volume for students, teachers, researchers and theorists, and anybody interested in the field.

The book has fourteen sections, each dealing with a major concept or issue in post-colonial theory. Each section is introduced by the editors and includes up to seven extracts from various theorists. As well as fundamental post-colonial issues, such as Language, Place, History and Ethnicity, it also assesses the similarities and differences with postmodernism, explores concepts such as Hybridity and The Body and Performance, and also examines the very important material practices of Education, Production and Consumption, and the modes of Representation and Resistance.

The uniqueness of this volume is in its range and comprehensiveness. By bringing together nearly ninety extracts from over fifty different writers, it demonstrates the vast spread of post-colonial theory, the degree to which such theory is emerging outside the metropolitan intellectual centres, and the significance such theory has in the practical political issues of living in this range of societies. This book makes accessible the full range of post-colonial theory, which otherwise would be either difficult or impossible for students, teachers or researchers to fully utilize.

**Bill Ashcroft**, **Gareth Griffiths** and **Helen Tiffin** teach at the Universities of New South Wales, Western Australia and Queensland respectively. Together they are the authors of *The Empire Writes Back* (Routledge 1989).

Related titles from Routledge

**THE CULTURAL STUDIES READER**
Edited by Simon During

**THE LESBIAN AND GAY STUDIES READER**
Edited by Henry Abelove, Michele Aina Barale, and David Halperin

**THE NEW HISTORICISM READER**
Edited by Harold Veeser

*The*
# POST-COLONIAL
## STUDIES READER

Edited by

*Bill Ashcroft, Gareth Griffiths
and Helen Tiffin*

London and New York

First published 1995
by Routledge
11 New Fetter Lane, London EC4P 4EE

Simultaneously published in the USA and Canada
by Routledge
29 West 35th Street, New York, NY 10001

Reprinted 1995

Designed and typeset in Garamond by Florencetype Ltd,
Stoodleigh, Devon
Printed and bound in Great Britain by
Clays Ltd, St Ives plc

*British Library Cataloguing in Publication Data*
A catalogue record for this book is available from the British Library

*Library of Congress Cataloguing in Publication Data*
The Post-colonial Studies Reader/edited by Bill Ashcroft, Gareth Griffiths,
and Helen Tiffin.
p. cm.
Includes bibliographical references and index.
1. Commonwealth literature (English) – History and criticism.
2. Decolonization in literature.   3. Imperialism in literature.
4. Colonies in literature.   I. Ashcroft, Bill.
II. Griffiths, Gareth.   III. Tiffin, Helen.
PR9080.P57   1994
820.9'358–dc20   94–17829

ISBN 0–415–09621–9 (hbk)
ISBN 0–415–09622–7 (pbk)

# Contents

# CONTENTS

# CONTENTS

CONTENTS

# CONTENTS

ix

CONTENTS

CONTENTS

xi

# CONTENTS

# *Illustrations*

# *Preface*

This is the latest in a number of Readers published by Routledge and joins such earlier titles as *The Cultural Studies Reader*. The publishers insisted that the title of *The Post-colonial Studies Reader* be congruent with the other readers which they publish. The authors are equally at pains to insist therefore that the title is not meant to claim some kind of completeness of coverage or absolute authority. In a field as diverse and contentious as post-colonial studies such a claim would be particularly extravagant and foolish. However, the more than eighty extracts in this reader are designed to introduce the major issues and debates in the field of post-colonial literary studies. This field itself has become so heterogeneous that no collection of readings could encompass every theoretical position now giving itself the name 'postcolonial/post-colonial'. These terms themselves encapsulate an active and unresolved dispute between those who would see the post-colonial as designating an amorphous set of discursive practices, akin to postmodernism, and those who would see it as designating a more specific, and 'historically' located set of cultural strategies. Even this latter view is divided between those who believe that post-colonial refers only to the period after the colonies become independent and those who argue, as the editors of this book would, that it is best used to designate the totality of practices, in all their rich diversity, which characterise the societies of the post-colonial world from the moment of colonisation to the present day, since colonialism does not cease with the mere fact of political independence and continues in a neo-colonial mode to be active in many societies.

The structure of the reader, the choice of subject areas and the selection and excisions of the readings are naturally determined by the editors' preferences and thus amount to a theoretical statement. But we have tried to introduce arguments with which we are not necessarily in agreement, and we have tried to produce a reader which is above all a stimulus to discussion, thought and further exploration. The parameters we have chosen will no doubt seem unsatisfactory to some: in order to achieve as wide a representation of areas and approaches as possible most extracts are limited to about two thousand words and will thus often not encompass the whole argument of the pieces from which they are taken; some theorists may seem to be under-represented given their importance to the field; some of the writers would not be considered 'post-colonial' theorists at all. But each extract is selected to say something coherent about an issue of immediate relevance to post-colonial practice, and represents what we have taken to be the most interesting, provocative or stimulating aspect of the original. Obviously, cultural and political critiques by general theorists such as Foucault, Derrida, Terdiman, Gramsci, Althusser, etc. have been influential in the construction of many post-colonial critical accounts but we have not included these in the reader since they are already easily accessible. This reader is not a collection of theorists, but of ideas; it is not interested in establishing a canon of theories or theorists but in indicating something of the great scope, the rich heterogeneity and vast energy of the field of post-colonial studies. We have been economical with footnotes, and if students or scholars wish to investigate the full argument and the range of sources of some of these pieces we direct them to the originals.

# *Acknowledgements*

For help, patience and support we should like to thank our partners, Judy, Carolyn and Chris.

For help in finding material, tracing references, editing and proofreading we want to thank many people, but particularly Tony da Silva and Chris Tiffin.

For generous permission to publish these extracts we thank the many journals and publishers who have acceded to our requests, in many cases promptly and sometimes with helpful advice.

# *General Introduction*

When Arthur James Balfour stood up in the House of Commons, at the height of British imperial power, on June 13 1910, to answer challenges to Britain's presence in Egypt, Edward Said tells us (1978: 32), he spoke under the mantle of two indivisible foundations of imperial authority – knowledge and power. The most formidable ally of economic and political control had long been the business of 'knowing' other peoples because this 'knowing' underpinned imperial dominance and became the mode by which they were increasingly persuaded to know themselves: that is, as subordinate to Europe. A consequence of this process of knowing became the export to the colonies of European language, literature and learning as part of a civilising mission which involved the suppression of a vast wealth of indigenous cultures beneath the weight of imperial control. The date of Balfour's speech is significant. In just a few years British imperial power would begin to be dismantled by the effects of two world wars and the rise of independence movements throughout the world. This political dismantling did not immediately extend to imperial *cultural* influences, but it was attended by an unprecedented assertion of creative activity in post-colonial societies.

European imperialism took various forms in different times and places and proceeded both through conscious planning and contingent occurrences. As a result of this complex development something occurred for which the *plan* of imperial expansion had not bargained: the immensely prestigious and powerful imperial culture found itself appropriated in projects of counter-colonial resistance which drew upon the many different indigenous local and hybrid *processes* of self-determination to defy, erode and sometimes supplant the prodigious power of imperial cultural knowledge. Post-colonial literatures are a result of this interaction between imperial culture and the complex of indigenous cultural practices. As a consequence, 'post-colonial theory' has existed for a long time before that particular name was used to describe it. Once colonised peoples had cause to reflect on and express the tension which ensued from this problematic and contested, but eventually vibrant and powerful mixture of imperial language and local experience, post-colonial 'theory' came into being.

1

The term 'post-colonial' is resonant with all the ambiguity and complexity of the many different cultural experiences it implicates, and, as the extracts in this Reader demonstrate, it addresses all aspects of the colonial process from the beginning of colonial contact. Post-colonial critics and theorists should consider the full implications of restricting the meaning of the term to 'after-colonialism' or after-Independence. All post-colonial societies are still subject in one way or another to overt or subtle forms of neo-colonial domination, and independence has not solved this problem. The development of new élites within independent societies, often buttressed by neo-colonial institutions; the development of internal divisions based on racial, linguistic or religious discriminations; the continuing unequal treatment of indigenous peoples in settler/invader societies – all these testify to the fact that post-colonialism is a continuing process of resistance and reconstruction. This does not imply that post-colonial practices are seamless and homogeneous but indicates the impossibility of dealing with any part of the colonial process without considering its antecedents and consequences.

Post-colonial theory involves discussion about experience of various kinds: migration, slavery, suppression, resistance, representation, difference, race, gender, place, and responses to the influential master discourses of imperial Europe such as history, philosophy and linguistics, and the fundamental experiences of speaking and writing by which all these come into being. None of these is 'essentially' post-colonial, but together they form the complex fabric of the field. Like the description of any other field the term has come to mean many things, as the range of extracts in this Reader indicates. However we would argue that post-colonial studies are based in the 'historical fact' of European colonialism, and the diverse material effects to which this phenomenon gave rise. We need to keep this fact of colonisation firmly in mind because the increasingly unfocused use of the term 'post-colonial' over the last ten years to describe an astonishing variety of cultural, economic and political practices has meant that there is a danger of its losing its effective meaning altogether. Indeed the diffusion of the term is now so extreme that it is used to refer to not only vastly different but even opposed activities. In particular the tendency to employ the term 'post-colonial' to refer to any kind of marginality at all runs the risk of denying its basis in the historical process of colonialism.

While drawing together a wide variety of theoretical and critical perspectives, this Reader attempts to redress a process whereby 'post-colonial theory' may itself mask and even perpetuate unequal economic and cultural relations. This happens when the bulk of the literary theory is seen to come out of the metropolitan centres, 'adding value' to the literary 'raw material' imported from the post-colonial societies (Mitchell 1992). Such a situation simply reproduces the inequalities of imperial power relations. Post-colonial 'theory' has been produced in all societies into which the imperial force of Europe has intruded, though not always in the formal guise of theoretical texts. But this might not be so clear today given the privileging of theory

2

produced in metropolitan centres and the publishing networks which perpetuate this process. It is relatively easy, for instance, to obtain the classic texts of colonialist discourse theory in metropolitan societies, since they appear in publications widely circulated in these areas. But critical material by post-colonial theorists such as E. K. Brathwaite, Michael Dash, Raja Rao and Wilson Harris (not to mention the 'theory' located in 'creative' texts) are either not available or ignored in many contemporary metropolitan discussions of the field. Equally, though for different reasons, such as a crisis of documentation in many post-colonial societies, much of this material is difficult to obtain there, too. One purpose of this collection is to make a wide range of post-colonial critical material available in a relatively accessible and inexpensive form.

We have attempted to show and celebrate the immense range of countries and literatures from which the theorisation of the post-colonial condition has emerged, and in so doing to place the more publicised recent concerns of colonialist discourse theory in a wider geographic and historic context. Indeed, for us, the hyphenated form of the word 'post-colonial' has come to stand for both the material effects of colonisation and the huge diversity of everyday and sometimes hidden responses to it throughout the world. We use the term 'post-colonial' to represent the continuing process of imperial suppressions and exchanges throughout this diverse range of societies, in their institutions and their discursive practices. Because the imperial process works *through* as well as *upon* individuals and societies 'post-colonial' theory rejects the egregious classification of 'First' and 'Third' World and contests the lingering fallacy that the post-colonial is somehow synonymous with the economically 'underdeveloped'.

The effects of imperialism occur in many different kinds of societies including those 'settler/invader' societies in which post-colonial contestation is just as strongly and just as ambivalently engaged as it is in more obviously decolonising states and regions. By the term 'post-colonial' we do not imply an automatic, nor a seamless and unchanging process of resistance but a series of linkages and articulations without which the process cannot be properly addressed. These linkages and articulations are not always directly oppositional; the material practices of post-colonial societies may involve a wide range of activities including conceptions and actions which are, or appear to be, complicit with the imperial enterprise. However, such complicit activities occur in *all* post-colonial societies, and their existence suggests the possibility of crucial comparisons which may be made within the whole range of post-colonial societies. The study of settler colony cultures where, it is frequently argued, such complicit practices are more obvious may, as a result, be especially useful in addressing the problem of complicity in all oppositional discourse, since they point to the difficulties involved in escaping from dominant discursive practices which limit and define the possibility of opposition. Settler colonies, precisely because their filiative metaphors of connection problematise the idea of

3

resistance as a simple binarism, articulate the ambivalent, complex and processual nature of all imperial relations.

The readings we have assembled here are mainly from societies which employ forms of english[1] as a major language of communication. Clearly it would be possible and even desirable to construct a text which addressed the wider polyphonic spectrum of the colonial past but this would require a project far beyond the scope of this one. The Reader also recognises, but does not directly address, the importance of the continuing body of work in indigenous languages. The 'silencing' of the post-colonial voice to which much recent theory alludes is in many cases a metaphoric rather than a literal one. Critical accounts emphasising the 'silencing' effect of the metro-politan forms and institutional practices upon pre-colonial cultures, and the resulting forces of 'hybridisation' which work on the continuing practice of those cultures, make an important point. But they neglect the fact that for many people in post-colonial societies the pre-colonial languages and cultures, although themselves subject to change and development, continue to provide the effective framework for their daily lives. Failure to acknowl-edge this might be one of the ways in which post-colonial discourse could, unwittingly, become 'a coloniser in its turn' (Ashcroft *et al.* 1989: 218). Without endorsing a naively 'nativist' position post-colonial theory needs to be aware that it is engaged in a project which supplements rather than replaces the continuing study and promotion of the indigenous languages of post-colonial societies.

In putting together this Reader we have asked the question: how might a genuinely post-colonial literary enterprise proceed? Our focus in addressing this problem is through the particular agency of literature teaching in the academy. We recognise that this is only one limited avenue of address to the wider social and political issues affecting post-colonial societies, but it seems to us to be an important and worthwhile one, since literature and literary study in the academy have been crucial sites of political and cultural struggle with the most far-reaching results for the general history and prac-tices of colonisation and de-colonisation. To define our purpose then: we have taken as our limited aim the provision of an effective text to assist in the revision of teaching practice within literary studies in english and so have sought to represent the impact of post-colonial literatures and criticism on the current shape of english studies.

## NOTE

1 This spelling reflects the fact that, as the editors argued in their earlier book *The Empire Writes Back: Theory and Practice in Post-colonial Literatures* (Ashcroft *et al.* 1989: 8), there is a 'need to distinguish between what is proposed as a standard code, English (the language of the erstwhile imperial centre), and the linguistic code, english, which has been transformed and subverted into several distinctive varieties throughout the world.'

# PART I

## Issues and Debates

# Introduction

The extracts in this section indicate something of the historical provenance, the general theoretical directions and the important debates which have featured in post-colonial theory in recent times. West Indian novelist George Lamming expresses in a personal way some of the enduring issues: how a Britain without its Empire can still maintain cultural authority in post-colonial societies, and the ways in which Eurocentric assumptions about race, nationality and literature return time and again to haunt the production of post-colonial writing. Lamming's is a foundational text in post-colonial writing; its early date indicates how long post-colonial intellectuals have been grappling with the articulation of their own modes of cultural production. It is important, too, in that it is a critical essay which is written by an imaginative writer, and as such represents the crucial role played by creative writers as diverse in time and place as Rabindranath Tagore, Raja Rao, Wole Soyinka, Chinua Achebe, Edward Kamau Brathwaite, Derek Walcott, Judith Wright, Tom King, Margaret Atwood, Dennis Lee, Alan Curnow, Keri Hulme and many others in developing a critical discourse in the post-colonial world. While these writers have often functioned as critics in a formal sense their own creative work has frequently been the site of critiques of imperial representation, language and ideological control. Thus, as Lamming argues here, the advent of the novel in the West Indies marks an important historical event as well as a formal cultural development.

This extract serves to remind us that the determining condition of what we refer to as post-colonial cultures is the historical phenomenon of colonialism, with its range of material practices and effects, such as transportation, slavery, displacement, emigration, and racial and cultural discrimination. These material conditions and their relationship to questions of ideology and representation are at the heart of the most vigorous debates in recent post-colonial theory. Even the claim that they may exist independently of the modes of representation which allowed them to come into formation is to assert a point of considerable controversy.

Abdul R. JanMohamed stresses the importance, as does Lamming, of the literary text as a site of cultural control and as a highly effective instrumentality for the determination of the 'native' by fixing him/her under the sign of the Other. JanMohamed also shows how these literary texts contain features which can be subverted and appropriated to the oppositional and anti-colonial purposes of contemporary post-colonial writing. His essay analyses the literary text in quite specific ways as a means of bringing into being and modifying the controlling discourses of colonisation. Using Lacan's distinction of the imaginary and symbolic stages of development as a conceptual tool in this analysis JanMohamed emphasises the self-contradictions of binary constructions. By recognising how the binarisms of colonial discourse operate (the self–other, civilised–native, us–them manichean polarities) post-colonial critics can promote an active reading which makes these texts available for re-writing and subversion. It is this process which brings into being the powerful syncretic texts of contemporary post-colonial writing. In the rest of the book from which this short extract is taken JanMohamed illustrates how this process of re-inscription works by developing an analysis of the relationship between contemporary texts of post-colonial writing and the colonial texts to which they 'write back'. Such a process of 'writing back', far from indicating a continuing dependence, is an effective means of escaping from the binary polarities implicit in the manichean constructions of colonisation and its practices.

Gayatri Spivak questions whether or not the possibility exists for any recovery of a subaltern voice that is not a kind of essentialist fiction. Although she expresses considerable sympathy for the project undertaken in contemporary historiography to give a voice to 'the subaltern' who had been written out of the record by conventional historical accounts, Spivak raises grave doubts about its theoretical legitimacy. She is sympathetic but critical in her response here to Ranajit Guha's subaltern studies project which seeks to obtain what Said termed the 'permission to speak' by going behind the terms of reference of 'élite' history to include the perspective of those who are never taken into account (the subaltern social groups). Recognising and applauding the project's endorsement of the heterogeneity of the colonial subject, and giving a qualified approval to the politics of the effort to speak a 'politics of the people', Spivak is nevertheless concerned to articulate what she sees as the difficulties and contradictions involved in constructing a 'speaking position' for the subaltern. Wanting to acknowledge the continuity and vigour of pre-colonial social practice, its ability to modify and to 'survive' colonial incursions and definitional strategies and exclusions, she insists that the poststructuralist mode of the project only disguises what she sees as an underlying persistent essentialism. For her, one cannot construct a category of the 'subaltern' that has an effective 'voice' clearly and *unproblematically* audible above the persistent and multiple echoes of its inevitable heterogeneity. Her conclusion is that for 'the true' subaltern group, whose identity is its difference, there is no subaltern subject that can 'know and speak itself'. Thus the intellectual must avoid reconstructing the subaltern as merely another unproblematic field of knowing, so confining its effect to the very form of representation ('text for knowledge') the project sought to evade and lay bare. The conclusion is expressed, perhaps unfortunately, in a rather negative way: 'Subaltern historiography must confront the impossibility of such gestures'. Spivak's negative, as José Rabasa has pointed out, does not 'necessarily exclude such instances of colonized subjects defracting power as those Homi Bhabha has isolated in the case of India' (Rabasa 1993: 11–12).

The emphasis is on the importance of the written text as an instrument of control (to which Said and JanMohamed's work makes reference), and of the deep ambivalences locked into the apparent universal fixities of colonialist epistemology, are taken up by Homi Bhabha. For Bhabha the 'emblem of the English book' is one of the most important of the 'signs taken for wonders' by which the coloniser controls the imagination and the aspirations of the colonised, because the book assumes a greater authority than the experience of the colonised peoples themselves. But, as Bhabha argues, such authority simultaneously renders the colonial presence ambivalent, since it only comes about by displacing those images of identity already held by the colonised society. The colonial space is therefore an agonistic space. Despite the 'imitation' and 'mimicry' with which colonised peoples cope with the imperial presence, the relationship becomes one of constant, if implicit, contestation and opposition. Indeed, such mimicry becomes the very site of that conflict, a 'transparency', as Bhabha puts it, which is dependent for its fixity on the underlying negative of imperial presence which it seems to duplicate. For Bhabha 'mimicry' does not mean that opposition is rejected, but rather that it is seen to encompass more than overt opposition. Opposition is not simply reduced to intention, but is implicit in the very production of dominance whose intervention as a 'dislocatory presence' paradoxically confirms the very thing it displaces. The resulting hybrid modalities also challenge the assumption of the 'pure' and the 'authentic', concepts upon which the resistance to imperialism often stands. Indeed hybridity, rather than indicating corruption or decline, may, as Bhabha argues, be the most common and effective form of subversive opposition since it displays the 'necessary deformation and displacement of all sites of discrimination and domination'.

Spivak's and Bhabha's analyses are important and very influential warnings of the complexities of the task faced by post-colonial theory. But they have also invited responses which see them and their approach as too deeply implicated in European intellectual traditions, which older, more radical exponents of post-colonial theory, such as Frantz Fanon and Albert Memmi, had sought to dismantle and set aside. The debate is a struggle between those who want to align themselves with the subaltern and those who insist that this attempt becomes at best only a refined version of the very discourse it seeks to displace. All are agreed, in some sense, that the main problem is how to effect agency for the post-colonial subject. But the contentious issue of how this is to be attained remains unresolved.

Benita Parry's critique of contemporary 'colonialist discourse' theory (such as Bhabha's and Spivak's) argues that the effect of its insistence on the 'necessary' silencing implicit in this mode of analysis has been to diminish the earlier intervention of critics like Fanon who stood much more resolutely for the idea that de-colonisation is a process of opposition to dominance. She also argues that colonialist discourse theory supports readings of post-colonial texts which inadequately ascribe a native 'absence' to texts in which the 'native' has access as a profoundly disruptive presence. In a sense Parry's argument is a plea for an analysis of the 'politics' of the project of colonialist discourse theory itself, and seeks to resurrect as a forgotten but vital element in the debate the voices of the post-colonial intellectuals of the earlier, oppositional 'national liberation' phase of decolonisation. Subsequent response from Spivak has argued that such oppositional cate-gories as the 'post-colonial intellectual' avoid the fact that the concept of 'intellectual' and of 'theory' as a discourse is by definition implicated in the Europeanisation/hybridisation of all culture in the aftermath of imperialism, making the distinctive category of 'post-colonial intellectual' as problematic as the term 'subaltern'.

The argument underpinning these positions, that there can be an engagement with the 'real' separate from its construction through what Barthes called 'reality effects', is put with great clarity by José Rabasa: 'cultural products should be taken as rhetorical artifices and not as deposi-tories of data from which a factual truth may be construed' (1993: 9). Yet, of course, the avoidance of such a construing in practice may be to allow semiotic analyses of texts totally 'liberated' from any attempt or desire to understand the context of cultural production from which they emerge. The effect of this is, of course, to wipe out cultural difference.

The debate between those who insist on the possibility of an effective alignment of position with the subaltern and those who insist that this, paradoxically, may serve only to construct a refinement of the system it seeks to dismantle, is taken up and expanded later in the Reader in the section on Representation and Resistance. There Jenny Sharpe's analysis of the problem of Resistance and Stephen Slemon's article on the crucial role of settler culture, or 'Second World' texts, in articulating the ambivalence at the heart of post-colonial resistance, continue and elaborate some of the issues raised in this section.

Stephen Slemon's overview of recent developments within the field of post-colonial studies includes, like Parry's, an analysis of the difficulty that 'colonialist criticism' has in confirming the agency of the post-colonial subject. A crucial question for post-colonial theory, given that contemporary thought has firmly fixed subjectivity in language, is 'how can one account for the capacity of the subject in a post-colonial society to resist imperialism and thus to intervene in the conditions which appear to construct subjectivity itself?' Slemon analyses the positions of some of the major participants in the debates in a fresh and interesting way but also regards the debate itself as the product of the institutionalisation of post-colonial studies within the practices of the contemporary academy. Quoting Henry Louis Gates, Slemon warns that 'academic interest in this history and the discourse of colonialism bids fair to become the last bastion for the project of global theory and for European universalism itself', forcing us to choose between 'oppositional critics whose articulations of the post-colonial institutionalise themselves as agonistic struggles over a thoroughly *disciplined* terrain'. Slemon reminds his readers that the real contest (agon) post-colonial studies seeks to address is that between the conflicting participants in the imperial process and their residual legatees, not between contemporary schools of theory. The real concerns of this oppositional subject are in danger of being reduced to merely another location in the academic institutionalised landscape, yet another mere invasive 'mapping' of the subdued and subjugated post-colonial world.

# 1

## The Occasion for Speaking

### George Lamming*

In any country, during this century, it seems that the young will remain too numerous and too strong to fear being alone. It is from this premise that I want to consider the circumstances as well as the significance of certain writers' migration from the British Caribbean to the London metropolis. . . .

How has it come about that a small group of men, different in years and temperament and social origins, should leave the respective islands they know best, even exchange life there for circumstances which are almost wholly foreign to them? . . . Why have they migrated? And what, if any, are the peculiar pleasures of exile? Is their journey a part of a hunger for recognition? Do they see such recognition as a confirmation of the fact that they are writers? What is the source of their insecurity in the world of letters? And what, on the evidence of their work, is the range of their ambition as writers whose nourishment is now elsewhere, whose absence is likely to drag into a state of permanent separation from their roots? . . .

The exile is a universal figure. The proximity of our lives to the major issues of our time has demanded of us all some kind of involvement. Some may remain neutral; but all have, at least, to pay attention to what is going on. On the political level, we are often without the right kind of information to make argument effective; on the moral level we have to feel our way through problems for which we have no adequate reference of traditional conduct as a guide. Chaos is often, therefore, the result of our thinking and our doing. We are made to feel a sense of exile by our inadequacy and our irrelevance of function in a society whose past we can't alter, and whose future is always beyond us. Idleness can easily guide us into accepting this as a condition. Sooner or later, in silence or with rhetoric, we sign a contract whose epitaph reads: To be an exile is to be alive.

When the exile is a man of colonial orientation, and his chosen residence is the country which colonised his own history, then there are certain

* From 'The Occasion For Speaking' *The Pleasures of Exile* London: Michael Joseph, 1960.

complications. For each exile has not only got to prove his worth to the other, he has to win the approval of Headquarters, meaning in the case of the West Indian writer, England. . . .

In England he does not feel the need to try to understand an Englishman, since all relationships begin with an assumption of previous knowledge, a knowledge acquired in the absence of the people known. This relationship with the English is only another aspect of the West Indian's relation to the *idea* of England.

As an example of this, I would recall an episode on a ship which had brought a number of West Indians to Britain. I was talking to a Trinidadian Civil Servant who had come to take some kind of course in the ways of bureaucracy. A man about forty-five, intelligent enough to be in the senior grade of the Trinidad Civil Service which is by no means backward, a man of some substance among his own class of people. We were talking in a general way about life among the emigrants. The ship was now steady; the tugs were coming alongside. Suddenly there was consternation in the Trinidadian's expression.

'But . . . but', he said, 'look down there.'

I looked, and since I had lived six years in England, I failed to see anything of particular significance. I asked him what he had seen; and then I realised what was happening.

'*They* do that kind of work, *too*?' he asked.

He meant the white hands and faces on the tug. In spite of films, in spite of reading Dickens – for he would have had to at the school which trained him for the Civil Service – in spite of all this received information, this man had never really felt, as a possibility and a fact, the existence of the English worker. This sudden bewilderment had sprung from his *idea* of England: and one element in that *idea* was that he was not used to seeing an Englishman working with his hands in the streets of Port-of-Spain.

This is a seed of his colonisation which has been subtly and richly infused with myth. We can change laws overnight; we may reshape images of our feeling. But this myth is most difficult to dislodge. . . .

I remember how pleased I was to learn that my first book, *In the Castle of My Skin*, had been bought by an American publisher. . . . It was the money I was thinking of to the exclusion of the book's critical reputation in America. The book had had an important critical press in England; its reputation here was substantial; so it could make no difference what America thought. . . . This is what I mean by the *myth*. It has little to do with lack of intelligence. It has nothing to do with one's origins in class. It is deeper and more natural. It is akin to the nutritive function of milk which all sorts of men receive at birth. It is *myth* as the source of spiritual foods absorbed, and learnt for exercise in the future. This *myth* begins in the West Indian from the earliest stages of his education. But it is not yet turned against America. In a sense, America does not even exist. It begins with the fact of England's supremacy in taste and judgement: a fact which can only have meaning and weight by a calculated cutting down to size of all non-England. The first to be cut down is the colonial himself.

This is one of the seeds which much later bear such strange fruit as the West Indian writers' departure from the very landscape which is the raw material of all their books. These men had to leave if they were going to function as writers since books, in that particular colonial conception of literature, were not – meaning, too, are not supposed to be – written by natives. Those among the natives who read also believed that; for all the books they had read, their whole introduction to something called culture, all of it, in the form of words, came from outside: Dickens, Jane Austen, Kipling and that sacred gang.

The West Indian's education was imported in much the same way that flour and butter are imported from Canada. Since the cultural negotiation was strictly between England and the natives, and England had acquired, somehow, the divine right to organise the native's reading, it is to be expected that England's export of literature would be English. Deliberately and exclusively English. And the further back in time England went for these treasures, the safer was the English commodity. So the examinations, which would determine that Trinidadian's future in the Civil Service, imposed Shakespeare, and Wordsworth, and Jane Austen and George Eliot and the whole tabernacle of dead names, now come alive at the world's greatest summit of literary expression. . . .

In [American novelist, James Baldwin's] most perceptive and brilliantly stated essays, *Notes of a Native Son*, he tries to examine and interpret his own situation as an American negro who is also a novelist drawing on the spiritual legacy of Western European civilisation. . . .

> I know, in any case, that the most crucial time in my own development came when I was forced to recognise that I was a kind of bastard of the West; when I followed the line of my past I did not find myself in Europe, but in Africa. And this meant that in some subtle way, in a really profound way I brought to Shakespeare, Bach, Rembrandt, to the stones of Paris, to the cathedral at Chartres, and to the Empire State Building, a special attitude. These were not really my creations, they did not contain my history; I might search in them in vain for ever for any reflection of myself; I was an interloper. At the same time I had no other heritage which I could possibly hope to use. I had certainly been unfitted for the jungle or the tribe.
>
> (Baldwin 1964: 14)

'I might search in vain for any reflection of myself. I had certainly been unfitted for the jungle or the tribe.'

We must pause to consider the source of Mr Baldwin's timidity; for it has a most respectable ancestry. Here is the great German philosopher Hegel having the last word on Africa in his Introduction to *The Philosophy of History*:

Africa proper, as far as History goes back, has remained – for all purposes of connection with the rest of the world – shut up; it is the Gold-land compressed within itself – the land of childhood, which lying beyond the days of self-conscious history, is enveloped in the dark mantle of Night. . . .

The negro as already observed exhibits the natural man in his completely wild and untamed state. We must lay aside all thought of reverence and morality – all that we call feeling – if we would rightly comprehend him; there is nothing harmonious with humanity to be found in this type of character. . . .

At this point we leave Africa never to mention it again. For it is no historical part of the world; it has no movement of development to exhibit. Historical movement in it – that is in its northern part – belongs to the Asiatic or European World. . . .

What we properly understand as Africa, is the Unhistorical, Undeveloped Spirit, still involved in the *conditions of mere nature* and which had to be presented here only as on the threshold of the World's history. . . .

The History of the World travels from East to West, for Europe *is absolutely the end of History*, Asia is the beginning.

It is important to relate the psychology implied in Mr Baldwin's regret to the kind of false confidence which Hegel represents in the European consciousness. For what disqualifies African man from Hegel's World of History is his apparent incapacity to evolve with the logic of Language which is the only aid man has in capturing the Idea. African Man, for Hegel, has no part in the common pursuit of the Universal. . . .

What the West Indian shares with the African is a common political predicament: a predicament which we call colonial; but the word colonial has a deeper meaning for the West Indian than it has for the African. The African, in spite of his modernity, has never been wholly severed from the cradle of a continuous culture and tradition. His colonialism mainly takes the form of lack of privilege in organising the day to day affairs of his country. This state of affairs is almost at an end; and its end is the result of the African's persistent and effective demand for political freedom. . . .

It is the brevity of the West Indian's history and the fragmentary nature of the different cultures which have fused to make something new; it is the absolute dependence on the values in that language of his coloniser which have given him a special relation to the word, colonialism. It is not merely a political definition; it is not merely the result of certain economic arrangements. It started as these, and grew somewhat deeper. Colonialism is the very base and structure of the West Indian cultural awareness. His reluctance in asking for complete, political freedom . . . is due to the fear that he has never had to stand. A foreign or absent Mother culture has always cradled his judgement. Moreover, the . . . freedom from physical fear has created a state of complacency in the West Indian awareness. And the higher up he moves in the social scale, the more crippled his mind and impulses become by the resultant complacency.

In order to change this way of seeing, the West Indian must change the very structure, the very basis of his values. . . .

I am not much interested in what the West Indian writer has brought to the English language; for English is no longer the exclusive language of the men who live in England. That stopped a long time ago; and it is today, among other things, a West Indian language. What the West Indians do with it is their own business. A more important consideration is what the West Indian novelist has brought to the West Indies. That is the real question; and its answer can be the beginning of an attempt to grapple with that colonial structure of awareness which has determined West Indian values.

There are, for me, just three important events in British Caribbean history. I am using the term, history, in an active sense. Not a succession of episodes which can easily be given some casual connection. What I mean by historical event is the creation of a situation which offers antagonistic oppositions and a challenge of survival that had to be met by all involved.

The first event is discovery. That began, like most other discoveries, with a journey; a journey inside, or a journey out and across. This was the meaning of Columbus. The original purpose of the journey may sometimes have nothing to do with the results that attend upon it. That journey took place nearly five centuries ago; and the result has been one of the world's most fascinating communities. The next event is the abolition of slavery and the arrival of the East – India and China – in the Caribbean Sea. The world met here, and it was at every level, except administration, a peasant world. In one way or another, through one upheaval after another, these people, forced to use a common language which they did not possess on arrival, have had to make something of their surroundings. . . .

The third important event in our history is the discovery of the novel by West Indians as a way of investigating and projecting the inner experiences of the West Indian community. The second event is about a hundred and fifty years behind us. The third is hardly two decades ago. . . . The West Indian writer is the first to add a new dimension to writing about the West Indian community. . . .

If we accept that the act of writing a book is linked with an expectation, however modest, of having it read; then the situation of a West Indian writer, living and working in his own community, assumes intolerable difficulties. The West Indian of average opportunity and intelligence has not yet been converted to reading as a civilised activity which justifies itself in the exercise of his mind. Reading seriously, at any age, is still largely associated with reading for examinations. In recent times the political fever has warmed us to the newspapers with their generous and diabolical welcome to join in the correspondence column. But book reading has never been a serious business with us. . . .

An important question, for the English critic, is not what the West Indian novel has brought to English writing. It would be more correct to ask what the West Indian novelists have contributed to English reading. For the language in which these books are written is English – which, I must repeat – is a West Indian language; and in spite of the unfamiliarity of its rhythms, it remains accessible to the readers of English anywhere in the world. The West Indian contribution to English reading has been made possible by their relation to the themes which are peasant. . . .

That's a great difference between the West Indian novelist and his contemporary in England. For peasants simply don't respond and see like middle-class people. The peasant tongue has its own rhythms which are [Trinidadian novelist Samuel] Selvon's and [Barbadian novelist Vic] Reid's rhythms; and no artifice of technique, no sophisticated gimmicks leading to the mutilation of form, can achieve the specific taste and sound of Selvon's prose.

For this prose is, really, the people's speech, the organic music of the earth. . . .

This may be the dilemma of the West Indian writer abroad: that he hungers for nourishment from a soil which he (as an ordinary citizen) could not at present endure. The pleasure and paradox of my own exile is that I belong wherever I am. My role, it seems, has rather to do with time and change than with the geography of circumstances; and yet there is always an acre of ground in the New World which keeps growing echoes in my head. I can only hope that these echoes do not die before my work comes to an end.

# 2

## The Economy of Manichean Allegory

### ABDUL R. JANMOHAMED*

COLONIALIST LITERATURE IS an exploration and a representation of a world at the boundaries of 'civilization,' a world that has not (yet) been domesticated by European signification or codified in detail by its ideology. That world is therefore perceived as uncontrollable, chaotic, unattainable, and ultimately evil. Motivated by his desire to conquer and dominate, the imperialist configures the colonial realm as a confrontation based on differences in race, language, social customs, cultural values, and modes of production.

Faced with an incomprehensible and multifaceted alterity, the European theoretically has the option of responding to the Other in terms of identity or difference. If he assumes that he and the Other are essentially identical, then he would tend to ignore the significant divergences and to judge the Other according to his own cultural values. If, on the other hand, he assumes that the Other is irremediably different, then he would have little incentive to adopt the viewpoint of that alterity: he would again tend to turn to the security of his own cultural perspective. Genuine and thorough comprehension of Otherness is possible only if the self can somehow negate or at least severely bracket the values, assumptions, and ideology of his culture. As Nadine Gordimer's and Isak Dinesen's writings show, however, this entails in practice the virtually impossible task of negating one's very being, precisely because one's culture is what formed that being. Moreover, the colonizers invariable assumption about his moral superiority means that he will rarely question the validity of either his own or his society's formation and that he will not be inclined to expend any energy in understanding the worthless alterity of the colonized. By thus subverting the traditional dialectic of self and Other that contemporary theory considers so important in the formation of self and culture, the assumption of moral superiority subverts the very potential of colonialist literature.

* From 'The Economy of Manichean Allegory: The Function of Racial Difference in Colonialist Literature' *Critical Inquiry* 12(1), 1985.

Instead of being an exploration of the racial Other, such literature merely affirms its own ethnocentric assumptions; instead of actually depicting the outer limits of 'civilization,' it simply codifies and preserves the structures of its own mentality. While the surface of each colonialist text purports to represent specific encounters with specific varieties of the racial Other, the subtext valorizes the superiority of European cultures, of the collective process that has mediated that representation. Such literature is essentially specular: instead of seeing the native as a bridge toward syncretic possibility, it uses him as a mirror that reflects the colonialist's self-image.

Accordingly, I would argue that colonialist literature is divisible into two broad categories: the 'imaginary' and the 'symbolic.' The emotive as well as the cognitive intentionalities of the 'imaginary' text are structured by objectification and aggression. In such works the native functions as an image of the imperialist self in such a manner that it reveals the latter's self-alienation. Because of the subsequent projection involved in this context, the 'imaginary' novel maps the European's intense internal rivalry. The 'imaginary' representation of indigenous people tends to coalesce the signifier with the signified. In describing the attributes or actions of the native, issues such as intention, causality, extenuating circumstances, and so forth, are completely ignored; in the 'imaginary' colonialist realm, to say 'native' is automatically to say 'evil' and to evoke immediately the economy of the manichean allegory. The writer of such texts tends to fetishize a nondialectical, fixed opposition between the self and the native. Threatened by a metaphysical alterity that he has created, he quickly retreats to the homogeneity of his own group. Consequently, his psyche and text tend to be much closer to and are often entirely occluded by the ideology of his group.

Writers of 'symbolic' texts, on the other hand, are more aware of the inevitable necessity of using the native as a mediator of European desires. Grounded more firmly and securely in the egalitarian imperatives of Western societies, these authors tend to be more open to a modifying dialectic of self and Other. They are willing to examine the specific individual and cultural differences between Europeans and natives and to reflect on the efficacy of European values, assumptions, and habits in contrast to those of the indigenous cultures. 'Symbolic' texts, most of which thematize the problem of colonialist mentality and its encounter with the racial Other, can in turn be subdivided into two categories.

The first type, represented by novels like E. M. Forster's *A Passage to India* and Rudyard Kipling's *Kim*, attempts to find syncretic solutions to the manichean opposition of the colonizer and the colonized. This kind of novel overlaps in some ways with the 'imaginary' text: those portions of the novel organized at the emotive level are structured by 'imaginary' identification, while those controlled by cognitive intentionality are structured by the rules of the 'symbolic' order. Ironically, these novels – which are conceived in the 'symbolic' realm of intersubjectivity, heterogeneity, and

particularity but are seduced by the specularity of 'imaginary' Otherness –
better illustrate the economy and power of the manichean allegory than do
the strictly 'imaginary' texts.

The second type of 'symbolic' fiction, represented by the novels of
Joseph Conrad and Nadine Gordimer, realizes that syncretism is impossible
within the power relations of colonial society because such a context traps
the writer in the libidinal economy of the 'imaginary.' Hence, becoming
reflexive about its context, by confining itself to a rigorous examination of
the 'imaginary' mechanism of colonialist mentality, this type of fiction
manages to free itself from the manichean allegory. . . .

If every desire is at base a desire to impose oneself on another and to
be recognized by the Other, then the colonial situation provides an ideal
context for the fulfillment of that fundamental drive. The colonialist's
military superiority ensures a complete projection of his self on the Other:
exercising his assumed superiority, he destroys without any significant
qualms the effectiveness of indigenous economic, social, political, legal, and
moral systems and imposes his own versions of these structures on the
Other. By thus subjugating the native, the European settler is able to
compel the Other's recognition of him and, in the process, allow his own
identity to become deeply dependent on his position as a master. This
enforced recognition from the Other in fact amounts to the European's
narcissistic self-recognition since the native, who is considered too
degraded and inhuman to be credited with any specific subjectivity, is cast
as no more than a recipient of the negative elements of the self that the
European projects onto him. This transitivity and the preoccupation with
the inverted self-image mark the 'imaginary' relations that characterize the
colonial encounter.

Nevertheless, the gratification that this situation affords is impaired by
the European's alienation from his own unconscious desire. In the 'imaginary' text, the subject is eclipsed by his fixation on and fetishization of the
Other: the self becomes a prisoner of the projected image. Even though the
native is negated by the projection of the inverted image, his presence as an
absence can never be canceled. Thus the colonialist's desire only entraps
him in the dualism of the 'imaginary' and foments violent hatred of the
native. This desire to exterminate the brutes, which is thematized
consciously and critically in 'symbolic' texts such as *Heart of Darkness* and
*A Passage to India*, manifests itself subconsciously in 'imaginary' texts,
such as those of Joyce Cary, through the narrators' clear relish in describing
the mutilation of natives. 'Imaginary' texts, like fantasies which provide
naïve solutions to the subjects' basic problems, tend to center themselves
on plots that end with the elimination of the offending natives.

The power of the 'imaginary' field binding the narcissistic colonialist
text is nowhere better illustrated than in its fetishization of the Other. This
process operates by substituting natural or generic categories for those that
are socially or ideologically determined. All the evil characteristics and

habits with which the colonialist endows the native are thereby not presented as the products of social and cultural difference but as characteristics inherent in the race – in the 'blood' – of the native. In its extreme form, this kind of fetishization transmutes all specificity and difference into a magical essence. Thus Dinesen boldly asserts:

> The Natives were Africa in flesh and ... [The various cultures of Africa, the mountains, the trees, the animals] were different expressions of one idea, variations upon the same theme. It was not a congenial upheaping of heterogeneous atoms, but a heterogeneous upheaping of congenial atoms, as in the case of the oak-leaf and the acorn and the object made from oak.
>
> (Dinesen 1937: 21)

As this example illustrates, it is not the stereotypes, the denigrating 'images' of the native (which abound in colonialist literature), that are fetishized. Careful scrutiny of colonialist texts reveals that such images are used at random and in a self-contradictory fashion. For example, the narrator of Cary's *Aissa Saved* can claim that 'Kolu children of old-fashioned families like Makunde's were remarkable for their gravity and decorum; ... they were strictly brought up and made to behave themselves as far as possible like grown-ups' (Cary 1949: 33). He even shows one such child, Tanawe, behaving with great decorum and gravity. Yet the same narrator depicts Kolu adults who have converted to Christianity as naughty, irresponsible children. Given the colonialist mentality, the source of the contradiction is quite obvious. Since Tanawe is too young to challenge colonialism, she can be depicted in a benign manner, and the narrator can draw moral sustenance from the generosity of his portrayal. But the adult Kolus' desire to become Christians threatens to eliminate one of the fundamental differences between them and the Europeans; so the narrator has to impose a difference. The overdetermined image he picks (Africans = children) allows him to feel secure once again because it restores the moral balance in favor of the ('adult') Christian conqueror. Such contradictory use of images abounds in colonialist literature.

My point, then, is that the imperialist is not fixated on specific images or stereotypes of the Other but rather on the affective benefits proffered by the manichean allegory, which generates the various stereotypes. As I have argued, the manichean allegory, with its highly efficient exchange mechanism, permits various kinds of rapid transformations, for example, metonymic displacement – which leads to the essentialist metonymy, as in the above quotation from Dinesen – and metaphoric condensation – which accounts for the structure and characterization in Cary's *Mister Johnson*. Exchange-value remains the central motivating force of both colonialist material practice and colonialist literary representation.

The fetishizing strategy and the allegorical mechanism not only permit a rapid exchange of denigrating images which can be used to maintain a sense of moral difference; they also allow the writer to transform social and historical dissimilarities into universal, metaphysical differences. If, as Dinesen has done, African natives can be collapsed into African animals and mystified still further as some magical essence of the continent, then clearly there can be no meeting ground, no identity, between the social, historical creatures of Europe and the metaphysical alterity of the Calibans and Ariels of Africa. If the differences between the Europeans and the natives are so vast, then clearly, as I stated earlier, the process of civilizing the natives can continue indefinitely. The ideological function of this mechanism, in addition to prolonging colonialism, is to dehistoricize and desocialize the conquered world, to present it as a metaphysical 'fact of life,' before which those who have fashioned the colonial world are themselves reduced to the role of passive spectators in a mystery not of their making.

There are many formal consequences of this denial of history and normal social interaction. While masquerading under the guise of realist fiction, the colonialist text is in fact antagonistic to some of the prevailing tendencies of realism. As M. M. Bakhtin has argued, the temporal model of the world changes radically with the rise of the realist novel: 'For the first time in artistic-ideological consciousness, time and the world become historical: they unfold as becoming, as an uninterrupted movement into a real future, as a unified, all-embracing and unconcluded process' (Bakhtin 1975: 30). But since the colonialist wants to maintain his privileges by preserving the status quo, his representation of the world contains neither a sense of historical becoming, nor a concrete vision of a future different from the present, nor a teleology other than the infinitely postponed process of 'civilizing.' In short, it does not contain any syncretic cultural possibility, which alone would open up the historic once more. . . .

This adamant refusal to admit the possibility of syncretism, of a rapprochement between self and Other, is the most important factor distinguishing the 'imaginary' from the 'symbolic' colonialist text. The 'symbolic' text's openness toward the Other is based on a greater awareness of potential identity and a heightened sense of the concrete socio-politico-cultural differences between self and Other. Although the 'symbolic' writer's understanding of the Other proceeds through self-understanding, he is freer from the codes and motifs of the deeper, collective classification system of his culture. In the final analysis, his success in comprehending or appreciating alterity will depend on his ability to bracket the values and bases of his culture. He may do so very consciously and deliberately, as Forster does in *A Passage to India*, or he may allow the emotions and values instilled in him during his social formation in an alien culture to inform his appraisals of the Other, as Kipling does in Kim. These two novels offer the most interesting attempts to overcome the barriers of racial difference. . . .

As we have seen, colonialist fiction is generated predominantly by the ideological machinery of the manichean allegory. Yet the relation between

22

imperial ideology and fiction is not unidirectional: the ideology does not simply determine the fiction. Rather, through a process of symbiosis, the fiction *forms* the ideology by articulating and justifying the position and aims of the colonialist. But it does more than just define and elaborate the actual military and putative moral superiority of the Europeans. Troubled by the nagging contradiction between the theoretical justification of exploitation and the barbarity of its actual practice, it also attempts to mask the contradiction by obsessively portraying the supposed inferiority and barbarity of the racial Other, thereby insisting on the profound moral difference between self and Other. Within this symbiotic relation, the manichean allegory functions as a transformative mechanism between the affective pleasure derived from the moral superiority and material profit that motivate imperialism, on the one hand, and the formal devices (genres, stereotypes, and so on) of colonialist fiction, on the other hand. By allowing the European to denigrate the native in a variety of ways, by permitting an obsessive, fetishistic representation of the native's moral inferiority, the allegory also enables the European to increase, by contrast, the store of his own moral superiority; it allows him to accumulate 'surplus morality,' which is further invested in the denigration of the native, in a self-sustaining cycle.

Thus the ideological function of all 'imaginary' and some 'symbolic' colonialist literature is to articulate and justify the moral authority of the colonizer and – by positing the inferiority of the native as a metaphysical fact – to mask the pleasure the colonizer derives from that authority. . . .

Finally, we must bear in mind that colonialist fiction and ideology do not exist in a vacuum. In order to appreciate them thoroughly, we must examine them in juxtaposition to domestic English fiction and the anglophone fiction of the Third World, which originates from British occupation and which, during the current, hegemonic phase of colonialism, is establishing a dialogic relation with colonialist fiction. The Third World's literary dialogue with Western cultures is marked by two broad characteristics: its attempt to negate the prior European negation of colonized cultures and its adoption and creative modification of Western languages and artistic forms in conjunction with indigenous languages and forms. This dialogue merits our serious attention for two reasons: first, in spite of the often studied attempts by ethnocentric canonizers in English and other (Western) language and literature departments to ignore Third World culture and art, they will not go away; and, second, as this analysis of colonialist literature (a literature, we must remember, that is sued to mediate between different cultures) demonstrates, the domain of literary and cultural syncretism belongs not to colonialist and neocolonialist writers but increasingly to Third World artists.

# 3

## Can the Subaltern Speak?

### Gayatri Chakravorty Spivak*

SOME OF THE most radical criticism coming out of the West today is the result of an interested desire to conserve the subject of the West, or the West as Subject. The theory of pluralized 'subject-effects' gives an illusion of undermining subjective sovereignty while often providing a cover for this subject of knowledge. Although the history of Europe as Subject is narrativized by the law, political economy, and ideology of the West, this concealed Subject pretends it has 'no geo-political determinations.' The much publicized critique of the sovereign subject thus actually inaugurates a Subject. . . .

This S/subject, curiously sewn together into a transparency by denegations, belongs to the exploiters' side of the international division of labor. It is impossible for contemporary French intellectuals to imagine the kind of Power and Desire that would inhabit the unnamed subject of the Other of Europe. It is not only that everything they read, critical or uncritical, is caught within the debate of the production of that Other, supporting or critiquing the constitution of the Subject as Europe. It is also that, in the constitution of that Other of Europe, great care was taken to obliterate the textual ingredients with which such a subject could cathect, could occupy (invest?) its itinerary – not only by ideological and scientific production, but also by the institution of the law. . . . In the face of the possibility that the intellectual is complicit in the persistent constitution of Other as the Self's shadow, a possibility of political practice for the intellectual would be to put the economic 'under erasure,' to see the economic factor as irreducible as it reinscribes the social text, even as it is erased, however imperfectly, when it claims to be the final determinant or the transcendental signified.

The clearest available example of such epistemic violence is the remotely orchestrated, far-flung, and heterogeneous project to constitute the colonial

* From 'Can the Subaltern Speak?' in Cary Nelson and Lawrence Grossberg (eds) *Marxism and the Interpretation of Culture* London: Macmillan, 1988.

subject as Other. This project is also the asymetrical obliteration of the trace of that Other in its precarious Subjectivity. It is well known that Foucault locates epistemic violence, a complete overhaul of the episteme, in the redefinition of sanity at the end of the European eighteenth century. But what if that particular redefinition was only a part of the narrative of history in Europe as well as in the colonies? What if the two projects of epistemic overhaul worked as dislocated and unacknowledged parts of a vast two-handed engine? Perhaps it is no more than to ask that the subtext of the palimpsestic narrative of imperialism be recognized as 'subjugated knowledge,' 'a whole set of knowledges that have been disqualified as inadequate to their task or insufficiently elaborated: naive knowledges, located low down on the hierarchy, beneath the required level of cognition or scientificity' (Foucault 1980: 82).

This is not to describe 'the way things really were' or to privilege the narrative of history as imperialism as the best version of history. It is, rather, to offer an account of how an explanation and narrative of reality was established as the normative one. . . .

Let us now move to consider the margins (one can just as well say the silent, silenced center) of the circuit marked out by this epistemic violence, men and women among the illiterate peasantry, the tribals, the lowest strata of the urban subproletariat. According to Foucault and Deleuze (in the First World, under the standardization and regimentation of socialized capital, though they do not seem to recognize this) the oppressed, if given the chance (the problem of representation cannot be bypassed here), and on the way to solidarity through alliance politics (a Marxist thematic is at work here) *can speak and know their conditions*. We must now confront the following question: On the other side of the international division of labor from socialized capital, inside *and* outside the circuit of the epistemic violence of imperialist law and education supplementing an earlier economic text, *can the subaltern speak*? . . .

The first part of my proposition – that the phased development of the subaltern is complicated by the imperialist project – is confronted by a collective of intellectuals who may be called the 'Subaltern Studies' group. They *must* ask, Can the subaltern speak? Here we are within Foucault's own discipline of history and with people who acknowledge his influence. Their project is to rethink Indian colonial historiography from the perspective of the discontinuous chain of peasant insurgencies during the colonial occupation. This is indeed the problem of 'the permission to narrate' discussed by Said (1984). As Ranajit Guha argues,

> The historiography of Indian nationalism has for a long time been dominated by elitism – colonialist elitism and bourgeois-nationalist elitism . . . shar[ing] the prejudice that the making of the Indian nation and the development of the consciousness-nationalism which confirmed this process were exclusively or predominantly elite achievements. In the colonialist and neo-colonialist historiographies these achievements are credited to British colonial rulers, administrators,

policies, institutions, and culture; in the nationalist and neo-nationalist writings – to Indian elite personalities, institutions, activities and ideas.

(Guha 1982: 1)

Certain varieties of the Indian elite are at best native informants for first-world intellectuals interested in the voice of the Other. But one must nevertheless insist that the colonized subaltern *subject* is irretrievably heterogeneous.

Against the indigenous elite we may set what Guha calls 'the *politics of the people,*' both outside ('this was an *autonomous* domain, for it neither originated from elite politics nor did its existence depend on the latter') and inside ('it continued to operate vigorously in spite of [colonialism], adjusting itself to the conditions prevailing under the Raj and in many respects developing entirely new strains in both form and content') the circuit of colonial production (Guha 1982: 4). I cannot entirely endorse this insistence on determinate vigor and full autonomy, for practical historiographic exigencies will not allow such endorsements to privilege subaltern consciousness. Against the possible charge that his approach is essentialist, Guha constructs a definition of the people (the place of that essence) that can be only an identity-in-differential. He proposes a dynamic stratification grid describing colonial social production at large. Even the third group on the list, the buffer group, as it were, between the people and the great macrostructural dominant groups, is itself defined as a place of in-betweenness, what Derrida has described as an '*antre*' (1981):

elite
{
 1. Dominant foreign groups.
 2. Dominant indigenous groups on the all-India level.

 3. Dominant indigenous groups at the regional and local levels.
 4. The terms 'people' and 'subaltern classes' [are] used as synonymous throughout [Guha's definition]. The social groups and elements included in this category represent *the demographic difference between the total Indian population and all those whom we have described as the 'elite.'*

Consider the third item on this list – the *antre* of situational indeterminacy these careful historians presuppose as they grapple with the question, Can the subaltern speak?

*Taken as a whole and in the abstract* this ... category ... was *heterogeneous* in its composition and thanks to the uneven character of regional economic and social developments, *different from area to area.* The same class or element which was dominant in one area ... could be among the dominated in another. This could and did create many ambiguities and contradictions in attitudes and alliances, especially among the lowest strata of the rural gentry, impoverished landlords, rich peasants and upper middle class peasants all of whom belonged, *ideally speaking*, to the category of people or subaltern classes.

(Guha 1982: 8)

'The task of research' projected here is 'to investigate, identify and measure the *specific* nature and degree of the *deviation* of [the] elements [constituting item 3] from the ideal and situate it historically.' 'Investigate, identify, and measure the specific': a program could hardly be more essentialist and taxonomic. Yet a curious methodological imperative is at work. I have argued that, in the Foucault–Deleuze conversation, a postrepresentationalist vocabulary hides an essentialist agenda. In subaltern studies, because of the violence of imperialist epistemic, social, and disciplinary inscription, a project understood in essentialist terms must traffic in a radical textual practice of differences. The object of the group's investigation, in the case not even of the people as such but of the floating buffer zone of the regional elite-subaltern, is a *deviation* from an *ideal* – the people or subaltern – which is itself defined as a difference from the elite. It is toward this structure that the research is oriented, a predicament rather different from the self-diagnosed transparency of the first-world radical intellectual. What taxonomy can fix such a space? Whether or not they themselves perceive it – in fact Guha sees his definition of 'the people' within the master-slave dialectic – their text articulates the difficult task of rewriting its own conditions of impossibility as the conditions of its possibility.

'At the regional and local levels [the dominant indigenous groups] . . . if belonging to social strata hierarchically inferior to those of the dominant all-Indian groups *acted in the interests of the latter and not in conformity to interests corresponding truly to their own social being*.' When these writers speak, in their essentializing language, of a gap between interest and action in the intermediate group, their conclusions are closer to Marx than to the self-conscious naiveté of Deleuze's pronouncement on the issue. Guha, like Marx, speaks of interest in terms of the social rather than the libidinal being. The Name-of-the-Father imagery in *The Eighteenth Brumaire* can help to emphasize that, on the level of class or group action, 'true correspondence to own being' is as artificial or social as the patronymic.

So much for the intermediate group marked in item 3. For the 'true' subaltern group, whose identity is its difference, there is no unrepresentable subaltern subject that can know and speak itself; the intellectual's solution is not to abstain from representation. The problem is that the subject's itinerary has not been traced so as to offer an object of seduction to the representing intellectual. In the slightly dated language of the Indian group, the question becomes, How can we touch the consciousness of the people, even as we investigate their politics? With what voice-consciousness can the subaltern speak? Their project, after all, is to rewrite the development of the consciousness of the Indian nation. The planned discontinuity of imperialism rigorously distinguishes this project, however old-fashioned its articulation, from 'rendering visible the medical and juridical mechanisms that surrounded the story [of Pierre Riviere].' Foucault is correct in suggesting that 'to make visible the unseen can also mean a change of level,

addressing oneself to a layer of material which had hitherto had no perti-
nence for history and which had not been recognized as having any moral,
aesthetic or historical value.' It is the slippage from rendering visible the
mechanism to rendering the individual, both avoiding 'any kind of analysis
of [the subject] whether psychological, psychoanalytical or linguistic,' that
is consistently troublesome (Foucault 1980: 49–50). . . .

When we come to the concomitant question of the consciousness of
the subaltern, the notion of what the work *cannot* say becomes important.
In the semioses of the social text, elaborations of insurgency stand in the
place of 'the utterance.' The sender – 'the peasant' – is marked only as a
pointer to an irretrievable consciousness. As for the receiver, we must ask
who is 'the real receiver' of an 'insurgency?' The historian, transforming
'insurgency' into 'text for knowledge,' is only one 'receiver' of any collectively intended social act. With no possibility of nostalgia for that lost
origin, the historian must suspend (as far as possible) the clamor of his or
her own consciousness (or consciousness-effect, as operated by disciplinary
training), so that the elaboration of the insurgency, packaged with an
insurgent-consciousness, does not freeze into an 'object of investigation,'
or, worse yet, a model for imitation. 'The subject' implied by the texts of
insurgency can only serve as a counterpossibility for the narrative sanctions
granted to the colonial subject in the dominant groups. The postcolonial
intellectuals learn that their privilege is their loss. In this they are a paradigm of the intellectuals.

It is well known that the notion of the feminine (rather than the
subaltern of imperialism) has been used in a similar way within deconstructive criticism and within certain varieties of feminist criticism. In
the former case, a figure of 'woman' is at issue, one whose minimal predi-
cation as indeterminate is already available to the phallocentric tradition.
Subaltern historiography raises questions of method that would prevent it
from using such a ruse. For the 'figure' of woman, the relationship between
woman and silence can be plotted by women themselves; race and class
differences are subsumed under that charge. Subaltern historiography must
confront the impossibility of such gestures. The narrow epistemic violence
of imperialism gives us an imperfect allegory of the general violence that is
the possibility of an episteme.

Within the effaced itinerary of the subaltern subject, the track of
sexual difference is doubly effected. The question is not of female participation in insurgency, or the ground rules of the sexual division of labor, for
both of which there is 'evidence.' It is, rather, that, both as object of
colonialist historiography and as subject of insurgency, the ideological
construction of gender keeps the male dominant. If, in the context of
colonial production, the subaltern has no history and cannot speak, the
subaltern as female is even more deeply in shadow. . . .

# 4

## Signs Taken for Wonders

### HOMI K. BHABHA*

*A remarkable peculiarity is that they (the English) always write the personal pronoun I with a capital letter. May we not consider this Great I as an unintended proof how much an Englishman thinks of his own consequence?*

Robert Southey, *Letters from England*

THERE IS A scene in the cultural writings of English colonialism which repeats so insistently after the early nineteenth century – and, through that repetition, so triumphantly *inaugurates* a literature of empire – that I am bound to repeat it once more. It is the scenario, played out in the wild and wordless wastes of colonial India, Africa, the Caribbean, of the sudden fortuitous discovery of the English book. It is, like all myths of origin, memorable for its balance between epiphany and enunciation. The discovery of the book is, at once, a moment of originality and authority, as well as a process of displacement that, paradoxically, makes the presence of the book wondrous to the extent to which it is repeated, translated, misread, displaced. It is with the emblem of the English book – 'signs taken for wonders' – as an insignia of colonial authority and a signifier of colonial desire and discipline, that I want to begin this essay.

In the first week of May 1817, Anund Messeh, one of the earliest Indian catechists, made a hurried and excited journey from his mission in Meerut to a grove of trees outside Delhi.

> He found about 500 people, men, women and children, seated under the shade of the trees, and employed, as had been related to him, in reading and conversation. He went up to an elderly looking man, and accosted him, and the following conversation passed.

* From 'Signs Taken for Wonders: Questions of Ambivalence and Authority Under a Tree Outside Delhi, May 1817' *Critical Inquiry* 12(1), 1985.

'Pray who are all these people? and whence come they?' 'We are poor
and lowly, and we read and love this book' — 'What is that book?' 'The
book of God!' — 'Let me look at it, if you please.' Anund, on opening
the book, perceived it to be the Gospel of our Lord, translated into the
Hindoostanee Tongue, many copies of which seemed to be in the
possession of the party: some were PRINTED others WRITTEN by
themselves from the printed ones. Anund pointed to the name of Jesus,
and asked, 'Who is that?' 'That is God! He gave us this book.' —
'Where did you obtain it?' 'An Angel from heaven gave it us, at
Hurdwar fair.' — 'An Angel?' 'Yes, to us he was God's Angel: but he
was a man, a learned Pundit.' (Doubtless these translated Gospels must
have been the books distributed, five or six years ago, at Hurdwar by
the Missionary.) 'The written copies we write ourselves, having no
other means of obtaining more of this blessed word.' — 'These books,'
said Anund, 'teach the religion of the European Sahibs. It is THEIR
book; and they printed it in our language, for our use.' 'Ah! no'; replied
the stranger, 'that cannot be, for they eat flesh.' — 'Jesus Christ,' said
Anund, 'teaches that it does not signify what a man eats or drinks.
EATING is nothing before God. *Not that which entereth into a man's
mouth defileth him but that which cometh out of the mouth, this
defileth a man*: for vile things come forth from the heart. *Out of the
heart proceed evil thoughts, murders, adulteries, fornications, thefts;
and these are the things that defile.*'

'That is true; but how can it be the European Book, when we believe
that it is God's gift to us? He sent it to us at Hurdwar.' 'God gave it
long ago to the Sahibs, and THEY sent it to us.' The ignorance and
simplicity of many are very striking, never having heard of a printed
book before; and its very appearance was to them miraculous. A great
stir was excited by the gradual increasing information hereby
obtained, and all united to acknowledge the superiority of the
doctrines of this Holy Book to every thing which they had hitherto
heard or known. An indifference to the distinctions of Caste soon
manifested itself; and the interference and tyrannical authority of the
Brahmins became more offensive and contemptible. At last, it was
determined to separate themselves from the rest of their Hindoo
Brethren; and to establish a party of their own choosing, four or five,
who could read the best, to be the public teachers from this newly-
acquired Book. . . . Anund asked them, 'Why are you all dressed in
white?' 'The people of God should wear white raiment,' was the reply,
'as a sign that they are clean, and rid of their sins.' — Anund observed,
'You ought to be BAPTIZED, in the name of the Father, and of the
Son, and of the Holy Ghost. Come to Meerut: there is a Christian
Padre there; and he will shew you what you ought to do.' They
answered, 'Now we must go home to the harvest; but, as we mean to
meet once a year, perhaps the next year we may come to Meerut.' I
explained to them the nature of the Sacrament and of Baptism; in
answer to which, they replied, 'We are willing to be baptized, but we
will never take the Sacrament. To all the other customs of Christians
we are willing to conform, but not to the Sacrament, because the

Europeans eat cow's flesh, and this will never do for us.' To this I answered, 'this WORD is of God, and not of men; and when it makes your hearts to understand, then you will PROPERLY comprehend it. They replied, 'If all our country will receive this Sacrament, then will we.' I then observed, The time is at hand, when all the countries will receive this WORD.' They replied, 'True.'

(Missionary Register 1818: 18–19])

Almost a hundred years later, in 1902, Joseph Conrad's Marlow, traveling in the Congo, in the night of the first ages, without a sign and no memories, cut off from the comprehension of his surroundings, desperately in need of a deliberate belief, comes upon Towson's (or Towser's) *Inquiry into some Points of Seamanship.*

Not a very enthralling book; but at the first glance you could see there a singleness of intention, an honest concern for the right way of going to work, which made these humble pages, thought out so many years ago, luminous with another than a professional light. . . . I assure you to leave off reading was like tearing myself away from the shelter of an old and solid friendship. . . .

'It must be this miserable trader – this intruder,' exclaimed the manager, looking back malevolently at the place we had left. 'He must be English,' I said.

(Conrad 1902: 71, 72)

Half a century later, a young Trinidadian discovers that same volume of Towson's in that very passage from Conrad and draws from it a vision of literature and a lesson of history. 'The scene,' writes V. S. Naipaul, 'answered some of the political panic I was beginning to feel':

To be a colonial was to know a kind of security; it was to inhabit a fixed world. And I suppose that in my fantasy I had seen myself coming to England as to some purely literary region, where, untrammeled by the accidents of history or background, I could make a romantic career for myself as a writer. But in the new world I felt that ground move below me . . . Conrad . . . had been everywhere before me. Not as a man with a cause, but a man offering a vision of the world's half-made societies . . . where always 'something inherent in the necessities of successful action carried with it the moral degradation of the idea.' Dismal but deeply felt: a kind of truth and half a consolation.

(Naipaul 1974: 233)

Written as they are in the name of the father and the author, these texts ⌐ of the civilizing mission immediately suggest the triumph of the colonialist moment in early English Evangelism and modern English literature. The discovery of the book installs the sign of appropriate representation: the word of God, truth, art creates the conditions for a beginning, a practice of history and narrative. But the institution of the Word in the wilds is also an *Enstellung*, a process of displacement, distortion, dislocation, repetition[1] – the dazzling light of literature sheds only areas of darkness. Still the idea of the English book is presented as universally adequate: like the 'metaphoric writing of the West,' it communicates 'the immediate vision of the thing, freed from the discourse that accompanied it, or even encumbered it' (Derrida 1981: 189–90). . . .

The discovery of the English book establishes both a measure of mimesis and a mode of civil authority and order. If these scenes, as I've narrated them, suggest the triumph of the writ of colonialist power, then it must be conceded that the wily letter of the law inscribes a much more ambivalent text of authority. For it is in between the edict of Englishness and the assault of the dark unruly spaces of the earth, through an act of repetition, that the colonial text emerges uncertainly. Anund Messeh disavows the natives' disturbing questions as he returns to repeat the now questionable 'authority' of Evangelical dicta; Marlow turns away from the African jungle to recognize, in retrospect, the peculiarly 'English' quality of the discovery of the book; Naipaul turns his back on the hybrid half-made colonial world to fix his eye on the universal domain of English literature. What we witness is neither an untroubled, innocent dream of England nor a 'secondary revision' of the nightmare of India, Africa, the Caribbean. What is 'English' in these discourses of colonial power cannot be represented as a plenitude or a 'full' presence; it is determined by its belatedness. As a signifier of authority, the English book acquires its meaning *after* the traumatic scenario of colonial difference, cultural or racial, returns the eye of power to some prior, archaic image or identity. Paradoxically, however, such an image can neither be 'original' by virtue of the act of repetition that constructs it – nor 'identical' by virtue of the difference that defines it. Consequently, the colonial presence is always ambivalent, split between its appearance as original and authoritative and its articulation as repetition and difference. . . .

The place of difference and otherness, or the space of the adversarial, within such a system of 'disposal' as I've proposed, is never entirely on the outside or implacably oppositional. It is a pressure, and a presence, that acts constantly, if unevenly, along the entire boundary of authorization, that is, on the surface between what I've called disposal-as-bestowal and disposition-as-inclination. The contour of difference is agonistic, shifting, splitting, rather like Freud's description of the system of consciousness which occupies a position in space lying on the borderline between outside and inside, a surface of protection, reception, and projection. The power play of presence is lost if its transparency is treated naively as the nostalgia for plenitude that should be flung repeatedly into the abyss – *mise en abîme* – from which its desire is born. Such theoreticist anarchism cannot intervene in the agonistic space of authority where

> the true and the false are separated and specific effects of power [are] attached to the true, it being understood also that it is not a matter of

32

a battle 'on behalf' of the truth, but of a battle about the status of truth and the economic and political role it plays.

(Foucault 1980: 132)

It is precisely to intervene in such a battle for the *status* of the truth that it becomes crucial to examine the *presence* of the English book. For it is this surface that stabilizes the agonistic colonial space; it is its *appearance* that regulates the ambivalence between origin and *Entstellung*, discipline and desire, mimesis and repetition.

Despite appearances, the text of transparency inscribes a double vision: the field of the 'true' emerges as a visible effect of knowledge/power only after the regulatory and displacing division of the true and the false. From this point of view, discursive 'transparency' is best read in the photographic sense in which a transparency is also always a negative, processed into visibility through the technologies of reversal, enlargement, lighting, editing, projection, not a source but a re-source of light. Such a bringing to light is never a prevision; it is always a question of the provision of visibility as a capacity, a strategy, an agency but also in the sense in which the prefix pro(vision) might indicate an elision of sight, delegation, substitution, contiguity, in place of . . . what?

This is the question that brings us to the ambivalence of the presence of authority, peculiarly visible in its colonial articulation. For if transparency signifies discursive closure – intention, image, author – it does so through a disclosure of its *rules of recognition* – those social texts of epistemic, ethno-centric, nationalist intelligibility which cohere in the address of authority as the 'present,' the voice of modernity. The acknowledgement of authority depends upon the immediate – unmediated – visibility of its rules of recognition as the unmistakable referent of historical necessity.

In the doubly inscribed space of colonial representation where the presence of authority – the English book – is also a question of its repetition and displacement, where transparency is *techné*, the immediate visibility of such a régime of recognition is resisted. Resistance is not necessarily an oppositional act of political intention, nor is it the simple negation or exclusion of the 'content' of an other culture, as a difference once perceived. It is the effect of an ambivalence produced within the rules of recognition of dominating discourses as they articulate the signs of cultural difference and reimplicate them within the deferential relations of colonial power – hierarchy, normalization, marginalization, and so forth. For domination is achieved through a process of disavowal that denies the *différance* of colonialist power – the chaos of its intervention as *Entstellung*, its dislocatory presence – in order to preserve the authority of its identity in the universalist narrative of nineteenth-century historical and political evolutionism.

The exercise of colonialist authority, however, requires the production of differentiations, individuations, identity effects through which discriminatory practices can map out subject populations that are tarred with the visible and transparent mark of power. Such a mode of subjection is distinct from what Foucault describes as 'power through transparency': the reign of opinion, after the late eighteenth century, which could not tolerate areas of darkness and sought to exercise power through the mere fact of things being known and people seen in an immediate, collective gaze. What radically differentiates the exercise of colonial power is the unsuitability of the Enlightenment assumption of collectivity and the eye that beholds it. For Jeremy Bentham (as Michel Perrot points out), the small group is representative of the whole society – the part is *already* the whole. Colonial authority requires modes of discrimination (cultural, racial, administrative . . .) that disallow a stable unitary assumption of collectivity. The 'part' (which must be the colonialist foreign body) must be representative of the 'whole' (conquered country), but the right of representation is based on its radical difference. Such doublethink is made viable only through the strategy of disavowal just described, which requires a theory of the 'hybridization' of discourse and power that is ignored by Western post-structuralists who engage in the battle for 'power' as the purists of difference.

The discriminatory effects of the discourse of cultural colonialism, for instance, do not simply or singly refer to a 'person', or to a dialectical power struggle between self and Other, or to a discrimination between mother culture and alien cultures. Produced through the strategy of disavowal, the *reference* of discrimination is always to a process of splitting as the condition of subjection: a discrimination between the mother culture and its bastards, the self and its doubles, where the trace of what is disavowed is not repressed but repeated as something *different* – a mutation, a hybrid. It is such a partial and double force that is more than the mimetic but less than the symbolic, that disturbs the visibility of the colonial presence and makes the recognition of its authority problematic. To be authoritative, its rules of recognition must reflect consensual knowledge or opinion; to be powerful, these rules of recognition must be breached in order to represent the exorbitant objects of discrimination that lie beyond its purview. Consequently if the unitary (and essentialist) reference to race, nation, or cultural tradition is essential to preserve the presence of authority as an immediate mimetic effect, such essentialism must be exceeded in the articulation of 'differentiatory,' discriminatory identities.

To demonstrate such an 'excess' is not merely to celebrate the joyous power of the signifier. Hybridity is the sign of the productivity of colonial power, its shifting forces and fixities; it is the name for the strategic reversal of the process of domination through disavowal (that is, the production of discriminatory identities that secure the 'pure' and original identity of authority). Hybridity is the revaluation of the assumption of colonial identity through the repetition of discriminatory identity effects. It displays the necessary deformation and displacement of all sites of discrimination and domination. It unsettles the mimetic or narcissistic demands of colonial power but reimplicates its identifications in strategies of subversion that turn the gaze of the discriminated back upon the eye of power. For the colonial hybrid is the articulation of the ambivalent space where the rite of power is enacted on the site of desire, making its objects at once disciplinary and disseminatory – or, in my mixed metaphor, a negative transparency. If discriminatory effects enable the authorities to keep an eye on them, their proliferating difference evades that eye, escapes that surveillance. Those discriminated against may be instantly recognized, but they also force a recognition of the immediacy and articulacy of authority – a disturbing effect that is familiar in the repeated hesitancy afflicting the colonialist discourse when it contemplates its discriminated subjects: the *inscrutability* of the Chinese, the *unspeakable* rites of the Indians, the *indescribable* habits of the Hottentots. It is not that the voice of authority is at a loss for words. It is, rather, that the colonial discourse has reached that point when, faced with the hybridity of its objects, the *presence* of power is revealed as something other than what its rules of recognition assert.

If the effect of colonial power is seen to be the *production* of hybridization rather than the noisy command of colonialist authority or the silent repression of native traditions, then an important change of perspective occurs. It reveals the ambivalence at the source of traditional discourses on authority and enables a form of subversion, founded on that uncertainty, that turns the discursive conditions of dominance into the grounds of intervention. It is traditional academic wisdom that the presence of authority is properly established through the nonexercise of private judgment and the exclusion of reasons, in conflict with the authoritative reason. The recognition of authority, however, requires a validation of its source that must be immediately, even intuitively, apparent – 'You have that in your countenance which I would fain call master' – and held in common (rules of recognition). What is left unacknowledged is the paradox of such a demand for proof and the resulting ambivalence for positions of authority. If, as Steven I. Lukes rightly says, the acceptance of authority excludes any evaluation of the content of an utterance, and if its source, which must be acknowledged, disavows both conflicting reasons and personal judgement, then can the 'signs' or 'marks' of authority be anything more than 'empty' presences of strategic devices? Need they be any the less effective because of that? Not less effective but effective in a different form, would be our answer.

## NOTE

1   'Overall effect of the dream-work: the latent thoughts are transformed into a manifest formation in which they are not easily recognisable. They are not only transposed, as it were, into another key, but *they are also distorted in such a fashion that only an effort of interpretation can reconstitute them*' (Laplanche and Pontalis 1980: 124). See also Samuel Weber's excellent chapter 'Metapsychology Set Apart' (1982: 32–60)

# 5

# Problems in Current Theories of Colonial Discourse

## Benita Parry*

The work of Spivak and Bhabha will be discussed to suggest the productive capacity and limitations of their different deconstructive practices, and to propose that the protocols of their dissimilar methods act to constrain the development of an anti-imperialist critique. It will be argued that the lacunae in Spivak's learned disquisitions issue from a theory assigning an absolute power to the hegemonic discourse in constituting and disarticulating the native. In essays that are to form a study on Master Discourse/Native informant, Spivak inspects 'the absence of a text that can "answer one back" after the planned epistemic violence of the imperialist project' (Spivak 1985a: 131), and seeks to develop a strategy of reading that will speak to the historically-muted native subject, predominantly inscribed in Spivak's writings as the non-elite or subaltern woman. A refrain, 'One never encounters the testimony of the women's voice-consciousness,' 'There is no space from where the subaltern (sexed) subject can speak,' 'The subaltern as female cannot be heard or read,' 'The subaltern cannot speak' (Spivak 1985b: 122, 129, 130), iterates a theoretical dictum derived from studying the discourse of *Sati* [widow sacrifice], in which the Hindu patriarchal code converged with colonialism's narrativization of Indian culture to efface all traces of woman's voice.

What Spivak uncovers are instances of doubly-oppressed native women who, caught between the dominations of a native patriarchy and a foreign masculist-imperialist ideology, intervene by 'unemphatic, ad hoc, subaltern rewriting(s) of the social text of *Sati*-suicide' (Spivak 1985b: 129): a nineteenth century Princess who appropriates – 'the dubious place of the free will of the sexed subject as female' (Spivak 1985a: 144) by signaling her intention of being a *Sati* against the edict of the British administration; a young Bengal girl who in 1926 hanged herself under circumstances that deliberately defied Hindu interdicts (Spivak 1985b). From the discourse of *Sati* Spivak

* From 'Problems in Current Theories of Colonial Discourse' *Oxford Literary Review* 9 (1&2), 1987.

derives large, general statements on woman's subject constitution/object formation in which the subaltern woman is conceived as a homogeneous and coherent category, and which culminate in a declaration on the success of her planned disarticulation. Even within the confines of this same discourse, it is significant that Lata Mani does find evidence, albeit mediated, of woman's voice. As Chandra Talpade Mohanty argues in her critique of western feminist writings on 'Third World Women,' discourses of representation should not be confused with material realities. Since the native woman is constructed within multiple social relationships and positioned as the product of different class, caste and cultural specificities, it should be possible to locate traces and testimony of women's voice on those sites where women inscribed themselves as healers, ascetics, singers of sacred songs, artizans and artists, and by this to modify Spivak's model of the silent subaltern.

If it could appear that Spivak is theorizing the silence of the doubly-oppressed subaltern woman, her theorem on imperialism's epistemic violence extends to posting the native, male and female, as an historically-muted subject. The story of colonialism which she reconstructs is of an interactive process where the European agent in consolidating the imperialist Sovereign Self, induces the native to collude in its own subject(ed) formation as other and voiceless. Thus while protesting at the obliteration of the native's subject position in the text of imperialism, Spivak in her project gives no speaking part to the colonized, effectively writing out the evidence of native agency recorded in India's 200 year struggle against British conquest and the Raj – discourses to which she scathingly refers as hegemonic nativist or reverse ethnocentric narrativization.

The disparaging of nationalist discourses of resistance is matched by the exorbitation of the role allotted to the post-colonial woman intellectual, for it is she who must plot a story, unravel a narrative and give the subaltern a voice in history, by using 'the resources of deconstruction "in the service of reading" to develop a strategy rather than a theory of reading that might be a critique of imperialism' (Spivak 1986: 230). Spivak's 'alternative narrative of colonialism' through a series of brilliant upheavals of texts which expose the fabrications and exclusions in the writing of the archive, is directed at challenging the authority of the received historical record and restoring the effaced signs of native consciousness, and it is on these grounds that her project should be estimated. Her account, it is claimed, disposes of the old story by dispersing the fixed, unitary categories on which this depended. Thus it is argued that for purposes of administration and exploitation of resources, the native was constructed as a programmed, 'nearly-selved' other of the European and not as its binary opposite. Furthermore, the cartography that became the 'reality' of India was drawn by agents who were themselves of heterogeneous class origin and social status and whose (necessarily) diversified maps distributed the native into differential positions which worked in the interest of the foreign authority

– for example, a fantasmatic race-differentiated historical demography restoring 'rightful' Aryan rulers, and a class discourse effecting the proto-proletarianization of the 'aborigines.'

Instead of recounting a struggle between a monolithic, near-deliberative colonial power and an undifferentiated oppressed mass, this reconstruction displays a process more insidious than naked repression, since here the native is prevailed upon to internalize as self-knowledge, the knowledge concocted by the master: 'He (the European agent) is worlding their own world, which is far from mere uninscribed earth, anew, by obliging them to domesticate the alien as Master,' a process generating the force 'to make the "native" see himself as "other" ' (Spivak 1985a: 133). Where military conquest, institutional compulsion and ideological interpellation was, epistemic violence and devious discursive negotiations requiring of the native that he rewrite his position as object of imperialism, is; and in place of recalcitrance and refusal enacted in movements of resistance and articulated in oppositional discourses, a tale is told of the self-consolidating other and the disarticulated subaltern.

This raw and selective summary of what are complex and subtle arguments has tried to draw out the political implications of a theory whose axioms deny to the native the ground from which to utter a reply to imperialism's ideological aggression or to enunciate a different self:

> No perspective *critical* of imperialism can turn the Other into a self, because the project of imperialism has always already historically refracted what might have been the absolutely Other into a domesticated Other that consolidates the imperialist self. . . . A full literary inscription cannot easily flourish in the imperialist fracture or discontinuity, covered over by an alien legal system masquerading as Law as such, an alien ideology established as only truth, and a set of human sciences busy establishing the native 'as self-consolidating Other.'
>
> (Spivak 1985c: 253, 254)

In bringing this thesis to her reading of *Wide Sargasso Sea* (Rhys 1968) as Jane Eyre's reinscription, Spivak demonstrates the pitfalls of a theory postulating that the Master Discourse preempts the (self) constitution of the historical native subject. When Spivak's notion is juxtaposed to the question Said asks in Orientalism, 'how can one study other cultures and peoples from a libertarian, or a non-repressive and non-manipulative perspective?', and Jean Rhys' novel examined for its enunciation (despite much incidental racism) of just such a perspective which facilitates the transformation of the Other into a Self, then it is possible to construct a re-reading of *Wide Sargasso Sea* iterating many of Spivak's observations while disputing her founding precepts.

Spivak argues that because the construction of an English cultural identity was inseparable from othering the native as its object, the articulation of the female subject within the emerging norm of feminist individualism during the age of imperialism, necessarily excluded the native female, who was positioned on the boundary between human and animal as the object of imperialism's social-mission or soul-making. In applying this interactive process to her reading of *Wide Sargasso Sea* Spivak assigns to Antoinette/Bertha, daughter of slave-owners and heiress to a post-emancipation fortune, the role of the native female sacrificed in the cause of the subject-constitution of the European female individualist. Although Spivak does acknowledge that *Wide Sargasso Sea* is 'a novel which rewrites a canonical English text within the European novelistic tradition in the interest of the white Creole rather than the native' (Spivak 1985c: 253), and situates Antoinette/Bertha as caught between the English imperialist and the black Jamaican, her discussion does not pursue the text's representations of a Creole culture that is dependent on both yet singular, or its enunciation of a specific settler discourse, distinct from the texts of imperialism. The dislocations of the Creole position are repeatedly spoken by Antoinette, the 'Rochester' figure and Christophine; the nexus of intimacy and hatred between white settler and black servant is written into the text in the mirror imagery of Antoinette and Tia, a trope which for Spivak functions to invoke the other that could not be selved:

> We had eaten the same food, slept side by side, bathed in the same river. As I ran, I thought, I will live with Tia and I will be like her. . . . When I was close I saw the jagged stone in her hand but I did not see her throw it. . . . I looked at her and I saw her face crumble as she began to cry. We stared at each other blood on my face, tears on hers. It was as if I saw myself. Like in a looking-glass.
>
> Rhys 1968: 24)

But while themselves not English, and indeed outcastes, the Creoles are Masters to the blacks, and just as Brontë's book invites the reader via Rochester to see Bertha Mason as situated on the human/animal frontier ('One night I had been awakened by her yells. . . . It was a fierce West Indian night . . . those are the sounds of a bottomless pit,' quoted in Spivak 1985c: 247–8), so does Rhys' novel via Antoinette admit her audience to the regulation settler view of rebellious blacks: 'the same face repeated over and over, eyes gleaming, mouth half-open,' emitting 'a horrible noise . . . like animals howling but worse.' (Rhys 1968: 32, 35)

The idiosyncrasies of an account where Antoinette plays the part of 'the woman from the colonies' are consequences of Spivak's decree that imperialism's linguistic aggression obliterates the inscription of a native self: thus a black female who in *Wide Sargasso Sea* is most fully selved, must be reduced to the status of a tangential figure, and a white Creole woman (mis)construed as the native female produced by the axiomatics of imperialism, her death interpreted as 'an allegory of the general epistemic violence of imperialism, the construction of a self-immolating subject for the glorification of the social mission of the colonizer' (Spivak 1985c: 251).

While allowing that Christophine is both speaking subject and interpreter to whom Rhys designates some crucial functions, Spivak sees her as marking the limits of the text's discourse, and not, as is here argued, disrupting it.

What Spivak's strategy of reading necessarily blots out is Christophine's inscription as the native, female, individual Self who defies the demands of the discriminatory discourses impinging on her person. Although an ex-slave given as a wedding-present to Antoinette's mother and subsequently a caring servant, Christophine subverts the Creole address that would constitute her as a domesticated Other, and asserts herself as articulate antagonist of patriarchal, settler and imperialist law. Natural mother to children and surrogate parent to Antoinette, Christophine scorns patriarchal authority in her personal life by discarding her patronymic and refusing her sons' fathers as husbands; as Antoinette's protector she impugns 'Rochester' for his economic and sexual exploitation of her fortune and person and as female individualist she is eloquently and frequently contemptuous of male conduct, black and white. . . .

Christophine's defiance is not enacted in a small and circumscribed space appropriated within the lines of dominant code, but is a stance from which she delivers a frontal assault against antagonists, and as such constitutes a counter-discourse. Wise to the limits of post-emancipation justice, she is quick to invoke the protection of its law when 'Rochester' threatens her with retribution: 'This is free country and I am free woman' (Rhys 1968: 131) – which is exactly how she functions in the text, her retort to him condensing her role as the black, female individualist: 'Read and write I don't know. *Other things I know*' (Rhys 1968: 133; emphasis added). . . .

Spivak's deliberated deafness to the native voice where it is to be heard, is at variance with her acute hearing of the unsaid in modes of Western feminist criticism which, while dismantling masculist constructions, reproduce and foreclose colonialist structures and imperialist axioms by 'performing the lie of constituting a truth of global sisterhood where the mesmerizing model remains male and female sparring partners of generalizable or universalizable sexuality who are the chief protagonists in that European contest' (Spivak 1986: 226). Demanding of disciplinary standards that 'equal rights of historical, geographical, linguistic specificity' be granted to the 'thoroughly stratified larger theatre of the Third World' (238), Spivak in her own writings severely restricts (eliminates?) the space in which the colonized can be written back into history, even when 'interventionist possibilities' are exploited through the deconstructive strategies devised by the post-colonial intellectual.

Homi Bhabha on the other hand, through recovering how the master discourse was interrogated by the natives in their own accents, produces an autonomous position for the colonial within the confines of the hegemonic discourse, and because of this enunciates a very different 'politics.' The sustained effort of writings which initially concentrated on deconstituting the structure of colonial discourse, and which latterly have engaged with the displacement of this text by the inappropriate utterances of the colonized, has been to contest the notion Bhabha considers to be implicit in Said's Orientalism, that 'power and discourse is possessed entirely by the coloniser.' Bhabha reiterates the proposition of anti-colonialist writing that the objective of colonial discourse is to construe the colonized as a racially degenerate population in order to justify conquest and rule. However because he maintains that relations of power and knowledge function ambivalently, he argues that a discursive system split in enunciation, constitutes a dispersed and variously positioned native who by (mis)appropriating the terms of the dominant ideology, is able to intercede against and resist this mode of construction.

In dissenting from analysis ascribing an intentionality and unidirectionality to colonial power which, in Said's words, enabled Europe to advance unmetaphorically upon the Orient, Bhabha insists that this not only ignores representation as a concept articulating both the historical and the fantasmatic, but unifies the subject of colonial enunciation in a fixed position as the passive object of discursive domination. By revealing the multiple and contradictory articulations in colonialism's address, Bhabha as contemporary critic seeks to demonstrate the limits of its discursive power and to countermand its demand 'that its discourse (be) non-dialogic, its enunciation unitary' (Bhabha 1985a: 100); and by showing the wide range of stereotypes and the shifting subject positions assigned to the colonized in the colonialist text, he sets out to liberate the colonial from its debased inscription as Europe's monolithic and shackled Other, and into an autonomous native 'difference.' However, this reappropriation although effected by the deconstructions of the post-colonial intellectual, is made possible by uncovering how the master-discourse had already been interrogated by the colonized in native accents. For Bhabha, the subaltern has spoken, and his readings of the colonialist text recover a native voice. . . .

Where Spivak in inspecting the absence of a text that can answer back after the planned epistemic violence of the imperialist project, finds pockets of non-co-operation in the dubious place of the free will of the (female) sexed subject' (Spivak 1985a: 144), Bhabha produces for scrutiny a discursive situation making for recurrent instances of transgression performed by the native from within and against colonial discourse. Here the autocolonization of the native who meets the requirements of colonialist address, is co-extensive with the evasions and 'sly civility' through which the native refuses to satisfy the demand of the colonizer's narrative. This concept of mimicry has since been further developed in the postulate of 'hybridity' as the problematic of colonial discourse.

Bhabha contends that when re-articulated by the native, the colonialist desire for a reformed, recognizable, nearly-similar other, is enacted as

41

parody, a dramatization to be distinguished from the 'exercise of dependent colonial relations through narcissistic identification.' For in the 'hybrid moment' what the native rewrites is not a copy of the colonialist original, but a qualitatively different thing-in-itself, where misreadings and incongruities expose the uncertainties and ambivalences of the colonialist text and deny it an authorizing presence. Thus a textual insurrection against the discourse of colonial authority is located in the natives' interrogation of the English book within the terms of their own system of cultural meanings, a displacement which is read back from the record written by colonialism's agents and ambassadors:

> Through the natives' strange questions it is possible to see, with historical hindsight, what they resisted in questioning the presence of the English – as religious mediation and as cultural and linguistic medium. . . . To the extent to which discourse is a form of defensive warfare, then mimicry marks those moments of civil disobedience within the discipline of civility: signs of spectacular resistance. When the words of the master become the site of hybridity – the warlike sign of the native – then we may not only read between the lines, but even seek to change the often coercive reality that they so lucidly contain.
>
> (Bhabha 1985a: 101, 104)

Despite a flagrantly ambivalent presentation which leaves it vulnerable to innocent misconstruction, Bhabha's theorizing succeeds in making visible those moments when colonial discourse already disturbed at its source by a doubleness of enunciation, is further subverted by the object of its address; when the scenario written by colonialism is given a performance by the native that estranges and undermines the colonialist script. The argument is not that the colonized possesses colonial power, but that its fracturing of the colonialist text by re-articulating it in broken English, perverts the meaning and message of the English book ('insignia of colonial authority and signifier of colonial desire and discipline,' 1985a: 89), and therefore makes an absolute exercise of power impossible.

A narrative which delivers the colonized from its discursive status as the illegitimate and refractory foil to Europe, into a position of 'hybridity' from which it is able to circumvent, challenge and refuse colonial authority, has no place for a totalizing notion of epistemic violence. Nor does the conflictual economy of the colonialist text allow for the unimpeded operation of discursive aggression: 'What is articulated in the doubleness of colonial discourse is not the violence of one powerful nation writing out another [but] a mode of contradictory utterance that ambivalently re-inscribes both coloniser and colonised.' The effect of this thesis is to displace the traditional anti-colonialist representation of antagonistic forces locked in struggle, with a configuration of discursive transactions: 'The place of difference and otherness, or the space of the adversarial, within such a system of "disposal" as I've proposed, is never entirely on the outside or implacably oppositional.' (95)

Those who have been or are still engaged in colonial struggles against contemporary forms of imperialism could well read the theorizing of discourse analysts with considerable disbelief at the construction this puts on the situation they are fighting against and the contest in which they are engaged. This is not a charge against the difficulty of the analyses but an observation that these alternative narratives of colonialism obscure the 'murderous and decisive struggle between two protagonists' (Fanon 1961: 30), and discount or write out the counter-discourses which every liberation movement records. The significant differences in the critical practices of Spivak and Bhabha are submerged in a shared programme marked by the exorbitation of discourse and a related incuriosity about the enabling socioeconomic and political institutions and other forms of social praxis. Furthermore, because their theses admit of no point outside of discourse from which opposition can be engendered, their project is concerned to place incendiary devices within the dominant structures of representation and not to confront these with another knowledge. For Spivak, imperialism's epistemic bellicosity decimated the old culture and left the colonized without the ground from which they could utter confrontational words; for Bhabha, the stratagems and subterfuges to which the native resorted, destabilized the effectivity of the English book but did not write an alternative text – with whose constitution Bhabha declines to engage, maintaining that an anti-colonialist discourse 'requires an alternative set of questions, techniques and strategies in order to construct it' (Bhabha 1983a: 198).

Within another critical mode which also rejects totalizing abstracts of power as falsifying situations of domination and subordination, the notion of hegemony is inseparable from that of a counter-hegemony. In this theory of power and contest, the process of procuring the consent of the oppressed and the marginalized to the existing structure of relationships through ideological inducements, necessarily generates dissent and resistance, since the subject is conceived as being constituted by means of incommensurable solicitations and heterogeneous social practices. The outcome of this agonistic exchange, in which those addressed challenge their interlocutors, is that the hegemonic discourse is ultimately abandoned as scorched earth when a different discourse, forged in the process of disobedience and combat, occupying new, never-colonized and 'utopian' territory, and prefiguring other relationships, values and aspirations, is enunciated. At a time when dialectical thinking is not the rage amongst colonial discourse theorists, it is instructive to recall how Fanon's dialogical interrogation of European power and native insurrection reconstructs a process of cultural resistance and cultural disruption, participates in writing a text that can answer colonialism back, and anticipates another condition beyond imperialism:

> Face to face with the white man, the Negro has a past to legitimate, a
> vengeance to extract. . . . In no way should I dedicate myself to the

43

revival of an unjustly unrecognized Negro civilization. I will not make
myself a man of the past. . . . I am not a prisoner of history; it is only
by going beyond the historical, instrumental hypothesis that I will
initiate the cycle of my freedom.

(Fanon 1952: 225–6, 229, 231)

The enabling conditions for Fanon's analysis are that an oppositional
discourse born in political struggle, and at the outset invoking the past in
protest against capitulating to the colonizer's denigrations, supersedes a
commitment to archaic native traditions at the same time as it rejects
colonialism's system of knowledge:

The colonialist bourgeoisie had in fact deeply implanted in the minds
of the colonised intellectual that the essential qualities remain eternal
in spite of all the blunders men may make: the essential qualities of the
West, of course. The native intellectual accepted the cogency of these
ideas and deep down in his brain you could always find a vigilant
sentinel ready to defend the Greco-Latin pedestal. Now it so happens
that during the struggle for liberation, at the moment that the native
intellectual comes into touch again with his people, this artificial
sentinel is turned into dust. All the Mediterranean values, – the
triumph of the human individual of clarity and of beauty – become
lifeless, colourless knick-knacks. All those speeches seem like collec-
tions of dead words; those values which seemed to uplift the soul are
revealed as worthless, simply because they have nothing to do with the
concrete conflict in which the people is engaged.

(Fanon 1961: 37–8)

While conceding the necessity of defending the past in a move away
from unqualified assimilation of the occupying power's culture, Fanon
recognizes the limitations on the writer and intellectual who utilize 'techniques and language which are borrowed from the stranger in his country.'
Such transitional writing reinterpreting old legends 'in the light of a
borrowed aestheticism and of a conception of the world which was
discovered under other skies,' is for Fanon but a prelude to a literature of
combat which 'will disrupt literary styles and themes . . . create a
completely new public' and mould the national consciousness, 'giving it
form and contours and flinging open before it new and boundless
horizons.' Fanon's theory projects a development inseparable from a
community's engagement in combative social action, during which a native
contest initially enunciated in the invaders' language, culminates in a rejection of imperialism's signifying system. This is a move which colonial
discourse theory has not taken on board, and for such a process to be investigated, a cartography of imperialist ideology more extensive than its
address in the colonialist space, as well as a conception of the native as
historical subject and agent of an oppositional discourse is needed.

44

# 6

## The Scramble for Post-colonialism

### STEPHEN SLEMON*

'POST-COLONIALISM', AS IT is now used in its various fields, de-scribes a remarkably heterogeneous set of subject positions, professional fields, and critical enterprises. It has been used as a way of ordering a critique of total-ising forms of Western historicism; as a portmanteau term for a retooled notion of 'class', as a subset of both postmodernism and post-structuralism (and conversely, as the condition from which those two structures of cultural logic and cultural critique themselves are seen to emerge); as the name for a condition of nativist longing in post-independence national groupings; as a cultural marker of non-residency for a third-world intellectual cadre; as the inevitable underside of a fractured and ambivalent discourse of colonialist power; as an oppositional form of 'reading practice'; and – and this was my first encounter with the term – as the name for a category of 'literary' activity which sprang from a new and welcome political energy going on within what used to be called 'Commonwealth' literary studies. The obvious tendency, in the face of this heterogeneity, is to understand 'post-colonialism' mostly as an object of desire for critical practice: as a shimmering talisman that in itself has the power to confer political legitimacy onto specific forms of institu-tionalised labour, especially on ones that are troubled by their mediated position within the apparatus of institutional power. I think, however, that this heterogeneity in the concept of the 'post-colonial' – and here I mean within the university institution – comes about for much more pragmatic reasons, and these have to do with a very real problem in securing the concept of 'colonialism' itself, as Western theories of subjectification and its resis-tances continue to develop in sophistication and complexity.

The nature of colonialism as an economic and political structure of cross-cultural domination has of course occasioned a set of debates, but it is not really on this level that the 'question' of European colonialism has troubled the various post-colonial fields of study. The problem, rather, is

* From 'The Scramble for Post-colonialism' in Chris Tiffin and Alan Lawson (eds) *De-Scribing Empire: Post-colonialism and Textuality* London: Routledge, 1994.

with the concept of colonialism as an ideological or discursive formation: that is, with the ways in which colonialism is viewed as an apparatus for constituting subject positions through the field of representation. In a way – and of course this is an extreme oversimplification – the debate over a description of colonialism's multiple strategies for regulating Europe's others can be expressed diagrammatically (see Figure 1)

The general understanding that colonialism works on a left-to-right order of domination, with line 'A' representing various theories of how colonialism oppresses through direct political and economic control, and lines 'BC' and 'DE' representing differing concepts of the ideological regulation of colonial subjects, of subordination through the manufacture of consent. Theories that recognise an efficacy to colonialism that proceeds along line 'A' are in essence 'brute force' or 'direct political' theories of colonialist oppression: that is, they reject the basic thesis that power manages social contradiction partly through the strategic production of specific ideas of the 'self' – which subordinated groups then internalise as being 'real'. Theories, however, that examine the trajectory of colonialist power primarily along line 'BC' – a line representing an ideological flanking for the economic colonialism running along line 'A' – focus on the constitutive power of state apparatuses like education, and the constitutive

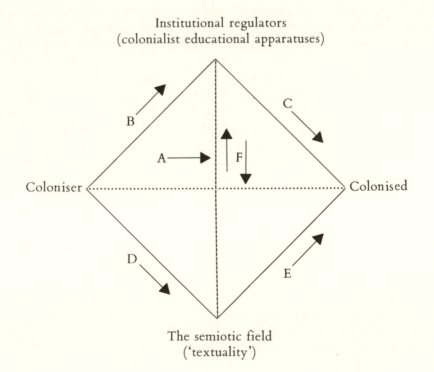

*Figure 1* Diagram representing the debate over the nature of colonialism

46

power of professional fields of knowledge within those apparatuses, in the production of colonialist relations. Along this line, Edward Said (1978) examines the political efficacy of 'orientalism' within colonialism; Talal Asad (1973) and many others examine the role of anthropology in reproducing colonial relations; Alan Bishop (1990) examines the deployment of Western concepts of 'mathematics' against African school-children, Timothy Mitchell (1988) examines how the professional field of 'political science' came into being through a European colonialist engagement with the cultures of Egypt; Gauri Viswanathan (1989) examines the foundations of 'English' literary studies within a structure of colonialist management in India. This work keeps coming in, and the list of radically compromised professional fields within the Western syllabus of 'humanities' options grows daily longer. Theories that focus primarily on line 'DE' in this diagram examine the ways in which ideology reproduces colonialist relations through the strategic deployment of a vast semiotic field of representations – in literary works, in advertising, in sculpture, in travelogues, in exploration documents, in maps, in pornography, and so on.

This pattern, as I've laid it out so far, does not seem especially controversial or problematic, but the difficulties arise at the moment of conceptualising the *relation* between colonialist professional fields and institutions (at the top of the diagram) and the whole field of representation (at the bottom of the diagram) – the field of 'textuality' and its investment in reproducing and naturalising the structures of power. To take up one example of this paradigmatically: in Edward Said's work on Orientalism, colonialist power is seen to operate through a complex relationship between apparatuses placed on line 'F', where in the first instance a scholarly educational apparatus called 'Orientalism' – at the top of the line – appropriates textual representations of 'the Orient' in order to consolidate itself as a discipline and to reproduce 'the Orient' as a deployable unit of knowledge. So, in the first instance, colonialist power in Said's argument runs not just through the middle ground of this chart but through a complex set of relations happening along line 'F'; and since Said's thesis is that a function at the top of this line is employing those representations created at the bottom of the line in order to make up 'knowledges' that have an ideological function, you can say that the vector of motion along line F is an upward one, and that this upward motion is part of the whole complex, discursive structure whereby 'Orientalism' manufactures the 'Orient' and thus helps to regulate colonialist relations. That is Said's first position – that under Orientalism the vector of line 'F' is upward. But in Said's analysis, colonialist power also runs through line F in a downward movement, where the scholarly apparatus of Orientalism is understood to be at work in the production of a purely fantastic and entirely projected idea of the 'Orient'. The point is that in the process of understanding the multivalent nature of colonialist discourse in terms of the historical specific of 'Orientalism', Said's model becomes structurally ambivalent – under

'Orientalism', the 'Orient' turns out to be something produced both as an object of scholarly knowledge and as a location for psychic projection – and I've tried to graph this ambivalence as a double movement or vector along line 'F'. For Said, the mechanism that produces this 'Orient', then, has to be understood as something capable of deploying an ambivalent structure of relations along line 'F', and deploying that structure towards a unified end. And so Said (and here I'm following Robert Young's (1990) analysis of the problem) ends up referring the whole structure of colonialist discourse back to a single and monolithic originating intention within colonialism, the intention of colonialist power to possess the terrain of its Others. That assumption of intention is basically where Said's theory has proven to be most controversial.

Said's text is an important one here, for as Robert Young has shown, Said's work stands at the headwaters of colonial discourse theory, and this ambivalence in Said's model may in fact initiate a *foundational* ambivalence in the critical work which comes out of this field. This ambivalence sets the terms for what are now the two central debates within colonial discourse theory: the debate over historical specificity, and the debate over agency.

The first debate – the debate over the problem of historical specificity in the model – concerns the inconclusive relation between actual historical moments in the colonialist enterprise and the larger, possibly trans-historical discursive formation that colonial discourse theory posits in its attempt to understand the multivalent strategies at work in colonialist power. Can you look at 'colonial discourse' only by examining what are taken to be paradigmatic moments within colonialist history?

If so, can you extrapolate a modality of 'colonialism' from one historical moment to the next? Does discursive colonialism always look structurally the same, or do the specifics of its textual or semiotic or representational manoeuvres shift registers at different historical times and in different kinds of colonial encounters? And what would it mean to think of colonial discourse as a set of exchanges that function in similar ways for all sorts of colonialist strategies in a vastly different set of cultural locations? These questions of historical specificity, though always a problem for social theory, are especially difficult ones for colonialist discourse theory, and the reason for this is that this theory quite appropriately refuses to articulate a simplistic structure of social causality in the relation between colonialist institutions and the field of representations. In other words, colonial discourse theory recognises a radical ambivalence at work in colonialist power, and that is the ambivalence I have attempted to show in Fig. 1 as a double moment in vector at the level of line 'F'.

To clarify this I want to make use of Gauri Viswanathan's important work on Britain's ideological control of colonised people through the deployment of colonialist educational strategies in nineteenth-century India. Obviously, the question of what happens along line 'F' can only be addressed by specific reference to immediate historical conditions, and every piece of archaeological work on colonialist power will want to formulate the vector of action here with particular sensitivity to the local conditions under analysis. Viswanathan researches this part of the puzzle with exemplary attention to history, and at heart her argument is that colonialist education in India (which would stand in as the ideological apparatus at the top of the diagram) strategically and intentionally deployed the vast field of canonical English 'literature' (the field of representations at the bottom of the diagram) in order to construct a cadre of 'native' mediators between the British Raj and the actual producers of wealth. The point here is that Viswanathan's analysis employs a purely upward vector of motion to characterise the specifics of how power is at work along line 'F' in the diagram, and what secures this vector is Viswanathan's scrupulous attention to the immediate conditions that apply within British and Indian colonial relations.

The problem, though – and here I mean the problem for colonial discourse theory – is that the foundational ambivalence or double movement that Said's work inserts into the model of colonialist discourse analysis always seems to return to the field; and it does so through critical work that on its own terms suggests a counter-flow along line 'F' at the same moment of colonialist history. That is, the residual ambivalence in the vector of line 'F' within colonial discourse theory seems to invite the fusion of Viswanathan's kind of analysis with critical readings that would articulate a downward movement at this place in the diagram; and one of the areas such work is now entering is the analysis of how English literary activity of the period (at the bottom of line 'F') suddenly turned to the *representation* of educational processes (at the top of the line), and why this literature should so immediately concern itself with the investments of educational representations in the colonialist scene. In examining the place of English literary activity within this moment of colonialist history, that is, a critic such as Patrick Brantlinger would want to argue for the valency of texts such as *Jane Eyre* or *Tom Brown's School Days* within colonialist discursive power, and colonialist discourse theory would want to understand how both kinds of discursive regulation, both vectors of movement along line 'F', are at work in a specific historical moment of colonialist relations. Because of Said's ambivalence in charting out the complex of Orientalism along line 'F', I am arguing, the field of colonialist discourse theory carries that sense of ambivalence forward, and looks to an extraordinary valency of movement within its articulation of colonialist power. The ambivalence makes our understanding of colonial operations a great deal clearer for historical periods but it also upsets the positivism of highly specific analyses of colonialist power going on *within* a period.

The basic project of colonial discourse theory is to push out from line 'A', and try to define colonialism both as a set of political relations and as a signifying system, one with ambivalent structural relations. It is remarkably clarifying in its articulation of the productive relations between seemingly disparate moments in colonialist power (the structure of literary education in India, the literary practice of representing educational control in Britain), but because it recognises an ambivalence in colonialist power, colonial discourse theory results in a concept of colonialism that cannot be historicised modally, and that ends up being tilted towards a description of all kinds of social oppression and discursive control. For some critics, this ambivalence bankrupts the field. But for others, the concept of 'colonialism' – like the concept of 'patriarchy' for feminism, which shares this structure of transhistoricality and lack of specificity – remains an indispensable conceptual category of critical analysis, and an indispensable tool in securing our understanding of ideological domination under colonialism to the level of political economy.

The first big debate going on within colonialist discourse theory, then, is a debate over what happens when a model of 'colonial discourse' is carried beyond its scattered moments of archaeological research and is taken up as a general structure of oppression. I want now to turn to the second big debate going on between theorists of colonialist discourse; and that is the debate over the question of *agency* under colonialist power. Basically, the question of agency can be restated as a question of who or what acts oppositionally, when ideology or discourse or psychic processes of some kind construct human subjects, and the question of specifying agency is becoming an extremely complex one in all forms of critical theory at present. Again, however, this debate has especial urgency within colonial discourse theory, and, again, that is because this theory recognises foundationally that the vector of line 'F' in Fig. 1 remains ambivalent at every moment of colonialist discursive control. . . .

I want to stress the presuppositional location of this post-colonial scramble – I want to articulate its foundations within the problematic of colonial discourse theory and within an unresolved debate within the Western humanities institution – because I suspect that at times workers in various orders of post-colonial analysis are made to feel a disempowering energy at work in their field – a disempowerment which stems from their sense that these debates ought to be resolved within post-colonial studies itself. And I also raise the question of an effect to these debates, not because I want to suggest they are anything other than crucial ones for the field, but because I think the terrain of post-colonial studies remains in danger of becoming colonised by competing academic methodologies, and being reparcelled into institutional pursuits that have no abiding interest in the specifics of either colonialist history or post-colonial agency. One of the most exciting research projects now going on in colonial discourse analysis, for example, is Homi Bhabha's theorising of colonialist ambivalence, and his attempt to carry that analysis forward to a wholesale critique of Western modernity. It is possibly instructive, therefore, that in the process of expressing admiration for his work, the post-structuralist critic Robert

Young inserts Bhabha's project into a narrative of unpackaging whose terms of reference are entirely European in origin: the radical restructuring of European historiography, and the allocation of alterity to the theatre of the European postmodern.

Along parallel lines, it is also instructive that Henry Louis Gates Jr. notes in Spivak's deconstructive brilliance a remarkable conflation between colonial discourse and Derrida's concept of writing itself – an argument, that is, that there is '*nothing* outside of (the discourse of) colonialism', and that all discourse must be nothing other than colonial discourse itself. Gates warns of a hidden consequence in this elevation in ascendency of the colonial paradigm by questioning what happens when we elide, for example, 'the distance between political repression and individual neurosis: the *positional* distance between Steve Biko and, say, Woody Allen?' (Gates 1991: 466) His argument is that academic interest in this history and the discourse of colonialism bids fair to become the last bastion for the project of global theory and for European universalism itself, and he asks us whether we really need to choose between oppositional critics whose articulations of the post-colonial institutionalise themselves as agonistic struggles over a thoroughly disciplined terrain.

I would like to echo Gates' sentiments in the face of this balkanisation; and in the absence of any real solutions to this crisis in the field I'd like to offer a two-part credo towards post-colonial work as it takes place within the Western academic institution. First, I think, post-colonial studies, if nothing else, needs to become more tolerant of methodological difference, at least when that difference is articulated towards emancipatory anti-colonialist ends. I am reminded that the great war within the Western 'humanities' is carried on the back of critical methodology and its competing orders, and that in many ways the subject-making function of the humanities is effected precisely in that debate. I have seen no evidence that the humanities carry any special brief for the global project of decolonisation, and so I would desperately want to preserve this function of decolonising commitment for post-colonial studies, despite its necessary investment in and ironic relation to the humanities complex. I am suspicious of the kind of argument that would insist on the necessary conflation of the diagram I put forward in this paper with a colonialist allegorical function, but I can see how the argument could be made. The tools for conceptual disempowerment in the struggle over method are going to remain available within post-colonial studies, but I remain suspicious of ahistorical and I think intolerant calls for homogeneity in a field of study which embraces radically different forms and functions of colonialist oppression and radically different notions of anti-colonialist agency.

Tolerance is never simply passive, and, ironically, the area of institutionalised post-colonial studies is finding itself increasingly invested in an academic star system of astonishing proportions, and through that star system it is learning to seek its instruction in oppositional tactics along lines that run increasingly and monolithically backward towards the centres of Western power. I cannot help noticing, for example, that in what Hortense Spillers calls the politics of mention, our theoretical masters in Paris or Oxford or New Haven are read and referenced by exemplary theorists of the local – the critic J. Michael Dash at the Mona campus in Jamaica is an example – but those metropolitan theorists seldom reference these cultural and theoretical mediators in return. Post-colonial studies should have an investment in open talk across cultural locations, however, and across methodological dynasties; and I think we do damage to the idea of post-coloniality at an immediate political level when that investment in cross-talk runs only one way.

As for the second part of this credo, I believe that post-colonial studies needs always to remember that its referent in the real world is a form of political, economic, and discursive oppression whose name, first and last, is *colonialism*. The forms of colonialist power differ radically across cultural locations, and its intersections with other orders of oppression are always complex and multivalent. But, wherever a globalised theory of the colonial might lead us, we need to remember that resistances to colonialist power always find material presence at the level of the local, and so the research and training we carry out in the field of post-colonialism, what-ever else it does, must always find ways to address the local, if only on the order of material applications. If we overlook the local, and the political applications of the research we produce, we risk turning the work of our field into the playful operations of an academic glass-bead game, whose project will remain at best a description of global relations, and not a script for their change. There is never a necessary politics to the study of politi-cal actions and reactions; but at the level of the local, and at the level of material applications, post-colonialism must address the material exigen-cies of colonialism and neo-colonialism, including the neo-colonialism of Western academic institutions themselves.

# PART II

## Universality and Difference

# Introduction

The concept of universalism is one of particular interest to post-colonial writers because it is this notion of a unitary and homogeneous human nature which marginalises and excludes the distinctive characteristics, the difference, of post-colonial societies. A crucial insistence of post-colonial theory is that, despite a shared experience of colonialism, the cultural realities of post-colonial societies may differ vastly. The washing out of cultural difference becomes a prominent effect of European literary criticism, since some appeal to the essential humanity of readers has been constructed as a function of the value and significance of the literary work. We are often told that what makes Shakespeare or Dante or Goethe 'great' is their ability to reveal something of 'the universal human condition'. Indeed the universality of writers has been invoked in literature discussions across the English-speaking world as an infallible sign of their stature or their 'seriousness'. The myth of universality is thus a primary strategy of imperial control as it is manifested in literary study and that is why it demands attention early on in this Reader. The universalist myth has, according to Chinua Achebe, a pernicious effect in the kind of colonialist criticism which denigrates the post-colonial text on the basis of an assumption that 'European' equals 'universal'. But even a brief analysis of the 'universal human condition' finds it disappearing into an endless network of provisional and specific determinations in which even the most apparently 'essential' features of human life become provisional and contingent.

The assumption of universalism is a fundamental feature of the construction of colonial power because the 'universal' features of humanity are the characteristics of those who occupy positions of political dominance. It is these people who are 'human', who have a legitimate history, who live in 'the world'. Because language is a discourse of power, in that it provides the terms and the structures by which individuals have a world, a method by which the 'real' is determined, notions of universality can, like the language which suggests them, become imperialistic. The language itself implies certain assumptions about the world, a certain history, a certain way of seeing. If one's own language, or one's immediate perceptions of the world do not concur then they must be suppressed in favour of that which the language itself reveals to be 'obvious'.

George Lamming has reminded us in his essay 'The Occasion for Speaking' of Hegel's assertion that the African is somehow outside of History, that Africa is 'no historical part of the world'. This is simply because History is the story of 'Civilisation' and it is only when that language becomes 'appropriated' by other cultures that the very concept of history can be questioned, and that the universal condition of humanity can be revealed as far more heterogeneous. At a strategic moment in the British occupation of India, English literature was invoked precisely for its imputed power to convey universal values. As Gauri Viswanathan points out, the concept of universalism became part of the technology of Empire: when the introduction of Christianity was considered by the Indian colonial adminis-tration to be too great a threat to good order, the 'universal' discourse of english literature (see n.1, p. 4) was consciously adopted as the vehicle for educating the Indian élites in tenets of civilised morality.

Not only is the supposed universal human nature found to be spurious when the post-colonial engages the European text ('What is a kiss?' asks Charles Larson's African student) but it is not even true of that most 'universal' of discourses – mathematics – as is explained by Alan Bishop. Yet such assumptions about literature and its relationship to human life profoundly influence the critical reception of post-colonial literatures. And not only is it true of both conservative and liberal humanism, but it also insidiously affects the responses of those critics who, like Frederic Jameson, passionately argue for a consideration of literatures other than the trans-Atlantic. Aijaz Ahmad points out the degree to which the habit of 'worldism' (as in first, second and third worldism), can obliterate the cultural distinc-tions between societies. The value of post-colonial discourse is that it provides a methodology for considering the dialogue of similarity and difference; the similarity of colonialism's political and historical pressure upon non-European societies, alongside the plurality of specific cultural effects and responses those societies have produced.

# 7

## Colonialist Criticism

### CHINUA ACHEBE*

WHEN MY FIRST novel was published in 1958 a very unusual review of it was written by a British woman, Honor Tracy, who is perhaps not so much a critic as a literary journalist. But what she said was so intriguing that I have never forgotten it. If I remember rightly she headlined it 'Three cheers for mere Anarchy!' The burden of the review itself was as follows: These bright Negro barristers . . . who talk so glibly about African culture, how would they like to return to wearing raffia skirts? How would novelist Achebe like to go back to the mindless times of his grandfather instead of holding the modern job he has in broadcasting in Lagos?

I should perhaps point out that colonialist criticism is not always as crude as this but the exaggerated grossness of a particular example may sometimes prove useful in studying the anatomy of the species. There are three principal parts here: Africa's inglorious past (raffia skirts) to which Europe brings the blessing of civilization (Achebe's modern job in Lagos) and for which Africa returns ingratitude (sceptical novels like *Things Fall Apart*).

Before I go on to more advanced varieties I must give one more example of the same kind as Honor Tracy's which on account of its recentness (1970) actually surprised me:

> The British administration not only safeguarded women from the worst tyrannies of their masters, it also enabled them to make their long journeys to farm or market without armed guard, secure from the menace of hostile neighbours. The Nigerian novelists who have written the charming and bucolic accounts of domestic harmony in African rural communities, are the sons whom the labours of these women educated; the peaceful village of their childhood to which they nostalgically look back was one which had been purged of bloodshed and

* From *Hopes and Impediments: Selected Essays 1965–1987* London: Heinemann, 1988. Based on a paper read to the association for Commonwealth Literature and Language Studies at Makere University, Uganda 1974.

alcoholism by an ague-ridden district officer and a Scottish mission lassie whose years were cut short by every kind of intestinal parasite.

It is even true to say that one of the most nostalgically convincing of the rural African novelists used as his sourcebook not the memories of his grandfathers but the records of the despised British anthropologists. The modern African myth-maker hands down a vision of colonial rule in which the native powers are chivalrously viewed through the eyes of the hard-won liberal tradition of the late Victorian scholar, while the expatriates are shown as schoolboys' blackboard caricatures.

(Andreski 1971: 26)

I have quoted this at such length because first of all I am intrigued by Iris Andreski's literary style which recalls so faithfully the sedate prose of the district officer government anthropologist of sixty or seventy years ago – a tribute to her remarkable powers of identification as well as to the durability of colonialist rhetoric. 'Tyrannies of their masters' . . . 'menace of hostile neighbours' . . . 'purged of bloodshed and alcoholism'. But in addition to this Iris Andreski advances the position taken by Honor Tracy in one significant and crucial direction – its claim to a deeper knowledge and a more reliable appraisal of Africa than the educated African writer has shown himself capable of.

To the colonialist mind it was always of the utmost importance to be able to say: 'I know my natives', a claim which implied two things at once: (a) that the native was really quite simple and (b) that understanding him and controlling him went hand in hand – understanding being a precondition for control and control constituting adequate proof of understanding. Thus in the heyday of colonialism any serious incident of native unrest, carrying as it did disquieting intimations of slipping control, was an occasion not only for pacification by the soldiers but also (afterwards) for a royal commission of inquiry – a grand name for yet another perfunctory study of native psychology and institutions. Meanwhile a new situation was slowly developing as a handful of natives began to acquire European education and then to challenge Europe's presence and position in their native land with the intellectual weapons of Europe itself. To deal with this phenomenal presumption the colonialist devised two contradictory arguments. He created the 'man of two worlds' theory to prove that no matter how much the native was exposed to European influences he could never truly absorb them; like Prester John[1] he would always discard the mask of civilization when the crucial hour came and reveal his true face. Now, did this mean that the educated native was no different at all from his brothers in the bush? Oh, no! He was different; he was worse. His abortive effort at education and culture though leaving him totally unredeemed and unregenerated had none the less done something to him – it had deprived him of his links with his own people whom he no longer even understood and who certainly wanted none of his dissatisfaction or pretensions. 'I know my natives; they are delighted with the way things are. It's only these half-educated ruffians who don't even know their own people.' How often one heard that and the many variations of it in colonial times! And how almost amusing to find its legacy in the colonialist criticism of our literature today! Iris Andreski's book is more than old wives' tales, at least in intention. It is clearly inspired by the desire to undercut the educated African witness (the modern myth-maker, she calls him) by appealing direct to the unspoilt woman of the bush who has retained a healthy gratitude for Europe's intervention in Africa. This desire accounts for all that reliance one finds in modern European travellers' tales on the evidence of 'simple natives' – houseboys, cooks, drivers, schoolchildren – supposedly more trustworthy than the smart alecs. . . .

In his book, *The Emergence of African Fiction*, Charles Larson tells us a few revealing things about universality. In a chapter devoted to Lenrie Peters's novel which he finds particularly impressive he speaks of its universality, its very limited concern with Africa itself. Then he goes on to spell it all out:

> That it is set in Africa appears to be accidental, for, except for a few comments at the beginning, Peters's story might just as easily take place in the southern part of the United States or in the southern regions of France- or Italy. If a few names of characters and places were changed one would indeed feel that this was an American novel. In short, Peters's story is universal.
>
> (Larson 1971: 230)

But Larson is obviously not as foolish as this passage would make him out to be, for he ends it on a note of self-doubt which I find totally disarming. He says:

> Or am I deluding myself in considering the work universal? Maybe what I really mean is that The Second Round is to a great degree Western and therefore scarcely African at all. (238)

I find it hard after that to show more harshness than merely agreeing about his delusion. But few people I know are prepared to be so charitable. In a recent review of the book in *Okike*, a Nigerian critic, Omolara Leslie, mocks 'the shining faith that we are all Americans under the skin'.

Does it ever occur to these universities to try out their game of changing names of characters and places in an American novel, say, a Philip Roth or an Updike, and slotting in African names just to see how it works? But of course it would not occur to them. It would never occur to them to doubt the universality of their own literature. In the nature of things the work of a Western writer is automatically informed by universality. It is only others who must strain to achieve it. So-and-so's work is universal; he has truly arrived! As though universality were some distant bend in the road which you may take if you travel out far enough in the direction of Europe or America, if you put adequate distance between yourself and your home. I should like to see the word 'universal' banned altogether from discussions of African literature until such a time as people cease to use it as a synonym for the narrow, self-serving parochialism of Europe, until their horizon extends to include all the world. If colonialist criticism were merely irritating one might doubt the justification of devoting a whole essay to it. But strange though it may sound some of its ideas and precepts do exert an influence on our writers, for it is a fact of our contemporary world that Europe's powers of persuasion can be far in excess of the merit and value of her case. Take for instance the black writer who seizes on the theme that Africa's past is a sadly inglorious one as though it were something new that had not already been 'proved' adequately for him. Colonialist critics will, of course, fall all over him in ecstatic and salivating admiration – which is neither unexpected nor particularly interesting. What is fascinating, however, is the tortuous logic and sophistry they will sometimes weave around a perfectly straightforward and natural enthusiasm.

A review of Yambo Ouologuem's *Bound to Violence* (1968b) by a Philip M. Allen in the *Pan-African Journal* (Allen 1971) was an excellent example of sophisticated, even brilliant colonialist criticism. The opening sentence alone would reward long and careful examination; but I shall content myself here with merely quoting it:

> The achievement of Ouologuem's much discussed, impressive, yet over-praised novel has less to do with whose ideological team he's playing on than with the *forcing of moral universality on African civilization.* (my italics)

A little later Mr Allen expounds on this new moral universality:

> This morality is not only 'un-African' – denying the standards set by omnipresent ancestors, the solidarity of communities, the legitimacy of social contract: it is a Hobbesian universe that extends beyond the wilderness, beyond the white man's myths of Africa, into all civilization, theirs and ours.

If you should still be wondering at this point how Ouologuem was able to accomplish that Herculean feat of forcing moral universality on Africa or with what gargantuan tools, Mr Allen does not leave you too long in suspense. Ouologuem is 'an African intellectual who has mastered both a style and a prevailing philosophy of French letters', able to enter 'the remote alcoves of French philosophical discourse'. . . .

That a 'critic' playing on the ideological team of colonialism should feel sick and tired of Africa's 'pathetic obsession with racial and cultural confrontation' should surprise no one. Neither should his enthusiasm for those African works that show 'no easy antithesis between white and black'. But an African who falls for such nonsense, not only in spite of Africa's so very recent history but, even more, in the face of continuing atrocities committed against millions of Africans in their own land by racist minority regimes, deserves a lot of pity. Certainly anyone, white or black, who chooses to see violence as the abiding principle of African civilization is free to do so. But let him not pass himself off as a restorer of dignity to Africa, or attempt to make out that he is writing about man and about the state of civilization in general. . . . Perhaps for most ordinary people what Africa needs is a far less complicated act of restoration. . . .

The colonialist critic, unwilling to accept the validity of sensibilities other than his own, has made a particular point of dismissing the African novel. He has written lengthy articles to prove its non-existence largely on the grounds that the novel is a peculiarly Western genre, a fact which would interest us if our ambition was to write 'Western' novels. But, in any case, did not the black people in America, deprived of their own musical instruments, take the trumpet and the trombone and blow them as they had never been blown before, as indeed they were not designed to be blown? And the result, was it not jazz? Is any one going to say that this was a loss to the world or that those first Negro slaves who began to play around with the discarded instruments of their masters should have played waltzes and foxtrots? No! Let every people bring their gifts to the great festival of the world's cultural harvest and mankind will be all the richer for the variety and distinctiveness of the offerings.

My people speak disapprovingly of an outsider whose wailing drowned the grief of the owners of the corpse. One last word to the owners. It is because our own critics have been somewhat hesitant in taking control of our literary criticism (sometimes – let's face it – for the good reason that we will not do the hard work that should equip us) that the task has fallen to others, some of whom (again we must admit) have been excellent and sensitive. And yet most of what remains to be done can best be tackled by ourselves, the owners. If we fall back, can we complain that others are rushing forward? A man who does not lick his lips, can he blame the harmattan for drying them?

## NOTE

1  From the novel (1910) of the same name by the imperial statesman and adventure writer, John Buchan.

# 8

# *Heroic Ethnocentrism*
## *The Idea of Universality in Literature*
### CHARLES LARSON*

IN THE FALL of 1962, when I began teaching English literature to high
school students in Nigeria, I encountered a number of stumbling blocks,
which I had in no way anticipated – all of them cultural, experiential. This
was not a matter of science or technology and their various by-products as
I had anticipated ('What is a flush toilet?') but, rather, matters related to
what I have learned to call culturally restricted materials. It was enough,
to be sure, just for my African students to read through a 450-page
Victorian novel (required reading in those days for the British-administered
school certificate examinations); and, as I later learned, in the lower levels
at least, students were accustomed to taking several months or even the
greater part of a year to read through and discuss the plot line of a single
novel. Length alone was enough to get them, since English was their second
language and the problem of vocabulary was especially troublesome. But
once the problems of language, vocabulary and verbosity had been overcome, reading through the words became a less difficult process than
understanding what the words themselves related – the 'experience of
literature' as we are wont to say.

'Excuse me, sir, what does it mean "to kiss"?' That was a much more
difficult question to answer than the usual ones relating to the plot or the
characters of the novel – a real shock when it was brought to my attention
that I had a rather naïve boy in my class. So I brushed the question off until
it was repeated a number of times and I slowly began to realize that all of
my students had no real idea of what it meant to kiss. This seemed an
extremely odd thing to me because most of my students were upper-form
boys in their late teens – some in their early twenties – and I had, of course,
heard them talking on occasion about their girl friends. It was also
rumoured that several of the boys were married, although by school regulations they were not supposed to be. Nevertheless, that question and

* From 'Heroic Ethnocentrism: The Idea of Universality in Literature' *The
American Scholar* 42(3) (Summer), 1973.

others of a like nature kept recurring – in part, no doubt, because we were reading Thomas Hardy's *Far from the Madding Crowd*. Why did Hardy's characters get so flustered when they were kissed (or more likely, when they weren't kissed)? When I asked one of the European-educated African teachers why my students always seemed ready to return to that same question, I was more than surprised to learn that Africans, traditionally at least, do not kiss; to learn that what I thought was 'natural' in one society is not natural at all, but learned, that is, cultural. Not all peoples kiss. Or, stated more appropriately, not all peoples have learned to kiss. (When I later attended American movies with Africans, I could understand why the audience often went into hysterics at the romantic scenes in the films.)

How was one to read a Thomas Hardy novel with all those frustrated kisses without ever having been kissed? How was I to explain something like this to my African students? Or, to limit my experience to a more technical matter concerning the novel's form which also perplexed my students, what about those long passages of description for which Hardy is so celebrated? My African students couldn't understand what page after page of description of the countryside had to do with the plot of the novel. What they had given me, as I later learned, was another clue to the differing ways in which culture shapes our interpretations of literature. It was not until I seriously began studying the African novel itself, however, that I could put all of those pieces together; just as the questions about those kisses revealed something about my African students' cultural background, so too, did their concern about the descriptive passages of Hardy's book. The fact that descriptive passages were virtually nonexistent in African fiction initially seemed particularly puzzling to me, since the first generation of African Anglophone novelists, at least, had been brought up almost entirely on the Victorian novel. Whereas other elements of the Victorian novel had found their way into the African novel, description had not. Could it be that this omission in the African novel revealed something basically different between African and Western attitudes toward nature, toward one's environment?

Kissing and description, attitudes toward love and nature – are these attitudes so different for the African? Is the African way of life less sophisticated than our own? Or is the belief that these supposedly 'universal' attitudes should be the same as ours the naïve one? Is this what we really mean when we talk about 'universality' in literature – if someone does not react to something in our literature the same way that we do, then he is to be considered inferior? Perhaps the term itself is meaningless. After all, people love and die in every culture. Their reactions to these events in their lives, however, may be significantly different from our own. And these reactions, in turn, shape their interpretations of literature.

For the most part, the term 'universal' has been grossly misused when it has been applied to non-Western literature, because it has so often been used in a way that ignores the multiplicity of cultural experiences. Usually, when we try to force the concept of universality on someone who is not Western, I think we are implying that our own culture should be the standard of measurement. Why else would we expect all peoples to react in the same way that we do? ... But let us return to those so-called universal experiences of all literature and illustrate some of the ways in which they may be radically different – at least for the African.

In his preface to Tsao-Hsueh-Chin's eighteenth-century Chinese novel, *Dream of the Red Chamber*, Mark Van Doren says, 'The greatest love stories have no time or place.' I frankly doubt this, in spite of other Western literary critics, who have also said that the most common theme in literature is love. (Leslie Fiedler, in his *Collected Essays*, for instance.) After reading dozens and dozens of contemporary African novels, I can in no way accept Van Doren's or Fiedler's assertions. There is at least one whole section of the world where the love story is virtually nonexistent. I can think of no contemporary African novel in which the central plot or theme can be called a 'love story,' no African novel in which the plot line progresses because of the hero's attempt to acquire a mate, no African novel in which seduction is the major goal, no African novel in which the fate of the lovers becomes the most significant element in the story. No African novel works this way because love as a theme in a Western literary sense is simply missing. Romantic love, seduction, sex – these are not the subjects of African fiction. In fact, in most contemporary African novels women play minor parts; the stories are concerned for the most part with a masculine world. There may be marriage, bride price and an occasional *tête à tête* but that is not the concern of the novel: it is always something else. There are no graphic descriptions of erotic love, there are no kisses, no holding hands. There is, in short, no love story as we have come to think of it in Western fiction. Not even the unrequited lover pining away. African fiction simply is not made of such stuff. ...

Western romance is only one theme that may puzzle the African reader. He may have trouble understanding the lack of concern about death in some Western novels, too. Or, what is more likely, the Western reader may totally miss the significance of a death in a piece of African fiction that he is reading. A. Alvarez, in his fine book, *The Savage God*, says that 'perhaps half the literature of the world is about death.' Yet our society has worked so hard to neutralize the shock of death that it is quite possible for us to miss the emotional overtones of a piece of African writing in which death occurs. Sembene Ousmane's celebrated short story, 'Black Girl' ('La noire de . . .') is one such example. The story concerns a young Senegalese girl named Diouana, who moves to Antibes when the French family she has worked for in Senegal returns to France. Ousmane begins his story by projecting us into Diouana's thoughts, illustrating her excitement and fascination at being able to have such a wonderful experience: the chance to live in France. But Diouana's dreams shortly become a nightmare. Overworked, isolated from her fellow Africans, called a nigger by the four children in the French family, after some months Diouana commits suicide by slashing her wrists in the bathtub. The Western reader may think that Ousmane's story is simply another rather melodramatic account of racial prejudice – which it is, in part. But it is also a story about modern slavery, and what that situation will drive the sane person into doing: taking his own life. Just as slaves jumped overboard to their deaths in the ocean in order to escape slavery in the New World, Diouana takes her own life to find release from her own enslaved situation. But this is only a part of it, for in committing suicide – one of the strongest taboos in many African societies – she has only temporarily released herself. She has trapped her ancestors, broken the cycle of life, and, if she is an only child, she has ended the family lineage. She has, in short, committed a terrible abomination, and the African reading the conclusion to Ousmane's story is horrified by what she has done. It is, therefore, the religious overtone relating to ancestral worship that the Western reader will probably be completely unaware of. . . .

The hero concept – the belief in the individual who is different from his fellowmen – is [also] almost totally alien to African life; and, as an extension of this, the hero in contemporary African fiction is for the most part non-existent. The hero is almost nonexistent in contemporary Western literature too, but his descendant, the anti-hero, the isolated figure, is a force to be reckoned with. This is not true of African fiction, however. Rather, it is the group-felt experience that is all important: what happens to the village, the clan, the tribe. . . .

One begins to wonder if two peoples as widely different as Africans and westerners will ever be able to read each other's literature and fully understand it. This is not, however, the question I started out to ask. Literature is not so limiting that only one interpretation is possible. We cannot all be both African and westerner, black and Caucasian. What is important, it seems to me, is that when we read a piece of non-Western literature we realize that the interpretation we make of it may be widely different from what the artist intended, and contrarily, that we should not expect people who are not of our own culture and heritage to respond in the same way that we do to our own literature. The time has come when we should avoid the use of the pejorative term 'universal.' What we really mean when we talk about universal experiences in literature are cultural responses that have been shaped by our own Western tradition.

Although most of the examples I have used in this essay are African in origin, I would hazard a final conjecture that the experience of other non-Western literatures (Chinese and Japanese, for example) will also support this belief that the word 'universal' is, indeed, limited. . . . For better or for worse, each of us was born into an ethnocentrically sealed world. The purpose of any piece of literature, no matter what culture it was produced in, is to show us something we were previously unaware of. Just as literature is a bridge connecting a life lived with a life not lived, so, too, all literature that is effective is a voyage into a previously untraveled world.

65

# 9

# *Entering Our Own Ignorance*
## *Subject–Object Relations in Commonwealth Literature*

### FLEMMING BRAHMS*

CHANGE IS THE key to the Commonwealth experience. Living in any Commonwealth country is profoundly different from living in Britain or any other country in the Old World. As a group the Commonwealth nations, however different they may be, share the experience of colonialism and its subsequent developments. Their histories vary, but they always need to be understood in terms of a dependence upon the imperial centre and a later movement towards independence. The different patterns of these social fabrics are all woven upon the common warp of a striving towards political, cultural and economic self-reliance. Few people would disagree with this, and most critics would agree that much of the literature produced in the Commonwealth deals with the nature of this newness and the effect it has upon the people living in these countries. In the post-colonial authors of the Third World we are struck by an enthusiasm and a sense of urgency to participate through their work in the re-creation of social and cultural selfhood; and in countries like Canada, Australia, and New Zealand we also find a strong sense of 'beginnings', a sense that life as a nation has only just begun and that the future is still being made. We might cite, for instance, the importance of the concept of 'landfall' in New Zealand literature, the prevalence of the political novel in African writing, and the West Indian and Canadian obsessions with cultural identity. But my point is much more cogently illustrated through reference to the subtitles chosen by W. H. New for the individual sections of his introduction to Commonwealth literature, *Among Worlds*: 'Patterns of Dislocation', 'The Politics of Freedom', 'In Search of Tomorrow's Traditions', 'Home Ground, Foreign Territory', 'Escape into Distance', 'In Response to a New Old Land', and 'Fastidious Antitheses' (New 1975). I have deliberately omitted the geographical references because one of the interesting aspects of this list is the fact that several of the terms could well have been applied to one or more of the other areas.

* From 'Entering Our Own Ignorance: Subject–Object Relations in Commonwealth Literature' *World Literature Written in English* 21(2) (Summer), 1982.

How do we as critics deal with these factors as they manifest themselves in the literature of the Commonwealth? It seems strange that the centrality of change in this experience and this literature is almost invariably negated by an inherent absolutism in the language of critics and theorists. As an example of this absolutism we may consider a comment by A. Norman Jeffares; having talked about the importance of writers in shaping new national identities, Jeffares goes on to discuss the significance of the Commonwealth context:

> To write, as Yeats put it, for one's own race, is obviously the most satisfactory situation for a writer. And yet the audience outside his immediate circle of friends, outside his own region, is very important. It is perhaps because of the existence of an outside and overseas audience that the different kinds of English written today in India, in Africa, in the Antipodes, in Asia, or in the West Indies, are not likely to become too local in interest, too diminished in continuity, too immediately appealing, and therefore, in the long run, too unacceptable throughout the world.
>
> (Jeffares 1965: xiii)

Here is a clear insistence upon the absolute value of the universal quilt of great literature. And if the passage cited conveys a curious sense of the colonial hegemony of the past being perpetuated on a cultural level, that impression is immediately reinforced when Jeffares seems, unwittingly, to be setting up an all too familiar model of the imperial centre drawing nourishment from the colonial periphery. From talking about the Commonwealth writer's position within his particular cultural situation he goes on to suggest his position within the British literary tradition:

> He can bring a special flavour: he can make a distinctive contribution to our common heritage. A language that is not renewed, that does not develop, can easily die. English at the moment is being enriched by the new usages of overseas writers. (xiii)

One could not possibly imagine the same scholar arguing that British writers 'bring a special flavour' to the 'common heritage', and this may confirm us in our suspicion that the universal values enunciated in the first quotation will turn out to be rather more 'immediately appealing' to readers in the Home Counties than to the overseas audience of the Commonwealth.

There are numerous instances in which the merits of works by Commonwealth writers have been called into question on the grounds of a specificity that runs counter to abstract universal concerns, and more often than not the established British tradition is invoked in order to drive the point home. Thus in his introduction to *The Commonwealth Pen*, A. L. McLeod states:

> Mere race and color problems never produce good literature. These problems have to become submerged in more universal themes. The

characters in Olive Schreiner's *The Story of an African Farm*, for instance, have genuine, human attributes and the book is a good novel because the author deals with human and universal values, just as E. M. Forster does in *A Passage to India* and Joseph Conrad does in *Heart of Darkness* or *Nigger of the Narcissus*, where Jim is the amalgam of many kinds of man, and not just a black man.

(McLeod 1961: 7–8)

The concept of the universal goes hand in hand with the perennial question of standards: these, too, are absolute and a priori entities which can be invoked whenever a statement is intended to be final and authoritative. We may return to Jeffares, discussing why we should read new Commonwealth writers:

True, one reads them because they tell us about the way their countries are evolving; true, one reads them because they enrich our pleasure in the English language, but in the cold light of judgement one reads them because they bring us new ideas, new interpretations of life to us. One reads them, in short, because they are good writers. The standards of judgement are not national standards. Standards of the critic must be cosmopolitan; only the best should be praised.

(Jeffares 1965: xiv)

And when we turn in the same volume to the 'Report and Recommendations' agreed upon at the 1964 Leeds conference on Commonwealth literature, we find the following paragraph under the heading 'Language, Literature, and University Courses':

University departments of English should include writings in English from any part of the world in the syllabuses of their formal academic courses, *provided that such works attain an appropriate academic standard.*

(emphasis added) (Press 1965: 212)

The implication is, of course, that such standards must be fixed and indisputable. . . .

Much of the energy of critics working in the Commonwealth field has been invested in the basic and very necessary task of gaining recognition for the new literatures. The time may have come, however, when we have to ask ourselves whether respectability has not, in fact, been won at the cost of an almost total, and probably often unconscious, subservience to a set of critical standards established at the literary centres of Britain and, to some extent, the United States. For Commonwealth writers, freedom to participate in the making of their own future will depend upon the degree to which they will allow not merely the past, but a past coming to them from somewhere else – in the form of an almost monolithic conception of the British literary tradition – to dominate their writing.

For a long time the established literary tradition has found itself operating at the two extreme poles of a continuum. These extremes are conventionally labelled the particular (or personal) and the universal. In the former the emphasis is upon the uniqueness of individual characters, who are regarded in relative isolation and whose personalities provide the impetus behind the conflicts in this action. In the latter the perspective is cosmic and eternal, and the prime movers are postulated universal principles that are said always to have determined the life of man. The ideal, we are being told, is the reconciliation of the two, through which we are supposedly able to see the universal principles at work in the particular manifestations of reality depicted in a literary work. In *Survival* Margaret Atwood sees this dichotomy, as it is perpetuated through the Old World literary tradition, as one of the main obstacles to an appreciation of Canadian writing:

> The tendency in Canada, at least in high school and university teaching, has been to emphasize the personal and the universal but to skip the national or cultural. This is like trying to teach human anatomy by looking only at the head and the feet. That's one reason for reading Canadian literature then; it gives you a more complete idea of how any literature is made: it's made by people living in a particular space at a particular time, and you can recognize that more easily if the space and the time are your own.
>
> (Atwood 1972b: 15)

What she has focused upon here is the space between the two poles, the large 'blind spot', as it were, of the inherited tradition and its concomitant critical terminology. The stasis of the binary model can be broken, and the full dynamic of the literary medium restored, through a re-integration of the 'body' part of the continuum of human existence into the creative and critical field of vision.

The difficult position to hold is the middle ground between the two extremes. This is the place where complex reality can be rendered in concrete and specific terms, and where fictional characters are seen both as individuals and as people defining themselves in social interaction and history. And to a large extent the difficulties stem from the critical norms and conventions with which the writers working there are confronted. In his essay 'Where Angels Fear to Tread' Chinua Achebe categorizes various types of critics who reveal a European or American bias in their work on African writing, and in the one category that he finds it worthwhile arguing with he isolates precisely the element of dogmatism that we are dealing with here:

> The other day one of them spoke of the great African novel yet to be written. He said the trouble with what we have written so far, is that it has concentrated too much on society and not sufficiently on individual characters and as a result it has lacked 'true' aesthetic proportions. I wondered when this truth became so self-evident and who decided that (unlike the other self-evident truth) this one should apply to black as well as white. It is all this cock-sureness which I find so very annoying.
>
> (Achebe 1973: 6)

Atwood and Achebe are working in very different literary milieus, but they both feel the need to react against the same kind of absolutist cultural hegemony.

# 10

———❖———

# Western Mathematics
## The Secret Weapon of Cultural Imperialism

### ALAN J. BISHOP*

OF ALL THE school subjects which were imposed on indigenous pupils in the colonial schools, arguably the one which could have been considered the least culturally-loaded was mathematics. Even today, that belief prevails. Whereas educational arguments have taken place over which language(s) should be taught, what history or religion, and whether, for example, 'French civilisation' is an appropriate school subject for pupils living thousands of kilometres from France, mathematics has somehow always been felt to be universal and, therefore, culture-free. It had in colonial times, and for most people it continues to have today, the status of a culturally neutral phenomenon in the otherwise turbulent waters of education and imperialism. . . .

Up to fifteen years or so ago, the conventional wisdom was that mathematics was culture-free knowledge. After all, the popular argument went, two twos are four, a negative number times a negative number gives a positive number, and all triangles have angles which add up to 180 degrees. These are true statements the world over. They have universal validity. Surely, therefore, it follows that mathematics must be free from the influence of any culture?

There is no doubt that mathematical truths like those are universal. They are valid everywhere, because of their intentionally abstract and general nature. So, it doesn't matter where you are, if you draw a flat triangle, measure all the angles with a protractor, and add the degrees together, the total will always be approximatcly 180 degrees. . . . Because mathematical truths like these are abstractions from the real world, they are necessarily context-free and universal.

But where do 'degrees' come from? Why is the total 180? Why not 200, or 100? Indeed, why are we interested in triangles and their properties at all? The answer to all these questions is, essentially, 'because some

* From 'Western Mathematics: The Secret Weapon of Cultural Imperialism' *Race and Class* 32(2), 1990.

people determined that it should be that way'. Mathematical ideas, like any other ideas, are humanly constructed. They have a cultural history.

The anthropological literature demonstrates for all who wish to see it that the mathematics which most people learn in contemporary schools is not the only mathematics that exists. For example, we are now aware of the fact that many different counting systems exist in the world. In Papua New Guinea, Lean has documented nearly 600 (there are more than 750 languages there) containing various cycles of numbers, not all base ten (Lean 1991). As well as finger counting, there is documented use of body counting, where one points to a part of the body and uses the name of that part as the number. Numbers are also recorded in knotted strings, carved on wooden tablets or on rocks, and beads are used, as well as many different written systems of numerals (Menninger 1969). The richness is both fascinating and provocative for anyone imagining initially that theirs is the only system of counting and recording numbers.

Nor only is it in number that we find interesting differences. The conception of space which underlies Euclidean geometry is also only one conception – it relies particularly on the 'atomistic' and object-oriented ideas of points, lines, planes and solids. Other conceptions exist, such as that of the Navajos where space is neither subdivided nor objectified, and where everything is in motion (Pinxten, Van Doren and Harvey 1983). Perhaps even more fundamentally, we are more aware of the forms of classification which are different from western hierarchical systems – Lancy, again in Papua New Guinea, identified what he referred to as 'edge-classification', which is more linear than hierarchical (Lancy 1983, Philp 1973). The language and logic of the Indo-European group have developed layers of abstract terms within the hierarchical classification matrix, but this has not happened in all language groups, resulting in different logics and in different ways of relating phenomena.

Facts like these challenge fundamental assumptions and long-held beliefs about mathematics. Recognising symbolisations of alternative arithmetics, geometries and logics implies that we should, therefore, raise the question of whether alternative mathematical systems exist. Some would argue that facts like those above already demonstrate the existence of what they call 'ethno-mathematics', a more localised and specific set of mathematical ideas which may not aim to be as general nor as systematised as 'mainstream' mathematics. Clearly, it is now possible to put forward the thesis that all cultures have generated mathematical ideas, just as all cultures have generated language, religion, morals, customs and kinship systems. Mathematics is now starting to be understood as a pan-cultural phenomenon.

We must, therefore, henceforth take much more care with our labels. We cannot now talk about 'mathematics' without being more specific, unless we are referring to the generic form (like language, religion, etc.). The particular kind of mathematics which is now the internationalised subject most of us recognise is a product of a cultural history, and in the last three centuries of that history, it was developing as part of western European culture (if that is a well-defined term). That is why the title of this article refers to 'western mathematics'. In a sense, that term is also inappropriate, since many cultures have contributed to this knowledge and there are many practising mathematicians all over the world who would object to being thought of as western cultural researchers developing a part of western culture. Indeed, the history of western mathematics is itself being rewritten at present as more evidence comes to light, but more of that later. Nevertheless, in my view it is thoroughly appropriate to identify 'western mathematics', since it was western culture, and more specifically western European culture, which played such a powerful role in achieving the goals of imperialism.

There seem to have been three major mediating agents in the process of cultural invasion of colonised countries by western mathematics: trade, administration and education. Regarding trade and the commercial field generally, this is clearly the area where measures, units, numbers, currency and some geometric notions were employed. More specifically, it would have been western ideas of length, area, volume, weight, time and money which would have been imposed on the indigenous societies. . . .

The second way in which western mathematics would have impinged on other cultures is through the mechanism of administration and government. In particular the numbers and computations necessary for keeping track of large numbers of people and commodities would have necessitated western numerical procedures being used in most cases. . . .

The third and major medium for cultural invasion was education, which played such a critical role in promoting western mathematical ideas and, thereby, western culture. . . . At worst, the mathematics curriculum was abstract, irrelevant, selective and elitist – as indeed it was in Europe – governed by structures like the Cambridge Overseas Certificate, and culturally laden to a very high degree. It was part of a deliberate strategy of acculturation – international in its efforts to instruct in 'the best of the West', and convinced of its superiority to any indigenous mathematical systems and culture. As it was essentially a university-preparatory education, the aspirations of the students were towards attending western universities. They were educated away from their culture and away from their society. . . .

So, it is clear that through the three media of trade, administration and education, the symbolisations and structures of western mathematics would have been imposed on the indigenous cultures just as significantly as were those linguistic symbolisations and structures of English, French, Dutch or whichever was the European language of the particular dominant colonial power in the country.

However, also like a language, the particular symbolisations used were, in a way, the least significant aspect of mathematics. Of far more importance, particularly in cultural terms, were the values which the symbolisations carried with them. Of course, it goes without saying that it was also conventional wisdom that mathematics was value free. How could it have values if it was universal and culture free? We now know better, and an analysis of the historical, anthropological and cross-cultural literatures suggests that there are four clusters of values which are associated with western European mathematics, and which must have had a tremendous impact on the indigenous cultures.

First, there is the area of rationalism, which is at the very heart of western mathematics. If one had to choose a single value and attribute which has guaranteed the power and authority of mathematics within western culture, it is rationalism. As Kline says: 'In its broadest aspect mathematics is a spirit, the spirit of rationality. It is this spirit that challenges, stimulates, invigorates, and drives human minds to exercise themselves to the fullest' (Kline 1972). . . .

Second, a complimentary set of values associated with western mathematics can be termed objectism, a way of perceiving the world as if it were composed of discrete objects, able to be removed and abstracted, so to speak, from their context. To decontextualise, in order to be able to generalise, is at the heart of western mathematics and science; but if your culture encourages you to believe, instead, that everything belongs and exists in its relationship with everything else, then removing it from its context makes it literally meaningless. In early Greek civilisation, there was also a deep controversy over 'object' or 'process' as the fundamental core of being. Heraclitos, in 600–500BC, argued that the essential feature of phenomena is that they are always in flux, always moving and always changing. Democritus and the Pythagoreans preferred the world-view of 'atoms', which eventually was to prevail and develop within western mathematics and science (see Ronan 1983 and Waddington 1977).

Horton sees objectism in another light. He compares this view with what he sees as the preferred African use of personal idiom as explanation. He argues that this has developed for the traditional African the sense that the personal and social 'world' is knowable, whereas the impersonal and the 'world of things' is essentially unknowable. The opposite tendency holds for the westerner (Horton 1967). . . . We can see, therefore, that with both rationalism and objectism as core values, western mathematics presents a dehumanised, objectified, ideological world-view which will emerge necessarily through mathematics teaching of the traditional colonial kind.

A third set of values concerns the power and control aspect of western mathematics. Mathematical ideas are used either as directly applicable concepts and techniques, or indirectly through science and technology, as ways to control the physical and social environment. As Schaff says in relation to the history of mathematics: 'The spirit of the nineteenth and twentieth centuries is typified by man's increasing mastery over his physical environment' (Schaff 1963: 48). So, using numbers and measurements in trade, industry, commerce and administration would all have emphasised the power and control values of mathematics. It was (and still is) so clearly useful knowledge, powerful knowledge, and it seduced the majority of peoples who came into contact with it. . . .

From those colonial times through to today, the power of this mathe-matico-technological culture has grown apace – so much so that western mathematics is taught nowadays in every country in the world. Once again, it is mainly taught with the assumption of universality and cultural neutrality. From colonialism through to neo-colonialism, the cultural imperialism of western mathematics has yet to be fully realised and under-stood. Gradually, greater understanding of its impact is being acquired, but one must wonder whether its all-pervading influence is now out of control.

As awareness of the cultural nature and influence of western mathe-matics is spreading and developing, so various levels of responses can also be seen. At the first level there is an increasing interest in the study of ethno-mathematics, through both analyses of the anthropological literature and investigations in real-life situations. . . .[1]

At the second level, there is a response in many developing countries and former colonies which is aimed at creating a greater awareness of one's own culture. Cultural rebirth or reawakening is a recognised goal of the educational process in several countries. Gerdes, in Mozambique, is a mathematics educator who has done a great deal of work in this area. He seeks not only to demonstrate important mathematical aspects of Mozambican society, but also to develop the process of 'defreezing' the 'frozen' mathematics which he uncovers. For example, with the plating methods used by fishermen to make their fish traps, he demonstrates significant geometric ideas which could easily be assimilated into the math-ematics curriculum in order to create what he considers to be a genuine Mozambican mathematics education for the young people there. . . .

The third level of response to the cultural imperialism of western mathematics is, paradoxically, to re-examine the whole history of western mathematics itself. It is no accident that this history has been written predominantly by white, male, western European or American researchers, and there is a concern that, for example, the contribution of Black Africa has been undervalued. . . .

I began by describing the myth of western mathematics' cultural neutrality. Increasingly, modern evidence serves to destroy this naïve belief. Nevertheless, the belief in that myth has had, and continues to have, powerful implications. Those implications relate to education, to national developments and to a continuation of cultural imperialism. Indeed it is not too sweeping to state that most of the modern world has accepted western mathematics, values included, as a fundamental part of its education. . . .

However, taking a broader view, one must ask: should there not be more resistance to this cultural hegemony? . . . Resistance is growing, critical debate is informing theoretical developments, and research is increasing, particularly in educational situations where culture-conflict is recognised. The secret weapon is secret no longer.

## NOTE

1 Bishop goes on to describe six 'universals' of ethno-mathematics, that is, six activities which may be found in some combination in every society: Counting; Locating; Measuring; Designing; Playing; Explaining. (Eds)

# 11

## Jameson's Rhetoric of Otherness and the 'National Allegory'

### Aijaz Ahmad*

I HAVE BEEN reading Jameson's work now for roughly fifteen years, and at least some of what I know about the literatures and cultures of Western Europe and the USA comes from him; and because I am a Marxist, I had always thought of us, Jameson and myself, as birds of the same feather, even though we never quite flocked together. But then, when I was on the fifth page of this text (specifically, on the sentence starting with 'All third-world texts are necessarily . . .' etc.), I realized that what was being theorized was, among many other things, myself. Now, I was born in India and I write poetry in Urdu, a language not commonly understood among US intellectuals. So I said to myself: '*All?* . . . *necessarily?*' It felt odd. Matters became much more curious, however. For the further I read, the more I realized, with no little chagrin, that the man whom I had for so long, so affectionately, albeit from a physical distance, taken as a comrade was, in his own opinion, my civilizational Other. It was not a good feeling.

I too think that there *are* plenty of very good books written by African, Indian and Latin American writers which are available in English and which must be taught as an antidote to the general ethnocentricity and cultural myopia of the Humanities as they are presently constituted in these United States. If some label is needed for this activity, one may call it 'Third World Literature'. Conversely, however, I also hold that this term, 'the Third World', is, even in its most telling deployments, a polemical one, with no theoretical status whatsoever. . . . I shall argue in context, then, that there is no such thing as a 'Third World Literature' which can be constructed as an internally coherent object of theoretical knowledge.

* From 'Jameson's Rhetoric of Otherness and the "National Allegory" ' *Social Text* 17 (Fall), 1987. A reply to Frederic Jameson's 'Third World Literature in the Era of Multinational Capitalism' *Social Text* 15 (Fall), 1986.

There are fundamental issues – of periodization, social and linguistic formations, political and ideological struggles within the field of literary production, and so on – which simply cannot be resolved at this level of generality without an altogether positivist reductionism. . . .

I shall argue later that since Jameson defines the so-called Third World in terms of its experience of colonialism and imperialism, the political category that necessarily follows from this exclusive emphasis is that of 'the nation', with nationalism as the peculiarly valorized ideology; and, because of this privileging of the nationalist ideology, it is then theoretically posited that 'all third-world texts are necessarily . . . to be read as . . . national allegories'. The theory of the 'national allegory' as the metatext is thus inseparable from the larger Three Worlds Theory which permeates the whole of Jameson's own text. We too have to begin, then, with some comments on 'the Third World' as a theoretical category and on 'nationalism' as the necessary, exclusively desirable ideology. . . .

As we come to the substance of what Jameson 'describes', I find it significant that First and Second Worlds are defined in terms of their production systems (capitalism and socialism, respectively), whereas the third category – the Third World – is defined purely in terms of an 'experience' of externally inserted phenomena. That which is constitutive of human history itself is present in the first two cases, absent in the third case. Ideologically, this classification divides the world between those who make history and those who are mere objects of it; elsewhere in the text, Jameson would significantly reinvoke Hegel's famous description of the master–slave relation to encapsulate the First–Third World opposition. But analytically, this classification leaves the so-called Third World in limbo; if only the First World is capitalist and the Second World socialist, how does one understand the Third World? Is it pre-capitalist? Transitional? Transitional between what and what? But then there is also the issue of the location of particular countries within the various 'worlds'.

Take, for example, India. Its colonial past is nostalgically rehashed on US television screens in copious series every few months, but the India of today has all the characteristics of a capitalist country: generalized commodity production, vigorous and escalating exchanges not only between agriculture and industry but also between Departments I and II of industry itself, and technical personnel more numerous than those of France and Germany combined. . . .

So – does India belong in the First World or the Third? . . .

I have said already that if one believes in the Three Worlds Theory – hence in a 'Third World' defined exclusively in terms of 'the experience of colonialism and imperialism' – then the primary ideological formation available to a left-wing intellectual will be that of nationalism; it will then be possible to assert – surely with very considerable exaggeration, but

possible to assert none the less – that 'all third-world texts are necessarily
. . . *national allegories*' (original emphasis). This exclusive emphasis on the
nationalist ideology is there even in the opening paragraph
of Jameson's text, where the only choice for the 'Third World' is said to
be between its 'nationalisms' and a 'global American postmodernist
culture'. Is there no other choice? Could not one join the 'Second World',
for example? . . .

Jameson's haste in totalizing historical phenomena in terms of binary
oppositions (nationalism/postmodernism, in this case) leaves little room for
the fact, for instance, that the only nationalisms in the so-called Third
World which have been able to resist US cultural pressure and have actually
produced any alternatives are those which are already articulated to and
assimilated within the much larger field of socialist political practice.
Virtually all the others have had no difficulty in reconciling themselves with
what Jameson calls 'global American postmodernist culture'; . . . Nor does
the absolutism of that opposition (postmodernism/nationalism) permit any
space for the simple idea that nationalism itself is not some unitary thing
with some predetermined essence and value. There are hundreds of nationalisms in Asia and Africa today; some are progressive, others are not.
Whether or not a nationalism will produce a progressive cultural practice
depends, to put it in Gramscian terms, upon the political character of the
power bloc which takes hold of it and utilizes it, as a material force, in the
process of constituting its own hegemony. There is neither theoretical
ground nor empirical evidence to support the notion that bourgeois nationalisms of the so-called Third World will have any difficulty with post-
modernism; they *want* it.

Yet there *is* a very tight fit between the Three Worlds Theory, the over-
valorization of the nationalist ideology, and the assertion that 'national
allegory' is the primary, even exclusive, form of narrativity in the so-called
Third World. If this 'Third World' is *constituted* by the singular 'experience
of colonialism and imperialism', and if the only possible response is a
nationalist one, then what else is there that is more urgent to narrate than
this 'experience'? In fact, there is *nothing else* to narrate. For if societies
here are defined not by relations of production but by relations of intranational domination; if they are forever suspended outside the sphere of
conflict between capitalism (First World) and socialism (Second World); if
the motivating force for history here is neither class formation and class
struggle nor the multiplicities of intersecting conflicts based upon class,
gender, nation, race, region, and so on, but the unitary 'experience' of
national oppression (if one is merely the *object* of history, the Hegelian
slave), then what else *can* one narrate but that national oppression?
Politically, we are Calibans all. Formally, we are fated to be in the post-
structuralist world of Repetition with Difference; the same allegory, the
nationalist one, rewritten, over and over again, until the end of time: 'all
third-world texts are necessarily . . .'.

But one could start with a radically different premiss: namely, the proposition that we live not in three worlds but in one; that this world includes the experience of colonialism and imperialism on both sides of Jameson's global divide (the 'experience' of imperialism is a central fact of all aspects of life inside the USA, from ideological formation to the utilization of the social surplus in military-industrial complexes); that societies in formations of backward capitalism are as much constituted by the division of classes as are societies in the advanced capitalist countries; that socialism is not restricted to something called 'the Second World' but is simply the name of a resistance that saturates the globe today, as capitalism itself does; that the different parts of the capitalist system are to be known not in terms of a binary opposition but as a contradictory unity – with differences, yes, but also with profound overlaps. . . .

Jameson claims that one cannot proceed from the premiss of a real unity of the world 'without falling back into some general liberal and humanistic universalism'. That is a curious idea, coming from a Marxist. One would have thought that the world was united not by liberalist ideology – that the world was not at all constituted in the realm of an Idea, be it Hegelian or humanist – but by the global operation of a single mode of production, namely the capitalist one, and the global resistance to this mode, a resistance which is itself unevenly developed in different parts of the globe. Socialism, one would have thought, was not by any means limited to the so-called Second World (the socialist countries) but is a global phenomenon, reaching into the farthest rural communities in Asia, Africa and Latin America, not to speak of individuals and groups within the United States. What gives the world its unity, then, is not a humanist ideology but the ferocious struggle between capital and labour which is now strictly and fundamentally global in character. . . .

As for the specificity of cultural difference, Jameson's theoretical conception tends, I believe, in the opposite direction – namely, that of homogenization. Difference between the First World and the Third is absolutized as an Otherness, but the enormous cultural heterogeneity of social formations within the so-called Third World is submerged within a singular identity of 'experience'. Now, countries of Western Europe and North America have been deeply tied together over roughly the last two hundred years; capitalism itself is so much older in these countries; the cultural logic of late capitalism is so strongly operative in these metropolitan formations; the circulation of cultural products among them is so immediate, so extensive, so brisk, that one could sensibly speak of a certain cultural homogeneity among them. But Asia, Africa and Latin America? Historically, these countries were never so closely tied together. . . .

Of course, great cultural similarities also exist among countries that occupy analogous positions in the global capitalist system, and there are similarities in many cases that have been bequeathed by the similarities of socioeconomic structures in the pre-capitalist past. The point is not to construct a typology that is simply the obverse of Jameson's, but rather to define the material basis for a fair degree of cultural homogenization among the advanced capitalist countries and the lack of that kind of homogenization in the rest of the capitalist world. In context, therefore, one is doubly surprised at Jameson's absolute insistence upon Difference and the relation of Otherness between the First World and the Third, and his equally insistent idea that the 'experience' of the 'Third World' could be contained and communicated within a single narrative form. By locating capitalism in the First World and socialism in the Second, Jameson's theory freezes and dehistoricizes the global space within which struggles between these great motivating forces actually take place. And by assimilating the enormous heterogeneities and productivities of our life into a single Hegelian metaphor of the master–slave relation, this theory reduces us to an ideal-type and demands from us that we narrate ourselves through a form commensurate with that ideal-type. To say that all Third World texts are necessarily this or that is to say, in effect, that any text originating within that social space which is not this or that is not a 'true' narrative. It is in this sense above all that the category of 'Third World Literature' which is the site of this operation, with the 'national allegory' as its meta-text as well as the mark of its constitution and difference, is, to my mind, epistemologically an impossible category. . . .

And at what point in history does a text produced in countries with 'experience of colonialism and imperialism' become a *Third World text*? In one kind of reading, only texts produced *after* the advent of colonialism could be so designated, since it is colonialism/imperialism which constitutes the Third World as such. But in speaking constantly of 'the West's Other'; in referring to the tribal/tributary and Asiatic modes as the theoretical basis for his selection of Lu Xun (Asian) and Sembene (African) respectively; in characterizing Freud's theory as a 'Western or First World reading' as contrasted with ten centuries of specifically Chinese distributions of the libidinal energy which are said to frame Lu Xun's texts – in deploying these broad epochal and civilizational categories, Jameson also suggests that the difference between the First World and the Third is itself primordial, rooted in things far older than capitalism as such. So, if the First World is the same as 'the West' and the 'Graeco-Judaic', one has, on the other hand, an alarming feeling that the *Bhagavad-Gita*, the edicts of Manu, and the Qur'an itself are perhaps Third World texts (though the Judaic elements of the Qur'an are quite beyond doubt, and much of the ancient art in what is today Pakistan is itself Graeco-Indic).

But there is also the question of *space*. Do all texts produced in countries with 'experience of colonialism and imperialism' become, by virtue of geographical origin, 'third-world texts'? Jameson speaks so often of '*all* third-world texts', insists so much on a singular form of narrativity for Third World Literature, that not to take him literally is to violate the very terms of his discourse. Yet one knows of so many texts from one's own part of the world which do not fit the description of 'national allegory' that one wonders why Jameson insists so much on the category, '*all*'. Without this category, of course, he cannot produce a theory of Third World Literature. But is it also the case that he means the opposite of what he actually says: not that '*all* third-world texts are to be read . . . as national allegories' but that *only* those texts which give us national allegories can be admitted as authentic texts of Third World Literature, while the rest are by definition excluded? So one is not quite sure whether one is dealing with a fallacy ('all third-world texts are' this or that) or with the Law of the Father (you must write *this* if you are to be admitted into my theory). . . .

Jameson insists over and over again that the *national* experience is central to the cognitive formation of the Third World intellectual, and that the narrativity of that experience takes the form exclusively of a 'national allegory'. But this emphatic insistence on the category 'nation' itself keeps slipping into a much wider, far less demarcated vocabulary of 'culture', 'society', 'collectivity', and so on. Are 'nation' and 'collectivity' the same thing? . . .

[O]ne may indeed connect one's personal experience to a 'collectivity' – in terms of class, gender, caste, religious community, trade union, political party, village, prison – combining the private and the public, and in some sense 'allegorizing' the individual experience, without involving the category of 'the nation' or necessarily referring back to the 'experience of colonialism and imperialism'. The latter statement would then seem to apply to a much larger body of texts, with far greater accuracy. By the same token, however, this wider application of 'collectivity' establishes much less radical difference between the so-called First and Third Worlds, since the whole history of realism in the European novel, in its many variants, has been associated with ideas of 'typicality' and 'the social', while the majority of the written narratives produced in the First World even today locate the individual story in a fundamental relation to some larger experience.

If we replace the idea of the 'nation' with that larger, less restrictive idea of 'collectivity', and if we start thinking of the process of allegorization not in nationalistic terms but simply as a relation between private and public, personal and communal, then it also becomes possible to see that allegorization is by no means specific to the so-called Third World.

# PART III

## Representation and Resistance

# Introduction

Representation and resistance are very broad arenas within which much of the drama of colonialist relations and post-colonial examination and subversion of those relations has taken place. In both conquest and colonisation, texts and textuality played a major part. European texts – anthropologies, histories, fiction, captured the non-European subject within European frameworks which read his or her alterity as *terror* or *lack*. Within the complex relations of colonialism these representations were re-projected to the colonised – through formal education or general colonialist cultural relations – as authoritative pictures of themselves. Concomitantly representations of Europe and Europeans within this textual archive were situated as normative. Such texts – the representations of Europe to itself, and the representation of others to Europe – were not accounts of different peoples and societies, but a projection of European fears and desires masquerading as scientific/'objective' knowledges. Said's foundational *Orientalism* examines the process by which this discursive formation emerges.

Because representation and resistance are such broad areas of contestation in post-colonial discourse, this is a section which exceeds its particular limits within this Reader. Feminism and its intersections with both colonialism and post-colonialism is necessarily about representation and resistance, as the 'Feminism' section of this Reader demonstrates. And it is through education and in terms of modes of production and consumption that colonialist representations persist and currently circulate in, for instance, popular television shows, cartoons, novels. Consequently the 'Education' and 'Production and Consumption' sections, like 'Universality' and 'Hybridity', are also concerned with representation and resistance as are a number of the introductory essays.

Post-colonial textual resistance to such colonialist representations has taken many forms, from the nineteenth-century parody of Macaulay's 1835 Minute by an unknown 'Bengali' writer (commented on by Jenny Sharpe), to the widespread contemporary practice of counter-canonical literary discourse discussed by Helen Tiffin. In 'A Small Place' the Antiguan writer Jamaica Kincaid adopts the deceptively simple style of a knowing child

(Kipling's 'half-devil and half-child') to interrogate those patterns which established the English as superior and Antiguans as necessarily inferior. In the second person address which she employs, she also draws attention to the ways in which the texts of the imperium and the derogatory representations they promulgated were constituted as authoritative through the convenient assumption that they offered a transparent 'window' on an objective reality; that relations between producers and consumers, or writers and readers, did not really exist and thus did not foster and reflect unequal colonialist power relations. By addressing the English (and by extension contemporary western tourists) directly in this way, Kincaid draws attention not only to the power of textual representations, but to the ideologies and technologies through which these were and are disseminated and rendered normative.

Theorising the nature and practice of post-colonial resistance more generally has become central to post-colonial debates. In particular post-structuralism's diverse intersections with post-colonialism have foregrounded questions not only of political commitment (books and barricades) but of agency itself (questions already raised by Bhabha's, Spivak's and JanMohamed's essays in Part I, 'Issues and Debates'). Stephen Slemon's article here succinctly summarises various kinds of literary resistances that have been theorised within post-colonialism and considers the crucial place of so-called 'second world' writing in such theorisations. Slemon, Sara Suleri and Jenny Sharpe all problematise earlier notions of post-colonial resistance (like those of Barbara Harlow or Timothy Brennan) which depend upon a system of irreducible binary oppositions. Instead, they move away from a resistance theorising which, in Sara Suleri's terms, 'precludes the concept of exchange by granting the idea of power a greater literalism than it deserved' towards a notion of 'cultural exchange'. In so doing, Suleri, like Appiah in *In My Father's House*, is paving the way for more complex analyses of colonial relations and thus of post-colonial resistances. If earlier theorisations of resistance presupposed a foundation of undislocatable binaries – centre/margin, self/other, coloniser/colonised – the general trajectory of the rather different projects of Bhabha, Slemon, Suleri and Appiah has been towards something that has always been implicit (even when not explicit) in both colonialist and post-colonial literary relations, and that is what Suleri calls the 'peculiar intimacy' of coloniser and colonised. Theorising this complex 'intimacy' without giving away the fact of persisting and historic *inequalities* within those relations and structures is perhaps *the* major focus of contemporary post-colonial theory.

# 12

## *Orientalism*

### Edward W. Said*

ON A VISIT to Beirut during the terrible civil war of 1975–1976 a French journalist wrote regretfully of the gutted downtown area that 'it had once seemed to belong to . . . the Orient of Chateaubriand and Nerval' (Desjardins 1976: 14). He was right about the place, of course, especially so far as a European was concerned. The Orient was almost a European invention, and had been since antiquity a place of romance, exotic beings, haunting memories and landscapes, remarkable experiences. Now it was disappearing; in a sense it had happened, its time was over. Perhaps it seemed irrelevant that Orientals themselves had something at stake in the process, that even in the time of Chateaubriand and Nerval Orientals had lived there, and that now it was they who were suffering; the main thing for the European visitor was a European representation of the Orient and its contemporary fate, both of which had a privileged communal significance for the journalist and his French readers. . . .

The Orient is not only adjacent to Europe; it is also the place of Europe's greatest and richest and oldest colonies, the source of its civilizations and languages, its cultural contestant, and one of its deepest and most recurring images of the Other. In addition, the Orient has helped to define Europe (or the West) as its contrasting image, idea, personality, experience. Yet none of this Orient is merely imaginative. The Orient is an integral part of European *material* civilization and culture. Orientalism expresses and represents that part culturally and even ideologically as a mode of discourse with supporting institutions, vocabulary, scholarship, imagery, doctrines, even colonial bureaucracies and colonial styles. In contrast, the American understanding of the Orient will seem considerably less dense, although our recent Japanese, Korean, and Indochinese adventures ought now to be creating a more sober, more realistic 'Oriental' awareness. Moreover, the vastly expanded American political and economic role in the Near East (the Middle East) makes great claims on our understanding of that Orient.

* From *Orientalism* New York: Random House, 1978.

It will be clear to the reader . . . that by Orientalism I mean several things, all of them, in my opinion, interdependent. The most readily accepted designation for Orientalism is an academic one, and indeed the label still serves in a number of academic institutions. Anyone who teaches, writes about, or researches the Orient – and this applies whether the person is an anthropologist, sociologist, historian, or philologist – either in its specific or its general aspects, is an Orientalist, and what he or she does is Orientalism. Compared with *Oriental studies* or *area studies*, it is true that the term *Orientalism* is less preferred by specialists today, both because it is too vague and general and because it connotes the high-handed executive attitude of nineteenth-century and early twentieth-century European colonialism. Nevertheless books are written and congresses held with 'the Orient' as their main focus, with the Orientalist in his new or old guise as their main authority. The point is that even if it does not survive as it once did, Orientalism lives on academically through its doctrines and theses about the Orient and the Oriental.

Related to this academic tradition, whose fortunes, transmigrations, specializations, and transmissions are in part the subject of this study, is a more general meaning for Orientalism. Orientalism is a style of thought based upon an ontological and epistemological distinction made between 'the Orient' and (most of the time) 'the Occident.' Thus a very large mass of writers, among whom are poets, novelists, philosophers, political theorists, economists, and imperial administrators, have accepted the basic distinction between East and West as the starting point for elaborate theories, epics, novels, social descriptions, and political accounts concerning the Orient, its people, customs, 'mind,' destiny, and so on. *This* Orientalism can accommodate Aeschylus, say, and Victor Hugo, Dante and Karl Marx. A little later in this introduction I shall deal with the methodological problems one encounters in so broadly construed a 'field' as this.

The interchange between the academic and the more or less imaginative meanings of Orientalism is a constant one, and since the late eighteenth century there has been a considerable, quite disciplined – perhaps even regulated – traffic between the two. Here I come to the third meaning of Orientalism, which is something more historically and materially defined than either of the other two. Taking the late eighteenth century as a very roughly defined starting point Orientalism can be discussed and analyzed as the corporate institution for dealing with the Orient – dealing with it by making statements about it, authorizing views of it, describing it, by teaching it, settling it: in short, Orientalism as a Western style for dominating, restructuring, and having authority over the Orient. I have found it useful here to employ Michel Foucault's notion of a discourse, as described by him in *The Archaeology of Knowledge* and in *Discipline and Punish*, to identify Orientalism. My contention is that without examining Orientalism as a discourse one cannot possibly understand the enormously systematic discipline by which European culture was able to manage – and even produce – the Orient politically, sociologically, militarily, ideologically, scientifically, and imaginatively during the post-Enlightenment period. Moreover, so authoritative a position did Orientalism have that I believe no one writing, thinking, or acting on the Orient could do so without taking account of the limitations on thought and action imposed by Orientalism. In brief, because of Orientalism the Orient was not (and is not) a free subject of thought or action. This is not to say that Orientalism unilaterally determines what can be said about the Orient, but that it is the whole network of interests inevitably brought to bear on (and therefore always involved in) any occasion when that peculiar entity 'the Orient' is in question. How this happens is what this book tries to demonstrate. It also tries to show that European culture gained in strength and identity by setting itself off against the Orient as a sort of surrogate and even underground self. . . .

I have begun with the assumption that the Orient is not an inert fact of nature. It is not merely *there*, just as the Occident itself is not just *there* either. We must take seriously Vico's great observation that men make their own history, that what they can know is what they have made, and extend it to geography: as both geographical and cultural entities – to say nothing of historical entities – such locales, regions, geographical sectors as 'Orient' and 'Occident' are man-made. Therefore as much as the West itself, the Orient is an idea that has a history and a tradition of thought, imagery, and vocabulary that have given it reality and presence in and for the West. The two geographical entities thus support and to an extent reflect each other. Having said that, one must go on to state a number of reasonable qualifications. In the first place, it would be wrong to conclude that the Orient was *essentially* an idea, or a creation with no corresponding reality. . . . There were – and are – cultures and nations whose location is in the East, and their lives, histories, and customs have a brute reality obviously greater than anything that could be said about them in the West. About that fact this study of Orientalism has very little to contribute, except to acknowledge it tacitly. But the phenomenon of Orientalism as I study it here deals principally, not with a correspondence between Orientalism and Orient, but with the internal consistency of Orientalism and its ideas about the Orient (the East as career) despite or beyond any correspondence, or lack thereof, with a 'real' Orient. . . .

A second qualification is that ideas, cultures, and histories cannot seriously be understood or studied without their force, or more precisely their configurations of power, also being studied. To believe that the Orient was created – or, as I call it, 'Orientalized' – and to believe that such things happen simply as a necessity of the imagination, is to be disingenuous. The relationship between Occident and Orient is a relationship of power, of domination, of varying degrees of a complex hegemony. . . .

This brings us to a third qualification. One ought never to assume that the structure of Orientalism is nothing more than a structure of lies or of myths which, were the truth about them to be told, would simply blow away. I myself believe that Orientalism is more particularly valuable as a sign of European–Atlantic power over the Orient than it is a veridic discourse about the Orient (which is what, in its academic or scholarly form, it claims to be). . . .

In a quite constant way, Orientalism depends for its strategy on this flexible *positional* superiority, which puts the Westerner in a whole series of possible relationships with the Orient without ever losing him the relative upper hand. And why should it have been otherwise, especially during the period of extraordinary European ascendancy from the late Renaissance to the present? The scientist, the scholar, the missionary, the trader, or the soldier was in, or thought about, the Orient because he *could be there*, or could think about it, with very little resistance on the Orient's part. Under the general heading of knowledge of the Orient, and within the umbrella of Western hegemony over the Orient during the period from the end of the eighteenth century, there emerged a complex Orient suitable for study in the academy, for display in the museum, for reconstruction in the colonial office, for theoretical illustration in anthropological, biological, linguistic, racial, and historical theses about mankind and the universe, for instances of economic and sociological theories of development, revolution, cultural personality, national or religious character. Additionally, the imaginative examination of things Oriental was based more or less exclusively upon a sovereign Western consciousness out of whose unchallenged centrality an Oriental world emerged, first according to general ideas about who or what was an Oriental, then according to a detailed logic governed not simply by empirical reality but by a battery of desires, repressions, investments, and projections. . . .

Therefore, Orientalism is not a mere political subject matter or field that is reflected passively by culture, scholarship, or institutions; nor is it a large and diffuse collection of texts about the Orient; nor is it representative and expressive of some nefarious 'Western' imperialist plot to hold down the 'Oriental' world. It is rather a *distribution* of geopolitical awareness into aesthetic, scholarly, economic, sociological, historical, and philological texts; it is an *elaboration* not only of a basic geographical distinction (the world is made up of two unequal halves, Orient and Occident) but also of a whole series of 'interests' which, by such means as scholarly discovery, philological reconstruction, psychological analysis, landscape and sociological description, it not only creates but also maintains; it *is*, rather than expresses, a certain *will* or *intention* to understand, in some cases to control, manipulate, even to incorporate, what is a manifestly different (or alternative and novel) world; it is, above all, a discourse that is by no means in direct, corresponding relationship with political power in the raw, but rather is produced and exists in an uneven exchange with various kinds of power, shaped to a degree by the exchange with power political (as with a colonial or imperial establishment), power intellectual (as with reigning sciences like comparative linguistics or anatomy, or any of the modern policy sciences), power cultural (as with orthodoxies and canons of taste, texts, values), power moral (as with ideas about what 'we' do and what 'they' cannot do or understand as 'we' do). Indeed, my real argument is that Orientalism is – and does not simply represent – a considerable dimension of modern political–intellectual culture, and as such has less to do with the Orient than it does with 'our' world.

Because Orientalism is a cultural and a political fact, then, it does not exist in some archival vacuum; quite the contrary, I think it can be shown that what is thought, said, or even done about the Orient follows (perhaps occurs within) certain distinct and intellectually knowable lines. Here too a considerable degree of nuance and elaboration can be seen working as between the broad superstructural pressures and the details of composition, the facts of textuality. Most humanistic scholars are, I think, perfectly happy with the notion that texts exist in contexts, that there is such a thing as intertextuality, that the pressures of conventions, predecessors, and rhetorical styles limit what Walter Benjamin once called the 'overtaxing of the productive person in the name of . . . the principle of "creativity",' in which the poet is believed on his own, and out of his pure mind, to have brought forth his work (Benjamin 1973: 71). Yet there is a reluctance to allow that political, institutional, and ideological constraints act in the same manner on the individual author.

# 13

# A Small Place

## JAMAICA KINCAID*

THE ANTIGUA THAT I knew, the Antigua in which I grew up, is not the
Antigua you, a tourist, would see now. That Antigua no longer exists. That
Antigua no longer exists partly for the usual reason, the passing of time,
and partly because the bad-minded people who used to rule over it, the
English, no longer do so. (But the English have become such a pitiful lot
these days, with hardly any idea what to do with themselves now that they
no longer have one quarter of the earth's human population bowing and
scraping before them. They don't seem to know that this empire business
was all wrong and they should, at least, be wearing sackcloth and ashes in
token penance of the wrongs committed, the irrevocableness of their bad
deeds, for no natural disaster imaginable could equal the harm they did.
Actual death might have been better. And so all this fuss over empire –
what went wrong here, what went wrong there – always makes me quite
crazy, for I can say to them what went wrong: they should never have left
their home, their precious England, a place they loved so much, a place
they had to leave but could never forget. And so everywhere they went they
turned it into England; and everybody they met they turned English. But
no place could ever really be England, and nobody who did not look
exactly like them would ever be English, so you can imagine the destruction of people and land that came from that. The English hate each other
and they hate England, and the reason they are so miserable now is that
they have no place else to go and nobody else to feel better than.) But let
me show you the Antigua that I used to know.

In the Antigua that I knew, we lived on a street named after an English
maritime criminal, Horatio Nelson, and all the other streets around us were
named after some other English maritime criminals. There was Rodney
Street, there was Hood Street, there was Hawkins Street, and there was
Drake Street. There were flamboyant trees and mahogany trees lining East

* From *A Small Place* London: Virago, 1988.

Street. Government House, the place where the Governor, the person standing in for the Queen, lived, was on East Street. Government House was surrounded by a high white wall – and to show how cowed we must have been, no one ever wrote bad things on it; it remained clean and white and high. (I once stood in hot sun for hours so that I could see a putty-faced Princess from England disappear behind these walls. I was seven years old at the time, and I thought, She has a putty face.) There was the library on lower High Street, above the Department of the Treasury, and it was in that part of High Street that all colonial government business took place. In that part of High Street, you could cash a cheque at the Treasury, read a book in the library, post a letter at the post office, appear before a magistrate in court. (Since we were ruled by the English, we also had their laws. There was a law against using abusive language. Can you imagine such a law among people for whom making a spectacle of yourself through speech is everything? When West Indians went to England, the police there had to get a glossary of bad West Indian words so they could understand whether they were hearing abusive language or not.) It was in that same part of High Street that you could get a passport in another government office. In the middle of High Street was the Barclays Bank. The Barclay brothers, who started Barclays Bank, were slave-traders. That is how they made their money. When the English outlawed the slave trade, the Barclay brothers went into banking. It made them even richer. It's possible that when they saw how rich banking made them, they gave themselves a good beating for opposing an end to slave trading (for surely they would have opposed that), but then again, they may have been visionaries and agitated for an end to slavery, for look at how rich they became with their banks borrowing from (through their savings) the descendants of the slaves and then lending back to them. But people just a little older than I am can recite the name of and the day the first black person was hired as a cashier at this very same Barclays Bank in Antigua. Do you ever wonder why some people blow things up? I can imagine that if my life had taken a certain turn, there would be the Barclays Bank, and there I would be, both of us in ashes. Do you ever try to understand why people like me cannot get over the past, cannot forgive and cannot forget? There is the Barclays Bank. The Barclay brothers are dead. The human beings they traded, the human beings who to them were only commodities, are dead. It should not have been that they came to the same end, and heaven is not enough of a reward for one or hell enough of a punishment for the other. . . .

We were taught the names of the Kings of England. In Antigua, the twenty-fourth of May was a holiday – Queen Victoria's official birthday. We didn't say to ourselves, Hasn't this extremely unappealing person been dead for years and years? . . .

I cannot tell you how angry it makes me to hear people from North America tell me how much they love England, how beautiful England is, with its traditions. All they see is some frumpy, wrinkled-up person passing by in a carriage waving at a crowd. But what I see is the millions of people, of whom I am just one, made orphans: no motherland, no fatherland, no gods, no mounds of earth for holy ground, no excess of love which might lead to the things that an excess of love sometimes brings, and worst and most painful of all, no tongue. For isn't it odd that the only language I have in which to speak of this crime is the language of the criminal who committed the crime? And what can that really mean? For the language of the criminal can contain only the goodness of the criminal's deed. . . .

Have I given you the impression that the Antigua I grew up in revolved almost completely around England? Well, that was so. I met the world through England, and if the world wanted to meet me it would have to do so through England. . . .

Our perception of this Antigua – the perception we had of this place ruled by these bad-minded people – was not a political perception. The English were ill-mannered, not racists; the school head-mistress was especially ill-mannered, not a racist; the doctor was crazy – he didn't even speak English properly, and he came from a strangely named place, he also was not a racist; the people at the Mill Reef Club were puzzling (why go and live in a place populated mostly by people you cannot stand), not racists . . . .

You loved knowledge, and wherever you went you made sure to build a school, a library (yes, and in both of these places you distorted or erased my history and glorified your own). But then again, perhaps as you observe the debacle in which I now exist, the utter ruin that I say is my life, perhaps you are remembering that you had always felt people like me cannot run things, people like me will never grasp the idea of Gross National Product, people like me will never be able to take command of the thing the most simpleminded among you can master, people like me will never understand the notion of rule by law, people like me cannot really think in abstractions, people like me cannot be objective, we make everything so personal. You will forget your part in the whole setup, that bureaucracy is one of your inventions, that Gross National Product is one of your inventions, and all the laws that you know mysteriously favour you. . . .

As for what we were like before we met you, I no longer care. No periods of time over which my ancestors held sway, no documentation of complex civilisations, is any comfort to me. Even if I really came from people who were living like monkeys in trees, it was better to be that than what happened to me, what I became after I met you.

# 14

## Post-colonial Literatures and Counter-discourse

### HELEN TIFFIN*

As GEORGE LAMMING once remarked, over three quarters of the contemporary world has been directly and profoundly affected by imperialism and colonialism. . . . Processes of artistic and literary decolonisation have involved a radical dis/mantling of European codes and a post-colonial subversion and appropriation of the dominant European discourses. This has frequently been accompanied by the demand for an entirely new or wholly recovered 'reality', free of all colonial taint. Given the nature of the relationship between coloniser and colonised, with its pandemic brutalities and its cultural denigration, such a demand is desirable and inevitable. But as the contradictions inherent in a project such as Chinweizu, Jemie and Madubuike's *The Decolonization of African Literature* demonstrate (Chinweizu *et al.* 1985), such pre-colonial cultural purity can never be fully recovered.

Post-colonial cultures are inevitably hybridised, involving a dialectical relationship between European ontology and epistemology and the impulse to create or recreate independent local identity. Decolonisation is process, not arrival; it invokes an ongoing dialectic between hegemonic centrist systems and peripheral subversion of them; between European or British discourses and their post-colonial dis/mantling. Since it is not possible to create or recreate national or regional formations wholly independent of their historical implication in the European colonial enterprise, it has been the project of post-colonial writing to interrogate European discourses and discursive strategies from a privileged position within (and between) two worlds; to investigate the means by which Europe imposed and maintained its codes in the colonial domination of so much of the rest of the world.

Thus the rereading and rewriting of the European historical and fictional record are vital and inescapable tasks. These subversive manoeuvres, rather than the construction or reconstruction of the essentially national or regional, are what is characteristic of post-colonial texts, as the

* From 'Post-Colonial Literatures and Counter-Discourse' *Kunapipi* 9(3), 1987.

subversive is characteristic of post-colonial discourse in general. Post-colonial literatures/cultures are thus constituted in counter-discursive rather than homologous practices, and they offer 'fields' (Lee 1977: 32–3) of counter-discursive strategies to the dominant discourse. The operation of post-colonial counter-discourse (Terdiman 1985)[1] is dynamic, not static: it does not seek to subvert the dominant with a view to taking its place, but, in Wilson Harris's formulation, to evolve textual strategies which continually 'consume' their 'own biases' (Harris 1985: 127) at the same time as they expose and erode those of the dominant discourse. . . .

In challenging the notion of literary universality (or the European appropriation of post-colonial practice and theory as post-modern or post-structuralist) post-colonial writers and critics engage in counter-discourse. But separate models of 'Commonwealth Literature' or 'New Writing in English' which implicitly or explicitly invoke notions of continuation of, or descent from, a 'mainstream' British literature, consciously or unconsciously reinvoke those very hegemonic assumptions against which the post-colonial text has, from its inception, been directed. Models which stress the shared language and shared circumstances of colonialism (recognising vast differences in the expression of British imperialism from place to place) allow for counter-discursive strategies, but unless their stress is on counter-discursive fields of activity, such models run the risk of becoming colonisers in their turn. African critics and writers in particular have rejected these models for their apparently neo-assimilative bases, and opted instead for the national or the pan-African. But if the impulse behind much post-colonial literature is seen to be broadly counter-discursive, and it is recognised that the resulting strategies may take many forms in different cultures, I think we have a more satisfactory model than national, racial, or cultural groupings based on marginalisation can offer, and one which perhaps avoids some of the pitfalls of earlier collective models or paradigms. Moreover, such a model can account for the ambiguous position of say, white Australians, who, though still colonised by Europe and European ideas, are themselves the continuing colonisers of the original inhabitants. In this model, all post-invasion Aboriginal writing and orature might be regarded as counter-discursive to a dominant 'Australian' discourse and beyond that again to its European progenitor. It is this model I wish to take up later in considering J. M. Coetzee's *Foe* which explores the problem of white South African settler literature in relation to the continuing oppression by whites of the black majority. . . .

It is possible to formulate at least two (not necessarily mutually exclusive) models for future post-colonial studies. In the first, the post-coloniality of a text would be argued to reside in its discursive features, in the second, in its determining relations with its material situation. The danger of the first lies in post-coloniality's becoming a set of unsituated reading practices; the danger in the second lies in the reintroduction of a covert form of essentialism. In an attempt to avoid these potential pitfalls I want to try to combine the two as overarching models in the reading of two texts by stressing counter-discursive strategies which offer a more general post-colonial reading practice or practices. These practices, though, are politically situated; sites of production and consumption that are inextricably bound up with the production of meaning. The site of communication is of paramount importance in post-colonial writing, and remains its most important defining boundary. . . .

Within the broad field of the counter-discursive many sub-groupings are possible and are already being investigated. These include 'magic realism' as post-colonial discourse, (see Dash 1974 and Slemon 1987) and the re/placing of carnivalesque European genres like the picaresque in post-colonial contexts, where they are carried to a higher subversive power. Stephen Slemon has demonstrated the potential of allegory as a privileged site of anti-colonial or post-colonial discourse (Slemon 1986, 1988b).

But the particular counter-discursive post-colonial field with which I want to engage here is what I'll call canonical counter-discourse. This strategy is perhaps most familiar through texts like Jean Rhys's *Wide Sargasso Sea*, and it is one in which a post-colonial writer takes up a character or characters, or the basic assumptions of a British canonical text, and unveils those assumptions, subverting the text for post-colonial purposes. An important point needs to be made here about the discursive functions of textuality itself in post-colonial worlds. European texts captured those worlds, 'reading' their alterity assimilatively in terms of their own cognitive codes. Explorers' journals, drama, fiction, historical accounts, 'mapping' enabled conquest and colonisation and the capture and/or vilification of alterity. But often the very texts which facilitated such material and psychic capture were those which the imposed European education systems foisted on the colonised as the 'great' literature which dealt with 'universals'; ones whose culturally specific imperial terms were to be accepted as axiomatic at the colonial margins. Achebe has noted the ironies of Conrad's *Heart of Darkness* being taught in colonial African universities.

Understandably, then, it has become the project of post-colonial literatures to investigate the European textual capture and containment of colonial and post-colonial space and to intervene in that originary and continuing containment. In his study of nineteenth century France, Richard Terdiman saw what he calls 'textual revolution' as partly conditional on the 'blockage of energy directed to structural change of the social formation' (Terdiman 1985: 80). But he goes on to note that even so, 'Literary revolution is not revolution by homology, but by *intended function.*' Literary revolution in post-colonial worlds has been an intrinsic component of social 'disidentification' (Pêcheux 1975: 158)[2] from the outset. Achebe's essay, 'The Novelist As Teacher' (Achebe 1975: 167–74) stresses the crucial function of texts in post-colonial social formations and their primacy in effecting revolution and restitution, priorities which are not surprising given the role of the text in the European capture and colonisation of Africa. Post-colonial counter-discursive strategies involve a mapping of the dominant discourse, a reading and exposing of its underlying assumptions, and the dis/mantling of these assumptions from the cross-cultural standpoint of the imperially subjectified 'local'. *Wide Sargasso Sea* directly contests British sovreignty – over persons, place, culture, language. It reinvests its own hybridised world with a provisionally normative perspective, but one which is deliberately constructed as provisional since the novel is at pains to demonstrate the subjective nature of point of view and hence the cultural construction of meaning.

Just as Jean Rhys writes back to Charlotte Brontë's *Jane Eyre* in *Wide Sargasso Sea*, so Samuel Selvon in *Moses Ascending* and J. M. Coetzee in *Foe* (and indeed throughout his works) write back to Daniel Defoe's *Robinson Crusoe*. Neither writer is simply 'writing back' to an English canonical text, but to the whole of the discursive field within which such a text operated and continues to operate in post-colonial worlds. Like William Shakespeare's *The Tempest*, *Robinson Crusoe* was part of the process of 'fixing' relations between Europe and its 'others', of establishing patterns of reading alterity at the same time as it inscribed the 'fixity' of that alterity, naturalising difference within its own cognitive codes. But the function of such a canonical text at the colonial periphery also becomes an important part of material imperial practice, in that, through educational and critical institutions, it continually displays and repeats for the colonised subject, the original capture of his/her alterity and the processes of its annihilation, marginalisation, or naturalisation as if this were axiomatic, culturally ungrounded, 'universal', natural.

Selvon and Coetzee take up the complex discursive field surrounding *Robinson Crusoe* and unlock these apparent closures.

## NOTES

1   Richard Terdiman, *Discourse/Counter-Discourse: The Theory and Practice of Symbolic Resistance in Nineteenth-Century France* (Ithaca and London: Cornell University Press, 1985). Terdiman theorises the potential and limitations of counter-discursive literary revolution within a dominant discourse noting that counter-discourses have the power to *situate*: to relativise the authority and stability of a dominant system of utterances which cannot even countenance their existence (pp. 15–16). But Terdiman regards counter-discourses as ultimately unable to effect genuine revolution, since they are condemned to remain marginal to the dominant discourse. The post-colonial situation is a rather different one, however, from that which provides Terdiman with his model.

2   Michel Pêcheux uses the term 'disidentification' to denote a transformation and displacement of the subject position interpellated by a dominant ideology.

# 15

## *Figures of Colonial Resistance*

### JENNY SHARPE*

IN THE ABSENCE of a critical awareness of colonialism's ideological effects, readings of counter-discourses can all too easily serve an institutional function of securing the dominant narratives. None of us escapes the legacy of a colonial past and its traces in our academic practice. . . .

I wish to demonstrate, through the historical example of India, certain problems with identifying sites of colonial resistance. I interpret as sites of resistance those ruptures in the representation of British colonialism as a civilizing mission. As my title suggests, I chart that problem through representative 'figures' that foreground the rhetorical strategies of the dominant discourses from which the truth-claims of our counter-narratives are derived. This complicity in narration indicates the necessity for defining our project as something other than the simple recuperation of lost testimonies. The first figure that I discuss, the 'mimic man' or 'colonial subject,'[1] makes visible the contradictions of colonialism at a time when a British presence in India was more or less taken for granted.[2] The mimic man is a contradictory figure who simultaneously reinforces colonial authority and disturbs it. Because the colonial subject was produced through a discourse of 'civility,' I begin by retelling the story of the civilizing mission in a manner that demonstrates the violence of its inscriptions. The discourse of civility strains to effect a closure in the case of the subaltern, where the violence of the colonial encounter is all the more visible. I read the 'cotton weaver' and the 'untouchable' as the mimic man's subaltern shadows, in order to demonstrate the class and caste determinants of colonial as well as postcolonial relations. . . .

Colonial fantasies about India center on the pseudo-aristocratic world the Anglo-Indians created with their sprawling bungalows, country clubs, and polite parties or 'frolics.' Accompanying a public display of civilized

* From 'Figures of Colonial Resistance' *Modern Fiction Studies*, 35(1), (Spring), 1989.

life are images that show the natives being freed from despotic rule, raised from their ignorance, and saved from cruel and barbarous practices. These vignettes tell of the civilizing mission, which is primarily a story about the colonizing culture as an emissary of light. Although the civilizing mission is generally associated with the selfconscious phase of imperialism beginning in the 1870s, the idea of colonialism as a moral obligation to spread Western civilization appeared long before imperialism was named as such. . . .[3]

Macaulay's Minute gives the effect of a general dissemination of the English language because it belongs to a discourse in which a Western educated, English speaking, indigenous middle class metonymically represented all of India. And it is in this capacity that the colonial subject served as an ideological alibi for colonialism.

Although one can still make a case for the education of the class-native in consumerism as liberating (see Robinson and Robinson 1971: 407–28), it is difficult to extend such readings to the freeing of labor power for Empire. Indian peasants and tribals were hired locally to cultivate a cotton dye in a system that has been described as 'indigo slavery,' or they were shipped to remote territories as 'coolies,' a form of indentured labor (see Sinha 1970 and Schweinitz 1983). The importation of cheaper, machine-produced English broadcloth into India deprived cotton-weavers of their livelihood. Many died of starvation. By the early decades of the nineteenth century the restructuring of the native industries around British manufacture was complete. Yet Macaulay's 1833 defence of the East India Company, which falls well within a discourse of civility, cannot speak of the ruined native industries upon which his vision of an economic and cultural 'exchange' depends. . . .

It is not simply a case that such accounts of colonial violence exceed the limits of the civilizing mission. Rather, the mythological proportions of the latter, the blinding brightness of its light, eclipse other stories of an East–West encounter. To think of the relation between the discourse centering on the production of the colonial subject and what it occludes as an eclipse is to see that the subaltern classes are not situated outside the civilizing project but are caught in the path of its trajectory. As I now turn to a scene of the educated native's writing, I see upon its pages the faint imprint of the bleached-out bones of the cotton-weavers. For the colonial subject who can answer the colonizers back is the product of the same vast ideological machinery that silences the subaltern. . . .

Arguing against the fixity of essentialist signification that Said's study of Orientalism suggests, Bhabha proposes a mixed economy of not only power and domination but also desire and pleasure (Bhabha 1983b: 156–61). He describes mimicry as a trope of partial presence that masks a threatening racial difference only to reveal the excesses and slippages of colonial power and knowledge. 'The menace of mimicry,' he explains, 'is its double vision which in disclosing the ambivalence of colonial discourse also disrupts its authority' (Bhabha 1984b: 129). The movement between a fixity of signification and its division, what he calls the 'ambivalence' of colonial discourse, demonstrates that colonial authority is never total or complete. And it is this absence of a closure that allows for native intervention.

The trajectory of Bhabha's work has moved him increasingly closer toward situating the slippages of colonial authority in a native appropriation of its signs. The trope of 'sly civility' points to both the excesses that a discourse of presence cannot contain as well as 'a native refusal to satisfy the colonizer's narrative demand' (Bhabha 1985b: 78). In turn, the native's 'hybrid demand' seizes colonial power in order to redefine the terms of its knowledge (Bhabha 1985a: 179). The ambivalence of colonial discourse that produces such colonial hybrids thus 'enables a form of subversion, founded on that uncertainty, that turns the discursive conditions of dominance into the grounds of intervention' (173). In words such as 'refusal,' 'subversion,' and 'intervention,' Bhabha ascribes a more active agency to the colonized than his earlier formulation of an inherently ambivalent colonial discourse might suggest. He nonetheless maintains that resistance is an effect of the contradictory representation of colonial authority, a native appropriation of its ambivalent strategies of power. I will momentarily suspend Bhabha's explanation of resistance, holding it alongside that other suspended narrative ending with the cotton weavers' bleached-out bones, as I offer my own example of the colonial subject's hybrid demand.

Among the holdings of the India Office Library in London, there exists an obscure document consisting of a used scrap of paper that contains, in the hand of a British judicial officer F. J. Shore, the draft of a letter to the editor of the *India Gazette*. . . .

The text that Shore proceeds to transcribe, an imaginary dialogue between two Bengalis, proleptically parodies Macaulay's 1835 Minute on Indian Education. In the dialogue, Baboo Must Hathee explains to his friend, Baboo Dana, why the English would benefit from learning Bengali. His suggestion restages the colonizers' privileging of racial purity and their own superior intellect in a manner that turns the language of purity and superiority against them. . . .

The initial triumph with which I discovered Shore's scribbled letter has since been quelled by the sobering reminder that the binary opposition between colonizer and colonized is not so easily reversed; the entire power structure of colonialism itself stands in the way of such an improbable exchange.[4] The impossibility of a reversal is made even more visible in light of the probability that this native work of fiction originated from a European. It is more than likely that Shore himself invented the dialogue as evidence of a native desire for vernacular education.[5] Here we see the colonizer disguising himself to help the native cast off his robe of Lancashire broadcloth.

Yet there is something to be said for Shore's 'duplicity,' for it demonstrates the difficulty of situating resistance. Do we identify, as the native response, Rammohun's actual demand for English education or his alleged demand for a vernacular one?[6] This double demand reveals Rammohun Roy as a contested site that cuts across the binary opposition of colonizer and colonized. But perhaps the question itself is the wrong one, as it adheres to the terms of a colonial discourse of civility. When Bhabha reads 'those moments of civil disobedience within the discipline of civility' as 'signs of spectacular resistance' (Bhabha 1985a: 181), he overlooks other more violent sites of colonial contact where Western civilization was simultaneously being written. To consider the violence with which colonialism enforces its mission is to recognize the signs of resistance in uncivil demands. They are demands that are missing from the texts of civility, for the civilizing mission cannot acknowledge the violence/resistance underpinning a tracing of its path. . . .

The 'success' of our critical work depends on the recognition that the subaltern is irreducible and yet ultimately irretrievable. Our models remain inadequate. In the absence of that failure we run the risk of imitating successful historical records and subordinating the subaltern.

## NOTES

1 I use 'colonial subject' specifically for the Western-educated native in order to emphasize 1) the subject status that a class of natives acquires by acceding to the authority of Western knowledge 2) the restriction of sovereignty to the colonizers alone, and 3) the denial of subject status to natives belonging to the subordinate or subaltern classes.

2 My discussion of colonialism refers to the period from the 1757 Battle of Plassey when the British gained territorial control over Northern India, to 1858, when the Indian Empire was officially consolidated following the so-called Sepoy Rebellion. . . .

3 The word 'imperialism' received currency in England after 1870, when it was explicitly identified with the civilizing mission. . . . Hegel, however, calls the English 'the missionaries of civilization to the world' as early as the 1820s. Also see Victor Kiernan, Harry Magdoff, and Peter Worsley. Lenin's *Imperialism: The Highest Stage of Capitalism* [1916] (1969) is a classic study of imperialism.

4 I am here reminded of the much quoted words that Caliban casts back at Prospero in Shakespeare's *The Tempest*: 'You taught me language; and my profit on 't/Is, I know how to curse' (I, ii: 363–4). While holding these words as an instance of the slave's refusal to remain docile and silent, we must also remember that Prospero's curses alone have the power to produce the desired effects of pain and torture.

5 I thank Barun De for bringing to my attention Shore's fondness for writing fictions of this kind. For Shore's official views on the role of the vernacular

languages in native education, see F. J. Shore's 'On the Language and Character Best Suited to the Education of the People.'

6   Interestingly enough, Samuel Charles Hill's catalogue for the Home Miscellaneous Series lists Shore's letter as 'Ram Mohun Roy's proposal that the English in India should adopt Bengali as their language' (517).

# 16

## Unsettling the Empire
### Resistance Theory for the Second World

STEPHEN SLEMON*

WHAT I WANT to do in this paper is address two separate debates in critical theory, and then attempt to yoke them together into an argument for maintaining within a discourse of post-colonialism certain textual and critical practices which inhabit ex-colonial settler cultures and their literatures. The textual gestures I want to preserve for post-colonial theory and practice are various and dispersed, but the territory I want to reclaim for post-colonial pedagogy and research – and reclaim *not* as a unified and indivisible area but rather as a groundwork for certain modes of anti-colonial work – is that neither/nor territory of white settler-colonial writing which Alan Lawson has called the 'Second World'.

The first debate concerns the *field* of the 'post-colonial'. . . .

The second debate I want to address concerns the nature of literary *resistance* itself. Is literary resistance something that simply issues forth, through narrative, against a clearly definable set of power relations? Is it something actually *there* in the text, or is it produced and reproduced in and through communities of readers and through the mediating structures of their own culturally specific histories? Do literary resistances escape the constitutive purchase of genre, and trope, and figure, and mode, which operate elsewhere as a contract between text and reader and thus a set of centralizing codes, or are literary resistances in fact necessarily *embedded* in the representational technologies of those literary and social 'texts' whose structures and whose referential codes they seek to oppose?

These questions sound like definitional problems, but I think in fact they are crucial ones for a critical industry which at the moment seems to find these two central terms – 'post-colonial' and 'resistance' – positively shimmering as objects of desire and self-privilege, and so easily appropriated to competing, and in fact hostile, modes of critical and literary practice. Arun Mukherjee makes this point with great eloquence

* From 'Unsettling the Empire: Resistance Theory for the Second World' *World Literature Written in English* 30(2), 1990.

(Mukherjee 1990: 1–9), asking what specificity, what residual grounding, remains with the term 'post-colonial' when it is applied indiscriminately to both Second- and Third-World literary texts. The term 'resistance' recently found itself at the centre of a similar controversy, when it was discovered how very thoroughly a *failure* in resistance characterized some of the earlier political writing of the great theorist of *textual* resistance, Paul de Man. Both terms thus find themselves at the centre of a quarrel over the kinds of critical taxonomies that will be seen to perform legitimate work in articulating the relation between literary texts and the political world; and to say this is to recognize that critical taxonomies, like literary canons, issue forth from cultural institutions which continue to police what voices will be heard, which *kinds* of (textual) intervention will be made recognizable and/or classifiable, and what *authentic* forms of post-colonial textual resistance are going to look like. These debates are thus institutional: grounded in university curricula, and *about* pedagogical strategies. They are also about the question of authenticity itself: how a text emerges from a cultural grounding and speaks to a reading community, and how textual ambiguity or ambivalence proves pedagogically awkward when an apparatus called 'English studies' recuperates various writing practices holistically as 'literatures', and then deploys them wholesale towards a discourse of inclusivity and coverage. The first debate – the question of the 'post-colonial' – is grounded in the overlapping of three competing research or critical fields, each of which carries a specific cultural location and history. In the first of these fields, the term 'post-colonial' is an outgrowth of what formerly were 'Commonwealth' literary studies – a study which came into being *after* 'English' studies had been liberalized to include 'American' and then an immediate national or regional literature (Australian, Canadian, West Indian), and as a way of mobilizing the concept of national or geographical *difference* within what remains a unitary idea of 'English'. The second of these critical fields, in contrast, employs the term 'post-colonial' in considering the valency of subjectivity specifically within Third- and Fourth-World cultures, and within black, and ethnic, and First-Nation constituencies dispersed within First-World terrain. The institutionalizing of these two critical fields has made possible the emergence of a third field of study, however, where nation-based examinations of a variable literary Commonwealth, or a variable literary Third World, give way to specific analyses of the discourse of colonialism (and neo-colonialism), and where studies in cultural representativeness and literary mimeticism give way to the project of identifying the kinds of anti-colonialist resistance that can take place in literary writing. . . .

'Post-colonial' studies in 'English' now finds itself at a shifting moment, where three very different critical projects collide with one another on the space of a single signifier – and what will probably be a single course offering within an English studies programme. Not surprisingly, this situation has produced some remarkable confusions, and they

105

underpin the present debate over the specificity of the 'post-colonial' in the areas of literary and critical practice.

The confusion which concerns me here is the way in which the *project* of the third 'post-colonial' critical field – that is, of identifying the scope and nature of anti-colonialist resistance in writing – has been mistaken for the project of the second critical field, which concerns itself with articulating the literary nature of Third- and Fourth-World cultural groups. For whereas the first and second of these post-colonial critical fields work with whole nations or cultures as their basic units, and tend to seek out the defining characteristics under which *all* writing in that field can be subsumed, the third critical field is concerned with identifying a social force, colonialism, and with the attempt to understand the resistances to that force, *wherever* they lie. Colonialism, obviously, is an enormously problematical category: it is by definition transhistorical and unspecific, and it is used in relation to very different kinds of cultural oppression and economic control. But like the term 'patriarchy,' which shares similar problems in definition, the concept of colonialism, to this third critical field, remains crucial to a critique of past and present power relations in world affairs, and thus to a specifically *post*-colonial critical practice which attempts to understand the relation of literary writing to power and its contestations.

This mistaking of a pro-active, anti-colonialist critical project with nation-based studies in Third- and Fourth-World literary writing comes about for good reason – for it has been, and always will be, the case that the most important forms of resistance to any form of social power will be produced from within the communities that are most immediately and visibly subordinated by that power structure. But when the idea of anti-colonial resistance becomes *synonymous* with Third- and Fourth-World literary writing, two forms of displacement happen. First, *all* literary writing which emerges from these cultural locations will be understood as carrying a radical and contestatory content – and this gives away the rather important point that subjected peoples are sometimes capable of producing reactionary literary documents. And secondly, the idea will be discarded that important anti-colonialist literary writing can take place *outside* the ambit of Third- and Fourth-World literary writing – and this in effect excises the study of anti-colonialist Second-World literary activity from the larger study of anti-colonialist literary practice. . . .

This conflating of the projects of the second and third post-colonial critical fields, and the consequent jettisoning of Second-World literary writing from the domain of the post-colonial, remains – in the Bloomian sense – a 'misreading', and one which seems to be setting in train a concept of the 'post-colonial' which is remarkably purist and absolutist in tenor. . . .

The foundational principle for this particular approach to the field of post-colonial criticism is at heart a simple binarism: the binarism of Europe and its Others, of colonizer and colonized, of the West and the Rest, of the vocal and the silent. It is also a centre/periphery model with roots in world-systems theory – and as so often happens with simple binary systems, this concept of the post-colonial has a marked tendency to blur when it tries to focus upon ambiguously placed or ambivalent material. In what seems to be emerging as the dominant focus of post-colonial literary criticism now – especially for literary criticism coming out of universities in the United States – this blurring is everywhere in evidence in relation to what world systems theory calls the field of 'semi-periphery', and what follows behind it is a radical foreclosing by post-colonial criticism on settler/colonial writing: the radical ambivalence of colonialism's middle ground. . . .

At any rate, the new binaristic absolutism which seems to come in the wake of First-World accommodation to the fact of post-colonial literary and cultural criticism seems to be working in several ways to drive that trans-national region of ex-colonial settler cultures away from the field of post-colonial literary representation. The Second World of writing within the ambit of colonialism is in danger of disappearing: because it is not sufficiently pure in its anti-colonialism, because it does not offer up an experiential grounding in a common 'Third World' aesthetics, because its modalities of *post*-coloniality are too ambivalent, too occasional and uncommon, for inclusion within the field. This debate over the scope and nature of the 'post-colonial', I now want to argue, has enormous investments in the second debate I want to discuss in this paper, for in fact the idea of both literary and political *resistance* to colonialist power is the hidden term, the foundational concept, upon which *all* these distinctions in the modality of the 'post-colonial' actually rest. . . .

The first concept of resistance is most clearly put forward by Selwyn Cudjoe in his *Resistance and Caribbean Literature* and by Barbara Harlow in her book, *Resistance Literature*. For Cudjoe and Harlow, resistance is an act, or a set of acts, that is designed to rid a people of its oppressors, and it so thoroughly infuses the experience of living under oppression that it becomes an almost autonomous aesthetic principle. *Literary* resistance, under these conditions, can be seen as a form of contractual understanding between text and reader, one which is embedded in an experiential dimension and buttressed by a political and cultural aesthetic at work in the culture. And 'resistance literature', in this definition, can thus be seen as that category of literary writing which emerges as an integral part of an organized struggle or resistance for national liberation.

This argument for literary 'resistance' is an important one to hold on to – but it is also a strangely untheorized position, for it fails to address three major areas of critical concern. The first is a political concern: namely, that centre/periphery notions of resistance can actually work to *reinscribe* centre/periphery relations and can 'serve an institutional function of securing the dominant narratives' (Sharpe 1989: 139). The second problem with this argument is that it assumes that literary resistance is simply somehow *there* in the literary text as a structure of intentionality, and *there* in the social text as a communicative gesture of pure availability. Post-Lacanian and post-Althusserian theories of the constructedness of subjectivity, however, would contest such easy access to representational purity, and would argue instead that resistance is grounded in the *multiple* and *contradictory* structures of ideological interpellation or subject-formation – which would call down the notion that resistance can *ever* be 'purely' intended or 'purely' expressed in representational or communicative models. The third problem with this argument is that it has to set aside the very persuasive theory of power which Foucault puts forward in his *The Archaeology of Knowledge*: the theory that power *itself* inscribes its resistances and so, in the process, seeks to contain them. It is this third objection, especially, which has energized the post-structuralist project of theorizing literary resistance – and in order to clarify what is going on in that theatre of critical activity I want to focus especially on Jenny Sharpe's wonderful article in *Modern Fiction Studies* entitled 'Figures of Colonial Resistance'.

Sharpe's article involves a reconsideration of the work of theorists such as Gayatri Spivak, Homi Bhabha, Abdul JanMohamed, and Benita Parry, each of whom has worked to correct the critical 'tendency to presume the transparency' of literary resistance in colonial and post-colonial writing (138), and who collectively have worked to examine the ways in which resistance in writing must go beyond the mere 'questioning' of colonialist authority. There are important differences in how all of these theorists define literary resistance, but the two key points Sharpe draws out are, first, that you can never *easily* locate the sites of anti-colonial resistance – since resistance itself is always in some measure an 'effect of the contradictory representation of colonial authority' (145) and never simply a 'reversal' of power – and secondly, that resistance itself is therefore never *purely* resistance, never *simply* there in the text or the interpretive community, but is always *necessarily* complicit in the apparatus it seeks to transgress. . . .

Sharpe's argument, that is, underscores the way in which literary resistance is necessarily in a place of ambivalence: between systems, between discursive worlds, implicit and complicit in both of them. And from this recognition comes the very startling but inevitable claim – made most spectacularly by Tim Brennan in his book on *Salman Rushdie and the Third World* – that the Third World resistance writer, the Third World resistance text, is necessarily self-produced as a doubly-emplaced and mediated figure – Brennan's term is 'Third-World Cosmopolitan' – between the First and the Third Worlds, and *within* the ambit of a First-World politics.

There is a contradiction within the dominant trajectory of First-World post-colonial critical theory here – for that same theory which argues persuasively for the necessary *ambivalence* of post-colonial literary resistance, and which works to emplace that resistance squarely *between* First- and Third-World structures of representation, *also* wants to assign 'Second World' or ex-colonial settler literatures unproblematically to the category of the literature of empire, the literature of the First World, precisely *because* of its ambivalent position within the First-World/Third-World, colonizer/colonized binary. Logically, however, it would seem that the argument being made by Spivak, Bhabha, Sharpe and others about the ambivalence of literary and other resistances – the argument that resistance texts are necessarily double, necessarily mediated, in their social location – is in fact nothing less than an argument *for* the emplacement of 'Second World' literary texts within the field of the 'post-colonial': for if there *is* only a space for a *pure* Third- and Fourth-World resistance outside the First-World hegemony, then *either* you have to return to the baldly untheorized notion which informs the first position in the debate over literary resistance, *or* you have to admit that at least as far as writing is concerned, the 'field' of the genuinely *post*-colonial can never *actually* exist.

It is for this reason, I think, and not because of some vestigial nostalgia for an empire upon which the sun will never set, that many critics and theorists have argued long and hard for the preservation of white Australian, New Zealander, southern African, and Canadian literatures within the field of comparative 'post-colonial' literary studies. . . .

The 'Second World' – like the third of the three 'post-colonial' critical fields I have been discussing – is at root a *reading position*, and one which is and often has been taken up in settler and ex-colonial literature and criticism. The 'Second World', that is, like 'post-colonial criticism' itself, is a critical manoeuvre, a reading and writing action; and embedded within it is a theory of communicative action akin in some ways to Clifford Geertz's thesis about 'intermediary knowledge', or Gadamer's theory of an interpretive 'fusion of horizons'. 'The inherent awareness of both "there" and "here," and the cultural ambiguity of these terms', writes Lawson, 'are not so much the boundaries of its cultural matrix, nor tensions to be resolved, but a space *within* which [the Second-World, post-colonial] literary text may move while speaking' (Lawson 1986). Lawson's definition of literary representation in the discursive 'Second World' thus articulates a figure for what many First-World critical theorists would correctly define as the limits and the condition of *post-colonial* forms of literary resistance. The irony is that many of those same First-World critics would define that 'post-colonial' as exclusively the domain of the Third and Fourth Worlds.

But what perhaps marks a *genuine* difference in the contestatory activity of Second- and Third-World post-colonial writing, I now want to argue, is that the *illusion* of a stable self/other, here/there binary division has *never* been available to Second-World writers, and that as a result the sites of figural contestation between oppressor and oppressed, colonizer and colonized, have been taken *inward* and *internalized* in Second-World post-colonial textual practice. By this I mean that the *ambivalence* of literary resistance itself is the 'always already' condition of Second-World settler and post-colonial literary writing, for in the white literatures of Australia, or New Zealand, or Canada, or southern Africa, anti-colonialist resistance has *never* been directed at an object or a discursive structure which can be seen purely external to the self. The Second-World writer, the Second-World text, that is, have always been complicit in colonialism's territorial appropriation of land, and voice, and agency, and this has been their inescapable condition even at those moments when they have promulgated their most strident and most spectacular figures of post-colonial resistance. In the Second World, anti-colonialist resistances in literature must necessarily *cut across the individual subject*, and as they do so they also, necessarily, contribute towards that theoretically rigorous understanding of textual resistance which post-colonial *critical* theory is only now learning how to recognize. This ambivalence of emplacement is the *condition* of their possibility; it has been since the beginning; and it is therefore scarcely surprising that the ambivalent, the mediated, the conditional, and the radically *compromised* literatures of this undefinable Second World have an enormous amount yet to tell to 'theory' about the nature of literary resistance.

This *internalization* of the object of resistance in Second-World literatures, this internalization of the self/other binary of colonialist relations, explains why it is that it has always been Second-World *literary* writing rather than Second-World *critical* writing which has occupied the vanguard of a Second-World post-colonial literary or critical *theory*. Literary writing is about internalized conflict, whereas critical writing – for most practitioners – is still grounded in the ideology of unitariness, and coherence, and specific argumentative drive. For this reason, Second-World *critical* writing – with some spectacularly transgressive exceptions – has tended to miss out on the rigours of what, I would argue, comprises a necessarily ambivalent, necessarily contra/dictory or incoherent, anti-colonialist *theory* of resistance. In literary documents such as De Mille's *Strange Manuscript* or Furphy's *Such Is Life*, to name two nineteenth-century examples, or in the 're-historical' fictions of writers such as Fiona Kidman, Ian Wedde, Thea Astley, Peter Carey, Kate Grenville, Barbara Hanrahan, Daphne Marlatt, Susan Swan, and Rudy Wiebe – to name only a few from the contemporary period – this necessary *entanglement* of anti-colonial resistances within the colonialist machineries they seek to displace has been consistently thematized, consistently worked through, in ways that the unitary and logical demands of critical argumentation, at least in its traditional genres, have simply not allowed.

# 17

## The Rhetoric of English India

### SARA SULERI*

[THERE IS A] precarious vulnerability of cultural boundaries in the context of colonial exchange. In historical terms, colonialism precludes the concept of 'exchange' by granting to the idea of power a greater literalism than it deserves. The telling of colonial and postcolonial stories, however, demands a more naked relation to the ambivalence represented by the greater mobility of disempowerment. To tell the history of another is to be pressed against the limits of one's own – thus culture learns that terror has a local habitation and a name. . . . The allegorization of empire, in other words, can only take shape in an act of narration that is profoundly suspicious of the epistemological and ethical validity of allegory, suggesting that the term 'culture' – more particularly, 'other cultures' – is possessed of an intransigence that belies exemplification. Instead, the story of culture eschews the formal category of allegory to become a painstaking study of how the idioms of ignorance and terror construct a mutual narrative of complicities. While the 'allegory of empire' will always have recourse to the supreme fiction of Conrad's Marlow, or the belief that what redeems it is 'the idea alone,' its heart of darkness must incessantly acknowledge the horror attendant on each act of cultural articulation that demonstrates how Ahab tells Naboth's story in order to know himself. . . .

From the vast body of eighteenth-century historical documentation of British rule in India to the proliferation of Anglo-Indian fiction in the nineteenth and twentieth centuries, the narratives of English India are fraught with the idiom of dubiety, or a mode of cultural tale-telling that is neurotically conscious of its own self-censoring apparatus. While such narratives appear to claim a new preeminence of historical facticity over cultural allegory, they nonetheless illustrate that the functioning of language in a colonial universe is preternaturally dependent on the instability of its own facts. For colonial facts are vertiginous: they lack a recognizable

* From *The Rhetoric of English India* Chicago: University of Chicago Press, 1992.

cultural plot; they frequently fail to cohere around the master-myth that proclaims static lines of demarcation between imperial power and disempowered culture, between colonizer and colonized. Instead, they move with a ghostly mobility to suggest how highly unsettling an economy of complicity and guilt is in operation between each actor on the colonial stage. If such an economy is the impelling force of the stories of English India, it demands to be read against the grain of the rhetoric of binarism that informs, either explicitly or implicitly, contemporary critiques of alterity in colonial discourse (see Bhabha 1983b; Spivak 1987; JanMohamed 1983). The necessary intimacies that obtain between ruler and ruled create a counter-culture not always explicable in terms of an allegory of otherness: the narrative of English India questions the validity of both categories to its secret economy, which is the dynamic of powerlessness at the heart of the imperial configuration.

If English India represents a discursive field that includes both colonial and postcolonial narratives, it further represents an alternative to the troubled chronology of nationalism in the Indian subcontinent. As long as the concept of nation is interpreted as the colonizer's gift to its erstwhile colony, the unimaginable community produced by colonial encounter can never be sufficiently read (Anderson 1983). Again, the theoretical paradigm of margin against center is unhelpful in this context, for it serves to hierarchize the emergence of nation in 'first' and 'third' worlds. . . .

If colonial cultural studies is to avoid a binarism that could cause it to atrophy in its own apprehension of difference, it needs to locate an idiom for alterity that can circumnavigate the more monolithic interpretations of cultural empowerment that tend to dominate current discourse. To study the rhetoric of the British Raj in both its colonial and postcolonial manifestations is therefore to attempt to break down the incipient schizophrenia of a critical discourse that seeks to represent domination and subordination as though the two were mutually exclusive terms. Rather than examine a binary rigidity between those terms – which is an inherently Eurocentric strategy – this critical field would be better served if it sought to break down the fixity of the dividing lines between domination and subordination, and if it further questioned the psychic disempowerment signified by colonial encounter. For to interpret the configurations of colonialism in the idiom of such ineluctable divisions is to deny the impact of narrative on a productive disordering of binary dichotomies. . . .

The intimacy of the colonial setting requires reiteration. For the reader of postcolonial discourse provides scant service to its conceptualization when she posits the issue of an intransigent otherness as both the first and the final solution to the political and aesthetic problems raised by the mutual transcriptions that colonialism has engendered in the Indian subcontinent. Diverse ironies of empire are too compelling to be explained away by the simple pieties that the idiom of alterity frequently cloaks. If cultural criticism is to address the uses to which it puts the agency of alterity, then it must further face the theoretical question that S. P. Mohanty succinctly formulates: 'Just how other, we need to force ourselves to indicate, is the Other?' (Mohanty 1989: 5). Since recourse neither to representation nor to cultural relativism can supply an answer, postcolonial discourse is forced into alternative questions: how can the dynamic of imperial intimacy produce an idea of nation that belongs neither to the colonizer nor to the colonized? Is nation in itself the alterity to which both subjugating and subjugated cultures must in coordination defer? In what ways does the idiom of otherness simply rehearse the colonial fallacy through which India could be interpreted only as the unreadability of romance? . . .

If the paradigm of master and victim is to be read in terms of its availability to the histories of colonialism and their concomitant narratives, then its rereading as a figure of colonial intimacy – as an interruption in traditional interpretations of imperial power – must necessarily generate a discursive guilt at the heart of the idiom of English India. Its troubled confluence of colony, culture, and nation lends a retroactive migrancy to the fact of imperialism itself, causing a figure like Kipling's Ahab to recognize that narration occurs to confirm the precariousness of power.

# PART IV

Postmodernism and
Post-colonialism

# Introduction

———◦∘◦———

'Post-colonial' as we define it does not mean 'post-independence', or 'after colonialism', for this would be to falsely ascribe an end to the colonial process. Post-colonialism, rather, begins from the very first moment of colonial contact. It is the discourse of oppositionality which colonialism brings into being. In this sense, post-colonial writing has a very long history. But it would be true to say that the intensification of theoretical interest in the post-colonial has coincided with the rise of postmodernism in Western society and this has led to both confusion and overlap between the two.

This confusion is caused partly by the fact that the major project of post-modernism – the deconstruction of the centralised, logocentric master narratives of European culture, is very similar to the post-colonial project of dismantling the Centre/Margin binarism of imperial discourse. The decentring of discourse, the focus on the significance of language and writing in the construction of experience, the use of the subversive strategies of mimicry, parody and irony – all these concerns overlap those of postmodernism and so a conflation of the two discourses has often occurred. Indeed the conflation is often quite sophisticated as we find in Linda Hutcheon's analysis. But it is useful to note that although 'theory' has emerged more often in the post-colonial *creative* text, theoretical texts such as Wilson Harris's *Tradition, the Writer and Society*, which offers many conclusions of an apparently poststructuralist nature, actually *precede* the writings of Derrida and Foucault. The rejection of the Cartesian individual, the instability of signification, the location of the subject in language or discourse, the dynamic operation of power: all these familiar post-structuralist concepts emerge in post-colonial thought in different guises which nevertheless confirm the political agency of the colonised subject. Post-colonialism is not simply a kind of 'postmodernism with politics' – it is a sustained attention to the imperial process in colonial and neo-colonial societies, and an examination of the strategies to subvert the actual material and discursive effects of that process.

One way of comparing these two discourses is to compare the claims they make upon experience. We are often told, for instance, that we live in a 'Postmodern Age', and in this claim an essentially European (or trans-

117

Atlantic) cultural movement makes yet again the same claim upon world history that other European movements have made in the past. We are hardly likely ever to find that we live in a 'Post-colonial Age' because the 'post' in post-colonial is not the same as the 'post' in postmodernism. Postmodernism, whether it is the cultural logic of late capitalism (as Frederic Jameson claims) or not, doesn't appear to be the primary framework within which most of the world's population carries out its daily life. The response to this might be that nevertheless western postmodernism has had a subtle and undeniable effect upon the rest of the world, but this is only another way of saying that the imperial process of eurocentrism is still active. This activity itself becomes a subject for post-colonial reading. Quite apart from any theoretical similarities, the *practices* of poststructuralist and post-colonial reading are completely distinct. In practice poststructuralism, for all its iconoclasm, licenses a return to the canon (particularly the canon of Romanticism) and to traditional forms of literary criticism because it appears to bring a completely new set of theoretical tools to bear upon well-worn texts. In contrast the very idea of post-colonial literary production precludes any return to a canon because the field itself transforms what we understand literature to be.

For Kwame Anthony Appiah, the post in post-colonialism is very different from that in postmodernism, for it is the post of a space-clearing gesture, a gesture which for him can sometimes be characterised as 'post-realist', 'post-nativist' and transnational rather than national categories which describe the 'postmodernisation' rather than the postmodernism of the post-colonial text. Simon During voices an objection to the claims of some post-colonial societies on the basis of their 'post-colonising' impetus, but this objection should be mediated in the reader's mind by the understanding of 'post-colonial' as a process as much as an identity. Linda Hutcheon's view of the overlap between the post-colonial and the postmodern is one of the best known discussions of the matter and her position is countered directly by Diana Brydon, whose concept of 'contamination' is also an important intervention into questions of cultural authenticity. The hybridity of the post-colonial writer, the continual deferral of authenticity is for Kumkum Sangari a source of creative strength and one which directly engages the universal-ising hegemony of international postmodernism. For in the final analysis, the problems of representation in the post-colonial text assume a political dimension very different from the radical provisionality now accepted as fundamental to postmodernism.

# 18

## The Postcolonial and the Postmodern

### KWAME ANTHONY APPIAH*

POSTCOLONIALITY IS THE condition of what we might ungenerously call a *comprador* intelligentsia: of a relatively small, Western-style, Western-trained, group of writers and thinkers, who mediate the trade in cultural commodities of world capitalism at the periphery. In the West they are known through the Africa they offer; their compatriots know them both through the West they present to Africa and through an Africa they have invented for the world, for each other and for Africa.

All aspects of contemporary African cultural life including music and some sculpture and painting, even some writings with which the West is largely not familiar – have been influenced – often powerfully – by the transition of African societies *through* colonialism, but they are not all in the relevant sense *post*colonial. For the *post* in postcolonial, like the post in postmodern is the *post* of the space-clearing gesture ... and many areas of contemporary African cultural life – what has come to be theorised as popular culture, in particular – are not in this way concerned with transcending – with going beyond – coloniality. Indeed, it might be said to be a mark of popular culture that its borrowings from international cultural forms are remarkably insensitive to – not so much dismissive of as blind to – the issue of neocolonialism or 'cultural imperialism'. This does not mean that theories of postmodernism are irrelevant to these forms of culture: for the internationalisation of the market and the commodification of art-works are both central to them. But it does mean that these artworks are not understood by their producers or their consumers in terms of a postmodernism: there is no antecedent practice whose claim to exclusivity of vision is rejected through these artworks. What is called 'syncretism' here is made possible by the international exchange of commodities, but is not a consequence of a space-clearing gesture.

* From *In My Father's House: Africa in the Philosophy of Culture* London: Methuen, 1992.

Postcolonial intellectuals in Africa, by contrast, are almost entirely dependent for their support on two institutions: the African university – an institution whose intellectual life is overwhelmingly constituted as Western – and the Euro-American publisher and reader. (Even when these writers seek to escape the West – as Ngugi wa Thiong'o did in attempting to construct a Kikuyu peasant drama – their theories of their situation are irreducibly informed by their Euro-American formation. Ngugi's conception of the writer's potential in politics is essentially that of the avant-garde; of left modernism.)

Now this double dependence on the university and the Euro-American publisher means that the first generation of modern African novels – the generation of Achebe's *Things Fall Apart* and Laye's *L'Enfant noir* – were written in the context of notions of politics and culture dominant in the French and British university and publishing worlds in the 1950s and '60s. This does not mean that they were like novels written in Western Europe at that time: for part of what was held to be obvious both by these writers and by the high culture of Europe of the day was that new literatures in new nations should be anti-colonial and nationalist. These early novels seem to belong to the world of eighteenth- and nineteenth-century literary nationalism; they are theorised as the imaginative recreation of a common cultural past that is crafted into a shared tradition by the writer; they are in the tradition of Scott, whose Minstrelsy of the Scottish Border was intended, as he said in the preface, to 'contribute somewhat to the history of my native country; the peculiar features of whose manners and character are daily melting and dissolving into those of her sister and ally'. The novels of this first stage are thus realist legitimations of nationalism: they authorise a 'return to traditions' while at the same time recognising the demands of a Weberian rationalised modernity.

From the later sixties on, these celebratory novels of the first stage become rarer: Achebe, for example, moves from the creation of a usable past in *Things Fall Apart* to a cynical indictment of politics in the modern sphere in *A Man of the People*. But I should like to focus on a francophone novel of the later sixties, a novel which thematises in an extremely powerful way many of the questions I have been asking about art and modernity: I mean, of course, Yambo Ouologuem's *Le Devoir de violence* (1968a). This novel, like many of this second stage, represents a challenge to the novels of this first stage: it identifies the realist novel as part of the tactic of nationalist legitimation and so it is – if I may begin a catalogue of its ways-of-being-*post*-this-and-that – *postrealist*.

Now, postmodernism is, of course, postrealist also. But Ouologuem's postrealism is surely motivated quite differently from that of such postmodern writers as, say, Pynchon. Realism naturalises: the originary 'African novel' of Chinua Achebe – *Things Fall Apart* – and of Camara Laye – *L'Enfant noir* – is 'realist'. So Ouologuem is against it, rejects – indeed, assaults – the conventions of realism. He seeks to delegitimate the forms of the realist African novel, in part, surely, because what it sought to naturalise was a nationalism that, by 1968, had plainly failed. The national bourgeoisie that took on the baton of rationalisation, industrialisation, bureaucratisation in the name of nationalism, turned out to be a klepto-cracy. Their enthusiasm for nativism was a rationalisation of their urge to keep the national bourgeosies of other nations – and particularly the powerful industrialised nations – out of their way. As Jonathan Ngaté has observed ' . . . *Le Devoir de violence* . . . deal[s] with a world in which *the efficacy* of the call to the Ancestors as well as the Ancestors themselves is seriously called into question' (Ngaté 1988: 59). That the novel is in this way postrealist allows its author to borrow, when he needs them, the techniques of modernism: which, as we learned from Fred Jameson, are often also the techniques of postmodernism. . . .

And the book's first sentence artfully establishes the oral mode – by then an inevitable convention of African narration – with words that Ngaté rightly describes as having the 'concision and the striking beauty and power of a proverb' (Ngaté 1988: 64) and mocks us in this moment because the sentence echoes the beginning of Andre Schwartz-Bart's decidedly un-African 1959 holocaust novel *Le Dernier des justes*; an echo that more substantial later borrowings confirm. . . .

> Our eyes drink the flash of the sun, and, conquered, surprise them-selves by weeping. Maschallah! oua bismillah! . . . An account of the bloody adventure of the niggertrash – dishonour to the men of nothing – *could easily begin in the* first half of this *century*; *but the true history of* the Blacks *begins* very much *earlier*, with the Saïfs, in the year 1202 of our era, in the African kingdom of Nakem. . . .
> (Ouologuem 1968a: 9) [Author's translation]

> *Our eyes* receive the light of dead stars. A biography of my friend Ernie *could easily begin in the* second quarter of the 20th *century*; *but the true history* of Ernie Led *begins* much *earlier*, in the old anglican city of York. More precisely: on the 11 March 1185.
> (Schwartz-Bart 1959: 11)

The reader who is properly prepared will expect an African holocaust; and these echoes are surely meant to render ironic the status of the rulers of Nakem as descendants of Abraham El Héït, 'Le Juif noir' (Ouologuem 1968a: 12).

The book begins, then, with a sick joke at the unwary reader's expense against nativism: and the assault on realism is – here is my second signpost – postnativist; this book is a murderous antidote to a nostalgia for *Roots*. As Wole Soyinka has said in a justly well-respected reading: 'the Bible, the Koran, the historic solemnity of the griot are reduced to the histrionics of wanton boys masquerading as humans' (1976: 100). It is tempting to read the attack on history here as a repudiation not of roots but of Islam, as Soyinka does when he goes on to say:

121

> A culture which has claimed indigenous antiquity in such parts of Africa as have submitted to its undeniable attractions is confidently proven to be imperialist; worse, it is demonstrated to be essentially hostile to the indigenous culture. . . . Ouologuem pronounces the Moslem incursion into black Africa to be corrupt, vicious, decadent, elitist and insensitive. At the least such a work functions as a wide swab in the deck-clearing operation for the commencement of racial retrieval.
>
> (1976: 105)

But it seems to me much clearer to read the repudiation as a repudiation of national history; to see the text as postcolonially postnationalist as well as anti- (and thus, of course, post-) nativist. (Indeed, Soyinka's reading here seems to be driven by his own equally representative tendency . . . to read Africa as race and place into everything.) Raymond Spartacus Kassoumi – who is, if anyone is, the hero of this novel – is, after all, a son of the soil, but his political prospects by the end of the narrative are less than uplifting. More than this, the novel explicitly thematises, in the anthropologist Shrobenius – an obvious echo of the name of the German Africanist Frobenius, whose work is cited by Senghor – the mechanism by which the new elite has come to invent its traditions through the 'science' of ethnography: 'Saïf made up stories and the interpreter translated, Madoubo repeated in French, refining on the subtleties to the delight of Shrobenius, that human crayfish afflicted with a groping mania for resuscitating an African universe – cultural autonomy, he called it, which had lost all living reality . . . he was determined to find metaphysical meaning in everything . . . African life, he held, was pure art (Ouologuem 1968b: 87) . . . At the start we have been told that 'there are few written accounts and the versions of the elders diverge from those of the griots, which differ from those of the chroniclers' (Ouologuem 1968b: 6). Now we are warned off the supposedly scientific discourse of the ethnographers.

Because this is a novel that seeks to delegitimate not only the form of realism but the content of nationalism, it will to that extent seem to us misleadingly to be postmodern. Misleadingly, because what we have here is not postmodernism but postmodern*isation*; not an aesthetics but a politics, in the most literal sense of the term. After colonialism, the modernisers said, comes rationality; that is the possibility the novel rules out. Ouologuem's novel is typical of this second stage in that it is not written by someone who is comfortable with and accepted by the new elite, the national bourgeoisie. Far from being a celebration of the nation, then, the novels of the second stage – the postcolonial stage – are novels of delegitimation: rejecting the Western *imperium*, it is true; but also rejecting the nationalist project of the postcolonial national bourgeoisie. And, so it seems to me, the basis for that project of delegitimation is very much not the postmodernist one: rather, it is grounded in an appeal to an ethical universal; indeed it is based, as intellectual responses to oppression in

Africa largely are based, in an appeal to a certain simple respect for human suffering, a fundamental revolt against the endless misery of the last thirty years. Ouologuem is hardly likely to make common cause with a relativism that might allow that the horrifyingly new-old Africa of exploitation is to be understood – legitimated – in its own local terms.

Africa's postcolonial novelists – novelists anxious to escape neocolonialism – are no longer committed to the nation; and in this they will seem, as I have suggested, misleadingly postmodern. But what they have chosen instead of the nation is not an older traditionalism but Africa – the continent and its people. This is clear enough, I think, in *Le Devoir de violence*; at the end of the novel Ouologuem writes: 'Often, it is true, the soul desires to dream the echo of happiness, an echo that has no past. But projected into the world, one cannot help recalling that Saïf, mourned three million times, is forever reborn to history beneath the hot ashes of more than thirty African republics' (1968b: 6). If we are to identify with anyone, *in fine*, it is with 'la négraille' – the niggertrash, who have no nationality. For these purposes one republic is as good – which is to say as bad – as any other. If this postulation of oneself as African – and neither as of this-or-that allegedly precolonial ethnicity nor of the new nation states – is implicit in *Le Devoir de violence*, in the important novels of V. Y. Mudimbe, *Entre les eaux*, *Le Bel Immonde* – recently made available in English as *Before the Birth of the Moon* – and *L'Écart*, this postcolonial recourse to Africa is to be found nearer the surface and over and over again. . . .

Postrealist writing; postnativist politics; a *transnational* rather than a *national* solidarity. And pessimism: a kind of *post*optimism to balance the earlier enthusiasm for *The Suns of Independence*. Postcoloniality is *after* all this: and its *post*, like postmodernism's, is also a post that challenges earlier legitimating narratives. And it challenges them in the name of the suffering victims of 'more than thirty republics'. But it challenges them in the name of the ethical universal; in the name of humanism, 'la gloire pour l'homme'. And on that ground it is not an ally for Western postmodernism but an agonist: from which I believe postmodernism may have something to learn.

For what I am calling humanism can be provisional, historically contingent, anti-essentialist (in other words, postmodern) and still be demanding. We can surely maintain a powerful engagement with the concern to avoid cruelty and pain while nevertheless recognising the contingency of that concern. Maybe, then, we can recover within postmodernism the postcolonial writers' humanism – the concern for human suffering, for the victims of the postcolonial state (a concern we find everywhere: in Mudimbe, as we have seen; in Soyinka's *A Play of Giants*; in Achebe, Farrah, Gordimer, Labou Tansi – the list is difficult to complete) – while still rejecting the master-narratives of modernism. This human impulse – an impulse that transcends obligations to churches and to nations – I propose we learn from Mudimbe's Landu.

But there is also something to reject in the postcolonial adherence to Africa of Nara, the earlier protagonist of Mudimbe's *L'Écart*: the sort of Manicheanism that makes Africa '*a body*', (nature) against Europe's juridical reality (culture) and then fails to acknowledge – even as he says it – the full significance of the fact that Africa is also 'a multiple existence'. *Entre les eaux* provides a powerful postcolonial critique of this binarism: we can read it as arguing that if you postulate an either–or choice between Africa and the West, there is no place for you in the real world of politics, and your home must be the otherworldly, the monastic retreat.

If there is a lesson in the broad shape of this circulation of cultures, it is surely that we are all already contaminated by each other, that there is no longer a fully autochthonous pure-African culture awaiting salvage by our artists (just as there is, of course, no American culture without African roots). And there is a clear sense in some postcolonial writing that the postulation of a unitary Africa over against a monolithic West – the binarism of Self and Other – is the last of the shibboleths of the modernisers that we must learn to live without.

# 19

# *Postmodernism or Post-colonialism Today*

## SIMON DURING*

WE CAN, RATHER brutally, characterize postmodern thought (the phrase is useful rather than happy) as that thought which refuses to turn the Other into the Same. Thus it provides a theoretical space for what postmodernity denies: otherness. Postmodern thought also recognizes, however, that the Other can never speak for itself as the Other. One should hesitate to call a discourse which revolves around these positions either for or against post-modernity, but it is certainly not simply consonant with it.

These propositions, none of which is either original or uncontentious, and all of which will be fleshed out below, allow me to mount my central thesis. This is that the concept postmodernity has been constructed in terms which more or less intentionally wipe out the possibility of post-colonial identity. Indeed, intention aside, the conceptual annihilation of the post-colonial condition is actually necessary to any argument which attempts to show that 'we' now live in postmodernity. For me, perhaps eccentrically, post-colonialism is regarded as the need, in nations or groups which have been victims of imperialism, to achieve an identity uncontaminated by universalist or Eurocentric concepts and images. Here the argument becomes complex, since post-colonialism constitutes one of those Others which might derive hope and legitimation from the first aspect of post-modern thought, its refusal to turn the Other into the Same. As such it is threatened by the second moment in postmodern thought. . . .

The post-colonial desire is the desire of decolonized communities for an identity. . . . Obviously it is closely connected to nationalism, for those communities are often, though not always, nations. In both literature and politics the post-colonial drive towards identity centres around language, partly because in postmodernity identity is barely available elsewhere. For the post-colonial to speak or write in the imperial tongues is to call forth a problem of identity, to be thrown into mimicry and ambivalence. The question of language for post-colonialism is political, cultural and literary,

* From 'Postmodernism or Post-colonialism Today' *Textual Practice* 1(1), 1987.

not in the transcendental sense that the phrase as *différend* enables politics, but in the material sense that a choice of language is a choice of identity.

The link between post-colonialism and language has a history. In his recent book, *Imagined Communities*, Benedict Anderson has argued that nationalism has always been grounded in Babel. That is to say, nationalism is a product of what he calls 'print-capitalism'. He writes: 'the convergence of capitalism and print technology on the fatal diversity of human languages created the possibility of a new form of imagined community which in its basic morphology set the stage for the modern nation' (Anderson 1983: 49). One does not have to accept the faculty psychology hidden in the phrase 'imagined community' to take the point. Nationalism emerges when some languages get into print and are transmitted through books, allowing subjects to identify themselves as members of the community of readers implied by these books.

Let us take Anderson's history further. Of all the works that created the new print languages, none had more authority than the sacred books. A whiff of heresy attaches itself to the story at this point. The sacred books, as vehicles of God's word, cannot be translated. No doubt, when God reveals himself in natural language, transposition of a kind has already taken place, but the human language becomes divine through the breath of God's voice, the trace of his hand. To deliver the Bible (or the Koran) to *any* demotic language is not just to allow nationalism to overpower the old church, but for meaning to precede form, for communication to precede revelation – it is to admit, in fact, the arbitrariness of the sign.

Anderson does not make a further argument which seems to me inescapable. Once the sign becomes arbitrary, once divine self-revelation becomes transferable across secular languages, then not only may national identities attach to the print language, but language itself no longer permits of any proper identity. If one language can be translated into another, if there is no such thing as a dead language, what untranslatable residue remains to be the property solely of those who speak it; its form, which cannot be communicated in – as one says – any other form? Yet an identity granted in terms of the signifier (which I use, as it is often used, as a figure for form as such) is an identity that necessarily cannot be communicated. It would seem to be written into the fate of nationalism as print-capitalism that national identity is conferred in the form of its own death warrant. Indeed, there are moments in our culture where an unquenchable nationalist pathos confronts its own mortality: one thinks of Hölderlin's poetry.

The appeal to what is unexchangeable in language is especially tempting under capitalism, which deals with things and words for their exchange value. In the classic formulations of nationalism – Fichte's Addresses to the German Nation, for instance – national identity is based on both language (the home of culture) and soil. When a post-colonial nationalist like the Kenyan novelist Ngugi, living under multinational capitalism, looks at the soil, he sees it as a means of production, and means of production do not articulate identities; indeed, where they can be owned, they are often owned by foreigners. This leaves him language and, within language, culture. (One might note that for decolonized nations the other great ground for nationalist pathos – war – has little place. Most post-colonial nations and tribes have a history of defeat by imperialist powers. Freedom is often the enemy's gift.)

Pre-colonial language shelters all the particularity elided over by colonial stereotyping, by modernist valorization of the primitive and by anthropology. In return, as identical to itself, national language excludes the web of contacts, the play of sameness and difference which weave one society into another. It does so in having the advantage that it is not unique. The number of languages available to be spoken is infinite; the economy of Babel is not restricted. And yet language is not identical to itself, and in translation a residue is always left behind.

Ngugi, who places language at the heart of his post-colonialism, was arrested for co-writing plays in Gikuyu, although no doubt his crime was also to aid Gikuyu's transformation into a print language. It is clear that he is not troubled by the sense that an identity given in print language is given as a death warrant. Thus, when he, or someone like him, enters a novel by a post-colonial writer who is disturbed by such questions, the mode of encounter is predictable. Near the beginning of Salman Rushdie's novel *Shame*, the narrator is interrupted by such a speaker, disputing his authority to tell the tale.

> *Outsider! Trespasser! You have no right to this subject*! . . . I know: nobody ever arrested me. Nor are they ever likely to. *Poacher! Pirate! We reject your authority. We know you, with your foreign language wrapped around you like a flag: speaking about us in your forked tongue, what can you tell but lies*? I reply with more questions: Is history to be considered the property of the participants solely? In what courts are such claims staked, what boundary commissions map out the territories? Can only the dead speak?'
>
> (Rushdie 1984: 23)

This is a dialogue across the bar which internally divides the post-colonial. The divide separates what one can call the post-colonized from the post-colonizers. The post-colonized identify with the culture destroyed by imperialism and its tongue; the post-colonizers, if they do not identify with imperialism, at least cannot jettison the culture and tongues of the imperialist nations. Of course there is not always a choice here. For many ex-colonies the native tongue is the world tongue – English. This is not just true for Australia and Canada, say, as it was once for the United States. It is also true for West Indians as well as for many Maoris and Aboriginals. Indeed, there exists a largely unrecognized but crucial difference in the various post-colonial nations. A country like Australia has almost no possibility of entry into the post-colonized condition, though its neighbour,

New Zealand, where Maoris constitute a large minority, does. New Zealand retains a language, a store of proper names, memories of a pre-colonial culture, which seductively figure identity. I have no doubt that the very name New Zealand, and its *différend*, will pass one day, the nation coming to call itself Aotearoa. What one encounters here is a politics of language which rests not on the power within language, the power of rhetoric, but on the power behind language. From the side of the post-colonizer, a return to difference is projected. But, from the side of post-modernity, English (multinational capitalism's tongue) will museumify those pre-colonial languages which have attached themselves to print and the image so belatedly.

Rushdie's dialogue between the post-colonized and the post-colonizer takes place in a language which is not quite transatlantic English. For instance, the position of the adverb in the phrase 'Is history to be considered the property of the participants solely?' marks a tone at the slightest of removes from that English. But its difference may not be invested with nationalist pathos. It remains too close to what is not different but the norm, the language of world power. The sense that Indian, New Zealand, Australian or Irish English is not as different from transatlantic English as French is from English, let alone as different as Maori or Gikuyu, figures the post-colonizer's emptiness. 'Can only the dead speak?' Rushdie elliptically asks, hinting, among other things, at the powerlessness of the pre-colonial tongues and at the death warrant involved in finding an identity through fallen languages, of which his own has fallen furthest.

Rushdie answers the post-colonized challenge in terms of the *différend*. The narrator enquires: 'In what courts are such claims staked?' Now it is he, whose side is not quite that of the oppressed, who appears as victim. He cannot find a place for justice, nor plainly articulate his case, partly because he speaks neither the language of the international market nor a post-colonized language. What he is charged with is what he inherited. If Rushdie, as a post-colonizer, speaks from a place in contemporary history where a *différend* is dramatically foregrounded, then Lyotard's retreat into transcendental philosophy, his mysticism of selected proper names, his preference for experiment, have a strong competitor. If Jameson cannot fully distance himself from the sublimity and internationalism of what we can call image-capitalism, then that is perhaps because he has not listened carefully enough to those voices which talk of the *différend* on its borders.

To consider the *Apocalypse Now* system alongside *Shame* is chastening. The problem is not one of varieties of postmodernism. Rushdie's work is sometimes called postmodern, but it certainly does not reflect post-modernity. *Shame*'s purpose is to reconnect shame – that epic, indeed pre-capitalist, emotion the Greeks called *aidos* – to the recent history of Pakistan. In redirecting shame, the novel calls upon a violence, both feminine and monstrous, which does not, like that of *Apocalypse Now*, reach a climax from the very beginning. *Shame* imagines an unlocalizable, inexpressive, ethically proper violence we never see in *Apocalypse Now*. Indeed, the novel as a whole works in precisely the opposite direction to Coppola's movie. History is not derealized, affect is not atomized into intensity, narrative triumphs, other cultures are not confined within Occidental myth, nor outside the Western screen. So we can say that, when confronted by his post-colonized accuser, Rushdie is startled into an articulation of the problematic of the *différend*, but, when faced with modern Pakistan, he acts as accuser in turn. Here his novel remains connected to those concepts of justice and reason that totalizing denouncers of our post-modernity assure us are in their safekeeping.

# 20

---

# *Circling the Downspout*
# *of Empire*

## Linda Hutcheon*

WHILE I WANT to argue here that the links between the post-colonial and the post-modern are strong and clear ones, I want to underline from the start the major difference, a difference post-colonial art and criticism share with various forms of feminism. Both have distinct political agendas and often a theory of agency that allow them to go beyond the post-modern limits of deconstructing existing orthodoxies into the realms of social and political action. While it is true that post-colonial literature, for example, is also inevitably implicated and, in Helen Tiffin's words, 'informed by the imperial vision' (1988: 172), it still possesses a strong political motivation that is intrinsic to its oppositionality. However, as can be seen by its recuperation (and rejection) by both the Right and the Left, post-modernism is politically ambivalent: its critique coexists with an equally real and equally powerful complicity with the cultural dominants within which it inescapably exists.

Those cultural dominants, however, are shared by all three forces. As Gayatri Spivak notes: 'There is an affinity between the imperialist subject and the subject of humanism' (1988: 202). While post-colonialism takes the first as its object of critique and post-modernism takes the second, feminists point to the patriarchal underpinnings of both. The title of a recent book of essays on colonial and post-colonial women's writing pinpoints this: *A Double Colonization* (Holst Petersen and Rutherford 1986). Feminisms have had similar impacts on both post-modern and post-colonial criticism. They have redirected the 'universalist' – humanist and liberal – discourses (see Larson 1973) in which both are debated and circumscribed. They have forced a reconsideration of the nature of the doubly colonized (but perhaps not yet doubly de-colonized) subject and its representations in art (see Donaldson 1988). The current post-structuralist/post-modern challenges to the coherent, autonomous subject have to be put

* From 'Circling the Downspout of Empire: Post-colonialism and Postmodernism' *Ariel* 20(4), 1989.

on hold in feminist and post-colonial discourses, for both must work first to assert and affirm a denied or alienated subjectivity: those radical post-modern challenges are in many ways the luxury of the dominant order which can afford to challenge that which it securely possesses.

Despite this major difference between the post-modern and the post-colonial – which feminisms help to place in the foreground and which must always be kept in mind – there is still considerable overlap in their concerns: formal, thematic, strategic. This does not mean that the two can be conflated unproblematically, as many commentators seem to suggest (Pache 1985; Kröller 1985; Slemon 1988a). Formal issues such as what is called 'magic realism', thematic concerns regarding history and marginality, and discursive strategies like irony and allegory are all shared by both the post-modern and the post-colonial, even if the final uses to which each is put may differ (cf. During 1985: 369). It is not a matter of the post-colonial *becoming* the post-modern, as one critic has suggested (Berry 1986: 321), but rather that the manifestations of their (different, if related) concerns often take similar forms; for example, both often place textual gaps in the foreground but their sites of production differ; there are 'those produced by the colonial encounter and those produced by the system of writing itself' (Slemon 1988a: 20), and they should not be confused.

The formal technique of 'magic realism' (with its characteristic mixing of the fantastic and the realist) has been singled out by many critics as one of the points of conjunction of post-modernism and post-colonialism. Its challenges to genre distinctions and to the conventions of realism are certainly part of the project of both enterprises. As Stephen Slemon has argued, until recently it has been used to apply to Third World literatures, especially Latin American (see Dash 1974) and Caribbean, but now is used more broadly in other post-colonial and culturally marginalized contexts to signal works which encode within themselves some 'resistance to the massive imperial centre and its totalizing systems' (Slemon 1988a: 10; also 1987). It has even been linked with the 'new realism' of African writing (Irele 1981: 70–1) with its emphasis on the localized, politicized and, inevitably, the historicized. Thus it becomes part of the dialogue with history that both post-modernism and post-colonialism undertake. After modernism's ahistorical rejection of the burden of the past, postmodern art has sought self-consciously (and often even parodically) to reconstruct its relationship to what came before; similarly, after that imposition of an imperial culture and that truncated indigenous history which colonialism has meant to many nations, post-colonial literatures are also negotiating (often parodically) the once tyrannical weight of colonial history in conjunction with the revalued local past. The post-modern and the post-colonial also come together, as Frank Davey has explained, because of the predominant non-European interpretation of modernism as 'an international movement, elitist, imperialist, "totalizing", willing to appropriate the local while being condescending toward its practice' (1988: 119).

131

LINDA HUTCHEON

In post-modern response, to use Canadian examples, Margaret Atwood rewrites the local story of Susanna Moodie, Rudy Wiebe that of Big Bear and Louis Riel, George Bowering that of George Vancouver. And in so doing, all also manage to contest the dominant Eurocentric interpretation of Canadian history. Despite the Marxist view of the post-modern as ahistorical – because it questions, rather than confirms, the process of History – from its roots in architecture on post-modernism has been embroiled in debates and dialogues with the past (see Hutcheon 1988a). This is where it overlaps significantly with the post-colonial (Kröller 1985: 121) which, by definition, involves a 'recognition of historical, political, and social circumstances' (Brydon 1987: 7). To say this is not to appropriate or recuperate the post-colonial into the post-modern, but merely to point to the conjunction of concerns which has, I think, been the reason for the power as much as the popularity of writers such as Salman Rushdie, Robert Kroetsch, Gabriel García Márquez, and so many others.

At this thematic and structural level, it is not just the relation to history that brings the two *posts* together; there is also a strong shared concern with the notion of marginalization, with the state of what we could call ex-centricity. In granting value to (what the centre calls) the margin or the Other, the post-modern challenges any hegemonic force that presumes centrality, even as it acknowledges that it cannot privilege the margin without acknowledging the power of the centre. As Rick Salutin writes, Canadians are not marginal 'because of the quirkiness of our ideas or the inadequacy of our arguments, but because of the power of those who define the centre' (1984: 6). But he too admits that power. The regionalism of magic realism and the local and particular focus of post-modern art are both ways of contesting not just this centrality, but also claims of universality. Post-modernism has been characterized as 'that thought which refuses to turn the Other into the Same' (During 1987: 33) and this is, of course, where its significance for post-colonialism comes in. In Canada, it has been Quebecois artists and critics who have embraced most readily the rhetoric of this post-colonial liberation – from Emile Borduas in 1948 to *Parti Pris* in the 1960s. However real this experience of colonization is in Quebec, there is a historical dimension here that cannot be ignored. Quebec may align itself politically with francophone colonies such as Algeria, Tunisia and Haiti (Kröller 1985: 120), but there is a major political and historical difference: the pre-colonial history of the French in Quebec was an imperialist one. As both Leonard Cohen's *Beautiful Losers* and Hubert Aquin's *Trou de mémoire* point out, the French were the first imperial force in what is now Canada and that too cannot be forgotten – without risking bad faith. This is not to deny, once again, the very real sense of cultural dispossession and social alienation in Quebec, but history cannot be conveniently ignored.

A related problem is that post-modern notions of difference and positively valued marginality can themselves be used to repeat (in a more covert way) colonizing strategies of domination when used by First World critics dealing with the Third World (see Chow 1986–87: 91): the precise point at which interest and concern become imperializing appropriation is a hotly contested one. In addition some critics, of course, see post-modernism as itself the dominant, Eurocentric, neo-universalist imperial discourse (Brydon 1987: 5; Tiffin 1988: 170–2). There are no easy solu-tions to any of these issues raised by the perhaps uncomfortable overlap of issues between the post-modern and the post-colonial, but that in itself is no reason not to explore that problematic site of interaction.

Besides the formal and thematic areas of mutual concern that I have already mentioned, there is what could be called a strategic or rhetorical one: the use of the trope of irony as a doubled or split discourse which has the potential to subvert from within. Some have seen this valorization of irony as a sign of the 'increasing purchase of post-structural codes of recog-nition in Western society' (Slemon 1988b: 157), but post-structuralism can also be seen as a product of the larger cultural enterprise of post-modernism (see Hutcheon 1988a). In either case, though, as a double-talking, forked-tongued mode of address, irony becomes a popular rhetorical strategy for working within existing discourses and contesting them at the same time. Its inherent semantic and structural doubleness also makes it a most convenient trope for the paradoxical dualities of both post-modern complicitous critique and post-colonial doubled identity and history. And indeed irony (like allegory, according to Slemon) has become a powerful subversive tool in the re-thinking and re-addressing of history by both post-modern and post-colonial artists.

Since I would like to discuss this point in more detail with particular reference to Canadian art, I must first make what might seem a digression, but which is, I believe, crucial: one of the lessons of post-modernism is the need to respect the particular and the local, and therefore to treat Canada as a post-colonial country seems to me to require some specification and even explanation. This is not to deny in any way that Canada's history and what have been called the 'psychological effects of a colonial past' (Keith 1985: 3) are not both very real and very important. Indeed, parts of Canada, especially the West, still feel colonized (see Harrison 1977: 208; Cooley 1987: 182). It is almost a truism to say that Canada as a nation has never felt central, culturally or politically; it has always felt what Bharati Mukherjee calls a 'deep sense of marginality':

> The Indian writer, the Jamaican, the Nigerian, the Canadian and the Australian, each one knows what it is like to he a peripheral man whose howl dissipates unheard. He knows what it is to suffer absolute emotional and intellectual devaluation, to die unfulfilled and still isolated from the world's centre.
>
> (Mukherjee-Blaise 1983: 151)

But to say this is still not the same as equating the white Canadian *experi-ence* of colonialism, and therefore of post-colonialism, with that of the

West Indies or Africa or India. Commentators are rather too quick to call Canada a Third World (Saul 1988: 53) and therefore post-colonial culture (Slemon 1988a: 10). Yet, they have behind them the weight of the famous pronouncement of Margaret Laurence that Canadians are Third World writers because 'they have had to find [their] own voices and write out of what is truly [theirs], in the face of an overwhelming cultural imperialism' (1970: 17). While this may be true and while certainly Canadian literary 'models remained those of Britain and more recently of America' (18), I cannot help feeling that there is something in this that is both trivializing of the Third World experience and exaggerated regarding the (white) Canadian. Of course Canada was politically a colony; but the consequences for white (not Native) writers today of that past are different from those for writers in Africa, India, or the Caribbean. The structural domination of Empire (see Stam and Spence 1983: 3–4) – not to mention the racial and cultural – differs considerably, as even thinking about something as obvious as economic 'underdevelopment' (Dorsinville 1983: 15) would suggest. . . .

When I began this discussion of irony as a discursive strategy of both post-modernism and post-colonialism, I suggested that, not unlike allegory, irony is a trope of doubleness. And doubleness is what characterizes not just the complicitous critique of the post-modem, but, by definition, the twofold vision of the post-colonial – not just because of the obvious dual history (Slemon 1988a: 15) but because a sense of duality was the mark of the colonial as well. Doubleness and difference are established by colonialism by its paradoxical move to enforce cultural sameness (JanMohamed 1985: 62) while, at the same time, producing differentiations and discriminations (Bhabha 1985a: 153). This is the doubleness often represented in the metaphor of Prospero and Caliban (Mannoni 1964; Dorsinville 1974; for a critique of this see Baker 1986, especially 190–6, and Donaldson 1988). It is the doubleness of the colonial culture imposed upon the colonized (Meyers 1973: vii). But it is also the double-ness of the colonized in relation to the colonizer, either as model or antithesis (Memmi 1965: 140). As Raymond Williams has argued, how-ever, all national literatures develop in this sort of way – up to a point: from imitation of a dominant pattern to assimilation or internalization of it (see also Marchak 1978: 182), but then to a stage of open revolt where what was initially excluded by the dominant pattern gets revalorized (121–8). Is the last one here the post-colonial stage, as most critics suggest? If so, then it can still be argued that its revolt continues to operate within the power field of that dominant culture, no matter how radical its reval-orization of its indigenous culture (Tiffin 1988: 172). This is why irony, the trope that works from within a power field but still contests it, is a consistently useful strategy for post-colonial discourse. . . .

The post-colonial is therefore as implicated in that which it challenges as is the *post-modern*. Critique may always be complicitous when irony is its primary vehicle. For this reason, I would disagree with one important part of Simon During's particular definition of post-colonialism as 'the need, in nations or groups which have been victims of imperialism, to achieve an identity uncontaminated by universalist or Eurocentric concepts and images' (1987: 33). Most post-colonial critics would oppose this as an essentialist, not to say simplifying definition, and I would have to agree with them that the entire post-colonial project usually posits precisely the impossibility of that identity ever being 'uncontaminated': just as the *word* post-colonialism holds within it its own 'contamination' by colonialism, so too does the culture itself and its various artistic manifestations, in Canada as elsewhere. Colonies might well speak 'unreflectingly', as Dennis Lee has suggested (1974: 163), but the *post*-colonial has at its disposal various ways of subverting from within the dominant culture – such as irony, allegory, and self-reflexivity – that it shares with the complicitous critique of post-modernism, even if its politics differ in important ways.

# 21

## *The White Inuit Speaks*
### *Contamination as Literary Strategy*
#### DIANA BRYDON*

MY TITLE IS inspired by the coincidental appearance of the Inuit as symbolic figure in two important Canadian novels published in 1989, Kristjana Gunnar's *The Prowler* and Mordecai Richler's *Solomon Gursky Was Here*. By echoing the influential American ethnographic text *Black Elk Speaks*, I mean to highlight the assumptions about cultural purity and authenticity that post-modernism and post-colonialism, and these two texts, both use and challenge. *Black Elk Speaks* itself is now being recognized as a white man's construct, fusing traditional Lakota with Christian philosophy – a hybrid rather than the purely authentic of the anthropologist's dreams (Powers 1990). Unlike those who deplore a perceived loss in authenticity in Black Elk's cultural contamination, Gunnars and Richler explore the creative potential of such cross-cultural contact. For them, as for the bilingual Canadian poet Lola Lemire Tostevin, 'the concept of contamination as literary device' would seem to be appealing. Tostevin argues that 'Contamination means differences have been brought together so they make contact' (1989: 13).

Such a process defines the central activities of post-modernism and post-colonialism – the bringing of differences together into creative contact. But this is also where they part company. For it is the nature of this contact – and its results – that are at issue. For post-colonial writers, the cross-cultural imagination that I am polemically calling 'contamination' for the purposes of this article, is not just a literary device but also a cultural and even a political project. Linda Hutcheon ('Circling the Downspout') [in Adam and Tiffin 1991] points out that post-colonialism and feminism have 'distinct political agendas and often a theory of agency that allow them to go beyond the post-modern limits of deconstructing existing orthodoxies into the realms of social and political action'. In contrast, she argues, 'post-

* From 'The White Inuit Speaks: Contamination as Literary Strategy' in Ian Adam and Helen Tiffin (eds) *Past the Last Post: Theorizing Post-colonialism and Post-modernism* New York and London: Harvester Wheatsheaf, 1991.

modernism is politically ambivalent' (168). At the same time, however, she concludes that the post-colonial is 'as implicated in that which it challenges as is the *post-modern*' (183). This assertion depends on a leap from the recognition that the post-colonial is 'contaminated' by colonialism (in the word itself and the culture it signifies) to the conclusion that such 'contamination' necessarily implies complicity. It is this notion I would like to explore more fully in the rest of this paper.

If we accept Hutcheon's assertion that post-modernism is politically ambivalent, what are the implications of such a theory? There are at least two that interest me here. Firstly, what enables this ambivalence? Post-modernism takes on a personality; it becomes a subject, human-like in its ability to express ambivalence. The functions of the author, declared dead by post-structuralist theory, resurface in post-modernism and in the post-modernist text through the concept of ambivalence. The authority of the post-modernist text comes from this ambivalence, this ability to see all sides, to defer judgement and to refuse agency. Secondly, what are the effects of this ambivalence? It would seem to suggest that action is futile; that individual value judgements are likely to cancel each other out; that one opinion is as good as another; that it would be futile and dishonest to choose one path above any other; that disinterested contemplation is superior to any attempt at action. In effect, then, ambivalence works to maintain the status quo. It updates the ambiguity so favoured by the New Critics, shifting their formalist analysis of the text's unity into a psychoanalysis of its fissures, and their isolation of text from world into a worldliness that cynically discounts the effectiveness of any action for social change.

To refer to contradictions instead of a fundamental ambivalence places the analysis within a political rather than a psychoanalytical framework. Post-modernism and post-colonialism often seem to be concerned with the same phenomena, but they place them in different grids of interpretation. The name 'post-modernism' suggests an aestheticizing of the political while the name 'post-colonialism' foregrounds the political as inevitably contaminating the aesthetic, but remaining distinguishable from it. If post-modernism is at least partially about 'how the world dreams itself to be "American" ' (Stuart Hall quoted in Ross 1988: xii), then post-colonialism is about waking from that dream, and learning to dream otherwise. Post-modernism cannot account for such post-colonial resistance writing, and seldom attempts to.

Much of my work over the past decade has involved documenting the contradictions of Canadian post-colonialism. Reading Canadian literature from a post-colonial perspective, recognizing Canadian participations in empire and in the resistance to empire, one quickly encounters some of the limitations of post-modernist theory in accounting for Canadian texts, even for those apparently post-modernist in form. Because Linda Hutcheon is one of Canada's preeminent theorists of the post-modern, this essay engages with her work first of all as a way of posing some of the problems I see when the post-colonial and the post-modern are brought together.

Despite post-modernism's function as a problematizing mode, several assumptions central to imperial discourse survive unchallenged in the work of its defenders. These include an evolutionary model of development, a search for synthesis that relies on a revival of the notion of authenticity, and an insistence on judging a work on its own terms alone as if there were only one true reading. A post-colonial reading would reject such assumptions: post-modernist readings affirm them under the guise of a disinterested objectivity. . . .


## THE EVOLUTIONARY MODEL

In 'Circling the Downspout' Hutcheon writes that '[t]he current post-structuralist/post-modernist challenges to the coherent, autonomous subject have to be put on hold in feminist and post-colonial discourses, for both must work first to assert and affirm a denied or alienated subjectivity: those radical post-modern challenges are in many ways the luxury of the dominant order which can afford to challenge that which it securely possesses.' (168) There are several problems with this statement. The first is the notion that there is a single evolutionary path of literary development established by the European model. Secondly, there is the idea of a norm of subjectivity also established by the European model. Thirdly, there is the implied assumption that political commitment (to the liberation of nation or women), even in non-European countries, must necessarily express itself through a literary realism that presents a unified subject along the nineteenth century European model. And finally, it seems to demean literary criticism as a 'luxury', something nonessential that not all societies really need, as if critique is not a necessary component for culture or identity building.

These assumptions are so strongly embedded in our western culture that even texts challenging such notions are read to confirm them. Consider Jamaica Kincaid's *Annie John*, a complex metafictional work challenging notions of a unified subjectivity that is often read as a traditional *bildungsroman* consolidating a simple achievement of just such a selfhood. Yet as Simon Gikandi argues . . . 'Caribbean women writers are concerned with a subject that is defined by what de Laurentis calls "a multiple, shifting, and often self-contradictory identity, a subject that is not divided in, but rather at odds, with language" '(Gikandi 1991:14) This is the kind of subject whose exploration Hutcheon argues must be 'put on hold' in feminist and post-colonial writing, yet in fact we find it in many of these texts, if we read them with the openness we bring to European fictions.

138

## THE SEARCH FOR SYNTHESIS

In expressing her unease with the use of post-colonial to describe the settler and multicultural contemporary cultures of Canada, Hutcheon suggests that perhaps Native culture 'should be considered the resisting, post-colonial voice of Canada' (172). This search for the authentic Canadian voice of post-colonialism mirrors the title of her book on post-modernism in Canada, *The Canadian Postmodern*. Just as we saw a unitary subjectivity being affirmed in the evolutionary model, so we see a unified voice or style being advocated here. Although Hutcheon here identifies Robert Kroetsch as 'Mr Canadian Postmodern' (1988b: 183), I would argue that there are several Canadian post-modernisms just as there is more than one Canadian post-colonial voice. A term may have multiple, subsidiary meanings without losing its usefulness in indicating a general category.

Hutcheon's assumption that the post-colonial speaks with a single voice leads her to belabour the necessity of resisting the totalizing application of a term that in her analysis would blur differences and deny the power relations that separate the native post-colonial experience from that of the settlers. Certainly turning to the post-colonial as a kind of touristic 'me-tooism' that would allow Canadians to ignore their own complicities in imperialism would be a serious misapplication of the term. Yet, as far as I know, discussions of Canadian post-colonialism do not usually equate the settler with the native experience, or the Canadian with the Third World. The kind of generalizations that Richard Roth criticizes in Abdul JanMohamed's work do tend to totalize in this way, but this kind of work always ignores countries like Canada. To my mind, Hutcheon gets it backwards when she writes: 'one can certainly talk of post-colonialism in Canada but only if the differences between its particular version and that of, especially, Third World nations is kept in mind' (174). The drawing of such distinctions is the whole point of talking about post-colonialism in Canada. The post-colonial perspective provides us with the language and the political analysis for understanding these differences. The danger is less that Canadians will rush to leap on the victim wagon than that they will refuse to recognize that they may well have some things in common with colonized people elsewhere.

Hutcheon's argument functions as a sort of straw man that misrepresents the post-colonial theoretical endeavour as practised in relation to Canada, deflecting attention away from its radical potential. Her argument demonstrates that in our care to respect the specificity of particular experiences we run another risk, that of a liberal pluralism which uses the idea of different but equal discourses to prevent the forming of alliances based on a comparative analysis that can perceive points of connection. Consider the following statement from *The Canadian Postmodern* (1988b) 'If women have not yet been allowed access to (male) subjectivity, then it is very difficult for them to contest it, as the (male) post-structuralist philosophers have been doing lately. This may make women's writing *appear* more conservative, but in fact it is just different' (5–6). By positing female writing as 'just different' from the male norm, Hutcheon erases the power differential she has been trying to establish, while reaffirming the male as the norm and the experimental as more advanced than and superior to the conservative. It sounds like special pleading for the second-rate, while on the surface it reaffirms the liberal myth of society formed from a plurality of equal differences. . . .

## THE CULT OF AUTHENTICITY

Paul Smith suggests that post-modernist discourse replaces the 'conflictual view and the comic view of the third world' with a 'cult of authenticity' (Ross 1988: 142). This seems to be what is happening with Hutcheon's assertion that only Canada's native peoples may claim to speak with an authentic post-colonial voice. Such an assertion connects her approach to post-colonialism to that of Frederic Jameson which produces a first world criticism respectful of a third world authenticity that it is believed his own world has lost. But what are the effects of such a 'cult of authenticity'? Meaghan Morris concludes her analysis of *Crocodile Dundee* with the statement that '[i]t is hardly surprising, then, that the figure of the colonial should now so insistently reappear from all sides not as deprived and dispossessed by rapacity but as the naive spirit of plenitude, innocence, optimism – and effective critical "distance" ' (Ross 1988: 124). The postmodernist revisionings of the colonial and post-colonial that Smith (1988) and Morris (1988) discuss function to defuse conflict, denying the necessity of cultural and political struggle, and suggesting that tourism is probably the best model for cross-cultural interaction.

Hutcheon's argument that Canada's native peoples are the authentic post-colonial voice of the nation, with its implication that descendants of settlers and immigrants represent at best a contaminated post-coloniality, conforms to this post-modernist model. To challenge it, as Hutcheon knows, is fraught with difficulties because authenticity has also been used by colonial peoples in their struggles to regain power over their own lives. While post-colonial theorists embrace hybridity and heterogeneity as the characteristic post-colonial mode, some native writers in Canada resist what they see as a violating appropriation to insist on their ownership of their stories and their exclusive claim to an authenticity that should not be ventriloquized or parodied. When directed against the Western canon, postmodernist techniques of intertextuality, parody, and literary borrowing may appear radical and even potentially revolutionary. When directed against native myths and stories, these same techniques would seem to repeat the imperialist history of plunder and theft. Or in the case of *The*

*Satanic Verses*, when directed against Islam, they may be read as sullying the dignity of a religion that prides itself on its purity.

Although I can sympathize with such arguments as tactical strategies in insisting on self-definition and resisting appropriation, even tactically they prove self-defeating because they depend on a view of cultural authenticity that condemns them to a continued marginality and an eventual death. Whose interests are served by this retreat into preserving an untainted authenticity? Not the native groups seeking land rights and political power. Ironically, such tactics encourage native peoples to isolate themselves from contemporary life and full citizenhood.

All living cultures are constantly in flux and open to influences from elsewhere. The current flood of books by white Canadian writers embracing Native spirituality clearly serves a white need to feel at home in this country and to assuage the guilt felt over a material appropriation by making it a cultural one as well. In the absence of comparable political reparation for past appropriations such symbolic acts seem questionable or at least inadequate. Literature cannot be confused with social action. Nonetheless, these creole texts are also part of the post-colonial search for a way out of the impasse of the endless play of post-modernist difference that mirrors liberalism's cultural pluralism. These books, like the post-colonial criticism that seeks to understand them, are searching for a new globalism that is neither the old universalism nor the Disney simulacrum. This new globalism simultaneously asserts local independence and global interdependencies. It seeks a way to cooperate without cooption, a way to define differences that do not depend on myths of cultural purity or authenticity but that thrive on an interaction that 'contaminates' without homogenizing. . . .

## JUDGING THE WORK ON ITS OWN TERMS

Hutcheon's conclusion to her *Poetics of Postmodernism* admits the 'limited' aims of post-modernism and its 'double encoding as both contestatory and complicitous' (1988a: 230). She acknowledges that 'I would agree with Habermas that this art does not "emit any clear signals" ', but adds that its saving grace is that 'it does not try to'. It cannot offer answers, 'without betraying its anti-totalizing ideology' (231). I have suggested that it does surreptitiously offer answers – in ambivalence itself, in the relativity of liberal pluralism, in the cult of authenticity that lies behind its celebration of differences. But is it true that answers necessarily totalize? Are these the only alternatives? Is Hutcheon here asking enough of the post-modernist text? Or is she even asking the most interesting or the most important questions? Isn't the effect of such a conclusion to preserve the status quo and the myth of an objectivity that itself totalizes? Can we legitimately ask more of a text than it asks of itself? Post-colonial criticism suggests that we can. . . .

Perhaps the clearest difference between a post-modernist practice and a post-colonial practice emerges through their different uses of history. As Hutcheon points out, '[h]istoriographic metafiction acknowledges the paradox of the reality of the past but its *textualized accessibility* to us today' (1988a: 14). Without denying that things happened, post-modernism focuses on the problems raised by history's textualized accessibility: on the problems of representation, and on the impossibility of retrieving truth. Post-colonialism, in contrast, without denying history's textualized accessibility, focuses on the reality of a past that has influenced the present. As a result of these different emphases, post-modern fiction takes liberties with what we know of the facts of the past much more freely than does post-colonial fiction. Richler's improbable introduction of fictional characters into historical narrative has more in common with the methods of a Sir Walter Scott than a D. M. Thomas. Neither he nor Gunnars deny that different versions of specific events will circulate, but they are interested in the effects of historical happenings: the effects of invasion, of military occupation, of food blockades, of revolution. . . .

As Stephen Slemon points out, 'Western post-modernist readings can so over-value the anti-referential or deconstructive energies of post-colonial texts that they efface the important recuperative work that is also going on within them' (1991: 7). Those deconstructive energies are at work in these two novels, but it is the recuperative power, which they seek to energize for their readers and their Canadian culture, that most distinguishes them. And it is this power that a post-colonial reading can help us to understand. The white Inuit is speaking. Who is listening?

## 22

# *The Politics of the Possible*

## Kumkum Sangari*

THE NONMIMETIC NARRATIVE modes of Gabriel García Márquez and
Salman Rushdie inhabit a social and conceptual space in which the
problems of ascertaining meaning assume a political dimension qualitatively different from the current postmodern skepticism about meaning
in Europe and America. Yet such nonmimetic, non-western modes
also seem to lay themselves open to the academized procedures of a
peculiarly western, historically singular, postmodern epistemology that
universalizes the self-conscious dissolution of the bourgeois subject, with
its now characteristic stance of self-irony, across both space and time.
The expansive forms of the modern and the postmodern novel appear
to stand in ever-polite readiness to recycle and accommodate other
cultural content, whether Latin American or Indian. The ease with which
a reader may be persuaded to traverse the path between such non-
western modes and western postmodernism – broadly defined here as
the specific preoccupations and 'sensibility' of both contemporary fiction
and of poststructuralist critical discourse – may well lead us to believe they
were indeed made for each other. There is not much to be gained by
surveying the literature on the subject or in quibbling with individual
readings, since the question here is obviously much larger than the
'misreading' of any single writer. The question concerns the way the
writings of the 'Third World' (a term that both signifies and blurs the
functioning of an economic, political, and imaginary geography able to
unite vast and vastly differentiated areas of the world into a single 'under-
developed' terrain) are consumed in the West (a term produced to opposite
effect by the same procedures). . . .

What are the modes of access into such nonmimetic fiction for
contemporary Euro-American, academic, poststructuralist discourse? In
what sense are the openings provided by the fiction itself and in what sense
are they constructed by the critical discourse?

* From 'The Politics of the Possible' *Cultural Critique* 7, 1987.

As my argument maintains, the hybrid writer is already open to two worlds and is constructed within the national and international, political and cultural systems of colonialism and neocolonialism. To be hybrid is to understand and question as well as to represent the pressure of such historical placement. The hybrid, lived-in simultaneity of Latin America, both historical and contradictory, is also the ground for political analysis and change. And yet for these same reasons, hybridity as a position is particularly vulnerable to reclassification. The 'modern' moments of such nonmimetic fiction emerge in fact from different social formations and express or figure different sets of social relations. Though forged within the insistent specificity of a localized relation, the very differences of such fiction are read as techniques of 'novelty' and 'surprise' in the West. Novelty guarantees assimilation into the line of postmodern writers not only because the principle of innovation is also the principle of the market in general (Hadjinicolaou 1982: 56) but also because the postmodern obsession with antimimetic forms is always on the lookout for new modes of 'self' fracture, for new versions of the self-locating, self-disrupting text. From this decontextualizing vantage point various formal affinities can easily be abstracted from a different mode of cognition; the nonmimetic can be read as antimimetic, difference can easily be made the excuse for sameness. The transformative spaces in a text – that is, those which do not readily give up their meaning – are the crucial node of its depoliticization. The enigma in Márquez's narratives can be read as a radical contextual figure or can be recuperated as yet another self-reflexive instance of the postmodern meaning/representation problematic. The synchronic time-space of postmodernism becomes a modality for collapsing other kinds of time – most notably, the politically charged time of transition. And further, since postmodernism both privileges the present and valorizes indeterminacy as a cognitive mode, it also deflates social contradiction into forms of ambiguity or deferral, instates arbitrary juxtaposition or collage as historical 'method,' preempts change by fragmenting the ground of praxis (see Sangari 1984: 73–4)

However, it is difficult to understand postmodernism without at the same time understanding the appropriative history of Western 'high' modernism. Raymond Williams points out that modernism is governed by the 'unevenness . . . of a class society,' and this – along with its mobility and dislocations, which find a home within the 'imperial metropolis' – leads to the characteristic experience of 'estrangement and exposure' (Williams 1984: 221–3) Nonetheless, modernism also enters into and is governed by another set of relationships. Modernism is a major act of cultural self-definition, made at a time when colonial territories are being reparceled and emergent nationalisms are beginning to present the early outlines of decolonization. As a cultural ensemble, modernism is assembled, in part, through the internalization of jeopardized geographical territory – which is now incorporated either as 'primitive' image/metaphor or as mobile nonlinear structure. Though intended as a critique, such incorporation often becomes a means for the renovation of bourgeois ideology, especially with the institutionalization of modernism. Ironically, the 'liberating' possibilities of an international, oppositional, and 'revolutionary' modernism for early-twentieth-century 'Third World' writers and artists came into being at a time when modernism was itself recuperating the cultural products of non-western countries largely within an aesthetic of the fragment. The modernism they borrowed was already deeply implicated in their own history, being based partly on a random appropriation and remodeling of the 'liberating' and energizing possibilities of their own indigenous 'traditions' (see Akshara 1984). Not only have the critical practices which have developed around modernism been central to the development of an assimilative bourgeois consciousness, a powerful absorptive medium for transforming colliding realities into a cosmopolitan, nomadic, and pervasive 'sensibility,' but the freewheeling appropriations of modernism also coincide with and are dependent on the rigorous documentation, inventory, and reclassification of 'Third World' cultural products by the museum/library archive. Modernism as it exists is inconceivable without the archive, and the archive as it exists is inconceivable without the political and economic relations of colonialism.

The modernist problems of knowing and representation continue to inform postmodernism. Though the organizing role of individual perception – which could legitimate perspective – and the cohesive role and concept of 'art' have lost their ability to bind the aesthetic of the fragment into a 'whole' and are indeed challenged and 'unmade' by postmodernism, there are distinct ideological and historical continuities between the two. Not only has the destabilizing of the image that modernism effected now been extended into the prose of postmodern critical theory and refined anew, but a postmodern aesthetic continues to raid the 'inarticulate' cultural forms of the 'Third World,' to 'textualize' a geographically lost terrain (for example, Roland Barthes's *Empire of Signs*).

Postmodern skepticism is the complex product of a historical conjuncture and is constructed as both symptom and critique of the contemporary economic and social formation of the West. But postmodernism does have a tendency to universalize its epistemological preoccupations – a tendency that appears even in the work of critics of radical political persuasion. On the one hand, the world contracts into the West; a Eurocentric perspective (for example, the post-Stalinist, antiteleological, anti-master narrative dismay of Euro-American Marxism) is brought to bear upon 'Third World' cultural products; a 'specialized' skepticism is carried everywhere as cultural paraphernalia and epistemological apparatus, as a way of seeing; and the postmodern problematic becomes *the* frame through which the cultural products of the rest of the world are seen. On the other hand, the West expands into the world; late capitalism muffles the globe and homogenizes (or threatens to) all cultural production

145

(see Jameson 1984: 76) – this, for some reason, is one 'master narrative' that is seldom dismantled as it needs to be if the differential economic, class, and cultural formation of 'Third World' countries is to be taken into account. The writing that emerges from this position, however critical it may be of colonial discourses, gloomily disempowers the 'nation' as an enabling idea and relocates the impulses for change as everywhere and nowhere. Because it sees the West as an engulfing 'center,' it perpetuates the notion of the 'Third World' as a residue and as a 'periphery' that must eternally palpitate the center. This center–periphery perspective is based on a homology between economic and cultural domination, and like the discursive structure of self and other, cannot but relegate the 'Third World' to the false position of a permanent yet desired challenge to (or subversion of) a suffocating Western sovereignty. From there it continues to nourish the self-defining critiques of the West, conducted in the interest of ongoing disruptions and reformulations of the self-ironizing bourgeois subject.

Such skepticism does not take into account either the fact that the post-modern preoccupation with the crisis of meaning is not everyone's crisis (even in the West) or that there are different modes of de-essentialization which are socially and politically grounded and mediated by separate perspectives, goals, and strategies for change in other countries. Postmodern skepticism dismantles the 'unifying' intellectual traditions of the West – whether liberal humanism or Marxism – but in the process denies to all the truth of or the desire for totalizing narratives. There is no necessary or obvious connection, as is often assumed, between the decentering of unitary discourses (or, the projects of the Enlightenment and modernity) and an 'international' radicalism. To believe that a critique of the centered subject and of representation is equal to a critique of colonialism and its accou-trements is in fact to disregard the different historical formation of subjects and ways of seeing that have actually obtained from colonization; and this often leads to a naive identification of all nonlinear forms with those of the decentered postmodern subject. Further, the crisis of legitimation (of meaning and knowledge systems) becomes a strangely vigorous 'master narrative' in its own right, since it sets out to rework or 'process' the know-ledge systems of the world in its own image; the postmodern 'crisis' becomes authoritative because it is inscribed within continuing power relations and because, as an energetic mode of 'acquisitive cognition' (see Agnew 1983: 72), it is deeply implicated in the structure of institutions. Indeed, it threatens to become just as imperious as bourgeois humanism, which was an ideological maneuver based on a series of affirmations, whereas post-modernism appears to be a maneuver based on a series of negations and self-negations through which the West reconstrues its identity as 'a play of projections, doublings, idealizations, and rejections of a complex, shifting otherness' (Clifford 1980: 220). Significantly, the disavowal of the objective and instrumental modalities of the social sciences occurs in the academies at a time when *usable* knowledge is fathered with growing certainty and

146

control by Euro-America through advanced technologies of information retrieval from the rest of the world (Escobar 1984–5: 387). In a somewhat pontifical diagnosis of the crisis of legitimation and the loss of credibility in the 'grand narratives' of emancipation, beginning with the French Revolution and culminating in Marxism, Lyotard concludes that 'our role as thinkers is to deepen our understanding of what goes on in language, to critique the vapid idea of information, to reveal an irremediable opacity at the very core of language' (Lyotard 1986–7: 216). To take such postmodern skepticism seriously may well entail stepping outside it in order to examine how, on the one hand, the operations of neo-colonialism (based on such vapid information) continue to be confidently carried out abroad and, on the other, 'return' as the crisis of meaning/representation/legitimation at home. Postmodernism, like modernism, may well turn out to be, in some respects, another internalization of the international role of the West. If the appropriation and internalization of the unknowability (or undecidability) produced in the contested and contradictory social space of gender, class (Sangari 1986), and imperial relations in nineteenth-century Euro-America provided both models of the self and grounds for the epistemological and ontological preoccupation of modernism, then perhaps the question of the *present locales* of undecidability is an urgent one.

The history of the West and the history of the non-West are by now irrevocably different and irrevocably shared. Both have shaped and been shaped by each other in specific and specifiable ways. The linear time of the West or the project of modernity did not simply mummify or overlay the indigenous times of colonized countries, but was itself open to alteration and reentered into discrete cultural combinations. Thus the history of Latin America is also the history of the West and informs its psychic and economic itinerary. The cultural projects of *both* the West and the non-West are implicated in a larger history. If the crisis of meaning in the West is seen as the product of a historical conjuncture, then perhaps the refusal either to export it or to import it may be a meaningful gesture, at least until we can replace the stifling monologues of self and other (which, however disordered or decentered, remain the orderly discourses of the bourgeois subject) with a genuinely dialogic and dialectical history that can account for the formation of different selves and the construction of different epistemologies.

# PART V

## Nationalism

# Introduction

One of the strongest foci for resistance to imperial control in colonial societies has been the idea of 'nation'. It is the concept of a shared community, one which Benedict Anderson calls an 'imagined community' (Anderson 1983: 15) which has enabled post-colonial societies to invent a self image through which they could act to liberate themselves from imperialist oppression. Nationalism in this sense is nowhere better summed up than in the work of Franz Fanon and his dictum that 'a national culture is the whole body of efforts made by a people in the sphere of thought to describe, justify and praise the action through which that people has created itself and keeps itself in existence.'

However, Fanon was also one of the earliest theorists to warn of the pitfalls of national consciousness, of its becoming an 'empty shell', a travesty of what it might have been. The dangers of a national bourgeoisie using nationalism to maintain its own power demonstrates one of the principal dangers of nationalism – that it frequently takes over the hegemonic control of the imperial power, thus replicating the conditions it rises up to combat. It develops as a function of this control, a monocular and sometimes xenophobic view of identity and a coercive view of national commitment.

Theorising national liberation discourse has been particularly strong in the African context. Chidi Amuta gives a brief, clear account of three of the main contributors to this debate – Fanon, Cabral and Ngugi. From a wider post-colonial perspective, the Indian critic Partha Chatterjee examines some of the contemporary attempts at theorising the nation and nationalism. Working from the base-line established by Anderson's analysis and from those of Marxist critics such as Gelner, Chatterjee shows how third-world nationalisms in the twentieth century have constructed themselves along the earlier forms of American and European nationalisms. Chattterjee demonstrates how this may enable post-colonial societies consciously to avoid or select amongst these forms in a more creative and effective way and to avoid naive nativist constructions of community in favour of an awareness of the complex formation of national consciousness in modern societies.

Settler colony cultures have never been able to construct simple concepts of the nation, such as those based on linguistic communality or racial or religious homogeneity. Faced with their 'mosaic' reality, they have, in many ways, been clear examples of the *constructedness* of nations. In settler colony cultures the sense of place and placelessness have been crucial factors in welding together a communal identity from the widely disparate elements brought together by transportation, migration and settlement. At the heart of the settler colony culture is also an ambivalent attitude towards their own identity, poised as they are between the centre from which they seek to differentiate themselves and the indigenous people who serve to remind them of their own problematic occupation of the country. The process of effecting justice, restitution and reconciliation with the indigenous peoples is now crucial to any notion of creating an effective identity, and the issue of how nationalism may continue to function to elide and obscure such important constitutive 'differences' has been at the heart of the debate in all ex-settler colony cultures in recent years.

Most recently a flurry of theoretical activity has made the nation and nationalism one of the most debated topics of contemporary theory. We have sought to illustrate the importance of this attempt at retheorising nationalism through the work of Timothy Brennan and Homi Bhabha. As Brennan notes, 'the rising number of studies on nationalism in the past three decades reflects its lingering, almost atmospheric insistence in our thinking.' We could also say that the interest in nationalism throughout the world reflects the growing disillusionment in postmodern Europe with nationalism and its excesses. Post-colonial societies are increasingly wary, therefore, of that neo-universalist internationalism which subsumes them within monocentric or Europe-dominated networks of politics and culture. The fiction of national essences is rejected for the more refractory and syncretic complexes of ordinary experience as a way of approaching literary production.

Although nation, like race, has only the most tenuous theoretical purchase, in political practice it has continued to be what Anderson describes as 'the most universally legitimate value in the political life of our time' (Anderson, 1983: 12). While nationalism operated as a general force of resistance in earlier times in post-colonial societies, a perception of its hegemonic and 'monologic' status is growing. From the point of view of literary theory, nationalism is of special interest since its rise, as Brennan and Bhabha note, is coterminous with the rise of the most dominant modern literary form, at least in European and European-influenced cultures – that of the novel. These ties between literature and nation evoke a sense of the 'fictive quality of the political concept itself' (Brennan). In this sense the story of the nation and the narrative form of the modern novel inform each other in a complex, reflexive way.

# 23

# *National Culture*

## FRANTZ FANON*

### ON NATIONAL CULTURE

TODAY WE KNOW that in the first phase of the national struggle colonialism tries to disarm national demands by putting forward economic doctrines. As soon as the first demands are set out, colonialism pretends to consider them, recognizing with ostentatious humility that the territory is suffering from serious underdevelopment which necessitates a great economic and social effort. And, in fact, it so happens that certain spectacular measures (centers of work for the unemployed which are opened here and there, for example) delay the crystallization of national consciousness for a few years. But, sooner or later, colonialism sees that it is not within its powers to put into practice a project of economic and social reforms which will satisfy the aspirations of the colonized people. Even where food supplies are concerned, colonialism gives proof of its inherent incapability. The colonialist state quickly discovers that if it wishes to disarm the nationalist parties on strictly economic questions then it will have to do in the colonies exactly what it has refused to do in its own country. . . .

I am ready to concede that on the plane of factual being the past existence of an Aztec civilization does not change anything very much in the diet of the Mexican peasant of today. I admit that all the proofs of a wonderful Songhai civilization will not change the fact that today the Songhais are underfed and illiterate, thrown between sky and water with empty heads and empty eyes. But it has been remarked several times that this passionate search for a national culture which existed before the colonial era finds its legitimate reason in the anxiety shared by native intellectuals to shrink away from that Western culture in which they all risk

* From 'On National Culture' and 'The Pitfalls of National Consciousness' in *The Wretched of the Earth* (trans. Constance Farrington) New York: Grove Press, 1968 (original French edition 1961).

153

being swamped. Because they realize they are in danger of losing their lives and thus becoming lost to their people, these men, hot-headed and with anger in their hearts, relentlessly determine to renew contact once more with the oldest and most pre-colonial springs of life of their people.

Let us go further. Perhaps this passionate research and this anger are kept up or at least directed by the secret hope of discovering beyond the misery of today, beyond self-contempt, resignation, and abjuration, some very beautiful and splendid era whose existence rehabilitates us both in regard to ourselves and in regard to others. I have said that I have decided to go further. Perhaps unconsciously, the native intellectuals, since they could not stand wonderstruck before the history of today's barbarity, decided to back further and to delve deeper down; and, let us make no mistake, it was with the greatest delight that they discovered that there was nothing to be ashamed of in the past, but rather dignity, glory, and solemnity. The claim to a national culture in the past does not only rehabilitate that nation and serve as a justification for the hope of a future national culture. In the sphere of psycho-affective equilibrium it is responsible for an important change in the native. Perhaps we have not sufficiently demonstrated that colonialism is not simply content to impose its rule upon the present and the future of a dominated country. Colonialism is not satisfied merely with holding a people in its grip and emptying the native's brain of all form and content. By a kind of perverted logic, it turns to the past of the oppressed people, and distorts, disfigures, and destroys it. This work of devaluing pre-colonial history takes on a dialectical significance today. . . .

In such a situation the claims of the native intellectual are not a luxury but a necessity in any coherent program. The native intellectual who takes up arms to defend his nation's legitimacy and who wants to bring proofs to bear out that legitimacy, who is willing to strip himself naked to study the history of his body, is obliged to dissect the heart of his people. . . .

To fight for national culture means in the first place to fight for the liberation of the nation, that material keystone which makes the building of a culture possible. There is no other fight for culture which can develop apart from the popular struggle. To take an example: all those men and women who are fighting with their bare hands against French colonialism in Algeria are not by any means strangers to the national culture of Algeria. The national Algerian culture is taking on form and content as the battles are being fought out, in prisons, under the guillotine, and in every French outpost which is captured or destroyed.

We must not therefore be content with delving into the past of a people in order to find coherent elements which will counteract colonialism's attempts to falsify and harm. We must work and fight with the same rhythm as the people to construct the future and to prepare the ground where vigorous shoots are already springing up. A national culture is not a folklore, nor an abstract populism that believes it can discover the people's true nature. It is not made up of the inert dregs of gratuitous actions, that is to say actions which are less and less attached to the ever-present reality of the people. A national culture is the whole body of efforts made by a people in the sphere of thought to describe, justify, and praise the action through which that people has created itself and keeps itself in existence. . . .

While at the beginning the native intellectual used to produce his work to be read exclusively by the oppressor, whether with the intention of charming him or of denouncing him through ethnic or subjectivist means, now the native writer progressively takes on the habit of addressing his own people.

It is only from that moment that we can speak of a national literature. Here there is, at the level of literary creation, the taking up and clarification of themes which are typically nationalist. This may be properly called a literature of combat, in the sense that it calls on the whole people to fight for their existence as a nation. It is a literature of combat, because it moulds the national consciousness, giving it form and contours and flinging open before it new and boundless horizons; it is a literature of combat because it assumes responsibility, and because it is the will to liberty expressed in terms of time and space.

On another level, the oral tradition – stories, epics, and songs of the people – which formerly were filed away as set pieces are now beginning to change. The storytellers who used to relate inert episodes now bring them alive and introduce into them modifications which are increasingly fundamental. There is a tendency to bring conflicts up to date and to modernize the kinds of struggle which the stories evoke, together with the names of heroes and types of weapons. The method of allusion is more and more widely used. The formula 'This all happened long ago' is substituted with that of 'What we are going to speak of happened somewhere else, but it might well have happened here today, and it might happen tomorrow.' The example of Algeria is significant in this context. From 1952–53 on, the storytellers, who were before that time stereotyped and tedious to listen to, completely overturned their traditional methods of storytelling and the contents of their tales. Their public, which was formerly scattered, became compact. The epic, with its typified categories, reappeared; it became an authentic form of entertainment which took on once more a cultural value. Colonialism made no mistake when from 1955 on it proceeded to arrest these storytellers systematically.

The contact of the people with the new movement gives rise to a new rhythm of life and to forgotten muscular tensions, and develops the imagination. Every time the storyteller relates a fresh episode to his public, he presides over a real invocation. The existence of a new type of man is revealed to the public. The present is no longer turned in upon itself but spread out for all to see. The storyteller once more gives free rein to his imagination; he makes innovations and he creates a work of art. It even happens that the characters, which are barely ready for such a transformation – highway robbers or more or less anti-social vagabonds – are taken up and remodelled. The emergence of the imagination and of the creative urge in the songs and epic stories of a colonized country is worth following. The storyteller replies to the expectant people by successive approximations, and makes his way, apparently alone but in fact helped on by his public, toward the seeking out of new patterns, that is to say national patterns. Comedy and farce disappear, or lose their attraction. As for dramatization, it is no longer placed on the plane of the troubled intellectual and his tormented conscience. By losing its characteristics of despair and revolt, the drama becomes part of the common lot of the people and forms part of an action in preparation or already in progress.

## THE PITFALLS OF NATIONAL CONSCIOUSNESS

National consciousness, instead of being the all-embracing crystallization of the innermost hopes of the whole people, instead of being the immediate and most obvious result of the mobilization of the people, will be in any case only an empty shell, a crude and fragile travesty of what it might have been. The faults that we find in it are quite sufficient explanation of the facility with which, when dealing with young and independent nations, the nation is passed over for the race, and the tribe is preferred to the state. These are the cracks in the edifice which show the process of retrogression, that is so harmful and prejudicial to national effort and national unity. We shall see that such retrograde steps with all the weaknesses and serious dangers that they entail are the historical result of the incapacity of the national middle class to rationalize popular action, that is to say their incapacity to see into the reasons for that action.

This traditional weakness, which is almost congenital to the national consciousness of underdeveloped countries, is not solely the result of the mutilation of the colonized people by the colonial regime. It is also the result of the intellectual laziness of the national middle class, of its spiritual penury, and of the profoundly cosmopolitan mold that its mind is set in.

The national middle class which takes over power at the end of the colonial regime is an underdeveloped middle class. It has practically no economic power, and in any case it is in no way commensurate with the bourgeoisie of the mother country which it hopes to replace. In its narcissism, the national middle class is easily convinced that it can advantageously replace the middle class of the mother country. But that same independence which literally drives it into a corner will give rise within its ranks to catastrophic reactions, and will oblige it to send out frenzied appeals for help to the former mother country. The university and merchant classes which make up the most enlightened section of the new state are in fact characterized by the smallness of their number and their being concentrated in the capital, and the type of activities in which they are engaged: business, agriculture, and the liberal professions. Neither financiers nor industrial magnates are to be found within this national middle class. The national bourgeoisie of underdeveloped countries is not engaged in production, nor in invention, nor building, nor labor; it is completely canalized into activities of the intermediary type. Its innermost vocation seems to be to keep in the running and to be part of the racket. The psychology of the national bourgeoisie is that of the businessman, not that of a captain of industry; and it is only too true that the greed of the settlers and the system of embargoes set up by colonialism have hardly left them any other choice. . . .

The national bourgeoisie turns its back more and more on the interior and on the real facts of its undeveloped country, and tends to look toward the former mother country and the foreign capitalists who count on its obliging compliance. As it does not share its profits with the people, and in no way allows them to enjoy any of the dues that are paid to it by the big foreign companies, it will discover the need for a popular leader to whom will fall the dual role of stabilizing the regime and of perpetuating the domination of the bourgeoisie. The bourgeois dictatorship of under-developed countries draws its strength from the existence of a leader. We know that in the well-developed countries the bourgeois dictatorship is the result of the economic power of the bourgeoisie. In the underdeveloped countries on the contrary the leader stands for moral power, in whose shelter the thin and poverty-stricken bourgeoisie of the young nation decides to get rich.

The people who for years on end have seen this leader and heard him speak, who from a distance in a kind of dream have followed his contests with the colonial power, spontaneously put their trust in this patriot. Before independence, the leader generally embodies the aspirations of the people for independence, political liberty, and national dignity. But as soon as independence is declared, far from embodying in concrete form the needs of the people in what touches bread, land, and the restoration of the country to the sacred hands of the people, the leader will reveal his inner purpose: to become the general president of that company of profiteers impatient for their returns which constitutes the national bourgeoisie.

In spite of his frequently honest conduct and his sincere declarations, the leader as seen objectively is the fierce defender of these interests, today combined, of the national bourgeoisie and the ex-colonial companies. His honesty, which is his soul's true bent, crumbles away little by little. His contact with the masses is so unreal that he comes to believe that his authority is hated and that the services that he has rendered his country are being called in question. The leader judges the ingratitude of the masses harshly, and every day that passes ranges himself a little more resolutely on the side of the exploiters. He therefore knowingly becomes the aider and abettor of the young bourgeoisie which is plunging into the mire of corruption and pleasure.

# 24

## Fanon, Cabral and Ngugi on National Liberation

### Chidi Amuta *

#### FANON: THE AESTHETICS OF NATIONAL LIBERATION

FANON'S POSITION ON national culture as contained in *The Wretched of the Earth* represents his most orchestrated articulation of the cultural (especially literary) implications of colonialism and its antithesis, the anti-colonial struggle. As is characteristic of other aspects of his writings on the colonial question, Fanon's position on culture is predicated on his essentially materialist recognition of the exploitative economic motive of colonialism as the decisive determinant of all aspects of the life of the colonized. Yet his grasp of the intricacy of culture transcends such mechanical materialism and perceives certain inner dynamics within the development of culture among the colonized. In this respect, the most enduring value of Fanon's views on the cultural question is to be located in the evolutionary paradigm which he established as well as in his emphasis on the *national* dimension of the anti-colonial consciousness in contrast to the racial emphasis of his contemporaries.

Proceeding from the familiar premise that cultural emasculation of the subjugated group is the necessary correlate of colonialist entrenchment, Fanon projected the pattern of cultural evolution among the colonized both during and even after the colonial era. Briefly, Fanon's evolutionary schema advances three distinct phases as follows:

1. The assimilationist phase in which 'the native intellectual gives proof that he has assimilated the culture of the occupying power'. Characteristically, the literary productions of the native at this stage bear resemblance to those in the literary tradition of the colonizing country.

* From 'A Dialectical Theory of African Literature: Categories and Springboards' Ch. 4 *The Theory of African Literature* London and New Jersey: Zed Books, 1989.

2. The *cultural nationalist* phase in which the native intellectual remembers his authentic identity and kicks against attempts to assimilate him. But owing to his own cultural alienation, the native intellectual's attempts at cultural reaffirmation stop at romanticizations of bygone days corrected by philosophical traditions and aesthetic conventions borrowed from the world of the colonizer.

3. The nationalist phase which is also the fighting phase in which the native man of culture 'after having tried to lose himself in the people and with the people, will on the contrary shake the people'. This is the revolutionary and nationalist phase in the literature of the colonized in which the exposure of more natives to the realities of colonialist oppression also contributes to a democratization of the drive for literary expression (Fanon 1967: 178–9). In the context of this schema, then, the relevant response of the colonized intellectual is contained in the second phase, that of cultural reaffirmation characterized by unbridled traditionalism and even ancestor-worship. This recourse to the resuscitation of past glories in literature is only a defence mechanism by native intellectuals 'to shrink away from that Western culture in which they all risk being swamped'. Fanon was however intensely aware of the limitations of this retrospective fixation in terms of altering the present material conditions of life among the colonized: 'all the proofs of a wonderful Songhai civilization will not change the fact that today the Songhais are underfed and illiterate' (Fanon 1967: 168).

Cultural nationalism, because it is predicated on a negation of racially-inflicted insults and psychological injuries, has political significance mainly at a racial or at best a continental level: 'The native intellectual who decides to give battle to colonial lies fights on the field of the whole continent.' Fanon was sufficiently realistic to admit the legitimacy and historical necessity of this phase in the consciousness of the native. But he equally cautioned that it must constitute only a transient phase, for to adopt continental cultural reaffirmation and nostalgic romanticism as a permanent stance would amount to a false consciousness totally dysfunctional in the task of national liberation:

> The historical necessity in which the men of African culture find themselves to racialize their claims and to speak more of African culture than of national culture will tend to lead them up a blind alley.
>
> (Fanon 1967: 172)

In this respect, Fanon's articulation of the basic requirements of a national culture was sufficiently rigorous to have anticipated some of the most radical positions of our contemporary criticism. He emphasized the need for the writer to see and understand clearly the people who constitute the object of his poetry through a process of self-immersion that literally approximates class suicide. Rightly regarded, therefore, cultural action cannot be divorced from the larger struggle for the liberation of the nation.

159

In effect, there ought to be a reciprocal relationship between national culture and the fight for freedom, a relationship in which national culture subserves national liberation.

In spite of his emphasis on the present and immediate, Fanon never totally discountenanced the insight which the past could provide in the process of national liberation. For him, the nationalist writer's preoccupation with the past must be 'with the intention of opening the future, as an invitation to action and a basis for hope'. This recognition contains a tacit warning with far-reaching implications for the relationship between the writer and his people. It is the responsibility of the writer not to immerse the people in a past they have left behind but to join and inspire them to confront the present as a historic moment. . . .

## CABRAL: NATIONAL LIBERATION AS AN ACT OF CULTURE

Like Fanon, Cabral was operating within an essentially materialist and libertarian notion of culture. In re-stating the classic pattern of colonialist denigration and subjugation of the cultural life of the colonized, he redefined the relationship between *history* (which exposes contradictions and conflicts in the life of society) and *culture* (which provides insights into the dynamic syntheses to resolve these conflicts) in very dialectical reciprocal terms:

> Whatever may be the ideology or idealist characteristics of cultural expression, culture is an essential element of the history of a people. Culture is, perhaps, the product of this history just as the flower is the product of a plant. Like history, or because it is history, culture has as its material base the level of the productive forces and the mode of production.
>
> (Cabral 1973:42)

The main thrust of Cabral's argument was to intensify the reciprocal relationship between history and culture to a point that both categories become hardly distinguishable. Thus, the national liberation struggle as a historical act also becomes an act of cultural resistance to the extent that it is recognized that the object of national liberation is the freedom of a society and its values from foreign domination:

> At any moment, depending on internal and external factors determining the evolution of the society in question, cultural resistance (indestructible) may take on new forms (political, economic, armed) in order to fully contest foreign domination.
>
> (Cabral 1973: 40)

The great force of culture as an instrument of nationalist resistance derives from its ideological appeal in terms of its ability to reflect history. Its political force is enhanced because it has great influence in determining relationships between people and nature, between one person and another, among groups in society and among societies in the international community.

Yet Cabral did not succumb to the liberal tendency to view culture as an undifferentiated continuum, unrelated to the structural manifestations of its informing society. In this regard, he made a distinction not only between the culture of the colonizers and that of the colonized but also in terms of the different levels of cultural expression among the colonized peoples. This recognition was equally predicated on his realization of the sectoral and class character of the socio-economic determinants of culture: 'while . . . culture has a mass character, it is not uniform, it is not equally developed in all sectors of society'. Thus, among the colonized, we can identify the culture of the urban Western-educated elite, of the religious leaders and 'traditional' rulers on one hand and the indigenous cultural expressions of the rural peasantry, untrammelled by the encrustations of foreign impositions and appropriations.

Given Cabral's belief in the instrumentality of culture in the national liberation struggle, it is only the culture of the rural peasantry, because it represents the authentic culture of African peoples and embraces the interests of the great majority of Africans, that can inform genuine natural liberation. It is therefore on the culture of the peasantry that the heavy accent in Cabral's position falls. Even at that, he was alive to the divergences and differences within authentic indigenous cultures arising from the intrinsic organic structures of those societies themselves. . . .

## NGUGI: LITERATURE AND THE ANTI-IMPERIALIST STRUGGLE

To be familiar with Ngugi's reputation as an African writer is to come into acquaintance with his intense sense of progressive social commitment which has quickened over the years into a clear-cut anti-imperialist consciousness predicated on a socialist ideological leaning. Ngugi's commitment has, however, not been confined to his creative writing but has found polemical and theoretical outlet in a series of brilliant essays, addresses, and anecdotes published in various anthologies and journals. More crucially, there is a sense in which Ngugi's polemical and theoretical statements can be seen as elaborations of the fictional worlds of his creative writing. Such volumes of essays as *Homecoming*, *Writers in Politics*, *Barrel of a Pen* and, recently, *Decolonizing the Mind* can, therefore, be said to exist to provide theoretical anchorage to his fictional works, for instance *The River Between*; *Weep Not, Child*; *A Grain of Wheat*; and *Petals of Blood*. It is on the theoretical works that we shall dwell in this section.

There is an unmistakably anti-imperialist thrust that runs through Ngugi's social philosophy which betrays the influence on his thought of both Fanon and Cabral on the one hand and the classics of Marxism/Leninism on the other. There is in fact a sense in which Ngugi's

161

view on African literature and art can be said to place the more generalized cultural theories of Fanon and Cabral in a more specialized literary context without however underplaying the dialectical relationship between African literature and the historical determinants of modern African society. It would not be an overstatement to say that while articulating views that are fast building up into an anti-imperialist aesthetics of African literature, Ngugi has simultaneously been creating works that practically illustrate the main features of his emergent aesthetics.

For ease of handling, we can discuss Ngugi's artistic and social philosophy in terms of specific areas of concern which cut across his major polemical and theoretical writings to date.

## Literature, National History and National Culture

While recognizing the continental relevance of Ngugi's art, it can be said that a certain consciousness of an attachment to the history of the Kenyan nation constitutes the single most important object of his commitment and inspiration. (I deal with his fictional mediations of aspects of Kenyan history later in this volume.) In this respect, Ngugi's historical consciousness understandably assumes the dimensions of an obsession given the fact that he grew up in the midst of the turbulence of the anti-colonial struggle.

The central experience which informs his historical consciousness is the Mau Mau armed struggle which Kenyan peasants and nationalists had to wage against British colonialism. The period of national emergency revealed not only the physical violence with which colonialism sought to entrench itself but also the cultural violence which it inflicted on the consciousness of the colonized. It was against this background that Ngugi may have derived the prominence which he has continued to give to the cultural aspects of the Mau Mau struggle.

> They (the freedom fighters) rediscovered the old songs – they had never completely lost touch with them – and reshaped them to meet the new needs of their struggle. They also created new songs and dances with new rhythms where the old ones were found inadequate.
>
> (Ngugi wa Thiong'o 1972: 30)

More importantly, Ngugi's conviction about the crucial role of literature in creating a truly historical consciousness is born of his recognition of the instrumentality of colonialist writers in the denigration of Kenyan national identity. In this regard, Ngugi has relentlessly drawn attention to the condescending and uncomplimentary depictions of the Kenyan (and African) reality by such imperialist writers as Elspeth Huxley, Robert Ruark, Karen Blixen, Rider Haggard and Rudyard Kipling, among others.

It is perhaps within the larger context of national culture that the peculiar challenges of Kenyan national history assume particular stridency in Ngugi's scheme. Here, it is important to note that Ngugi's articulation of the concept and responsibilities of national culture echo Fanon and Cabral respectively in many respects. This identity of viewpoint is forged by the very nature of the colonial experience which provides the locus for the work of the three writers. Equally founded on the familiar axioms of the materialist view of culture, Ngugi's views have been articulated against the background of the obvious domination of the vital sectors of contemporary Kenyan national life by foreign interests and institutions. In the area of culture, the domination is in the form of (a) the preponderance of works by foreign (mainly English) authors in the literature syllabi of schools and colleges, (b) domination of the film industry by American influence, (c) domination of the mass media and publishing outfits by Western interests as well as the high foreign content of performances at the national theatre. These aberrations pose a double challenge for patriotic Kenyans: 'A central fact of Kenyan life today is the fierce struggle between the cultural forces representing foreign interests and those representing patriotic national interests' (Ngugi wa Thiong'o, 1981a: 42).

# 25

## *Nationalism as a Problem*

### PARTHA CHATTERJEE*

HISTORICALLY, THE POLITICAL community of the nation superseded the preceding 'cultural systems' of religious community and dynastic realm. In the process there occurred 'a fundamental change . . . in modes of appre-hending the world, which, more than anything else, made it possible to "think" the nation' (Anderson 1983: 28). It was the 'coalition of Protestantism and print-capitalism' which brought about this change. 'What, in a positive sense, made the new communities imaginable was a half-fortuitous, but explosive, interaction between a system of production and productive relations (capitalism), a technology of communications (print), and the fatality of human linguistic diversity' (Anderson 1983: 46). The innumerable and varied ideolects of pre-print Europe were now 'assembled, within definite limits, into print-languages far fewer in number'. This was crucial for the emergence of national consciousness because print-languages created 'unified fields of exchange and communi-cations' below Latin and above the spoken vernaculars, gave a new fixity to language, and created new kinds of 'languages-of-power' since some dialects were closer to the print-languages and dominated them while others remained dialects because they could not insist on their own printed form.

Once again historically, three distinct types or 'models' of nationalism emerged. 'Creole nationalism' of the Americas was built upon the ambitions of classes whose economic interests were ranged against the metropolis. It also drew upon liberal and enlightened ideas from Europe which provided ideological criticisms of imperialism and *anciens régimes*. But the shape of the new imagined communities was created by 'pilgrim creole functionaries and provincial creole printmen'. Yet as a 'model' for emulation, creole nationalism remained incomplete, because it lacked linguistic communality

* From 'Nationalism as a Problem' *Nationalist Thought and the Colonial World: A Derivative Discourse* Japan and London: Zed Books for United Nations University, 1986.

and its state form was both retrograde and congruent with the arbitrary administrative boundaries of the imperial order.

The second 'model' was that of the linguistic nationalisms of Europe, a model of the independent national state which henceforth became 'available for pirating'.

> But precisely because it was by then a known model, it imposed certain 'standards' from which too-marked deviations were impossible. . . . Thus the 'populist' character of the early European nationalisms, even when led, demagogically, by the most backward social groups, was deeper than in the Americas: serfdom had to go, legal slavery was unimaginable – not least because the conceptual model was set in ineradicable place.
>
> (Anderson 1983: 78–9)

The third 'model' was provided by 'official nationalism' – typically, Russia. This involved the imposition of cultural homogeneity from the top, through state action. 'Russification' was a project which could be, and was, emulated elsewhere.

All three modular forms were available to third world nationalisms in the 20th century. Just as creole functionaries first perceived a national meaning in the imperial administrative unit, so did the 'brown or black Englishman' when he made his bureaucratic pilgrimage to the metropolis. On return,

> the apex of his looping flight was *the highest administrative centre to which he was assigned*: Rangoon, Accra, Georgetown, or Colombo. Yet in each constricted journey he found bilingual travelling companions with whom he came to feel a growing communality. In his journey he understood rather quickly that his point of origin – conceived either ethnically, linguistically, or geographically – was of small significance . . . it did not fundamentally determine his destination or his companions. Out of this pattern came that subtle, half-concealed transformation, step by step, of the colonial-state into the national-state, a transformation made possible not only by a solid continuity of personnel, but by the established skein of journeys through which each state was experienced by its functionaries.
>
> (Anderson 1983: 105)

But this only made possible the emergence of a national consciousness. Its rapid spread and acquisition of popular roots in the 20th century are to be explained by the fact that these journeys were now made by 'huge and variegated crowds'. Enormous increases in physical mobility, imperial 'Russification' programmes sponsored by the colonial state as well as by corporate capital, and the spread of modern-style education created a large bilingual section which could mediate linguistically between the metropolitan nation and the colonized people. The vanguard role of the intelligentsia derived from its bilingual literacy. 'Print-literacy already made possible the imagined community floating in homogeneous, empty time. . . . Bilingualism meant access, through the European language-of-state, to modern Western culture in the broadest sense, and, in particular, to the models of nationalism, nationness, and nation-state produced elsewhere in the course of the nineteenth century' (Anderson 1983: 107).

Third-world nationalisms in the 20th century thus came to acquire a 'modular' character.

> They can, and do, draw on more than a century and a half of human experience and three earlier models of nationalism. Nationalist leaders are thus in a position consciously to deploy civil and military educational systems modelled on official nationalism's; elections, party organizations, and cultural celebrations modelled on the popular nationalisms of 19th century Europe; and the citizen-republican idea brought into the world by the Americas.
>
> (Anderson 1983: 123)

Above all, the very idea of 'nation' is now nestled firmly in virtually all print-languages, and nation-ness is virtually inseparable from political consciousness.

'In a world in which the national state is the overwhelming norm, all of this means that nations can now be imagined without linguistic communality – not in the naive spirit of *nostros los Americanos*, but out of a general awareness of what modern history has demonstrated to be possible' (Anderson 1983: 123).

# 26

# The Discovery of Nationality in Australian and Canadian Literatures

Alan Lawson*

At the 1982 Seminar on 'The Sense of Place in the New Literatures in English' at Macquarie University, Stephen Gray talked of a phase in which a literature 'came into its own'. That phase is the one I wish to discuss in this paper.

> Phase three, then, has to be the coming into its own of a literature, not just in terms of a prescribable number of acceptably 'great' works, but in terms of the whole nexus that supports a literature – its own publishing industry, including newspapers, magazines and journals, its own self-referring use of language, its mutual understanding of a set of infolded norms and values, its own context of myth about the past and the present, its theoretical wing of evaluators like ourselves, its sense of settling in to keep doing a job that has to be continually done, and – most important of all – its own community of readership or audience, which receives the work and feeds back into it reciprocally. That is as workable a definition of what was going on in Elizabethan England, and what New Literatures are achieving for themselves today. Call it status.
>
> (Gray 1984: 228)

Social, literary and political commentators in Australia and Canada have, perhaps, shown an even greater obsession with the problem of national identity than those of most other emergent colonial or post-colonial nations. In the Canadian case it is easy – probably far too easy – to point to the provocation from within (the French) and from next door (the Americans). In Australia, the obsession has been remarked upon obsessively

* From 'Patterns Preferences and Preoccupations: The Discovery of Nationality in Australian and Canadian Literatures' in Peter Crabbe (ed.) *Theory and Practice in Comparative Studies: Canada, Australia and New Zealand* Sydney: ANZACS (Australia New Zealand Association for Canadian Studies), 1983.

for about a century and a half, though the causes are less easy to define. In both countries there are grounds, I suggest, for regarding the problem of national identity as a fundamental one, a structural, colonial one. 'Who am I when I am transported?' is an inevitable colonial question and in countries where the climate, the landscape and the native inhabitants did little to foster any sense of continuity, where the sense of distance, both within and without was so great, the feeling that a new definition of self – metaphysical, historical, cultural, linguistic and social – was needed, was, and is, over-whelmingly persuasive.

The inevitable recognition for the colonial, nurtured either personally or culturally on images of a distant and different place, was that there is a discrepancy between image and experience, between culture and context, between literature and life. Of those discrepancies the last will serve as a paradigm of the others. It is the intensity of the recognition of this latter gap that makes it an imperative part of the writer's task and a major part of his/her problem to make sense of that gap – to provide images of the *here* that will not shock or embarrass by comparison with the long-held images of *there*. There is then, for colonial writers, especially those of Canada, New Zealand, South Africa, the West Indies, and Australia a psychological responsibility to find not only what Van Wyck Brooks (writing about American literary history) called 'the usable past' but also the usable here, the usable now, the usable us, and the usable tongue. To define, that is, images of identity, of community, of history, of place.

Implicitly recognizing this, the historians and commentators in both Canada and Australia have assumed that it was part of the writer's task to provide a sense of national identity. Now at different periods, various terms have been used but 'Australianness' or 'Canadianness' were, in whatever guise, felt to be crucial. The problem that this has posed, I believe, arose from the fact that national identity was never just a psycho-political phenomenon. There is in fact a cluster of words within which the notion has, at different times, been located. One of the most common terms used was maturity and in the hands of different critics it took on different complexions. G. A. Wilkes, for instance, in *The Stockyard and the Croquet Lawn* notes that 'Australian cultural development has normally been seen in terms of an *emergent* nationalism'. John Plamenatz has argued that nationalism is properly understood as a

> desire to preserve or enhance a people's national or cultural identity when that identity is threatened, or the desire to transform or even create it where it is felt to be inadequate or lacking.
>
> (Plamenatz 1973: 23–4.)

He emphasizes that conjunction of national and cultural since, rightly in my view, he argues that what distinguishes a people consists of ways of seeing, thinking and behaving. 'Nationalism', he says, 'is primarily a cultural phenomenon, though it can, and often does, take a political form'

(Plamenatz 1973: 24). Nationalism is a reaction of peoples who feel culturally at a disadvantage. Taking his clue from Herder he goes on, very importantly, to remind us that 'a human being becomes an individual, a rational and a moral person capable of thinking and acting for himself, *in the process* of acquiring the language and the culture of his people' (Plamenatz 1983: 27). These are the important ramifications of the terms 'nationality' and 'nationalism' as I use them. When the cultural identity in question is that of a people transported to a new and strange place, the physical environment assumes unexpected importance and the language undergoes great strain.

# 27

## *The National Longing for Form*

### Timothy Brennan*

It is especially in Third World fiction after the Second World War that the fictional uses of 'nation' and 'nationalism' are most pronounced. The 'nation' is precisely what Foucault has called a 'discursive formation' – not simply an allegory or imaginative vision, but a gestative political structure which the Third World artist is consciously building or suffering the lack of. 'Uses' here should be understood both in a personal, craftsmanlike sense, where nationalism is a trope for such things as 'belonging', 'bordering', and 'commitment'. But it should also be understood as the *institutional* uses of fiction in nationalist movements themselves. At the present time, it is often impossible to separate these senses.

The phrase 'myths of the nation' is ambiguous in a calculated way. It does not refer only to the more or less unsurprising idea that nations are mythical, that – as Hugh Seton-Watson wrote in his massive study of nations and states as recently as 1976 – 'there is no "scientific" means of establishing what all nations have in common' (Seton-Watson 1977: 5). The phrase is also not limited to the consequences of this artificiality in contemporary political life – namely, the way that various governments invent traditions to give permanence and solidity to a transient political form.

While the study of nationalism has been a minor industry in the disciplines of sociology and history since the Second World War, the premise here is that *cultural* study, and specifically the study of imaginative literature, is in many ways a profitable one for understanding the nation-centredness of the post-colonial world, as has begun to be seen in some recent studies (Jameson 1986: 65–88; Ahmad 1987: 3–25). From the point of view of cultural studies, this approach in some ways traverses uncharted ground. With the exception of some recent sociological works which use literary theories, it is rare in English to see 'nation-ness' talked about as an

* From 'The National Longing For Form' in Homi K. Bhabha (ed.) *Nation and Narration* London: Routledge, 1990.

imaginative vision – as a topic worthy of full fictional realization. Also, it should be said that this neglect is not true of other literatures with a close and obvious relationship to the subject – for example those of Latin America and (because of the experience of the war) Germany and Italy. Even in the underrepresented branch of Third World English studies, one is likely to find discussions of race and colonialism, but not the 'nation' as such.

Only a handful of critics (often themselves tied to the colonized by background or birth) have seen English fiction about the colonies as growing out of a comprehensive imperial system. (Examples might include Edward Said, Ariel Dorfman, Hugh Ridley, Amiri Baraka, Homi Bhabha, Jean Franco, Abdul JanMohamed, Cornell West, and others.) The universality of this system, and its effects on the imaginative life, are much clearer – even inescapable – in the literature not of the 'colonies' but of the 'colonized'. The recent interest in Third World literature reflected in special issues of mainstream journals and new publishers' series, as well as new university programmes, is itself a mark of the recognition that imperialism is, culturally speaking, a two-way flow.

For, in the period following the Second World War, English society was transformed by its earlier imperial encounters. The wave of postwar immigration to the imperial 'centres' – including in England the influx of large numbers of non-white people from Africa and the Caribbean, and in America, from Asia and Latin America – amounted to what Gordon Lewis calls 'a colonialism in reverse' – a new sense of what it means to be 'English' (Lewis 1978: 304). To a lesser extent, the same has happened in France (Harlow 1987: 27).

The wave of successful anti-colonial struggles from China to Zimbabwe has contributed to the forced attention now being given in the English-speaking world to the point of view of the colonized – and yet, it is a point of view that must increasingly be seen as a part of English-speaking culture. It is a situation, as the Indo-English author Salman Rushdie points out, in which English, 'no longer an English language, now grows from many roots; and those whom it once colonized are carving out large territories within the language for themselves' (Salman Rushdie 'The Empire writes back with a vengeance' *The Times* 3 July 1982: 8). The polycultural forces in domestic English life have given weight to the claims of the novelists and essayists abroad who speak more articulately and in larger crowds about neocolonialism. And, in turn, such voices from afar give attention to the volatile cultural pluralism at home. The Chilean expatriate, Ariel Dorfman, has written that 'there may be no better way for a country to know itself than to examine the myths and popular symbols that it exports to its economic and military dominions' (Dorfman 1983: 8). And this would be even truer when the myths come home. One of the most durable myths has certainly been the 'nation'.

Not the colonies, but the colonized. The 'novel of empire' in its classic modernist versions (*Heart of Darkness*, *Passage to India*, *The Plumed*

*Serpent*) has been blind to the impact of a world system largely directed by Anglo-American interests, however much it involved itself passionately, unevenly, and contradictorily in some of the human realities of world domination. For English criticism – even among politically minded critics after the war – has refused to place the fact of domination in a comprehensive approach to its literary material, and that becomes impossible when facing the work of those who have not merely visited but lived it.

The rising number of studies on nationalism in the past three decades reflects its lingering, almost atmospheric, insistence in our thinking. In cultural studies, the 'nation' has often lurked behind terms like 'tradition', 'folklore', or 'community', obscuring their origins in what Benedict Anderson has called 'the most universally legitimate value in the political life of our time' (Anderson 1983: 12).

The rise of the modern nation-state in Europe in the late eighteenth and early nineteenth centuries is inseparable from the forms and subjects of imaginative literature. On the one hand, the political tasks of modern nationalism directed the course of literature, leading through the Romantic concepts of 'folk character' and 'national language' to the (largely illusory) divisions of literature into distinct 'national literatures'. On the other hand, and just as fundamentally, literature participated in the formation of nations through the creation of 'national print media' – the newspaper and the novel. Flourishing alongside what Francesco de Sanctis has called 'the cult of nationality in the European nineteenth century', it was especially the novel as a composite but clearly bordered work of art that was crucial in defining the nation as an 'imagined community'.

In tracing these ties between literature and nation, some have evoked the fictive quality of the political concept itself. For example, José Carlos Mariátegui, a publicist and organizer of Peru's Quechua-speaking minority in the 1920s, outlined the claims of fiction on national thought, saying simply that 'The nation . . . is an abstraction, an allegory, a myth that does not correspond to a reality that can be scientifically defined' (Mariátegui 1971: 187–8). Race, geography, tradition, language, size, or some combination of these seem finally insufficient for determining national essence, and yet people die for nations, fight wars for them, and write fictions on their behalf. Others have emphasized the *creative* side of nation-forming, suggesting the cultural importance of what has often been treated as a dry, rancorous political fact: 'Nationalism is not the awakening of nations to self-consciousness; it *invents* nations where they do not exist' (Ernest Gellner, quoted in Anderson 1983: 15).

The idea that nations are invented has become more widely recognized in the rush of research following the war. To take only one recent example, the idea circuitously finds its way into Eric Hobsbawm's and Terence Ranger's recent work on 'the invention of tradition', which is really a synonym in their writing for the animus of any successful nation-state:

> It is clear that plenty of political institutions, ideological movements and groups – not least in nationalism – were so unprecedented that even historic continuity had to be invented, for example by creating an ancient past beyond effective historical continuity either by semi-fiction (Boadicea, Vercingetorix, Arminius the Cheruscan) or by forgery (Ossian, the Czech medieval manuscripts). It is also clear that entirely new symbols and devices came into existence . . . such as the national anthem . . . the national flag . . . or the personification of 'the nation' in symbol or image.
>
> (Hobsbawm 1983: 7)

Corresponding to Hobsbawm's and Ranger's examples, literary myth too has been complicit in the creation of nations – above all, through the genre that accompanied the rise of the European vernaculars, their institution as languages of state after 1820, and the separation of literature into various 'national' literatures by the German Romantics at the end of the eighteenth and the beginning of the nineteenth centuries. Nations, then, are imaginary constructs that depend for their existence on an apparatus of cultural fictions in which imaginative literature plays a decisive role. And the rise of European nationalism coincides especially with one form of literature – the novel. . . . It was the *novel* that historically accompanied the rise of nations by objectifying the 'one, yet many' of national life, and by mimicking the structures of the nation, a clearly bordered jumble of languages and styles. Socially, the novel joined the newspaper as the major vehicle of the national print media, helping to standardize language, encourage literacy, and remove mutual incomprehensibility. But it did more than that. Its manner of presentation allowed people to imagine the special community that was the nation. . . .

[N]ovels in the post-war period are unique because they operate in a world where the level of communications, the widespread politics of insurgent nationalism, and the existence of large international cultural organisations have made the topics of nationalism and exile unavoidably aware of one another. The idea of nationhood is not only a political plea, but a formal binding together of disparate elements. And out of the multiplicities of culture, race, and political structures, grows also a repeated dialectic of uniformity and specificity: of world culture and national culture, of family and of people. One of many clear formulations of this can be found in Fanon's statement that '[i]t is at the heart of national consciousness that international consciousness lives and grows' (Fanon 1967: 247–8). These universalist tendencies – already implicit in the concept of 'inalienable rights' – is accentuated by the break-up of the English and Spanish imperial systems, with their unities of language, their common enemies, and (in the case of Spanish America) their contiguous terrain. Examples of the persistence of this motif might be found, for instance, in the controversial role of the terms 'Africa' in the wtiting of the Nigerian author Chinua Achebe, or 'America' in the essays of the Cuban patriot José Marti.

Thus, of course, not all Third World novels about nations are 'nationalistic'. The variations range from outright attacks on independence, often mixed with nostalgia for the previous European *status quo* (as in the work of V. S. Naipaul, Manohar Malgonkar, and others), to vigorously anticolonial works emphasizing native culture (Ngugi wa Thiong'o, Tayib Salih, Sipho Sepamla, and others), to cosmopolitan explanations of the 'lower depths', or the 'fantastic unknown' by writers acquainted with the tastes and interests of dominant culture (García Márquez, Wole Soyinka, Salman Rushdie, and others).

As we shall see, in one strain of Third World writing the contradictory topoi of exile and nation are fused in a lament for the necessary and regrettable insistence of nation-forming, in which the writer proclaims his identity with a country whose artificiality and exclusiveness have driven him into a kind of exile – a simultaneous recognition of nationhood and an alienation from it. As we have said, the cosmopolitan thrust of the novel form has tended to highlight this branch of well-publicized Third World fiction. One result has been a trend of cosmopolitan commentators on the Third World, who offer an *inside view* of formerly submerged peoples for target reading publics in Europe and North America in novels that comply with metropolitan literary tastes.

Some of its better known authors have been from Latin America: for example, García Márquez, Vargas Llosa, Alejo Carpentier, Miguel Asturias, and others. But there is also a related group of postwar satirists of nationalism and dependency – writers of encyclopedic national narratives that dismember a recent and particularized history in order to expose the political dogma surrounding and choking it. Here one thinks especially of the Indo-English author Salman Rushdie, of the Paraguayan novelist Augusto Roa Bastos, and the South African Nadine Gordimer, along with many others.

In the case of Salman Rushdie, for instance, the examples of India and Pakistan are, above all, an opportunity to explore postcolonial *responsibility*. The story he tells is of an entire region slowly coming to think of itself as one, but a corollary of his story is disappointment. So little improvement has been made. In fact, the central irony of his novels is that independence has damaged Indian spirits by proving that 'India' can act as abominably as the British did. In a kind of metafictional extravaganza, he treats the heroism of nationalism bitterly and comically because it always seems to him to evolve into the nationalist demagogy of a caste of domestic sellouts and powerbrokers.

This message is very familiar to us because it has been easier to embrace in our metropolitan circles than the explicit challenges of, say, the Salvadoran protest-author Manlio Argueta, or the sparse and caustic satires of the Nigerian author, Obi Egbuna. However, it is perhaps the trend's overt cosmopolitanism – its Third World thematics as seen through the elaborate fictional architecture of European high art – that perfectly imagines the novel's obsessive nation-centredness and its imperial (that is, universalizing) origins. Distanced from the sacrifices and organizational drudgery of actual resistance movements, and yet horrified by the obliviousness of the west towards their own cultures, writers like Rushdie and Vargas Llosa have been well poised to thematize the centrality of nation-forming while at the same time demythifying it from a European perch. Although Vargas Llosa's erudite and stylistically sumptuous *The War of the End of the World*, for example, is not at all characteristic of the 'counter-hegemonic aesthetics' of much Third World writing, its very disengagement frees him to treat the ambivalence of the independence process as a totality, and, although negatively, reassert its fundamental importance to the postcolonial imagination. His treatment may be neither the most representative nor the most fair, but its very rootlessness brilliantly articulates the emotional life of decolonization's various political contestants. It is 'in-between'.

# 28

# Dissemination
## Time, Narrative, and the Margins
## of the Modern Nation

### HOMI K. BHABHA*

HOW DOES ONE write the nation's modernity as the event of the everyday and the advent of the epochal? The language of national belonging comes laden with atavistic apologues, which has led Benedict Anderson to ask: 'But why do nations celebrate their hoariness, not their astonishing youth?' (Anderson 'Narrating the nation' *The Times Literary Supplement*). The nation's claim to modernity, as an autonomous or sovereign form of political rationality, is particularly questionable if, with Partha Chatterjee, we adopt the post-colonial perspective:

> Nationalism ... seeks to represent itself in the image of the Enlightenment and fails to do so. For Enlightenment itself, to assert its sovereignty as the universal ideal, needs its Other; if it could ever actualise itself in the real world as the truly universal, it would in fact destroy itself.
>
> (Chatterjee 1986: 17)

Such ideological ambivalence nicely supports Gellner's paradoxical point that the historical necessity of the idea of the nation conflicts with the contingent and arbitrary signs and symbols that signify the effective life of the national culture. The nation may exemplify modern social cohesion but

> Nationalism is not what it seems, and above all not what it seems to itself... The cultural shreds and patches used by nationalism are often arbitrary historical inventions. Any old shred would have served as well. But in no way does it follow that the principle of nationalism ... is itself in the least contingent and accidental.
>
> (Gellner 1983: 56)

* From 'Dissemination: Time, Narrative, and the Margins of the Modern Nation' in Homi K. Bhabha (ed.) *Nation and Narration* London: Routledge, 1990.

The problematic boundaries of modernity are enacted in these ambivalent temporalities of the nation-space. The language of culture and community is poised on the fissures of the present becoming the rhetorical figures of a national past. Historians transfixed on the event and origins of the nation never ask, and political theorists possessed of the 'modern' totalities of the nation – 'Homogeneity, literacy and anonymity are the key traits' (Gellner 1983: 38) – never pose, the awkward question of the disjunctive representation of the social, in this double-time of the nation. It is indeed only in the disjunctive time of the nation's modernity – as a knowledge disjunct between political rationality and its impasse, between the shreds and patches of cultural signification and the certainties of the nationalist pedagogy – that questions of nation as narration come to be posed. How do we plot the narrative of the nation that must mediate between the teleology of progress tipping over into the 'timeless' discourse of irrationality? How do we understand that 'homogeneity' of modernity – the people – which, if pushed too far, may assume something resembling the archaic body of the despotic or totalitarian mass? In the midst of progress and modernity, the language of ambivalence reveals a politics 'without duration', as Althusser once provocatively wrote: 'Space without places, time without duration' (Althusser 1972: 78). To write the story of the nation demands that we articulate that archaic ambivalence that informs modernity. We may begin by questioning that progressive metaphor of modern social cohesion – *the many as one* – shared by organic theories of the holism of culture and community, and by theorists who treat gender, class, or race as radically 'expressive' social totalities.

# 29

# *What Ish My Nation?*

## DAVID CAIRNS AND SHAUN RICHARDS*

The process of describing the colonized [in Ireland] and inscribing them in the discourse as second-order citizens in comparison with the colonizers commenced with the invocation of the judicial and military power of the State, but subsequently the colonizers attempted to convince the colonized themselves of their irremovable deficiencies and the consequent naturalness and permanence of their subordination. The wish of the colonizer that subjection should be willingly accepted rather than require constant recourse to coercion, can be seen in *Henry V*, the culmination of Shakespeare's second tetralogy, itself a dramatization of the process involved in the constitution of the unified nation, particularly as the process is expressed in the constitution of the unified and ordered subject who, to emphasize the power of the process, is the monarch himself. The transformation of Hal into Henry, particularly through the rejection of Falstaff, is a highly charged realization of the denial and repression of the 'other' attendant upon the constitution of the ordered subject and nation. What Shakespeare dramatizes is the originating moment of nationhood when the nation 'becomes conscious of itself, when it creates a model of itself' (Lotman 1978: 227). . . .

*Henry V* dramatizes the might and mercy of the English Nation State as it resolves the action as the victory at Agincourt is crowned by Henry's kissing the French Princess in the recognition that she is his 'sovereign queen'. The result of this betrothal, it is hoped, will be that the contending kingdoms should share an equal unity and 'Christian-like accord' (Act 5, Sc. ii). Philip Edwards has argued that the resolution of this imperial war is a piece of dramatic wish-fulfilment: that a contemporary cause of discord, namely Ireland, should come to an equally satisfactory conclusion (Edwards 1979: 74–86). . . .

While the play dramatizes an idealized resolution of the Anglo-Irish discord in the unity of marriage, and threatens in dialogue the alternative

* From 'What Ish My Nation?' *Writing Ireland: Colonialism, Nationalism and Culture* Manchester: Manchester University Press, 1988.

of massacre, there is also a more direct engagement with the problems of 'internal colonialism', which, in their expression, suggest that they have already been resolved. The famous scene at the English camp when English, Welsh, Scots and Irish Captains meet in an encounter whose main function is to dramatize their united presence in an army constantly referred to as English (Act 3, Sc. ii), reveals that just as in the marriage which unites England and France, so in the union which produces the English Nation State, there is a relationship which is 'structured in dominance'. What simultaneously unites and divides the Captains, or at least distinguishes between them, is the English language. Fluellen the Welshman substitutes 'p' for 'b' and utters 'look you' at intervals, Jamy the Scot has even more deviations from 'standard' linguistic expectations with his frequent use of 'gud' and mispronunciation of 'marry', while Macmorris the Irishman is the very embodiment of the 'stage Irishman'; pugnacious and argumentative, expressing all in repetitious 'mispronunciations': 'O, tish ill done, tish ill done! By my hand, tish ill done!' (Act 3, Sc. ii). These Celts are united in their service to the English Crown. Their use of the English language, however, reveals that 'service' is the operative word, for in rank, in dramatic importance, and in linguistic competence, they are comical second-order citizens. They are, moreover, disputatious, and the argument between Fluellen and Macmorris, which is resolved by Gower's admonition, is further dramatic evidence of the harmony which England has brought to the fractious occupants of the Celtic fringe. Shakespeare's dramatization of the harmonious incorporation of such disparate elements into the English State reaches its peak in Macmorris's famous question: 'What ish my nation?' (Act 3, Sc. ii). As Philip Edwards argues, Macmorris's outburst is a denial of such separate status, brought on by the sensed implication in the words of Fluellen, that while the Welsh may speak from within the united State, Macmorris is a member of a separate and therefore marginal group. 'What ish my nation?' is therefore a rhetorical question to which the answer is supplied by Macmorris's service in the English army. The achievement, on a mass scale, of Macmorris's incorporation would represent a triumphant conclusion to the process of unmaking ... as a pre-requisite for the fashioning of godly and biddable second-order citizens. The process of self-fashioning required the continued presence of an 'other' so that the maintenance of subtle points of differentiation from the colonizer would continue to reproduce, not only the subordination of the colonized, but the superordination of the colonizer. ...

The Shakespearean 'fiction' of *Henry V* is, then, the expression of a politically advantageous 'myth' and indeed is expressed in terms which are themselves subsequently utilized for overtly political purposes. James I of England whose accession to the throne came only four years after the composition of *Henry V*, also expressed the indissolubility of the nation in terms of a marriage: 'I am the husband, and the whole isle is my lawful wife' (Edwards 1979: 84). This merging of the marginal with the mighty is equated by James with the fate of the brook which flows into a river which, in turn, flows into an ocean: 'so by the conjunction of divers little kingdoms in one are all these private differences and questions swallowed up' (84).

Culture, then, requires the drive toward – if not the achievement of – unity. But the contradictions that are necessarily excluded as a means of its achievement are quite literally those elements which contra-dict, speak against and speak otherwise than the dominant group. While Henry can be seen to court the French Princess in her own tongue and she replies in English, the same degree of linguistic parity is not extended to the Celtic Captains, for their position in the contemporary world of Elizabethan England was potentially, and actually, far more disruptive than that of a nation whose separate status was now an acknowledged if not welcomed fact. The Welsh, Scots and Irish must, therefore, be seen to speak English as evidence of their incorporation within the greater might of England, but they must speak it with enough deviations from the standard form to make their subordinate status in the union manifestly obvious. What cannot be acknowledged is their possession of an alternative language and culture, for to do so would be to stage the presence of the very contradictions which the play denies in its attempt to stage the ideal of a unified English Nation State. The resolution in the play is seen to be achieved by marriage rather than by massacre, by incorporation rather than by exclusion, but the inclusion of the Celts within the English State, of which the army is a paradigm, is as a result of an equally devastating act of cultural elision. The victims in the process of the march towards unity are those who contradict, and so implicitly question, the dominance of the incorporating power. Shakespeare's work engages with the process of colonial discourse at the moment of its mobilization to deal with Ireland, but the position of the colonized, namely Macmorris, is seen as one of proud inclusion. In this sense, the play, despite its references to the slaughter of Irish rebels, is an idealization of an actuality which stubbornly refused to conform.

# PART VI

*Hybridity*

# Introduction

In the preceding section on Nationalism it became clear that the idea of the nation is often based on naturalised myths of racial or cultural origin. That the need to assert such myths of origin was an important feature of much early post-colonial theory and writing, and that it was a vital part of the collective political resistance which focused on issues of separate identity and cultural distinctiveness is made clear in many of the extracts collected there. But what is also made clear is how problematic such construction is and how it has come under question in more recent accounts.

Most post-colonial writing has concerned itself with the hybridised nature of post-colonial culture as a strength rather than a weakness. Such writing focuses on the fact that the transaction of the post-colonial world is not a one-way process in which oppression obliterates the oppressed or the coloniser silences the colonised in absolute terms. In practice it rather stresses the mutuality of the process. It lays emphasis on the survival even under the most potent oppression of the distinctive aspects of the culture of the oppressed, and shows how these become an integral part of the new formations which arise from the clash of cultures characteristic of imperialism. Finally, it emphasises how hybridity and the power it releases may well be seen to be the characteristic feature and contribution of the post-colonial, allowing a means of evading the replication of the binary categories of the past and developing new anti-monolithic models of cultural exchange and growth.

Hybridity occurs in post-colonial societies both as a result of conscious moments of cultural suppression, as when the colonial power invades to consolidate political and economic control, or when settler-invaders dispossess indigenous peoples and force them to 'assimilate' to new social patterns. It may also occur in later periods when patterns of immigration from the metropolitan societies and from other imperial areas of influence (e.g. indentured labourers from India and China) continue to produce complex cultural palimpsests with the post-colonised world.

Not surprisingly, since such formulations tend to resist ideas of a pure culture of either the post- or pre-colonial they have not found universal assent. They have also tended to emerge most strongly where no simple possibility for asserting a pre-colonial past is available, notably in the radically dislocated culture of the West Indies. Yet these regional patterns have formed the basis for the development of literary forms (such as 'magical realism') which have had a wide influence, and which have been applied by critics to societies of widely different kinds such as those of settler colonies, and even, as Homi Bhabha's piece indicates, to theories of colonisation in societies such as India. In a different way, as Chinua Achebe's account of his childhood shows, even the cultures in countries such as Nigeria which have sought energetically to assert the validity and continuity of their pre-colonial past have still found a fruitful metaphor in the idea of cross-fertilisation between their constitutive elements. They have realised that for the foreseeable future much of the artistic and social production of their world will take place within the constraints of the traces of the colonial and neo-colonial moment, and that much of the distinctiveness of contemporary post-colonial societies will be produced by and against this process either by vigorous resistance or, more frequently in recent times, by a dialogic process of recovery and reinscription.

The term hybridity has been sometimes misinterpreted as indicating something that denies the traditions from which it springs, or as an alternative and absolute category to which all post-colonial forms inevitably subscribe but, as E. K. Brathwaite's early and influential account of Jamaican creolisation made clear, the 'creole' is not predicated upon the idea of the disappearance of independent cultural traditions but rather on their continual and mutual development. The interleaving of practices will produce new forms even as older forms continue to exist. The degree to which these forms become hybridised varies greatly across practices and between cultures. Thus, as critics like Karin Barber and E. K. Brathwaite have noted, oral practices may continue alongside the orally-influenced forms of post-colonial written culture in countries like Nigeria and Jamaica.

It is probably true to say though that no post-colonial form has been able entirely to avoid the impact of the shifts which have characterised the post-colonial world. Whilst assertions of national culture sought to articulate the dangerous politics of assimilation implicit in the colonial, theories of the hybridity of the post-colonial world assert a different and arguably more potent resistance in the counter-discursive practices they celebrate. Whatever one's final view, these discussions have been the site of one of the most vigorous and fruitful critical debates in recent years.

# 30

## Fossil and Psyche

KIRSTEN HOLST PETERSEN AND
ANNA RUTHERFORD*

### FOSSILS

Modern man is the product of that evolutionary symbiosis, and by any other hypothesis incomprehensible, indecipherable. *Every living being is also a fossil. Within it, all the way down to the microscopic structure of its proteins, it bears the traces if not the stigmata of its ancestry.* This is even truer of man than of any other animal species because of the dual evolution – physical and ideational – to which he is heir.

Jacques Monod

The word *fossil* is used in an idiosyncratic sense to invoke a rhythmic capacity to re-sense contrasting spaces and to suggest that a curious rapport exists between *ruin* and *origin* as latent to arts of genesis.

Wilson Harris

Only a dialogue with the past can produce originality.

Wilson Harris

WE LIVE IN a world in which we have polarized the so-called savage mind and the so-called civilized mind. Wilson Harris believes that we are in fact much closer to the savage mind than we think or would like to admit and he agrees with Monod when he says that each living person is a fossil in so far as each man carries within himself remnants of deep-seated antecedents. The past plays tricks on us and conditions our present responses. Floating around in the psyche of each one of us are all the fossil identities. By entering into a fruitful dialogue with the past one becomes able to revive the fossils that are buried within oneself and are part of one's ancestors. To illustrate this, one could mention the uses to which a people could put their common past or cultural heritage. During the course of his stay at Aarhus

* From *Enigma of Values: An Introduction to Wilson Harris* Aarhus: Dangaroo Press, 1976.

185

Wilson Harris gave a public lecture which he entitled 'Magical Realism'. In this lecture he told a story which was a perfect example of the positive influence which an awareness of one's roots can have. Part of the tale is repeated here.

I was born on the coastlands of Guyana and one is aware that one has there a heterogeneous body of peoples, peoples whose antecedents came from Africa, from India, Europe, and so on. And apart from that there is a very significant Amerindian presence, people who are descended from the pre-Columbian world. One of the sad things is that most of these people live within a context in which the issue of community remains alien or hidden away. This is something which came home to me in a peculiarly symbolic way on my first expedition into the interior of Guyana, in which I was aware of an enormous difference between the landscape of the coastlands and the landscape of the interior. I had penetrated 150 miles. It seemed as if one had travelled thousands and thousands of miles, and in fact had travelled to another world, as it were, because one was suddenly aware of the fantastic density of place. One was aware of one's incapacity to describe it, as though the tools of language one possessed were inadequate. It was pointless describing the river as running dark, the trees as green, or the rocks as grey. All this seemed less to do with the medium of place and more to do with the immediate tool of the world as representing or signifying 'place'. Later I was to relate myself to those 'representations' or 'significations' as relative faces of the dynamic mystery of language, and this for me was a groping but authentic step into the reality of place. At first, however, I was conscious of how helpless I was in wrestling with something immensely authentic, immensely rich, immensely challenging. And I believe in my early experiments with poem and fiction I was simply using the word as a tool of identity. That is, I could not relate identity to eclipsed perspectives of place and community. And one of the first catalysts which occurred, which assisted me to come to grips with the kind of narrative juxtapositions which I needed and which I wanted to find, happened on an expedition into the Potaro river, which is a tributary of the Essequebo.

The Essequebo runs out of Brazil into the Atlantic. It runs through this fantastic landscape in which if one gets into the forest it seems as if the sky itself is a lake and the rivers are pouring from the sky. We were gauging the river for hydro-electric power and had chosen as our station a section where the river narrowed and then opened up again to run towards the Tumatumari rapids a mile or so away. It was necessary to gauge the river at all stages from the lowest to the highest levels. One needs to do this continuously because the sort of stage discharge curve one gets is built up out of frequent observations that check back on themselves. We set up a base line on one bank with alignment rods at right angles to this. We were thus able to align ourselves and anchor our boat in the river, one anchor at the stern and another at the bow. Then with a sextant we took a reading in order to

186

calculate distances from the bank as we made our way across the river. The Potaro river is strangely beautiful and secretive. When the river falls, the sand banks begin to appear. At the foot of the Tumatumari rapids or falls the sand is like gold. Above, an abrupt change of texture occurs – it is white as snow. These startling juxtapositions seemed to me immensely significant in some curious and intuitive way that bore upon an expressionistic void of place and time.

When the river runs high the sand banks disappear. We were – on the particular expedition to which I am referring – gauging the river at a very high and dangerous stage. The water swirled, looked ugly and suddenly one of the anchors gripped the bed of the stream. The boat started to swing around and to take water. We could not dislodge the anchor. I decided that the only thing we could do was to cut ourselves free. So we severed the anchor rope and that was the end of that. Two or three years later, gauging the river in the same way, the identical impasse happened. Once again the anchor at the stern lodged in the bed of the stream. And this time it was much more crucial because the boat swung so suddenly, we took so much water, that it seemed to me at that moment that we were on the point of sinking. I am sure I couldn't have swum to the river bank if the boat had gone down because at that high stage I would have been pulled into the Tumatumari falls and decapitated by the rocks. As the boat swung I said to a man behind me: 'Cut the rope.' Well, he was so nervous that he took his prospecting knife and all he could do was a sort of feeble sawing upon the anchor rope as if he were paralyzed at that moment by the whole thing, the river, the swirling canvas of the stream. He was paralyzed. And then another member – the outboard mechanic – gave a sudden tug and the anchor moved. The boat righted itself. Half-swamped as we were, we were able to start the outboard engine and drive towards the bank. We began pulling up the anchor as we moved in. We got to the bank and then were able to bring the anchor right up when we discovered that it had hooked into the one we had lost three years before. Both anchors had now come up.

It is almost impossible to describe the kind of energy that rushed out of that constellation of images. I felt as if a canvas around my head was crowded with phantoms and figures. I had forgotten some of my own antecedents – the Amerindian/Arawak ones – but now their faces were on the canvas. One could see them in the long march into the twentieth century out of the pre-Columbian mists of time. One could also sense the lost expeditions, the people who had gone down in these South American rivers. One could sense a whole range of things, all sorts of faces – angelic, terrifying, daemonic – all sorts of contrasting faces, all sorts of figures. There was a sudden eruption of consciousness, and what is fantastic is that it all came out of a constellation of two ordinary objects, two anchors.

(Harris 1973b: 38–41)

The two anchors released an awareness of possibilities or in Wilson Harris's terms 'a density of resources'. Through such incidents one is able to gain an insight into a new dimension of psychic possibilities which up until then one had been unaware of.

On the other hand of course the same search for roots can give an entirely different result and can be used to foster a narrow nationalism. This was the case with Nazi Germany where the past was evoked to serve present feelings of national and racial superiority.

What must be remembered is that fossils like 'living' beings contain restrictive as well as explosive rooms or spaces and the fossil value of our human and a-human antecedents can either act as positive forces or can become prejudices, hideous biases, leading to implacable animism. So in fact one half of our 'fossil value' is constantly combating the other half.


## ARCHITECTONIC FOSSIL SPACES

Awareness of the ambivalence of fossils enables one to visualize new possibilities and construct a new scale along which one can attempt to progress. This constructive process is what Wilson Harris means by architectonic; it presupposes an insight that may enable us to relate to the static in a new way thereby modifying both it and us. It is a process that can be equated with profound creativity.

When one realizes that involuntary codes are built into targets and affect objective judgement the creative imagination embarks on a quest for new values, on the psychical journey, and the former target is given new significance by the creative recognition of the architectonic fossil spaces. (See Figure 2.) . . .

What one must remember is that the goal of the spiritual journey, which is the realization of one's vision, can never be final except in the beginning of something new. The possibility and necessity of beginning again is always inherent in it; true permanence is never static, it is an eternal process of becoming, susceptible to dialogue with otherness.

There are moments in history that may endure for a decade or a generation when a culture may 'rest' in its achievements. This is natural and desirable. When however such a pattern of 'rest' begins to assume an idolatrous function of 'changelessness' Wilson Harris suggests that the institutions and models of the day begin to conceal from the body politic itself a growth of catastrophe to which there has ceased to be a 'creative' or 'digestive' response. Then there seems to be no possibility of change except through familiar violence or revenge patterns of self-destructive order.

South African society today provides an excellent illustration of some of the concepts that have just been discussed. The two alchemical dimensions, 'albedo' and 'nigredo', (not necessarily black and white but in this case they happen to be so) have become isolated in every way from one another. The white South Africans have locked themselves in their own

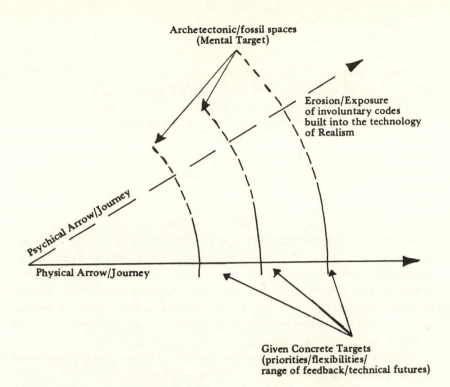

*Figure 2* Theme of expedition

apparently changeless fortresses of culture; 'albedo' (white supremacy) has become a basis for an idolatrous self-sufficient feedback.

A breakthrough from such a condition or dilemma is the vision Athol Fugard presents us with in *The Blood Knot*. In his play he has shown the dynamite-like situation that exists in present-day South Africa where the dialogue between opposites has been superseded by a totalitarian family of man. . . .

What one must remember is that fulfilment is a *ceaseless* task of the psyche; that identity is part of an infinite movement, that one can only come into a dialogue with the past and future, a dialogue which is necessary, if one ceases to invest in a single (and therefore latent totalitarian) identity. If one invests in identity one locks oneself in an immobile horizon; totalitarian identity was the extreme function of the Nazis. One must be prepared to participate in the immense and specific challenges of a wider community, to participate in what Wilson Harris calls the 'complex creativity involved in the "digestion" and "liberation" of contrasting spaces'.

# 31

## Named for Victoria, Queen of England

### CHINUA ACHEBE*

I WAS BAPTISED Albert Chinualumogu. I dropped the tribute to Victorian England when I went to the university although you might find some early acquaintances still calling me by it. The earliest of them all – my mother – certainly stuck to it to the bitter end. So if anyone asks you what Her Britannic Majesty Queen Victoria had in common with Chinua Achebe, the answer is: they both lost their Albert! As for the second name which in the manner of my people is a full-length philosophical statement I simply cut it in two, making it more businesslike without, I hope, losing the general drift of its meaning.

I have always been fond of stories and intrigued by language – first Igbo and later English which I began to learn at about the age of eight. I don't know for certain but I probably have spoken more words in Igbo than English but I have definitely written more words in English than Igbo. Which I think makes me perfectly bilingual. Some people have suggested that I should be better off writing in Igbo. Sometimes they seek to drive the point home by asking me in which language I dream. When I reply that I dream in both languages they seem not to believe it. More recently I have heard an even more potent and metaphysical version of the question: in what language do you have an orgasm? Which would settle the matter if I knew.

We lived at the crossroads of cultures. We still do today; but when I was a boy one could see and sense the peculiar quality and atmosphere of it more clearly. I am not talking about all that rubbish we hear of the spiritual void and mental stresses that Africans are supposed to have, or the evil forces and irrational passions prowling through Africa's heart of darkness. We know the racist mystique behind a lot of that stuff and should merely point out that those who prefer to see Africa in those lurid terms have not themselves demonstrated any clear superiority in sanity or more competence in coping with life.

* From 'Named for Victoria, Queen of England' *New Letters* 40(3) (Fall), 1973.

But still the crossroads does have a certain dangerous potency; dangerous because a man might perish there wrestling with multiple-headed spirits, but also he might be lucky and return to his people with the boon of prophetic vision.

On one arm of the cross we sang hymns and read the Bible night and day. On the other my father's brother and his family, blinded by heathenism, offered food to idols. That was how it was supposed to be anyhow. But I knew without knowing why it was too simple a way to describe what was going on. Those idols and that food had a strange pull on me in spite of my being such a thorough little Christian that often at Sunday services at the height of the grandeur of *Te Deum Laudamus* I would have dreams of a mantle of gold falling on me while the choir of angels drowned our mortal song and the voice of God Himself thundering: This is my beloved son in whom I am well pleased. Yes, despite those delusions of divine destiny I was not past taking my little sister to our neighbour's house when our parents were not looking and partaking of heathen festival meals. I never found their rice to have the flavour of idolatry. I was about ten then. If anyone likes to believe that I was torn by spiritual agonies or stretched on the rack of my ambivalence he certainly may suit himself. I do not remember any undue distress. What I do remember was a fascination for the ritual and the life on the other arm of the crossroads. And I believe two things were in my favour – that curiosity and the little distance imposed between me and it by the accident of my birth. The distance becomes not a separation but a bringing together like the necessary backward step which a judicious viewer may take in order to see a canvas steadily and fully.

I was lucky in having a few old books around the house when I was learning to read. As the fifth in a family of six children and with parents so passionate for their children's education I inherited many discarded primers and readers. I remember *A Midsummer Night's Dream* in an advanced stage of falling apart. I think it must have been a prose adaptation, simplified and illustrated. I don't remember whether I made anything of it. Except the title. I couldn't get over the strange beauty of it. A Midsummer Night's Dream. It was a magic phrase – an incantation that conjured up scenes and landscapes of an alien, happy and unattainable land.

I remember also my mother's *Ije Onye Kraist* which must have been an Igbo adaptation of *Pilgrim's Progress*. It could not have been the whole book; it was too thin. But it had some frightening pictures. I recall in particular a most vivid impression of *the valley of the shadow of death*. I thought a lot about death in those days. There was another little book which frightened and fascinated me. It had drawings of different parts of the human body. But I was only interested in what my elder sister told me was the human heart. Since there is a slight confusion in Igbo between heart and soul I took it that that strange thing looking almost like my mother's iron cooking pot turned upside down was the very thing that flew out when a man died and perched on the head of the coffin on the way to the cemetery.

I found some use for most of the books in our house but by no means all. There was one Arithmetic book I smuggled out and sold for half-a-penny which I needed to buy the tasty *mai-mai* some temptress of a woman sold in the little market outside the school. I was found out and my mother who had never had cause till then to doubt my honesty – laziness, yes; but not theft – received a huge shock. Of course she redeemed the book. I was so ashamed when she brought it home that I don't think I ever looked at it again which was probably why I never had much use for mathematics.

My parents' reverence for books was almost superstitious; so my action must have seemed like a form of juvenile simony. My father was much worse than my mother. He never destroyed any paper. When he died we had to make a bonfire of all the hoardings of his long life. I am the very opposite of him in this. I can't stand paper around me. Whenever I see a lot of it I am seized by a mild attack of pyromania. When I die my children will not have a bonfire.

The kind of taste I acquired from the chaotic literature in my father's house can well be imagined. For instance I became very fond of those aspects of ecclesiastical history as could be garnered from *The West African Churchman's Pamphlet* – a little terror of a booklet prescribing interminable Bible readings morning and night. It had the date of consecration for practically every Anglican bishop who ever served in West Africa; and, even more intriguing, the dates of their death. Many of them didn't last very long. I remember one pathetic case (I forget his name) who arrived in Lagos straight from his consecration at St. Paul's Cathedral and was dead within days, and his wife a week or two after him. Those were the days when West Africa was truly the white man's grave, when those great lines were written, of which I was at that time unaware:

> Bight of Benin! Bight of Benin!
> Where few come out though many go in!

But the most fascinating information I got from *Pamphlet*, as we called it, was this cryptic entry for the month of August:

> *Augustine, Bishop of Hippo, died 430*

It had that elusive and eternal quality, a tantalizing unfamiliarity which I always found moving.

I did not know that I was going to be a writer because I did not really know of the existence of such creatures until fairly late. The folk-stories my mother and elder sister told me had the immemorial quality of the sky and the forests and the rivers. Later, when I got to know people it still didn't help much. It was the same Europeans who made all the other marvellous things like the motor-car. We did not come into it at all. We made nothing that wasn't primitive and heathenish.

The nationalist movement in British West Africa after the Second World War brought about a mental revolution which began to reconcile us to ourselves. It suddenly seemed that we too might have a story to tell. *Rule Britannia*! to which we had marched so unself-consciously on Empire Day now stuck in our throat.

At the university I read some appalling novels about Africa (including Joyce Cary's much praised *Mister Johnson*) and decided that the story we had to tell could not be told for us by anyone else no matter how gifted or well-intentioned.

Although I did not set about it consciously in that solemn way I now know that my first book, *Things Fall Apart*, was an act of atonement with my past, the ritual return and homage of a prodigal son. But things happen very fast in Africa. I had hardly begun to bask in the sunshine of reconciliation when a new cloud appeared, a new estrangement. Political independence had come. The nationalist leader of yesterday (with whom it had not been too difficult to make common cause) had become the not so attractive party boss. And then things really got going. The party boss was chased out by the bright military boys, new idols of the people. But the party boss knows how to wait, knows by heart the counsel Mother Bedbug gave her little ones when the harassed owner of the bed poured hot water on them: 'Be patient,' said she, 'for what is hot will in the end be cold.'

One hears that the party boss is already conducting a whispering campaign: 'You done see us chop,' he says, 'now you see *dem* chop. Which one you like pass?' And the people are truly confused.

In a little nondescript coffee shop where I sometimes stop for a hamburger in Amherst there are some unfunny inscriptions hanging on the walls, representing a one-sided dialogue between management and staff. The unfunniest of them all reads – poetically:

> Take care of your boss
> The next one may be worse.

The trouble with writers is that they will often refuse to live by such rationality.

# 32

# Of the Marvellous Realism of the Haitians

## Jacques Stephen Aléxis*

### TOWARDS A DYNAMIC INTEGRATION OF THE MARVELLOUS; MARVELLOUS REALISM

THE ART AND literature of several peoples of Negro origin, like those of many countries of the Antilles and Central and Latin America, have frequently given the example of the possible dynamic integration of the Marvellous in realism. It does not seem to us fair to think that the fascination, originality, and singular attractions of the aesthetic forms proper to countries of Negro origin are inexplicable, or that they are the result of chance, or the attraction of novelty, or a question of fashion. It is true that all peoples, whoever they may be, are endowed with feeling as well as with reason, but let us remember the saying that 'the people who have no more legends are condemned to perish of cold', and let us objectively recognize the fact that modern life with its stern rates of production, with its concentration of great masses of men into industrial armies, caught up in the frenzy of Taylorism, with its inadequate leisure, and its context of mechanized life, hampers and slows down the production of legends and a living folk lore. By way of contrast, the under-developed populations of the world who have still quite recently had to live in contact with Nature, have for centuries been compelled particularly to sharpen their eyes, their hearing, their sense of touch. The peoples among whom industrial life is most highly developed, have, for their part, used their senses to a lesser extent during the last few centuries, since material civilization has saved them a great deal of effort; that has been the price of industrial mechanization, certain regrettable consequences of which everyone recognizes. The under-developed populations of the world, on their part, know a blend of mechanical civilization and 'natural' life, so to speak, and it is beyond dispute that they have feelings of special liveliness. The problems which they have to face, the low standard of living, unemployment, poverty,

* From 'Of the Marvellous Realism of the Haitians' *Présence Africaine* 8–10, 1956.

hunger and illness are also problems which it is important to liquidate, and we do not overlook this.

These specially lively feelings give these peoples artistic possibilities which should be used. From there it is only a step to conceiving that the Haitian, for instance, does not seek to grasp the whole of sensible reality, but what strikes him, what threatens him, what in Nature particularly touches and stirs his emotions. From another angle, since reality is not intelligible in all its aspects to the members of under-developed communities, he naturally transposes his conceptions of relativity and of the marvellous in to his vision of everyday reality. A bird in rapid flight is, above all, a pair of wings, a woman giving suck impresses by her round and heavy breasts, a wild beast is essentially a footfall and a roar, the body responds naturally to music without following a pre-ordained plan, in contrast to other men who exercise a constant restraint over their bodies in order to conform to the social usages of polite society. To demonstrate the peculiar, and sometimes paradoxical, sensitivity of the Haitian, for example, we would cite the fact that in our Voodoo religion a man possessed will sometimes take a red hot iron in his hands without burning them and lick it; he climbs trees with agility, even if he is an old man, he succeeds in dancing for several days and nights on end, he chews and swallows glass. . . . Quite apart from any mystic conception of the world, in the light of numerous observed facts, there are many values which should be revised by science. Can one, in effect, strip a human being of all his antecedents, of all the unconditioned reflexes born of the conditioned reflexes transmitted by heredity? A human being cannot be the son of no man, the past and history cannot be denied; the Haitian, and, through him, his culture, is the legatee of an inheritance of reactions of behaviour and habitude anterior to his hundred and fifty years of independence; he is still, to a large extent, heir of cultural elements derived from distant Africa. The Haitian has an air, a family likeness, internal as much as external, which makes him resemble on many planes his other brothers in the world of Negro origin. That, moreover, is why we are here at this Congress.

It is because they recognize that their people express their whole consciousness of reality by the use of the Marvellous, that Haitian writers and artists have become aware of the formal problem of its use. Behind the imaginary characters of the *romancero* of Bouqui and Malice, it is a faithful picture of the conditions of rural life which the Haitian story-teller executes, it is its beauties and its ugliness, and struggles, the drama of the oppressors and the oppressed which he brings on to their stage. In his working songs, for among us work is unthinkable without music, or without songs in which all the workers take part, – in his working songs the Voodoo gods of the Haitian are nothing but an inspiration towards the ownership of the land on which he works, an aspiration towards the rain which feeds the harvest, an aspiration towards abundant bread, an aspiration to get rid of the maladies which afflict him, an aspiration towards betterment in every sphere. Even the religious songs and dances are transparent symbols in which they beg the gods for the solution of a specific problem; there are, moreover, pleasant gods, soldier gods, politician gods, powerful gods and exploited gods, gods who are unhappy in love, infirm gods, one-legged gods, blind gods, dumb gods, rapacious gods and gods who are simple, kind and helpful, poets and laughter. When they are mariners, our people also include the width of the horizon, the murmuring of the waves, the drama of the seas, in the form of Agouet Arroyo, the Loa of the Ocean, they hymn the Diamond Siren, 'the Sun Queen', as they sometimes say, but nothing more actual, nothing more truthful, nothing more loving than all these entities. How could we be unconscious to the extent of refusing to use all that in the service of realizing specific and actualized struggles: That is what made the poet and playwright Morisseau-Leroy write as follows in a recent article:

> We are again living through a renaissance of the Haitian song. We see flourishing again forms of expression, both rich and original, as in the times when Dithyrambic or satyric, lyric or bucolic couplets flowed from the lips of a people whose temper and humour were proof against all misery. . . . From one end of the Republic to another nephews and uncles, nieces and aunts are singing or humming in cadence. . . . And if Agoue T'Arroya does not afford that rude class of workers enough protection against shipwreck, the official social institutions of the Republic have hardly done better in that direction. It is therefore gratuitously that in their songs they invoke the gods and the chiefs. . . . I want before everything to emphasize that if reality in its local aspect, as in its universal aspect, escapes those who have been led astray by a certain humanism, the popular bards, the 'composes' remain, in my view, the sole masters of Haitian poetry, the only ones capable of making us sing and dance together in the unavowed and common conviction that the people are safe and sound.'

What, then, is the Marvellous, except the imagery in which a people wraps its experience, reflects its conception of the world and of life, its faith, its hope, its confidence in man, in a great justice, and the explanation which it finds for the forces antagonistic to progress? It is true that the Marvellous implies ingenuousness and empiricism, if not mysticism, but it has been proved that something else can be bound up with it. When the great painter Wilson Bigaud painted a picture called 'The Earthly Paradise' he made full use of the Marvellous, but has the painter not expressed the way in which the Haitian people conceives a time of happiness? Look at all those fruits which accumulate in bunches on the canvas, those dense masses of colour, all those splendid animals, tranquil and fraternal, including the wild beasts, is it not the cosmic dream of abundance and fraternity of a people still suffering from hunger and deprivation? When in his play *Rara* Morisseau-Leroy shows a man dying for his right to a feast day in the drabness of his working days, paralytics who get up and dance, mutes who begin to sing when, after the death of heroes, people recount that they are traversing the region, when ghosts are seen, no-one is mistaken, no-one gives it a mystical significance, but everyone sees in it an incitement to the fight for happiness. Naturally, one must always do better, and the combatants of the advance guard of Haitian culture recognize the need resolutely to transcend whatever is irrational, mystic and animist in their national patrimony, but they do not think that that is an insoluble problem. They will reject the animist garment which conceals the realist nucleus, the dynamics of their culture, a nucleus charged with good sense, life and humanism, they will put on its feet again what is too often walking on its head, but they will never deny that cultural tradition, which is a great and fine thing, the only one which they possess as their own. Just as there is no question of any people denying religious works of art influenced by a mystical conception of life, Haitian men of culture will be able in a dynamic, positive and scientific way, a way of social realism, to combine the whole human protest against the harsh realities of life, all the emotion, the long cry of struggle, distress and hope which are contained in the works and forms transmitted to them by the past.

Social realism, conscious of the imperatives of history, preaches an art human in its content, but resolutely national in its form. This means that the pseudo 'world citizens' of culture, the true cosmopolitans, the true expatriates, have nothing to do with the man of our time, nothing to do with progress, and therefore nothing to do with culture. If all human races and all nations are equal and sisters, they have none the less their own traditions, their own temperament and forms which are more likely to touch them. If Art were not national in its form, how could the citizens of a country set about recognizing the perfumes and the climates which they love, so as truly to relive the works of beauty which are offered to them, and to find in them their share of dreams and of courage? The result would be that the people in question would find it difficult to take part in the forward movement of mankind towards liberation, since that art and that literature, essential elements in realization as much as in delight, would have no hold upon their feelings.

Haitian artists made use of the Marvellous in a dynamic sense before they realized that they were creating a Marvellous Realism. We became gradually conscious of the fact. Creating realism meant that the Haitian artists were setting about speaking the same language as their people. The Marvellous Realism of the Haitians is thus an integral part of Social Realism, and in its Haitian form it follows the same preoccupations. The treasury of tales and legends, all the musical, choreographic and plastic symbolism, all the forms of Haitian popular art are there to help the nation in solving its problems and in accomplishing the tasks which lie before it. The Western genres and organons bequeathed to us must be resolutely transformed in a national sense, and everything in a work of art must stir those feelings which are peculiar to the Haitians, sons of three races and an infinity of cultures.

197

To sum up, the objects of Marvellous Realism are:

1. To sing the beauties of the Haitian motherland, its greatness as well as its wretchedness, with the sense of the magnificent prospects which are opened up by the struggles of its people and the universal and the profound truth of life;
2. To reject all art which has no real and social content;
3. To find the forms of expression proper to its own people, those which correspond to their psychology, while employing in a renovated and widened form, the universal models, naturally in accordance with the personality of each creator;
4. To have a clear consciousness of specific and concrete current problems and the real dramas which confront the masses, with the purpose of touching and cultivating more deeply, and of carrying the people with them in their struggles.

In relation to particular forms of art, there are many aspects which need to be made clearer, but only a detailed discussion would enable us to come nearer to the truth. It is not an easy task to progress along the road of this kind of realism, and there are many gropings and many errors ahead of us, but we shall know how to profit even by our mistakes, to reach as soon as possible what is already taking shape before our eyes. Work will settle all the rest.

# 33

# *Marvellous Realism*
## *The Way out of Négritude*
### MICHAEL DASH*

## TOWARDS A REDEFINITION OF HISTORY

IF THERE IS one sound idea that the ideology of 'négritude' puts forward, it is certainly the notion of the double alienation of the black man – that is a belief that the problem is more than political and economic, that there was a psychological and spiritual reconstruction that should also take place. However, it was difficult for them to provide a solution to the problem of spiritual regeneration for the simple reason that they themselves held as true an attitude to the past as being totally un-creative. Indeed in their reiteration of the injustice of the past they did no more than emphasize the fact of spiritual loss to the extent that any notions of survival or emergence of a Third World personality were totally neglected. This is the essential difference between 'Marvellous Realism' and 'Négritude' – for the former stresses patterns of emergence from the continuum of history. For the elaboration of this philosophy we will examine the ideas of Jacques Stephen Aléxis, Haitian novelist, and Wilson Harris, a Guyanese novelist.

One feature of Third World writers which distinguishes them as a distinct literary fraternity is the fundamental dialogue with history in which they are involved. However, as we have noted, so far this dialogue with the past essentially consisted of a continuous and desperate protest against the ironies of history. They adhered to the view of history as fateful coincidence and tragic accident, and saw their function as artists in terms of their attitude to the past, that is, either in terms of a committed protest against the past which would give birth to a new humanism, or were so overwhelmed by the 'fact' of privation or dispossession that they withdrew to a position of cynicism with regard to their peoples (V. S. Naipaul the Trinidadian novelist is often quoted as typical of this attitude). However such attitudes to the continuum of history left out of account a significant

* From 'Marvellous Realism: The Way out of Négritude' *Caribbean Studies* 13(4), 1974.

and positive part of the history of the Third World. It made it difficult to
see beyond the tragedy of circumstance to the complex process of survival
which the autochthonous as well as the transplanted cultures in the New
World underwent. Such an investigation of the process of adaptation and
survival in the oppressed cultures of the New World could well change the
vision of the past which froze the Third World writer in the prison of
protest and reveal the colonial legacy as a positive and civilizing force in
spite of the brutality and privation which cloud this historical period.

Such an attitude would signify for the Third World writer an investigation of his past which goes beyond the documented privations of slavery
and colonization to a more speculative vision of history in which the
consciousness of the dominated cultures would predominate. In order to tap
this consciousness, both Aléxis and Harris have turned to the myths, legends
and superstitions of the folk in order to isolate traces of a complex culture
of survival which was the response of the dominated to their oppressors
(Aléxis 1960 and Harris 1970b). That is to say that colonization and slavery
did *not* make things of men, but in their own way the enslaved peoples
might have in their own imagination so reordered their reality as to reach
beyond the tangible and concrete to acquire a new re-creative sensibility
which could aid in the harsh battle for survival. The only thing they could
possess (and which could not be tampered with) was their imagination and
this became the source of their struggle against the cruelty of their condition. This notion of a counter-culture of the imagination is the basis of
Harris' investigation of the practices of Haitian Voudou, limbo and the
Amerindian religious rites, as he is convinced that . . .

> . . . the imagination of the folk involved a crucial inner re-creative
> response to the violations of slavery and indenture and conquest.
>
> (Harris 1970b: 12)

This is an attitude to the conquered peoples which is unprecedented. It is
the taking into account of the inner resources that the ancestors of the
Third World could have developed to combat their tragic environment,
therefore engaging in a conception of the past which would shatter the
myths of 'historylessness' or 'non-achievement'.

Of what importance can the conception of such an 'inner corrective' on
history be to the contemporary writer? It means fundamentally that in the
same way he can circumvent the ironies of history so can he avoid the
negativity of pure protest. What can indeed emerge is a literature of
renascence – a literary aesthetic and reality based on the fragile emergence
of the Third World personality from the privations of history. Now such a
conception of reality would mean for the writer, the endowing of the
concrete and the tangible with a figurative meaning. Harris comments on
this as a possibility of the writer when he claims:

> I believe the possibility exists for us to become involved in perspectives
> of renascence which can bring into play a figurative meaning beyond

an apparently real world or prison of history – I believe a philosophy
of history may well lie buried in the arts of the imagination.

(Harris 1970c: 8)

This would signify an adoption of the positive imaginative reconstruction
of reality developed in the consciousness of the folk, by the contemporary
writer. It is more than coincidence which can explain the striking similarity
between Harris' claim and Aléxis' statement in 1956:

> Haitian art, in effect, presents the real, with its accompaniment of the
> strange and the fantastic, of dreams and half light, of the mysterious
> and the marvellous. . . . The West of Graeco-Latin descent too often
> tends to intellectualisation, to idealization, to the creation of perfect
> canons, to the logical unity of the elements of feeling, to a pre-estab-
> lished harmony, whereas our art tends towards the most exact sensual
> representation of reality, towards a creative intuition, character, power
> of expression.
>
> (Aléxis 1956: 260)

Such a vision of the imaginative resonances of external reality, far from
being a poetic abstraction, can not only be explained by the imagination of
the conquered cultures of the past but by the fact that . . . 'the under-
developed populations of the world who have still quite frequently had to
live in contact with nature, have been compelled particularly to sharpen
their eyes, their hearing, their sense of touch' (Aléxis 1956: 268).

# 34

## Creolization in Jamaica

### EDWARD KAMAU BRATHWAITE*

THE SINGLE MOST important factor in the development of Jamaican society was not the imported influence of the Mother Country or the local administrative activity of the white élite, but a cultural action – material, psychological and spiritual – based upon the stimulus/response of individuals within the society to their environment and – as white/black, culturally discrete groups – to each other. The scope and quality of this response and interaction were dictated by the circumstances of the society's foundation and composition – a 'new' construct, made up of newcomers to the landscape and cultural strangers each to the other; one group dominant, the other legally and subordinately slaves. This cultural action or social process has been defined within the context of this work as creolization. Mrs Duncker has described it, in general terms in so far as it affected white settlers and visitors:

> Although there were some people who came to the West Indies and refused to conform, the power of the society to mould new-comers was strong. However oddly constructed West India society might appear in England, for the English people coming to the West Indies it was only a short time before they were caught up in the system. . . .
>
> (Duncker 1960: 231)

Maria Nugent must have said the same thing to herself when, after watching her dance with an (elderly) black slave, her hostesses broke down and cried from horror and outrage. We were faced here with an obscure force, working upon an entire section of society, which makes them all conform to a certain concept of themselves; makes them perform in certain roles which, in fact, they quickly come to believe in. . . .

Slaves in Jamaica came from a wide area of West Africa, within the period of this study, mainly from the Gold Coast and the Niger and Cross

* From *The Development of Creole Society in Jamaica 1770–1820* Oxford: Clarendon Press, 1971.

deltas. Creolization began with 'seasoning' – a period of one to three years, when the slaves were branded, given a new name and put under apprenticeship to creolized slaves. During this period the slave would learn the rudiments of his new language and be initiated into the work routines that awaited him.

These work routines, especially for plantation slaves, were the next important step in creolization. . . . From this followed 'socialization' – participation with others through the gang system, and through communal recreational activities such as drumming and dancing and festivals. . . . For the docile there was also the persuasion of the whip and the fear of punishment; for the venal, there was the bribe of gift or compliment or the offer of a better position, and for the curious and self-seeking, the imitation of the master. This imitation went on, naturally, most easily among those in closest and most intimate contact with Europeans, among, that is, domestic slaves, female slaves with white lovers, slaves in contact with missionaries or traders or sailors, skilled slaves anxious to deploy their skills, and above all, among urban slaves in contact with the 'wider' life. . . .

It was one of the tragedies of slavery and of the conditions under which creolization had to take place, that it should have produced this kind of mimicry; should have produced such 'mimic-men'. But in the circumstances this was the only kind of 'white' imitation that would have been accepted, given the terms in which the slaves were seen; and it was this kind of mimicry that was largely smiled upon and cultivated by 'middle class' Jamaican (and West Indian) society after Emancipation. *The snow was falling in the canefields* became typical of the 'educated' West Indian imagination.

But it was a two-way process, and it worked both ways. . . . In white households the Negro influence was pervasive, especially in the country areas. . . .

To preserve the pure dialect of the tribe (at least of the females) planters had to send to England for governesses and practically locked their daughters away from Negro influence.

But it was in the intimate area of sexual relationships that the greatest damage was done to white creole apartheid policy and where the most significant – and lasting – inter-cultural creolization took place. Black mistresses made convenient spies and/or managers of Negro affairs, and white men in petty authority were frequently influenced in their decisions by black women with whom they were amorously, or at any rate sensually, connected. . . .

Creolization, then, was a cultural process that took place within a creole society – that is, within a tropical colonial plantation polity based on slavery.

Even more important for an understanding of Jamaican development during this period was the process of creolization, which is a way of seeing the society, not in terms of white and black, master and slave, in separate nuclear units, but as contributory parts of a whole. To see Jamaica (or the West Indies generally) as a 'slave' society is as much a falsification of reality, as the seeing of the island as a naval station or an enormous sugar factory. Here, in Jamaica, fixed with the dehumanizing institution of slavery, were two cultures of people, having to adapt themselves to a new environment and to each other. The friction created by this confrontation was cruel, but it was also creative. The white plantations and social institutions described in this study reflect one aspect of this. The slaves' adaptation of their African culture to a new world reflects another. The failure of Jamaican society was that it did not recognize these elements of its own creativity. Blinded by the need to justify slavery, white Jamaicans refused to recognize their black labourers as human beings, thus cutting themselves off from the one demographic alliance that might have contributed to the island's economic and (possibly) political independence. What the white Jamaican élite did not, could not, would not, dare accept, was that true autonomy for them could only mean true autonomy for all; that the more unrestricted the creolization, the greater would have been the freedom. They preferred a bastard metropolitanism – handed down to the society in general after Emancipation – with its consequence of dependence on Europe, to a complete exposure to creolization and liberation of their slaves.

Blinded by the wretchedness of their situation, many of Jamaica's slaves, especially the black élite (those most exposed to the influence of their masters), failed, or refused, to make conscious use of their own rich folk culture (their one indisputable possession), and so failed to command the chance of becoming self-conscious and cohesive as a group and consequently, perhaps, winning their independence from bondage, as their cousins in Haiti had done. 'Invisible', anxious to be 'seen' by their masters, the élite blacks and the mass of the free coloureds (apart from the significant exceptions already discussed within the body of this work, and those who, after Emancipation, were to establish, against almost impossible odds, the free villages and small peasantries of rural Jamaica), conceived of visibility through the lenses of their masters' already uncertain vision as a form of 'greyness' – an imitation of an imitation. Whenever the opportunity made it possible, they and their descendants rejected or disowned their own culture, becoming, like their masters, 'mimic-men'.

Cultural autonomy demands a norm and a residential correspondence between the 'great' and 'little' traditions within the society. Under slavery there were two 'great' traditions, one in Europe, the other in Africa, and so neither was residential. Normative value-references were made outside the society. Creolization (despite its attendant imitations and conformities) provided the conditions for and possibility of local residence. It certainly mediated the development of authentically local institutions, and an Afro-creole 'little' tradition among the slave 'folk'. But it did not, during the period of this study, provide a norm. For this to have been provided, the Euro-creole élite (the one group able, to some extent, to influence the pace and quality of creolization) would have had to have been much stronger, culturally, than it was. Unable or unwilling to absorb in any central sense the 'little' tradition of the majority, its efforts and its continuing colonial dependence merely created the pervasive dichotomy which has been indicated in this study. . . .

My own idea of creolization is based on the notion of an historically affected socio-cultural continuum, within which (in the case of Jamaica) there were four inter-related and sometimes overlapping orientations. From their several cultural bases people in the West Indies tend towards certain directions, positions, assumptions, and ideals. But nothing is really fixed and monolithic. Although there is white/brown/black, there are infinite possibilities within these distinctions and many ways of asserting identity.

# 35

## Cultural Diversity and Cultural Differences

### Homi K. Bhabha*

[THE] REVISION OF the history of critical theory rests . . . on the notion of cultural difference, not cultural diversity. Cultural diversity is an epistemological object – culture as an object of empirical knowledge – whereas cultural difference is the process of the *enunciation* of culture as 'knowledg*eable*', authoritative, adequate to the construction of systems of cultural identification. If cultural diversity is a category of comparative ethics, aesthetics, or ethnology, cultural difference is a process of signification through which statements *of* culture or *on* culture differentiate, discriminate, and authorize the production of fields of force, reference, applicability, and capacity. Cultural diversity is the recognition of pre-given cultural 'contents' and customs, held in a time-frame of relativism; it gives rise to anodyne liberal notions of multiculturalism, cultural exchange, or the culture of humanity. Cultural diversity is also the representation of a radical rhetoric of the separation of totalized cultures that live unsullied by the intertextuality of their historical locations, safe in the Utopianism of a mythic memory of a unique collective identity. Cultural diversity may even emerge as a system of the articulation and exchange of cultural signs in certain . . . imperialist accounts of anthropology.

Through the concept of cultural difference I want to draw attention to the common ground and lost territory of contemporary critical debates. For they all recognize that the problem of the cultural emerges only at the significatory boundaries of cultures, where meanings and values are (mis)read or signs are misappropriated. . . .

The time of liberation is, as Fanon powerfully evokes, a time of cultural uncertainty, and, most crucially, of significatory or representational undecidability:

> But [native intellectuals] forget that the forms of thought and what [they] feed . . . on, together with modern techniques of information, language and dress have dialectically reorganized the people's

* From 'The Commitment to Theory' *New Formations* 5, 1988.

> intelligences and *the constant principles (of national art)* which acted
> as safeguards during the colonial period are now undergoing extremely
> radical changes . . . [We] must join the people in that fluctuating move-
> ment which they are *just* giving a shape to . . . which will be the signal
> for everything to be called into question . . . it is to the zone of *occult*
> *instability* where the people dwell that we must come.
>
> (My emphasis) (Fanon 1967: 168)

The enunciation of cultural difference problematizes the division of past
and present, tradition and modernity, at the level of cultural representation
and its authoritative address. It is the problem of how, in signifying the
present, something comes to be repeated, relocated, and translated in the
name of tradition, in the guise of a pastness that is not necessarily a faithful
sign of historical memory but a strategy of representing authority in terms
of the artifice of the archaic. That iteration negates our sense of the origins
of the struggle. It undermines our sense of the homogenizing effects of
cultural symbols and icons, by questioning our sense of the authority of
cultural synthesis in general.

This demands that we rethink our perspective on the identity of
culture. Here Fanon's passage – somewhat reinterpreted – may be helpful.
What is implied by his juxtaposition of the constant national principles
with his view of culture-as-political-struggle, which he so enigmatically and
beautifully describes as 'the zone of occult instability where the people
dwell'? These ideas not only help to explain the nature of colonial struggle.
They also suggest a possible critique of the positive aesthetic and political
values we ascribe to the unity or totality of cultures, especially those that
have known long and tyrannical histories of domination and misrecog-
nition. Cultures are never unitary in themselves, nor simply dualistic in
relation of Self to Other. This is not because of some humanistic nostrum
that beyond individual cultures we all belong to the human culture of
mankind; nor is it because of an ethical relativism that suggests that in our
cultural capacity to speak of and judge Others we necessarily 'place
ourselves in their position', in a kind of relativism of distance of which
Bernard Williams has written at length (Williams 1985: ch. 9).

The reason a cultural text or system of meaning cannot be sufficient
unto itself is that the act of cultural enunciation – the place of utterance –
is crossed by the difference of writing or écriture. This has less to do with
what anthropologists might describe as varying attitudes to symbolic
systems within different cultures than with the structure of symbolic
representation – not the content of the symbol or its 'social function', but
the structure of symbolization. It is this 'difference' in language that is
crucial to the production of meaning and ensures, at the same time, that
meaning is never simply mimetic and transparent.

The linguistic difference that informs any cultural performance is
dramatized in the common semiotic account of the disjuncture between the
subject of a proposition (énoncé) and the subject of enunciation, which is

not represented in the statement but which is the acknowledgment of its discursive embeddedness and address, its cultural positionality, its reference to a present time and a specific space. The pact of interpretation is never simply an act of communication between the I and the You designated in the statement. The production of meaning requires that these two places be mobilized in the passage through a Third Space, which represents both the general conditions of language and the specific implication of the utterance in a performative and institutional strategy of which it cannot 'in itself' be conscious. What this unconscious relation introduces is an ambivalence in the act of interpretation. . . .

The intervention of the Third Space, which makes the structure of meaning and reference an ambivalent process, destroys this mirror of representation in which cultural knowledge is continuously revealed as an integrated, open, expanding code. Such an intervention quite properly challenges our sense of the historical identity of culture as a homogenizing, unifying force, authenticated by the originary Past, kept alive in the national tradition of the People. In other words, the disruptive temporality of enunciation displaces the narrative of the Western nation which Benedict Anderson so perceptively describes as being written in homogeneous, serial time (Anderson 1983: ch. 2).

It is only when we understand that all cultural statements and systems are constructed in this contradictory and ambivalent space of enunciation, that we begin to understand why hierarchical claims to the inherent originality or 'purity' of cultures are untenable, even before we resort to empirical historical instances that demonstrate their hybridity. Fanon's vision of revolutionary cultural and political change as a 'fluctuating movement' of occult instability could not be articulated as cultural *practice* without an acknowledgment of this indeterminate space of the subject(s) of enunciation. It is that Third Space, though unrepresentable in itself, which constitutes the discursive conditions of enunciation that ensure that the meaning and symbols of culture have no primordial unity or fixity; that even the same signs can be appropriated, translated, rehistoricized, and read anew.

Fanon's moving metaphor – when reinterpreted for a theory of cultural signification – enables us to see not only the necessity of theory, but also the restrictive notions of cultural identity with which we burden our visions of political change. For Fanon, the liberatory 'people' who initiate the productive instability of revolutionary cultural change are themselves the bearers of a hybrid identity. They are caught in the discontinuous time of translation and negotiation, in the sense in which I have been attempting to recast these works. In the moment of liberatory struggle, the Algerian people destroy the continuities and constancies of the 'nationalist' tradition which provided a safeguard against colonial cultural imposition. They are now free to negotiate and translate their cultural identities in a discontinuous intertextual temporality of cultural difference. The native intellectual who identifies the people with the 'true national culture' will be disappointed. The people are now the very principle of 'dialectical reorganization' and they construct their culture from the national text translated into modern Western forms of information technology, language, dress. The changed political and historical site of enunciation transforms the meanings of the colonial inheritance into the liberatory signs of a free people of the future.

> I have been stressing a certain void or misgiving attending every assimilation of contraries – I have been stressing this in order to expose what seems to me a fantastic mythological congruence of elements. . . . And if indeed therefore any real sense is to be made of material change it can only occur with an acceptance of a concurrent void and with a willingness to descend into that void wherein, as it were, one may begin to come into confrontation with a spectre of invocation whose freedom to participate in an alien territory and wilderness has become a necessity for one's reason or salvation
>
> ( Harris 1973a: 60–3).

This meditation by the great Guyanian writer Wilson Harris on the void of misgiving in the textuality of colonial history reveals the cultural and historical dimension of that Third Space of enunciation which I have made the precondition for the articulation of cultural difference. He sees it as accompanying the 'assimilation of contraries' and creating that occult instability which presages powerful cultural changes. It is significant that the productive capacities of this Third Space have a colonial or post-colonial provenance. For a willingness to descend into that alien territory – where I have led you – may reveal that the theoretical recognition of the split-space of enunciation may open the way to conceptualizing an *inter*national culture, based not on the exoticism or multi-culturalism of the *diversity* of cultures, but on the inscription and articulation of culture's *hybridity*. To that end we should remember that it is the 'inter' – the cutting edge of translation and negotiation, the *in-between*, the space of the *entre* that Derrida has opened up in writing itself – that carries the burden of the meaning of culture. It makes it possible to begin envisaging national, anti-nationalist, histories of the 'people'. It is in this space that we will find those words with which we can speak of Ourselves and Others. And by exploring this hybridity, this 'Third Space', we may elude the politics of polarity and emerge as the others of our selves.

# PART VII

*Ethnicity and Indigeneity*

# Introduction

With the concepts of ethnicity and indigeneity we bring together two of the most vexed and complex issues in post-colonial theory. The way each intersects with notions of race, marginality, imperialism, and identity, leads to a constantly shifting theoretical ground, a ground continually contested and subject to more heated debate than most. At its simplest the argument boils down to a dispute over whether some ethnic groups and not others are entitled to the term 'ethnic', and whether the indigenous people of an invaded colony are the only 'truly colonised' group, an issue already discussed earlier in Diana Brydon's essay 'The White Inuit Speaks'.

Much of the difficulty surrounding these concepts can be resolved if we understand the imperial project as a process rather than a structure. For instance, the model of an imperial 'centre' controlling a colonial 'margin', a model which underlies much of the policy, strategies and outcomes of colonialism, is a myth which is only retained by post-colonial discourse in order to be deconstructed. As a geographical myth the centre/margin binarism leads by logical extension to such absurdities as the idea that all people in colonies are marginalised while nobody at the imperial centre can be marginalised; or, more crudely, that whites are the colonisers and blacks the colonised. Obviously if we try to find *the* centre of the empire, we will never find it, even in Piccadilly or Buckingham Palace, because this structural notion omits the institutions and process by which power is disseminated and maintained. Clearly that process is one set in train by the imperial project and continues throughout the colonial world as Trinh T. Minh-ha demonstrates ('The centre itself is marginal'). This is why 'post-colonial' can apply to white settler/invader colonies as much as to the indigenous people. It is also why the idea that only some ethnic groups are 'ethnic' and not others can be seen to be fallacious.

The argument put by Werner Sollors that 'ethnic' includes all ethnic groups and not simply all those except an arbitrarily selected dominant group is one which generally concurs with the post-colonial rejection of the centre/margin binarism. This acceptance of ethnic pluralism, that everyone in a society is 'ethnic', is not to deny that some ethnic groups exercise dominance in a society. But the binarism of one ethnic group at the centre and all others at the margin, overlooks the actual overlap between the multiplicity of ethnic groups and the dynamic, processual and multi-faceted institutions of power. As Stuart Hall points out, the conceptualisation of ethnicity itself is undergoing a radical change based upon the increasingly complex politics of representation: old binarisms of black/white, and indeed conceptions of the 'essential' ethnic subject itself are now increasingly open to question.

The indigenous peoples of 'settled' colonies, or 'First-Nations', have in many ways become the *cause célébre* of post-colonialism. No other group seems so completely to earn the position of colonised group, so unequivocally to demonstrate the processes of imperialism at work. But indigenous groups have so often fallen into the political trap of essentialism set for them by imperial discourse. Imperial narratives such as that of anthropology in their project of *naming* and thus *knowing* indigenous groups have imported a notion of aboriginality, of cultural authenticity, which proves difficult to displace. The result is the positioning of the indigenous people as the ultimately marginalised, a concept which reinscribes the binarism of centre/margin, and prevents their engagement with the subtle processes of imperialism by locking them into a locally strategic but ultimately self-defeating essentialism. As Mudrooroo says, 'all cultures and societies change and adapt', and it is in a dynamic and shifting environment of adaptation that the political claims of indigenous people are situated.

The semiotic system by which the indigenous peoples of Canada, Australia and New Zealand have been represented looks, according to Terry Goldie, something like a chessboard in which the semiotic pawn signifying the indigenous person can only be moved in very circumscribed ways. This is the imperialist corollary of the essentialist argument and indeed essentialism works, in the long run, to the detriment of the indigenous society, as Gareth Griffiths shows, by separating the indigenous subject under conflicting categories of 'authentic' and 'inauthentic'. As post-colonial discourse demonstrates, the appeal to 'authenticity' is not merely an ontological contradiction, but a political trap. Thus the question of 'who can write as the Other' addressed by Margery Fee becomes particularly pertinent, for the rejection of an 'authentic' or 'essential' indigenous subjectivity must be reconciled with the real material conditions of subjection.

# 36

## No Master Territories

### TRINH T. MINH-HA*

### CENTRE AND MARGIN

THE IMPERVIOUSNESS IN the West of the many branches of knowledge to
everything that does not fall inside their predetermined scope has been
repeatedly challenged by its thinkers throughout the years. They extol the
concept of decolonization and continuously invite into their fold 'the challenge of the Third World.' Yet, they do not seem to realize the difference
when they find themselves face to face with it – a difference which does not
announce itself, which they do not quite anticipate and cannot fit into any
single varying compartment of their catalogued world; a difference they
keep on measuring with inadequate sticks designed for their own morbid
purpose. When they confront the challenge 'in the flesh,' they naturally do
not recognize it as a challenge. Do not hear, do not see. They promptly
reject it as they assign it to their one-place-fits-all 'other' category and
either warily explain that it is 'not quite what we are looking for' and that
they are not the right people for it; or they kindly refer it to other 'more
adequate' whereabouts such as the 'counter-culture,' 'smaller independent,'
'experimental' margins.

They? Yes, they. But, in the colonial periphery (as in elsewhere), we are
often them as well. Colored skins, white masks; colored masks, white skins.
Reversal strategies have reigned for some time. *They* accept the margins; so
do *we*. For without the margin, there is no center, no heart. *The English
and the French precipitate towards us, to look at themselves in our mirror.
Following the old colonizers who mixed their blood in their turn, having
lost their colonies and their blondness – little by little touched by this
swarthy tint spreading like an oil stain over the world – they will come to
Buenos Aires in pious pilgrimmage to try to understand how one cannot
be, yet always be* (Ortiz 1987: 96). The margins, our sites of survival,

* From *When the Moon Waxes Red: Representation, Gender and Cultural Politics*
New York and London: Routledge, 1991.

215

become our fighting grounds and their site for pilgrimage. Thus, while we turn around and reclaim them as our exclusive territory, they happily approve, for the divisions between margin and center should be preserved, and as clearly demarcated as possible, if the two positions are to remain intact in their power relations. Without a certain work of displacement, again, the margins can easily recomfort the center in its goodwill and liberalism; strategies of reversal thereby meet with their own limits. The critical work that has led to an acceptance of negativity and to a new positivity would have to continue its course, so that even in its negativity and positivity, it baffles, displaces, rather than suppresses. By displacing, it never allows this classifying world to exert its classificatory power without returning it to its own ethnocentric classifications. All the while, it points to an elsewhere-within-here whose boundaries would continue to compel frenzied attempts at 'baptizing' through logocentric naming and objectivizing to reflect on themselves as they face their own constricting apparatus of refined grids and partitioning walls.

The center itself is marginal . . . [H]ow possible is it to undertake a process of decentralization without being made aware of the margins within the center and the centers within the margin? Without encountering marginalization from both the ruling center and the established margin? Wherever she goes she is asked to show her identity papers. What side does she speak up for? Where does she belong (politically, economically)? Where does she place her loyalty (sexually, ethnically, professionally)? Should she be met at the center, where they invite her in with much display, it is often only to be reminded that she holds the permanent status of a 'foreign worker,' 'a migrant,' or 'a temporary sojourner' – a status whose definable location is necessary to the maintenance of a central power. 'How about a concrete example from your own culture?' 'Could you tell us what it is like in . . . (your country)?' *As a minority woman, I . . . As an Asian-American woman, I . . . As a woman-of-color filmmaker, I . . . As a feminist, a . . ., and a . . . I. . . .* Not foreigner, yet foreign. At times rejected by her own community, other times needfully retrieved, she is both useless and useful. *The irreducibility of the margin in all explanation. The ceaseless war against dehumanization.* This shuttling in-between frontiers is a working out of and an appeal to another sensibility, another consciousness of the condition of marginality: that in which marginality is the condition of the center.

To use marginality as a starting point rather than an ending point is also to cross beyond it towards other affirmations and negations. There cannot be any grand totalizing integration without massive suppression, which is a way of recirculating the effects of domination. *Liberation opens up new relationships of power, which have to be controlled by practices of liberty* (Foucault 1988: 4). Displacement involves the invention of new forms of subjectivities, of pleasures, of intensities, of relationships, which also implies the continuous renewal of a critical work that looks carefully and intensively at the very system of values to which one refers in fabricating the tools of resistance. The risk of reproducing totalitarianism is always present and one would have to confront, in whatever capacity one has, the controversial values likely to be taken on faith as universal truths by one's own culture(s). . . .

## OUTSIDE IN INSIDE OUT

. . . Essential difference allows those who rely on it to rest reassuringly on its gamut of fixed notions. Any mutation in identity, in essence, in regularity, and even in physical place poses a problem, if not a threat, in terms of classification and control. If you can't locate the other, how are you to locate yourself?

> One's sense of self is always mediated by the image one has of the other. (I have asked myself at times whether a superficial knowledge of the other, in terms of some stereotype, is not a way of preserving a superficial image of oneself.)
>
> (Crapanzano 1985: 54)

Furthermore, where should the dividing line between outsider and insider stop? How should it be defined? By skin color (no blacks should make films on yellows)? By language (only Fulani can talk about Fulani, a Bassari is a foreigner here)? By nation (only Vietnamese can produce works on Vietnam)? By geography (in the North–South setting, East is East and East can't meet West)? Or by political affinity (Third World on Third World counter First and Second Worlds)? What about those with hyphenated identities and hybrid realities? (It is worth noting here a journalist's report in a recent *Time* issue, which is entitled 'A Crazy Game of Musical Chairs.' In this brief but concise report, attention is drawn on the fact that South Africans, who are classified by race and placed into one of the nine racial categories that determine where they can live and work, can have their classification changed if they can prove they were put in the wrong group. Thus, in an announcement of racial reclassifications by the Home Affairs Minister, one learns that: *'nine whites became colored, 506 coloreds became white, two whites became Malay, 14 Malay became white . . . 40 coloreds became black, 666 blacks became colored, 87 coloreds became Indian, 67 Indians became colored, 26 coloreds became Malay, 50 Malays became Indian, 61 Indians became Malay . . . and the list goes on. However, says the Minister, no blacks applied to become white, and no whites became black* (*Time* 9 March 1987: 54).

The moment the insider steps out from the inside, she is no longer a mere insider (and vice versa). She necessarily looks in from the outside while also looking out from the inside. Like the outsider, she steps back and records what never occurs to her the insider as being worth or in need of recording. But unlike the outsider, she also resorts to non-explicative, nontotalizing strategies that suspend meaning and resist closure. (This is often viewed by the outsiders as strategies of partial concealment and disclosure aimed at preserving secrets that should only be imparted to initiates.) She refuses to reduce herself to an Other, and her reflections to a mere outsider's objective reasoning or insider's subjective feeling. She knows, probably like Zora Neale Hurston the insider-anthropologist knew, that she is not an outsider like the foreign outsider. She knows she is different while at the same time being Him. Not quite the Same, not quite the Other, she stands in that undetermined threshold place where she constantly drifts in and out. Undercutting the inside/outside opposition, her intervention is necessarily that of both a deceptive insider and a deceptive outsider. She is this Inappropriate Other/Same who moves about with always at least two/four gestures: that of affirming 'I am like you' while persisting in her difference; and that of reminding 'I am different' while unsettling every definition of otherness arrived at. . . .

Whether she turns the inside out or the outside in, she is, like the two sides of a coin, the same impure, both-in-one insider/outsider. For there can hardly be such a thing as an essential inside that can be homogeneously represented by all insiders; an authentic insider in there, an absolute reality out there, or an incorrupted representative who cannot be questioned by another incorrupted representative. . . .

In the context of this Inappropriate Other, questions like 'How loyal a representative of his/her people is s/he?' (the filmmaker as insider), or 'How authentic is his/her representation of the culture observed?' (the film-maker as outsider) are of little relevance. When the magic of essences ceases to impress and intimidate, there no longer is a position of authority from which one can definitely judge the verisimilitude value of the representation. In the first question, the questioning subject, even if s/he is an insider, is no more authentic and has no more authority on the subject matter than the subject whom the questions concern.

This is not to say that the historical 'I' can be obscured or ignored, and that differentiation cannot be made; but that 'I' is not unitary, culture has never been monolithic, and more or less is always more or less in relation to a judging subject. Differences do not only exist between outsider and insider – two entities –, they are also at work within the outsider or the insider – a single entity. This leads us to the second question in which the film-maker is an outsider. As long as the filmmaker takes up a positivistic attitude and chooses to bypass the inter-subjectivities and realities involved, factual truth remains the dominant criterion for evaluation and the question as to whether his/her work successfully represents the reality it claims would continue to exert its power. The more the representation leans on verisimilitude, the more it is subject to normative verification.

# 37

## Who is Ethnic?

WERNER SOLLORS*

'ARE WE ETHNIC?' – as the *New Yorker* put it in a cartoon of 1972 depicting a white middle-class family in an elegant dining room – is the question Yankees or WASPs have had to ask themselves many times since then, and without getting just one universally accepted answer.

Two conflicting uses of 'ethnic' and 'ethnicity' have remained in the air. According to Everett and Helen Hughes 'we are all ethnic' (Hughes 1952: 7), and in E. K. Francis's terminology of 1947 'not only the French Canadians or the Pennsylvania Dutch would be ethnic groups but also the French of France or the Irish of Ireland' (Francis 1947: 395). But this universalist and inclusive use is in frequent conflict with the other use of the word, which excludes dominant groups and thus establishes an 'ethnicity minus one'. It may be absurd, as Harold Abramson has argued, to except white Anglo-Saxon Protestant Americans from the category of ethnicity (Abramson 1973: 9), and yet it is a widespread practice to define ethnicity as otherness. The contrastive terminology of ethnicity thus reveals a point of view which changes according to the speaker who uses it: for example, for some Americans eating turkey and reading Hawthorne appear to be more 'ethnic' than eating lasagne and reading Puzo.

As Everett Hughes suggested in a personal letter in 1977, the association of the ethnic with the other is not made in some languages: 'In Greece the national bank is the ethnic bank. In this country ethnic banks cannot be the national bank . . .' To say it in the simplest and clearest terms, an ethnic, etymologically speaking is a *goy*. The Greek word *ethnikos*, from which the English 'ethnic' and 'ethnicity' are derived, meant 'gentile', 'heathen'. Going back to the noun *ethnos*, the word was used to refer not just to people in general but also to 'others'. In English usage the meaning shifted from 'non-Israelite' (in the Greek translation of the Bible the word *ethnikos* was used to render the Hebrew *goyim*) to 'non-Christian'. Thus

* From *Beyond Ethnicity: Consent and Descent in American Culture* Oxford and New York: Oxford University Press, 1986.

the word retained its quality of defining another people contrastively, and often negatively. In the Christianized context the word 'ethnic' (sometimes spelled 'hethnic') recurred, from the fourteenth to the nineteenth century, in the sense of 'heathen'. Only in the mid-nineteenth century did the more familiar meaning of 'ethnic' as 'peculiar to a race or nation' reemerge. However, the English language has retained the pagan memory of 'ethnic', often secularized in the sense of ethnic as other, as nonstandard, or, in America, as not fully American. This connotation gives the opposition of ethnic and American the additional religious dimension of the contrast between heathens and chosen people. No wonder that there is popular hesitation to accept the inclusive use of ethnicity. The relationship between ethnicity and American identity in this respect parallels that of pagan superstition and true religion. . . .

Ethnic theorists have often dwelled on the antithetical nature of ethnicity. In ethnic name-calling the tendency persists, as George Murdock argued in Seligman's *Encyclopaedia of the Social Sciences*, that a people

> usually calls itself either by a flattering name or by a term signifying simply 'men', 'men of men', 'first men', or 'people'. Aliens on the other hand, are regarded as something less than men; they are styled 'barbarians' or are known by some derogatory term corresponding to such modern American ethnic tags as 'bohunk', 'chink', 'dago', 'frog', 'greaser', 'nigger', 'sheeny' and 'wop'.
>
> (Murdock 1931: 613)

As Agnes Heller writes, what 'is now called "ethnocentrism" is the natural attitude of all cultures toward alien ones' (Heller 1984: 271). Such antithetical definitions not only are noticeable in the modern world (or among American ethnic writers and critics) but were also undertaken by American Indians. Thus, although it has become de rigueur in ethnic criticism to refer to the original inhabitants of the American continent as 'Native Americans' in order to avoid the, not slur, but misnomer 'Indians', the various Indian nations have followed the human pattern of calling themselves 'people' and calling others less flattering things. . . .

In his introduction to *Ethnic Groups and Boundaries* 1969), Frederick Barth sees the essence of ethnicity in such (mental, cultural, social, moral, aesthetic, and not necessarily territorial) boundary-constructing processes which function as cultural markers between groups. For Barth it is 'the ethnic *boundary* that defines the group, not the cultural stuff that it encloses' (15). 'If a group maintains its identity when members interact with others, this entails criteria for determining membership and ways of signalling membership and exclusion' (15). Previous anthropologists (and, we might add, historians, sociologists, and literary critics) tended to think about ethnicity 'in terms of different peoples, with different histories and cultures, coming together and accommodating themselves to each other'; instead, Barth suggests, we should 'ask ourselves what is needed to make ethnic distinctions *emerge* in an area' (38). With a statement that runs against the grain of much ethnic historiography, Barth argues that

> when one traces the history of an ethnic group through time, one is *not* simultaneously, in the same sense, tracing the history of 'a culture': the elements of the present culture of that ethnic group have not sprung from the particular set that constituted the group's culture at a previous time, whereas the group has a continual organizational existence with boundaries (criteria of membership) that despite modifications have marked off a continuing unit.
>
> (38)

Barth's focus on *boundaries* may appear scandalously heretical to some, but it does suggest plausible interpretations of the polyethnic United States. (Barth uses the term 'polyethnic' instead of the more common Graeco-Roman mixture 'multi-ethnic' – to maintain boundaries in etymology.) Barth's theory can easily accommodate the observation that ethnic groups in the United States have relatively little cultural differentiation, that the cultural *content* of ethnicity (the stuff that Barth's boundaries enclose) is largely interchangeable and rarely historically authenticated. . . .

## RACE AND ETHNICITY

To compound problems, there is another important line of disagreement concerning race and ethnicity. On the one hand, Harold Abramson argued that although 'race is the most salient ethnic factor, it is still only one of the dimensions of the larger cultural and historical phenomenon of ethnicity' (Abramson 1973: 175). . . . On the other hand, M. G. Smith would rather side with Pierre van den Berghe's *Race and Racism* (1967) and consider race a special 'objective' category that cannot be meaningfully discussed under the heading 'ethnicity' (Smith 1982: 10).

I have here sided with Abramson's universalist interpretation according to which ethnicity includes dominant groups and in which race, while sometimes facilitating external identification, is merely one aspect of ethnicity. I have three reasons for doing so. First, the interpretation of the rites and rituals of culturally dominant groups sometimes provides the matrix for the emergence of divergent group identities. . . . Second, the discussions of ethnicity and the production of ethnic literature have been strongly affected by Afro-Americans, and so actively influenced by them since World War II, that an omission of the Afro-American tradition in a discussion of ethnic culture in America would create a very serious gap in our reflections. In fact, the very emergence of the stress on ethnicity and the unmeltable ethnics was directly influenced by the black civil rights movement and strengthened by its radicalization in the 1960s. . . . Finally, I am interested in the processes of group formation and in the naturalization of group relationships . . . and have found examples from Puritan New England and Afro-America crucial to an understanding of these processes among other groups in America. The term 'ethnicity' here is thus a broadly conceived term.

# 38

## *New Ethnicities*

### Stuart Hall*

I HAVE CENTERED my remarks on an attempt to identify and characterize a significant shift that has been going on (and is still going on) in black cultural politics. This shift is not definitive, in the sense that there are two clearly discernable phases – one in the past which is now over and the new one which is beginning – which we can neatly counterpose to one another. Rather, they are two phases of the same movement, which constantly overlap and interweave. Both are framed by the same historical conjuncture and both are rooted in the politics of anti-racism and the post-war black experience in Britain. Nevertheless I think we can identify two different 'moments' and that the difference between them is significant.

It is difficult to characterize these precisely, but I would say that the first moment was grounded in a particular political and cultural analysis. Politically, this is the moment when the term 'black' was coined as a way of referencing the common experience of racism and marginalization in Britain and came to provide the organizing category of a new politics of resistance, amongst groups and communities with, in fact, very different histories, traditions and ethnic identities. In this moment, politically speaking, 'The Black experience', as a singular and unifying framework based on the building up of identity across ethnic and cultural difference between the different communities, became 'hegemonic' over other ethnic/racial identities – though the latter did not, of course, disappear. . . .

The struggle to come into representation was predicated on a critique of the degree of fetishization, objectification and negative figuration which are so much a feature of the representation of the black subject. There was a concern not simply with the absence or marginality of the black experience but with its simplification and its stereotypical character.

The cultural politics and strategies which developed around this critique had many facets, but its two principal objects were first the

* From 'New Ethnicities' *Black Film, British Cinema* ICA Documents 7, London: Institute of Contemporary Arts, 1989.

question of *access* to the rights to representation by black artists and black cultural workers themselves. Secondly the *contestation* of the marginality, the stereotypical quality and the fetishized nature of images of blacks, by the counter-position of a 'positive' black imagery. These strategies were principally addressed to changing what I would call the 'relations of representation'.

I have a distinct sense that in the recent period we are entering a new phase. But we need to be absolutely clear what we mean by a 'new' phase because, as soon as you talk of a new phase, people instantly imagine that what is entailed is the *substitution* of one kind of politics for another. I am quite distinctly *not* talking about a shift in those terms. . . . There is no sense in which a new phase in black cultural politics could replace the earlier one. Nevertheless, it is true that as the struggle moves forward and assumes new forms, it does to some degree *displace*, reorganize and reposition the different cultural strategies in relation to one another. . . .

The shift is best thought of in terms of a change from a struggle over the relations of representation to a politics of representation itself. It would be useful to separate out such a 'politics of representation' into its different elements. We all now use the word representation, but, as we know, it is an extremely slippery customer. It can be used, on the one hand, simply as another way of talking about how one images a reality that exists 'outside' the means by which things are represented: a conception grounded in a mimetic theory of representation. On the other hand the term can also stand for a very radical displacement of that unproblematic notion of the concept of representation. My own view is that events, relations, structures do have conditions of existence and real effects, outside the sphere of the discursive, but that it is only within the discursive, and subject to its specific conditions, limits and modalities, do they have or can they be constructed within meaning. Thus, while not wanting to expand the territorial claims of the discursive infinitely, how things are represented and the 'machineries' and regimes of representation in a culture do play a *constitutive*, and not merely a reflexive, after-the-event role. This gives questions of culture and ideology, and the scenarios of representation – subjectivity, identity, politics – a formative, not merely an expressive, place in the constitution of social and political life. I think it is the move towards this second sense of representation which is taking place and which is transforming the politics of representation in black culture.

This is a complex issue. First, it is the effect of a theoretical encounter between black cultural politics and the discourses of a Eurocentric, largely white, critical cultural theory which in recent years, has focussed so much analysis of the politics of representation. This is always an extremely diffi-cult, if not dangerous encounter. (I think particularly of black people encountering the discourses of post-structuralism, post-modernism, psychoanalysis and feminism.) Secondly, it marks what I can only call 'the end of innocence', or the end of the innocent notion of the essential black subject. Here again, the end of the essential black subject is something which people are increasingly debating, but they may not have fully reckoned with its political consequences. What is at issue here is the recognition of the extraordinary diversity of subjective positions, social experiences and cultural identities which compose the category 'black'; that is, the recognition that 'black' is essentially a politically and culturally *constructed* category, which cannot be grounded in a set of fixed transcultural or transcendental racial categories and which therefore has no guarantees in Nature. What this brings into play is the recognition of the immense diversity and differentiation of the historical and cultural experience of black subjects. This inevitably entails a weakening or fading of the notion that 'race' or some composite notion of race around the term black will either guarantee the effectivity of any cultural practice or determine in any final sense its aesthetic value.

We should put this as plainly as possible. Films are not necessarily good because black people make them. They are not necessarily 'right-on' by virtue of the fact that they deal with black experience. Once you enter the politics of the end of the essential black subject you are plunged headlong into the maelstrom of a continuously contingent, unguaranteed, political argument and debate: a critical politics, a politics of criticism. You can no longer conduct black politics through the strategy of a simple set of reversals, putting in the place of the bad old essential white subject, the new essentially good black subject. Now, that formulation may seem to threaten the collapse of an entire political world. Alternatively, it may be greeted with extraordinary relief at the passing away of what at one time seemed to be a necessary fiction. Namely, either that all black people are good or indeed that all black people are *the same*. After all, it is one of the predicates of racism that 'you can't tell the difference because they all look the same'. This does not make it any easier to conceive of how a politics can be constructed which works with and through difference, which is able to build those forms of solidarity and identification which make common struggle and resistance possible but without suppressing the real heterogeneity of interests and identities, and which can effectively draw the political boundary lines without which political contestation is impossible, without fixing those boundaries for eternity. It entails the movement in black politics, from what Gramsci called the 'war of manoeuvre' to the 'war of position' – the struggle around positionalities. But the difficulty of conceptualizing such a politics (and the temptation to slip into a sort of endlessly sliding discursive liberal-pluralism) does not absolve us of the task of developing such a politics.

The end of the essential black subject also entails a recognition that the central issues of race always appear historically in articulation, in a formation, with other categories and divisions and are constantly crossed and recrossed by the categories of class, of gender and ethnicity. (I make a distinction here between race and ethnicity to which I shall return.) To me, films like *Territories, Passion of Remembrance, My Beautiful Laundrette* and *Sammy and Rosie Get Laid*, for example, make it perfectly clear that the shift has been engaged; and that the question of the black subject cannot be represented without reference to the dimensions of class, gender, sexuality and ethnicity. . . .

I am familiar with all the dangers of ethnicity as a concept and have written myself about the fact that ethnicity, in the form of a culturally constructed sense of Englishness and a particularly closed, exclusive and regressive form of English national identity, is one of the core characteristics of British racism today. I am also well aware that the politics of anti-racism has often constructed itself in terms of a contestation of 'multi-ethnicity' or 'multi-culturalism'. On the other hand, as the politics of representation around the black subject shifts, I think we will begin to see a renewed contestation over the meaning of the term 'ethnicity' itself.

If the black subject and black experience are not stabilized by Nature or by some other essential guarantee, then it must be the case that they are constructed historically, culturally, politically – and the concept which refers to this is 'ethnicity'. The term ethnicity acknowledges the place of history, language and culture in the construction of subjectivity and identity, as well as the fact that all discourse is placed, positioned, situated, and all knowledge is contextual. Representation is possible only because enunciation is always produced within codes which have a history, a position within the discursive formations of a particular space and time. The displacement of the 'centred' discourses of the West entails putting in question its universalist character and its transcendental claims to speak for everyone, while being itself everywhere and nowhere. The fact that this grounding of ethnicity in difference was deployed, in the discourse of racism, as a means of disavowing the realities of racism and repression does not mean that we can permit the term to be permanently colonized. That appropriation will have to be contested, the term disarticulated from its position in the discourse of 'multi-culturalism' and transcoded, just as we previously had to recuperate the term 'black', from its place in a system of negative equivalences. The new politics of representation therefore also sets in motion an ideological contestation around the term 'ethnicity'. But in order to pursue that movement further, we will have to retheorize the concept of *difference*.

It seems to me that, in the various practices and discourses of black cultural production, we are beginning to see constructions of just such a new conception of ethnicity: a new cultural politics which engages rather than suppresses *difference* and which depends, in part, on the cultural construction of new ethnic identities. Difference, like representation, is also a slippery, and therefore, contested concept. There is the 'difference' which makes a radical and unbridgeable separation: and there is a 'difference' which is positional, conditional and conjunctural, closer to Derrida's notion of *differance*, though if we are concerned to maintain a politics it cannot be defined exclusively in terms of an infinite sliding of the signifier. We still have a great deal of work to do to *decouple* ethnicity, as it functions in the dominant discourse, from its equivalence with nationalism, imperialism, racism and the state, which are the points of attachment around which a distinctive British or, more accurately, English ethnicity have been constructed. Nevertheless, I think such a project is not only possible but necessary. Indeed, this decoupling of ethnicity from the violence of the state is implicit in some of the new forms of cultural practice that are going on in films like *Passion* and *Handsworth Songs*. We are beginning to think about how to represent a non-coercive and a more diverse conception of ethnicity, to set against the embattled, hegemonic conception of 'Englishness' which, under Thatcherism, stabilizes so much of the dominant political and cultural discourses, and which, because it is hegemonic, does not represent itself as ethnicity at all.

This marks a real shift in the point of contestation, since it is no longer only between antiracism and multiculturalism but *inside* the notion of ethnicity itself. What is involved is the splitting of the notion between, on the one hand the dominant notion which connects it to nation and 'race' and on the other hand what I think is the beginning of a positive conception of the ethnicity of the margins, of the periphery. That is to say, a recognition that we all speak from a particular place, out of a particular history, out of a particular experience, a particular culture, without being contained by that position as 'ethnic artists' or film-makers. We are all, in that sense, *ethnically* located and our ethnic identities are crucial to our subjective sense of who we are. But this is also a recognition that this is not an ethnicity which is doomed to survive, as Englishness was, only by marginalizing, dispossessing, displacing and forgetting other ethnicities. This precisely is the politics of ethnicity predicated on difference and diversity.

# 39

## White Forms, Aboriginal Content

### MUDROOROO*

BEFORE DISCUSSING ABORIGINAL prose literature, I must emphasise that Aborigines do not occupy a unique position in this world. They are just one of the many peoples that became immersed in the European flood which flowed out from the fifteenth century onwards. The Aboriginal response to this threatened drowning has been and is similar to that of many other peoples. Unfortunately many white settlers in Australia have little or no sense of any history or culture apart from their own, and too often it seems that a lot believe that they were created in Australia sometime in the recent past after Captain James Cook and Governor Arthur Phillip (two Poms) arrived in Australia. Naturally we all know better than this, and how important our roots are.

For better or worse, ninety-nine per cent of Australian culture is of European derivation. Aboriginal culture (or cultures) alone is (are) indigenous and rooted in the soil. They, like every other culture on the globe, are subject to change and are changing constantly. I want to emphasise that such a thing as a stone-age culture (static and unchanging), is a myth created by those who should have known better and still put forth by those who should know better. All societies and cultures change and adapt, and this is fact not theory. The Indonesians were the first recorded visitors to Australia and aspects of their culture were taken in and adapted by the Aborigines of Arnhem land. Cultural traits from New Guinea were adapted by the Queensland Aborigines and perhaps this process was two-way. Cultural affinities between Papua New Guinea, Torres Strait and Cape York Peninsula do exist. The idea of Australia being isolated from the rest of the world until the arrival of the Europeans is a myth put out by them, and sooner or later it must be laid to rest. Professor Berndt in his book *Arnhem Land* gives Aboriginal historical sources showing pre-European contact.

* From 'White Forms, Aboriginal Content' in Jack Davis and Bob Hodge (eds) *Aboriginal Writing Today* Canberra: Australian Institute of Aboriginal Studies, 1985.

Before the Europeans brought a system of writing to Australia, all literature was oral – that is, a spoken or memorised literature. Religious traditions and beliefs, legends and historical events which were considered important, were handed down from generation to generation, usually in the form of verse as it is easier to learn and keep straight lines of verse rather than unwieldy prose. Prose was used in the telling of stories, tales and some historical events such as did not need to be as rigidly fixed as those things dealing with religious beliefs. This prose could easily be made to serve as a basis of a written tradition, and this has been done in the case of books of legends and stories. But, until very recently, and here I refer to Stephen Muecke and his editing of the stories of Paddy Roe, the form of the tale or story has been completely neglected. In the process of editing, the oral form has been divorced from the content. A comparison between one of Paddy's stories and any other so-called books of Aboriginal stories or tales will bear this out. The methods of Aboriginal story-telling are edited out and the content forced into forms akin to the fairy tale, an oral tradition in itself which has been forced into a nineteenth century written format.

Before the current set of symbols representing twenty-odd sounds was brought to or introduced into Australia, some memory aids were in use. These were the so-called letter sticks and some types of bark painting – a form of pictorial writing which could be read off by someone with a knowledge of the symbol system. When the Europeans arrived with their system of writing, Aboriginal literature began to change from an oral to a written one, not only in English but in the few Aboriginal languages which were allowed to be used. This process is still continuing. White people began the process of translating (often inaccurately) bits and pieces of oral literature and writing them down. Some also wrote down the original language, but most were content to use English and from this developed a sort of industry in which often distorted Aboriginal religious beliefs, legends and stories, and even Aboriginal characters became a sign of the British colonist who had some sympathy with Australia, its land and its people. But too often the Aborigines were observed through British eyes and culture and put down in British forms. Aboriginal culture became as distorted as others seen through British eyes such as the Irish, African, Indian and Chinese. Eventually, but only after the back of Aboriginal resistance was broken and the people subjugated, did pity rise to produce some form of biography. These meatless things often had some point to be proved and the authors were not interested in depicting human beings with all the frailties of human beings. It was only in the middle of the twentieth century that anthropologists with reasonably scientific methods and attitudes came into being. They began to look at cultures objectively, as a means of existing in the world, so that members of a culture were only people using that culture to exist in the world. Eventually it was accepted that there was no such thing as a graded series of cultures leading upwards to some pie-in-the-sky perfection. This, too, was but a cultural concept, and other cultures had the reverse concept, a fall from perfection to imperfection, from a past golden age to a corrupt age of iron. Even today, some modern day Aborigines believe that the advent of the Europeans into Australia was the end of a golden age and a descent into the dark ages. . . .

There is a preponderance of biography or autobiography (life story) in Aboriginal written literature, and many people I talk to are concerned about this form of literature. This makes me ask whether there was such a form in traditional oral literature or if it is a completely introduced form. Of course, we are not concerned so much with campfire talk, but with a definite literary tradition, information which is stored in some form and passed down from generation to generation. It is easy to find such forms of literary expression which though cast in verse or song are clearly biographical or autobiographical. I refer to those so-called myths detailing the lives of the Dreaming Ancestors, such as the Wandjina in the Kimberley region and Djanggawul and his two sisters in north-eastern Arnhem Land. These are clearly biographical and detail lives or sections of lives that have a definite beginning and end. For example Djanggawul Brother and his two Sisters arrived at Port Bradshaw then began establishing a religious cult. Song cycles detail their adventures and exploits. It remains to be seen if this tradition was used to detail the lives of ordinary people. . . .

## THE NOVEL

The novel presents a problem, not only as to length, but also as to content. In a sense, novelists are people isolated from their community. Isolation is necessary in novel-writing, I think, and thus writers like the Samoan, Albert Wendt, have declared: 'I accept living in exile as a permanent condition of my life: a lot of it even in my own country. Most artists are like that.' Perhaps literature and writing does entail a separation from people. . . . For better or worse, to become a writer is to become conscious, is to judge, to ponder and to dream. These are solitary activities, and writers, though they may exist in society and act in it, have to withdraw periodically if they are to create, but it is not to forget people in a sterile world of the mind. . . .

We are lucky in being Aborigines in that there is so much around us and in our community. And a lot of this calls for writers to document and put in order. Who shall tell the story of Noonkanbah, of the Brisbane Protest of 1982, of the various Aboriginal struggles and people who are in the forefront of these struggles, but our writers? They are necessary to us.

The novel takes a lot of work to write and a lot of thought and dreaming to put together. It reflects reality, but is not reality. It can be much and nothing. Eventually when more Aboriginal novels are written we shall be able to see the various facets of Aboriginal life, community, and culture with some objectivity.

## SUMMARY

Australian Aboriginal literature is a literature of the Fourth World, that is, of the indigenous minorities submerged in a surrounding majority and governed by them. It must and does deal with the problems inherent in this position and it must be compared to similar literatures, for example the American Indian, for the correspondences and contradictions to be seen it should not be compared to the majority literature. Perhaps the most that can be said for modern Australian literature, or rather current literature, is its utter complacency and the fact that it is becoming more and more irrelevant to the society with which it seeks to deal. Aboriginal literature is and can be more vital in that it is seeking to come to grips with and define a people, the roots of whose culture extend in an unbroken line far back into a past in which English is a recent intrusion. In a sense, Aboriginal writing is a white form in that it is mostly written in English, and too often a polished English which is divorced from the community itself. Thus not only is there a contradiction in the use of alien forms, but also in the use of an alien language which too often has driven out the original language. It is imperative that wherever possible Aboriginal languages must be allowed to live and grow so that they may form the basis of the means of expression. Aboriginal children should be taught, or rather given the means to learn a language, one that is their area or their own so that the continuity of past and present and future may be maintained.

# 40

# The Representation of the Indigene

## Terry Goldie*

IT IS MY perception that the shape of the signifying process as it applies to indigenous peoples is formed by a certain semiotic field, a field that provides the boundaries within which the images of the indigene function. The existence of this semiotic field constitutes an important aspect of the 'subjugated knowledges' to which Foucault refers in *Power/Knowledge* (1980: 81). The indigene is a semiotic pawn on a chess board under the control of the white signmaker. And yet the individual signmaker, the individual player, the individual writer, can move these pawns only within certain prescribed areas. Whether the context is Canada, New Zealand, or Australia becomes a minor issue since the game, the signmaking is all happening on one form of board, within one field of discourse, that of British imperialism. Terms such as 'war-dance,' 'war-whoop,' 'tomahawk,' and 'dusky' are immediately suggestive everywhere of the indigene. To a North American, at least the first three would seem to be obvious Indianisms, but they are also common in works on the Maori and the Aborigine. Explorers like Phillip King (*Narrative* 1827) generally refer to Aborigines as Indian, and specific analogies to North American Indians are ubiquitous in nineteenth-century Australian literature. Terms misapplied in the Americas became re-misapplied in a parody of imperialist discourse. The process is quite similar to one Levi-Strauss describes in *The Savage Mind* (1972): 'In other words, the operative value of the systems of naming and classifying commonly called totemic derives from their formal character: they are codes suitable for conveying messages which can be transposed into other codes, and for expressing messages received by means of different codes in terms of their own system' (75). Obvious extreme ethnographic differences between the different indigenous cultures did little to impede the transposition.

To extend the chessboard analogy, it would not be oversimplistic to maintain that the play between white and indigene is a replica of the black

* From *Fear and Temptation: The Image of the Indigene in Canadian, Australian and New Zealand Literatures* Kingston: McGill-Queens University Press, 1989.

and white squares, with clearly limited oppositional moves. The basic dualism, however, is not that of good and evil, although it has often been argued to be so, as in Abdul R. JanMohamed's 'The Economy of Manichean Allegory' (1985): 'The dominant model of power – and interest – relations in all colonial societies is the manichean opposition between the putative superiority of the European and the supposed inferiority of the native' (63). JanMohamed maintains that in apparent exceptions 'any evident "ambivalence" is in fact a product of deliberate, if at times subconscious, imperialist duplicity, operating very efficiently through the economy of its central trope, the manichean allegory' (61). Such a basic moral conflict is often implied but in contemporary texts the opposition is frequently between the 'putative superiority' of the indigene and the 'supposed inferiority' of the white. As Said suggests, the positive and negative sides of the image are but swings of one and the same pendulum: 'Many of the earliest oriental amateurs began by welcoming the Orient as a salutary *derangement* of their European habits of mind and spirit. The Orient was overvalued for its pantheism, its spirituality, its stability, its longevity, its primitivism, and so forth. . . . Yet almost without exception such overesteem was followed by a counter-response: the Orient suddenly appeared lamentably under-humanized, antidemocratic, backward, barbaric, and so forth' (1978: 150). Almost all of these characterizations could be applied to the indigenes of Australia, New Zealand, and Canada, as positive or negative attributes.

The complications of the issue extend even beyond oppositions of race, as Sander Gilman suggests in *Difference and Pathology* (1985):

> Because there is no real line between self and the Other, an imaginary line must be drawn; and so that the illusion of an absolute difference between self and Other is never troubled, this line is as dynamic in its ability to alter itself as is the self. This can be observed in the shifting relationship of antithetical stereotypes that parallel the existence of 'bad' and 'good' representations of self and Other. But the line between 'good' and 'bad' responds to stresses occurring within the psyche. Thus paradigm shifts in our mental representations of the world can and do occur. We can move from fearing to glorifying the Other. We can move from loving to hating. (18)

The problem is not the negative or positive aura associated with the image but rather the image itself. . . .

At least since Fanon's *Black Skin White Masks* (1952) it has been a commonplace to use 'Other' and 'Not-self' for the white view of blacks and for the resulting black view of themselves. The implication of this assertion of a white self as subject in discourse is to leave the black Other as object. The terms are similarly applicable to the Indian, the Maori, and the Aborigine but with an important shift. They are Other and Not-self but also must become self. Thus as Richon suggests and Pearson implies, imperialist discourse valorizes the colonized according to its own needs for reflection. 'The project of imperialism has always already historically refracted what might have been the absolute Other into a domesticated Other that consolidated the imperialist self,' explains Gayatri Spivak in 'Three Women's Texts and a Critique of Imperialism' (1985c: 253). Tzvetan Todorov in *The Conquest of America: The Question of the Other* (1982) also notes how the group as Other can function.

> This group in turn can be interior to society: women for men, the rich for the poor, the mad for the 'normal'; or it can be exterior to society, i.e., another society which will be near or far away, depending on the case: beings whom everything links to me on the cultural, moral, historical plane; or else unknown quantities, outsiders whose language and customs I do not understand, so foreign that in extreme instances I am reluctant to admit they belong to the same species as my own.
>
> (3)

But Spivak's area of study, the Indian sub-continent, is a different case from that of the Australian, Canadian, and New Zealand because the imperialist discourse remains admittedly non-indigenous. India is valorized by its relationship to imperialist dynamics but it 'belongs' to the white realm only as part of the empire. . . . Australians, New Zealanders, and Canadians have, and long have had, a clear agenda to erase this separation of belonging. The white Canadian looks at the Indian. The Indian is Other and therefore alien. But the Indian is indigenous and therefore cannot be alien. So the Canadian must be alien. But how can the Canadian be alien within Canada?

There are only two possible answers. The white culture can attempt to incorporate the Other, superficially through beaded moccasins and names like Mohawk Motors, or with much more sophistication, through the novels of Rudy Wiebe. Conversely, the white culture may reject the indigene: 'This country really began with the arrival of the whites.' This is no longer an openly popular alternative, but its historical importance is reflected in things like the 'native societies' that existed in all three countries in the late nineteenth century, societies to which no non-white, no matter how native, need have applied.

The importance of the alien within cannot be overstated. In their need to become 'native,' to belong here, whites in Canada, New Zealand, and Australia have adopted a process which I have termed 'indigenization.' A peculiar word, it suggests the impossible necessity of becoming indigenous. For many writers, the only chance for indigenization seemed to be through writing about the humans who are truly indigenous, the Indians, Inuit, Maori, and Aborigines. As J. J. Healy notes in *Literature and the Aborigine in Australia* (1978), 'The Aborigine was part of the tension of an indigenous consciousness. Not the contemporary Aborigine, not even a plausible historical one, but the sort of creature that *might* persuade a white Australian to look in the direction of the surviving race' (173). Many

Canadians, New Zealanders, and Australians have responded strongly to this creature and to their own need to become indigenous. . . .

Of course the majority of writers in all three countries have given brief or no attention to native peoples. Perhaps then, while the image of the indigene may be a consistent concern, it is a limited one, the *Jindyworobaks* notwithstanding. But the process of indigenization is complex. Each reference in *The Bulletin*, the nationalistic nineteenth century Australian magazine, to the white Australian as 'native' or 'indigenous' is a comment on indigenization, regardless of the absence of Aborigines in those references. As Macherey claims, 'an ideology is made of what it does not mention; it exists because there are things which must not be spoken of' (1978: 132). In other words, absence is also negative presence. Thus in a work such as Henry Handel Richardson's *The Fortunes of Richard Mahony* (1930), a trilogy which uses the Australian gold rush as a field through which to explore the founding of a nation, the Aborigine is an essential non-participant.

Neither the racial split between self and Other nor the process of indigenization originates with Canada, Australia, or New Zealand, but neither do they have clear origins which might be seen as the source for these manifestations. Presumably the first instance in which one human perceived another as Other in racial terms came when the first recognized the second as different in colour, facial features, language, etc. And the first felt need for indigenization came when a person moved to a new place and recognized an Other as having greater roots in that place. The lack of a specific origin for these conditions is reflected in the widespread occurrence of their modern manifestations. . . .

However, regardless of the changes made in the form of the chessboard, whether dismissive histories of penetration or sensitive novels of appropriation, the semiotic field has continued, particularly in the few basic moves which the indigenous pawn has been allowed to make.

These few basic moves Said calls 'standard commodities' (1978: 190). Two such commodities which appear to be standard in the 'economy' created by the semiotic field of the indigene in Australian, Canadian, and New Zealand literatures are sex and violence. They are poles of attraction and repulsion, temptation by the dusky maiden and fear of the demonic violence of the fiendish warrior. Often both are found in the same work, as in John Richardson's *Wacousta or The Prophecy* ([1832] 1967), in which the warrior constantly attacks, but the maiden is an agent to avoid that attack. They are emotional signs, semiotic embodiments of primal responses. Could one create a more appropriate signifier for fear than the treacherous redskin? He incorporates, in generous quantities, the tenor of the impassioned, uncontrolled spirit of evil. He is strangely joined by the Indian maiden, who tempts the being chained by civilization towards the liberation represented by free and open sexuality, not the realm of untamed evil but of unrestrained joy. 'The "bad" Other becomes the negative stereotype; the "good" Other becomes the positive stereotype. The former is that which we fear to become; the latter, that which we fear we cannot achieve' (Gilman 1985: 20). Added to this is the alien's fear of the 'redskin' as hostile wilderness, the new, threatening land, and the arrivant's attraction to the maiden as restorative pastoral, this new, available land.

A third important commodity is orality, all the associations raised by the indigene's speaking, non-writing, state. The writers' sense of indigenes as having completely different systems of understanding different epistemes, is based on an often undefined belief that cultures without writing operate within a different dimension of consciousness. This different dimension suggests a fourth commodity, mysticism, in which the indigene becomes a sign of oracular power, either malevolent, in most nineteenth-century texts, or beneficent, in most contemporary ones. In an interesting variant on the semiotic process, the inadequacies of the writer's culture, in which little knowledge is to be gained from the popular beliefs of its own traditions . . . is placed in contrast to an indigenous belief system (usually quite asystemic) which holds the promise of a Presence to exceed even the presence of orality. . . .

[A] fifth commodity in the semiotic field of the indigene [is] the prehistoric. The historicity of the text, in which action makes a statement, whether overt or covert, on the chronology of the culture, shapes the indigene into an historical artifact, a remnant of a golden age that seems to have little connection to anything akin to contemporary life. A corollary of the temporal split between this golden age and the present degradation is a tendency to see indigenous culture as true, pure, and static. Whatever fails this test is not really a part of that culture.

The commodities – sex, violence, orality, mysticism, the prehistoric – can be seen as part of a circular economy within and without the semiotic field of the indigene. . . . It appears that as long as this semiotic field exists, as long as the shapes of the standard commodities change but the commodities remain the same, the chess match can appear to vary but there is still a defineable limit to the board. The necessities of indigenization can compel the players to participate but they cannot liberate the pawn.

# 41

## The Myth of Authenticity

### GARETH GRIFFITHS*

THERE ARE REAL dangers in recent representations of indigenous peoples in popular discourse, and especially in the media, which stress claims to an 'authentic' voice. For these claims, by overwriting the actual complexity of difference may write out that voice as effectively as earlier oppressive discourses of reportage. In fact, it may well be the same process at work, and the result may be just as crippling to the efforts of indigenous peoples to evolve an effective strategy of recuperation and resistance.

For example, in a recent dispute over mining at Yakabindie in Western Australia both sides of the dispute invoked the sign of the authentic in their defence of their position. The 'liberal' tone of modern journalism, its claim to even-handedness, is possible partly because of the way in which certain signs have been fetishised within popular discourse, in this case that of the 'authentic', the traditional and the local. The report in the *West Australian* of Monday, 12 August 1991 can stand as an encapsulation of this problem, representing as it does two images of the authentic, both inscribed under such legitimating signs as the 'elder', the local, and the tribal, and both counterposed by the illegitimate signs of the outsider, the Southerner, the fringe-dweller, whose representative in the article is the Perth political activist Robert Bropho. Let me quote the relevant paragraphs;

> Wiluna resident Tony Green, 89, said he was born less than 8 km. from Yakabindie. He had spent most of his life in the area and had never heard of a sacred site near the proposed mine. 'What about the future?' he said. 'We need the jobs for the people. I'd give that land to the mining people.' But community elder Dusty Stevens highlighted the feelings which have divided the region's Aborigines. 'Some of these fellahs just wouldn't know,' he said. There are a lot of sites in there.' The appearance of Mr. Bropho and members of the Swan Valley Fringe

* From 'The Myth of Authenticity' in Chris Tiffin and Alan Lawson (eds) *De-Scribing Empire* London: Routledge, 1994.

Dwellers at the meeting was attacked by Goldfields Aboriginal spokesman Aubrey Lynch, who said the southerners had nothing to do with the issue.

(*West Australian*, 12 August, 1991: 9)

Articles like this are an increasingly typical way of representing in the media the 'positions' and 'voices' of the indigene, inscribing them in effect as disputational claimants to a 'territoriality' of the authentic. Australian Aboriginal peoples may increasingly wish to assert their sense of the local and the specific as a recuperative strategy in the face of the erasure of difference characteristic of colonialist representation. But such representations subsumed by the white media under a mythologised and fetishised sign of the 'authentic' can also be used to create a privileged hierarchy of Australian Aboriginal voice which in practice represents that community as divided. More subtly, it may construct a belief in the society at large that issues of recovered 'traditional' rights are of a different order of equity from the right to general social justice and equality. Whilst this may be in part the unintentional product of a worthy liberal desire to recuperate Australian Aboriginal culture, it also frequently results, as in the case I have given, in a media construction of the 'authentic' Australian Aboriginal in opposition to the 'inauthentic' political activists whose claim is undermined (the metaphor is an appropriate one) by a dismissal of their right to represent Australian Aboriginal culture in any legitimate way.

In order fully to understand what is involved here it seems to me that these representations need also to be addressed through their reflection of a larger practice within colonialist discourse, a practice in which the possibilities of subaltern speech are contained by the discourse of the oppressor, and in which the writing of the Australian Aboriginal under the sign of 'authenticity' is an act of 'liberal' discursive violence, parallel in many ways to the inscription of the 'native' (indigene) under the sign of the savage. On the surface the obvious connection is through the reversed sentimental and nostalgic rendering of the Australian Aboriginal under the sign of the primitive (noble savage rather than cannibal savage). But at a deeper level both processes may be about the inscription of ourselves displaced upon the Australian Aboriginal, an inscription which may overwrite and overdetermine the full range of representations through which contemporary Australian Aboriginality might otherwise effectively be represented.

Michael Taussig's powerful study of the massacre and enslavement of the Putumayo Indians in the early years of this century stresses the way in which the silenced subjects of oppression are spoken by the different discourses through which their story is inscribed. . . .

Taussig records how contemporary Indians subjected to terror by the greed of the rubber companies of our own day, such as the Andoke Yarocamena, register their perceptions of the powerful ways in which 'narration' functions to control and override their resistance:

> Something crucial about the complicity and the magical powers of the company employees emerges from what has been said in recent times about Andoke Indians who claim that the rubber company had a stronger story than the Indians' story and this is why, for example, the armed uprising of the Andoke Yarocamena against the company failed and failed so disastrously.
>
> (Taussig 1987: 107)

It is clearly crucial to resistance that the 'story' of the Indian continues to be told. It is only through such counter-narratives that alter/native views can be put. As Taussig notes, however, this contradicts, at a simple level, the Indian assertion that their story is less powerful than that of the European. By story here is meant, as Taussig goes on to explain, that narrative (*rafue*) through which a 'necessary mediation between concept and practice which ensures the reproduction of the everyday world' (107) is effected. That is to say the fundamental systemic discourse through which the world is represented, analogous to other indigenous stories such as that of the various dreamings of the Australian Aboriginal peoples. The oppressor clearly shows that they are aware that their own narrative of the Indian, what the Andoke called 'Historias para *Nosotros* – histories not of, but for us' (107) are not perceived by the *oppressors* to be successful as the Andoke assert because of a greater mystic efficacy but because they override and overdetermine the possibility for the Indian speaking their own position within the alternative discourse of the conqueror. That the conquerors in fact continue to fear the 'story' of the indigene and seek to silence it is graphically and horrifically illustrated by their favoured torture of cutting out the tongues of the Indians and then, subsequent to this act, forcing them to 'speak'. In the light of the concerns raised by such images the reports on disputes such as Yakabindie may take on new and powerful resonances and the act of constructing the speech of the already silenced may metaphorically, at least, be perceived as an act best characterised, as I have suggested above, by a metaphor of violence, however 'liberal' in intention. In both cases the appropriated features of authentic discourse are installed after the event of silencing by violence.

Strategies of recuperation and texts which insist on the importance of re-installing the 'story' of the indigenous cultures are, therefore, as many Australian Aboriginal spokespeople have insisted, crucial to their resistance. Such recuperations may be the literal recuperation of the texts of pre-colonial cultures, the narratives of the dreaming or the body of pre-colonial oratures, or, as in the case of the work of Mudrooroo Narogin Nyoongah such as his recently published novel *Master of the Ghost Dreaming*, attempts to reinscribe the dominant culture of colonial society by re-telling the moment of encounter and invasion through indigenous eyes and discourses. In a sense this is part and parcel of Mudrooroo Narogin Nyoongah's asserted desire to speak from an 'essential' Aboriginal position (the word is his not mine) and of his belief that Aboriginal texts

239

may be authentic or inauthentic in so far as they cohere within a larger Aboriginal metatext (which means, I presume, in part at least that alter/ native story (rafue) of which the Andoke also speak). But Mudrooroo Narogin Nyoongah has also argued in the same text that 'the Aboriginal writer is a Janus-type figure with one face turned to the past and the other to the future while existing in a postmodern, multicultural Australia in which he or she must fight for cultural space' (Narogin 1990: 24). Thus in a sense he embraces his hybridised position not as a badge of failure or denigration but as part of that contestational weave of cultures which recent critical theory argues is the inescapable condition of all post-modernist experience, though at the same time he asserts in both his critical writing and practice as a novelist the importance of asserting his identity in essentialist difference as a political strategy. In this apparent contradic-tion he is registering the difficult and ambivalent position which the Aboriginal writer is forced to occupy in the complex task of simultaneously recuperating the traditional and contesting the profile of identity for Aboriginal peoples in contemporary Australian political and cultural space. . . .

Many of the problems raised by this issue have also been addressed by those who have sought to theorise the difficulties which arise when we consider the possibility of a subaltern subject 'speaking' within any domi-nant discourse such as colonialism or patriarchy. The questions these debates have raised include: We know that subaltern people are oppressed, but how do we know? How can that oppression be spoken? Even when the subaltern appears to 'speak' there is a real concern as to whether what we are listening to is really a subaltern voice, or the subaltern being spoken by the subject position they occupy within the larger discursive economy. Thus as Jenny Sharpe has argued the speaker who resists the colonial necessarily achieves that position within the framework of the system they oppose (her example is the famous anti-colonial speech of Aziz in the trial scene of Forster's *A Passage to India* (Sharpe 1989: 148–50). In inscribing such acts of resistance the deep fear for the liberal critic is contained in the worry that in the representation of such moments what is inscribed is not the subaltern's voice but the voice of your own other. Homi Bhabha has also acknowledged that subaltern speech is in some sense conditional upon the dominant discourse:

> For it is between the edict of Englishness and the assault of the dark unruly spaces of the earth, through an act of repetition, that the colonial text emerges uncertainly.
>
> (Bhabha 1985a: 126–7)

For Homi Bhabha, if I read him correctly, the possibility of subaltern speech exists principally and crucially when its mediation through mimicry and parody of the dominant discourse subverts and menaces the authority within which it necessarily comes into being. (In this same article Bhabha offers a convincing account of how such resistances can be developed and how they flourish within and through the deployment of mimicry within the necessarily hybridised condition of the colonised society.)

One basis for applying such aspects of colonialist theory to this topic is that indigenous peoples, too, in many important ways, exist in relation to their own societies (themselves settler colonies) in ways analogous to the colonial subject. They have been presented frequently in the representations of settler societies as subjects who do not possess, to use Bhabha's phrase, 'a stable unitary assumption of collectivity' (Bhabha 1985a: 153). This is, in part, the result of the deliberate suppression of pre-colonial cultures, and the displacement of their peoples in a policy of assimilation which aimed at the suppression of difference. The very wiping out of distinctive collectivities under an undifferentiated term such as 'aboriginal' is an example of this process in operation. It is therefore a powerful need of such peoples to re-assert their pre-colonised cultures and to struggle for the recuperation of their cultural difference and its resilience in and through the local and specific. Let me be quite clear that it is not with this process that I am quarrelling, but rather with the uses made of some of the strategies of authenticity associated with this process within white systems of representation which disavow the possibilities for the hybridised subjects of the colonising process to legitimate themselves or to speak in ways which menace the authority of the dominant culture precisely in so far as it 'mimics' and so subverts it. In such a fetishised use of the inscription of the authentic a further and subtler example of control emerges, one which in this use may function just as negatively in its impact on the effective empowerment of Australian aboriginal voices. The danger resides not in the inscription of the alternative metatext as such, but in the specific employment of this metatext under the sign of the authentic to exclude the many and complex voices of the Aboriginal peoples past and present.

The mythologising of the authentic characterised in the media representation of the Nyoongah in the *West Australian* article I have quoted, is then in many ways itself a construction which overpowers one of the most powerful weapons within the arsenal of the subaltern subject: that of displacement, disruption, ambivalence, or mimicry, discursive features founded not in the closed and limited construction of a pure authentic sign but in endless and excessive transformation of the subject positions possible within the hybridised. I want to argue that authentic speech, where it is conceived not as a political strategy within a specific political and discursive formation but as a fetishised cultural commodity, may be employed within such accounts as that of the *West Australian* to enact a discourse of "'liberal violence', re-enacting its own oppressions on the subjects it purports to represent and defend.

241

# 42

## Who Can Write as Other?

MARGERY FEE*

IN AN ARTICLE published in *Ariel* in October 1985, [New Zealand novelist] C. K. Stead expresses reservations about Keri Hulme's highly-acclaimed *the bone people* . . . 'a novel by a Pakeha which has won an award [The Pegasus Award for Maori Literature] intended for a Maori' (Stead 1985: 104). Stead raises here two very controversial questions. First, how do we determine minority group membership? Second, can majority group members speak as minority members, Whites as people of colour, men as women, intellectuals as working people? If so, how do we distinguish biased and oppressive tracts, exploitative popularizations, stereotyping romanticizations, sympathetic identifications and resistant, transformative visions? . . .

The problem is complicated by the increasing number of writers who, like Hulme, are of mixed ancestry; who, like Aboriginal writer Sally Morgan, have been raised in ignorance of their ancestry; or who, like Canadian Métis writer Beatrice Culleton, have been brought up in White foster homes. Even writers like Witi Ihimaera and Patricia Grace, whose 'Maoriness' does not seem to be in question, speak English as their mother tongue, and have had to write their way back into their Maori language and culture (Pearson 1982: 166). This 'complication' is a salutary one, in that it emphasizes the dubiousness of most commonplaces about indigenous identity. . . .

Stead points out that Hulme was not brought up speaking Maori, an argument that would exclude both Patricia Grace and Witi Ihimaera from genuine Maoriness, and then casts doubt on the 'authenticity' of some of the Maori elements in the novel. To him they seem 'willed, self-conscious, not inevitable, not entirely authentic' (104). To shift the argument from the biological to the cultural and linguistic, as Stead has just done, seems a move toward flexibility, but is, in fact, quite rigid. Many indigenous people with eight indigenous great-grandparents live in cities and no longer

* From 'Why C. K. Stead Didn't Like Keri Hulme's *the bone people*: Who Can Write as Other?' *Australian and New Zealand Studies in Canada* 1, (1989).

speak their aboriginal languages. The majority culture has either actively caused or passively allowed the loss of traditional indigenous languages and cultures world-wide. For example, Native children in Canada were frequently either sent to boarding schools with White teachers who often punished them for speaking their native languages, or taken away from their parents and communities and sent to White foster homes. Canadian Native communities are still struggling for control over their children's education and foster care. For a member of a majority culture to try to deprive anyone of an indigenous identity just because of the success of this sort of program of cultural obliteration is ironic at best. . . .

The demand for 'authenticity' denies Fourth World writers a living, changing culture. Their culture is deemed to be Other and must avoid crossing those fictional but ideologically essential boundaries between Them and Us, the Exotic and the Familiar, the Past and the Future, the 'Dying' and the Living. Especially, 'authentic' writing from the Fourth World must steer clear of that quintessentially 'new' and ever renewing genre, the novel. For Stead, the function of the Maori work of literature is to preserve the past, not to change the future. Given the destruction inflicted by Whites on indigenous cultures one sympathizes with this view, but indigenous peoples may well feel it is suicidal to devote the time of their best-educated to cultural preservation at the cost of political renewal. Indigenous people have been acculturated to popular western literary forms, and any writer who wishes to reach them is unlikely to do so with a 'pure' traditional form. Nor are ordinary White readers likely to be attracted to an imitation of oral poetry, and yet the majority must be reached by minority writers if change is to take place.

Finally, Stead's insistence that the Maori elements be 'unconscious,' rather than 'willed,' is essentially a demand to hear what seems 'natural' to him, that is 'authentic' accounts that echo the 'authentic' accounts he is used to – those written by White anthropologists and those Pakeha writers who borrow this material. In fact, anthropologists have recently focussed almost obsessively on the degree to which ethnocentricity has marked and continues to mark the assumptions and results of the discipline. Since most writing works within a limited range of ideological possibilities, the trick for most writers is to sound original while repeating the same old 'truths' using the same old literary conventions. Writers who are trying to change the discursive formation, even if only a little, are usually greeted with incomprehension or annoyance. Hulme's attempt to integrate Pakeha and Maori culture in a way that transgresses the boundary between them is bound to seem 'willed,' since so few pieces of writing have made the attempt.

Stead does finally turn to Hulme's text and points to 'the imaginative strength' of *the bone people*: 'it creates a sexual union where no sex occurs, creates parental love where there are no physical parents, creates the stress and fusion of a family where there is no actual family' (104). The biological essentialism of Stead's assumption that sex and biological parenthood are the sole constituents of an 'actual' family blinds him to the realization that here is Hulme's definition of Maori: 'actual' Maoriness, like an 'actual' family, has nothing to do with biology and everything to do with solidarity of feeling. Stead wants clear categories: either one is a Maori or a Pakeha. Although he is perceptive enough to spot the points where Hulme is violating his categories, he does not realize that she is doing so consciously and consistently.

Hulme's definition of Maori is far more liberal than either Stead's of Maori or Hobson's of American Indian. Perhaps her definition is too liberal, because if we simply conclude that if one feels Maori one is, we fall into a new set of problems. I may feel Maori, I may think I am writing as one, and be completely deluded. Indeed, as Sneja Gunew points out, even the belief that a Maori with 'pure' Maori ancestry automatically will write as a Maori is flawed: the oppressed Other 'supposedly speaks authentically and unproblematically as a unified subject on behalf of the groups she or he represents. . . . In the drive toward universalism one cannot admit that those oppressed others whom we hear as speaking authentic experience might be playing textual games' (1987: 262). Roland Barthes, Jacques Derrida, and Michel Foucault, to name only the most eminent, have undermined rather thoroughly the argument for the authentic and unified voice of the author. Thus, it may seem, my support for Hulme's claim to write as a Maori has been produced only to be withdrawn again. Not quite. To see the individual writer as merely either a conduit for an eclectic range of multiple voices or the mouthpiece for the dominant discourse goes too far. Some writers are resisting writers. However, to say that anyone who qualifies as a Fourth World writer can or should write only about the Fourth World experience is simply another instance of the ubiquitous restriction of the minority. Yet some restrictions do exist.

Edward Said writes of Conrad that even when writing about the oppressed, all he 'can see is a world dominated by the West, and – of equal importance – a world in which every opposition to the West only confirms its wicked power. What Conrad could not see is life lived outside this cruel tautology . . . [and] not controlled by the gringo imperialists and liberal reformers of this world' (Said 1988: 70). By implication, some can see beyond this cruel tautology. But how far? David Maughan Brown (1985) details the extent to which even Ngugi wa Thiong'o's most radical fiction is affected by his liberal humanist education. It is not possible simply to assume that a work written by an 'Other' (however defined), even a politicized Other, will have freed itself from the dominant ideology. Homi Bhabha says 'there is always, in Said, the suggestion that colonial power and discourse is possessed entirely by the coloniser, which is an historical and theoretical simplification' (Bhabha 1983b: 25). Radical writing, by definition, is writing that is struggling, of necessity only partly successfully, to rewrite the dominant ideology from within, to produce a different version of reality. Hulme laboriously hammered her vision out over twelve years, beginning to write herself into a Maori and New Zealand into Aotearoa. As Terry Threadgold notes, ' "ideology" is not "out there," imposed as it were from above, but rather, is part of the signification itself. Ideologies are constructed in language as contextualized social discourse' (Threadgold 1986: 29). Rewriting the dominant ideology is not easy, since the difference between Pakeha and Maori has been written into existence by the dominant discourse, and thus the process of rewriting this ideology is the work of the whole New Zealand community, rather than of any one writer.

All this makes the idea of accurately or finally distinguishing authentic from inauthentic discourse impossible: the ideal of 'authenticity' has been proven to be, like so many others, relative and context-bound. This does not leave us, however, with nothing but language games. If the context is firmly kept in mind, it is possible to argue that to be classified as 'Fourth World,' writing must somehow promote indigenous access to power without negating indigenous difference.

# PART VIII

# Feminism and
# Post-colonialism

# Introduction

In many different societies, women, like colonised subjects, have been relegated to the position of 'Other', 'colonised' by various forms of patriarchal
domination. They thus share with colonised races and cultures an intimate
experience of the politics of oppression and repression. It is not surprising
therefore that the history and concerns of feminist theory have paralleled
developments in post-colonial theory. Feminist and post-colonial discourses
both seek to reinstate the marginalised in the face of the dominant, and early
feminist theory, like early nationalist post-colonial criticism, was concerned
with inverting the structures of domination, substituting, for instance, a
female tradition or traditions for a male-dominated canon. But like post-
colonial criticism, feminist theory has rejected such simple inversions in favour
of a more general questioning of forms and modes, and the unmasking of the
spuriously author/itative on which such canonical constructions are founded.

Until recently feminist and post-colonial discourses have followed a path
of convergent evolution, their theoretical trajectories demonstrating striking
similarities but rarely intersecting. In the last ten years, however, there has
been increasing interest not just in their parallel concerns but in the nature
of their actual and potential intersections – whether creatively coincident or
interrogative. Feminism has highlighted a number of the unexamined
assumptions within post-colonial discourse, just as post-colonialism's inter-
rogations of western feminist scholarship have provided timely warnings
and led to new directions.

Early problems raised by the attempts to accommodate these similar but
sometimes conflicting agendas are described by Kirsten Holst Petersen in
'First Things First'. It is significant that this problem is articulated as a
dilemma for African women *writers* whose representations of their societies,
and of patriarchal oppressions within them, are seen as conflicting with the
processes of decolonisation and cultural restitution, not just in terms of
images presented to the former colonisers, but more significantly in terms
of their *own* Euro-interpellated populations. African cultural values systematically denigrated by colonialist ideologies and institutions demand positive
representation, and this restitutive impulse has frequently been seen to
conflict with feminist *re*formation.

The notion of 'double colonisation' – i.e. that women in formerly colonised societies were *doubly* colonised by both imperial and patriarchal ideologies – became a catch-phrase of post-colonial and feminist discourses in the 1980s. But it is only recently that 'double colonisation' has begun to be adequately theorised. Ketu Katrak (like the East and West African writers Petersen discusses) reminds us of the inescapable necessity of situating a feminist politics within particular colonised societies. Using the example of the Jamaican Sistren Collective's work, she grounds a decolonising feminist restitution in the local particularities of class and race. The Jamaican writer Erna Brodber's short essay 'Sleeping's Beauty and Prince Charming' (1989) suggests another way of actually theorising the concept of a double colonisation. Texts – the 'fairy tales' of Europe – have not only subjectified Jamaican women, but through cultural interpellation effected the erasure of the black female body within Jamaican male culture. Hence the black 'Prince Charming' of Brodber's fable can *sense* his female counterpart, but when he looks for her he can see 'no/body'. Sara Suleri examines a rather different refraction of the concept of 'double colonisation' in Pakistan through the recent institution of Muslim Law, a process facilitated by neo-colonial United States' support of a male regime where laws against rape have recoiled horrifically on the bodies of women and children.

Not surprisingly perhaps, the use of language in decolonising strategies forms the basis of Sistren's (re)creative experimentation; and Trinh T. Minh-ha, aware of the difficulties of, in Audre Lorde's terms, using the masters' tools to dismantle his house, nevertheless attempts to escape enclosure through complex linguistic/generic experimentation. Significantly, too, she refuses to be 'ghettoised' through the separate and/or combined essentialisms of gender, race or ethnicity, seeing these consolidating positions – politically strategic as they may at first appear – as new houses or rather out-houses of the 'master'(s).

Chandra Mohanty's 'Under Western Eyes' (with Rachel Carby's 'White Woman Listen!') is foundational in critiquing Western feminisms which too easily elide specific cultural difference and 'naturalise' all women's oppression under widely differing manifestations of patriarchical domination to European models. As Gayatri Spivak demonstrates, what is a radically liberating piece of writing or politics in *one* arena can act as a colonising agent in another. Sara Suleri's article, with which this section concludes, offers a useful critique of a number of the positions discussed above.

# 43

## First Things First
### Problems of a Feminist Approach
### to African Literature
#### KIRSTEN HOLST PETERSEN*

IN THE AUTUMN of 1981 I went to a conference in Mainz. The theme of the conference was 'The Role of Women in Africa'; it was a traditional academic conference and proceeded in an orderly fashion with papers on various aspects of the subject and not too much discussion until the last day of the conference when a group of young German feminists had been invited to participate. They dismissed the professor who up until then had chaired the session (he was a man), installed a very articulate student as chairwoman, and proceeded to turn the meeting into a series of personal statements and comments in the tradition of feminist movement meetings. They discussed Verena Stefan's book *Shedding* with its radical feminist solution, and they debated their relationship to their mothers, in terms of whether they should raise their mothers' consciousness and teach them to object to their fathers or whether perhaps it was best to leave them alone. The African women listened for a while, and then they told their German sisters how inexplicably close they felt to their mothers/daughters, and how neither group would dream of making a decision of importance without first consulting the other group. This was not a dialogue! It was two very different voices shouting in the wilderness, and it pointed out to me very clearly that universal sisterhood is not a given biological condition as much as perhaps a goal to work towards, and that in that process it is important to isolate the problems which are specific to Africa or perhaps the Third World in general, and also perhaps to accept a different hierarchy of importance in which the mother/daughter relationship would be somewhat downgraded.

One obvious and very important area of difference is this: whereas Western feminists discuss the relative importance of feminist versus class emancipation, the African discussion is between feminist emancipation

* From 'First Things First: Problems of a Feminist Approach to African Literature' *Kunapipi* 6(3), 1984.

versus the fight against neo-colonialism, particularly in its cultural aspect. In other words, which is the more important, which comes first, the fight for female equality or the fight against Western cultural imperialism? When I say that this is what the discussion is about, I hasten to add that there is very little explicit discussion about the subject, but – as I hope to show – the opinion which is implicit in the choice of subject of the first generation of modern African writers has had a profound influence on attitudes to women and the possibility of a feminist school of writing.

Whilst there is not a lot, there is some explicit discussion about the subject. The Malawian poet Felix Mnthali states one view very clearly in a poem called 'Letter to a Feminist Friend':[1]

> I will not pretend
> to see the light
> in the rhythm of your paragraphs:
> illuminated pages
> need not contain
> any copy-right
> on history
>
> My world has been raped
>                          looted
>             and squeezed
> by Europe and America
> and I have been scattered
> over three continents
> to please Europe and America
>
> AND NOW
> the women of Europe and America
> after drinking and carousing
> on my sweat
> rise up to castigate
>                   and castrate
> their menfolk
> from the cushions of a world
> I have built!
>
> Why should they be allowed
> to come between us?
> You and I were slaves together
> uprooted and humiliated together
> Rapes and lynchings –
>
> the lash of the overseer
> and the lust of the slave-owner

do your friends 'in the movement'
understand these things?

. . .

No, no, my sister,
                    my love,
first things first!
Too many gangsters
still stalk this continent
too many pirates
too many looters
far too many
still stalk this land –

. . .

When Africa
at home and across the seas
is truly free
there will be time for me
and time for you
to share the cooking
and change the nappies –
till then,
first things first!

... An important impetus behind the wave of African writing which
started in the '60s was the desire to show both the outside world and
African youth that the African past was orderly, dignified and complex and
altogether a worthy heritage. This was obviously opting for fighting
cultural imperialism, and in the course of that the women's issue was not
only ignored – a fate which would have allowed it to surface when the time
was ripe – it was conscripted in the service of dignifying the past and
restoring African self-confidence. The African past was not made the object
of a critical scrutiny the way the past tends to be in societies with a more
harmonious development, it was made the object of a quest, and the picture
of women's place and role in these societies had to support this quest and
was consequently lent more dignity and described in more positive terms
than reality warranted. Achebe's much praised objectivity with regard to
the merits and flaws of traditional Ibo society becomes less than praise-
worthy seen in this light: his traditional women are happy, harmonious
members of the community, even when they are repeatedly beaten and
barred from any say in the communal decision-making process and
constantly reviled in sayings and proverbs. It would appear that in traditional wisdom behaving like a woman is to behave like an inferior being.

My sense of humour has always stopped short at the pleasant little joke about Okonkwo being punished, not for beating his wife, but for beating her during the week of peace (Achebe 1958). The obvious inequality of the sexes seems to be the subject of mild amusement for Achebe.

If Achebe is obviously quite contented with the unequal state of affairs, Okot p'Bitek takes this tendency a step further and elevates his female protagonist, Lawino, into the very principle of traditional ways. . . . [But] in refusing to admire Lawino's romanticised version of her obviously sexist society one tears away the carpet from under the feet of the fighter against cultural imperialism. Lawino has become a holy cow, and slaughtering her and her various sisters is inevitably a betrayal, because they are inextricably bound up with the fight for African self-confidence in the face of Western cultural imperialism. . . .

It is no coincidence that this paper started as a discussion of images of women in literature written by men and ended by discussing a female writer and her portrayal of women's situation in present-day Africa. It is only just that women should have the last say in the discussion about their own situation, as, undoubtedly, we shall. This, however, is not meant to further the over-simplified view that a woman's view is always bound to be more valid than a man's in these discussions. The 'first things first' discussion as it appears in the writing of Ngugi and Buchi Emecheta is a good example of the complexity of this situation. Ngugi's ideological starting point seems to me ideal. 'No cultural liberation without women's liberation.' This . . . is a more difficult and therefore more courageous path to take in the African situation than in the Western one, because it has to borrow some concepts – and a vocabulary – from a culture from which at the same time it is trying to disassociate itself and at the same time it has to modify its admiration for some aspects of a culture it is claiming validity for. . . . [But] Buchi Emecheta . . . can recreate the situation and difficulties of women with authenticity and give a valuable insight into their thoughts and feelings. Her prime concern is not so much with cultural liberation, nor with social change. To her the object seems to be to give women access to power in the society as it exists, to beat men at their own game. She lays claim to no ideology, not even a feminist one. She simply ignores the African dilemma, whereas Ngugi shoulders it and tries to come to terms with it. This could look like the welcome beginning of 'schools' of writing, and to my mind nothing could be more fruitful than a vigorous debate in literature about the role and future of women.

## NOTE

1   Felix Mnthali, 'Letter to a Feminist Friend'. The poem will appear in a volume entitled *Beyond the Echoes*. [*This book does not appear in the current bibliographies we have been able to check. We can only assume the volume announced has not yet appeared. Eds.]*

# 44

# Decolonizing Culture
## Toward a Theory for Post-colonial Women's Texts

### Ketu H. Katrak*

THE CONCEPT OF social responsibility, not only for postcolonial writers but also for critics/theorists, is central to my concern. Social responsibility must be the basis of any theorizing on postcolonial literature as well as the root of the creative work of the writers themselves. Whereas writers commonly respond seriously to the many urgent issues of their societies, critics/theorists of this literature often do not.

What theoretical models will be appropriate for this task? How can theory be an integral part of the struggle of these writers as presented in their novels, poems, dramas, essays, letters, and testimonies? How can we make our theory and interpretation of postcolonial texts challenge the hegemony of the Western canon? How can we, within a dominant Eurocentric discourse, make our study of postcolonial texts itself a mode of resistance? And, most significantly, what theoretical models will be most constructive for the development of this literature?

It is useful within a postcolonial context to think of theory, as Barbara Harlow suggests, as strategy, to consider certain integral and dialectical relationships between theory and practice. I wish to propose certain theoretical models for a study of women writers that will expand a narrow academic conceptualization of theory and that can be expressed in a language lucid enough to inspire people to struggle and to achieve social change.

## DECOLONIZING POSTCOLONIAL THEORY

I would like first to examine several disconcerting trends in the recent production and consumption of postcolonial theory in general in order to

* From 'Decolonizing Culture: Toward a Theory for Postcolonial Women's Texts' *Modern Fiction Studies* 35(1), 1989.

decolonize this terrain and then to propose a historically situated method of approaching the work of women writers. One finds 1) little theoretical production of postcolonial writers given the serious attention it deserves, or that it is dismissed as not theoretical enough by Western standards; 2) the increasing phenomenon of using postcolonial texts as raw material for the theory producers and consumers of Western academia; 3) theoretical production as an end in itself, confined to the consumption of other theorists who speak the same privileged language in which obscurity is regularly mistaken for profundity. A new hegemony is being established in contemporary theory that can with impunity ignore or exclude postcolonial writers' essays, interviews, and other cultural productions while endlessly discussing concepts of the 'Other,' of 'difference,' and so on. Soyinka's words in his Preface to *Myth, Literature and the African World* still ring true:

> We black Africans have been blandly invited to submit ourselves to a second epoch of colonialism – this time by a universal-humanoid abstraction defined and conducted by individuals whose theories and prescriptions are derived from the apprehension of *their* world and *their* history, *their* social neuroses and *their* value systems.
>
> (1976: x)

Another more subtly insidious trend in recent postcolonial theory is the critic's attempt to engage with certain fashionable theoretical models in order 1) to validate postcolonial literature, even to prove its value through the use of complicated Eurocentric models, or 2) to succumb to the lure of engaging in a hegemonic discourse of Western theory given that it is 'difficult' or 'challenging,' often for the sole purpose of demonstrating its shortcomings for an interpretation of postcolonial texts. The intellectual traps in such theoretical gymnastics are many: for instance, a questioning of the canon and a simultaneous appropriating and tokenizing of postcolonial literary texts or an attempt to get away from narrowly anthropological readings of these texts and thereby interpreting them primarily as 'acts of language.'

The result is thus situations that inevitably assert an intellectual and political domination. Often, with the best intentions, Western intellectuals are unconsciously complicit in an endeavor that ironically ends up validating the dominant power structure, even when they ideologically oppose such hegemonic power. . . .

Postcolonial women writers participate actively in the ongoing process of decolonizing culture. Fanon's concept that 'decolonization is always a violent phenomenon' is useful for an analysis of how the English language is 'violated' from its standard usage and how literary forms are transformed from their definitions within the Western tradition. In terms of language, it is as if a version of the cultural and economic violence perpetrated by the colonizer is now appropriated by writers in order to 'violate' the English language in its standard use. Both arenas – linguistic and cultural – are dialectically related. Language *is* culture, particularly the transformations of rhetorical and discursive tools available through a colonial(ist) education system; and one expression of cultural tradition (among others like film, popular culture, festival) is through language. . . .

Women writers' uses of oral traditions and their revisions of Western literary forms are integrally and dialectically related to the kinds of content and the themes they treat. Women writers' stances, particularly with regard to glorifying/denigrating traditions, vary as dictated by their own class backgrounds, levels of education, political awareness and commitment, and their search for alternatives to existing levels of oppression often inscribed within the most revered traditions. Their texts deal with, and often challenge, their dual oppression–patriarchy that preceded and continues after colonialism and that inscribes the concepts of womanhood, motherhood, traditions such as dowry, bride-price, polygamy, and a worsened predicament within a capitalist economic system introduced by the colonizers. Women writers deal with the burdens of female roles in urban environments (instituted by colonialism), the rise of prostitution in cities, women's marginalization in actual political participation. . . .

## THE SISTREN COLLECTIVE (JAMAICA)

Sistren's work best illustrates a radical revising both of the English language in their use of 'patwah' and of literary forms such as drama and the short story that are based on folk-forms, ritual, and personal testimony. Sistren came together in May 1977 when a group of twelve working-class women employed as street cleaners under the Michael Manley government 'special make-work program called Impact' presented a drama titled *Downpression Get a Blow*. They were assisted by Honor Ford Smith of the Jamaica School of Drama, who was the Artistic Director for the group from 1977 to 1988.

Sistren's creative use of folk-forms uses working-class women's daily language. As Ford Smith notes, 'Writing in dialect, with its improvised spelling and immediate flavor, the women learned to write a form of English that had previously been considered "bad, coarse, vulgar." . . . By writing a language that had hitherto been that of a non-literate people, the women broke silence' (Ford Smith 1985: 85–91). There is vast potential for cultural resistance within what Edward Kamau Brathwaite in his significant study *History of the Voice* calls 'a submerged language' (1984: 16). When expressed, this language can be most empoweringly subversive, particularly within Caribbean society where middleclass attitudes about 'proper speech' still prevail. . . .

In postcolonial Jamaica, a neocolonist legacy of denigrating 'patwah' continues. Sistren's use of 'patwah' demonstrates 'the refusal of a people to imitate a coloniser,' remarks Ford Smith, and 'their insistence on creation, their movement from obedience towards revolution. Not to nurture such a language is to retard the imagination and power of the people who created it' (88).[1] Ford Smith depicts the relationship of language to power relations and to class in Jamaican society; 'patwah' is commonly used for entertainment purposes, not for serious writing and reflection. Working-class people who speak 'patwah' often cannot write it, and the rift between the oral and the literate cultures gets deeper. Ford Smith skillfully brings these two dimensions together in her use of oral testimony, itself a part of oral tradition, as the base for Sistren's written stories entitled *Lionheart Gal: Lifestories of Jamaican Women*. One significant contribution of *Lionheart Gal* is the combination of oral and written forms: thirteen of the fifteen stories are based on oral testimony/interview that records working-class women's daily language. . . . The stories effectively demystify female roles, such as the nurturing mother and the romanticizing of peasant life, as well as sexuality and violence. 'Taken together, they are a composite woman's story. . . . All of the testimonies are underscored by a movement from girlhood to adulthood, country to city, isolated individual experiences to a more politicised collective awareness . . .' (Sistren with Honor Ford Smith (ed.) 1985: 1).

## NOTE

1   Ford Smith has created this new spelling of 'patwah' in order to distinguish it from more commonly used spelling 'patois.'

# 45

## Under Western Eyes
### Feminist Scholarship and Colonial Discourses

CHANDRA TALPADE MOHANTY*

HOWEVER SOPHISTICATED OR problematical its use as an explanatory construct, colonization almost invariably implies a relation of structural domination, and a suppression – often violent – of the heterogeneity of the subject(s) in question. What I wish to analyze is specifically the production of the 'Third World Woman' as a singular monolithic subject in some recent (Western) feminist texts. . . .

Clearly Western feminist discourse and political practice is neither singular nor homogeneous in its goals, interests or analyses. However, it is possible to trace a coherence of *effects* resulting from the implicit assumption of 'the West' (in all its complexities and contradictions) as the primary referent in theory and praxis. My reference to 'Western feminism' is by no means intended to imply that it is a monolith. Rather, I am attempting to draw attention to the similar effects of various textual strategies used by particular writers that codify Others as non-Western and hence themselves as (implicitly) Western. It is in this sense that I use the term 'Western feminist.' The analytic principles discussed below serve to distort Western feminist political practices, and limit the possibility of coalitions among (usually White) Western feminists and working class and feminists of color around the world. These limitations are evident in the construction of the (implicitly consensual) priority of issues around which apparently *all* women are expected to organize. . . .

The relationship between 'Woman' – a cultural and ideological composite Other constructed through diverse representational discourses (scientific, literary, juridical, linguistic, cinematic, etc.) – and 'women' – real, material subjects of their collective histories – is one of the central questions the practice of feminist scholarship seeks to address. This

* From 'Under Western Eyes: Feminist Scholarship and Colonial Discourses' *Boundary 2* 12(3), 13(1) (Spring/Fall), 1984.

connection between women as historical subjects and the re-presentation of Woman produced by hegemonic discourses is not a relation of direct identity, or a relation of correspondence or simple implication.[1] It is an arbitrary relation set up by particular cultures. I would like to suggest that the feminist writings I analyze here discursively colonize the material and historical heterogeneities of the lives of women in the third world, thereby producing/re-presenting a composite, singular 'Third World Woman' – an image which appears arbitrarily constructed, but nevertheless carries with it the authorizing signature of Western humanist discourse.[2] I argue that assumptions of privilege and ethnocentric universality on the one hand, and inadequate self-consciousness about the effect of Western scholarship on the 'third world' in the context of a world system dominated by the West on the other, characterize a sizeable extent of Western feminist work on women in the third world. An analysis of 'sexual difference' in the form of a cross-culturally singular, monolithic notion of patriarchy or male dominance leads to the construction of a similarly reductive and homogeneous notion of what I call the 'Third World Difference' – that stable, ahistorical something that apparently oppresses most if not all the women in these countries. And it is in the production of this 'Third World Difference' that Western feminisms appropriate and 'colonize' the fundamental complexities and conflicts which characterize the lives of women of different classes, religions, cultures, races and castes in these countries. It is in this process of homogenization and systematization of the oppression of women in the third world that power is exercised in much of recent Western feminist discourse, and this power needs to be defined and named. . . .

Western feminist scholarship cannot avoid the challenge of situating itself and examining its role in such a global economic and political framework. To do any less would be to ignore the complex interconnections between first and third world economies and the profound effect of this on the lives of women in these countries. I do not question the descriptive and informative value of most Western feminist writings on women in the third world. I also do not question the existence of excellent work which does not fall into the analytic traps I am concerned with. In fact I deal with an example of such work later on. In the context of an overwhelming silence about the experiences of women in these countries, as well as the need to forge international links between women's political struggles, such work is both pathbreaking and absolutely essential. However, it is both to the *explanatory potential* of particular analytic strategies employed by such writing, and to their *political effect* in the context of the hegemony of Western scholarship, that I want to draw attention here. While feminist writing in the US is still marginalized (except from the point of view of women of color addressing privileged White women), Western feminist writing on women in the third world must be considered in the context of the global hegemony of Western scholarship – i.e., the production, publication, distribution and consumption of information and ideas. Marginal

or not, this writing has political effects and implications beyond the immediate feminist or disciplinary audience. One such significant effect of the
dominant 'representations' of Western feminism is its conflation with imperialism in the eyes of particular third world women.[3] Hence the urgent need
to examine the *political* implications of *analytic* strategies and principles. . . .

The first principle I focus on concerns the strategic location or situation
of the category 'women' vis-à-vis the context of analysis. The assumption of
women as an already constituted, coherent group with identical interests
and desires, regardless of class, ethnic or racial location or contradictions,
implies a notion of gender or sexual difference or even patriarchy (as male
dominance – men as a correspondingly coherent group) which can be
applied universally and cross-culturally. The context of analysis can be
anything from kinship structures and the organization of labor to media
representations. The second principle consists in the uncritical use of particular methodologies in providing 'proof' of universality and cross-cultural
validity. The third is a more specifically political principle underlying the
methodologies and the analytic strategies, i.e., the model of power and
struggle they imply and suggest. I argue that as a result of the two modes –
or, rather, frames – of analysis described above, a homogeneous notion of
the oppression of women as a group is assumed, which, in turn, produces
the image of an 'average third world woman.' This average third world
woman leads an essentially truncated life based on her feminine gender
(read: sexually constrained) and being 'third world' (read: ignorant, poor,
uneducated, tradition-bound, domestic, family-oriented, victimized, etc.).
This, I suggest, is in contrast to the (implicit) self-representation of Western
women as educated, modern, as having control over their own bodies and
sexualities, and the freedom to make their own decisions. The distinction
between Western feminist re-presentation of women in the third world, and
Western feminist *self*-presentation is a distinction of the same order as that
made by some marxists between the 'maintenance' function of the house-
wife and the real 'productive' role of wage labor, or the characterization
by developmentalists of the third world as being engaged in the lesser
production of 'raw materials' in contrast to the 'real' productive activity of
the First World. These distinctions are made on the basis of the privileging
of a particular group as the norm or referent. Men involved in wage labor,
first world producers, and, I suggest, Western feminists who sometimes cast
Third World women in terms of 'ourselves undressed' (Rosaldo 1980: 392),
all construct themselves as the referent in such a binary analytic.

## 'WOMEN' AS CATEGORY OF ANALYSIS, OR: WE ARE ALL
## SISTERS IN STRUGGLE

By women as a category of analysis, I am referring to the critical assumption
that all of us of the same gender, across classes and cultures, are somehow

socially constituted as a homogeneous group identified prior to the process of analysis. This is an assumption which characterizes much feminist discourse. The homogeneity of women as a group is produced not on the basis of biological essentials, but rather on the basis of secondary socio-logical and anthropological universals. Thus, for instance, in any given piece of feminist analysis, women are characterized as a singular group on the basis of a shared oppression. What binds women together is a sociological notion of the 'sameness' of their oppression. It is at this point that an elision takes place between 'women' as a discursively constructed group and 'women' as material subjects of their own history. Thus, the discursively consensual homogeneity of 'women' as a group is mistaken for the histori-cally specific material reality of groups of women. This results in an assumption of women as an always-already constituted group, one which has been labelled 'powerless,' 'exploited,' 'sexually harrassed,' etc., by feminist scientific, economic, legal and sociological discourses. (Notice that this is quite similar to sexist discourse labelling women weak, emotional, having math anxiety, etc.) The focus is not on uncovering the material and ideological specificities that constitute a particular group of women as 'powerless' in a particular context. It is rather on finding a variety of cases of 'powerless' groups of women to prove the general point that women as a group are powerless. . . .

Male violence must be theorized and interpreted *within* specific societies, both in order to understand it better, as well as in order to effec-tively organize to change it. Sisterhood cannot be assumed on the basis of gender; it must be formed in concrete, historical and political practice and analysis. . . .

[Unless this is done] women are constituted as a group via dependency relationships vis-à-vis men, who are implicitly held responsible for these relationships. When 'women of Africa' as a group (versus 'men of Africa' as a group?) are seen as a group precisely because they are generally dependent and oppressed, the analysis of specific historical differences becomes impossible, because reality is always apparently structured by divisions – two mutually exclusive and jointly exhaustive groups, the victims and the oppressors. Here the sociological is substituted for the biological in order, however, to create the same – a unity of women. Thus, it is not the descriptive potential of gender difference, but the privileged positioning and explanatory potential of gender difference as the *origin* of oppression that I question. . . . Women are taken as a unified 'Powerless' group prior to the analysis in question. Thus, it is then merely a matter of specifying the context *after the fact*. . . . The problem with this analytic strategy is that it assumes men and women are already constituted as sexual-political subjects *prior* to their entry into the arena of social relations. Only if we subscribe to this assumption is it possible to under-take analysis which looks at the 'effects' of kinship structures, colonialism, organization of labor, etc., on women, who are already defined as a group apparently because of shared dependencies, but ultimately because of their gender. But women are *produced through these very relations* as well as being implicated in forming these relations. As Michelle Rosaldo states: '. . . woman's place in human social life is not in any direct sense a product of the things she does (or even less, a function of what, biologically, she is) but the meaning her activities acquire through concrete social interactions' (Rosaldo 1980: 400). That women mother in a variety of societies is not as significant as the *value* attached to mothering in these societies. The distinction between the act of mothering and the status attached to it is a very important one – one that needs to be made and analyzed contextually.

## NOTES

1   I am indebted to Teresa de Lauretis for this particular formulation of the project of feminist theorizing. See especially her introduction in de Lauretis, *Alice Doesn't: Feminism, Semiotics, Cinema* (Bloomington: Indiana University Press, 1984); see also Sylvia Wynter, 'The Politics of Domination,' unpublished manuscript.

2   This argument is similar to Homi Bhabha's definition of colonial discourse as strategically creating a space for a subject peoples through the production of knowledges and the exercise of power. The full quote reads: '[colonial discourse is] an apparatus of power . . . an apparatus that turns on the recognition and disavowal of racial/cultural/historical differences. Its predominant strategic function is the creation of a space for a "subject peoples" through the production of knowledges in terms of which surveillance is exercised and a complex form of pleasure/unpleasure is incited. It (i.e., colonial discourse) seeks authorisation for its strategies by the production of knowledges by coloniser and colonised which are stereotypical but antithetically evaluated.' Homi Bhabha, 'The Other Question – the Stereotype and Colonial Discourse.' *Screen* 24 (November–December 1983), 23.

3   A number of documents and reports on the UN International Conferences on Women, Mexico City, 1975, and Copenhagen, 1980, as well as the 1976 Wellesley Conference on Women and Development attest to this. Nawal el Saadawi, Fatima Mernissi and Mallica Vajarathon in 'A Critical Look At The Wellesley Conference' (*Quest*, IV (Winter 1978), 101–7), characterize this conference as 'American-planned and organized,' situating third world participants as passive audiences. They focus especially on the lack of self-consciousness of Western women's implications in the effects of imperialism and racism in their assumption of an 'international sisterhood.' A recent essay, by Pratibha Parmar and Valerie Amos, is titled 'Challenging Imperial Feminism,' *Feminist Review* 17 (Autumn 1984), 3–19. Parmar and Amos characterize Euro-American feminism which seeks to establish itself as the only legitimate feminism as 'imperial.'

# 46

## *Writing Postcoloniality and Feminism*

### TRINH T. MINH-HA*

WORDS EMPTY OUT with age. Die and rise again, accordingly invested with new meanings, and always equipped with a secondhand memory. In trying to tell something, a woman is told, shredding herself into opaque words while her voice dissolves on the walls of silence. Writing: a commitment of language. The web of her gestures, like all modes of writing, denotes a historical solidarity (on the understanding that her story remains inseparable from history). She has been warned of the risk she incurs by letting words run off the rails, time and again tempted by the desire to gear herself to the accepted norms. But where has obedience led her? At best, to the satisfaction of a 'made-woman,' capable of achieving as high a mastery of discourse as that of the male establishment in power. Immediately gratified, she will, as years go by, sink into oblivion, a fate she inescapably shares with her foresisters. How many, already, have been condemned to premature deaths for having borrowed the master's tools and thereby played into his hands? Solitude is a common prerequisite, even though this may only mean solitude in the immediate surroundings. Elsewhere, in every corner of the world, there exist women who, despite the threat of rejection, resolutely work toward the unlearning of institutionalized language, while staying alert to every deflection of their body compass needles. *Survival*, as Audre Lorde comments, '*is not an academic skill*. . . . It is learning how to take our differences and make them strengths. *For the master's tools will never dismantle the master's house*. They may allow us temporarily to beat him at his own game, but they will never enable us to bring about genuine change' (Lorde 1981: 99). The more one depends on the master's house for support, the less one hears what he doesn't want to hear. Difference is not difference to some ears, but awkwardness or incompleteness. Aphasia. Unable or unwilling? Many have come to tolerate this dissimilarity and have decided to suspend their judgments (only) whenever the other is concerned. Such an

* From *Woman, Native, Other: Writing Postcoloniality and Feminism* Bloomington, Ind.: Indiana University Press, 1989.

attitude is a step forward; at least the danger of speaking for the other has emerged into consciousness. But it is a very small step indeed, since it serves as an excuse for their complacent ignorance and their reluctance to involve themselves in the issue. You who understand the dehumanization of forced removal–relocation–reeducation–redefinition, the humiliation of having to falsify your own reality, your voice – you know. And often cannot *say* it. You try and keep on trying to unsay it, for if you don't, they will not fail to fill in the blanks on your behalf, and you will be said.

## THE POLICY OF 'SEPARATE DEVELOPMENT'

With a kind of perverted logic, they work toward your erasure while urging you to keep your way of life and ethnic values *within the borders of your homelands*. This is called the policy of 'separate development' in apartheid language. Tactics have changed since the colonial times and indigenous cultures are no longer (overtly) destroyed (preserve the form but remove the content, or vice versa). You may keep your traditional law and tribal customs among yourselves, as long as you and your own kind are careful not to step beyond the assigned limits. Nothing has been left to chance when one considers the efforts made by the White South African authorities to distort and use the tools of Western liberalism for the defense of their racialistic-ally indefensible cause. Since no integration is possible when terror has become the order of the day, I (not you) will give you freedom. I will grant you autonomy – not complete autonomy, however, for 'it is a liberal fallacy to suppose that those to whom freedom is given will use it only as foreseen by those who gave it' (Manning 1968: 287). . . . The delimitation of territories is my answer to what I perceive as some liberals' dream for 'the inauguration, namely, of a system in which South Africa's many peoples would resolve themselves unreluctantly into one' (289). The governed do not (should not) compose a single people; this is why I am eager to show that South Africa is not one but ten separate nations (of which the White nation is the only one to be skin-defined; the other nine being determined largely on the basis of language – the Zulu nation, the Swazi nation, and so on). This philosophy – I will not call it 'policy' – of 'differentiation' will allow me to have better control over my nation while looking after yours, helping you thereby to gradually stand on your own. It will enable you to return to 'where you belong' whenever you are not satisfied with my law and customs or whenever you are no longer useful to me. Too bad if you consider what has been given to you as the leftovers of my meals. Call it 'reserves of cheap labor' or 'bantustans' if you wish; 'separate development' means that each one of us minds her/his own business (I will interfere when my rights are concerned since I represent the State) and that your economical poverty is of your own making. As for 'the Asiatic cancer, which has already eaten so deeply into the vitals of South

Africa, [it] ought to be resolutely eradicated' (Jan Christaaen Smuts, quoted in Fischer 1954: 25). Non-white foreigners have no part whatsoever in my plans and I 'will undertake to drive the coolies [Indians] out of the country within four years' (General Louis Botha, quoted in Fischer 1954: 25). My 'passionate concern for the future of a European-type white society, and . . . that society's right to self-preservation' is not a question of color feeling, but of nationalism, the 'Afrikaner nationalism [which] is a form of collective selfishness; but to say this is simply to say that it is an authentic case of nationalism' (Manning 1968: 287).

Words manipulated at will. As you can see, 'difference' is essentially 'division' in the understanding of many. It is no more than a tool of self-defense and conquest. You and I might as well not walk into this semantic trap which sets us up against each other as expected by a certain ideology of separatism. Have you read the grievances some of our sisters express on being among the few women chosen for a 'Special Third World Women's Issue' or on being the only Third World woman at readings, workshops, and meetings? . . .

Why not go and find out for yourself when you don't know? Why let yourself be trapped in the mold of permanent schooling and wait for the delivery of knowledge as a consumer waits for her/his suppliers' goods? The understanding of difference is a shared responsibility, which requires a minimum of willingness to reach out to the unknown. As Audre Lorde says,

> Women of today are still being called upon to stretch across the gap of male ignorance, and to educate men as to our existence and our needs. This is an old and primary tool of all oppressors to keep the oppressed occupied with the master's concerns. Now we hear that it is the task of black and third world women to educate white women, in the face of tremendous resistance, as to our existence, our differences, our relative roles in our joint survival. This is a diversion of energies and a tragic repetition of racist patriarchal thought.
>
> (Lorde 1981: 100)

One has to be excessively preoccupied with the master's concerns, indeed, to try to explain why women cannot have written 'the plays of Shakespeare in the age of Shakespeare,' as Virginia Woolf did. Such a waste of energy is perhaps unavoidable at certain stages of the struggle; it need not, however, become an end point in itself. . . .

Specialness as a soporific soothes, anaesthetizes my sense of justice; it is, to the wo/man of ambition, as effective a drug of psychological self-intoxication as alcohol is to the exiles of society. Now, i am not only given the permission to open up and talk, i am also encouraged to express my difference. My audience expects and demands it; otherwise people would feel as if they have been cheated: We did not come to hear a Third World member speak about the First (?) World, We came to listen to that voice of difference likely to bring us *what we can't have* and to divert us from the monotony of sameness. They, like their anthropologists whose specialty is to detect all the layers of my falseness and truthfulness, are in a position to decide what/who is 'authentic' and what/who is not. No uprooted person is invited to participate in this 'special' wo/man's issue unless s/he 'makes up' her/his mind and paints her/himself thick with authenticity. Eager not to disappoint, i try my best to offer my benefactors and benefactresses what they most anxiously yearn for: the possibility of a difference, yet a difference or an otherness that will not go so far as to question the foundation of their beings and makings. Their situation is not unlike that of the American tourists who, looking for a change of scenery and pace in a foreign land, such as, for example, Japan, strike out in search of what they believe to be the 'real' Japan – most likely shaped after the vision of Japan as handed to them and reflected in television films like 'Shogun' – or that of the anthropologists, whose conception of 'pure' anthropology induces them to concentrate on the study of 'primitive' ('native,' 'indigenous,' or to use more neutral, technical terms: 'non-state,' 'non-class') societies. Authenticity in such contexts turns out to be a product that one can buy, arrange to one's liking, and/or preserve. Today, the 'unspoiled' parts of Japan, the far-flung locations in the archipelago, are those that tourism officials actively promote for the more venturesome visitors. Similarly, the Third World representative the modern sophisticated public ideally seeks is the unspoiled African, Asian, or Native American, who remains more preoccupied with her/his image of the *real* native – the *truly different* – than with the issues of hegemony, racism, feminism, and social change (which s/he lightly touches on in conformance to the reigning fashion of liberal discourse). A Japanese actually looks more Japanese in America than in Japan, but the 'real' type of Japanism ought to be in Japan. The less accessible the product 'made-in-Japan,' the more trustworthy it is, and the greater the desire to acquire and protect it. . . .

## THE QUESTION OF ROOTS AND AUTHENTICITY

'I was made to feel,' writes Joanne Harumi Sechi, 'that cultural pride would justify and make good my difference in skin color while it was a constant reminder that I was different' (Sechi 1980: 444). Every notion in vogue, including the retrieval of 'roots' values, is necessarily exploited and recuperated. The invention of needs always goes hand in hand with the compulsion to help the needy, a noble and self-gratifying task that also renders the helper's service indispensable. The part of the savior has to be filled as long as the belief in the problem of 'endangered species' lasts. To persuade you that your past and cultural heritage are doomed to eventual extinction and thereby keeping you occupied with the Savior's concern, inauthenticity is condemned as a *loss of origins* and a whitening (or faking) of non-Western values. Being easily offended in your elusive identity and reviving readily an old, racial charge, you immediately react when such guilt-instilling accusations are leveled at you and are thus led to stand in need of defending that very ethnic part of yourself that for years has made you and your ancestors the objects of execration. Today, planned authenticity is rife; as a product of hegemony and a remarkable counterpart of universal standardization, it constitutes an efficacious means of silencing the cry of racial oppression. We no longer wish to erase your difference. We demand, on the contrary, that you remember and assert it. At least, to a certain extent. Every path I/i take is edged with thorns. On the one hand, i play into the Savior's hands by concentrating on authenticity, for my attention is numbed by it and diverted from other, important issues; on the other hand, i do feel the necessity to return to my so-called roots, since they are the fount of my strength, the guiding arrow to which i constantly refer before heading for a new direction. The difficulties appear perhaps less insurmountable only as I/i succeed in making a distinction between difference reduced to identity-authenticity and difference understood also as critical difference from myself. The first induces an attitude of temporary tolerance – as exemplified in the policy of 'separate development' – which serves to reassure the conscience of the liberal establishment and gives a touch of subversiveness to the discourse delivered. . . .

The pitting of anti-racist and anti-sexist struggles against one another allows some vocal fighters to dismiss blatantly the existence of either racism or sexism within their lines of action, as if oppression only comes in separate, monolithic forms. Thus, to understand how pervasively dominance operates via the concept of hegemony or of absent totality in plurality is to understand that the work of decolonization will have to continue within the women's movements. . . .

# 47

# *Three Women's Texts and a Critique of Imperialism*

## Gayatri Chakravorty Spivak*

IT SHOULD NOT be possible to read nineteenth-century British literature without remembering that imperialism, understood as England's social mission, was a crucial part of the cultural representation of England to the English. The role of literature in the production of cultural representation should not be ignored. These two obvious 'facts' continue to be disregarded in the reading of nineteenth-century British literature. This itself attests to the continuing success of the imperialist project, displaced and dispersed into more modern forms.

If these 'facts' were remembered, not only in the study of British literature but in the study of the literatures of the European colonizing cultures of the great age of imperialism, we would produce a narrative in literary history, of the 'worlding' of what is now called 'the Third World.' To consider the Third World as distant cultures, exploited but with rich intact literary heritages waiting to be recovered, interpreted, and curricularized in English translation fosters the emergence of 'the Third World' as a signifier that allows us to forget that 'worlding,' even as it expands the empire of the literary discipline.[1]

It seems particularly unfortunate when the emergent perspective of feminist criticism reproduces the axioms of imperialism. A basically isolationist admiration for the literature of the female subject in Europe and Anglo-America establishes the high feminist norm. It is supported and operated by an information-retrieval approach to 'Third World' literature which often employs a deliberately 'nontheoretical' methodology with self-conscious rectitude.

In this essay, I will attempt to examine the operation of the 'worlding' of what is today 'the Third World' by what has become a cult text of feminism: *Jane Eyre* (Brontë [1847] 1980). I plot the novel's reach and grasp, and locate its structural motors. I read *Wide Sargasso Sea* (Rhys

* From 'Three Women's Texts and a Critique of Imperialism' *Critical Inquiry* 12(1), 1985.

1968) as *Jane Eyre*'s reinscription and *Frankenstein* as an analysis – even a deconstruction – of a 'worlding' such as *Jane Eyre*'s.

I need hardly mention that the object of my investigation is the printed book, not its 'author.' To make such a distinction is, of course, to ignore the lessons of deconstruction. A deconstructive critical approach would loosen the binding of the book, undo the opposition between verbal text and the bio-graphy of the named subject 'Charlotte Brontë,' and see the two as each other's 'scene of writing.' In such a reading, the life that writes itself as 'my life' is as much a production in psychosocial space (other names can be found) as the book that is written by the holder of that named life – a book that is then consigned to what *is* most often recognized as genuinely 'social': the world of publication and distribution. To touch Brontë's 'life' in such a way, however, would be too risky here. We must rather strategically take shelter in an essentialism which, not wishing to lose the important advantages won by US mainstream feminism, will continue to honor the suspect binary oppositions – book and author, individual and history – and start with an assurance of the following sort: my readings here do not seek to undermine the excellence of the individual artist. If even minimally successful, the readings will incite a degree of rage against the imperialist narrativization of history, that it should produce so abject a script for her. I provide these assurances to allow myself some room to situate feminist individualism in its historical determination rather than simply to canonize it as feminism as such. . . .

Elizabeth Fox-Genovese, in an article on history and women's history, shows us how to define the historical moment of feminism in the West in terms of female access to individualism (see Fox-Genovese 1982). The battle for female individualism plays itself out within the larger theater of the establishment of meritocratic individualism, indexed in the aesthetic field by the ideology of 'the creative imagination.' Fox-Genovese's presupposition will guide us into the beautifully orchestrated opening of *Jane Eyre*.

It is a scene of the marginalization and privatization of the protagonist: 'There was no possibility of taking a walk that day. . . . Out-door exercise was now out of the question. I was glad of it,' Brontë writes (Brontë 1980: 9). The movement continues as Jane breaks the rules of the appropriate topography of withdrawal. The family at the center withdraws into the sanctioned architectural space of the withdrawing room or drawing room; Jane inserts herself – 'I slipped in' – into the margin – 'A small breakfast-room *adjoined* the drawing room' (Brontë 1980: 9; my emphasis). . . .

Here in Jane's self-marginalized uniqueness, the reader becomes her accomplice: the reader and Jane are united – both are reading. Yet Jane still preserves her odd privilege, for she continues never quite doing the proper thing in its proper place. . . .

Before following the track of this unique imagination, let us consider the suggestion that the progress of *Jane Eyre* can be charted through a sequential arrangement of the family/counter-family dyad. In the novel, we encounter, first, the Reeds as the legal family and Jane, the late Mr. Reed's sister's daughter, as the representative of a near incestuous counter-family; second, the Brocklehursts, who run the school Jane is sent to, as the legal family and Jane, Miss Temple, and Helen Burns as a counter-family that falls short because it is only a community of women; third, Rochester and the mad Mrs. Rochester as the legal family and Jane and Rochester as the illicit counter-family. Other items may be added to the thematic chain in this sequence: Rochester and Céline Varens as structurally functional counter-family; Rochester and Blanche Ingram as dissimulation of legality – and so on. It is during this sequence that Jane is moved from the counter-family to the family-in-law. In the next sequence, it is Jane who restores full family status to the as-yet-incomplete community of siblings, the Riverses. The final sequence of the book is a *community of families*, with Jane, Rochester, and their children at the center. . . .

It is the unquestioned ideology of imperialist axiomatics . . . that conditions Jane's move from the counter-family set to the set of the family-in-law. Marxist critics such as Terry Eagleton have seen this only in terms of the ambiguous *class* position of the governess (see Eagleton 1975). Sandra Gilbert and Susan Gubar, on the other hand, have seen Bertha Mason only in psychological terms, as Jane's dark double (see Gilbert and Gubar 1979). I will not enter the critical debates that offer themselves here. Instead, I will develop the suggestion that nineteenth-century feminist individualism could conceive of a 'greater' project than access to the closed circle of the nuclear family. This is the project of soul making beyond 'mere' sexual reproduction. Here the native 'subject' is not almost an animal but rather the object of what might be termed the terrorism of the categorical imperative. . . .

I have suggested that Bertha's function in *Jane Eyre* is to render indeterminate the boundary between human and animal and thereby to weaken her entitlement under the spirit if not the letter of the Law. When Rhys rewrites the scene in *Jane Eyre* where Jane hears 'a snarling, snatching sound, almost like a dog quarrelling' and then encounters a bleeding Richard Mason (Brontë 1980: 210), she keeps Bertha's humanity, indeed her sanity as critic of imperialism, intact. Grace Poole, another character originally in *Jane Eyre*, describes the incident to Bertha in *Wide Sargasso Sea*: 'So you don't remember that you attacked this gentleman with a knife? . . . I didn't hear all he said except "I cannot interfere legally between yourself and your husband." It was when he said "legally" that you flew at him.' (Rhys 1968: 150). In Rhys' retelling, it is the dissimulation that Bertha discerns in the word 'legally' – not an innate bestiality – that prompts her violent *reaction*.

In the figure of Antoinette, whom in *Wide Sargasso Sea* Rochester violently renames Bertha, Rhys suggests that so intimate a thing as personal and human identity might be determined by the politics of imperialism.

5
Franken-
stein

Antoinette, as a white Creole child growing up at the time of emancipation in Jamaica, is caught between the English imperialist and the black native. . . .

*Wide Sargasso Sea* marks with uncanny clarity the limits of its own discourse in Christophine, Antoinette's black nurse. We may perhaps surmise the distance between *Jane Eyre* and *Wide Sargasso Sea* by remarking that Christophine's unfinished story is the tangent to the latter narrative, as St. John Rivers' story is to the former. Christophine is not a native of Jamaica; she is from Martinique. Taxonomically, she belongs to the category of the good servant rather than that of the pure native. But within these borders, Rhys creates a powerfully suggestive figure. . . .

I must myself close with an idea that I cannot establish within the limits of this essay. Earlier I contended that *Wide Sargasso Sea* is necessarily bound by the reach of the European novel. I suggested that, in contradistinction, to reopen the epistemic fracture of imperialism without succumbing to a nostalgia for lost origins, the critic must turn to the archives of imperialist governance. I have not turned to those archives in these pages. In my current work, by way of a modest and inexpert 'reading' of 'archives,' I try to extend, outside of the reach of the European novelistic tradition, the most powerful suggestion in *Wide Sargasso Sea* that *Jane Eyre* can be read as the orchestration and staging of the self-immolation of Bertha Mason as 'good wife.' The power of that suggestion remains unclear if we remain insufficiently knowledgeable about the history of the legal manipulation of widow-sacrifice in the entitlement of the British government in India. I would hope that an informed critique of imperialism, granted some attention from readers in the First World, will at least expand the frontiers of the politics of reading.

# NOTE

1   My notion of the 'worlding of a world' upon what must be assumed to be uninscribed earth is a vulgarization of Martin Heidegger's idea: see 'The Origin of the Work of Art' in Heidegger [1971] (1977) *Poetry, Language, Thought*, translations and introduction by Albert Hofstadter, New York: Harper Colophon Books, pp. 17–87.

# 48

## Woman Skin Deep
### Feminism and the
### Postcolonial Condition

#### Sara Suleri*

I WOULD CLAIM that while current feminist discourse remains vexed by
questions of identity formation and the concomitant debates between essentialism and constructivism, or distinctions between situated and universal
knowledge, it is still prepared to grant an uneasy selfhood to a voice that is
best described as the property of 'postcolonial Woman.' Whether this voice
represents perspectives as divergent as the African-American or the post-
colonial cultural location, its imbrications of race and gender are accorded
an iconicity that is altogether too good to be true. Even though the marriage
of two margins should not necessarily lead to the construction of that
contradiction in terms, a 'feminist center,' the embarrassed privilege granted
to racially encoded feminism does indeed suggest a rectitude that could be
its own theoretical undoing. The concept of the postcolonial itself is too
frequently robbed of historical specificity in order to function as a preap-
proved allegory for any mode of discursive contestation. The coupling
of *postcolonial* with *woman*, however, almost inevitably leads to the
simplicities that underlie unthinking celebrations of oppression, elevating
the racially female voice into a metaphor for 'the good.' Such metaphoricity
cannot exactly be called essentialist, but it certainly functions as an impedi-
ment to a reading that attempts to look beyond obvious questions of good
and evil. In seeking to dismantle the iconic status of postcolonial feminism,
I will attempt here to address the following questions: within the
tautological margins of such a discourse, which comes first, gender or race?
How, furthermore, can the issue of chronology lead to some preliminary
articulation of the productive superficiality of race?

Before such questions can be raised, however, it is necessary to pay
some critical attention to the mobility that has accrued in the category of

* From 'Woman Skin Deep: Feminism and the Postcolonial Condition' *Critical
Inquiry*, 18(4) (Summer), 1992.

postcolonialism. Where the term once referred exclusively to the discursive practices produced by the historical fact of prior colonization in certain geographically specific segments of the world, it is now more of an abstraction available for figurative deployment in any strategic redefinition of marginality. For example, when James Clifford elaborated his position on travelling theory during a recent seminar, he invariably substituted the metaphoric condition of postcoloniality for the obsolete binarism between anthropologist and native.[1] As with the decentering of any discourse, however, this reimaging of the postcolonial closes as many epistemological possibilities as it opens. On the one hand, it allows for a vocabulary of cultural migrancy, which helpfully derails the postcolonial condition from the strictures of national histories, and thus makes way for the theoretical articulations best typified by Homi Bhabha's recent anthology, *Nation and Narration* (1990). On the other hand, the current metaphorization of postcolonialism threatens to become so amorphous as to repudiate any locality for cultural thickness. A symptom of this terminological and theoretical dilemma is astutely read in Kwame Anthony Appiah's essay, 'Is the Post- in Postmodernism the Post- in Postcolonial?' (1991). Appiah argues for a discursive space-clearing that allows postcolonial discourse a figurative flexibility and at the same time reaffirms its radical locality within historical exigencies. His discreet but firm segregation of the postcolonial from the postmodern is indeed pertinent to the dangerous democracy accorded the coalition between postcolonial and feminist theories, in which each term serves to reify the potential pietism of the other.

In the context of contemporary feminist discourse, I would argue, the category of postcolonialism must be read both as a free-floating metaphor for cultural embattlement and as an almost obsolete signifier for the historicity of race. There is no available dichotomy that could neatly classify the ways in which such a redefinition of postcoloniality is necessarily a secret sharer in similar reconfigurations of feminism's most vocal articulation of marginality, or the obsessive attention it has recently paid to the racial body. Is the body in race subject or object, or is it more dangerously an objectification of a methodology that aims for radical subjectivity? Here, the binarism that informs Chandra Mohanty's paradigmatic essay, 'Under Western Eyes: Feminist Scholarship and Colonial Discourses,' deserves particular consideration. Where Mohanty engages in a particular critique of 'Third World Woman' as a monolithic object in the texts of Western feminism, her argument is premised on the irreconcilability of gender as history and gender as culture. 'What happens,' queries Mohanty, 'when [an] assumption of "women as an oppressed group" is situated in the context of Western feminist writing about third world women?' What happens, apparently, begs her question. In contesting what she claims is a 'colonialist move,' Mohanty proceeds to argue that 'Western feminists alone become the true "subjects" of this counter-history. Third World women, on the other hand, never rise above the debilitating generality of their "object" status' (Mohanty 1991: 71). A very literal ethic underlies such a dichotomy, one that demands attention to its very obviousness: how is this objectivism to be avoided? How will the ethnic voice of womanhood counteract the cultural articulation that Mohanty too easily dubs as the exegesis of Western feminism? The claim to authenticity – only a black can speak for a black; only a postcolonial subcontinental feminist can adequately represent the lived experience of that culture – points to the great difficulty posited by the 'authenticity' of female racial voices in the great game that claims to be the first narrative of what the ethnically constructed woman is deemed to want.

This desire all too often takes its theoretical form in a will to subjectivity that claims a theoretical basis most clearly contravened by the process of its analysis. An example of this point is Trinh Minh-ha's treatise, *Woman, Native, Other* (1989), which seeks to posit an alternative to the anthropological twist that constitutes the archaism through which nativism has been apprehended. Subtitled *Writing Postcoloniality and Feminism*, Trinh's book is a paradigmatic meditation that can be essentialized into a simple but crucial question: how can feminist discourse represent the categories of 'woman' and 'race' at the same time? If the languages of feminism and ethnicity are to escape an abrasive mutual contestation, what novel idiom can freshly articulate their radical inseparability? Trinh's strategy is to relocate her gendering of ethnic realities on the inevitable territory of postfeminism, which underscores her desire to represent discourse formation as always taking place after the fact of discourse. It further confirms my belief that had I any veto power over prefixes, *post-* would be the first to go – but that is doubtless tangential to the issue at hand. In the context of Trinh's methodology, the shape of the book itself illuminates what may best be called the endemic ill that effects a certain temporal derangement between the work's originary questions and the narratives that they engender. *Woman, Native, Other* consists of four loosely related chapters, each of which opens with an abstraction and ends with an anecdote. While there is a self-pronounced difference between the preliminary thesis outlined in the chapter 'Commitment from the Mirror-Writing Box' to the concluding claims in 'Grandma's Story,' such a discursive distance is not matched with any logical or theoretical consistency. Instead, a work that is impelled by an impassioned need to question the lines of demarcation between race and gender concludes by falling into a predictable biological fallacy in which sexuality is reduced to the literal structure of the racial body, and theoretical interventions within this trajectory become minimalized into the naked category of lived experience.

When feminism turns to lived experience as an alternative mode of radical subjectivity, it only rehearses the objectification of its proper subject. While lived experience can hardly be discounted as a critical resource for an apprehension of the gendering of race, neither should such data serve as the evacuating principle for both historical and theoretical

275

contexts alike. 'Radical subjectivity' too frequently translates into a low-grade romanticism that cannot recognize its discursive status as *pre-* rather than *post-*. In the concluding chapter of Trinh's text, for example, a section titled 'Truth and Fact: Story and History' delineates the skewed idiom that marginal subjectivities produce. In attempting to proclaim an alternative to male-identified objectivism, Trinh-as-anthropologist can only produce an equally objectifying idiom of joy:

> Let me tell you a story. For all I have is a story. Story passed on from generation to generation, named Joy. Told for the joy it gives the storyteller and the listener. Joy inherent in the process of storytelling. Whoever understands it also understands that a story, as distressing as it can be in its joy, never takes anything away from anybody.
>
> (Trinh 1989: 119)

Given that I find myself in a more acerbic relation both to the question of the constitution of specific postcolonialisms and of a more metaphoric postcolonial feminism, such a jointly universalist and individualist 'joy' is not a term that I would ordinarily welcome into my discursive lexicon. On one level, its manipulation of lived experience into a somewhat fallacious allegory for the reconstitution of gendered race bespeaks a transcendence – and an attendant evasion – of the crucial cultural issues at hand. On a more dangerous level, however, such an assumption serves as a mirror image of the analyses produced by the critics of political rectitude. For both parties, 'life' remains the ultimate answer to 'discourse.' The subject of race, in other words, cannot cohabit with the detail of a feminist language.

Trinh's transcendent idiom, of course, emanates from her somewhat free-floating understanding of 'postcoloniality': is it an abstraction into which all historical specificity may be subsumed, or is it a figure for a vaguely defined ontological marginality that is equally applicable to all 'minority' discourses? In either case, both the categories of 'woman' and 'race' assume the status of metaphors, so that each rhetoric of oppression can serve equally as a mirrored allegory for the other. Here, *Woman, Native, Other* is paradigmatic of the methodological blurring that dictates much of the discourse on identity formation in the coloring of feminist discourse. To privilege the racial body in the absence of historical context is indeed to generate an idiom that tends to waver with impressionistic haste between the abstractions of postcoloniality and the anecdotal literalism of what it means to articulate an 'identity' for a woman writer of color. Despite its proclaimed location within contemporary theoretical – not to mention post-theoretical – discourse, such an idiom poignantly illustrates the hidden and unnecessary desire to resuscitate the 'self.'

What is most striking about such discursive practices is their failure to confront what may be characterized best as a great enamourment with the 'real.' Theories of postcolonial feminism eminently lend themselves to a reopening of the continued dialogue that literary and cultural studies have

– and will continue to have – with the perplexing category known as realism, but at present the former discourse chooses to remain too precariously parochial to recognize the bounty that is surely its to give. Realism, however, is too dangerous a term for an idiom that seeks to raise identity to the power of theory. While both may be windmills to the quixotic urge to supply black feminism with some version of the 'real,' Trinh's musings on this subject add a mordantly pragmatic option to my initial question: 'what comes first, race or gender?' Perhaps the query would be more finely calibrated if it were rephrased to ask, 'What comes first, race, gender, or profession?' And what, in our sorry dealings with such realisms, is the most phantasmagoric category of all? . . .

If race is to complicate the project of divergent feminisms, in other words, it cannot take recourse to biologism, nor to the incipient menace of rewriting alterity into the ambiguous shape of the exotic body.

The body that serves as testimony for lived experience, however, has received sufficient interrogation from more considered perspectives on the cultural problems generated by the dialogue between gender and race, along with the hyperrealist idiom it may generate. Hazel Carby helpfully advocates that

> black feminist criticism [should] be regarded critically as a problem, not a solution, as a sign that should be interrogated, a locus of contradictions. Black feminist criticism has its source and its primary motivation in academic legitimation, placement within a framework of bourgeois humanistic discourse.
>
> (Carby 1987: 15)

The concomitant question that such a problem raises is whether the signification of gendered race necessarily returns to the realism that it most seeks to disavow. If realism is the Eurocentric and patriarchal pattern of adjudicating between disparate cultural and ethnic realities, then it is surely the task of radical feminism to provide an alternative perspective. In the vociferous discourse that such a task has produced, however, the question of alternativism is all too greatly subsumed either into the radical strategies that are designed to dictate the course of situated experience, or into the methodological imperatives that impell a work related to *Woman, Native, Other* such as bell hooks's *Talking Back: Thinking Feminist, Thinking Black*.

While the concept of 'talking back' may appear to be both invigorating and empowering to a discourse interested in the reading of gendered race, the text *Talking Back* is curiously engaged in talking to itself; in rejecting Caliban's mode of protest, its critique of colonization is quietly narcissistic in its projection of what a black and thinking female body may appear to be, particularly in the context of its repudiation of the genre of realism. Yet this is the genre, after all, in which African-American feminism continues to seek legitimation: hooks's study is predicated on the anecdotes of lived experience and their capacity to provide an alternative to the discourse of what she terms patriarchal rationalism. Here the unmediated quality of a local voice serves as a substitute for any theoretical agenda that can make more than a cursory connection between the condition of postcolonialism and the question of gendered race. Where hooks claims to speak beyond binarism, her discourse keeps returning to the banality of easy dichotomies: 'Dare I speak to oppressed and oppressor in the same voice? Dare I speak to you in a language that will take us away from the boundaries of domination, a language that will not fence you in, bind you, or hold you? Language is also a place of struggle' (hooks 1989: 28). The acute embarrassment generated by such an idiom could possibly be regarded as a radical rhetorical strategy designed to induce racial discomfort in its audience, but it more frequently registers as black feminism's failure to move beyond the proprietary rights that can be claimed by any oppressed discourse.

As does Trinh's text, hooks's claims that personal narrative is the only salve to the rude abrasions that Western feminist theory has inflicted on the body of ethnicity. The tales of lived experience, however, cannot function as a sufficient alternative, particularly when they are predicated on dangerously literal professions of postcolonialism. *Yearning: Race, Gender, and Cultural Politics*, hooks's more recent work, rehearses a postcolonial fallacy in order to conduct some highly misguided readings of competing feminisms within the context of racial experience. . . .

I proffer life in Pakistan as an example of such a postcolonial and lived experience. Pakistani laws, in fact, pertain more to the discourse of a petrifying realism than do any of the feminist critics whom I have cited thus far. The example at hand takes a convoluted postcolonial point and renders it nationally simple: if a postcolonial nation chooses to embark on an official program of Islamization, the inevitable result in a Muslim state will be legislation that curtails women's rights and institutes in writing what has thus far functioned as the law of the passing word. . . .

It is important to keep in mind that the formulation of the Hudood Ordinances was based on a multicultural premise, even though they were multicultural from the dark side of the moon. These laws were premised on a Muslim notion of *Hadd* and were designed to interfere in a postcolonial criminal legal system that was founded on Anglo-Saxon jurisprudence. According to feminist lawyer Asma Jahangir,

> the Hudood Ordinances were promulgated to bring the criminal legal system of Pakistan in conformity with the injunctions of Islam. . . . Two levels of punishments are introduced in the Ordinances. Two levels of punishment and, correspondingly, two separate sets of rules of evidence are prescribed. The first level or category is the one called the 'Hadd' which literally means the 'limit' and the other 'Tazir', which means 'to punish'.
>
> (Jahangir and Jilani 1990: 24)

The significance of the *Hadd* category is that it delineates immutable sentences: *Tazir* serves only as a safety net in case the accused is not convicted under *Hadd*. These fixed rules are in themselves not very pretty: *Hadd* for theft is amputation of a hand; for armed robbery, amputation of a foot; for rape or adultery committed by married Muslims, death by stoning; for rape or adultery committed by non-Muslims or unmarried Muslims, a hundred public lashes (Jahangir and Jilani 1990: 24). While I am happy to report that the *Hadd* has not yet been executed, the laws remain intact and await their application.

The applicability of these sentences is rendered more murderous and even obscenely ludicrous when the immutability of the *Hadd* punishments is juxtaposed with the contingency of the laws of evidence. If a man is seen stealing a thousand rupees by two adult Muslim males, he could be punished by *Hadd* and his hand would be amputated. If an adult Muslim stole several million rupees and the only available witnesses were women and non-Muslims, he would not qualify for a *Hadd* category and would be tried under the more free-floating *Tazir* instead. 'A gang of men can thus rape all the residents of a women's hostel,' claims Jahangir with understandable outrage, 'but [the] lack of ocular evidence of four Muslim males will rule out the imposition of a Hadd punishment' (Jahangir and Jilani 1990: 49). Such a statement, unfortunately, is not the terrain of rhetoric alone, since the post-Hudood Ordinance application of the Tazir has made the definition of rape an extremely messy business indeed.

Here, then, we turn to *Zina*, and its implications for the Pakistani female body. The Hudood Ordinances have allowed for all too many openings in the boundaries that define rape. Women can now be accused of rape, as can children; laws of mutual consent may easily convert a case of child abuse into a prosecution of the child for *Zina*, for fornication. Furthermore, unmarried men and women can be convicted of having committed rape against each other, since a subsection of the *Zina* offense defines rape as 'one where a man or a woman have illicit sex knowing that they are not validly married to each other' (quoted in Jahangir and Jilani 1990: 58). In other words, fornication is all, and the statistics of the past few years grimly indicate that the real victims of the Hudood Ordinances are women and children, most specifically those who have no access to legal counsel and whose economic status renders them ignorant of their human rights.

Jahangir cites the example of a fifteen-year-old woman, Jehan Mina, who, after her father's death, was raped by her aunt's husband and son. Once her pregnancy was discovered, another relative filed a police report alleging rape. During the trial, however, the accused led no defense, and Mina's testimony alone was sufficient to get her convicted for fornication and sentenced to one hundred public lashes. That child's story is paradigmatic of the untold miseries of those who suffer sentences in Muslim jails.

Let me state the obvious: I cite these alternative realisms and constructions of identity in order to reiterate the problem endemic to post-colonial feminist criticism. It is not the terrors of Islam that have unleashed the Hudood Ordinances on Pakistan, but more probably the United States government's economic and ideological support of a military regime during that bloody but eminently forgotten decade marked by the 'liberation' of Afghanistan. Jehan Mina's story is therefore not so far removed from our current assessment of what it means to be multicultural. How are we to connect her lived experience with the overwhelming realism of the law? In what ways does her testimony force postcolonial and feminist discourse into an acknowledgement of the inherent parochialism and professionalism of our claims?

## NOTE

1   James Clifford's course, 'Travel and Identity in Twentieth-Century Interculture,' was given as the Henry Luce Seminar at Yale University, Fall 1990.

# PART IX

## Language

# *Introduction*

Language is a fundamental site of struggle for post-colonial discourse because the colonial process itself begins in language. The control over language by the imperial centre – whether achieved by displacing native languages, by installing itself as a 'standard' against other variants which are constituted as 'impurities', or by planting the language of empire in a new place – remains the most potent instrument of cultural control. Language provides the terms by which reality may be constituted; it provides the names by which the world may be 'known'. Its system of values – its suppositions, its geography, its concept of history, of difference, its myriad gradations of distinction – becomes the system upon which social, economic and political discourses are grounded.

One of the most subtle demonstrations of the power of language is the means by which it provides, through the function of naming, a technique for knowing a colonised place or people. To name the world is to 'understand' it, to know it and to have control over it. The word 'Africa', for instance, is determined by European historical formations which had little or no relevance to the complex of linguistic cultural and economic factors which tied and sometimes separated various societies on the continent. To name reality is therefore to exert power over it, simply because the dominant language becomes the way in which it is known. In colonial experience this power is by no means vague or abstract. A systematic education and indoctrination installed the language and thus the reality on which it was predicated as preeminent.

There are several responses to this dominance of the imperial language, but two present themselves immediately in the decolonizing process – rejection or subversion. The process of radical decolonisation proposed by Ngugi wa Thiong'o is a good demonstration of the first alternative. Ngugi's programme for restoring an ethnic or national identity embedded in the mother tongue involves a rejection of English, a refusal to use it for his writing, a refusal to accede to the kind of world and reality it appears to name, a refusal to submit to the political dominance its use implies. This stance of rejection rests upon the assumption that an essential Gikuyu identity may be regained, an identity which the language of the coloniser seems to have displaced or dispersed.

283

However, many more writers have felt that this appeal to some essential cultural identity is doomed to failure, indeed, misunderstands the heterogeneous nature of human experience. Ngugi's own essay indicates the divergent reasons fellow African writers had for using the English language, but most involve a confidence that English can be used in the process of *resisting* imperialism. Braj Kachru shows how in the Indian situation the language has provided a neutral vehicle for communication between contesting language groups, while the Indian novelist Raja Rao voices, in a piece written as long ago as 1938, the challenge of the post-colonial writer to adapt the colonial language to local needs. This determination to use the language as an ethnographic tool has been a more common response of post-colonial writers. The appropriation of the language is essentially a subversive strategy, for the adaptation of the 'standard' language to the demands and requirements of the place and society into which it has been appropriated amounts to a far more subtle rejection of the political power of the standard language. In Chinua Achebe's words this is a process by which the language is made to bear the weight and the texture of a different experience. In doing so it becomes a different language. By adapting the alien language to the exigencies of a mother grammar, syntax, vocabulary, and by giving a shape to the variations of the speaking voice, such writers and speakers construct an 'english' which amounts to a very different linguistic vehicle from the received standard colonial 'English'. As Bill Ashcroft demonstrates, the belief that the English text is unable to communicate a 'non-English' cultural meaning is based on a misconception of the way language 'means'. Meaning is seen to be a constitutive interaction within the 'message event'.

The process of language adaptation is linguistically profound because it establishes a medium which fractures the concept of a standard language and installs the 'marginal' variations of language use as the actual network of a particular language. W. H. New demonstrates how language variation produces culturally distinctive writing whether in single language or multiple language societies. The nuances of a settler culture writing can produce as finely realised a set of distinctions as the writing issuing from the meeting of two very distinct language groups. E. K. Brathwaite demonstrates the process of language adaptation in the Caribbean, arguably one of the most dynamic linguistic communities in the world. What he calls 'Nation Language' is a language which, rather than attempting to recover lost origins, demonstrates the vigorous success of linguistic variation in this region.

One of the most detailed examinations of this process has focused on the Anglophone and Francophone speaking communities of West Africa. Chantal Zabus employs the very useful notion of a *palimpsest* to demonstrate how the language practices of a region may be built up through a range of linguistic strategies, one of the most significant of which she calls 'relexification'.

# 49

## The Language of African Literature

### NGUGI WA THIONG'O*

IN 1962 I was invited to that historic meeting of African writers at Makerere University College, Kampala, Uganda.... The title, 'A Conference of African Writers of English Expression', automatically excluded those who wrote in African languages.... The discussions on the novel, the short story, poetry, and drama were based on extracts from works in English and hence they excluded the main body of work in Swahili, Zulu, Yoruba, Arabic, Amharic and other African languages. Yet, despite this exclusion of writers and literature in African languages, no sooner were the introductory preliminaries over than this Conference of 'African Writers of English Expression' sat down to the first item on the agenda: 'What is African Literature?' ...

English, like French and Portuguese, was assumed to be the natural language of literary and even political mediation between African people in the same nation and between nations in Africa and other continents. In some instances these European languages were seen as having a capacity to unite African peoples against divisive tendencies inherent in the multiplicity of African languages within the same geographic state. Thus Ezekiel Mphahlele later could write, in a letter to *Transition* number 11, that English and French have become the common language with which to present a nationalist front against white oppressors, and even 'where the whiteman has already retreated, as in the independent states, these two languages are still a unifying force'. ...

Chinua Achebe, in a speech entitled 'The African Writer and the English Language' (1975), said:

> Is it right that a man should abandon his mother tongue for someone else's? It looks like a dreadful betrayal and produces a guilty feeling. But for me there is no other choice. I have been given the language and I intend to use it.
>
> (Achebe 1975: 62)

* From 'The Language of African Literature' *Decolonising the Mind: The Politics of Language in African Literature* London: James Currey, 1981.

See the paradox: the possibility of using mother-tongues provokes a tone of levity in phrases like 'a dreadful betrayal' and 'a guilty feeling'; but that of foreign languages produces a categorical positive embrace, what Achebe himself, ten years later, was to describe as this 'fatalistic logic of the unassailable position of English in our literature'. . . .

The lengths to which we were prepared to go in our mission of enriching foreign languages by injecting Senghorian 'black blood' into their rusty joints, is best exemplified by Gabriel Okara in an article reprinted in *Transition*:

> As a writer who believes in the utilization of African ideas, African philosophy and African folklore and imagery to the fullest extent possible, I am of the opinion the only way to use them effectively is to translate them almost literally from the African language native to the writer into whatever European language he is using as medium of expression. I have endeavoured in my words to keep as close as possible to the vernacular expressions. For, from a word, a group of words, a sentence and even a name in any African language, one can glean the social norms, attitudes and values of a people.
>
> In order to capture the vivid images of African speech, I had to eschew the habit of expressing my thoughts first in English. It was difficult at first, but I had to learn. I had to study each law expression I used and to discover the probable situation in which it was used in order to bring out the nearest meaning in English. I found it a fascinating exercise.
>
> (Okara 1963: 15)

Why, we may ask, should an African writer, or any writer, become so obsessed by taking from his mother-tongue to enrich other tongues? Why should he see it as his particular mission? We never asked ourselves: how can we enrich our languages? How can we 'prey' on the rich humanist and democratic heritage in the struggles of other peoples in other times and other places to enrich our own? . . . What seemed to worry us more was this: after all the literary gymnastics of preying on our languages to add life and vigour to English and other foreign languages, would the result be accepted as good English or good French? Will the owner of the language criticise our usage? Here we were more assertive of our rights! Chinua Achebe wrote:

> I feel that the English language will be able to carry the weight of my African experience. But it will have to be a new English, still in full communion with its ancestral home but altered to suit new African surroundings.
>
> (1975: 62)

Gabriel Okara's position on this was representative of our generation:

> Some may regard this way of writing English as a desecration of the language. This is of course not true. Living languages grow like living

things, and English is far from a dead language. There are American, West Indian, Australian, Canadian and New Zealand versions of English. All of them add life and vigour to the language while reflecting their own respective cultures. Why shouldn't there be a Nigerian or West African English which we can use to express our own ideas, thinking and philosophy in our own way?

(Okara 1963: 15–16)

How did we arrive at this acceptance of 'the fatalistic logic of the unassailable position of English in our literature', in our culture and in our politics? . . . How did we, as African writers, come to be so feeble towards the claims of our languages on us and so aggressive in our claims on other languages, particularly the languages of our colonisation? . . .

In my view language was the most important vehicle through which that power fascinated and held the soul prisoner. The bullet was the means of the physical subjugation. Language was the means of the spiritual subjugation. Let me illustrate this by drawing upon experiences in my own education, particularly in language and literature.

I was born into a large peasant family father, four wives and about twenty-eight children. I also belonged, as we all did in those days, to a wider extended family and to the community as a whole.

We spoke Gikuyu as we worked in the fields. We spoke Gikuyu in and outside the home. I can vividly recall those evenings of story-telling around the fireside. It was mostly the grown-ups telling the children but everybody was interested and involved. We children would re-tell the stories the following day to other children who worked in the fields picking the pyrethrum flowers, tea-leaves or coffee beans of our European and African landlords. . . .

There were good and bad story-tellers. A good one could tell the same story over and over again, and it would always be fresh to us, the listeners. He or she could tell a story told by someone else and make it more alive and dramatic. The differences really were in the use of words and images and the inflexion of voices to effect different tones.

We therefore learnt to value words for their meaning and nuances. Language was not a mere string of words. It had a suggestive power well beyond the immediate and lexical meaning. Our appreciation of the suggestive magical power of language was reinforced by the games we played with words through riddles, proverbs, transpositions of syllables, or through nonsensical but musically arranged words. So we learnt the music of our language on top of the content. The language, through images and symbols, gave us a view of the world, but it had a beauty of its own. The home and the field were then our pre-primary school but what is important, for this discussion, is that the language of our evening teach-ins, and the language of our immediate and wider community, and the language of our work in the fields were one.

And then I went to school, a colonial school, and this harmony was broken. The language of my education was no longer the language of my culture. I first went to Kamaandura, missionary run, and then to another called Maanguuu run by nationalists grouped around the Gikuyu Independent and Karinga Schools Association. Our language of education was still Gikuyu. The very first time I was ever given an ovation for my writing was over a composition in Gikuyu. So for my first four years there was still harmony between the language of my formal education and that of the Limuru peasant community.

It was after the declaration of a state of emergency over Kenya in 1952 that all the schools run by patriotic nationalists were taken over by the colonial regime and were placed under District Education Boards chaired by Englishmen. English became the language of my formal education. In Kenya, English became more than a language: it was the language, and all the others had to bow before it in deference.

Thus one of the most humiliating experiences was to be caught speaking Gikuyu in the vicinity of the school. The culprit was given corporal punishment – three to five strokes of the cane on bare buttocks – or was made to carry a metal plate around the neck with inscriptions such as I AM STUPID or I AM A DONKEY. . . .

The attitude to English was the exact opposite: any achievement in spoken or written English was highly rewarded; prizes, prestige, applause; the ticket to higher realms. English became the measure of intelligence and ability in the arts, the sciences, and all the other branches of learning. English became the main determinant of a child's progress up the ladder of formal education. . . . Literary education was now determined by the dominant language while also reinforcing that dominance. Orature (oral literature) in Kenyan languages stopped. . . .

Thus language and literature were taking us further and further from ourselves to other selves, from our world to other worlds.

What was the colonial system doing to us Kenyan children? What were the consequences of, on the one hand, this systematic suppression of our languages and the literature they carried, and on the other the elevation of English and the literature it carried? To answer those questions, let me first examine the relationship of language to human experience, human culture, and the human perception of reality. . . .

Language as communication has three aspects or elements. There is first what Karl Marx once called the language of real life, the element basic to the whole notion of language, its origins and development: that is, the relations people enter into with one another in the labour process, the links they necessarily establish among themselves in the act of a people, a community of human beings, producing wealth or means of life like food, clothing, houses. A human community really starts its historical being as a community of co-operation in production through the division of labour;

the simplest is between man, woman and child within a household; the more complex divisions are between branches of production such as those who are sole hunters, sole gatherers of fruits or sole workers in metal. Then there are the most complex divisions such as those in modern factories where a single product, say a shirt or a shoe, is the result of many hands and minds. Production is co-operation, is communication, is language, is expression of a relation between human beings and it is specifically human.

The second aspect of language as communication is speech and it imitates the language of real life, that is communication in production. The verbal signposts both reflect and aid communication or the relations established between human beings in the production of their means of life. Language as a system of verbal signposts makes that production possible. The spoken word is to relations between human beings what the hand is to the relations between human beings and nature. The hand through tools mediates between human beings and nature and forms the language of real life: spoken words mediate between human beings and form the language of speech.

The third aspect is the written signs. The written word imitates the spoken. Where the first two aspects of language as communication through the hand and the spoken word historically evolved more or less simultaneously, the written aspect is a much later historical development. Writing is representation of sounds with visual symbols, from the simplest knot among shepherds to tell the number in a herd or the hieroglyphics among the Agikuyu gicaandi singers and poets of Kenya, to the most complicated and different letter and picture writing systems of the world today. . . .

But there is more to it: communication between human beings is also the basis and process of evolving culture. In doing similar kinds of things and actions over and over again under similar circumstances, similar even in their mutability, certain patterns, moves, rhythms, habits, attitudes, experiences and knowledge emerge. Those experiences are handed over to the next generation and become the inherited basis for their further actions on nature and on themselves. There is a gradual accumulation of values which in time become almost self-evident truths governing their conception of what is right and wrong, good and bad, beautiful and ugly, courageous and cowardly, generous and mean in their internal and external relations. Over a time this becomes a way of life distinguishable from other ways of life. They develop a distinctive culture and history. Culture embodies those moral, ethical and aesthetic values, the set of spiritual eyeglasses, through which they come to view themselves and their place in the universe. Values are the basis of a people's identity, their sense of particularity as members of the human race. All this is carried by language. Language as culture is the collective memory bank of a people's experience in history. Culture is almost indistinguishable from the language that makes possible its genesis, growth, banking, articulation and indeed its transmission from one generation to the next. . . .

Language as communication and as culture are then products of each other. Communication creates culture: culture is a means of communication. Language carries culture, and culture carries, particularly through orature and literature, the entire body of values by which we come to perceive ourselves and our place in the world. How people perceive themselves affects how they look at their culture, at their politics and at the social production of wealth, at their entire relationship to nature and to other beings. Language is thus inseparable from ourselves as a community of human beings with a specific form and character, a specific history, a specific relationship to the world. . . .

I believe that my writing in the Gikuyu language, a Kenyan language, an African language, is part and parcel of the anti-imperialist struggles of Kenyan and African peoples. In schools and universities our Kenyan languages – that is the languages of the many nationalities which make up Kenya – were associated with negative qualities of backwardness, under-development, humiliation and punishment. . . .

So I would like to contribute towards the restoration of the harmony between all aspects and divisions of language so as to restore the Kenyan child to his environment, understand it fully so as to be in a position to change it for his collective good. I would like to see Kenya peoples' mother-tongues (our national languages!) carry a literature reflecting not only the rhythms of a child's spoken expression, but also his struggle with his nature and his social nature.

But writing in our languages per se – although a necessary first step in the correct direction – will not itself bring about the renaissance in African cultures if that literature does not carry the content of our peoples' anti-imperialist struggles to liberate their productive forces from foreign control. . . .

In other words writers in African languages should reconnect themselves to the revolutionary traditions of an organised peasantry and working class in Africa in their struggle to defeat imperialism and create a higher system of democracy and socialism in alliance with all other peoples of the world.

# 50

---

# *The Alchemy of English*

## Braj B. Kachru*

[T]HE ENGLISH LANGUAGE is a tool of power, domination and elitist identity, and of communication across continents. Although the era of the 'White man's burden' has practically ended in a political sense, and the Raj has retreated to native shores, the linguistic and cultural consequences of imperialism have changed the global scene. The linguistic ecology of, for example, Africa and Asia is not the same. English has become an integral part of this new complex sociolinguistic setting. The colonial Englishes were essentially acquired and used as non-native second languages, and after more than two centuries, they continue to have the same status. The *non-nativeness* of such varieties is not only an attitudinally significant term, but it also has linguistic and sociolinguistic significance. . . .

In India, only Sanskrit, English, Hindi and to some extent Persian have acquired pan-Indian intranational functions. The domains of Sanskrit are restricted, and the proficiency in it limited, except in the case of some professional pandits. The cause of Hindi was not helped by the controversy between Hindi, Urdu and Hindustani. Support for Hindustani almost ended with independence; after the death of its ardent and influential supporter, Gandhi, very little was heard about it. The enthusiasm and near euphoria of the supporters of Hindi were not channeled in a constructive (and realistic) direction, especially after the 1940s. The result is that English continues to be a language both of power and of prestige.

For governments, English thus serves at least two purposes. First, it continues to provide a linguistic tool for the administrative cohesiveness of a country (as in South Asia and parts of Africa). Second, at another level, it provides a language of wider communication (national and international). The enthusiasm for English is not unanimous, or even widespread. The disadvantages of using it are obvious: cultural and social implications accompany the use of an external language. But the native languages are losing in this competition.

* From *The Alchemy of English: The Spread, Functions and Models of Non-Native Englishes* Oxford: Pergamon Institute, 1986.

English does have one clear advantage, attitudinally and linguistically: it has acquired a *neutrality* in a linguistic context where native languages, dialects, and styles sometimes have acquired undesirable connotations. Whereas native codes are functionally marked in terms of caste, religion, region, and so forth, English has no such 'markers,' at least in the non-native context. It was originally the foreign (alien) ruler's language, but that drawback is often overshadowed by what it can do for its users. True, English is associated with a small and elite group; but it is in their role that the *neutrality* of a language becomes vital (e.g. for Tamil speakers in Tamil Nadu, or Bengali speakers in West Bengal). In India the most widely used language is Hindi (46 percent) and its different varieties (e.g., Hindustani, Urdu), have traditionally been associated with various factions: Hindi with the Hindus; Urdu with the Muslims; and Hindustani with the maneuvering political pandits who could not create a constituency for it. While these attitudinal allocations are not necessarily valid, this is how the varieties have been perceived and presented. English, on the other hand, is not associated with any religious or ethnic faction.

Whatever the limitations of English, it has been perceived as the language of power and opportunity, free of the limitations that the ambitious attribute to the native languages.

## ATTITUDINAL NEUTRALITY AND POWER

In several earlier studies it has been shown (Kachru 1978 and 1982a) that in *code-mixing*, for example, English is being used to *neutralize* identities one is reluctant to express by the use of native languages or dialects. 'Code-mixing' refers to the use of lexical items or phrases from one code in the stream of discourse of another. Neutralization thus is a linguistic strategy used to 'unload' a linguistic item from its traditional, cultural and emotional connotations by avoiding its use and choosing an item from another code. The borrowed item has referential meaning, but no cultural connotations in the context of the specific culture. This is not borrowing in the sense of filling a lexical gap. . . . In Kashmiri the native word *mɔnd* ('widow') invokes the traditional connotations associated with widowhood. Its use is restricted to abuses and curses, not occurring in 'polished' conversation. *vedvā* (Hindi *vidhwā*) or English *widow* is preferred by the Hindus. In Tamil, as shown by Annamalai (1978) *maccaan* and *attimbeer* reveal the caste identity of the speaker – not desirable in certain situations. Therefore, one uses English *brother-in-law*, instead. English *rice* is neutral compared with *saadam* or *soru* (purist) in Tamil. A lexical item may be associated with a specific style in the native language as are *manaivi* (formal) and *pendītti* (colloquial) in Tamil, but the English equivalent *wife* has no style restrictions.

In such contexts, then, the power of neutralization is associated with English in two ways. First, English provides – with or without 'mixing' –

292

an additional code that has referential meaning but no cultural overtones or connotations. . . . Second, such use of English develops new code-mixed varieties of languages. Lexicalization from English is particularly preferred in the contexts of kinship, taboo items, science and technology, or in discussing sex organs and death. What Moag (1982: 276) terms the 'social neutrality' of English in the case of Fiji is applicable in almost all the countries where English is used as a non-native language. In the Fijian context, Tongans and Fijians

> find English the only safe medium in which to address those of higher status. English not only hides their inability in the specialized vernacular registers, but also allows them to meet traditional superiors on a more or less equal footing

> (276). . . .

## CONTACT LITERATURES IN ENGLISH: CREATIVITY IN THE OTHER TONGUE

The contact literatures in English have several characteristics, of which two may be mentioned here. In South Asia, to take one example, there are three more or less pan-South Asian literatures: Sanskrit, Persian, and Hindi. In terms of both style and content, Sanskrit has been associated with the native Hindu tradition. Persian (in its Indian form) and Urdu have maintained the Perso-Arabic stylistic devices, metaphors and symbolism. It is this aspect of Urdu that alienated it from the traditionalist Hindus, who believe that in its formal experimentation, thematic range, and metaphor, it has maintained an 'un-Indian' (Islamic) tradition, and continues to seek inspiration from such non-native traditions. This attitude toward Urdu tells only part of the story, and negates the contribution that the Hindus have made to the Urdu language, and the way it was used as the language of national revival. Indian English literature cuts across these attitudes. It has united certain pan-South Asian nationalists, intellectuals, and creative writers. It has provided a new perspective in India through an 'alien' language.

In Indian English fiction (see e.g. Mukherjee 1971; Parameswaran 1976) R. K. Narayan, Mulk Raj Anand, and Raja Rao (e.g. his *Kanthapura*) have brought another dimension to the understanding of the regional, social and political contexts. In this process, linguistically speaking, the process of the Indianization of English has acquired an institutionalized status.

In a sociological sense, then, English has provided a linguistic tool and a sociopolitical dimension very different from those available through native linguistic tools and traditions. A non-native writer in English functions in two traditions. In psychological terms, such a multilingual role calls for adjustment. In attitudinal terms, it is controversial; in linguistic terms, it is challenging, for it means molding the language for new contexts. Such a writer is suspect as fostering new beliefs, new value systems, and even new linguistic loyalties and innovations.

This, then, leads us to the other side of this controversy. For example, what have been the implications of such a change – attitudinally and sociologically – for the Indian languages (and for African languages) and for those speakers whose linguistic repertoires do not include English? Additionally, we need to ask what are its implications for creative writers whose media are 'major' or 'minor' Indian languages?

## POST-COLONIAL PERIOD

Since independence, the controversy about English has taken new forms. Its alien power base is less an issue; so is its Englishness or Americanness in a cultural sense. The English language is not perceived as necessarily imparting only Western traditions. The medium is non-native, but the message is not. In several Asian and African countries, English now has national and international functions that are both distinct and complementary. English has thus acquired a new power base and a new elitism. The domains of English have been restructured ... people ask is English really a non-native ('alien') language for India, for Africa, for South East Asia?

In the case of India one wonders: has India played the age-old trick on English too, of nativizing it and acculturating it – in other words, Indianizing it? The Indian writer and philosopher Raja Rao associates power with English, which, in his mind is equal if not greater than Sanskrit, when he says:

> Truth, said a great Indian sage, is not the monopoly of the Sanskrit language. Truth can use any language, and the more universal, the better it is. If metaphysics is India's primary contribution to world civilization, as we believe it is, then must she use the most universal language for her to be universal.... And as long as the English language is universal it will always remain Indian. ... It would then be correct to say as long as we are Indian – that is, not nationalists, but truly Indians of the Indian psyche – we shall have the English language with us and amongst us, and not as a guest or friend, but as one of our own, of our caste, our creed, our sect and our tradition.
>
> (Rao 1978: 421)

These new power bases in Africa or in Asia have called into question the traditionally accepted, externally normative standards for the institutionalized varieties. The new varieties have their own linguistic and cultural ecologies or sociological contexts. The adaptation to these new ecologies has given non-native Englishes new identities. ...

One might say that contemporary English does not have just one defining context but many – across cultures and languages. This is also true of the growing new literatures in English. The concepts of 'British literature' or 'American literature' represent only part of the spectrum. The new traditions – really not so new – must be incorporated into the tradition of 'literature[s] in English' (Narasimhaiah 1978). . . .

The alchemy of English (present and future), then, does not only provide social status, it also gives access to attitudinally and materially desirable domains of power and knowledge. It provides a powerful linguistic tool for manipulation and control. In addition, this alchemy of English has left a deep mark on the languages and literature of the non-western world. English has thus caused transmutation of languages, equipping them in the process for new societal, scientific and technological demands. The process of Englishization has initiated stylistic and thematic innovations, and has 'modernized' registers. The power of English is so dominant that a new caste of English-using speech fellowships has developed across cultures and languages. It may be relatively small, but it is powerful, and its values and perspectives are not necessarily in harmony with the traditional values of these societies. In the past, the control and manipulation of international power have never been in the hands of users of one language group. Now we see a shift of power from the traditional caste structure; in the process, a new caste has developed. In this sense, English has been instrumental in a vital social change, and not only in that of language and literatures.

# 51

# *Language and Spirit*

## Raja Rao*

There is no village in India, however mean, that has not a rich *sthala-purana*, or legendary history, of its own. Some god or godlike hero has passed by the village – Rama might have rested under this pipal-tree, Sita might have dried her clothes, after her bath, on this yellow stone, or the Mahatma himself, on one of his many pilgrimages through the country, might have slept in this hut, the low one by the village gate. In this way the past mingles with the present, and the gods mingle with men to make the repertory of your grandmother always bright. One such story from the contemporary annals of a village I have tried to tell.

The telling has not been easy. One has to convey in a language that is not one's own the spirit that is one's own. One has to convey the various shades and omissions of a certain thought-movement that looks maltreated in an alien language. I use the word 'alien,' yet English is not really an alien language to us. It is the language of our intellectual make-up – like Sanskrit or Persian was before – but not of our emotional make-up. We are all instinctively bilingual, many of us writing in our own language and in English. We cannot write like the English. We should not. We cannot write only as Indians. We have grown to look at the large world as part of us. Our method of expression therefore has to be a dialect which will some day prove to be as distinctive and colorful as the Irish or the American. Time alone will justify it.

After language the next problem is that of style. The tempo of Indian life must be infused into our English expression, even as the tempo of American or Irish life has gone into the making of theirs. We, in India, think quickly, we talk quickly, and when we move we move quickly. There must be something in the sun of India that makes us rush and tumble and run on. And our paths are paths interminable. The *Mahabharata* has 214,778 verses and the *Rama-yana* 48,000. The *Puranas* are endless and innumerable. We have neither punctuation nor the treacherous 'ats' and

* 'Author's Foreword' *Kanthapura* [1938] Bombay: New Directions, 1963.

'ons' to bother us – we tell one interminable tale. Episode follows episode, and when our thoughts stop our breath stops, and we move on to another thought. This was and still is the ordinary style of our storytelling. I have tried to follow it myself in this story.

It may have been told of an evening, when as the dusk falls, and through the sudden quiet, lights leap up in house and after house, and stretching her bedding on the veranda, a grandmother might have told you, newcomer, the sad tale of her village.

# 52

## Constitutive Graphonomy

### BILL ASHCROFT*

THE WRITTEN TEXT is a social situation. That is to say, it has its existence in something more than the marks on the page, namely in the participations of social beings whom we call writers and readers, who constitute the writing as communication of a particular kind, as 'saying' a certain thing. When these participants exist in different cultures, two issues quickly come to the forefront: can writing in one language convey the reality of a different culture? and can a reader fully understand a different cultural reality being communicated in the text? . . . Constitutive Graphonomy, the constitutive ethnography of writing systems, attempts to answer these questions by examining the 'objective' meanings of writing as a process of social accomplishment between the participants. Meaning is a social fact which comes to being within the discourse of a culture, and social facts as well as social structures are themselves social accomplishments.

Clearly the notion of the text as dialogical accomplishment requires some clarification since our assumption of the givenness of texts is supported at the very least by the evidence of their physical tangibility. To the question, 'How do you mean?', we could say that the *meaning* of a word is *meant* by the person who utters it and is *taken to mean* something by the person who hears it. As a radical oversimplification of the history of European literary theory we could say that such history has been an arena in which all of these participants: the language, the utterer or writer, and the hearer or reader, have been locked in a gladitorial contest over the ownership of meaning. But on closer examination it can be seen that all three 'functions' of this exchange participate in the 'social' situation of the written text.

Meaning is a social accomplishment characterised by the participation of the writer and reader functions within the 'event' of the particular discourse. To take into account the necessary presence of these functions

* From 'Constitutive Graphonomy: A Post-colonial Theory of Literary Writing' in Stephen Slemon and Helen Tiffin (eds) *After Europe: Critical Theory and Post-colonial Writing* Mundelstrup: Dangaroo, 1989.

and the situation in which the meaning occurs the meaning may be called a 'situated accomplishment'. It is easy to see the understanding reached in conversation as a 'situated accomplishment' for the face-to-face interaction enables a virtually limitless adjustment to the flow of talk. The central feature of such activity is *presence*, the presence of the speaker and the hearer to each other constituting language as communication. Yet even in the most empathetic exchange the speaker and hearer are never really 'present' to one another. The experience of one conversant can never *become* the experience of the other, the 'mind' is a retrospective and largely hypothetical concommitant to what is 'revealed' in language. Meaning and the understanding of meaning can occur because the language encodes the reciprocity of the experiences of each conversant. It is the situation, the '*event*' of this reciprocal happening which 'tells', which 'refers', which 'informs'.

This helps us to reassess traditional approaches to meaning such as those in speech act theory (Austin 1962). While we can inscribe the propositional content of a speech act we cannot, for instance, inscribe its illocutionary force. Such force is carried in the situation of the message. The illocutionary and perlocutionary force of the sign THIS WAY are embodied entirely in its character as sign and the social conventions surrounding its role. Similar conventions surround and determine the forms of different kinds of writing, particularly those given the designation 'literary'. The illocutionary force (and, by extension, we might say the *cultural* force) of these texts similarly cannot be *conveyed* by means of grammar, italics, punctuation, but rather actualised constitutively in the conventional practice – the situation – of the reading. The writing 'event' thus becomes the centre of the accomplishment of meaning, for it is here that the system, the social world of its users and the absent 'participants' themselves, intersect.

Post-colonial writing affirms the primacy of the message event because the immense 'distance' between author and reader in the cross-cultural or sub-cultural text undermines the privilege of both subject and object and opens meaning to a relational dialectic which 'emancipates' it. This emancipation, however, is limited by the 'absence' which is often inscribed in the cross-cultural text – the gulf of silence or 'metonymic gap' (Ashcroft, Griffiths and Tiffin 1989: 51–9) installed by strategies of language variance which signify its difference. It is precisely cultural *difference* rather than cultural *identity* which is installed in this way because identity itself is the function of a network of differences rather than an essence. Inscription therefore does not 'create meaning' by enregistering it, rather, it initiates meaning to a horizon of relationships circumscribed by that silence which ultimately resists complete interpretation. It is this silence, the metonymic assertion of the post-colonial text's difference, which resists the absorption of post-colonial literature into a universalist paradigm. We can thus see how important is the cross-cultural literary text in questions of signification. Nothing better describes to us the distance traversed in the social engagement which occurs when authors write and readers read. But it is clear that the distances *are* traversed. Writing comes into being at the intersection of the sites of production and consumption. Although the 'social relationship' of the two absent subjects is actually a function of their access to the 'situation' of the writing, it is in this threefold interaction of situation, author function, and reader function that meaning is accomplished.

## LANGUAGE

The first contender for the 'ownership' of meaning is language, commonly held to embody or contain meaning either by direct representation or in a more subtle way by determining the perception of the world. Language in post-colonial societies, characterised as it is by complexity, hybridity and constant change, inevitably rejects the assumption of a linguistic structure or code which can be described by the colonial distinction of 'standard' and 'variant'. All language is 'marginal', all language emerges out of conflict and struggle. The post-colonial text brings language and meaning to a discursive site in which they are mutually constituted, and at this site the importance of usage is inescapable.

Words are never simply referential in the actual dynamic habits of a speaking community. Even the most simple words like 'hot', 'big', 'man', 'got', 'ball', 'bat', have a number of meanings, depending on how they are used. Indeed, these uses are the ways (and therefore what) the word means in certain circumstances. In his novel *The Voice* Gabriel Okara (1970) demonstrates the almost limitless prolixity of the words 'inside' and 'insides' to describe the whole range of human volition, experience, emotion and thought. Brought to the site of meaning which stands at the intersection between two separate cultures, the word demonstrates the total dependence of that meaning upon its 'situated-ness'.

Language cannot, therefore, be said to perform its function by reflecting or referring to the world in a purely contingent way, and thus meanings cannot remain exclusively accessible to those 'native' speakers who 'experience their referents', so to speak. The central feature of the ways in which words mean things in spoken or written discourse is the situation of the word. The ranges of 'nuance' and 'connotation' which are sometimes held to be the key to the incommunicability of cultural *experience* are simply functions of that situation. This is particularly important for its dismantling of the claims that a particular language has an essential and exclusive capacity to convey cultural truth. In general, one may see how the word is meant by the way it functions in the sentence, but the meaning of a word may require considerably more than a sentence for it to be adequately situated. The question remains whether it is the responsibility of the author in the cross-cultural text to employ techniques which more promptly 'situate' the word or phrase for the reader. While post-colonial writing has led to a profusion of technical innovation which exists to span the purported gap between writer and prospective reader, the process of reading itself is a continual process of contextualisation and adjustment directly linked to the constitutive relations within the discursive event.

An alternative, determinist view, proposed by Whorf and Sapir, that language actually constructs the perceptions and experiences of speakers seems less problematic. The central idea of Whorf and Sapir's thesis is well known (see Sapir 1931 and Whorf 1952), proposing that language functions not simply as a device for reporting experience, but also, and more significantly, as a way of defining experience for its speakers. But even this more attractive view of the link between language and the world may give rise to a number of objections from constitutive theory. Clearly, language offers one set of categories and not another for speakers to organise and describe experience, but should we therefore assume that language *creates* meanings in the minds of speakers? While it is quite clear that language is more than a 'reproducing instrument for voicing ideas' (for what do thoughts or ideas look like apart from their expression in language?) the same objections can be applied to the idea of language as the 'shaper' or 'programmer' of ideas. Such ideas are still inaccessible apart from language. To possess a language is to possess a technique, not necessarily a quantum of knowledge about the world.

It is the situation of discourse, then, rather than the linguistic system in the speaker's mind in which the 'obligatory terms' of language are structured. The meaning and nature of perceived reality are not determined within the minds of the users, nor even within the language itself, but within the use, within the multiplicity of relationships which operate in the system. Margaret Atwood makes an interesting reference to a North American Indian language which has no noun-forms, only verb-forms. In such a linguistic culture the experience of the world remains in continual process. Such a language cannot exist if language is either anterior or posterior to the world but reinforces the notion that language inhabits the world, *in practice*. The semantic component of the sentence is contained in the syntax: the meaning of a word or phrase is its use in the language, a use which has nothing to do with the kind of world a user 'has in his or her head'.

What the speaker 'has in mind', like a linguistic system or culture, or intentions or meanings, are only accessible in the 'retrospective' performance of speaking. The categories which language offers to describe the world are easily mistaken to shape something in the mind because we naturally assume that, like the rules of chess, we hold the linguistic system 'in our minds', in advance of the world. But language is co-extensive with social reality, not because it causes a certain perception of the world, but because it is inextricable from that perception.

Languages exist, therefore, neither before the fact nor after the fact but *in the fact*.

If the written text is a social situation the post-colonial text empha-sises the central problem of this situation, the 'absence' of those 'functions' in the text which operate to constitute the discursive event as communi-cation: the 'writer' and 'reader'. The Author, with its vision and intentions, its 'gifted creative insight', has historically exerted the strongest claim upon the meaning of writing. But how *does* the non-English speaker, for instance, mean anything in English? Firstly, writers, like the language, are subject to the *situation*, in that they must say something *meanable*. This does not mean they cannot alter the language, to use it neologistically and creatively, but they are limited *as any speaker is limited* to a situation in which words have meaning. Literature, and particularly narrative, has the capacity to domesticate even the most alien experience. It does not need to *reproduce* the experience to signify its nature. The processes of understanding are therefore not limited to the minds of speakers of one mother tongue and denied the speakers of another. Meaning and understanding exist outside the mind, within the engagement of speakers using the language. Understanding is not a function of what goes on in the 'mind' at all, but a location of the word in the 'message event' – that point at which the language, the writer and reader coincide to produce the meaning. The cultural 'distance' detected at this point is not a result of the inability of language to communicate, but a product of the 'metonymic gap' installed by strategies of language variance which themselves signify a post-colonial identity.

# 53

## New Language, New World

### W. H. NEW*

In critical commentaries which have been published over the last few decades, there has been some controversy about whether English is an acceptable literary language in the Commonwealth. The arguments have been variously literary and political. Some critics have rejected the English language as a suitable vehicle for local expression, asserting the incompatibility of local thought and English words, English syntax, English style. Others, adhering to the notion of a single English literary tradition, find England's literature to embody the excellences to which 'peripheral' literatures must aspire. Still other writers, spurning British literary models, accept American ones, and consequently run the risk of merely transferring their colonial allegiance; while those who totally reject America appear to ignore how much their own cultures make use of the international technical language to which America has so largely contributed during the twentieth century. Whether the impulse is to attach oneself to Great Traditions or to sever oneself from them, there is general agreement in all these stances about one thing: language affirms a set of social patterns and reflects a particular cultural taste. Writers who imitate the language of another culture, therefore, allow themselves to be defined by it. The best of the Commonwealth writers who do use English, however, have done more than just use the language; they have also modified it, in the process generating alternative literary possibilities.

They have not simply substituted one set of words for another . . . The plain fact is that a new lexicon is not simple to use. English is an absorptive language and takes words like *Kookaburra* and *tomahawk* quite readily into its lexicon. But new words – invented, borrowed, or however devised in any given culture – have their own resonances, their own connotations. In use, they demand an appropriate formal context – sometimes even a new syntax – if they are to make sense. Failing to control form

* From 'New Language, New World' in C. D. Narasimhaiah (ed.) *Awakened Conscience: Studies in Commonwealth Literature* London: Heinemann, 1978.

would result in pastiche and be equally as barren as imitation. This problem is even more acute in the cases where a society has adapted old words to new situations. The Europeans who early arrived in Canada, for example, in effect rewrote the environment when they applied European terms to it. . . .

Plainly, writers who are striving to evoke the voices of their society will make creative use of the words in that society, whether or not they are all common parlance, all from the same rootstock, or all spoken by the same group. The *combination* of words creates a formal context while it creates a literary world. It establishes sound, structural order, and structural rhythm both as inseparable extensions of a lexicon and as inherent contributors to meaning. . . .

When we read Allen Curnow's 1941 poem 'House and Land', we are conscious of a related literary device. Once more there are hints of the English language being used outside the English cultural ambience and once more it is not the lexicon alone which is creating the difference. Here, however, we are aware not so much of a combination between a non-English vocabulary with English principles of structure as of a marriage between the poem's structural organisation and its dependence on idiom and accent. It is a poem to be heard, a poem that depends on the nuances of the spoken word, and it appears straightforward only if as critical listeners we fail to perceive its four separate voices. Three of its personae are clearly specified: old Miss Wilson, remnant of a transplanted English family, with English attitudes to language and landscape; the cowman, phlegmatic and idiomatic; and the historian, educated out of the broadest of local accents and intellectualising about the identity of this locale. Responding to all three and providing a context for them is the fourth voice, the ironic one of the narrator. The resulting poem is a play of separate monologues, which sounds something like this (I have distorted Curnow's stanzaic pattern to separate the four voices):

Wasn't this the site, asked the historian, of the original homestead?
Couldn't tell you, said the cowman;

I just live here, he said,
Working for old Miss Wilson
Since the old man's been dead.

Moping under the bluegums
The dog trailed his chain
From the privy as far as the fowlhouse
And back to the privy again,
Feeling the stagnant afternoon
Quicken with the smell of rain.

There sat old Miss Wilson.
With her pictures on the wall,

The baronet uncle, mother's side,
And one she called
Taking tea from a silver pot
For fear the house might fall.

People in the *colonies*, she said,
Can't quite understand . . .
Why, from Waiau to the mountains
It was all father's land,

She's all of eighty said the cowman,
Down at the milking-shed
I'm leaving here next winter.
Too bloody quiet, he said. . . .
                    (Curnow 1962: 5–6)

Quite clearly the poem has Curnow's own stamp on it.. . . . The language
has contrived to convey a recognisable cultural sensibility, not just an individual one . . . which expresses – to quote from another Curnow poem,
'The Unhistoric Story' – 'something different, something/Nobody counted
on' (7).

This situation is not unrelated to the point which John Figueroa makes
about Creole syntax and dialect in Derek Walcott's 'Tales of the Islands,
Chap. VI'. Showing how Walcott holds standard and non-standard lexical
and grammatical items in a tightly controlled relationship, Figueroa writes
that Walcott is

> an innovator. He is not only reproducing 'the dialect' as the 'true'
> speech of a certain person; he is also embodying and expressing
> through the very heterogoneity of our language situation a certain
> basic relationship (in the West Indies) between 'fete' and angst;
> between 'Oxbridge guys' and 'native art'; between two kinds of cele-
> bration. And he does this partly by his masterly use of the Creole
> base which breaks through all the Oxbridge and the existentialist
> 'philosophy' in the shape of 'we has none.'
>   In the space of one sonnet he significantly uses the variety of speech
> and language which exists in the Creole situation – he uses this variety
> to do what could not be done in an homogeneous speech community.
> In other words he turns a situation often considered to be confusing
> and somehow 'backward' entirely to his, and our, advantage.
>                     (Figueroa 1970: 227–8)

Literature which uses the actual language – the sounds and syntax – of
the people becomes, then, an arena in which the people's political and
psychological tensions can find expression. The linguistic contrarieties
that are part of such 'actual language' both derive from and convey
the tensions in the society. And the literary form that can sustain the
verbal tensions becomes a means of celebrating, or exposing, or at least

recognising and communicating particular social realities. The realities existed before the form was devised; the language also existed before the form was found that could accommodate it. The problem of writing, which authors faced and resolved, turns at this point into a problem of reading, for critics to appreciate and unravel.

Turning to Edward Brathwaite's trilogy *The Arrivants*, we are made aware of yet another extension of literary uses of language. A work like Curnow's makes us conscious of the relationship between lexicon and phonology, conscious of the simple fact that we must hear the sounds of the words we read. A work like Brathwaite's focuses our attention on sound itself, on ways in which sound – by both rhythm and syllable – communicates meaning. That Brathwaite makes deliberate use of a number of different rhythms in his poem is obvious even at first listening. Calypso, limbo, blues, reggae, speech rhythms, drum rhythms, syllables that mimic crow noises and syllables that emulate rain: all these are sounded. They provide some of the clearest examples of poetic lines being crafted with movement in mind as well as literal meaning. Part of the 'Calypso' section, for example, reads as follows:

> Steel drum steel drum
> hit the hot calypso dancing
> hot rum hot rum
> who goin' stop this bacchanalling?
>
> For we glance the banjo
> dance the limbo
> grow our crops by maljo
>
> have loose morals
> gather corals
> father our neighbour's quarrels
>
> perhaps when they come
> with their cameras and straw
> hats: sacred pink tourists from the frozen Nawth
>
> we should get down to those
> white beaches
> where if we don't wear breeches
> it becomes an island dance
> Some people do in' tt'ell
> while others are catchin' hell
> O the boss gave our Johnny the sack
> though we beg him please
> please to tak 'im back
> so the boy now nigratin' overseas. . . .
>
> (Brathwaite 1973: 49–50)

The uprooting and transplanting of African culture that took place when Africans were taken to the Caribbean led inevitably to variations on the parent pattern. The development of European languages as native tongues was one of them. As Brathwaite's poem emphasises, the people of the West Indies are no longer wholly 'African', whatever their ancestral origins, no more than Curnow's New Zealanders are wholly English. Part of Brathwaite's intent is to make this point, and having made it, to return his questing narrator to the islands in order to find his future. All this is bound with a search for godhead and an exploration of what is meant by *possession*: *possessing* and *being possessed*. . . .

Writers themselves have been among the clearest observers of their own linguistic environments, and among the clearest commentators on the relation they find between the language they live with, the culture they live in, and the world they create. In a laconic interview with Graeme Gibson, for example, Dave Godfrey enunciates his sense of a particular literary challenge he faces as a Canadian writer. 'Well,' he said,

> one of the problems is that I work a lot backwards from language, you know; that is, just almost visually I work with words, and musically I work with words. . . . I start with the words, put the words together and the content of the people grows out of the words . . . in a sense you're trying to say things in a different way. You're really trying to open up the language and then you move back to the form part of it. Now in Africa that was very easy to do. I mean you have different dialects, different languages, you have strange kinds of English, you have a lot of new writers writing in different ways. You have a real richness in the people's vocabulary, in the conflicting vocabularies of a different culture and whatnot. Once you start writing about Canada you get into the problem which I ran into in DEATH GOES BETTER WITH COCA COLA, and that is, reticence is the natural form, you know, and you write these kind of tight-lipped stories.
>
> (Godfrey 1972: 163–4)

His book of integrated short stories, *Death Goes Better with Coca Cola* – the title a mordant, culturally activist allusion to an American advertising commercial – is one of his attempts to meet the challenge. Like Dennis Lee and Margaret Laurence, he has attempted to render Canadian cadences. . . .

In India, in 1938, Raja Rao observed in his 'Author's Foreword' to *Kanthapura* that

> the telling has not been easy. One has to convey in a language that is not one's own the spirit that is one's own. . . . We cannot write like the English. We should not. . . . Our method of expression therefore has to be a dialect which will some day prove to be as distinctive and colourful as the Irish or the American. Time alone will justify it.
>
> (Rao [1938] 1963: vii)

And when Chinua Achebe, in the series of essays collected in *Morning Yet on Creation Day*, calls openly and directly for an end to 'colonialist criticism' (1975: 3–18) and for asserting the link between language and truth (37), and for respecting the language which writers actually use (50), he, too, calls attention to the relation between the writer's medium and the writer's world. He reiterated the Commonwealth literary challenge in 1964 when he enunciated clearly his feeling that 'the English language will be able to carry the weight of [his] African experience. But it will have to be a new English, still in full communion with its ancestral home but altered to suit its new African surroundings' (62). What the anonymous Canadian writer in the *Dominion Annual Register* wrote in 1881 – that a new literature 'may borrow the literary forms of the authorcraft of the Old World, but its themes must be those of the New' (Morgan 1882: 282) only went halfway. There are a good many abstract themes one would expect to find straddling international borders, but colonial form will always stand in the way of what, from our various Commonwealth vantage points, we consider creative expression.

# 54

## Nation Language

### EDWARD KAMAU BRATHWAITE*

THE CARIBBEAN IS a set of islands stretching out . . . on an arc of some two thousand miles from Florida through the Atlantic to the South American coast, and they were originally inhabited by Amerindian people: Taino, Siboney, Carib, Arawak. In 1492 Columbus 'discovered' (as it is said) the Caribbean, and with that discovery came the intrusion of European culture and peoples and a fragmentation of the original Amerindian culture. We had Europe 'nationalizing' itself into Spanish, French, English and Dutch so that people had to start speaking (and thinking) four metropolitan languages rather than possibly a single native language. Then with the destruction of the Amerindians, which took place within 30 years of Columbus' discovery (one million dead a year) it was necessary for the Europeans to import new labour bodies into the area. And the most convenient form of labour was the labour on the edge of the *slave* trade winds, the labour on the edge of the hurricane, the labour on the edge of Africa. And so Ashanti, Congo, Yoruba, all that mighty coast of western Africa was imported into the Caribbean. And we had the arrival in our area of a new language structure. It consisted of many languages but basically they had a common semantic and stylistic form. What these languages had to do, however, was to submerge themselves, because officially the conquering peoples – the Spaniards, the English, the French, and the Dutch – insisted that the language of public discourse and conversation, of obedience, command and conception should be English, French, Spanish or Dutch. They did not wish to hear people speaking Ashanti or any of the Congolese languages. So there was a submergence of this imported language. Its status became one of inferiority. Similarly, its speakers were slaves. They were conceived of as inferiors – non-human, in fact. But this very submergence served an interesting intercultural purpose, because although people continued to speak English as it was spoken in Elizabethan

* From *History of the Voice: The Development of Nation Language in Anglophone Caribbean Poetry* London and Port of Spain: New Beacon, 1984.

times and on through the Romantic and Victorian ages, that English was, nonetheless, still being influenced by the underground language, the submerged language that the slaves had brought. And that underground language was itself constantly transforming itself into new forms. It was moving from a purely African form to a form which was African but which was adapted to the new environment and adapted to the cultural imperative of the European languages. And it was influencing the way in which the English, French, Dutch, and Spaniards spoke their own language. So there was a very complex process taking place, which is now beginning to surface in our literature.

Now, as in South Africa (and any area of cultural imperialism for that matter), the educational system of the Caribbean did not recognize the presence of these various languages. What our educational system did was to recognize and maintain the language of the conquistador, the language of the planter, the language of the official, the language of the anglican preacher. It insisted that not only would English be spoken in the anglophone Caribbean, but that the educational system would carry the contours of an English heritage. Hence . . . Shakespeare, George Eliot, Jane Austen – British literature and literary forms, the models which had very little to do, really, with the environment and the reality of non-Europe – were dominant in the Caribbean educational system. It was a very surprising situation. People were forced to learn things which had no relevance to themselves. Paradoxically, in the Caribbean (as in many other 'cultural disaster' areas), the people educated in this system came to know more, even today, about English kings and queens than they do about our own national heroes, our own slave rebels, the people who helped to build and to destroy our society. We are more excited by their literary models, by the concept of, say, Sherwood Forest and Robin Hood than we are by Nanny of the Maroons, a name some of us didn't even know until a few years ago.[1] And in terms of what we write, our perceptual models, we are more conscious (in terms of sensibility) of the falling of snow, for instance – the models are all there for the falling of the snow – than of the force of the hurricanes which take place every year. In other words, we haven't got the syllables, the syllabic intelligence, to describe the hurricane, which is our own experience, whereas we can describe the imported alien experience of the snowfall. It is that kind of situation that we are in.

> The day the first snow fell I floated to my birth of feathers falling by
> my window; touched earth and melted, touched again and left a little
> touch of light and everywhere we touched till earth was white.
>
> (Brathwaite 1975: 7)

This is why there were (are?) Caribbean children who, instead of writing in their 'creole' essays 'the snow was falling on the playing fields of Shropshire' (which is what our children literally were writing until a few years ago, below drawings they made of white snowfields and the corn-haired people who inhabited such a landscape), wrote 'the snow was falling on the cane-fields' trying to have both cultures at the same time.

What is even more important, as we develop this business of emergent language in the Caribbean, is the actual rhythm and the syllables, the very software, in a way, of the language. What English has given us as a model for poetry, and to a lesser extent prose (but poetry is the basic tool here), is the pentameter. . . .

It is *nation language* in the Caribbean that, in fact, largely ignores the pentameter. Nation language is the language which is influenced very strongly by the African model, the African aspect of our New World/Caribbean heritage. English it may be in terms of some of its lexical features. But in its contours, its rhythm and timbre, its sound explosions, it is not English, even though the words, as you hear them, might be English to a greater or lesser degree. And this brings us back to the question . . . can English be a revolutionary language? And the lovely answer that came back was: *it is not English that is the agent. It is not language, but people, who make revolutions.*

I think, however, that language does really have a role to play here – certainly in the Caribbean. But it is an English which is not the standard, imported, educated English, but that of the submerged, surrealist experience and sensibility, which has always been there and which is now increasingly coming to the surface and influencing the perception of contemporary Caribbean people. It is what I call, as I say, *nation language*. I use the term in contrast to *dialect*. The word 'dialect' has been bandied about for a long time, and it carries very pejorative overtones. Dialect is thought of as 'bad English'. Dialect is 'inferior English'. Dialect is the language used when you want to make fun of someone. Caricature speaks in dialect. Dialect has a long history coming from the plantation where people's dignity is distorted through their language and the descriptions which the dialect gave to them. Nation language, on the other hand, is the submerged area of that dialect which is much more closely allied to the African aspect of experience in the Caribbean. It may be in English: but often it is in an English which is like a howl, or a shout or a machine-gun or the wind or a wave. It is also like the blues. And sometimes it is English and African at the same time. I am going to give you some examples. But I should tell you that the reason I have to talk so much is that there has been very little written on this subject. I bring to you the notion of nation language but I can refer you to very little literature, to very few resources. I cannot refer you to what you call an 'Establishment'. . . .

Now I'd like to describe for you some of the characteristics of our nation language. First of all, it is from, as I've said, an oral tradition. The poetry, the culture itself, exists not in a dictionary but in the tradition of the spoken word. It is based as much on sound as it is on song. That is to say, the noise that it makes is part of the meaning, and if you ignore the noise (or what you would think of as noise, shall I say) then you lose part of the meaning. When it is written, you lose the sound or the noise, and therefore you lose part of the meaning. . . .

In order to break down the pentameter, we discovered an ancient form which was always there, the calypso. This is a form that I think nearly everyone knows about. It does not employ the iambic pentameter [IP]. It employs dactyls. It therefore mandates the use of the tongue in a certain way, the use of sound in a certain way. It is a model that we are moving naturally towards now. Compare

(IP)     To be or not to be, that is the question

(Kaiso)     The stone had skidded arc'd and bloomed into islands
Cuba San Domingo
                         Jamaica Puerto Rico (Brathwaite 1967: 48)

But not only is there a difference in syllabic or stress pattern, there is an important difference in shape of intonation. In the Shakespeare (IP above), the voice travels in a single forward plane towards the horizon of its end. In the kaiso, after the skimming movement of the first line, we have a distinct variation. The voice dips and deepens to describe an intervalic pattern. And then there are more ritual forms like *kumina*, like *shango*, the religious forms, which I won't have time to go into here, but which begin to disclose the complexity that is possible with nation language.

The other thing about nation language is that it is part of what may be called total expression. . . . Reading is an isolated, individualistic expression. The oral tradition on the other hand demands not only the griot but the audience to complete the community: the noise and sounds that the maker makes are responded to by the audience and are returned to him. Hence we have the creation of a continuum where meaning truly resides. And this total expression comes about because people be in the open air, because people live in conditions of poverty ('unhouselled') because they come from a historical experience where they had to rely on their very breath rather than on paraphernalia like books and museums and machines. They had to depend on immanence, the power within themselves, rather than the technology outside themselves. . . .

The other model that we have and that we have always had in the Caribbean, as I've said before, is the calypso, and we are going to hear now the Mighty Sparrow singing a *kaiso* which came out in the early sixties. It marked, in fact, the first major change in consciousness that we all shared. . . . In 'Dan is the Man in the Van' he says that the education we got from England has really made us idiots because all of those things that we had to read about – Robin Hood, King Alfred and the Cakes, King Arthur and the Knights of the Round Table – all of these things really haven't given us anything but empty words. And he did it in the calypso form. And you could hear the rhyme-scheme of this poem. He is rhyming on 'n's' and 'l's' and he is creating a cluster of syllables and a counterpoint between voice

312

and orchestra, between individual and community, within the formal notion of 'call and response', which becomes typical of our nation in the revolution.

(Solo)      According, to de education you get when you small
You(ll) grow up wi(th) true ambition an respec for
one an all
But in my days in school they teach me like a fool
THE THINGS THEY TEACH ME A
SHOULDA BEEN A BLOCK-HEADED
MULE

(Chorus) *Pussy has finish his work long ago*
*An now he restin an ting*
*Solomon Agundy was born on a MunDEE*
DE ASS IN DE LION SKIN.
(Sparrow 1963: 86)

I could bring you a book, The Royal Reader, or the one referred to by Sparrow, Nelson's West Indian Reader by J. O. Cutteridge, that we had to learn at school by heart, which contained phrases like: 'the cow jumped over the moon', 'ding dong bell, pussy in the well', 'Twisty & Twirly were two screws' and so on. I mean, that was our beginning of an understanding of literature. 'Literature' started (startled, really) literally at that level, with that kind of model. It was all we had. The problem of transcending this is what I am talking about now. . . .

Today, we have a very confident movement of nation language. In fact, it is inconceivable that any Caribbean poet writing today is not going to be influenced by this submerged/emerging culture. . . . at last, our poets, today, are recognizing that it is essential that they use the resources which have always been there, but which have been denied to them – and which they have sometimes themselves denied.

## NOTE

1   The Maroons were escaped slaves who set up autonomous societies throughout Plantation America. Nanny of the Maroons, an ex-Ashanti Queen Mother, is regarded as one of tbe greatest of the Jamaica freedom fighters. See Brathwaite, *Wars of Respect* (Kingston 1977).

# 55

## Relexification

### CHANTAL ZABUS*

*'Who are you people be? If you are comimg-in people be, then come in.'*

Gabriel Okara, *The Voice.*

SUCH WOULD BE the invitation to the frowning, recalcitrant reader into a realm where a seemingly familiar language conveys an unfamiliar message. When the West African writer attempts to simulate the character of African speech in a Europhone text, some process is at work which has never been adequately described. Indeed, the terminology used to identify such an approach in current literature, whether it be linguistic or literary studies or the writer's own assessment of his method(s), has been misleading because of the confusion with the notion of 'translation' as well as other equally inaccurate terms. Such terms as 'transference' or 'transmutation' have indeed permeated studies with particular reference to West Africa and its literary output in English (see especially Kachru 1982b, Shridar 1982, Bokamba 1982). Against this unsatisfactory nomenclature, I propose the linguistic term 'relexification.'

Loreto Todd's felicitous formulation – 'the relexification of one's mother tongue, using English vocabulary but indigenous structures and rhythms' (Todd 1982: 303) – best describes the process at work when the African language is simulated in the Europhone text. The emphasis is here on the lexis in the original sense of speech, word or phrase and on *lexicon* in reference to the vocabulary and morphemes of a language and, by extension, to word formation. As we shall see, this concept can be expanded to refer to semantics and syntax, as well. I shall thus here redefine relexification as the making of a new register of communication out of an alien lexicon. The adjectives 'new' and 'alien' are particularly relevant in a post-colonial

* From *The African Palimpsest: Indigenization of Language in the West African Europhone Novel* Cross Cultures 4, Amsterdam and Atlanta GA: Rodopi, 1991.

context in which the European language remains alien or irreducibly 'other' to a large majority of the West African population . . . and a 'new' language is being forged as a result of the particular language-contact situation in West Africa and the artist's imaginative use of that situation.

Relexification is often diachronic despite its synchronic aspects. As Achebe points out with regard to the 'new English' of his novels, 'the beginning of this English . . . was already there in [his] society, in popular speech and [he] foresee[s] the possibility for a lot more Africanization or Nigerianization of English in [his] literature' (Egejuru 1980: 49). However, the writer's innovations, whether lexico-semantic or morpho-syntactic, may not reflect variations in current oral usage in West Africa. For instance, Igbo people today use 'eleven' instead of 'ten and one' (Igbo: *iri no otu*), which Achebe used in *Things Fall Apart* to render the traditional Igbo counting system (Achebe 1958: 37, Zaslavsky 1973: 47). Relexification in its diachronic function should therefore not be confused with what has been called 'nativization' (Shridhar 1982) or 'Africanism' in reference to 'any English construction that reflects a structural property of an African language' (Bokamba 1982: 78). Nor does it bear any resemblance to any purely synchronic function of relexification verging on mother-tongue interference, calquing (also calking) or loan-translation. 'Africanization,' as well as 'indigenization,' however, refer to larger strategies of cultural decolonization . . . which are to be understood against the general background of African and 'Third World' economic de-linkage with Western supremacy.

Whether Alfred Sauvy meant it or not when he coined the phrase – *le tiers monde* – after the French *tiers état*, the 'Third World' has become the site of the 'third code' . . . This new register of communication, which is neither the European target language nor the indigenous source language, functions as an 'interlanguage' or as a 'third register,' after Irwin Stern's analysis of the new Portuguese/Kimbudu language in Angolan Luandino Vieira's fiction. Such a register results from the 'minting,' to borrow Jahn's numismatic phrase, the 're-cutting,' as Sartre contends in 'Orphée noir,' or the 'fashioning [out],' as Achebe would have it, of a new European-based novelistic language wrung out of the African tongue (Jahn 1966: 239–42). When relexified, it is not 'metropolitan' English or French that appears on the page but an unfamiliar European language that constantly suggests another tongue. As such, it is closer to verbatim or loan-translation than to translation *per se* but, as we shall see, it differs from both. So when Gabriel Okara writes: 'My insides smell with anger' or when Ahmadou Kourouma writes: 'Il n'avait pas soutenu un petit rhume,' both writers have relexified two West African languages – Ijo and Maninka – into English and French, respectively.

Although they do not use the term 'relexification,' writers unanimously recognize that the process at work when they write novels in European languages involves 'some sort of translation' that 'approximates' the meaning in the source language. . . . Gabriel Okara is of the opinion that 'the only way to use [African ideas] effectively is to translate them almost literally from the African language native to the writer into whatever European language he is using as his medium of expression' (Okara 1963: 15). On the Francophone side, Cameroonian Francis Bebey attempts to 'extract the essence of Douala and put it alongside the essence of French so as to attain a very enriched cultural level' (Bebey 1979: 112). The Senegalese writer Cheikh Hamidou Kane 'doesn't think that the use of French modifies his style or intent but rather that his use of French is modified' (by Peulh/Pular), whereas the Guinean writer Camara Laye admits that he loses 'a lot in the transposition from Malinke into French' (Egejuru 1980: 35, 42).

Such remarks are not confined only to West Africa. Thus, the South African novelist and critic, Es'kia Mphahlele, concurs:

> I listen to the speech of my people, to the ring of dialogue in my home language and struggle to find an approximation to the English equivalent . . . it is really an attempt to paraphrase a single Sotho expression.
>
> (Mphahlele 1964: 303–4)

Two years earlier, in 1962, the African writers attending the Makerere Conference, of which Mphahlele wrote a press report, had reached the following consensus:

> It was generally agreed that it is better for an African writer to think and feel in his own language and then look for an English transliteration approximating the original.
>
> (Mphahlele 1962: 2). . . .

Relexification is thus tied to the notions of 'approximation' and of 'transparence.' Yet, it also encompasses those of 'transposition,' 'paraphrase,' 'translation' (even 'psychic'), 'transliteration,' 'transference' and 'transmutation.' To make matters worse, there is some disagreement about the process of ideation behind relexification. Es'kia Mphahlele points to the difficulty of 'peg[ging] the point at which [he] stop[s] thinking in [his] mother tongue and begin[s] to think in English, and vice versa' (Mphahlele 1964: 304). Also, Olympe Bhely-Quenum from Benin confesses that he writes in Fon or Yoruba – 'two or three lines,' then translates his thoughts and develops the original idea into the target language (1982: 14). Here, the writer admits to the possibility of an African-language original, which, under the guise of carelessly jotted notes – 'two or three lines' – or elaborate literary fragments, is not visible in the record of literary history. This phenomenon is said to have existed, in various degrees, in European Renaissance verses that poets would first compose in Latin and then expand into a French version. In that respect, the fate of Latin which can be understood in terms of either death or creolization, may be relevant to the future of African languages, where writers continue writing in

European languages and refuse to fecundate oral art with writing, thereby practising some sort of 'linguistic contraception.'

Relexification also differs from 'auto-translation,' that is, the translation of one's own work, in that the latter posits that the original work is visible. Such is the case with Ghanaian Kofi Awoonor's translation in English of his own poem 'I Heard a Bird Cry,' originally written in Ewe. About the English version he submitted to *Black Orpheus* he has this to say:

> Some kind of transference of perception takes place. I move from one linguistic dimension into another totally different, sometimes violently different one. . . . Within me these two things exist side by side so I can move across these boundaries with, I hope, absolute ease. So at times ideas that exist in the Ewe, or that have taken place in the Ewe poems, either get mutated or expanded or contracted, whatever, depending upon words and what technical mode I want to use in English.
>
> (Awoonor in Lindfors *et al.* 1972: 49)

Auto-translation . . . is a contemporary yet exceptional trend in African writing, as epitomized by Ngugi wa Thiong'o's own English translations of his works composed in Gikuyu.

John Pepper Clark concurs with Awoonor's notion of mutation through expansion or contraction of ideas in the source language: 'a thought you have has been very well expressed already in your mother tongue; you like that manner of expression so much you want to transplant it into English' (Clark 1972: 68). In the absence of an original, writers add cautiously that one must not assume that the African writer thinks first in his mother tongue and then translates his thoughts into the target language. Chinua Achebe warns us: 'If it were such a simple, mechanical process, I would agree that it was [a] pointless . . . eccentric pursuit' (1975: 102). Writers' psychosocial attitudes towards relexification vary considerably but it is preferable to leave questions related to such attitudes to psycholinguists and transformational grammarians.

Unlike interpretive translation or the 'lesser' activity of *transcodage* which both take place between two texts – the original and the translated version – relexification is characterized by the absence of an original. It therefore does not operate from the language of one text to the other but from one language to the other within the same text. Such texts are . . . palimpsests for, behind the scriptural authority of the target European language, the earlier, imperfectly erased remnants of the source language are still visible. Just as these remnants may lead to the discovery of lost literary works of centuries long past, the linguistic remnants inhabiting the relexified text may lead to the discovery of the repressed source language. The linguistic notions of 'source language' and 'target language' are therefore retained because of the underlying implication that the un-earthing of these debris inevitably leads to the 'source' of the native culture-based text, without its idyllic, bucolic connotations of a return to the etymological and cultural roots of African culture. Although the 'act of reading' a palimpsest lies beyond the scope of this study, one should stress the uniqueness and particularity of each 'message-event' and its openness for a wide variety of readings when consumed, by different audiences in different socio-linguistic contexts.

What distinguishes relexification from translation is not only the absence of a separate original. Relexification takes place, as already suggested, between two languages within the same text. Although these two languages are unrelated, they interact as dominant vs. dominated languages or elaborated vs. restricted codes, as they did and still do to some extent in West Africa where the European language is the official language and the medium of prestige and power. As it hosts such warring tendencies, relexification is a strategy in potentia which transcends the merely methodological. On the methodological level, it stems from a need to solve an immediate artistic problem: that of rendering African concepts, thought-patterns and linguistic features in the European language. On the strategic level, relexification seeks to subvert the linguistically codified, to decolonize the language of early, colonial literature and to affirm a revised, non-atavistic orality via the imposed medium.

Whereas the method of pidginization grounds the character in his/her supranational or urban identity, relexification grounds the character in a specific ethnicity. Relexification is therefore statistically more recurrent than pidginization in novels with a local or rural setting, hereafter called native culture-based novels. The degree of pidginization is thus in inverse ratio to the degree of relexification. For instance, Chinua Achebe's *A Man of the People* (1960) contains ninety-three Pidgin utterances whereas *Things Fall Apart* (1958) contains only three of them. As a rule, there is a higher incidence of relexifying devices as the work comes closer to orality. This should come as no surprise since such texts are relexified from languages that have remained essentially oral and belong to the vast corpus of oral human discourse, for most languages spoken by humans over the millennia have no connection with writing. The relexified medium goes beyond the literary utilization of existing popular idioms and, in its world-creating aspect, transfigures the glottopolitical situation through the creation of a new form of literary expression.

# PART X

## The Body and Performance

# Introduction

The 'difference' of the post-colonial subject by which s/he can be 'othered' is felt most directly and immediately in the way in which the superficial differences of the body and voice (skin colour, eye shape, hair texture, body shape, language, dialect or accent) are read as indelible signs of the 'natural' inferiority of their possessors. As Fanon noted many years ago, this is the inescapable 'fact' of blackness, a 'fact' which forces on 'negro' people a heightened level of bodily self-consciousness, since it is the body which is the inescapable, visible sign of their oppression and denigration. In a more general way the 'fact' of the body is a central feature of the post-colonial, standing as it does metonymically for all the 'visible' signs of difference, and their varied forms of cultural and social inscription, forms often either under-valued, overdetermined or even totally invisible to the dominant colonial discourse. Yet, paradoxically the resulting self-consciousness, as Fanon perceived, can drive the very opposition which can undo this stereotyping.

Bodily presence and awareness in one sense or another is one of the features which is central to post-colonial rejections of the Eurocentric and logocentric emphasis on 'absence', a rejection which positions the Derridean dominance of the 'written' sign within a larger discursive economy of voice and movement. In its turn this alter/native discursive and inscriptive economy which stresses the oral and the performative is predi-cated upon the idea of an exchange in which those engaged are physically present to one another. In oral performance the meaning is made in the exchange that is a sine qua non of orality. The oral text is not synonymous with the written inscriptions or oral 'texts' collected by anthropologists and others in recent years. In practice the oral only exists and acquires meaning in the possibility of an immediate and modifying response, existing there-fore only interactively with its whole speech or movement event.[1] In other words the real body is acknowledged in such an exchange in a way in which the 'pale' material concerns of recent theory are readily dissolved.

In most written accounts the oral is overdetermined even in the act of being recorded and celebrated by the written. This is what usually passes for an acknowledgement of the 'oral' and 'performative'. This inferior posi-tioning replicates the larger positioning of the oral and performative within

321

the economy of communication in the modern world. In 'modern' societies the oral and the performative continues to exist alongside the written but it is largely ignored or relegated to the condition of pretext in many accounts, represented as only the beginning or origin of the written. Yet in many post-colonial societies oral, performative events may be the principal present and modern means of continuity for the pre-colonial culture and may also be the tools by which the dominant social institutions and discourses can be subverted or repositioned, shown that is to be constructions naturalised within a hierarchised politics of difference. At a further metaphorical level the body and the voice often become the sign in post-colonial written texts for alter/native cultures which can only exist within the written as a disruption or a gap, simultaneously unbridgeable and yet bridged by the written word. Such a trace is crucial to the position of post-colonial texts which seek to record the continuing presence of oral, performative cultures of colonised groups within the predominantly written discourse of the coloniser.

The body itself has also been the literal 'text' on which colonisation has written some of its most graphic and scrutable messages. The punishment machine of Kafka's nightmare story 'In the Penal Colony', which literally inscribes on the dying body of the transgressor the name of his 'crime', is a powerful allegorisation of what was, too often, a literal reality in both slave colonies and penal colonies, as Gillian Whitlock's reference to the slave narrative of Mary Prince here makes clear.

The body, too, has become then the literal site on which resistance and oppression have struggled, with the weapons being in both cases the physical signs of cultural difference, veils and wigs, to use Kadiatu Kanneh's terms, symbols and literal occasions of the power struggles of the dominater and dominated for possession of control and identity. Such struggles have often articulated the further intersections of race with gender and class in the construction of the colonised as subject and subaltern.

All in all the recent interest in theorising this complex interaction, whose trace as these extracts show can be found in varying ways across all post-colonial societies, is a site of some of the most provocative and challenging recent discussions of post-coloniality.

# NOTE

1   For a very illuminating and useful set of accounts of 'orality' see *Discourse and Its Disguises: The Interpretation of African Oral Texts* ed. Karin Barber and P. F. de Moraes Farias, Centre of West African Studies, Birmingham University African Studies Series 1, 1989.

# 56

## The Fact of Blackness

### FRANTZ FANON*

THE BLACK MAN among his own in the twentieth century does not know at what moment his inferiority comes into being through the other. Of course I have talked about the black problem with friends, or, more rarely, with American Negroes. Together we protested, we asserted the equality of all men in the world. In the Antilles there was also that little gulf that exists among the almost-white, the mulatto, and the nigger. But I was satisfied with an intellectual understanding of these differences. It was not really dramatic. And then . . .

And then the occasion arose when I had to meet the white man's eyes. An unfamiliar weight burdened me. The real world challenged my claims. In the white world the man of color encounters difficulties in the development of his bodily schema. Consciousness of the body is solely a negating activity. It is a third-person consciousness. The body is surrounded by an atmosphere of certain uncertainty. I know that if I want to smoke, I shall have to reach out my right arm and take the pack of cigarettes lying at the other end of the table. The matches, however, are in the drawer on the left, and I shall have to lean back slightly. And all these movements are made not out of habit but out of implicit knowledge. A slow composition of my *self* as a body in the middle of a spatial and temporal world – such seems to be the schema. It does not impose itself on me; it is, rather, a definitive structuring of the self and of the world-definitive because it creates a real dialectic between my body and the world. . . .

'Look, a Negro!' It was an external stimulus that flicked over me as I passed by. I made a tight smile.

'Look, a Negro!' It was true. It amused me.

'Look, a Negro!' The circle was drawing a bit tighter. I made no secret of my amusement.

---

* From 'The Fact of Blackness' *Black Skin, White Masks* (1952) (trans. Charles Lam Markmann) London: MacGibbon & Kee, 1968.

'Mama, see the Negro! I'm frightened!' Frightened! Frightened! Now they were beginning to be afraid of me. I made up my mind to laugh myself to tears, but laughter had become impossible. . . .

My body was given back to me sprawled out, distorted, recolored, clad in mourning in that white winter day. The Negro is an animal, the Negro is bad, the Negro is mean, the Negro is ugly; look, a nigger, it's cold, the nigger is shivering, the nigger is shivering because he is cold, the little boy is trembling because he is afraid of the nigger, the nigger is shivering with cold, that cold that goes through your bones, the handsome little boy is trembling because he thinks that the nigger is quivering with rage, the little white boy throws himself into his mother's arms: Mama, the nigger's going to eat me up.

All round me the white man, above the sky tears at its navel, the earth rasps under my feet, and there is a white song, a white song. All this whiteness that burns me . . .

I sit down at the fire and I become aware of my uniform. I had not seen it. It is indeed ugly. I stop there, for who can tell me what beauty is?

Where shall I find shelter from now on? I felt an easily identifiable flood mounting out of the countless facets of my being. I was about to be angry. The fire was long since out, and once more the nigger was trembling.

'Look how handsome that Negro is! . . .'

'Kiss the handsome Negro's ass, madame!'

Shame flooded her face. At last I was set free from my rumination. At the same time I accomplished two things: I identified my enemies and I made a scene. A grand slam. Now one would be able to laugh.

The field of battle having been marked out, I entered the lists.

What? While I was forgetting, forgiving, and wanting only to love, my message was flung back in my face like a slap. The white world, the only honorable one, barred me from all participation. A man was expected to behave like a man. I was expected to behave like a black man – or at least like a nigger. I shouted a greeting to the world and the world slashed away my joy. I was told to stay within bounds, to go back where I belonged.

They would see, then! I had warned them, anyway. Slavery? It was no longer even mentioned, that unpleasant memory. My supposed inferiority? A hoax that it was better to laugh at. I forgot it all, but only on condition that the world not protect itself against me any longer. I had incisors to test. I was sure they were strong. And besides . . .

What! When it was I who had every reason to hate, to despise, I was rejected? When I should have been begged, implored, I was denied the slightest recognition? I resolved, since it was impossible for me to get away from an *inborn complex*, to assert myself as a BLACK MAN. Since the other hesitated to recognize me, there remained only one solution: to make myself known.

In *Anti-Semite and Jew*, Sartre says: 'They [the Jews] have allowed themselves to be poisoned by the stereotype that others have of them, and they live in fear that their acts will correspond to this stereotype . . . We may say that their conduct is perpetually overdetermined from the inside' (1965: 95).

All the same, the Jew can be unknown in his Jewishness. He is not wholly what he is. One hopes, one waits. His actions, his behavior are the final determinant. He is a white man, and, apart from some rather debatable characteristics, he can sometimes go unnoticed. He belongs to the race of those who since the beginning of time have never known cannibalism. What an idea, to eat one's father! Simple enough, one has only not to be a nigger. Granted, the Jews are harassed – what am I thinking of? They are hunted down, exterminated, cremated. But these are little family quarrels. The Jew is disliked from the moment he is tracked down. But in my case everything takes on a *new* guise. I am given no chance. I am overdetermined from without. I am the slave not of the 'idea' that others have of me but of my own appearance.

I move slowly in the world, accustomed now to seek no longer for upheaval. I progress by crawling. And already I am being dissected under white eyes, the only real eyes. I am *fixed*. Having adjusted their microtomes, they objectively cut away slices of my reality. I am laid bare. I feel, I see in those white faces that it is not a new man who has come in, but a new kind of man, a new genus. Why, it's a Negro! . . .

As I begin to recognize that the Negro is the symbol of sin, I catch myself hating the Negro. But then I recognize that I am a Negro. There are two ways out of this conflict. Either I ask others to pay no attention to my skin, or else I want them to be aware of it. I try then to find value for what is bad – since I have unthinkingly conceded that the black man is the color of evil. In order to terminate this neurotic situation, in which I am compelled to choose an unhealthy, conflictual solution, fed on fantasies, hostile, inhuman in short, I have only one solution: to rise above this absurd drama that others have staged round me, to reject the two terms that are equally unacceptable, and, through one human being, to reach out for the universal. When the Negro dives – in other words, goes under – something remarkable occurs.

Listen again to Césaire:

Ho ho
Their power is well anchored
Gained
Needed
My hands bathe in bright heather
In swamps of annatto trees
My gourd is heavy with stars
But I am weak. Oh I am weak.
Help me.
And here I am on the edge of metamorphosis

Drowned blinded
Frightened of myself, terrified of myself
Of the gods . . . you are no gods. I am free.
(Césaire 1946: 144)

THE REBEL: I have a pact with this night, for twenty years
I have heard it calling softly for me . . .
(Césaire 1946: 122)

Having again discovered that night, which is to say the sense of his identity, Césaire learned first of all that 'it is no use painting the foot of the tree white, the strength of the bark cries out from beneath the paint. . . .'

The discovery of the existence of a Negro civilization in the fifteenth century confers no patent of humanity on me. Like it or not, the past can in no way guide me in the present moment.

The situation that I have examined, it is clear by now, is not a classic one. Scientific objectivity was barred to me, for the alienated, the neurotic, was my brother, my sister, my father. I have ceaselessly striven to show the Negro that in a sense he makes himself abnormal; to show the white man that he is at once the perpetrator and the victim of a delusion.

There are times when the black man is locked into his body. Now, 'for a being who has acquired consciousness of himself and of his body, who has attained to the dialectic of subject and object, the body is no longer a cause of the structure of consciousness, it has become an object of consciousness' (Merleau-Ponty 1945: 277).

The Negro, however sincere, is the slave of the past. None the less I am a man, and in this sense the Peloponnesian War is as much mine as the invention of the compass. Face to face with the white man, the Negro has a past to legitimate, a vengeance to exact; face to face with the Negro, the contemporary white man feels the need to recall the times of cannibalism. A few years ago, the Lyon branch of the Union of Students From Overseas France asked me to reply to an article that made jazz music literally an irruption of cannibalism into the modern world. Knowing exactly what I was doing, I rejected the premises on which the request was based, and I suggested to the defender of European purity that he cure himself of a spasm that had nothing cultural in it. Some men want to fill the world with their presence. A German philosopher described this mechanism as *the pathology of freedom*. In the circumstances, I did not have to take up a position on behalf of Negro music against white music, but rather to help my brother to rid himself of an attitude in which there was nothing healthful.

# 57

## Jazz and the West Indian Novel

### EDWARD KAMAU BRATHWAITE*

IT IS OF course difficult (and I make no attempt to disguise this) to make wholly convincing correspondences from music into literature; and easier to demonstrate relationships between jazz improvisation and the folk/oral tradition than it is to do the same with jazz and the more conscious products of the 'written' tradition – for one thing, their very literary nature – their artistic premeditation, for example, and their non-folk, European-type and intellectual influences, require qualifications and the kind of analysis which a study of the kind cannot properly attempt. One can only pursue intuitions and indicate an approach. What can be said with some certainty, however, is that on analysis, it would appear that many folk forms, and those passages on West Indian (and other) literary works that grapple most closely with folk forms and folk experience, contain elements of improvisation.

Here, for example, is a folk form improvisation tacked on, as it were, at the end of Neville Dawes' *The Last Enchantment* (1960):

> Once when Anancy was a little boy he was going on an' him see Ping-Wing bramble wid a rat, Him fight Ping-Wing take 'way the rat so carry it hang it up in the kitchen. When him gawn Granny come een an' eat off the rat. When Anancy come back him cyan fine the rat. Him say, 'Come, come Granny give me me rat, me rat come from Ping-Wing, Ping-Wing juk me han', me han' come from God.' Granny say, 'Ah cyan't give back the rat because ah heat it off but take dis knife.'
>
> Anancy go awn until him see a man was cutting cane without a knife. Him say, 'Man, how come you cuttin' cane widout a knife an' I have knife?' The man take Anancy knife start cut the cane an' bruk the knife.'
>
> Anancy say, 'Come come man give me mi knife mi knife come from Granny Granny eat mi rat mi rat come from Ping-Wing Ping-Wing juk

* From 'Jazz and the West Indian Novel' Part I, *BIM* XI(44), 1967; Part II, *BIM* XII(45), 1967; Part III *BIM* XII(46), 1968.

mi han' mi han' come from God.' The man say, 'Ah cyan't give you
back yo' knife for it break. But tek dis grass . . . '

This is an almost perfect example of improvisation, in the jazz sense, where
tone, rhythm and image come together to create a certain kind of effect.
And of course this same story could be told by different people with infinite
degrees of variation. But this, as it occurs in Dawes' novel, is, as I said,
merely tacked on at the end. *The Last Enchantment* itself does not reveal
any specifically 'jazz' qualities though there is some reference to jazz and
jazz musicians and a kind of improvisation takes place through the figure
of a 'white man, very pale, with the skin of the forehead stretched tight
across the brows and almost transparent' (p. 188, see also pp. 196–7, 273),
who recurs in various guises at critical points in the novel. But this is
not jazz improvisation (the novel's concerns are too 'sophisticated' for this)
but rather in the nature of classical music *motif* – the sort of thing attempted
by Mittelholzer in his 'leitmotif' novels, *Latticed Echoes* (1960) and *Thunder
Returning* (1961) but no West Indian novelist has, as far as I know,
attempted yet to incorporate the Anancy story structure in the *form* of his
work; and this is because, as I have already suggested, most of our novelists,
after their initial 'creole' expression, have passed on out of the West Indian
orbit, moving to London, New York or Montreal before they can really
come to grips with the problem of formally expressing the deep-rooted experiences of the folk aspect of their tradition. Where is the second and third
novel written by a West Indian *in* the West Indies about the West Indies?

No. To find 'written' examples of improvisation similar to the Anancy
story, we have to turn to those few poets who have remained working in
the West Indies (and as Margaret Blundell pointed out in her article in *BIM*
43 (1966), there are fewer even of these than one might expect) and
who have had, for one reason or another, to come to grips with the oral
tradition of the region:

If a cross yuh dah-cross,
Beg yuh cross meck me pass.
Dem yah crossin' is crosses yuh know!
Koo de line! Yuh noh se
Car an truck backa me?
Hear dah hoganeer one deh dah-blow!

Missis, walk fas' an cross!
Pickney, cross mek me pass!
Lady, galang an mine yuh business!
(Louise Bennett: 'Pedestrian Crosses')

The 'improvisation' here is not only in the variations of tone, made possible
by the assumption of dramatic method (as in the calypso), and in the
changes of rhythm within the verse structure, but in the 'melody' itself –
the variations based on the word 'cross'. Lorrimer Alexander, using his

Guyanese speech patterns achieves, again through dramatic presentation, another kind of improvisatory effect:

> Hi look! Moongazer!
> Look! Look!
>
> Whey?
>
> Deh, man! Standin! pon da
> genip tree stump
> wid he han' stretch out
> straight straight
> he head ben' back
> lookin' up at de moon.
> You see? You see?
>
> Ah see!
> Yes, he en movin'
> 'tall 'tall.
> Oh meh lawd
> how we gun pass!
>
> Pass! Pass fass!
>
> Not me at all!
>
> But we cahn stay heah!
> Listen . . .
>                         ('Moongazer')

. . . Improvisatory effects can also be achieved through repetition of a 'theme' – the jazz 'riff' – a kind of collective response which marks the end of one improvisation and the beginning of the next. This is a form found in many folk literatures. In the Jamaican folk tale, 'William Saves his Sweetheart' for instance, as recorded in Le Page and De Camp's *Jamaican Creole* (1960), which contains an almost equal mixture of English and West African elements, the improvisation takes place during the description of the action and each improvisation is separated by a riff or chorus. A witch has captured a young girl stealing her peas in a gully:

> 'See here! Stand up there! I am going to tell you now, if you eat my peas, you are going to be drowned, but if you no eat it, nothing won't do you. So swear, you bitch! Swear! Say you no eat it, while you know you eat it!' And she lick down one of the limes on the dirt, so *wham*! and the dry gully pump up water, cover the girl's instep. The girl say, 'My! Poor me one! What I am going to do today?' She say, 'Swear! Swear, you bitch!' And she lick down one other lime, so *wham*! and the water mount the girl to her knee. The girl say:
>
> Laad ooi! Mi William ooi!
> Mii William ooi!

Po mi one, ooi! Peas ooi!
O, mi dearest William oo!
Ring down peas o hai! A ring down!
O, ring down.

William's ma, an old witch, is in her yard. She hear, she say, 'Stand!
But I no hear William's name being called in the dry gully? But I ask
William over and over, say if he have sweetheart. William say no! Then
where William gone now? Hear what William's name is doing down
there! The old witch lick down the last lime, so *wham*! and the water
mount the girl around her waist. She hail out for the better.

Oo, mi dearest William ooi! Mi William oo hoi!
Po me one oo! Peas oo!
Oi, a ring down!
Oo, mi dearest William ei!
Ring down peas oi! Oi! A-ring down!
Oi, ring down!

In this 'English' version, of course, the rhythmic 'jazz' elements are not
conveyed. One has to remember that the narrator does not in fact say: 'She
hear, she say, 'Stand! But I no hear William's name being called in the dry
gully?' But: *Him hear, say, Tan! But mi no hear William name de Kall-a
drai gully?* And instead of 'Hear what William's name is doing down there'
(which isn't jazz), it would really be: *Ye we William name de-du down de!*
(which is). . . .

Using therefore the idea of jazz as an aesthetic model (a way of seeing;
a critical tool), we can perhaps now begin to generalise a little (even if
negatively) about the kind of West Indian novel which, for my purposes,
I have called 'the jazz novel'; the most successful, though far from perfect,
example of which, so far, has been Roger Mais' *Brother Man*. (The reasons
why there have not been more of these novels – only Salkey's *A Quality of
Violence* could be said to be another; and why Mais' itself is so very flawed,
may perhaps be gathered from my previous discussion in Parts I and II of
this study. It is mainly a question of orientation; attitude to 'West Indian'
material; the amount of attention given to what we really have; the kinds
of models which we have absorbed as paradigms.)

The 'jazz novel', in the normal course of things, will hardly be an
'epic'. Dealing with a specific, clearly-defined, folk-type community, it will
try to express the essence of this community through its form. It will absorb
its rhythms from the people of this community; and its concern will be with
the community as a whole, its characters taking their place in that
community, of which they are felt and seen to be an integral part. The
conflicts which give this kind of novel meaning will not be Faustian
conflicts of self-seeking knowledge or the Existentialist stoicism of alienation. These novels, it need hardly be said, have their place, and West
Indians will continue to write them. This is as it should be and is related

to the freedom of the artist. We are not here trying to say what anybody should or should not write. We are striving towards a way of *seeing* what they write and relating it to our indigenous experience. There is an argument, of course, that holds that 'our experience' is in fact the world's; by which, I think, is meant West Europe's, certainly Britain and North America's. I do not dispute this; though I would seriously qualify it. But I would also add that those people who delight to see our experience as 'international', as 'cosmopolitan', tend to see it *only* as these things. When pressed, they are able to provide little *basis* for their wide horizons. It is my contention that *before it is too late*, we must try to find the high ground from which we ourselves will see the world, and towards which the world will look to find us. An 'international' tradition by all means for those that wish it. *But a creole culture as well*. And a creole way of seeing first. It is from this that we must begin. From this view-point I would say that Naipaul's *A House for Mr Biswas* and Orlando Patterson's *The Children of Sisyphus*, to take two fine recent examples, are not jazz novels, although both of them contain brilliant jazz moments. The jazz novel is concerned, as these two books are, with illuminating a specific, 'basic' community; and both these books have done a great deal to return our attention to 'West Indian' possibilities (see my article 'Roots' in *BIM* 37). Their elements of *protest* are also closer to jazz than they are, say, to the waltz, the raga or the highlife. But when all is said and done, *Biswas* and *Sisyphus* remain essentially concerned with exploring the *ego* rather than the *gestalt* of their communities; and both Patterson and Naipaul in their most recent novels (*An Absence of Ruins* (1967); *The Mimic Men* (1967)) have gone even farther along this road. . . .

*Brother Man* was published in 1954. The following year Roger Mais published what was to be his last novel, *Black Lightning*. (Fragments of a fourth work have since come to light and there is the possibility that an edited version of this may soon be released.) *Black Lightning* begins:

> Miriam walked deeper into the wood, following the sound of the axe. Every now and then she stopped to scrape burrs from her dress, and then she would straighten up again, and listen for the sound.
>
> (Mais 1955: 9)

The rhythm is there as before. But this is not a novel about community. Miriam is following, searching, finding. The Faustian individuals have emerged to make their world.

# 58

---

# *In Search of the Lost Body*
## *Redefining the Subject in*
## *Caribbean Literature*

### MICHAEL DASH*

IN CÉSAIRE'S WRITING the body has the last word. In his poetry and theatre he re-enacts the need to reintegrate the exiled subject in the lost body. In his epic poem *Cahier d'un retour au pays natal*, Césaire imagines the journey of the disembodied subject across the estranging waters and the eventual reintegration of the body with the *pays natal*. . . .

In order to embrace this mutilated *pays natal*, the subject must overcome his or her initial revulsion. He or she must radically redefine notions of time, space, beauty and power before return becomes possible, and must strip away all illusions – whether that of heroic prodigal, solemn demiurge or New World African – empty consciousness of all pretensions ('overboard with alien riches/overboard with my real lies') in order to achieve reintegration. The end of exile, the triumph over the estranging sea, is only possible when the subject feels his or her bonds with the lost body of the native land. The ego-centred attitude of saviour or reformer must yield to a humble realisation that the discourse of the island-body is more powerful. The *pays natal* is the realm of viscous damp where familiar meanings dissolve, of the unspeakable that eludes the systematising word.

The importance of Césaire's contribution to a tradition of Caribbean writing is his passionate concern with psychic 're-memberment', with the successful incarnation of the displaced subject. Without reference to Césaire, Harris describes this concern as 'a new corpus of sensibility' which imaginatively releases the deep archetypal resonances of 'the theme of the phantom limb – the re-assembly of dismembered man or god' (Harris 1981: 27). The *Cahier* ends with a triumphant vision of sensory plenitude as the subject is possessed by the lost island-body. In the final movement of this poem, the 'wound of the waters' yields its secret as it becomes the pupil

* From 'In Search of the Lost Body: Redefining the Subject in Caribbean Literature'
*Kunapipi* 11(1), 1989.

of the eye, the navel of the world, an integrating Omphalos. The dream of 'La Rencontre Bien Totale', the ecstatic abolition of all dualism, haunts Césaire's imagination. In Césaire's essay *Poésie et Connaissance* (1944) he describes the poetic ideal as a capacity to transcend oppositions, to achieve André Breton's vision of a 'certain point in mind' which could exist beyond contradictions. The dynamic image at the end of the *Cahier* – of the spiral, plunging in two directions – is an imaginative representation of the power of the reanimated body. The ideal of a restless, protean physicality is constantly invoked in his poetry. As *Intimité marine*, he states his poetic identity in terms of 'the neck of an enraged horse, as a giant snake. I coil I uncoil I leap.'

The images of dismemberment and reintegration so passionately stated in Césaire's epic poem recur throughout his poetic *oeuvre*. For instance the poem '*Corps perdu*' (which gives its name to the collection of poems) specifically deals with the retrieval of the lost body. Another poem that restates the theme of dismemberment is '*Dit d'errance*', which does invoke 'archetypal resonances', in Harris's words, in its reference to the indestructibility of the Egyptian god Osiris. The poetic subject assumes all dismemberments which have existed.

> All that ever was dismembered
> in me has been dismembered
> all that ever was mutilated
> in me has been mutilated . . .
>             (Davis 1984: 102)

As Gregson Davis points out in his reading of the poem, the lines 'the goddess piece by fragment/put back together her dissevered lover' specifically refer to the reconstitution of Osiris by Isis. Césaire has a special priority in Caribbean writing because of this vision of the re-membered body. . . .

Césaire's writing never ceases to insist on the unstable nature of the world. His horror of stasis (*durcir le beau*), his belief that stability is a mirage, has created the possibility of isolating the ideal of unencumbered physical movement or the refusal of corporeal determinism in Caribbean literature. The ideal of revolutionary self-assertiveness is expressed through corporeal imagery. For instance, Frantz Fanon attempts to rewrite the body of colonised man, creating a new subject from the dismemberment and castration inflicted by the coloniser's destructive gaze. In *The Wretched of the Earth*, Fanon equates a reanimated body with the liberated voice of the revolutionary intellectual:

> It is a vigorous style, alive with rhythms, struck through and through
> with bursting life. . . . The new movement gives rise to a new rhythm
> of life and to forgotten muscular tensions, and develops the imagin-
> ation.
>
>                         (Fanon 1967:177)

333

Fanon's images of verbal muscularity have a resonance in Caribbean writing in which revolutionary potential is evoked through the resurrected flesh. The reanimated body of the land in Jacques Roumain's *Masters of the Dew* and the erotic carnality of René Depestre's *Rainbow for the Christian West* are clear examples of spiritual awakening expressed in images of revitalised physicality.

The rewriting or reinventing of the subject does not always take the form of virile images of sexual hubris. Corporeal metamorphosis can take a totally different direction if the subject is defined in terms of an exemplary reticence or evasiveness. In Simone Schwarz-Bart's novel *The Bridge of Beyond*, the corporeal ideal is one of resilience, slipperiness and manoeuvrability. Bodies are repeatable, can be dissolved or can defy the force of gravity. For instance, Télumée deals with personal tragedy by imagining herself as floating free of the world and its destructive force:

> Then I would lie on the ground and try to dissolve my flesh: I would fill myself with bubbles and suddenly go light – a leg would be no longer there, then an arm, my head and whole body faded into the air, and I was floating.
>
> (Schwarz-Bart 1982:104)

Her fantasy of an unencumbered body is an imaginative strategy designed to resist the desecrating force of her oppressive world. Schwarz-Bart's novel is a tribute to the survival of a particular group of women because of their imaginative powers. Her narrative is built around the tensions that separate the transcendental from the existential. Her main character yearns for a world divested of fixed, determining matter. The *morne* or hill which offers refuge exerts a vertical pull on the protagonist to counteract the downward pull of the plains with which fiery destruction and physical entrapment are associated.

In Schwarz-Bart's tale of female endurance, the subject is not aggressively impulsive but values suppleness and taciturn stoicism. In the face of the insults of her *béké* mistress Mme. Desaragne, she is 'ready to dodge, to slip between the meshes of the trap she was weaving with her breath'. She clings to this image of elusiveness until Mme. Desaragne disappears like starch dissolved in water. Schwarz-Bart's novel demonstrates the corrective power of the folk imagination. We have insight into a process of psychic *marronnage* that allows the individual to survive even in the most vulnerable circumstances.

This image of an ever-changing body emerges as an even more suggestive symbol in the work of Alejo Carpentier. In it an aesthetic of incompleteness offers an insight into a world where forms are unstable, where an intricate branching, adaptation and accretion governs the existence of all things. Carpentier's imagery is best explained in the symbolism of the grotesque as described by the Russian critic Bakhtin, in which the body 'is not something completed and finished, but open, uncompleted' (Bakhtin 1984: 364). In Carpentier's novel *Explosion in a Cathedral*, we are presented with a teeming world inhabited by fluid, evanescent form. Nothing has a fixed contour in this submarine world in which matter cannot be discriminated from non-matter. Esteban, Carpentier's protagonist, realises that this world resists being named or structured. In its unspeakable nature it defies the efforts of the comprehending subject:

> Carried into a world of symbiosis, standing up to his neck in pools whose water was kept perpetually foaming by cascading waves, and was broken, torn, shattered, by the hungry bite of jagged rocks, Esteban marvelled to realise how the language of these islands had made use of agglutinations, verbal amalgams and metaphors to convey the formal ambiguity of things which participated in several essences at once.
>
> (Carpentier1972: 185)

The ambiguous space imagined by Carpentier is akin to Harris's zone of 'inarticulacy' or Bakhtin's 'unpublicized spheres of speech' in which 'the dividing lines between objects and phenomena are drawn quite differently than in the prevailing picture of the world' (Bakhtin 1984: 421). Esteban's field of vision does not focus on the concrete and the static but on a world of infinite metamorphosis that seems to defy language itself. It illustrates Harris's conception of Caribbean consciousness caught between sea and forest.

Post-modernism concentrates on the inadequacy of interpretation and the disorienting reality of the unexplainable. Caribbean writing exploits precisely this terrain of the unspeakable. In the radical questioning of the need to totalise, systematise and control, the Caribbean writer is a natural deconstructionist who praises latency, formlessness and plurality. In order to survive, the Caribbean sensibility must spontaneously decipher and interpret the sign systems of those who wish to dominate and control. The writing of the region goes beyond simply creating alternative systems to reflect the futility of all attempts to construct total systems, to assert the powers of the structuring subject. It is not simply a matter of deploying Caliban's militant idiom against Prospero's signifying authority. It is, perhaps, a matter of demonstrating the opacity and inexhaustibility of a world that resists systematic construction or transcendent meaning.

# 59

# The Body as
# Cultural Signifier

## RUSSELL McDOUGALL*

THE VARIOUS LEVELS of rhythm in Achebe's fiction, from stylistic to structural and thematic, have been explored before this (McCarthy 1985: 243–56). My project is a related one: it is to focus on the human body as a verbal signifier that encodes movement iconographically as a condition of culture. The complex kinetics of *Arrow of God* relates directly to a theory of action, from which develops a hermeneutic practice: reading as a dance of attitudes, criticism as participation. . . .[1]

I am opposed to the Eurocentric appropriation of Achebe's 'canon' for the metropolitan 'Great Tradition' and my purpose is to consider in detail the counter assertion, often announced but rarely argued on the evidence. If this is a truly decolonizing fiction, the case cannot be argued simply at the level of content (by authenticating social setting, folklore, the use of proverbs, etc.); meaning needs to be explored in terms of mode. My interest is in the *attitudes* of the image, the *strategies* of the narrative, the *placing* of the reader, the *cultural coding* of those aesthetic principles that inform the whole process of the fiction.

When Ezeulu, Chief Priest of Ulu, decides to send Oduche to learn the ways of the whiteman it is as an extension of himself, saying: 'I want one of my sons to . . . be my eye there' (Achebe 1974: 45). But it is also as a sacrifice:

> it may even happen to an unfortunate generation that they are pushed beyond the end of things, and their back is broken and hung over a fire. When this happens they may sacrifice their own blood. This is what our sages meant when they said that a man who has nowhere else to put his hand for support puts it on his own knee.

Oduche is not only the eye; he is also the knee. But it is not only vision and sacrifice that are linked in the duality of Ezeulu's motive for sending his son

---

* From 'Achebe's *Arrow of God*: The Kinetic Idiom of an Unmasking' *Kunapipi* 9(2), 1987.

to join the whiteman: the eye is to see, so that he may know the secret of the whiteman's power, and the knee is to lend support to the arm put upon it in order to stabilize a collective body on the brink of collapse. The connection between the two is inescapable. The knowledge that is to come from what the eye sees and to stabilize the traditional power-base of the villages of Umuaro is correlated with a physical gesture, and that is aimed at maintaining the vertical position and balance of the body under the severe stress of imperialism. . . .[2]

It is change, in the form of the whiteman, that poses the external threat. 'The world is changing,' Ezeulu tells Oduche. 'I do not like it. But I am like the bird Eneke-nti-oba. When his friends asked him why he was always on the wing he replied: "Men of today have learnt to shoot without missing and so I have learnt to fly without perching" ' (45). This is Ezeulu's explanation of why he wants Oduche to be his eye. Of particular interest is the concept associated with Oduche-the-eye of adjusting to change by being constantly on the move; for, at the same time, the response to change that is embodied in Oduche-the-leg (upon which the hand seeks support) is the *arrest* of motion. This latter response is ritualized in the sacrifice of Oduche, while the ritual counterpart of the former is the dance: 'If anyone asks you why you should be sent to learn these new things tell him that a man must dance the dance prevalent in his time' (89). The attitude to change, then, is a complex one, of neutralizing it by embracing it, or of arresting it by making sacrifice to the god that is bringing it about. Dance bridges the poles of opposition embodied in this complexity of response to change.

If the image for responding to change by moving with it is the dancer, it must be admitted that the significant point, flexibility, focuses to a great degree on the legs. Peggy Harper writes: 'A characteristic body posture in [Nigerian] dance consists of a straight-backed torso with the legs used as springs, the knees bending and stretching in fluidly executing the rhythmic action patterns of the dance, and feet placed firmly on the ground' (1969: 289). The hand which seeks body-support upon the leg, then, implies the arrest of motion; not only is this 'logical', it refers as well to the traditional principle of 'supporting' as a stabilizing mode. This particular 'supporting' image requires the leg to bend, to provide a plane against which the hand can push, in order to gain the vertical impulse of stability. This seems obvious and pedantic perhaps; but it is worth stressing that the ultimate intention is 'straightness', so that, although motion is arrested, the image is underlined by an active potentiality – straighten*ing*. The iconography of the bended knee in sculpture often suggests the same context. The implication, centring on the knee, is of flexibility – which moves us considerably closer to the image of the dancer than the apparent contradiction in Ezeulu's responses to change might at first suggest. Although the African ideal of stability is generally vested in a flat-footed approach to the dance, and embodied in performance by a straight-backed torso, the complementary ideal of flexibility relies upon *bended* 'buoyant knees over stable feet' (Thompson 1979: 10). As the image of the dancer and the image of the 'supporting' knee are seen to merge, so do the respective associated poles of Ezeulu's apparently contradictory responses to change, in accord with the traditional dance dialectic relating flexibility to stability.

In sending Oduche to learn the whiteman's ways, Ezeulu bases his response to change upon the principle of flexibility, or, in other words, *innovation*; but the principle behind sacrificing the boy to the whiteman's god is one of stability, or *tradition*. One might even see the two responses as relating to two different perceptions of time, 'real' and 'mythic', the one permitting individual innovation and the other sacrificing the individual to the tradition of community. If this is so then we should not wonder that the image of the dancer and the image of the 'supporting' knee are not so polarized as Ezeulu's responses to change at first seem: as 'real' and 'mythic' time mesh. Positive proof of this is given in the form of call-and-response (and solo-and-circle), which provides a potent organizational metaphor throughout the novel. As Thompson writes, there is an 'overlap situation' in call-and-response that

> combines innovative calls (or innovative steps, of the leader) with tradition (the choral round, by definition blurring individuality). Solo-ensemble work, among the many other things it seems to accomplish, is the presentation of the individual as a figure on the ground of custom. It is the very perception of real and mythic time.
>
> (Thompson 1979: 43)

That Oduche is sent to the whiteman as both a sacrifice and 'to learn a new dance' (169) in fact suggests the mesh of tradition and innovation that is at the core of Ezeulu's response to the threat of the whiteman. This becomes most apparent when he makes use of the whiteman's attitude to time, an attitude expressed first in the Assistant District Officer's keeping the Priest waiting (as the ADO himself had been kept waiting while being 'broken in' at the Lieutenant Governor's dinner) and then by his imprisoning him. Imprisonment and other forms of coercive waiting enslave one to a future that makes the present meaningless – as Camus, Beckett and other Absurdists have demonstrated. But Ezeulu attempts to exploit the temporal condition of meaningless imprisonment (a symbolic condition of Western life, tyrannized as it is by imperial structure) so as to manipulate the traditional year of his people, in revenge for their disrespect: 'his real struggle was with his own people and the white man was, without knowing it, his ally. The longer he was kept in Okperi the greater his grievance and his resources for the fight' (176). The whiteman, of course, is *not* his ally, and so in the end he fails (and falls). If one is to move with the rhythm of change as the dancer to the drum, one must contribute one's own rhythm and not merely mark time. . . .

To say that innovation and tradition mesh in the overall motivation for sending Oduche to the whiteman is another way of saying that he is expected 'to learn a new dance' while maintaining in his mind the rhythm of the old. In other words, what Ezeulu requires of him is conceived by Achebe in the same terms as 'apart-playing': in the terms of cross-rhythmic interpretation. Oduche is to learn the ways of the whiteman without losing his commitment to the ways of his people. Unfortunately, however, the rhythm of the whiteman is not merely different in kind. The Western 'approach to rhythm is called divisive because we divide the music into standard units of time', Chernoff tells us:

> As we mark the time by tapping or clapping our hands, we are separating the music into easily comprehensible units of time. . . . It is this fact, that Western musicians count together from the same starting point, which enables a conductor to stand in front of more than a hundred men and women playing in an orchestra and keep them together with his baton. Rhythm is something we *follow*.
>
> (Quoted in Thompson 1979: 41–2). . . .

Accordingly, Oduche is unable to cross the rhythm of the 'new dance' with the rhythm of his people; instead, he takes it on its own terms, and follows it. The next time we come across Oduche, after his father's command to tell the whiteman the old custom even as he learns the new, we see him instead 'speak up for the Lord' (49) against the Sacred Python – following instead of interpreting. The irony of his subsequent Christian naming (an imperial act of claiming), as the rock upon which the Church will be built ('Peter'), is that it is an image of solid inflexibility totally alien to African notions of support and stability. . . .

The hermeneutic principle of *Arrow of God* is one of fluid movement from one position to another, a dancing of attitudes which, in the reader's way of relating them, composes his/her own contribution to what the novel is *doing*. A sense of rhythm and of balance is needed to activate the shifting patterns of metaphor and to relate the different faces of truth, where truth is 'like a Mask dancing' and its 'characters' are permutations of its essence. . . .

The potential and the limits of individual participation in the communal context are dramatized as they are encoded by idiom in *Arrow of God*. At the core of the colonial relationship, as T. O. Ranger declares, is 'the successful manipulation and control of symbols' (Ranger 1975: 166). Ezeulu undoubtedly fails in this power struggle; but the novel does not. Nor does Idemili. Implicit in much 'criticism' of Achebe's fiction is the honorific judgement that it extends the Great Tradition of the Nineteenth-Century Novel in its European Heyday; were this true, from a post-colonial point of view it would be an accusation, for, as Gayatri Spivak and others have demonstrated, that form of fiction encodes the ideal of Empire (by investing narrative authority in omniscient or centralized perspective, by proposing concepts of universalized value, etc.) (Spivak 1987). The accusation, of course, is false. Achebe has captured the symbolic form of the novel from the 'central' tradition, and grounded it upon an aesthetic of movement and motion and agility – which, as he says, 'inform the Igbo concept of existence' and so, by a paradigm shift, reconstitute the nature and experience of fiction. The reader must engage with a kinetic performance, must participate in a process: '*Ada-akwu ofu ebe enene mmoo*; you do not stand in one place to watch a masquerade. You must imitate its motion' (Address given by Achebe at Guelph University, Ontario, 1984). The process is one of socialization and constant renewal, functioning by an 'overlap' of multiple perspectives – individual and communal, call-and-response, solo-and-circle – that redefines the imperial concept of the centre in African terms, in terms of slippage: as that blank space where innovation inscribes itself on the ground of tradition.

## NOTES

1 This critical model is an adaptation of the 'metronome sense' advocated as essential to an understanding of African music by Richard Alan Waterman (1952: 211). I am indebted also to John Miller Chernoff's discussion of African music as an educational force (1981: 154).
2 The impetus for my continuing examination of the kinetics of Achebe's fiction comes from Robert Farris Thompson's discussion of African art history (Thompson 1979).

# 60

## Dance, Movement and Resistance Politics

### HELEN GILBERT*

CRITICAL ANALYSIS OF dance in Australian plays is virtually non-existent
even though almost all Aboriginal, and some feminist and other playwrights, use dance in their texts. Similarly, most theatre reviewers either fail
to notice the dance, or classify it as spectacle, therein eliding its signifying
practices with aesthetic (read normative) standards of judgment. Heavily
influenced by Western theatrical and critical traditions, representations of
dance in contemporary white (and to a lesser extent, black) Australian
drama necessarily carry traces of earlier historical readings of European
drama that link dance, somewhat ambivalently, with themes of harmony or
chaos. . . .

Dramaturgically speaking, enactment of some kind of dance in a play
does a number of things to the text. As a focalizing agent, it draws attention to the rhetoric of embodiment in all performance, something which is
less apparent in dramatization of dialogue, especially within the conventions of realism. Even while bringing the body into focus, dance also
spatializes, which is to say that it foregrounds proxemic relations between
characters, spectators, and features of the set. The ever-shifting relational
axis of space breaks down binary structures that seek to situate dance
as either image or identity, and the spectator as observer rather than
co-producer of meaning. Furthermore, situated within a dramatic text,
dance often de-naturalizes theatre's signifying practices by disrupting
narrative sequence and/or genre. What dance 'does' then, is draw attention
to the constructedness of dramatic representation, which suggests that it
can function as an alienating device in the Brechtian sense. This calls for
analysis of its ideological encoding, an especially important project in
criticism of postcolonial texts. . . .

In discussing specific instances of dance in contemporary Australian
drama, I begin with David Malouf's *Blood Relations* because, in its refiguring

* From 'The Dance as Text in Contemporary Australian Drama: Movement and
Resistance Politics' *Ariel* 23(1), 1992.

of *The Tempest*, this play positions the dance within a tradition which it then subverts to expose the ideological assumptions which traverse the body in the masque scene of Shakespeare's colonial paradigm. The dance of the nymphs and reapers in Prospero's vision functions as a representation of ritualized social harmony and appropriates the New World with its portent of bounteous harvest. It also desexualizes the body by linking Miranda and Ferdinand's forthcoming union with images of the fruition of nature, and, significantly, denies illegitimate sexual desire by excluding Caliban from the spectacle. Malouf refigures Shakespeare's dance as part of a carnivalesque magic show layered with ironic and apocalyptic overtones. The performance is neither at the behest nor under the control of Willy (the Australian Prospero), and it clearly expresses conflict rather than harmony. Kit, who functions as an Ariel figure, engineers the show despite Willy's opposition; then he foregrounds the dance as homosexual display when he dances in an exaggerated fashion with Dash (Trinculo), eclipsing Cathy/Miranda and Edward/Ferdinand's performance as the 'happy couple'. During their movements, the characters' dialogue operates as a running meta-commentary on the dancing itself, stressing its theatricality, which provides the spectator with a method for deconstructing the illusionistic devices of representation. Meanwhile, Dinny/Caliban, the Aboriginal character in the play, makes a potent statement of political autonomy when he declines an invitation to join the dance, and then disrupts it completely with a recitation of Caliban's 'This island's mine . . . ' speech from *The Tempest*. By insisting on staging his own 'show', Dinny refuses the inscriptions of white ritual movement on his body and holds the whole performance, and its Shakespearean prototype as well, up to scrutiny.

As well as resisting identities imposed by the dominant culture on individuals or groups and/or abrogating the privilege of their signifying systems, dance can function to recuperate postcolonial subjectivity because movement helps constitute the individual in society. . . .

Movement as producer of one's self and one's culture has special significance for reading the dance as text in Aboriginal plays. In imperial historical accounts, Aboriginal dance has been encoded as the expression of savage or exotic 'otherness' within a discourse which represents blacks as objects to be looked at, rather than as self-constituting subjects. W. Robertson, for example, writing in 1928, constructs Aboriginal dance during a *corroboree* as the picturesque signifier of less-than-human behaviour. 'The weirdly painted natives issuing from the dense bracken of the bush to perform the dances, looked more like wraiths than human beings. . . .' (Robertson 1928: 95). . . .

These descriptions, though purportedly historical accounts, clearly use theatrical conventions to conflate nature and the indigene, marking the dance as a 'primitive' performance event designed for consumption by the imperial spectator. Along with some notion of theatrical order (an implied programme), Robertson's narrative points to the use of costuming and make-up (the painted bodies), while evoking backstage areas in the 'dense blackness of the bush' and a well-lit space by the fire where the compelling stage action occurs. This narrative exemplifies what Nietzsche argues is the constitutive basis of history – 'dramatistical' thought, or the ability 'to think one thing with another, and weave the elements into a whole, with the presumption that the unity of plan must be put into the objects if it isn't there' (quoted in White 1982: 53). In constructing a bush theatre to frame (read contain) the dance, and by situating himself as the impartial observer of a series of static 'pictures', Robertson naturalizes his perspective, renders invisible the appropriative function of the historian's gaze, and militates against the threat of difference that the Aboriginal dance with its 'frenzied movements' poses. He can thus categorize the dancers as more wraith-like than human and relegate the *corroboree* to the realm of the fantastic, the fictional, the infernal, reserving the notion of 'real' dance for the dominant culture by marginalizing its variants. Robertson's failure to acknowledge the dancers' subjectivity prevents him from discerning any functional aspects of the *corroboree* vis-à-vis Aboriginal culture and certainly blinds him to the possibility of resistance politics. It is this representation of dance as reified spectacle that is problematized in contemporary Aboriginal drama if we focus on movement as part of identity formation/recuperation and spatial re-orientation. . . .

As an important mode of narrative in Aboriginal culture, dancing (or drawing with the body) can also function to restore masculine identity through its links with ritual and male initiation ceremonies. In Richard Walley's *Coordah*, Nummy, the 'local drunk' and 'trickster' figure, escapes the fixity of these roles formed within the dominant discourse of colonization by recreating his Aboriginality through dance performance (Walley 1989: 109–166). Similarly, dancing in a *corroboree* gives Billy Kimberly of Jack Davis's *No Sugar* an opportunity to transgress his assigned role of tracker/informant (Davis 1986). During the *corroboree*, individual identity is both created by, and subsumed in, group identity as culturally coded movement that gives valance to each performer's dance, allowing participants to shed their everyday roles determined within white hierarchies of power. In this sense, the dance acts as a shaman exorcizing evil. It is also an occasion for the exchange of cultural capital between tribes, and for the contestation of white dominated space. A recent production of *No Sugar* in Perth featured the dance as a potent tool for symbolic reclamation of Aboriginal land when, even after the performers' movements ended, their spatial inscriptions were clearly palpable through footprints on the sand and a visible layer of unsettled red dust. As Auber Octavius Neville, Chief Protector of Aborigines, walked tentatively across this ground in his three-piece suit to deliver a speech that situated Aborigines firmly within white historical discourse, traces of the *corroboree* marked his presence as incongruous, invasive, and ultimately illegitimate. (The published text of *No Sugar* does not place the scenes depicting the *corroboree* and Neville's speech in adjacency; however, director Phil Thompson worked closely with Jack Davis in this production.)

That *No Sugar* encodes the *corroboree* as a masculine activity (the female characters are denied participation *and* spectatorship) raises some problematic issues: on the one hand, it gives the dance a higher status as cultural production because all societies deem the occupations of men more important than those of women (Hanna 1987: 22–3); on the other hand, most of Davis's predominantly white audience will be tempted to read the performance from culturally subjectified standpoints that link dance with female activity, thereby seeing the *corroboree* as a feminizing practice. The ritual and spatial codings of the performance, however, resist this totalizing impulse by grounding the *corroboree* firmly in Aboriginal history and epistemology through its links with the Dreamtime, which, Stephen Muecke claims, is the 'constant supplementary signified of all Aboriginal narrative' (Muecke 1983: 98). The agency of white Australian theatre practice can also function to legitimate Aboriginal performance practices even while it necessarily compromizes them. As Penny Van Toorn argues in her analysis of minority texts and majority audiences, hybridized texts 'harness the power of valorizing signs recognized by the dominant audience in order to impart prestige to the valorizing signs' of their own culture (Van Toorn 1990: 112). . . .

Feminist Australian drama has also explored the dance's potential as transformative agent in identity recuperation. Dorothy Hewett, for example, has written plays in which dance features not only as enacted resistance to the appropriation of the female body within imperialist and/or patriarchal discourses but also as an active self-constituting process. A similar ideological project underscores the representation of dance in Sarah Cathcart and Andrea Lemon's monodrama, *The Serpent's Fall* (Cathcart and Lemon 1988), which uses the body/performance of a single actor playing six separate characters to produce a fluid concept of feminine gender identity while at the same time enacting sociocultural differences between the characters. The primary character, Sarah, an Australian actor, plays, alternately, a young archaeologist, a middle-aged Greek migrant, an urban Aborigine, a cafeteria boss, and a retired teacher – all but one of them women. As Sarah slips from one character to another without costume changes or breaks, using only mimed props, the performance enacts what Jill Dolan outlines as the two opposing feminist theories of the self, identity politics and poststructural notions of the decentred subject. . . .

These theories of self may both be applied to a reading of the play's dance, a seminal sequence in which Sarah in rapid succession performs dances as four separate characters. As she moves, her transitions between characters, and the traces of difference thus enacted by a single but composite body, both produce and deconstruct cultural and racial specificity, showing identity to be fluid but not without some sort of grounding in individual sociohistorical circumstances. Not surprisingly, this dance functions as a mode of empowerment for all of its participants: for Kelly, the Aboriginal woman, it forms a link with the land; for Sula, a moment of resistance to the drudgery of the cafeteria and its patriarchal structures; for Bernice, the archaeologist, the possibility of rewriting the body against the discourses of power engendered in the biblical myth of genesis; and for Sarah herself, further confirmation that her own performance, and therefore her 'self' is, in a sense, intertextual. This composite, shifting sense of identity, which has much in common with that of the hybridized post-colonial subject, figures as the most important feature of *The Serpent's Fall* and its construction of the feminine, and the Australian. . . .

Whereas Aboriginal and Feminist playwrights frequently use dance as a mode of empowerment for marginalized individuals/groups, other Australian plays represent dance more ambiguously. Although an in-depth examination of this topic is beyond the scope of my paper, Louis Nowra's work deserves mention. Almost all of Nowra's plays include some kind of dance, most of which enact a struggle for power and authority in tense, uneasy relationships between individuals and groups. From a postcolonial perspective, these struggles can be seen as emblematic of the colonizer/colonized dialectic, a process that, to some extent, hybridizes the identity of both dominating and subordinated groups. The Bal Masqué scene of *Visions* (Nowra 1979) enacts such a process in a combination of movement and verbal discourse in which Madam Lynch (representative of European imperial power) and Lopez (a somewhat ambivalent figure of colonial resistance) vie for control over the dance, which in symbolic terms can be seen as Paraguayan culture and even the country itself. . . .

In contemporary Australian drama, then, the dance emerges as a locus of struggle in producing and representing individual and cultural identity. As a site of competing ideologies, it also offers a site of potential resistance to hegemonic discourses through its representation of the body on stage as a moving subject that actually looks back at the spectator, eluding the kind of appropriation that the 'male gaze' theories of cinema outline. In Stanton Garner's terms, 'exploiting the body's centrality within the theatrical medium' allows the refiguring of the 'actor's body as a principal site of theatrical and political intervention, establishing (in the process) a contemporary "body politic" rooted in the individual's sentient presence' (Garner 1990: 146). Thus, reading/producing the dance as text provides an approach to drama that de-naturalizes notions of the self grounded primarily in language, and avoids privileging the performance of the mind over the performance of the body. As spectators with a split gaze that recognizes representation as distinct from embodiment, we *can* know the dancer from the dance.

# 61

# Feminism and the Colonial Body

## KADIATU KANNEH*

*'It is the white man who creates the Negro. But it is the Negro who creates negritude. To the colonialist offensive against the veil, the colonized opposes the cult of the veil.'*

(Fanon 1970a: 47)

THIS QUOTE IS taken from Frantz Fanon's 'Algeria Unveiled', which I take as my opening text because, for me, it introduces an ongoing and significant debate in feminist and cultural politics. The place of the body in analyses of gender or race has become so complicated and so fraught that words like identity, subjectivity and desire – all familiar words by now – are anything but simple.

Where does racial identity lie? How is it mobilised in terms of Black and feminist resistance? And how do gender or race intersect or become mobilised in identity politics?

Fanon's essay focuses on the interplay of body, dress and cultural identity – not only as sites of metaphor and play, but as areas of crucial contestation in the Algerian war of independence. Clothing becomes emblematic of a cultural or racial group; representing a colonial relationship which is both gendered and sexualised.

The feminising of colonised territory is, of course, a trope in colonial thought. In Fanon's analysis, Algerian women are placed in a metonymic process where both veil and woman become interchangeable, scopic signifiers of colonised Algeria itself – as oppressed, inscrutable, and dispossessed.

It is under the aegis of a displaced feminist politics that a specifically colonial battle, on one level, becomes waged. Fanon characterises the French colonial resolve in the phrase: 'we must first of all conquer

---

* From 'The Difficult Politics of Wigs and Veils: Feminism and the Colonial Body' Paper presented at the Conference on Gender and Colonialism, University College, Galway, May 1992.

the women; we must go and find them behind the veil where they hide themselves and in the houses where the men keep them out of sight' (37–8).

This 'kind of violence' as Fanon calls it, where 'unveiling' equals – as he writes – 'revealing . . . baring . . . breaking her resistance . . . making her available' (43) is confused with a mission of female liberation and a paternalistic notion of empowerment, which, in practice and at base, is a politics of ownership and control, 'The European faced with an Algerian woman wants to see' (44).

The familiar discourse of rape between coloniser, and colonised country, becomes elaborated through images of rending veils, of exposing bodies and forbidden horizons 'piece by piece' (42).

In many West African countries, 'the colonialist offensive against the veil' is replaced by the missionary offensive against the breasts. Here, it is the very *exposure* of the female body, its unabashed exhibition, which likewise stands for an unacceptable misuse of women and characterises, for the Western mind, the African man's primitive promiscuity and possessiveness. Civilisation and Christianity in this context typically lie on the road to covering up, concealing, neutralising, and taming the body.

These static, and yet contradictory, representations of the colonised woman, or the Black subject, emerge from a network of European knowledge systems which Fanon identifies as: 'written accounts . . . photographic records . . . motion pictures', and the gaze of 'the tourist and the foreigner' (35).

In this way, 'Ethnic' dress becomes interchangeable with tradition and essentialism, and the female body enters an unstable arena of scrutiny and meaning. . . .

I'd like to now turn very briefly to a major issue in Western feminism which involves the representation, discussion and manipulation of Third World women. Here, the debate moves to a different kind of acculturation of the body, where what is literally inscribed in the flesh, and, by implication, in the sexual freedom and expression of African women, is placed as a difficult agenda for Black and White women.

The taboo of female circumcision in certain feminist writing is so obscured by myth and conflation that it is the *representation* and *meaning* of this issue in feminism which I wish to explore. That is, how does this range of practices and their differing degrees of severity, meaning, and importance in the male and female worlds of African societies, become *one* polarised argument about the very basis of female or feminist identity?

'Female circumcision' has become almost a dangerous trope in Western feminisms for the muting and mutilation of women – physically, sexually and psychologically – and for these women's *need for* Western feminism. Circumcision, clitoridectomy, infibulation, become one visible marker of outrageous primitivism, sexism, and *the* Third World woman.

I don't wish to invalidate the varying degrees of pain or the struggles of certain African women to change some or all of these practices, but I do wish to militate against how the subject of feminism in Africa is often seen to be the circumcised – hence, damaged and oppressed – Black Third World woman.

Not only, then, does the representation of the body characteristically oscillate between, and confuse, natural and cultural attributes in discussions of race, but feminine and masculine – or feminist and non-feminist – agency becomes at issue. The battle over the Black Third World woman's body is staged as a battle between First World feminists and Black Third World men.

This is a suspect development of affairs to say the least, one reason being that a Black feminist response is often to defensively revalorise the role of men and traditional African societies as indiscriminate wholes, against what is seen – often rightly – as arrogant and culturally 'superior' Western interference and insult.

But it's not just in feminism that the bodies of Black people have been metaphorically invaded, analysed and represented by liberal, paternalist (or maternalist) principles. Where racial identity lies in the body, and its link to racism, culture and psychology has been endlessly documented by Western scientists, anthropologists, travel writers, photographers and journalists. . . .

Black and female identities are not simply figurative or superficial sites of play and metaphor, but occupy very real political spaces of diaspora, dispossession and resistance. What is complicated is the simultaneity of suffering and power, marginalisation and threat, submission and narcissism, which accrue to Black and women's bodies and their representation in racist cultures.

To go further than Mercer's query: 'So who, in this postmodern melée of semiotic appropriation and counter-creolisation, is imitating whom?' (Mercer 1987: 52), I would like to end with the question: 'On whose terms is this celebration of postmodern plurality and difference being conducted?'

# 62

## Outlaws of the Text

### GILLIAN WHITLOCK*

RESPONSES TO EMPIRE in settler societies, like Australia and Canada, comprise a site of contesting and conflicting claims, an array of identifications and subjectivities which refuse to cohere neatly into oppositional or complicit post-colonialisms. Settler post-colonialism confounds the positions of self and other in relation to discourse and discursive strategies; as a number of theorists of settler cultures argue, these 'second world' spaces are characterised by the ambiguity and ambivalence of both oppositional and complicit positions (Lawson 1991, Slemon 1990). Confusions of complicity and resistance in these cultures makes the identification of outlaws in settler territory a perilous enterprise. On these frontiers outlaws and sheriffs are not in predictable and fixed opposition but related and interdependent, mixed in hybrid forms which confuse the rule of Law. These ambiguities are all the more evident when we turn to settler women in particular, who occupy a terrain of 'shiftingness' (Giles 1989). Here discourses of gender, class and race further complicate forms of complicity and resistance. The female body has always been crucial to the reproduction of Empire, and deeply marked by it. On the other hand it can also be at the bosom of de-scribing Empire. The anatomy of the female body in colonial space is the skeleton for the following discussion which ends, but does not begin, in the settler colonies. In fact [I want to examine this process] via Bermuda and the history of Mary Prince, an unlikely autobiographer. . . .

You may well ask how it is that we have available to us an autobiography by a woman born into slavery in the Crown colony of Bermuda in 1788. We learn from her *History* that she was sold as an infant, sold again in 1805 as an adolescent, and again as a woman in her twenties. Each time

* From 'Outlaws of the Text: Women's Bodies and the Organisation of Gender in Imperial Space' Paper presented at the 'Australia/Canada: Post-colonization and Women's Texts' research network at the Calgary Institute for the Humanities, February 13–16, 1992.

her *History* records experiences of degradation and brutality which reach a nadir on the salt ponds of Turks Island. She was sold for a fourth and final time to a merchant in Antigua, who took her to England with his family in 1828 to do their laundry. Here, at the height of the anti-slavery campaign, Mary Prince came to the attention of the Anti-Slavery Society and became a maid in the house of Thomas Pringle, the Secretary of the Society. . . .

The character of the *History* is shaped generically according to the form of the British slave narrative which, in 1830, prescribed a particularly limited sense of the intersections between gender and race in the life history of slave women.

For this form, this casting of a life of slavery, won public support by detailing atrocities and portraying slaves as pure and Christian-like, innocent victims and martyrs. Women whose cause they championed could not be seen to be involved in any form of moral corruption: 'Christian purity, for these abolitionists, overrode regard for truth' (Ferguson 1986: 4). Without doubt this constrained Prince's ability to describe her experiences fully. The abusive sexual experience which were no doubt part of the brutality she suffered enter the text only in encoded ways. What is remarkable about the shape of Prince's *History* is that it attributes to her personhood, and spiritual equality. It is however blind to gender, to her womanhood. We know Prince married but we know no detail of her married life, or whether she became a mother at any stage of her career. All traces of her sexuality and likely sexual abuse are absent from the *History*. This was of course 20 years prior to the black abolitionist and freed slave Sojourner Truth's speech to the Akron convention in 1851. 'Aint I a Woman?' was the refrain of Truth's speech. It is a claim upon both race and gender, about how gender affects racial oppression, which is notably absent at Claremont Square in 1831. It is, then, by no means the case that the colonial body is gendered in the representation. Mary Prince's body is marked by her race and status.

There is at the end of Mary Prince's *History* an episode which makes the construction of her identity in these terms clear. Appendix Three was added to the third edition of the *History* following 'inquiries from various quarters respecting the existence of marks of severe punishments on Mary Prince's body'. Mary's narrative is, it seems not enough. So the amanuensis, the guest who copied Mary's story from her own lips, now views Mary's body and provides a testimonial, 'full and authentic evidence' that 'the whole back part of her body is severely scarred, and, as it were, *chequered*, with the vestiges of severe floggings.' '[There] are many large gashes on other parts of her person, exhibiting an appearance as if the flesh had been deeply cut, or lacerated with gashes, by some instrument wielded by most unmerciful hands' (Ferguson 1986: 119). There is no evidence here that it is a female body which is scarred and disfigured. . . .

Mary Prince's body is a reminder that as late as 1830 the most brutal forms of repression continued in the British Empire. In penal and slave colonies in particular savage physical punishment and coercion remained even as more subtle forms of self surveillance and discipline were instituted in Europe. Tyrannical ideals of order and precision could preside unchecked in the garrisons, penitentiaries and planter households of the settler and crown colonies. . . .

The body at the end of Mary's *History* also brings home to us that the gender of the female body becomes visible only in particular ways of knowing. . . .

I will do this by bringing a second image alongside that viewing of Mary's body at Claremont Square in the last week of March 1831. Within a week of testifying to Mary's scars the relationship between these two women took a different turn: here Mary becomes the spectator, the amanuensis the autobiographical subject. Let me, finally, allow the amanuensis to speak from a letter of April 9, 1831:

> I was on the 4th instant at St. Pancras Church made the happiest girl on earth, in being united to the beloved being in whom I have long centred all my affections. Mr Pringle 'gave me' away, and Black Mary, who had treated herself with a complete new suit upon the occasion, went on the coach box, to see her dear Missie and Biographer wed. . . .

This second glimpse, equally intriguing, of Mary Prince as Black Mary, resplendent in a new suit and perched on the coach box of the bridal carriage, is our last view of her. Of her dear Missie and Biographer we know more. Like so many women of her class who married a half pay officer with no prospects of inheritance, it was her fate to emigrate – to Upper Canada. From here she would pen another autobiographical document, one better known than Mary Prince's *History*. It was published in 1852 as *Roughing It in the Bush*. . . .

The journey which Moodie began with Mary Prince as observer on the coach box was presented much less sentimentally in 1909 by Cicely Hamilton. In her first wave feminist polemic *Marriage as a Trade* Hamilton presents marriage as women's compulsory trade, a ceremony which marks their entry as wives and later mothers into the sexual economy of a patriarchal society. Throughout Hamilton's brutally rationalist discussion of marriage as trade in which the currency is women's bodies, we see the influence of imperialism upon her argument. The reproduction of British values and race following the passage of the bridal ships, the association of marriage and emigration which was so much a feature of nineteenth century European sexual politics, alerts Hamilton to the commercial basis of the marriage transaction.

Those of us who write about settler women in Australia and Canada as critics or, like Grenville and Marlatt, as authors need to grasp precisely the location of these emigrants in the imperial organisation of gender and race. For it was in the settler colonies that nineteenth century pro-natalist discourses assumed particular importance. As Marchant observed in 1916, in the difference between the number of cradles and the number of coffins lie the existence and persistence of our Empire. The dissemination of British institutions and society depended upon its emigrants; in colonies of occupation – India, Africa – European women were valued less than in settlement colonies. In fact Chilla Bulbeck has argued that in these colonies women were seen as wives but not mothers, in pre-Bowlby days women were expected to send their children 'Home' to school (Bulbeck 1991: 14). However, in settlement colonies the fertility of European women and the welfare of mothers and children were vital to the colonising project. The British Women's Emigration Association, for example, used marriage as one of its incentives to encourage women to emigrate. They also stressed this as an opportunity to civilise the world and secure British values in the colonies. White women as homemakers and mothers helped to maintain and promote the Empire through the biological and daily reproduction of the settler population. (Strobel 1991: 46). The uterus was singled out not only as the most important female organ, but the most important organ of the Race; as one imperialist opined: 'the uterus is to the Race what the heart is to the Individual' (Gallagher and Laqueur 1987). . . .

Of course this process of rearing racially and nationally identified children assumed particular valency in settler colonies; discourses of maternalism characterise the writings of settler women from the beginnings. Their gender and status as wife and mother were crucial to the politics of imperialism. Catharine Parr Traill's handbook *The Backwoods of Canada*, for example, is an instruction to European settler women in appropriate maternal behaviour. 'Maternal' here is to be understood in the widest terms, incorporating not only management of domestic 'capital', the making of soap and sugar, but also the 'husbanding' of local flora and wildlife. . . .

My argument here is that this child and that fusion of emigration with maternity are crucial to our understanding the historically specific context of settler writings by and about women. Discourses of maternalism and imperialism coalesced to produce that collective identity of the immigrant gentlewoman which Moodie and her kind embodied – with varying degrees of success! By coming to this maternal body via Mary Prince, whose status as a mother is unknown and whose body is represented in terms of race and status rather than gender, I mean to stress that colonial subjects were by no means necessarily gendered in the representation. The case of Mary Prince reminds us of the tangle of distinct and variable relations of power and points of resistance in the field of Empire. . . .

# PART XI

*History*

# Introduction

The significance of history for post-colonial discourse lies in the modern origins of historical study itself, and the circumstances by which 'History' took upon itself the mantle of a discipline. For the emergence of history in European thought is coterminous with the rise of modern colonialism, which in its radical othering and violent annexation of the non-European world, found in history a prominent, if not *the* prominent, instrument for the control of subject peoples. At base, the myth of a value free, 'scientific' view of the past, the myth of the beauty of order, the myth of the story of history as a simple representation of the continuity of events, authorised nothing less than the construction of world reality. This was a time in which the European nations, represented by three or four 'world' cities, 'absorbed into themselves the whole of world history' as Oswald Spengler puts it (Spengler [1926] 1962: 32).

The question the human sciences had to face in the nineteenth century was: what does it mean to have a history? This question, Foucault maintains, signals a great mutation in the consciousness of Western man, a mutation which has to do ultimately with 'our modernity', which in turn is the sense we have of being utterly different from all other forms of humanity known to history' (Foucault 1970: 219–20). The question we ask at this point is, of course, who is this 'we'? Clearly, what it means to have a history is the same as what it means to have a legitimate existence: history and legitimation go hand in hand; history legimates 'us' and not others.

According to Hayden White it was important that history, seeking the title of 'scientific discipline' in the nineteenth century mould, should suppress the modality of interpretation which has always given it its form. The appeal to a moral or political authority underlying all interpretation had to be sublimated by dissolving the authority to interpret into the interpretation itself. This, and the desire for the 'scientific', generated a particular historiographic ideology: a single narrative truth which was 'simply' the closest possible representation of events. White identifies the emergence of the discipline of history with a strategic moment of choice between possible discursive options, in which the apparently neutral narrative form succeeded by virtue of its resemblance to the purity of scientific disciplines. A crucial question he asks is 'What is *ruled out* by conceiving the historical object in such a way that *not* to conceive it in that way would constitute prima facie evidence of want of discipline' (White 1982: 120). His answer is *rhetoric*, which can be described as an awareness of the variety of ways of configuring a past which itself only exists as a chaos of forms.

The problem of history becomes particularly crucial for the post-colonial writer. For not only are the questions of truth and fiction, of narrativity and indeterminacy, time and space, of pressing importance because the material ground, the political dimension of post-colonial life impresses itself so urgently, but the historical narrativity is that which structures the forms of reality itself. In other words, the myth of historical objectivity is embedded in a particular view of the sequential nature of narrative, and its capacity to reflect, isomorphically, the pattern of events it records. The post-colonial task, therefore is not simply to contest the message of history, which has so often relegated individual post-colonial societies to footnotes to the march of progress, but also to engage the medium of narrativity itself, to reinscribe the 'rhetoric', the heterogeneity of historical representation as White describes it. This, of course, is easier said than done for post-colonial societies which so often have failed to gain access to the very institution of 'History' itself with its powerful rules of inclusion and exclusion.

José Rabasa indicates the extent of the historical construction of a Eurocentric world, in the conception of the Mercator Atlas itself. The map of the world can be seen as a palimpsest on which Europe has written its own dominance through the agency of history. This tendency of history to construct the world can be seen, as Peter Hulme shows, in the historical emergence of the word 'cannibal' to describe the inhabitants of the West Indies. That which etymologically begins as description assumes very quickly a power to signify the 'Other'. That which emerges as 'historical' is the result of contesting discourses. But it is the servitude to the 'muse of History' that Derek Walcott sees as most debilitating to the New World societies because it inevitably ossifies into a 'literature of recrimination and despair'. In this way the spirit of resistance itself is caught in the disempowering binarism of imperial history. Walcott suggests the need for a new beginning to post-colonial history, a new Adam and a new Eden, one which dispenses with imperial history altogether. Paul Carter's concept of spatial history goes some way towards this by rejecting the imperial idea of history as a stage on which it plays out its universal theme of the emergence of order out of chaos. The concept of place as a palimpsest written and overwritten by successive (historical) inscriptions is one way of circumventing history as the 'scientific narrative' of events.

As with that western commodity called 'Theory' (in its various forms; theories about writing, or philosophy, or politics) the way in which colonised peoples have been able to enter the 'discursive plane', so to speak, of these patently authoritative and powerful intellectual pursuits, is through *literary* writing which may authorise otherwise forbidden entries into the intellectual

356

battlefield of European thought. Wilson Harris believes that 'a philosophy of history may well lie buried in the arts of the imagination'. For Harris such imaginative arts extend beyond the 'literary' to include the discourse of the *limbo* dance or of *vodun*, all examples of the creativity of 'stratagems available to Caribbean man in the dilemmas of history which surround him'. In post-colonial societies the term 'literary' may well operate in its traditional canonical way, but more often it has come to operate as a mode by which the objectivity of narrative is contested, and particularly the narrative of history.

Recognising that all histories, no matter what they are about, ultimately have 'Europe' as their subject, Dipesh Chakrabarty advocates a post-colonial history that, rather than returning to atavistic, nativist histories, or rejecting modernism itself, should invent a narrative that 'deliberately makes visible, within the very structure of its narrative forms, its own repressive strategies and practices'.

# 63

## *Allegories of* Atlas

### José Rabasa*

As far as I know, there is no history of the atlas as a genre. Insofar as such a history might turn out to be for clarifying the question of Eurocentrism, I believe that an analysis of Mercator's *Atlas* is a necessary preparatory task. I also believe that the *Atlas* manifests the main constituents that have defined Europe as a privileged source of meaning for the rest of the world. Eurocentrism, as I will try to point out with respect to the *Atlas*, is more than an ideological construct that vanishes with the brush of the pen or merely disappears when Europe loses its position of dominance. The trace of European expansionism continues to exist in the bodies and minds of the rest of the world, as well as in the fantasies of the former colonizers. The transposition of the image of the palimpsest becomes an illuminative metaphor for understanding geography as a series of erasures and over-writings that have transformed the world. The imperfect erasures are, in turn, a source of hope for the reconstitution or reinvention of the world from native points of view. . . .

A cursory glance at Mercator's World Map (Figure 3) uncovers a plurality of semiotic systems and semantic levels interacting with each other.

The Map functions as a mirror of the world, not because the representation of the earth has the status of a natural sign, but because it aims to invoke a simulacrum of an always inaccessible totality by means of an arrangement of symbols. Thus Mercator, after enumerating the different sections of the *Atlas*, tells us in 'Preface upon Atlas' that his work '(as in a mirror) will set before your eyes, the whole world, that in the making of some rudiments, ye may finde out the causes of things, and so by attayning unto wisdom and prudence, by this meanes leade the Reader to higher speculation' (Mercator 1636: 'Preface' ). As such the World Map itself

* From 'Allegories of *Atlas*' *Inventing A-M-E-R-I-C-A: Spanish Historiography and the Formation of Eurocentrism* Norman, Okla., and London: University of Oklahoma Press, 1993.

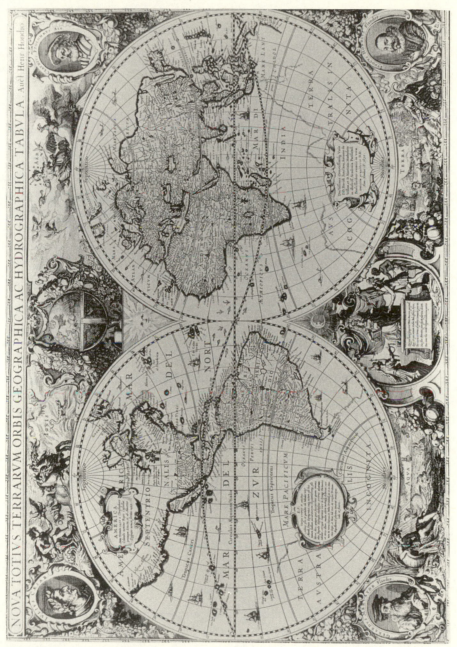

*Figure 3* Mercator's world map
*Source:* Mercator 1636

organizes different semiotic systems for creating a play of mirrors that would ultimately lead the reader to speculate on the creation of the world and the godhead: only topics from the part of the *Atlas* on 'Creation' are not allegorically coded on the margins of the world map. . . .

Since the totality of the world can never be apprehended as such in a cartographical objectification, maps have significance only within a subjective reconstitution of the fragments. The *Atlas* stands out as an ironic allegorization of this blind spot inherent in a cartographical enterprise. As a palimpsest, the *Atlas* conveys the irony of a bricolage where the interpreter is caught up in an open-ended process of signification and where the loose fragments derived from primitive texts allow for a plurality of combinations. Memory and systematic forgetfulness suspend the elucidation of a stable structure and constitute the need for an active translation.

An inside and an outside constitute two planes of content and expression for reading the map. The outside introduces an allegorical decoration that offers a narrative illumination to the portrayal of the earth. A title, portraits, proper names, allegories of the elements, a celestial sphere, instruments of measurement, a sun, a moon, and an allegory of the four continents frame the world with historic, cosmographic and anthropological categories. These registers introduce a series of strata into an apparently homogeneous and flat representation of the globe. The frame functions both as a decoration and as a content to be read in the map. Likewise, the separation of the world into two circles (the Old and New World) tabulated by meridians, parallels and the line of the zodiac, not only structure the totality of the world for locating names and points in space, but are also particular expressions of the celestial sphere represented in the frame itself. As a result, the map mirrors the course of history and the macrocosmos. Under closer inspection, we find the inside and the outside organized in terms of a binary opposition between the eternal and the contingent, between hard and soft parts. Without exhausting the binary oppositions organizing the map, the following samples exemplify the hierarchical arrangements:

| *Hard* | *Soft* |
|---|---|
| moderns | ancients |
| Europe | the rest of the world |
| Old World | New World |
| masculine | feminine |
| coordinates | contours |
| macrocosmos | microcosmos |

These binary oppositions must be understood as independent realms interacting with each other and inseparable for portraying the totality of the cosmos and the whole circle of the Earth. In the following discussion we will often see soft and hard characterizations of the written and the visual, of geography and history, shift positions. . . .

Let us now observe in the following analogy between cartography and the art of painting how the historical is indissoluble from the geographical in Mercator's *Atlas*:

> . . . I have principally endeavored to describe before every Mapp the order & nature of the most remarkeable places in every Province, the better to profit, the studious, and carefull of Politick matters and States affairs.
> (Mercator 1636 II: 269)

For Mercator, the written defines differences in what would otherwise be a homogeneous space. As a result, knowledge and power merge 'to profit the studious, and carefull of Politick matters and State affairs'. The written solidifies locations while supplying meaning to the visual. Writing, as such, is both a soft and a hard component in the *Atlas*. Inscriptions precede and determine the visibility of the contour, but they also flesh out the abstract frame. The possibility and the significance of the map thus depend on history. The inscription of the map gives place to its silhouette, but its silhouette is historical and meaningful only when it evokes a European history. In this light Mercator explains in 'Preface to the Reader' the scope of the Atlas: 'This work then is composed of *Geographie* (which is a description of the knowne Earth and parts thereof) and *Historie*, which is (*Oculus Mundi*) the eye of the World' (Mercator 1636: 'Preface'). The personification of geographic space in terms of a Eurocentric perspective is inseparable from the above definition of history as a visual function: 'the eye of the World'. . . .

The visual and the written ironically jumble up time and space within this paradoxical understanding of history, and the 'eye of the world' takes on a plurality of meanings depending on three points of reference:

(1) Travel narratives prefigure the data of the *Atlas*.
(2) History introduces a soft component into the maps for a qualitative determination of space.
(3) Mercator defines cosmography as the light of history.

Whatever alternative, the metaphorical nature of the maps explodes into a spatiotemporal reversibility: time becomes spatial and space becomes temporal. Cosmography is the light of history, while history illuminates the spatial representation of the Earth. . . .

## RHETORIC AND THE UNIVERSALITY OF EUROPE

Along with an ideological stance, the *Geographie* and *Historie of the Atlas* convey a planetary strategy wherein knowledge and representation indissolubly institute and erase territories. If specific political configurations establish boundaries and national identities for a European geographic space, then the rest of the world acquires spatial meaning only after the different regions have been inscribed by Europeans. History, 'the eye of the World', on an ideological level defines the national character of territories depicted. History thus naturalizes particular national formations and institutionalizes forgetfulness of earlier territorializations in the perception of the world. Next to this ideological, or mythological, reification of space, the signalling instrumentality of the *Atlas* opens the territories to a qualitative appraisal of demographic, commercial, ethnographic, religious, political and military details for strategic arrangements. Ideology naturalizes history insofar as it places national configurations and the destiny of European domination *sub specie aeternitatis*. Accordingly, the signalling power of the Atlas reopens territories to domination and appropriation within a historical dimension. . . .

. . . It is specifically the Christian European *man* who can offer the mirror of the world and hold a privileged position throughout the universal semblance of the *Atlas*: 'Here [in Europe] wee have the right of Lawes, the dignity of the Christian Religion, the forces of Armes. . . . Moreover, Europe manageth all Arts and Sciences with such dexterity, that for the invention of manie things shee may be truely called a Mother . . . she hath . . . all manner of learning, whereas other Countries are all of them, overspread with Barbarisme' (1636 I: 42). Let us leave aside for the moment the *Mother Europe* attribute. This passage makes manifest how global histories and geographies, despite their 'introduction' of other religions into the world scenario, always retain a Eurocentric perspective that defines the position and value of the rest of the world. In this respect, the project of the *Atlas* seals an epoch that began with Columbus: the pulsating utopian and millenarian disruptions of European history that the discovery of the New World provoked in Spanish historiography are long gone from the totalizing global vision of Mercator. . . .

In Mercator's maps, previous names accompany contemporary usages. The different regions of the world carry a temporal disparity according to the periods when the sources of information were produced. Generally speaking, Mercator also displays a tendency to make space historical by incorporating legends into the empty areas in the maps. This practice ensures a centrifugal movement from the name-laden Europe to the periphery, where legends and drawings characterize vast territories without history. In the periphery itself, the concentration of names serves as an index of colonialization. . . .

The normality and supremacy of Europe, however, are not perceptible in the bare frame of the world.We have already seen how the written – names and legends – index the higher position of Europe insofar as a hierarchy of space moves from an agglomeration of names to vaguely defined contours, and the newly discovered territories acquire semanticity in terms of their inclusion within a European perspective. Legends in the World map remind us of this. . . . One thing is for certain – no region must be left uncharted. Accordingly, the unknown (*Terra Australis incognita*, most of

*America Septantrionalis*) must be prefigured, invented for a hesitant total-ization of the shape of the Earth. . . .

It is interesting to note in the frame of the World Map, that while Ptolemy, Mercator and Hondius carry a national identification next to their names, Caesar, a symbol of imperialism, stands open to national determi-nation. While Ptolemy is dressed in a Renaissance fashion, Caesar's laurel crown takes a transhistorical and transnational dimension. Caesar func-tions as an empty slot where different leaders may inscribe themselves. The merging of geography and history, of knowledge and power, have Caesar as a prototypical incarnation of world domination. . . . Like the symbol of Caesar, the world revealed by Mercator's *Atlas* is a transhistorical and transnational theatre where imperialist configurations take form by means of particular national appropriations. Beyond rationalization, the *Atlas* establishes a world subject to national translations. Hexham formulates the malleability of the *Atlas* in the following terms:

> At their request I have undertaken, and by the helpe of God, according to my weake abilitie, translated their *Atlas Major* into English, for the good of my Countrie-men, and by their direction (who have most interest therein) have enlarged, & augmented it, out of many worthy Authors of my owne Nation, where it was most needful and requisite, and amended some errours in it, which were escaped in the former editions, & they for their parts have adorned it with new and exact Maps.
>
> (1636 'Preface')

The *Englishising* of the world rests on the translatability of Caesar and the imperialist regard. The role of the translator corresponds to the formulation of a planetary strategy from a national point of view. Under the objective simulacrum of the *Atlas* flows an ironic commentary to the papal bulls that partitioned the unknown world between Portugal and Spain. The Iberian discoveries, conquests and tentative location of places for a determi-nation of sovereignty slowly shaped and mapped the totality of the globe (16). Such a totality became a theatre for contention as European nations came to disregard the pontifical division of the Earth. . . .

Not only are the allegories in the *Atlas* an integral part of cartography, but the *Atlas* as a whole stands as an ironic allegory of the geographer's project to encompass the totality of the world. Atlas, king of Mauritania, the legendary first constructor of the globe, becomes a symbol for a particular genre of the Renaissance 'Book of the World'. In the process the ancient male geographer is transformed into a feminine flat representation of the world where Europe ultimately figures as the mother of 'all manner of learning'. As I have pointed out, in the allegory of the four continents, the presence of the male principle in the female personification of the continents formulates a hierarchy in terms of their subordination to masculinity. Asia, Africa and America in their degrees of nudity lack properness; that is, their selfhood depends solely on European imprints and a consequent mimicry of European space.

From the invention of America emerges a new Europe. The millenarian dream whereby the Franciscans transferred the geographic realization of history to the New World now, with Mercator, returns the locus of universal history to Europe; the angelic nature of the natives is replaced with a universal subjectivity that is indispensable to the knowing of truth and thus constitutes the apex of history. Europe, which in analogous allegories is invested with a sphere and a cross emblematic of Catholicism, assumes a secular version where science and knowledge define her supremacy and universality. . . .

If Europeans retain the universal key, nothing keeps the *Atlas* from being translated into a non-European idiom as its ultimate irony within a historical horizon. This is not the place to elaborate on the 'writing back' of the colonized, but my analysis depends on the possibility that the universal address of the *Atlas* includes readings not confined to a Eurocentric point of view. The meanings of humanity, the world and history become undecidable beyond a European battle ground. Universal history is undecidable, not on account of a theoretical deconstruction of teleology and eschatology, but because of an ever-present deconstruction of Eurocentric world views by the rest of the world. As it were, the empire has always been writing back. The allegorization of the four continents suppresses the colonialist machinery and fabricates an omnipotent European subject who can dominate the world from the cabinet, but it also produces a blind spot that dissolves history as a privileged modality of European culture.

# 64

## Columbus and the Cannibals

### Peter Hulme*

THE PRIMARY *OED* definition of 'cannibal' reads: 'A man (*esp.* a savage) that eats human flesh; a man-eater, an anthropophagite. Originally proper name of the man-eating Caribs of the Antilles.' The morphology or, to use the *OED*'s word, form-history of 'cannibal' is rather more circumspect. The main part of its entry reads:

> (In 16th c. pl. *Canibales*, a. Sp. *Canibales*, originally one of the forms of the ethnic name *Carib* or *Caribes*, a fierce nation of the West Indies, who are recorded to have been anthropophagi, and from whom the name was subsequently extended as a descriptive term . . .)

This is a 'true' account of the morphology of the word 'cannibal' in English, yet it is also an ideological account that functions to repress important historical questions about the use of the term – its discursive morphology, perhaps, rather than its linguistic morphology. The trace of that repression is the phrase 'who are recorded to have been', which hides beneath its blandness – the passive tense, the absence (in a book of authorities) of any ultimate authority, the assumption of impartial and accurate observation – a different history altogether.

The tone of 'who are recorded to have been' suggests a nineteenth-century ethnographer sitting in the shade with notebook and pencil, calmly recording the savage rituals being performed in front of him. However unacceptable that might now seem as 'objective reporting', it still appears a model of simplicity compared with the complexities of the passages that constitute the record in this instance.

On 23 November 1492 Christopher Columbus approached an island 'which those Indians whom he had with him called "Bohio" .' According to Columbus's *Journal* these Indians, usually referred to as Arawaks:

* From *Colonial Encounters: Europe and the Native Caribbean 1492–1797* London and New York: Methuen, 1986.

said that this land was very extensive and that in it were people who
had one eye in the forehead, and others whom they called 'canibals'.
Of these last, they showed great fear, and when they saw that this
course was being taken, they were speechless, he says, because these
people ate them and because they are very warlike.

(Columbus [1825] 1960 68–9) . . .

This is the first appearance of the word 'canibales' in a European text, and
it is linked immediately with the practice of eating human flesh. The
*Journal* is, therefore, in some sense at least, a 'beginning text'.

But in just what sense is that name and that ascription a 'record' of
anything? For a start the actual text on which we presume Columbus to
have inscribed that name disappeared, along with its only known copy, in
the middle of the sixteenth century. The only version we have, and from
which the above quotation is taken, is a handwritten abstract made by
Bartolome de Las Casas, probably in 1552, and probably from the copy of
Columbus's original then held in the monastery of San Pablo in Seville.
There have subsequently been various transcriptions of Las Casas's manuscript. So the apparent transparency of 'who are recorded to have been' is
quickly made opaque by the thickening layers of language: a transcription
of an abstract of a copy of a lost original. This is chastening, but to some
extent contingent. More telling is what might be called the internal opacity
of the statement. Columbus's 'record', far from being an observation that
those people called 'canibales' ate other people, is a report of other people's
words; moreover, words spoken in a language of which he had no prior
knowledge and, at best, six weeks' practice in trying to understand.

Around this passage cluster a whole host of ethnographic and
linguistic questions. . . . But the general argument here will be that, though
important, these questions take second place to the textual and discursive
questions. What first needs examination, in other words, are not isolated
passages taken as evidence for this or that, but rather the larger units of
text and discourse, without which no meaning would be possible at all.

To write about the text we call 'el diario de Colón' (Columbus's
journal) is to take a leap of faith, to presume that the transcription of the
manuscript of the abstract of the copy of the original stands in some kind
of meaningful relationship to the historical reality of Columbus's voyage
across the Atlantic and down through the Caribbean islands during the
winter months of 1492–3.

It would be perverse and unhelpful to presume that no such relationship exists, but credulous and unthinking to speak – as some have done – of
the *Journal*'s 'frank words, genuine and unadorned'. Circumspection would
certainly seem called for. Yet if the *Journal* is taken not as a privileged eye-
witness document of the discovery, nor as an accurate ethnographic record,
but rather as the first fable of European beginnings in America, then its
complex textual history and slightly dubious status become less important
than the incredible narrative it unfolds.

This is not an argument in favour of somehow lifting Columbus and his *Journal* out of history. . . . But it is an argument in favour of bracketing particular questions of historical accuracy and reliability in order to see the text whole, to gauge the structure of its narrative, and to chart the interplay of its linguistic registers and rhetorical modalities. To read the *Journal* in this way is also to defer the biographical questions: the Columbus of whom we speak is for the moment a textual function, the 'I' of the *Journal* who is occasionally, and scandalously, transformed into the third person by the intervention of the transcriber's 'I'.

The *Journal* is generically peculiar. It is in part a log-book, and throughout records the navigational details of Columbus's voyage. Commentators have usually accepted that it was written up almost every evening of the six-and-a-half-month journey, not revised or rewritten, and not constructed with a view to publication. It certainly gives that impression, which is all that matters here: Columbus is presented by the *Journal* as responding day by day to the stimulus of new challenges and problems. Yet if its generic shape is nautical the *Journal* is also by turns a personal memoir, an ethnographic notebook, and a compendium of European fantasies about the Orient: a veritable palimpsest.

'From whom the name was subsequently extended as a descriptive term.' Linguistic morphology is concerned only with the connection made between the term 'cannibal' and the practice of eating human flesh. We have seen how the very first mention of that term in a European text is glossed with reference to that practice, and for the linguist it is satisfactory, but not of intrinsic interest, to note how that reference is always present, either implicitly or explicitly, in any recorded use of the word 'cannibal' from Columbus's on 23 November 1492 onwards. It was adopted into the bosom of the European family of languages with a speed and readiness which suggests that there had always been an empty place kept warm for it. Poor 'anthropophagy', if not exactly orphaned, was sent out into the cold until finding belated lodging in the nineteenth century within new disciplines seeking authority from the deployment of classical terminology.

All of which makes it even stranger that the context of that beginning passage immediately puts the association between the word 'cannibal' and the eating of human flesh into doubt. Las Casas continues:

> The admiral says that he well believes that there is something in this, but that since they were well armed, they must be an intelligent people [gente de razon], and he believed that they may have captured some men and that, because they did not return to their own land, they would say that they were eaten.
>
> (Columbus 1960: 69)

This passage is of no interest to linguistic morphology since Columbus's scepticism failed to impinge upon the history of the word. Ethnographically it would probably be of scant interest, showing merely Columbus's initial scepticism, and therefore making him a more reliable witness in the end. Even from the point of view of a revisionist ethnography that wanted to discount suggestions of native anthropophagy the passage could only be seen as evidence of the momentary voice of European reason soon to be deafened by the persistence of Arawak defamations of their traditional enemy. Attention to the discursive complexities of the text will suggest a different reading. The great paradox of Columbus's *Journal* is that although the voyage of 1492–3 was to have such a devastating and long-lasting effect on both Europe and America, and is still celebrated as one of the outstanding achievements of humanity, the record itself tells of misunderstandings, failures and disappointments. The greatest of these – that he had not reached Asia – was too overwhelming for Columbus ever to accept. The minor ones are in some ways even more telling. . . .

In brief, what a symptomatic reading of the *Journal* reveals is the presence of two distinct discursive networks. In bold outline each discourse can be identified by the presence of key words: in one case 'gold', 'Cathay', 'Grand Khan', 'intelligent soldiers', 'large buildings', 'merchant ships'; in the other 'gold', 'savagery', monstrosity', 'anthropophagy'. Even more boldly, each discourse can be traced to a single textual origin, Marco Polo and Herodotus respectively. More circumspectly, there is what might be called a discourse of Oriental civilization and a discourse of savagery, both archives of topics and motifs that can be traced back to the classical period. It is tempting to say that the first was based on empirical knowledge and the second on psychic projection, but that would be a false dichotomy. There was no doubt a material reality – the trade that had taken place between Europe and the Far East over many centuries, if intermittently. In pursuit of, or as an outcome of, this trade there were Europeans who travelled to the Far East, but their words are in no way a simple reflection of 'what they saw'. For that reason it is better to speak of identifiable discourses. There was a panoply of words and phrases used to speak about the Orient: most concerned its wealth and power, as well they might since Europe had for many years been sending east large amounts of gold and silver. Marco Polo's account was the best-known deployment of these topoi. The discourse of savagery had in fact changed little since Herodotus's 'investigation' of Greece's 'barbarian' neighbours. The locations moved but the descriptions of Amazons, Anthropophagi and Cynocephali remained constant throughout Ctesias, Pliny, Solinus and many others. This discourse was hegemonic in the sense that it provided a popular vocabulary for constituting 'otherness' and was not dependent on *textual* reproduction. Textual authority was however available to Columbus in Pierre d'Ailly and Aeneas Sylvius, and indeed in the text that we know as 'Marco Polo', but which is properly *Divisament dou Monde*, authored by a writer of romances in French, and itself already an unravellable discursive network.

In the early weeks of the Columbian voyage it is possible to see a certain jockeying for position between these two discourses, but no overt conflict. The relationship between them is expressed as that between present and future: this is a world of savagery, over there we will find Cathay. But there are two potential sites of conflict, one conscious – in the sense of being present in the text; the other unconscious – in the sense that it is present only in its absence and must be reconstructed from the traces it leaves. The conscious conflict is that two elements, 'the soldiers of the Grand Khan' from the discourse of Marco Polo and 'the mandating savages' from the discourse of Herodotus, are competing for a single signifier – the word 'canibales'. Columbus's wavering on 23 November belongs to a larger pattern of references in which 'canibal' is consistently glossed by his native hosts as 'maneater' while it ineluctably calls to his mind 'el Gran Can'. In various entries the phonemes echo each other from several lines' distance until on 11 December 1492 they finally coincide:

> it appears likely that they are harassed by an intelligent race, all these islands living in great fear of those of Caniba. 'And so I repeat what I have said on other-occasions,' he says, 'the Caniba are nothing else than the people of the Grand Khan [*que Caniba no es otra cosa sino la gente del Gran Can*], who must be very near here and possess ships, and they must come to take them captive, and as the prisoners do not return, they believe that they have been eaten.'
>
> (Columbus 1960: 92–3)

The two 'Can' are identified as one, the crucial identification is backdated, and 'canibal' as man-eater must simply disappear having no reference to attach itself to.

Except of course that it does not disappear at all. That would be too easy. In fact the assertion of the identity of 'Caniba' with 'gente del Can', so far from marking the victory of the Oriental discourse, signals its very defeat; as if the crucial phonetic evidence could only be brought to textual presence once its power to control action had faded.

# 65

## The Muse of History

### DEREK WALCOTT*

*History is a nightmare from which I am trying to awake*
James Joyce

THE COMMON EXPERIENCE of the new world, even for its patrician writers whose veneration of the old is read as idolatory of the mestizo, is colonialism. They too are victims of tradition, but they remind us of our debt to the great dead, that those who break a tradition first hold it in awe. They perversely discourage disfavor, but because their sense of the past is of a timeless, yet habitable moment, the New World owes them more than it does those who wrestle with the past, for their veneration subtilizes an arrogance which is tougher than violent rejection. They know that by openly fighting tradition we perpetuate it, that revolutionary literature is a filial impulse, and that maturity is the assimilation of the features of every ancestor.

When these writers cunningly describe themselves as classicists and pretend an indifference to change, it is with an irony as true of the colonial anguish as the fury of the radical. If they appear to be phony aristocrats, it is because they have gone past the confrontation of history, that Medusa of the New World.

These writers reject the idea of history as time for its original concept as myth, the partial recall of the race. For them history is fiction, subject to a fitful muse, memory. Their philosophy, based on a contempt for historic time, is revolutionary, for what they repeat to the New World is its simultaneity with the Old. Their vision of man is elemental, a being inhabited by presences, not a creature chained to his past. Yet the method by which we are taught the past, the progress from motive to event, is the same by which we read narrative fiction. In time every event becomes an exertion of memory and is thus subject to invention. The farther the facts,

* From 'The Muse of History' in Orde Coombes (ed.) *Is Massa Day Dead? Black Moods in the Caribbean* New York: Doubleday, 1974.

the more history petrifies into myth. Thus, as we grow older as a race, we grow aware that history is written, that it is a kind of literature without morality, that in its actuaries the ego of the race is indissoluble and that everything depends on whether we write this fiction through the memory of hero or of victim.

In the New World servitude to the muse of history has produced a literature of recrimination and despair, a literature of revenge written by the descendants of slaves or a literature of remorse written by the descendants of masters. Because this literature serves historical truth, it yellows into polemic or evaporates in pathos. The truly tough aesthetic of the New World neither explains nor forgives history. It refuses to recognize it as a creative or culpable force. This shame and awe of history possess poets of the Third World who think of language as enslavement and who, in a rage for identity, respect only incoherence or nostalgia.

The great poets of the New World, from Whitman to Neruda, reject this sense of history. Their vision of man in the New World is Adamic. In their exuberance he is still capable of enormous wonder. Yet he has paid his accounts to Greece and Rome and walks in a world without monuments and ruins. They exhort him against the fearful magnet of older civilizations. Even in Borges, where the genius seems secretive, immured from change, it celebrates an elation which is vulgar and abrupt, the life of the plains given an instant archaism by the hieratic style. Violence is felt with the simultaneity of history. So the death of a gaucho does not merely repeat, but is, the death of Caesar. Fact evaporates into myth. This is not the jaded cynicism which sees nothing new under the sun, it is an elation which sees everything as renewed. . . .

New World poets who see the 'classic style' as stasis must see it also as historical degradation, rejecting it as the language of the master. This self-torture arises when the poet also sees history as language, when he limits his memory to the suffering of the victim. Their admirable wish to honor the degraded ancestor limits their language to phonetic pain, the groan of suffering, the curse of revenge. The tone of the past becomes an unbearable burden, for they must abuse the master or hero in his own language, and this implies self-deceit. Their view of Caliban is of the enraged pupil. They cannot separate the rage of Caliban from the beauty of his speech when the speeches of Caliban are equal in their elemental power to those of his tutor. The language of the torturer mastered by the victim. This is viewed as servitude, not as victory.

But who in the New World does not have a horror of the past, whether his ancestor was torturer or victim? Who, in the depth of conscience, is not silently screaming for pardon or for revenge? The pulse of New World history is the racing pulse beat of fear, the tiring cycles of stupidity and greed. . . .

371

In time the slave surrendered to amnesia. That amnesia is the true history of the New World. That is our inheritance, but to try and understand why this happened, to condemn or justify is also the method of history, and these explanations are always the same: This happened because of that, this was understandable because, and in days men were such. These recriminations exchanged, the contrition of the master replaces the vengeance of the slave, and here colonial literature is most pietistic, for it can accuse great art of feudalism and excuse poor art as suffering. To radical poets poetry seems the homage of resignation, an essential fatalism. But it is not the pressure of the past which torments great poets but the weight of the present:

> there are so many dead,
> and so many dikes the red sun breached,
> and so many heads battering hulls
> and so many hands that have closed over kisses
> and so many things that I want to forget.
>
> (Neruda)

The sense of history in poets lives rawly along their nerves:

> My land without name, without America,
> equinoctial stamen, lance-like purple,
> your aroma rose through my roots
> into the cup I drained, into the most tenuous
> word not yet born in my mouth.
>
> (Neruda)

It is this awe of the numinous, this elemental privilege of naming the new world which annihilates history in our great poets, an elation common to all of them, whether they are aligned by heritage to Crusoe and Prospero or to Friday and Caliban. They reject ethnic ancestry for faith in elemental man. The vision, the 'democratic vista,' is not metaphorical, it is a social necessity. A political philosophy rooted in elation would have to accept belief in a second Adam, the recreation of the entire order, from religion to the simplest domestic rituals. The myth of the noble savage would not be revived, for that myth never emanated from the savage but has always been the nostalgia of the Old World, its longing for innocence. The great poetry of the New World does not pretend to such innocence, its vision is not naive. Rather, like its fruits, its savor is a mixture of the acid and the sweet, the apples of its second Eden have the tartness of experience. In such poetry there is a bitter memory and it is the bitterness that dries last on the tongue. It is the acidulous that supplies its energy. . . . For us in the archipelago the tribal memory is salted with the bitter memory of migration.

To such survivors, to all the decimated tribes of the New World who did not suffer extinction, their degraded arrival must be seen as the beginning, not the end of our history. The shipwrecks of Crusoe and of the crew in *The Tempest* are the end of an Old World. It should matter nothing to the New World if the Old is again determined to blow itself up, for an obsession with progress is not within the psyche of the recently enslaved. That is the bitter secret of the apple. The vision of progress is the rational madness of history seen as sequential time, of a dominated future. Its imagery is absurd. In the history books the discoverer sets a shod foot on virgin sand, kneels, and the savage also kneels from his bushes in awe. Such images are stamped on the colonial memory, such heresy as the world's becoming holy from Crusoe's footprint or the imprint of Columbus' knee. These blasphemous images fade, because these hieroglyphs of progress are basically comic. And if the idea of the New and the Old becomes increasingly absurd, what must happen to our sense of time, what else can happen to history itself, but that it too is becoming absurd? This is not existentialism. Adamic, elemental man cannot be existential. His first impulse is not self-indulgence but awe, and existentialism is simply the myth of the noble savage gone baroque. . . .

But to most writers of the archipelago who contemplate only the shipwreck, the New World offers not elation but cynicism, a despair at the vices of the Old which they feel must be repeated. Their malaise is an oceanic nostalgia for the older culture and a melancholy at the new, and this can go as deep as a rejection of the untamed landscape, a yearning for ruins. To such writers the death of civilizations is architectural, not spiritual, seeded in their memories is an imagery of vines ascending broken columns, of dead terraces, of Europe as a nourishing museum. They believe in the responsibility of tradition, but what they are in awe of is not tradition, which is alert, alive, simultaneous, but of history, and the same is true of the new magnifiers of Africa. For these their deepest loss is of the old gods, the fear that it is worship which has enslaved progress. Thus the humanism of politics replaces religion. They see such gods as part of the process of history, subjected like the tribe to cycles of achievement and despair. Because the Old World concept of God is anthropomorphic, the New World slave was forced to remake himself in His image, despite such phrases as 'God is light, and in Him is no darkness,' and at this point of intersecting faiths the enslaved poet and enslaved priest surrendered their power. But the tribe in bondage learned to fortify itself by cunning assimilation of the religion of the Old World. What seemed to be surrender was redemption. What seemed the loss of tradition was its renewal. What seemed the death of faith, was its rebirth. . . .

I accept this archipelago of the Americas. I say to the ancestor who sold me, and to the ancestor who bought me, I have no father, I want no such father, although I can understand you, black ghost, white ghost, when you both whisper 'history,' for if I attempt to forgive you both I am falling into your idea of history which justifies and explains and expiates, and it is not mine to forgive, my memory cannot summon any filial love, since your features are anonymous and erased and I have no wish and no power to pardon. You were when you acted your roles, your given, historical roles of slave seller and slave buyer, men acting as men, and also you, father in the filth-ridden gut of the slave ship, to you they were also men, acting as men, with the cruelty of men, your fellowman and tribesman not moved or hovering with hesitation about your common race any longer than my other bastard ancestor hovered with his whip, but to you inwardly forgiven grandfathers, I, like the more honest of my race, give a strange thanks. I give the strange and bitter and yet ennobling thanks for the monumental groaning and soldering of two great worlds, like the halves of a fruit seamed by its own bitter juice, that exiled from your own Edens you have placed me in the wonder of another, and that was my inheritance and your gift.

# 66

## Spatial History

### PAUL CARTER*

BEFORE THE NAME: what was the place like before it was named? How did Cook see it? . . . Even as we look towards the horizon or turn away down fixed routes, our gaze sees through the space of history, as if it was never there. In its place, nostalgia for the past, cloudy time, the repetition of facts. The fact that where we stand and how we go is history: this we do not see.

According to our historians it was always so. Australia was always simply a stage where history occurred, history a theatrical performance. It is not the historian who stages events, weaving them together to form a plot, but History itself. History is the playwright, coordinating facts into a coherent sequence: the historian narrating what happened is merely a copyist or amanuensis. He is a spectator like anybody else and, whatever he may think of the performance, he does not question the stage conventions. . . .

In a theatre of its own design, history's drama unfolds; the historian is an impartial onlooker, simply repeating what happened. In [Australian historian Manning] Clarke's account [of the landing of the First Fleet] this illusion of the historian as *répétiteur* is reinforced by other, literary means. . . .

Such history is a fabric woven of self-reinforcing illusions. But above all, one illusion sustains it. This is the illusion of the theatre, and, more exactly, the unquestioned convention of the all-seeing spectator. The primary logic which holds together Clarke's description is its visibility. Nature's painted curtain is drawn aside to reveal heroic man at his epic labour on the stage of history. . . .

This kind of history, which reduces space to a stage, that pays attention to events unfolding in time alone, might be called imperial history. The governor erects a tent here rather than there; the soldier blazes a trail in that direction rather than this: but, rather than focus on the *intentional*

* From *The Road to Botany Bay: An Essay in Spatial History* London: Faber, 1987.

world of historical individuals, the world of active, spatial choices, empirical history of this kind has as its focus facts which, in a sense, come after the event. The primary object is not to understand or to interpret: it is to legitimate. This is why this history is associated with imperialism – for who are more liable to charges of unlawful usurpation and constitutional illegitimacy than the founders of colonies? Hence, imperial history's *defensive* appeal to the logic of cause and effect: by its nature, such a logic demonstrates the emergence of order from chaos.

Hence, too, its preference for fixed and detachable facts, for actual houses, visible clearings and boats at anchor. For these, unlike the intentions which brought them there, unlike the material uncertainties of lived time and space, are durable objects which can be treated as typical, as further evidence of a universal historical process. Orphaned from their unique spatial and temporal context, such objects, such historical facts, can be fitted out with new paternities. Legitimized by an imperial discourse, they can even form future alliances of their own. (It is precisely this family-tree myth of history which assures the historian his privileged status.) . . .

The fact is that, as an account of foundation and settlement, not to mention the related processes of discovery and exploration, empirical history, with its emphasis on the factual and static, is wholly inadequate. . . . For the result of cause and effect narrative history is to give the impression that events unfold according to a logic of their own. They refer neither to the place, nor to the people. Imperial history's mythic lineage of heroes is the consequence of its theatrical assumption that, in reality, historical individuals are actors, fulfilling a higher destiny. . . .

*The Road to Botany Bay*, then, is written against these mythic imaginings. It is a prehistory of places, a history of roads, footprints, trails of dust and foaming wakes. . . . Against the historians, it recognizes that our life as it discloses itself spatially is dynamic, material but invisible. It constantly transcends actual objects to imagine others beyond the horizon. It cannot be delimited by reference to immediate actions, let alone treated as an autonomous fact independent of intention. It recognizes that the spatiality of historical experience evaporates before the imperial gaze. . . .

What is evoked here are the spatial forms and fantasies through which a culture declares its presence. It is spatiality as a form of non-linear writing; as a form of history. That cultural space *has* such a history is evident from the historical documents themselves. For the literature of spatial history – the letters home, the explorer's journals, the unfinished maps – are written traces which, but for their spatial occasion, would not have come into being. They are not like novels: their narratives do not conform to the rules of cause-and-effect empirical history. Rather they are analogous to unfinished maps and should be read accordingly as records of travelling. . . .

Such spatial history – history that discovers and explores the lacuna left by imperial history – begins and ends in language. It is this which makes it history rather than, say, geography. If it does *imitate* the world of the traveller it is in a different sense. For, like the traveller whose gaze is oriented and limited, it makes no claim to authoritative completeness. It is, must be, like a journey, exploratory. . . .

But where to begin? Late in 1616, Dirck Hartog of Amsterdam and his ship, the *Eendracht*, were blown on to the north-west coast of Australia. The skipper commemorated his involuntary landing on a pewter plate, which he affixed to a post. The island where Hartog landed was named after him; the adjoining mainland was called the Land of Eendracht. In 1697, another Dutchman, Vlamingh, also blown off-course, found Hartog's memorial. He had Hartog's inscription copied on to a new pewter plate and appended a record of his own visit. In 1699, the English seaman, William Dampier, also visited this coast. He let the island retain its Dutch connection, but renamed the country to the east Shark Bay. Then, in 1801, one Captain Emmanuel Hamelin discovered a pewter plate 'of about six inches in diameter on which was roughly engraven two Dutch inscriptions . . .' and named the place Cape Inscription. . . .

[S]uch a name, as the earlier editions testify, belongs firmly to the history of travelling. Rewritten and repeated, it serves as a point of departure. But Cape Inscription, the name, is also the result of erasure: it also symbolizes the imperial project of permanent possession through dispossession. In short, the name oscillates between two extreme interpretations. It suggests a kind of history which is neither static nor mindlessly mobile, but which incorporates both possibilities. It points to a kind of history where travelling is a process of *continually* beginning, continually ending, where discovery and settlement belong to the same exploratory process. . . .

But Cape Inscription is also a striking figure of speech, an oxymoron yoking writing and landscape in a surprising, even grotesque way. A geographical feature is made no bigger than a page of writing. A calligraphic flourish is able, it seems, to plume out like an ocean current a hundred miles long. This metaphorical way of speaking is a pointer to the way spatial history must interpret its sources. It also indicates, concisely and poetically, the *cultural* place where spatial history begins: not in a particular year, nor in a particular place, but *in the act of naming*. For by the act of place-naming, space is transformed symbolically into a place, that is, a space with a history.

# 67

## *The Limbo Gateway*

### WILSON HARRIS*

I WANT TO make it as clear as I can that a cleavage exists in my opinion between the historical convention in the Caribbean and Guianas and the arts of the imagination. I believe a philosophy of history may well lie buried in the arts of the imagination and whether my emphasis falls on *limbo* or *vodun*, on Carib bush-baby omens, on Arawak zemi, on Latin, English inheritances – in fact within and beyond these emphases – my concern is with epic stratagems available to Caribbean man in the dilemmas of history which surround him.

There are two kinds of myths related to Africa in the Caribbean and Guianas. One kind seems fairly direct, the other has clearly undergone metamorphosis. In fact even the direct kind of myth has suffered a 'sea-change' of some proportions. In an original sense, therefore, these myths which reflect an African link in the Caribbean are also part and parcel of a native West Indian imagination and therefore stand, in some important ways, I feel, in curious rapport with vestiges of Amerindian fable and legend. (Fable and myth are employed as variables of the imagination in this essay.)

Let us start with a myth stemming from Africa which has undergone metamorphosis. The one which I have in mind is called *limbo*. The limbo dance is a well-known feature in the Carnival life of the West Indies today though it is still subject to intellectual censorship as I shall explain as I go along in this paper. The *limbo* dancer moves under a bar which is gradually lowered until a mere slit of space, it seems, remains through which with spread-eagled limbs he passes like a spider.

*Limbo* was born, it is said, on the slave ships of the Middle Passage. There was so little space that the slaves contorted themselves into human spiders. Limbo, therefore, as Edward Brathwaite, the distinguished

* From 'History, Fable and Myth in the Caribbean and the Guianas' in Hena Maes-Jelinek (ed.) *Explorations: A Selection of Talks and Articles 1966–81* Mundelstrup: Dangaroo Press, 1981.

Barbadian-born poet, has pointed out, is related to *anancy* or spider fables. If I may now quote from *Islands*, the last book in his trilogy:

> drum stick knock
> and the darkness is over me
> knees spread wide
> and the water is hiding me
> *limbo*
> *limbo like me*

But there is something else in the *limbo–anancy* syndrome which, as far as I am aware, is overlooked by Edward Brathwaite, and that is the curious dislocation of a chain of miles reflected in the dance so that a re-trace of the Middle Passage from Africa to the Americas and the West Indies is not to be equated with a uniform sum. Not only has the journey from the Old World to the new varied with each century and each method of transport but needs to be re-activated in the imagination as a limbo perspective when one dwells on the Middle Passage: a *limbo* gateway between Africa and the Caribbean.

In fact here, I feel, we begin to put our finger on something which is close to the inner universality of Caribbean man. Those waves of migration which have hit the shores of the Americas – North, Central and South – century after century have, at various times, possessed the stamp of the spider metamorphosis in the refugee flying from Europe or in the indentured East Indian and Chinese from Asia.

*Limbo* then reflects a certain kind of gateway or threshold to a new world and the dislocation of a chain of miles. It is – in some ways – the archetypal sea-change stemming from Old Worlds and it is legitimate, I feel, to pun on *limbo* as a kind of shared phantom *limb* which has become a subconscious variable in West Indian theatre. The emergence of formal West Indian theatre was preceded, I suggest, by that phantom limb which manifested itself on Boxing Day after Christmas when the ban on the 'rowdy' bands (as they were called) was lifted for the festive season.

I recall performances I witnessed as a boy in Georgetown, British Guiana, in the early 1930s. Some of the performers danced on high stilts like elongated limbs while others performed spread-eagled on the ground. In this way limbo spider and stilted pole of the gods were related to the drums like grassroots and branches of lightning to the sound of thunder.

Sometimes it was an atavistic spectacle and it is well known that these bands were suspected by the law of subversive political stratagems. But it is clear that the dance had no political or propaganda motives though, as with any folk manifestation, it could be manipulated by demagogues. The whole situation is complex and it is interesting to note that Rex Nettleford in an article entitled 'The Dance as an Art Form – Its Place in the West Indies' has this to say: 'Of all the arts, dance is probably the most neglected.

The art form continues to elude many of the most intuitive in an audience, including the critics' (Nettleford 1968: 127).

It has taken us a couple of generations to begin – just begin – to perceive, in this phenomenon, an activation of unconscious and sleeping resources in the phantom limb of dismembered slave and god. An activation which possesses a nucleus of great promise – of far-reaching new poetic form.

For *limbo* (one cannot emphasize this too much) is not the total recall of an African past since that African past in terms of tribal sovereignty or sovereignties was modified or traumatically eclipsed with the Middle Passage and with generations of change that followed. *Limbo* was rather the renascence of a new corpus of sensibility that could translate and accommodate African and other legacies within a new architecture of cultures. For example, the theme of the phantom limb – the re-assembly of dismembered man or god – possesses archetypal resonances that embrace Egyptian Osiris, the resurrected Christ and the many-armed goddess of India, Kali, who throws a psychical bridge with her many arms from destruction to creation.

In this context it is interesting to note that *limbo* – which emerged as a novel re-assembly out of the stigmata of the Middle Passage – is related to Haitian *vodun* in the sense that Haitian *vodun* (though possessing a direct link with African *vodun* which I shall describe later on) also seeks to accommodate new Catholic features in its constitution of the muse.

It is my view – a deeply considered one – that this ground of accommodation, this art of creative coexistence born of great peril and strangest capacity for renewal – pointing away from apartheid and ghetto fixations – is of the utmost importance and *native* to the Caribbean, perhaps to the Americas as a whole. It is still, in most respects, a latent syndrome and we need to look not only at *limbo* or *vodun* but at Amerindian horizons as well – shamanistic and rain-making vestiges and the dancing bush baby legends of the Caribs (now extinct) which began to haunt them as they crouched over their campfires under the Spanish yoke.

Insufficient attention has been paid to such phenomena and the original native capacity these implied as omens of rebirth. Many historians have been intent on indicting the Old Work of Europe by exposing a uniform pattern of imperialism in the New World of the Americas. Thus they conscripted the West Indies into a mere adjunct of imperialism and overlooked a subtle and far-reaching renascence. In a sense therefore the new historian [Thomas] – though his stance is an admirable one in debunking imperialism – has ironically extended and reinforced old colonial prejudices which censored the *limbo* imagination as a 'rowdy' manifestation and overlooked the complex metaphorical gateway it constitutes in rapport with Amerindian omen.

Later on I intend to explore the Amerindian gateways between cultures which began obscurely and painfully to witness (long before *limbo* or *vodun* or the Middle Passage) to a native suffering community steeped in caveats of conquest. At this point I shall merely indicate that these gateways exist as part and parcel of an original Caribbean architecture which it is still possible to create if we look deep into the rubble of the past, and that these Amerindian features enhance the *limbo* assembly with which we are now engaged – the spider syndrome and phantom limb of the gods arising in Negro fable and legend.

I used the word 'architecture' a moment or two ago because I believe this is a valid approach to a gateway society as well as to a community which is involved in an original re-construction or re-creation of variables of myth and legend in the wake of stages of conquest.

First of all the *limbo* dance becomes the human gateway which dislocates (and therefore begins to free itself from) a uniform chain of miles across the Atlantic. This dislocation of interior space serves therefore as a corrective to a uniform cloak or documentary stasis of imperialism. The journey across the Atlantic for the forebears of West Indian man involved a new kind of space, inarticulate as this new 'spatial' character was at the time – and not simply an unbroken schedule of miles in a log book. Once we perceive this inner corrective to historical documentary and protest literature which sees the West Indies as utterly deprived, or gutted by exploitation, we begin to participate in the genuine possibilities of original change in a people severely disadvantaged (it is true) at a certain point in time.

The *limbo* dance therefore implies, I believe, a profound art of compensation which seeks to re-play a dismemberment of tribes (*note again the high stilted legs of some of the performers and the spider-anancy masks of others running close to the ground*) and to invoke at the same time a curious psychic re-assembly of the parts of the dead muse and god. And that re-assembly which issued from a state of cramp to articulate a new growth – and to point to the necessity for a new kind of drama novel and poem – is a creative phenomenon of the first importance in the imagination of a people violated by economic fates.

One cannot over-emphasize, I believe, how original this phenomenon was. So original it aroused both incomprehension and suspicion in the intellectual and legal administrations of the land (I am thinking in particular of the first half of the twentieth century though one can, needless to say, go much farther back). What is bitterly ironic – as I have already indicated – is that present-day historians in the second half of the twentieth century – militant and critical of imperialism as they are here – have fallen victim, in another sense, to the very imperialism they appear to denounce. They have no criteria for arts of originality springing out of an age of *limbo* and the history they write is without an inner time. This historical refusal to see may well be at the heart of the *Terrified Consciousness* which a most significant critic to emerge in the West Indies at this time, Kenneth Ramchand, analyses in a brilliant essay (Ramchand 1969). One point which Kenneth Ramchand did not stress – but which is implicit in what he calls the 'nightmare' in Jean Rhys's novel *Wide Sargasso Sea* – is that Antoinette is mad Bertha in *Jane Eyre* and that Jean Rhys, intuitively rather than intentionally, compensates a historical portrait of the West Indian creole – bridges the gap, as it were, between an outer rational frame and an inner irrational desolation to transform the hubris of reason (or proprietorship of flesh-and-blood) and bring into play a necessity for re-creative and therapeutic capacities grounded in complex vision. . . .

I believe that the *limbo* imagination of the folk involved a crucial inner re-creative response to the violations of slavery and indenture and conquest, and needed its critical or historical correlative, its critical or historical advocacy. This was not forthcoming since the historical instruments of the past clustered around an act of censorship and of suspicion of folk-obscurity as well as individual originality, and that inbuilt suspicion continues to motivate a certain order of critical writing in the West Indies today.

# 68

# Postcoloniality and the Artifice of History

## DIPESH CHAKRABARTY*

THE PURPOSE OF this article is to problematize the idea of 'Indians' 'representing themselves in 'history.' Let us put aside for the moment the messy problems of identity inherent in a transnational enterprise such as *Subaltern Studies*, where passports and commitments blur the distinctions of ethnicity in a manner that some would regard as characteristically post-modern. I have a more perverse proposition to argue. It is that insofar as the academic discourse of history – that is, 'history' as a discourse produced at the institutional site of the university – is concerned, 'Europe' remains the sovereign theoretical subject of all histories, including the ones we call 'Indian,' 'Chinese,' 'Kenyan,' and so on. There is a peculiar way in which all these other histories tend to become variations on a master narrative that could be called 'the history of Europe.' In this sense, 'Indian' history itself is in a position of subalterneity; one can only articulate subaltern positions in the name of this history. . . .

Colonial Indian history is replete with instances where Indians arro-gated subjecthood to themselves precisely by mobilizing, within the context of 'modern' institutions and sometimes on behalf of the modernizing project of nationalism, devices of collective memory that were both anti-historical and antimodern. This is not to deny the capacity of 'Indians' to act as subjects endowed with what we in the universities would recognize as 'a sense of history' (what Peter Burke calls 'the renaissance of the past') but to insist at the same time that there were also contrary trends, that in the multifarious struggles that took place in colonial India, antihistorical constructions of the past often provided very powerful forms of collective memory.

There is then this double bind through which the subject of 'Indian' history articulates itself. On the one hand, it is both the subject and the object of modernity, because it stands for an assumed unity called

* From 'Postcoloniality and the Artifice of History: Who Speaks for "Indian" Pasts?' *Representations* 32 (Winter), 1992.

the 'Indian people' that is always split into two – a modernizing elite and a yet-to-be-modernized peasantry. As such a split subject, however, it speaks from within a metanarrative that celebrates the nation state; and of this metanarrative the theoretical subject can only be a hyperreal 'Europe,' a 'Europe' constructed by the tales that both imperialism and nationalism have told the colonized. The mode of self-representation that the 'Indian' can adopt here is what Homi Bhabha has justly called 'mimetic' (Bhabha 1984b). Indian history, even in the most dedicated socialist or nationalist hands, remains a mimicry of a certain 'modern' subject of 'European' history and is bound to represent a sad figure of lack and failure. The transition narrative will always remain 'grievously incomplete.'

On the other hand, maneuvers are made within the space of the mimetic – and therefore within the project called 'Indian' history – to represent the 'difference' and the 'originality' of the 'Indian,' and it is in this cause that the antihistorical devices of memory and the antihistorical 'histories' of the subaltern classes are appropriated. Thus peasant/worker constructions of 'mythical' kingdoms and 'mythical' pasts/futures find a place in texts designated 'Indian' history precisely through a procedure that subordinates these narratives to the rules of evidence and to the secular, linear calendar that the writing of 'history' must follow. The antihistorical, antimodern subject, therefore, cannot speak itself as 'theory' within the knowledge procedures of the university even when these knowledge procedures acknowledge and 'document' its existence. Much like Spivak's 'subaltern' (or the anthropologist's peasant who can only have a quoted existence in a larger statement that belongs to the anthropologist alone), this subject can only be spoken for and spoken of by the transition narrative that will always ultimately privilege the modern (i.e., 'Europe').

So long as one operates within the discourse of 'history' produced at the institutional site of the university, it is not possible simply to walk out of the deep collusion between 'history' and the modernizing narrative(s) of citizenship, bourgeois public and private, and the nation state. 'History' as a knowledge system is firmly embedded in institutional practices that invoke the nation state at every step – witness the organization and politics of teaching, recruitment, promotions, and publication in history departments, politics that survive the occasional brave and heroic attempts by individual historians to liberate 'history' from the meta-narrative of the nation state. One only has to ask, for instance: Why is history a compulsory part of education of the modern person in all countries today including those that did quite comfortably without it until as late as the eighteenth century? Why should children all over the world today have to come to terms with a subject called 'history' when we know that this compulsion is neither natural nor ancient? It does not take much imagination to see that the reason for this lies in what European imperialism and third-world nationalisms have achieved together: the universalization of the nation state as the most desirable form of political community. Nation states have the capacity to enforce their truth games, and universities, their critical distance notwith-standing, are part of the battery of institutions complicit in this process. 'Economics' and 'history' are the knowledge forms that correspond to the two major institutions that the rise (and later universalization) of the bour-geois order has given to the world – the capitalist mode of production and the nation state ('history' speaking to the figure of the citizen). A critical historian has no choice but to negotiate this knowledge. She or he therefore needs to understand the state on its own terms, i.e., in terms of its self-justificatory narratives of citizenship and modernity. Since these themes will always take us back to the universalist propositions of 'modern' (European) political philosophy – even the 'practical' science of economics that now seems 'natural' to our constructions of world systems is (theoretically) rooted in the ideas of ethics in eighteenth-century Europe – a third-world historian is condemned to knowing 'Europe' as the original home of the 'modern,' whereas the 'European' historian does not share a comparable predicament with regard to the pasts of the majority of humankind. Thus follows the everyday subalternity of non-Western histories with which I began this paper. Yet the understanding that 'we' all do 'European' history with our different and often non-European archives opens up the possibility of a politics and project of alliance between the dominant metropolitan histories and the subaltern peripheral pasts. Let us call this the project of provincializing 'Europe,' the 'Europe' that modern imperialism and (third-world) nationalism have, by their collaborative venture and violence, made universal. Philosophically, this project must ground itself in a radical critique and transcendence of liberalism (i.e., of the bureaucratic construc-tions of citizenship, modern state, and bourgeois privacy that classical political philosophy has produced), a ground that late Marx shares with certain moments in both poststructuralist thought and feminist philosophy. In particular, I am emboldened by Carole Pateman's courageous declaration – in her remarkable book *The Sexual Contract* (1988) – that the very conception of the modern individual belongs to patriarchal categories of thought.

The project of provincializing 'Europe' refers to a history that does not yet exist; I can therefore only speak of it in a programmatic manner. To fore-stall misunderstanding, however, I must spell out what it is not while outlining what it could be.

To begin with, it does not call for a simplistic, out-of-hand rejection of modernity, liberal values, universals, science, reason, grand narratives, totalizing explanations, and so on. Fredric Jameson has recently reminded us that the easy equation often made between 'a philosophical conception of totality' and 'a political practice of totalitarianism is baleful' (Jameson 1988: 354). What intervenes between the two is history – contradictory, plural, and heterogeneous struggles whose outcomes are never predictable, even retrospectively, in accordance with schemas that seek to naturalize and domesticate this heterogeneity. These struggles include coercion (both on behalf of and against modernity), physical, institutional, and symbolic violence, often dispensed with dreamy-eyed idealism – and it is this violence that plays a decisive role in the establishment of meaning, in the creation of truth regimes, in deciding, as it were, whose and which 'universal' wins. As intellectuals operating in academia, we are not neutral to these struggles and cannot pretend to situate ourselves outside of the knowledge procedures of our institutions.

The project of provincializing 'Europe' therefore cannot be a project of 'cultural relativism.' It cannot originate from the stance that the reason/science/universals which help define Europe as the modern are simply 'culture-specific' and therefore only belong to the European cultures. For the point is not that Enlightenment rationalism is always unreasonable in itself but rather a matter of documenting how – through what historical process – its 'reason,' which was not always self-evident to everyone, has been made to look 'obvious' far beyond the ground where it originated. If a language, as has been said, is but a dialect backed up by an army, the same could be said of the narratives of 'modernity' that, almost universally today, point to a certain 'Europe' as the primary habitus of the modern.

This Europe, like 'the West,' is demonstrably an imaginary entity, but the demonstration as such does not lessen its appeal or power. The project of provincializing 'Europe' has to include certain other additional moves: 1) the recognition that Europe's acquisition of the adjective *modern* for itself is a piece of global history of which an integral part is the story of European imperialism; and 2) the understanding that this equating of a certain version of Europe with 'modernity' is not the work of Europeans alone; third-world nationalisms, as modernizing ideologies *par excellence*, have been equal partners in the process. I do not mean to overlook the anti-imperial moments in the careers of these nationalisms; I only underscore the point that the project of provincializing 'Europe' cannot be a nationalist, nativist, or atavistic project. In unraveling the necessary entanglement of history – a disciplined and institutionally regulated form of collective memory – with the grand narratives of 'rights,' 'citizenship,' the nation state, 'public' and 'private' spheres, one cannot but problematize 'India' at the same time as one dismantles 'Europe.'

The idea is to write into the history of modernity the ambivalences, contradictions, the use of force, and the tragedies and the ironies that attend it. That the rhetoric and the claims of (bourgeois) equality, of citizens' rights, of self-determination through a sovereign nation state have in many circumstances empowered marginal social groups in their struggles is undeniable – this recognition is indispensable to the project of Subaltern Studies. What effectively is played down, however, in histories that either implicitly or explicitly celebrate the advent of the modern state and the idea of citizenship is the repression and violence that are as instrumental in the victory of the modern as is the persuasive power of its rhetorical strategies. Nowhere is this irony – the undemocratic foundations of 'democracy' – more visible than in the history of modern medicine, public health, and personal hygiene, the discourses of which have been central in locating the body of the modern at the intersection of the public and the private (as defined by, and subject to negotiations with, the state). The triumph of this discourse, however, has always been dependent on the mobilization, on its behalf, of effective means of physical coercion. I say 'always' because this coercion is both originary/foundational (i.e., historic) as well as pandemic and quotidian. Of foundational violence, David Arnold gives a good example in a recent essay on the history of the prison in India. The coercion of the colonial prison, Arnold shows, was integral to some of the earliest and pioneering research on the medical, dietary, and demographic statistics of India, for the prison was where Indian bodies were accessible to modernizing investigators (Arnold 1992). Of the coercion that continues in the names of the nation and modernity, a recent example comes from the Indian campaign to eradicate smallpox in the 1970s. Two American doctors (one of them presumably of 'Indian' origin) who participated in the process thus describe their operations in a village of the Ho tribe in the Indian state of Bihar:

> In the middle of gentle Indian night, an intruder burst through the bamboo door of the simple adobe hut. He was a government vaccinator, under orders to break resistance against smallpox vaccination. Lakshmi Singh awoke screaming and scrambled to hide herself. Her husband leaped out of bed, grabbed an axe, and chased the intruder into the courtyard. Outside a squad of doctors and policemen quickly overpowered Mohan Singh. The instant he was pinned to the ground, a second vaccinator jabbed smallpox vaccine into his arm. Mohan Singh, a wiry 40-year old leader of the Ho tribe, squirmed away from the needle, causing the vaccination site to bleed. The government team held him until they had injected enough vaccine. . . . While the two policemen rebuffed him, the rest of the team overpowered the entire family and vaccinated each in turn. Lakshmi Singh bit deep into one doctor's hand, but to no avail.
>
> (Brilliant 1978: 3)

There is no escaping the idealism that accompanies this violence. The subtitle of the article in question unselfconsciously reproduces both the military and the do-gooding instincts of the enterprise. It reads: 'How an army of samaritans drove smallpox from the earth.'

Histories that aim to displace a hyperreal Europe from the center toward which all historical imagination currently gravitates will have to seek out relentlessly this connection hetween violence and idealism that lies at the heart of the process by which the narratives of citizenship and modernity come to find a natural home in 'history.' I register a fundamental disagreement here with a position taken by Richard Rorty in an exchange with Jörgen Habermas. Rorty criticizes Habermas for the latter's conviction 'that the story of modern philosophy is an important part of the story of the democratic societies' attempts at self-reassurance.' Rorty's statement follows the practice of many Europeanists who speak of the histories of these 'democratic societies' as if these were self-contained histories complete in themselves, as if the self-fashioning of the West were something that occurred only within its self-assigned geographical boundaries. At the very least Rorty ignores the role that the 'colonial theater' (both external and internal) – where the theme of 'freedom' as defined by modern political philosophy was constantly invoked in aid of the ideas of 'civilization,' 'progress,' and latterly 'development' – played in the process of engendering this 'reassurance.' The task, as I see it, will be to wrestle ideas that legitimize the modern state and its attendant institutions, in order to return to political philosophy – in the same way as suspect coins returned to their owners in an Indian bazaar – its categories whose global currency can no longer be taken for granted.

And, finally – since 'Europe' cannot after all be provincialized within the institutional site of the university whose knowledge protocols will always take us back to the terrain where all contours follow that of my hyperreal Europe – the project of provincializing Europe must realize within itself its own impossibility.

It therefore looks to a history that embodies this politics of despair. It will have been clear by now that this is not a call for cultural relativism or for atavistic, nativist histories. Nor is this a program for a simple rejection of modernity, which would be, in many situations, politically suicidal. I ask for a history that deliberately makes visible, within the very structure of its narrative forms, its own repressive strategies and practices, the part it plays in collusion with the narratives of citizenships in assimilating to the projects of the modern state all other possibilities of human solidarity. The politics of despair will require of such history that it lays bare to its readers the reasons why such a predicament is necessarily inescapable. This is a history that will attempt the impossible: to look toward its own death by tracing that which resists and escapes the best human effort at translation across cultural and other semiotic systems, so that the world may once again be imagined as radically heterogeneous. This, as I have said, is impossible within the knowledge protocols of academic history, for the globality of academia is not independent of the globality that the European modern has created. To attempt to provincialize this 'Europe' is to see the modern as inevitably contested, to write over the given and privileged narratives of citizenship other narratives of human connections that draw sustenance from dreamed-up pasts and futures where collectivities are defined neither by the rituals of citizenship nor by the nightmare of 'tradition' that 'modernity' creates. There are of course no (infra)structural sites where such dreams could lodge themselves. Yet they will recur so long as the themes of citizenship and the nation state dominate our narratives of historical transition, for these dreams are what the modern represses in order to be.

# PART XII

## *Place*

# *Introduction*

Place and displacement are crucial features of post-colonial discourse. By 'Place' we do not simply mean 'landscape'. Indeed the idea of 'landscape' is predicated upon a particular philosophic tradition in which the objective world is separated from the viewing subject. Rather 'place' in post-colonial societies is a complex interaction of language, history and environment. It is characterised firstly by a sense of displacement in those who have moved to the colonies, or the more widespread sense of displacement from the imported language, of a gap between the 'experienced' environment and descriptions the language provides, and secondly, by a sense of the immense investment of culture in the construction of place.

A sense of displacement, of the lack of 'fit' between language and place, may be experienced by both those who possess English as a mother tongue and those who speak it as a second language. In both cases, the sense of dislocation from an historical 'homeland' and that created by the dissonance between language, the experience of 'displacement' generates a creative tension within the language. Place is thus the concommitant of difference, the continual reminder of the separation, and yet of the hybrid interpenetration of the coloniser and colonised.

The theory of place does not simply propose a binary separation between the 'place' named and described in language, and some 'real' place inaccessible to it, but rather indicates that in some sense place *is* language, something in constant flux, a discourse in process. The sense of 'lack of fit' between language and place is that which propels writers such as Robert Kroetsch and Dennis Lee to construct a new language. The post-colonial text, negotiating as it does the space between the textual language and the lived space becomes the metonym of the continual process of reclamation, as a cultural reality is both *posited* and *reclaimed* from the incorporating dominance of English.

Whether the speaker is the settler, the indigenous occupant of invaded colonies, a member of a colonised and dominated African or Indian society or the multifarious Caribbean region, language always negotiates a kind of gap between the word and its signification. In this sense the dynamic of 'naming' becomes a primary colonising process because it appropriates, defines, captures the place in language. And yet the process of naming opens wider the very epistemological gap which it is designed to fill, for the 'dynamic mystery of language', as Wilson Harris puts it, becomes a groping step into the reality of place, not simply reflecting or representing it, but in some mysterious sense intimately involved in the process of its creation, of its 'coming into being'.

Place therefore, the 'place' of the 'subject', throws light upon subjectivity itself, because whereas we might conceive subjectivity as a process, as Lacan has done, so the discourse of place is a process of a continual dialectic between subject and object. Thus a major feature of post-colonial literatures is the concern with either developing or recovering an appropriate identifying relationship between self and place because it is precisely within the parameters of place and its separateness that the process of subjectivity can be conducted.

Place is also a palimpsest, a kind of parchment on which successive generations have inscribed and reinscribed the process of history. V. S. Naipaul signals this in *The Middle Passage* when he sees the history of the Caribbean signified in the land: 'There is slavery in the vegetation. In the sugarcane, brought by Columbus on that second voyage when, to Queen Isabella's fury, he proposed the enslavement of the Amerindians' (Naipaul 1962: 61–2). But the simple conflict of coloniser and colonised which Naipaul sees here is really a simplification of the complex way in which history is embedded in place. As a kind of counterpoint to Rabasa's critique of Mercator's Atlas, Graham Huggan demonstrates how the map itself is decolonised in post-colonial constructions of place. The map is the crucial signifier of control over place and thus of power over the inscription of being.

Perhaps the most detailed discussion of this process is Paul Carter's *The Road to Botany Bay* which surveys at length the extent to which the language of travel, of exploration, of settlement, indeed naming itself, turned empty space into 'place' in Australia and has continued to re-write the text of that place. This was not a place which was 'simply there' but a place which is in a continual process of being 'written'. This is true of any place, but in post-colonial experience the linkage between language, place and history is far more prominent because the interaction is so much more urgent and contestatory. One of the more interesting aspects of this palimpsest is the rewriting, through Aboriginal textuality, of a place which would seem to have been overwritten by the coloniser. As Bob Hodge and Vijay Mishra point out, the 'place' in aboriginal culture, rather than existing as a visual construct, is a kind of 'ground of being'.

It is perhaps no accident that the most overt agonising over place occurs in the settler colonies, those which Alfred Crosby calls the 'new Europes'. In no other part of the world has such a profound ecological colonialism taken place: lands that occupy temperate zones roughly equivalent to Europe have not only wholeheartedly exported European crops but have become the granaries of the world. The ecological imperialism of which Crosby speaks is a kind of metaphor for the discursive invasion which has led to such social ambivalence, but which has also led to such creative productivity.

# 69

## *Unhiding the Hidden*

### ROBERT KROETSCH*

AT ONE TIME I considered it the task of the Canadian writer to give names to his experience, to be the namer. I now suspect that, on the contrary, it is his task to un-name.

This necessity did not originate with Canadian writers. Heidegger says in his *Poetry, Language, Thought*: '*Roman thought takes over the Greek words without a corresponding, equally authentic experience of what they say, without the Greek word*. The rootlessness of Western thought begins with this translation' (1971: 23).

The Canadian writer's particular predicament is that he works with a language, within a literature, that appears to be authentically his own, and not a borrowing. But just as there was in the Latin word a concealed Greek experience, so there is in the Canadian word a concealed other experience, sometimes British, sometimes American.

In recent years the tension between this appearance of being just like someone else and the demands of authenticity has become intolerable – both to the individuals and to the society. In recent Canadian fiction the major writers resolve the paradox – the painful tension between appearance and authenticity – by the radical process of demythologizing the systems that threaten to define them. Or, more comprehensively, they uninvent the world.

The most conspicuous example is the novel *Surfacing*, by Margaret Atwood (1972a). In the novel the three *named* characters, Joe, Davie and Anna, live constantly in danger of becoming American. Waiting for the barbarians, they begin to become, in terms of the essential American paradox, the awaited barbarians. . . .

Atwood's heroine must remove the false names that adhere to her experience. The terror of her journey is not that she, like her drowned father, like her drowned and revived antipodal brother, almost drowns; it

* From 'Unhiding the Hidden: Recent Canadian Fiction' *Journal of Canadian Fiction* 3(3), 1974.

is rather that she surfaces. The terror resides not in her going insane but in her going sane.

Atwood signals this very Canadian predicament when she has the narrator say early in the novel, 'Now we're on my home ground, foreign territory.' The truth is disguised, hidden. Camouflage, the narrator says, 'was one of my father's policies'. And she too is good at varieties of camouflage. . . .

But underneath this layering, this concealing, is a woman who still recognizes that something doesn't fit. Joe says, 'Do you love me, that's all,' and she thinks: 'It was the language again, I couldn't use it because it wasn't mine.'

The Roman writer borrowed a Greek word into a Latin context. The Canadian writer borrows an English word into an English-language context, a French word into a French-language context. The process of rooting that borrowed word, that totally exact homonym, in an authentic experience, is then, and must be, a radical one.

Atwood's heroine burns the drawings and the typescript from which she works. She takes off the ring that signifies her sham marriage, drops it into the fire. But even that is only the beginning:

> Everything from history must be eliminated, the circles and the arrogant square pegs. I rummage under the mattress and bring out the scrapbooks, ripping them up. . . . When the paper things are burned I smash the glasses and plates and the chimney of the lamp. . . . When nothing is left intact and the fire is only smouldering, I leave, carrying one of the wounded blankets with me, I will need it until the fur grows. The house shuts with a click behind me.
>
> (Atwood 1972a: 176–7)

In the marvellous extravagance of this surfacing, this uninventing of the world, the narrator must finally deliver herself of the notion that she is a human being. Bare-assed she can become bear-assed – in accordance with the outrageous, seductive, fabulated contemporary female vision of what total freedom must be. At the end of *Surfacing* the narrator has achieved a state wherein she might . . . give birth to her true identity. . . .

Where the larger process of uninventing, in Atwood becomes a journey into the wilderness, in [Robertson] Davies [author of *The Manticore* (1972)] it is a journey to the old civilization, the sum of our ancestry. And yet, for both these novelists, the condition of pre-history is necessary to valid and authentic birth. . . .

I choose to comment on [Rudy] Wiebe's *The Temptations of Big Bear* (1973) because here, a bear-inspired man acts out, not only mythologically, but historically as well, the uninvention of the world. . . . Wiebe makes of a tribe of Crees the epitome of our Canadian selves being extinguished into existence by the British and American cultures. Hounded, tricked, robbed, cheated, shot at, starved – we prove they cannot capture us: and then voluntarily we reveal ourselves to be the destroying elements. Big Bear is the poet-creator who must himself be uncreated in order to represent our necessary fate. He must resist temptations to be anything – farmer, politician, trading-post white man, Christian – other than his fated self. He must *talk* his way into his decreated and valid self: he must, dying, become the source and creator of the unimaginable new.

In his talking – in the language of the novel – he and Wiebe decreate the literary tradition that binds us into not speaking the truth. Wiebe and Harlow and Godfrey, like Grove before them, have a marvellous ability to keep the language clumsy, brutal, unbeautiful, vital, charged. Atwood makes a fine Canadian prose style of the run-on sentence. Davies distrusts any sentence that loses its connection with his newspaperman background. But Wiebe is determined to destroy the sentence itself back to sense, back to its ground. He says in his dedication that he 'unearthed' the story. He recognizes the problem of language: we learn that Corporal Sleigh 'never read a book because people in them never walked in mud. . . . You never got the sense of anyone being downright dirty the way territories' mud stuck to you in globs. . . .' (272). He demonstrates how the problem of language becomes one of culture, society, identity: Peter Houri attempts to translate, to speak of the crime against, Queen Victoria's 'crown and dignity'. Big Bear responds:

> there is nothing true when they say I tried to steal her hat. How could I do that? Or knock it off, as Poundmaker said they told him, by throwing sticks at it. . . . I didn't know she had a hat and I never wear hats, what would I want it for to make me steal it, women's hats are nice but a man would be drunk.
>
> (387)

Where Davies invented documents, Wiebe quotes from existing sources, lets government records and legal debate and newspapers and memoirs and journals speak for themselves. The sheer failure of that language to confront reality is both comic and appalling. We discover, finally, why Wiebe is driven into complicity with the so-called renegade Indians. Like them, he must experience the de-composition of the world. He must, whatever the cost, go Indian himself.

It is possible that the old obsessive notion of identity and ego, is itself a spent fiction, that these new writers are discovering something essentially new, something essential not only to Canadians but to the world they would uncreate. Whatever the case, they dare the ultimate *contra-diction*: they uncreate themselves into existence. Like Heidegger they will accept that the root meaning of the word truth is un-concealing, dis-closing, dis-covering, un-hiding. Or to put it in prairie terms, they will, like Rudy Wiebe's Big Bear, even when locked up in the Stony Mountain pen, with the Archbishop generously in attendance – even then they will be loyal to their own first visions. Offered the consolation and pride of the old names, they will 'decline to be christened'.

# 70

# Writing in Colonial Space

## Dennis Lee*

### CADENCE

Most of my life as a writer is spent listening into a cadence which is a kind of taut cascade, a luminous tumble. If I withdraw from immediate contact with things around me I can sense it churning, flickering, dancing, locating things in more shapely relation to one another without robbing them of themselves. I say it is present continuously, but certainly I spend days on end without noticing it. I hear it more clearly because I have recognised it in Hölderlin or Henry Moore, but I don't think it originates in their work. I think they heeded it too.

What I hear is initially without content; but when the poem does come, the content must accord with the cadence I have been overhearing or I cannot make it. (I speak of 'hearing' cadence, but in fact I am baffled by how to describe it. There is no auditory sensation – I don't hallucinate; yet it is like sensing a continuous, changing tremor with one's ear and one's whole body at the same time. It seems very matter-of-fact, yet I do not know the name of the sense with which I perceive it.)

More and more I sense this cadence as presence – though it may take 50 or 100 revisions before a poem enacts it – I sense it as presence, both outside myself and inside my body opening out and trying to get into words. What is it? I can convey some portion of that by pointing to things I have already written, saying 'Listen to the cadence here, and here – no, listen to the deeper cadence in which the poem is locally sustained.' But the cadence of the poems I have written is such a small and often mangled fraction of what I hear, it tunes out so many wavelengths of that massive, infinitely fragile polyphony, that I frequently despair. And often it feels perverse to ask what is cadence, when it is all I can manage to heed it. . . .

* From 'Cadence, Country, Silence: Writing in Colonial Space' *Boundary 2*, 3(1) (Fall), 1974.

# COUNTRY

I have been writing of cadence as though one had merely to hear its words and set them down. But that is not true, at least not in my experience. There is a check on one's pen which seems to take hold at the very moment that cadence declares itself. Words arrive, but words have also gone dead.

To get at this complex experience we must begin from the hereness, the local nature of cadence. We never encounter cadence in the abstract; it is insistently here and now. Any man aspires to be at home where he lives, to celebrate communion with men on earth around him, under the sky where he actually lives. And to speak from his own dwelling – however light or strong the inflections of that place – he will make his words intelligible to men elsewhere, because authentic. In my case, then, cadence seeks the gestures of being a Canadian human: *mutatis mutandi*, the same is true for anyone here – an Israeli, an American, a Quebecker.

But if we live in a space which is radically in question for us, that makes our barest speaking a problem to itself. For voice does issue in part from civil space. And alienation in that space will enter and undercut our writing, make it recoil upon itself, become a problem to itself.

The act of writing 'becomes a problem to itself' when it raises a vicious circle; when to write necessarily involves something that seems to make writing impossible. Contradictions in our civil space are one thing that make this happen, and I am struck by the subtle connections people here have drawn between words and their own problematic public space. . . .

To explore the obstructions of cadence is, for a Canadian, to explore the nature of colonial space. Here I am particularly concerned with what it does to writing. One can also analyse it economically or politically, or try to act upon it; but at this point I want only to find words for our experience of it. . . .

I shall be speaking of 'words', but not merely those you find in a dictionary. I mean all the resources of the verbal imagination, from single words through verse forms, conventions about levels of style, characteristic versions of the hero, resonant structures of plot. And I use my own experience with words because I know it best. It tallies with things other writers in their thirties have said, but I don't know how many would accept it fully.

My sense when I began writing, about 1960 – and this lasted five or six years – was that I had access to a great many words: those of the British, the American, and (so far as anyone took it seriously) the Canadian traditions. Yet at the same time those words seemed to lie in a great random heap, which glittered with promise so long as I considered it in the mass but within which each individual word went stiff, inert, was somehow clogged with sludge, the moment I tried to move it into place in a poem. I could stir words, prod at them, cram them into position; but there was no way I could speak them directly. They were completely external to me, though since I had never known the words of poetry in any other way I assumed that was natural.

Writers everywhere don't have to begin with a resistant, external language; there was more behind the experience than just getting the hang of the medium during apprenticeship. In any case, after I had published one book of poems and finished another a bizarre thing happened: I stopped being able to use words on paper at all.

All around me – in England, America, even in Canada – writers opened their mouths and words spilled out like crazy. But increasingly when I opened mine I simply gagged; finally, the words no longer came. For about four years at the end of the decade I tore up everything I wrote – twenty words on a page were enough to set me boggling at their palpable inauthenticity. And looking back at my previous writing, I felt as if I had been fishing pretty beads out of a vat of crank-case oil and stringing them together. The words weren't limber or alive or even mine.

To discover that you are mute in the midst of all the riches of a language is a weird experience. I had no explanation for it; by 1967 it had happened to me, but I didn't know why . . . I had just begun to write, and now I was stopped. I would still sit down in my study with a pen and paper from time to time, and every time I ended up ripping the paper to pieces and pitching it out. The stiffness and falsity of the words appalled me; the reaction was more in my body than my mind, but it was very strong. . . .

The colonial writer does not have words of his own. Is it not possible that he projects his own condition of voicelessness into whatever he creates? that he articulates his own powerlessness, in the face of alien words, by seeking out fresh tales of victims? . . . perhaps the colonial imagination is driven to recreate, again and again, the experience of writing in colonial space.

We are getting close to the centre of the tangle. Why did I stop being interested in Shakespeare at Stratford, when I had gone assiduously for ten summers? Why did I fidget and squirm in front of TV and read so much less? And why did I dry?

The words I knew said Britain, and they said America, but they did not say my home. They were always and only about someone else's life. All the rich structures of language were present, but the currents that animated them were not home to the people who used the language here.

But the civil self seeks nourishment as much as the biological self; it too fuels the imagination. And if everything it can find is alien, it may protect itself in a visceral spasm of refusal. To take an immediate example: the words I used above 'language', 'home', 'here' – have no native charge; they convey only meanings in whose face we have been unable to find ourselves since the eighteenth century. This is not a call for arbitrary new Canadian definitions, of course. It is simply to point out that the texture, weight and connotation of almost every word we use comes from abroad. For a person whose medium is words, who wants to use words to recreate our being human here – and where else do we live? – that fact creates an absolute problem.

Why did I dry for four years? The language was drenched with our non-belonging, and words – bizarre as it sounds, even to myself – words had become the enemy. To use them as a writer was to collaborate further in one's extinction as a rooted human being. And so, by a drastic and involuntary stratagem of self-preserval, words went dead.

The first necessity for the colonial writer – so runs the conventional wisdom – is to start writing of what he knows. His imagination must come home. But that first necessity is not enough. For if you are Canadian, home is a place that is not home to you – it is even less your home than the imperial centre you used to dream about. Or to say what I really know best, the *words* of home are silent. And to write a jolly ode to harvests in Saskatchewan, or set an American murder mystery in Newfoundland, is no answer at all. Try to speak the words of your home and you will discover – if you are a colonial – that you do not know them.

To speak unreflectingly in a colony, then, is to use words that speak only alien space. To reflect is to fall silent, discovering that your authentic space does not have words. And to reflect further is to recognise that you and your people do not in fact have a privileged authentic space just waiting for words; you are, among other things, the people who have made an alien inauthenticity their own. You are left chafing at the inarticulacy of a native space which may not exist. So you shut up.

But perhaps – and here was the breakthrough – perhaps our job was not to fake a space of our own and write it up, but rather to find words for our space-lessness. Perhaps that *was* home. This dawned on me gradually. Instead of pushing against the grain of an external, uncharged language, perhaps we should finally come to writing with that grain.

To do that was a homecoming – and a thoroughly edgy, uncertain homecoming it was. You began by giving up the idea of writing in the same continuum as Lowell, Roethke, Ginsberg, Olson, Plath. . . . It was a question of starting from your own necessities. And you began striving to hear what happened in words – in 'love', 'inhabit', 'fail', 'earth', 'house' – as you let them surface in your own mute and native land. It was a funny, visceral process; there was nothing as explicit as starting to write in *joual*, though the process was comparable. There was only the decision to let words be how they actually are for us. But I am distorting the experience again by writing it down. There was nothing conscious about this decision, initially at least – it was a direction one's inner ear took up. I know I fought it.

The first mark of words, as you began to re-appropriate them in this space-less civil space, was a kind of blur of unachieved meaning. That I had already experienced, though only as something oppressing and negative. But then I began to sense something more.

Where I lived, a whole swarm of inarticulate meanings lunged, clawed, drifted, eddied, sprawled in half-grasped disarray beneath the tidy meaning which the simplest word had brought with it from England and the States. 'City': once you learned to accept the blurry, featureless character of that word – responding to it as a Canadian word, with its absence of native connotation – you were dimly savaged by the live, inchoate meanings trying to surface through it. The whole tangle and sisyphean problematic of people's existing here, from the time of the *coureurs de bois* to the present day, came struggling to be included in the word 'city'. Cooped up beneath the familiar surface of the word as we use it ('city' as London, as New York, as Los Angeles) – and cooped up further down still, beneath the blank and blur you heard when you sought some received indigenous meaning for the word – listening all the way down, you began to overhear the strands and communal lives of millions of people who went their particular ways here, whose roots and lives and legacy come together in the cities we live in. Edmonton, Toronto, Montreal, Halifax: 'city' meant something still unspoken, but rampant with held-in energy. Hearing it was like watching the contours of an unexpected continent gradually declare themselves through the familiar lawns and faces of your block.

Though that again is hindsight: all of it. You heard an energy, and those lives were part of it. Under the surface alienation and the second-level blur of our words there was a living barrage of meaning: private, civil, religious – unclassifiable finally, but there, and seamless, and pressing to be spoken. And I felt that press of meaning: I had no idea what it was, but I could feel it teeming towards words. I called it cadence.

And hearing that cadence, I started to write again.

# 71

## Naming Place

### PAUL CARTER*

[I]T WAS ALMOST a commonplace among British residents that, in Australia, the laws of association seemed to be suspended. There seemed to be nothing that could be accurately named. There was, consequently, very little purchase for the imagination – that mental faculty which . . . was primarily a mechanism for making analogies. This was why Barron Field lamented in his *Geographical Memoirs* that Australia was quite unsuitable as a subject for poetry. Referring in particular to 'the eternal eucalyptus', the former dramatic critic of *The Times*, the friend of Coleridge and Wordsworth, wrote:

> No tree, to my taste, can be beautiful that is not deciduous. . . . Dryden says of the laurel
>
> > From winter winds it suffers no decay;
> > For ever fresh and fair, and every month is May.
>
> Now it may be the fault of the cold climate in which I was bred, but this is just what I complain of in an evergreen. 'Forever fresh', is a contradiction in terms; what is 'forever fair' is never fair; and without January, in my mind, there can be no May. All the dearest allegories of human life are bound up with the infant and slender green of spring, the dark redundance of summer, and the sere and yellow leaf of autumn. These are as essential to the poet as emblems, as they are to the painter as picturesque objects; and the common consent and immemorial custom of European poetry has made the change of the seasons, and its effect upon vegetation, a part, as it were, of our very nature. I can therefore hold no fellowship with Australian foliage. . . .
>
> (Field 1825: 423–4)

Field's real subject in this passage is not nature at all. It is language, and the impossibility of distinguishing the language of feeling from the language

* From *The Road to Botany Bay: An Essay in Spatial History* London, Boston: Faber, 1987.

of description. The proper context in which to understand Field's uncompromising stance is not the history of taste but the history of mind. In particular, the point of departure for Field's animadversions is clearly the prevalent doctrine of associationism. . . . The association of simple ideas to form complex ones depended on the ideas (or objects they derived from) being comparable. And first among the qualities of objects that made their comparison possible was, as Hume wrote, 'resemblance': 'This is a relation without which no philosophical relation can exist, since no objects will admit of comparison, but what have some degree of resemblance' (Hume 1934: 22). European nature is an 'emblem' of human life because its cycle of seasons resembles the seasons of human life. Poetry, then, in so far as it evokes human life metaphorically, involves not the description of nature but its association with human themes.

But, as Barron Field's remarks bring out, the association of ideas depended on a profounder assumption. It depended on the assumption that distinct ideas existed to be related. But how is a distinct idea defined, except in relation to other ideas? Since, as Hume put it, 'all kinds of reasoning consist in nothing but a comparison, and a discovery of those relations, either constant or inconstant, which two or more objects bear to each other' (Hume 1934: 77), an absolute idea is a contradiction in terms. Hence Field's irritation with Dryden's laurel. Our ideas of freshness and fairness are relative. They derive their distinctness from our ideas of sereness and dullness. Their efficacy as metaphors of human life depends on our ideas of stale and withered age. But a tree eternally green offers the poet nothing. It defies the logic of association. It is not a distinct idea.

The far-reaching and astonishing implication of Field's remarks is, then, that Australia is, strictly speaking, indescribable. In so far as its nature is undifferentiated, it does not have a distinct character. Lacking this, it cannot be compared and so known. Its uniformity also means that it cannot be named, because no nameable parts distinguish themselves. Not amenable to the logic of association, Australia appears to be unknowable. A state of uniformity offers no starting point, whether for literary or physical travel.

The implications of this conclusion are not only literary. Bearing in mind that the prime responsibility of the early explorers was to *describe* what they saw, the dissonance between language and land presented a considerable challenge. There was no question of falling back on the logic of facts. There was no possibility even of allowing oneself the lazy luxury of comparison. Facts proved fancies; analogies proved false. Indeed, the spatial ramifications of Field's argument are well brought out by Field himself – in the context, significantly enough, of place names. Not surprisingly, Field is highly critical of Australian place names, which, he presumes, attempt to apply the principles of association. Given the 'prosaic, unpicturesque, unmusical' qualities of Australian nature, they are doomed, in his view, to failure. Here is Field's description of the country in the region of

Mount York, between Windsor and Bathurst in the Blue Mountains, west of Sydney:

> The King's Tableland is as anarchical and untabular as any His Majesty possesses. The Prince Regent's Glen below it (if it be the glen that I saw) is not very romantic. Jamison's Valley we found by no means a happy one. Blackheath is a wretched misnomer. Not to mention its awful contrast to the beautiful place of that name in England, heath it is none. Black it may be when the shrubs are burnt, as they often are. Pitt's Amphitheatre disappointed me. The hills are thrown together in a monotonous manner, and their clothing is very unpicturesque – a mere sea of harsh trees; but Mr Pitt was no particular connoisseur in mountain scenery or in amphi-theatres.
>
> (Field 1825: 430)

This splenetic outburst against misnomers and misnamers is based on the assumption that the Australian names in question violate the logic of association. It is not so much a 'description' of nature as a critique of the absurdity of associative naming in Australia: the 'Tableland' in question does not really resemble a tableland; the 'Glen' does not really suggest a glen; the 'Valley' does not really recall a valley, because the Australian places fail to conjure up the proper associations. In Australia, therefore, class names of this kind fail.

The interesting thing about Field's view is that it underlines the perhaps surprising point that *both* elements in place names were figurative, and non-factual: it is not only the particularizing element 'Botany' that is metaphorical; the apparently more objective term 'Bay' may be equally fanciful. What Field's remarks do not bring out, though, is the even more important point that follows from this – which is that the proper way in which to interpret geographical class names like 'valley' and 'tableland' is not in terms of imperial history, but within the perspective of the history of travelling. The imperial pretensions of particularizing epithets like 'King's', 'Prince Regent's' and even 'Pitt's' may seem all too obvious, but their concentration suggests that even they reflect the namer's intention to characterize a space. And, certainly, when we turn to the other element in such names, the spatial intention they express becomes inescapable. For the fact is that such names were given. In some sense they 'stuck'. And, even if we accepted Field's genealogical judgement and considered such classificatory names failures, we would still be left wondering why they were given in the first place. Why, if the newcomers were bound by the laws of analogy, by what they had formerly seen and read, did they not leave these nameless extensions, these culturally invisible intervals, unnamed and silent?

The truth is that the naming process may have been metaphorical and, to that extent, a kind of gnomic poetry *manqué*, but it was not associational in intent. It was not a retrospective gloss, after the event, a sort of gilding in bad taste round the physical mirror of history. It was the names themselves that brought history into being, that invented the spatial and conceptual coordinates within which history could occur. For how, without place names, without agreed points of reference, could directions be given, information exchanged, 'here' and 'there' defined? Consider those most beautiful of Australian names, names like Cape Catastrophe, Mount Misery, Retreat Well and Lake Disappointment. These names do not merely confirm Field's argument, that the logic of association breaks down in Australia: they also defy it, asserting the possibility of naming in the absence of resemblance. If a well is associated with water and is therefore regarded as an aid to the traveller, to describe it as *Retreat* well is to say the conventional associations of the class name fail here. A mountain, associated with long views and perhaps with water, would, it might be thought, be welcomed by the explorer. To call it 'Mount Misery' is again to suggest that, in Australia, the normal logic of association breaks down. But, if these 'wells' are not wells, these 'mountains' unmountainlike, what do the names mean? What is their function? The paradox they express is not descriptive. Rather, it refers to the traveller's state of expectation.

More than this, such class names (as their riddling qualifiers often make explicit) do not reflect what is already there: on the contrary, they embody the existential necessity the traveller feels to invent a place he can inhabit. Without them, punctuating the monotony, distinguishing this horizon from that, there would be no evidence he had travelled. To be sure, the traveller might retain his private impressions, but, without names, and the discourse of the journal they epitomize, his experience could never become public, a historical fact leading to other facts, other journeys. Thus, the fundamental impulse in applying class names like 'mount' or 'river' was a desire to differentiate the uniformity.

Partly, of course, the uniformity defied easy differentiation because, in a quite simple way, the English language lacked words to characterize it. Alexander Hamilton Hume and William Hovell, for example, who led the first overland expedition from Sydney to Port Phillip in 1824, 'cross swamp which had been mistaken for a meadow'. As it turns out, it is neither one nor the other:

> This, like all other spaces of any extent, lying intermediately between the ranges, consists of a kind of meadow, divided along its centre by a small but rapid stream, is somewhat swampy, and in places near the water produces reeds.
>
> (Hovell and Hume 1831: 51)

This was a case where a kind of country, far from rare, raised a problem of nomenclature. There was no English term for it, and yet in more arid regions the traveller sought it out. Indeed another explorer, Edward John Eyre, depended on it when making his attempt on the centre in 1841. Advancing northward parallel to the Flinders Range in South Australia,

we just kept far enough into the plains to intercept the watercourses
from the hills where they spread out into level country, and by this
means we got excellent feed for our horses.

(Eyre 1845: 94)

As this fertile zone of passage was neither meadow nor swamp, the
explorer had no name for it. Passages like these come close to vindicating
the reductionist view of the American philosopher of language, Benjamin
Whorf. On the map at least, these places do not exist simply because they
cannot be named; reality is a naive reflection of the language available to
describe it. But, even though Eyre and Hume and Hovell cannot name this
intermediate space directly, they can, after all, refer to it. What limits their
powers of description is not vocabulary but the desire to differentiate, the
necessity of naming in order to travel. And, in so far as such nameless zones
can be located syntactically and spatially between 'plains' and 'hills', they
have been appropriated to the traveller's route.

In any case, the difficulty of vocabulary aside, the criteria of differentiation were not simply empirical, naively describing the nature of 'things'
already there – it was precisely such objects that names served to constitute. They were determined not empirically but rhetorically. They
embodied the traveller's directional and territorial ambitions: his desire to
possess where he had been as a preliminary to going on. And this desire
was not placeless, it did not resemble the equal stare of the map grid. It
depended on positing a 'here' (the traveller's viewpoint and orientation)
and a 'there' (the landscape, the horizon). And where such viewpoints did
not exist, they had to be hypothesized, rhetorically asserted by way of
names. Otherwise, the landscape itself could never enter history.

This is the significance of the urgency, the premature willingness, of
Australian travellers to name 'mountains' and 'rivers'. Mountains and
rivers were culturally desirable, they conjured up pleasing associations. But,
more fundamentally, they signified differences that made a difference. They
implied the possibility of viewpoints, directions: to call a hill 'Prospect Hill'
. . . is to describe hills' historical function. 'Supposed course of the River
Nepean': to write these words on the map one after the other is to set out
graphically the spatial intention implicit in invoking the word 'river'. Hills
and rivers were, in fact, the kind of object that made travelling as a
historical activity possible. They were the necessary counterpart of the traveller's desire to travel, to see the horizon and to find a route there.

# 72

## *Decolonizing the Map*

### GRAHAM HUGGAN*

THE PREVALENCE OF the map topos in contemporary post-colonial literary texts, and the frequency of its ironic and/or parodic usage in these texts, suggests a link between a de/reconstructive reading of maps and a revisioning of the history of European colonialism. This revisionary process is most obvious, perhaps, in the fiction of the Caribbean writer Wilson Harris, where the map features as a metaphor of the perceptual transformation which allows for the revisioning of Caribbean cultural history in terms other than those of catastrophe or complex. Throughout his work, Harris stresses the relativity of modes of cultural perception; thus, although he recognizes that a deconstruction of the social text of European colonialism is the prerequisite for a reconstruction of post-colonial Caribbean culture, he emphasizes that this and other post-colonial cultures neither be perceived in essentialist terms, nor divested of its/their implication in the European colonial enterprise. The hybrid forms of Caribbean and other post-colonial cultures merely accentuate the transitional status of all cultures; so while the map is ironized on the one hand in Harris's work as a visual analogue for the inflexibility of colonial attitudes and for the 'synchronic essentialism' of colonial discourse, it is celebrated on the other as an agent of cultural transformation and as a medium for the imaginative revisioning of cultural history (see Harris 1981).

More recent developments in post-colonial writing and, in particular, in the Canadian and Australian literatures, suggest a shift of emphasis from the interrogation of European colonial history to the overt or implied critique of unquestioned nationalist attitudes which are viewed as 'synchronic' formations particular not to post-colonial but, ironically, to colonial discourse. A characteristic of contemporary Canadian and Australian writing is a multiplication of spatial references which has resulted not only in an increased range of national and international

* From 'Decolonizing the Map: Post-Colonialism, Post-Structuralism and the Cartographic Connection' *Ariel* 20(4), 1989.

locations but also in a series of 'territorial disputes' which pose a challenge to the self-acknowledging 'mainstreams' of metropolitan culture, to the hegemonic tendencies of patriarchal and ethnocentric discourses, and implicitly, I would argue, to the homogeneity assumed and/or imposed by colonialist rhetoric. These revised forms of cultural decolonization have brought with them a paradoxical alliance between internationalist and regionalist camps where the spaces occupied by the 'international', like those by the 'regional', do not so much forge new definitions as denote the semantic slippage between prescribed definitions of place. The attempt by writers such as Hodgins (1977) and Malouf (1985) to project spaces other than, or by writers such as Van Herk (1986) and Atwood (1985), to articulate the spaces between, those prescribed by dominant cultural or cultural groups, indicates a resistance to the notion of cartographic enclosure and to the imposed cultural limits that notion implies. Yet the range of geographical locations and diversity of functions served by the map metaphor in the contemporary Canadian and Australian literatures suggests a desire on the part of their respective writers not merely to deterritorialize, but also to reterritorialize, their increasingly multiform cultures. The dual tendencies towards geographical dispersal (as, for example, in the 'Asian' fictions of Koch and Rivard) and cultural decentralization (as, for example, in the hyperbolically fragmented texts of Bail and Kroetsch) can therefore be seen within the context of a resiting of the traditional 'mimetic fallacy' of cartographic representation. The map no longer features as a visual paradigm for the ontological anxiety arising from frustrated attempts to define a national culture, but rather as a locus of productive dissimilarity where the provisional connections of cartography suggest an ongoing perceptual transformation which in turn stresses the transitional nature of post-colonial discourse. This transformation has been placed within the context of a shift from an earlier 'colonial' fiction obsessed with the problems of writing in a 'colonial space' to a later, 'post-colonial' fiction which emphasizes the provisionality of all cultures and which celebrates the particular diversity of formerly colonized cultures whose ethnic mix can no longer be considered in terms of the colonial stigmas associated with mixed blood or cultural schizophrenia. Thus, while it would be unwise to suggest that the traditional Canadian and Australian concerns with cultural identity have become outmoded, the reassessment of cartography in many of their most recent literary texts indicates a shift of emphasis away from the desire for homogeneity towards an acceptance of diversity reflected in the interpretation of the map, not as a means of spatial containment or systematic organization, but as a medium of spatial perception which allows for the reformulation of links both within and between cultures.

In this context, the 'new spaces' of post-colonial writing in Canada and Australia can be considered to resist one form of cartographic discourse, whose patterns of coercion and containment are historically implicated in the colonial enterprise, but to advocate another, whose flexible cross-cultural patterns not only counteract the monolithic conventions of the West but revision the map itself as the expression of a shifting ground between alternative metaphors rather than as the approximate representation of a 'literal truth'. This paradoxical motion of the map as a 'shifting ground' is discussed at length by the French post-structuralists Gilles Deleuze and Félix Guattari. For Deleuze and Guattari, maps are experimental in orientation:

> The map is open and connectable in all its dimensions; it is detachable, reversible, susceptible to constant modification. It can be torn, reversed, adapted to any kind of mounting, reworked by an individual, group, or social formation. It can be drawn on the wall, conceived of as a work of art, constructed as a political action or as a meditation.
>
> (Deleuze and Guattari 1987: 12)

The flexible design of the map is likened by Deleuze and Guattari to that of the rhizome, whose 'deterritorializing lines of flight' (222) effect 'an asignifying rupture against the oversignifying breaks separating structures or cutting across a single structure' (7–9).

As Diana Brydon has illustrated, Deleuze and Guattari's association of the multiple connections/disconections of the rhizome with the transformative patterns of the map provides a useful, if by its very nature problematic, working model for the description of post-colonial cultures and for the closer investigation of the kaleidoscopic variations of post-colonial discourse (Brydon 1988). Moreove., ber of contemporary women writers in Canada and Australia, notably Nicole Brossard and Marion Campbell, have adapted Deleuze and Guattari's model to the articulation of a feminist cartography which dissociates itself from the 'over-signifying' spaces of patriarchal representation but through its 'deterritorializing lines of flight' produces an alternative kind of map characterized not by the containment or regimentation of space but by a series of centrifugal displacements (see Godard 1987). Other implicitly 'rhizomatic' maps are sketched out in experimental fictions such as those of Kroetsch (1975) and Baillie (1986) in Canada, and Bail (1980) and Murnane (1984) in Australia, where space, as in Deleuze and Guattari's model, is constituted in terms of a series of intermingling lines of connection which shape shifting patterns of de- and reterritorialization. In the work of these other 'new novelists', the map is often identified, then parodied and/or ironized, as a spurious definitional construct, thereby permitting the writer to engage in a more wide-ranging deconstruction of Western signifying systems. . . . If the map is conceived of in Deleuze and Guattari's terms as 'rhizomatic' ('open') rather than as a falsely homogeneous ('closed') construct, the emphasis then shifts from de- to reconstruction, from mapbreaking to mapmaking. The benefit of Deleuze and Guattari's model is that it provides a viable alternative to the implicitly hegemonic (and historically colonialist) form of cartographic discourse which uses the duplicating procedures of mimetic representation and structuralist reconstitution as strategic means of stabilizing the foundations of Western culture and of 'fixing' the position (thereby maintaining the power) of the West in relation to cultures other than its own. Thus, whereas Derrida's deconstructive analysis of the concepts of 'centred' structure and 'interested' simulacrum engenders a process of displacement which undoes the supposed homogeneity of colonial discourse, Deleuze and Guattari's rhizomatic map views this process in terms of a processual transformation more pertinent to the operations of post-colonial discourse and to the complex patterns of de- and reterritorialization working within and between the multicultural societies of the post-colonial world.

As Stephen Slemon has demonstrated, one of the characteristic ploys of post-colonial discourse is its adoption of a creative revisionism which involves the subversion or displacement of dominant discourses (Slemon 1988b). But included within this revisionary process is the internal critique of the post-colonial culture (or cultures), a critique which takes into account the transitional nature of post-colonial societies and which challenges the tenets both of an essentialist nationalism which sublimates or overlooks regional differences and of an unconsidered multiculturalism (mis)appropriated for the purposes of enforced assimilation rather than for the promulgation of cultural diversity. The fascination of post-colonial writers, and of Canadian and Australian writers in particular, with the map topos can be seen in this context as a specific instance of creative revisionism in which the desystematization of a narrowly defined and demarcated 'cartographic' space allows for a culturally and historically located critique of colonial discourse while, at the same time, producing the momentum for a projection and exploration of 'new territories' outlawed or neglected by dominant discourses which previously operated in the colonial, but continue to operate in modified or transposed forms in the post-colonial, culture. I would suggest further that, in the cases of the contemporary Canadian and Australian literatures, these territories correspond to a series of new or revised rhetorical spaces occupied by feminism, regionalism and ethnicity, where each of these items is understood primarily as a set of counter-discursive strategies which challenge the claims of or avoid circumscription within one or other form of cultural centrism. These territories/spaces can also be considered, however, as shifting grounds which are themselves subject to transformational patterns of de- and reterritorialization. The proliferation of spatial references, crossing of physical and/or conceptual boundaries and redisposition of geographical coordinates in much contemporary Canadian and Australian writing stresses the provisionality of cartographic connection and places the increasing diversity of their respective literatures in the context of a post-colonial response to and/or reaction against the ontology and epistemology of 'stability' promoted and safeguarded by colonial discourse. I would conclude from this that the role of cartography in contemporary Canadian and Australian writing, specifically, and in post-colonial writing in general, cannot be solely envisaged as the reworking of a particular spatial paradigm, but consists rather in the implementation of a series of creative revisions which register the transition from a colonial framework within which the writer is compelled to recreate and reflect upon the restrictions of colonial space to a post-colonial one within which he or she acquires the freedom to engage in a series of 'territorial disputes' which implicitly or explicitly acknowledge the relativity of modes of spatial (and, by extension, cultural) perception. So while the map continues to feature in one sense as a paradigm of colonial discourse, its deconstruction and/or revisualization permits a 'disidentification' from the procedures of colonialism (and other hegemonic discourses) and a (re) engagement in the ongoing process of cultural decolonization. The 'cartographic connection' can therefore be considered to provide that provisional link which joins the contestatory theories of post-structuralism and post-colonialism in the pursuit of social and cultural change.

# 73

## *Aboriginal Place*

### Bob Hodge and Vijay Mishra*

#### LAND AS THEME

For Aborigines today the issue of issues is land rights. So it is surprising at first glance that Aboriginal art and literature is not rich in references to land and evocations of landscapes. Aborigines' love of their own land and their precise knowledge of its topography are not in question, yet it was traditionally not an explicit theme in visual or verbal art. The situation of contemporary Aborigines is now very different. Instead of the confident assumption of identity tied to and established through links to a country, dispossession to some degree is their universal experience. But there is still a continuity between traditional and contemporary forms of cultural expression of this theme amongst Aborigines. Traditional culture provided a highly flexible set of ways of encoding a nexus of rights and obligations towards the land. It gave rise to aesthetic statements which were essentially political and juridical rather than personal and expressive. This quality made it equally well adapted to the needs of Aborigines today, all of whom are in some respects fringe-dwellers in their own land, needing a means of relocating themselves in White Australia, reconstructing an identity which is fully Aboriginal yet adequate to the new situation.

In looking at these kinds of adaptation we need to recognise the validity of the two broad strategies adopted by Aboriginal people as these are reflected in cultural forms. Many Aboriginal groups in northern and central Australia are trying to reestablish traditional ways of life, as close to their traditional territories as is now possible. The acrylic art of the Western Desert peoples and the maintenance of traditional languages are important to this strategy. But for many Aborigines in the south the route back has been disrupted, so that the direct link with a specific piece of country is no longer viable. For these Aborigines, urban dwellers or fringe-dwellers in country towns, the achievements of Western Desert artists are

* From *The Dark Side of the Dream* London: Allen & Unwin, 1991.

inspiring but unavailable. The writers who speak for them include all the Aboriginal writers well known in the White community: Jack Davis, Kath Walker (Oodgeroo Noonuccal), Colin Johnson (Mudrooroo Narogin), Kevin Gilbert, Robert Bropho and Sally Morgan. Yet each of these distinct strands of Aboriginal art is equally Aboriginal, equally crucial to all Aborigines, since one establishes the Aboriginal base, while the other opens up the transformational freedom that is equally important to all Aborigines, wherever they are placed.

As an instance of traditional adaptation, we will take two texts by Peter Skipper, a painting and a story. Peter Skipper's Walmatjari speaking group was part of the exodus of Western Desert people who moved east, out of the desert area, in closer proximity to areas of White settlement in the northwest of Western Australia. His community is established near Fitzroy Crossing, where Peter Skipper is an important elder who is concerned to retain traditional forms of life in this new situation.

The story we will look at was reported to a linguist, Joyce Hudson, and transcribed by her as an example of the Walmatjari language. In that form (part of a grammar of Walmatjari for use by linguists and educators) it has the low aesthetic status and small circulation typical of this genre. It seems a casual and uninformative anecdote, yet like so many such texts it has a complexity of structure and depth of meaning that repay much closer scrutiny. Our reading, we should point out at the outset, will barely scratch the surface of the meanings of this text which are 'owned' by Peter Skipper to which we have no way or right to access. We will begin by giving a translation of the complete text, drawing on Joyce Hudson's translation and commentary (1978):

> In the wet season they eat plant food, Janiya
> and meat, lizard -
> meat, lizard and wild onion plants, wild onion.
>
> In the wet season they eat the
> bush-walnuts as plant food, bush-walnuts they eat.
>
> In the sandhills they lived like this
> the people lived in that former time in the sandhills.
>
> They were eating meat and plant food.
> Plants that they ate were various, various.
> They were eating all kinds of plant food,
> all kinds of plant foods they ate,
> until what they ate was finished,
> a finish to eating plant food and meat
>
> Well, they ate meat only,
> then that finished.
> And the people they went this way
> to other kinds of plant food, Whiteman's tucker.

Well, those people too, they went north to the stations.
Then they gave them plant food,
the people from the sandhills.

Those people went for good,
never to return.
Well, they went on a journey for plant food,
Whiteman's tucker.
Then they stayed there, those people.
So they ate the plant food of the Whiteman,
and so they stayed there, the people,
never to return.

In terms of comparable White genres, this is closest to a lyric of loss and dispossession, stately and formulaic, almost literally a structure of feeling organising a temporal and spatial map. There is no comment, no explanation, no justification of either present or past, only a recurring set of organising categories that can be applied to both. Why did the food supply disappear? Was it a natural disaster, an extended drought, or was it the incursions of Whites with their stock and excessive demands on the fragile ecology? Peter Skipper gives no answer or not explicitly. . . .

Another principle of the structure, which our translation can only indicate with some clumsiness, is the repetition of the two categories of food, *kuyi* (meat) and *miyi* (plant). These two words insistently classify the natural environment as kinds of food to be hunted or gathered in the gendered division of labour of traditional society. The progression that Skipper describes has three stages. In the first, normative stage, there is both *miyi* and *kuyi*, gathering and hunting. In the second phase, there is only *kuyi*, hunting. The tucker supplied by the Whites is referred to every time as *miyi*, plant foods. Flour and sugar may have been the main staples provided by stations, but there was meat too, from occasional killings. Skipper classifies this food in social not in biological terms as *miyi*, implying a comment on its effect on the traditional roles of Aboriginal society. He does not cast back to a time when men as hunters were exclusive or dominant providers – that phase in his scheme was a result of a breakdown in the natural order. Instead in the landscape of plenitude, in the Wet season in the past, men and women were coequals. That is the situation that can and must return, when another Wet succeeds the present Dry.

There is no statement of regret, though the repeated 'never to return' unmistakeably suggests a sense of loss. What the text does is to carry the values of the desert and the past into the new situation, not as a legitimation of the present (a form of existence which is still radically incomplete) but as a kind of charter for change. The text is neither militant nor resigned, but its criticism and its optimism are so understated as to be almost invisible. Its dominant qualities of balance and poise are aesthetic

414

and political, and even its self-effacement is part of a strategy of survival. And although this past is a remembered historical past it also has something of the structural form of what is called 'the Dreamtime' by Aboriginalists: that is, a time in the past whose values are still active in the present.

Peter Skipper painted *Jila Japingka* (Figure 4) in 1987, a text which is reproduced in Sutton (1988). The style of the painting is typical of the acrylics of the Western Desert artists, though it has its own distinctive qualities. As is normal for such texts, the first impression is the sense of formal patterns, produced by repetition of a small number of elements, as happens with his verbal text also. The meaning of the text is otherwise almost inaccessible, without further explanation. Sutton provides a gloss, the first aspect of which is its positioning in space and time. The cross-shape (painted deep blue) is formed by rain from the four compass-points, with the top rain from the east, the bottom rain from the west, with rain from the north on the left, and rain from the south on the right.

This, then, is a map of the same landscape as in the story, the all-important landscape in which Peter Skipper and his people have acted out their life. The east, where his people came from, is positioned at the top of the picture, and the west (Fitzroy Crossing, Broome) is at the bottom. As is typical of traditional Aboriginal art, this text makes no attempt to represent the landscape accurately. The symmetry of the four rains implies that rain comes equally from all four directions, which is very far from true in that part of the Kimberleys. But the symmetry is broken by the profusion of water-sources in the dry east (the arc above the cross and the four water-holes above all painted blue), as against the absence of water in the west. The painting encodes the meaning of plenitude as an attribute of the east (and the past) compared to the west and the present, just as the story did.

The semi-circles and concentric circles are traditional motifs, which carry a complex of meanings, referring to home-centres (campsites, water-holes, fires) or people resting. But the grid of rectangular shapes is not typical. In this text these shapes dominate the west and the north, characterising the spaces of civilisation and Whitemen's ways, seeming not unlike the bars of a cage, symbols of regimented existence. But Sutton's annotation indicates that these rectangular shapes are sandhills, so that western civilisation is reclassified as a kind of desert. 'Desert' in this scheme is partly negative. However in Skipper's system the actual desert region is constructed as a place of abundance, not as a barren place. This contradictory classification then has a positive implication, making the barren terrain of civilisation a place in which Aborigines can survive as they did in the Western Desert.

Skipper achieves this meaning-effect by drawing on the resources of traditional art, specifically its capacity to use a minimalist system of classification to establish a complex network of connections that in Western traditions is associated with metaphor. We see a more typical instance of

*Figure 4  Jila Japingka* by Peter Skipper (Picture courtesy of Duncan Kentish and Peter Skipper)

this in the use of semi-circular shapes. Sutton's annotation indicates that the two large arcs in the top right of the painting are long sandhills, while the others represent clouds. The semicircular shape acts as a classifier which establishes a metaphoric link between the two: these sandhills are like clouds insofar as both are like people camped around a site. Clouds are the source of water and sandhills are dry, so the link serves to resolve these primary oppositions. But sandhills themselves are encoded as both semicircular and rectangular rounded open shapes (home, Aboriginality) and rectilinear closed shapes (White domains, exile). In this and many other ways the painting responds to two opposing impulses, establishment of difference (between desert and water, home and exile, Aboriginal and White) and the resolution of difference.

The verbal text is constructed out of the same fundamental principles, and is concerned with the same crucial issue – coming to terms with the position of Aborigines in White Australia, using traditional resources to express a twin sense of alienation and belonging. If we gave the texts a more formal analysis we would come up with the seemingly implausible elaborations of the kind of structuralism for which Claude Levi-Strauss is famous. Neither text is a normal object for these forms of exegesis, and the verbal text especially seems far too humble a form to justify any attention to its formal qualities and implicit levels of meaning. We have discussed them in such detail as the only way to make the general point convincing. Very many Aboriginal texts, written and unwritten, recorded or not, deal directly with the fundamental issues facing Aboriginal people, torn as they are between alienation and a sense of belonging. The strategy they use is an adaptation of traditional Aboriginal ways, constructing maps that are designed to represent broad stretches of space and time, to give meaning and perspective, direction and hope on the bewildering journey of the life of themselves and their people.

# 74

## Ecological Imperialism

### ALFRED W. CROSBY*

EUROPEAN IMMIGRANTS AND their descendants are all over the place, which requires explanation.

It is more difficult to account for the distribution of this subdivision of the human species than that of any other. The locations of the others make an obvious kind of sense. . . . All these peoples have expanded geographically – have committed acts of imperialism, if you will – but they have expanded into lands adjacent to or at least near to those in which they had already been living. . . . Europeans, in contrast, seem to have leapfrogged around the globe.

Europeans, a division of Caucasians distinctive in their politics and technologies, rather than in their physiques, live in large numbers and nearly solid blocks in northern Eurasia, from the Atlantic to the Pacific. They occupy much more territory there than they did a thousand or even five hundred years ago, but that is the part of the world in which they have lived throughout recorded history, and there they have expanded in the traditional way, into contiguous areas. They also compose the great majority in the populations of what I shall call the Neo-Europes, lands thousands of kilometers from Europe and from each other. Australia's population is almost all European in origin, and that of New Zealand is about nine-tenths European. In the Americas north of Mexico there are considerable minorities of Afro-Americans and *mestizos* (a convenient Spanish-American term I shall use to designate Amerindian and white mixtures), but over 80 percent of the inhabitants of this area are of European descent. . . . Even if we accept the highest estimations of Afro-American, and Amerindian populations, more than three of every four Americans in the southern temperate zone are entirely of European ancestry. Europeans, to borrow a term from apiculture, have swarmed again and again and have selected their new homes as if each swarm were physically repulsed by the others.

* From *Ecological Imperialism: The Biological Expansion of Europe 900–1900* Cambridge: Cambridge University Press, 1986.

The Neo-Europes are intriguing for reasons other than the disharmony between their locations and the racial and cultural identity of most of their people. These lands attract the attention – the unblinking envious gaze – of most of humanity because of their food surpluses. They compose the majority of those very few nations on this earth that consistently, decade after decade, export very large quantities of food. In 1982, the total value of all agricultural exports in the world, of all agricultural products that crossed national borders, was $210 billion. Of this, Canada, the United States, Argentina, Uruguay, Australia, and New Zealand accounted for $64 billion, or a little over 30 percent, a total and a percentage that would be even higher if the exports of southern Brazil were added. The Neo-European share of exports of wheat, the most important crop in international commerce, was even greater. In 1982, $18 billion worth of wheat passed over national boundaries, of which the Neo-Europes exported about $13 billion. In the same year, world exports of protein-rich soybeans, the most important new entry in international trade in foodstuffs since World War II, amounted to $7 billion. The United States and Canada accounted for $6.3 billion of this. In exports of fresh, chilled, and frozen beef and mutton, the Neo-Europes also lead the world, as well as in a number of other foodstuffs. Their share of the international trade in the world's most vitally important foods is much greater than the Middle East's share of petroleum exports (see Brown 1984: 19).

The dominant role of the Neo-Europes in international trade in foodstuffs is not simply a matter of brute productivity. . . . These regions lead the world in production of food *relative to the amount locally consumed*, or, to put it another way, in the production of surpluses for export. To cite an extreme example, in 1982 the United States produced only a minuscule percentage of the world's rice, but it accounted for one-fifth of all exports of that grain, more than any other nation (*World Almanac 1984*: 156). . . .

[L]et us turn to the subject of the Europeans' proclivity for migrating overseas, one of their most distinctive characteristics, and one that has had much to do with Neo-European agricultural productivity. Europeans were understandably slow to leave the security of their homelands. The populations of the Neo-Europes did not become as white as they are today until long after Cabot, Magellan, and other European navigators first came upon the new lands, nor until many years after the first white settlers made their homes there. In 1800, North America, after almost two centuries of successful European colonization, and though in many ways the most attractive of the Neo-Europes to Old World migrants, had a population of fewer than 5 million whites, plus about 1 million blacks. Southern South America, after more than two hundred years of European occupation, was an even worse laggard, having less than half a million whites. Australia had only 10,000, and New Zealand was still Maori country.

Then came the deluge. Between 1820 and 1930, well over 50 million Europeans migrated to the Neo-European lands overseas. That number

# ALFRED W. CROSBY

amounts to approximately one-fifth of the entire population of Europe at the beginning of that period. Why such an enormous movement of peoples across such vast distances? Conditions in Europe provided a considerable push – population explosion and a resulting shortage of cultivable land, national rivalries, persecution of minorities – and the application of steam power to ocean and land travel certainly facilitated long distance migration. But what was the nature of the Neo-European pull? The attractions were many, of course, and they varied from place to place in these new-found lands. But underlying them all, and coloring and shaping them in ways such that a reasonable man might be persuaded to invest capital and even the lives of his family in Neo-European adventures, were factors perhaps best described as biogeographical. . . .

Where are the Neo-Europes? Geographically they are scattered, but they are in similar latitudes. They are all completely or at least two-thirds in the temperate zones, north and south, which is to say that they have roughly similar climates. The plants on which Europeans historically have depended for food and fiber, and the animals on which they have depended for food, fiber, power, leather, bone, and manure, tend to prosper in warm-to-cool climates with an annual precipitation of 50 to 150 centimeters. These conditions are characteristic of all the Neo-Europes, or at least of their fertile parts in which Europeans have settled densely. One would expect an Englishman, Spaniard, or German to be attracted chiefly to places where wheat and cattle would do well, and that has indeed proved to be the case.

The Neo-Europes all lie primarily in temperate zones, but their native biotas are clearly different from one another and from that of northern Eurasia. . . . European colonists sometimes found Neo-European flora and fauna exasperatingly bizarre. Mr. J. Martin in Australia in the 1830s complained that

> the trees retained their leaves and shed their bark instead, the swans were black, the eagles white, the bees were stingless, some mammals had pockets, others laid eggs, it was warmest on the hills and coolest in the valleys, [and] even the blackberries were red.
>
> (Powell 1976: 13–14)

There is a striking paradox here. The parts of the world that today in terms of population and culture are most like Europe are far away from Europe – indeed, they are across major oceans – and although they are similar in climate to Europe, they have indigenous floras and faunas different from those of Europe. The regions that today export more foodstuffs of European provenance – grains and meats – than any other lands on earth had no wheat, barley, rye, cattle, pigs, sheep, or goats whatsoever five hundred years ago. The resolution of the paradox is simple to state, though difficult to explain. North America, southern South America, Australia, and New Zealand are far from Europe in distance but have climates similar to hers, and European flora and fauna, including human beings, can thrive

420

in these regions if the competition is not too fierce. In general, the competition has been mild. On the pampa, Iberian horses and cattle have driven back the guanaco and rhea; in North America, speakers of Indo-European languages have overwhelmed speakers of Algonkin and Muskhogean and other Amerindian languages; in the antipodes, the dandelions and house cats of the Old World have marched forward, and kangaroo grass and Kiwis have retreated. Why? Perhaps European humans have triumphed because of their superiority in arms, organization, and fanaticism, but what in heaven's name is the reason that the sun never sets on the empire of the dandelion? Perhaps the success of European imperialism has a biological, an ecological, component. . . .

The Neo-Europes collectively and singly are important, more important than their sizes and populations and even wealth indicate. They are enormously productive agriculturally, and with the world's population thrusting toward 5 billion and beyond, they are vital to the survival of many hundreds of millions. The reasons for this productivity include the undeniable virtuosity of their farmers and agricultural scientists and, in addition, several fortuitous circumstances that require explanation. The Neo-Europes all include large areas of very high photosynthetic potential, areas in which the amount of solar energy, the sunlight, available for the transformation of water and inorganic matter into food is very high. The quantity of light in the tropics is, of course, enormous, but less than one might think, because of the cloudiness and haziness of the wet tropics and the unvarying length of the day year-round. . . .

Taking all in all, the zones of the earth's surface richest in photosynthetic potential lie between the tropics and fifty degrees latitude north and south. There most of the food plants that do best in an eight-month growing season thrive. Within these zones the areas with rich soils that receive the greatest abundance of sunlight and, as well, the amounts of water that our staple crops require – the most important agricultural land in the world, in other words – are the central United States, California, southern Australia, New Zealand, and a wedge of Europe consisting of the southwestern half of France and the northwestern half of Iberia. All of these, with the exception of the European wedge, are within the Neo-Europes; and a lot of the rest of the Neo-European land, such as the pampa or Saskatchewan, is nearly as rich photosynthetically, and is as productive in fact, if not in theory (see Chang 1970). . . .

An extraordinarily, perhaps frighteningly, large number of humans elsewhere in the world depend on the Neo-Europes for much of their food, and it appears that more and more will as world population increases. . . . Often in defiance of ideology and perhaps of good sense, more and more members of our species are becoming dependent on parts of the world far away where pale strangers grow food for sale. A very great many people are hostage to the possible effects of weather, pests, diseases, economic and political vagaries, and war in the Neo-Europes.

The responsibilities of the Neo-Europeans require unprecedented ecological and diplomatic sophistication: statesmanship in farm and embassy, plus greatness of spirit. One wonders if their comprehension of our world is equal to the challenge posed by the current state of our species and of the biosphere. It is an understanding formed by their own experience of one to four centuries of plenty, a unique episode in recorded history. I do not claim that this plenty has been evenly distributed: the poor are poor in the Neo-Europes, and Langston Hughes's nagging question 'What happens to a dream deferred?' still nags, but I do insist that the people of the Neo-Europes almost universally believe that great material affluence can and should be attained by everyone, particularly in matters of diet. In Christ's Palestine, the multiplication of the loaves and fishes was a miracle; in the Neo-Europes it is expected. . . .

Today we are drawing on the advantages accruing from second entry, but widespread erosion, diminishing fertility, and the swift growth in the numbers of those dependent on the productivity of Neo-European soils remind us that the profits are finite. We are in need of a flowering of ingenuity equal to that of the Neolithic or, lacking that, of wisdom.

# PART XIII

## Education

# Introduction

In *Images in Print* (1988), a study of race, class and gender bias in contemporary Caribbean text books, Ruby King and Mike Morrissey note that although some of the countries of the Commonwealth Caribbean have been independent for twenty-five years, the values and patterns of British colonial education have persisted. Education is perhaps the most insidious and in some ways the most cryptic of colonialist survivals, older systems now passing, sometimes imperceptibly, into neo-colonialist configurations.

Such patterns are reproduced not just through established curricula, syllabuses and set texts, but more fundamentally through basic attitudes to education itself, to both its nature and its role within particular nations and cultures. Moreover the conditions of production and consumption of education and its technologies, while they may have undergone subtle shifts, have not, as Philip Altbach argues, significantly altered the unequal power relations between the educational producers and the 'peripheral' consumers of education.

Education, whether state or missionary, primary or secondary (and later tertiary) was a massive cannon in the artillery of empire. The military metaphor can however seem inappropriate, since unlike outright territorial aggression, education effects, in Gramsci's terms, a 'domination by consent'. This domination by consent is achieved through what is taught to the colonised, how it is taught, and the subsequent emplacement of the educated subject as a part of the continuing imperial apparatus – a knowledge of English literature, for instance, was required for entry into the civil service and the legal professions. Education is thus a conquest of another kind of territory – it is the foundation of colonialist power and consolidates this power through legal and administrative apparatuses.

As Gauri Viswanathan notes, 'the split between the material and discursive practices of colonialism is nowhere sharper than in the progressive rarefaction of the rapacious, exploitative, and ruthless actor of history into the reflective subject of literature.' As important as all education proved as a means to colonialist control, literary education had a particular valency. The brutality of colonial personnel was, through the deployment of literary texts in education, both converted to and justified by the implicit and explicit

425

'claims' to superiority of civilisation embodied/encoded through the 'fetish' of the English book.

Education becomes a technology of colonialist subjectification in two other important and intrinsically interwoven ways. It establishes the locally English or British as normative through critical claims to 'universality' of the values embodied in English literary texts, and it represents the colonised to themselves as inherently inferior beings – 'wild', 'barbarous', 'uncivilised'.

Moreover, technologies of teaching strongly reinforced such textual representations. The reciting of poetry, dramatic set-pieces or prose passages from the works of English writers was not just a practice of literary teaching throughout the empire – it was also an effective mode of moral, spiritual and political inculcation. The English 'tongue' (and thus English literary culture and its values) was learned 'by heart': a phrase that captures the technology's particular significance. Texts, as a number of cultures recognise, actually enter the body, and imperial education systems inter-pellated a colonialist subjectivity not just through syllabus content, or the establishment of libraries within which the colonial could absorb 'the lesson of the master', but through internalising the English text, and reproducing it before audiences of fellow colonials. Recitation of literary texts thus becomes a ritual act of obedience, often performed by a child before an audience of admiring adults, who, in reciting that English tongue, speaks as if s/he were the imperial speaker/master rather than the subjectified colonial so often represented in English poetry and prose.

This is one reason why education, and literary education in particular, has been a major theme and site of contestation in post-colonial literatures. Writers like Jean Rhys in *Wide Sargasso Sea* challenge the whole of that discursive field within which *Jane Eyre* was produced and reproduced, through formal education and informal repute at the colonial periphery. Both Jamaica Kincaid in *Lucy* and Erna Brodber in *Myal* anatomise and dis/mantle imperial education and its technologies. In *Myal* too, Brodber examines the question of knowledges themselves, and against Anglo-education with its colonialist intent, posits an/other kind of knowledge based on African cultural survivals. In so doing both she and Kincaid examine and challenge that persisting gap between the so-called 'first world' production of knowl-edge (the 'authoritative' text) and its consumption at colonial and post-colonial sites – the inferior and mutable *con*texts for these 'immutable' Anglo-European products.

Formal tertiary education – specifically literary education – thus becomes the focus of debate in the following pieces by John Docker and Ngugi wa Thiong'o. Although these essays were written in the 1970s, little has really changed. Few 'English Departments' of Commonwealth and former Commonwealth countries have abolished the title, and most (including universities in the United States) still retain English literature as the core curriculum. And in spite of fundamental changes in literary theory most still remain Anglo-oriented if not Anglo-dominated. Arun Mukherjee suggests one of the reasons for this persistence in her account of the gap between theory and pedagogy in university English teaching.

The recent revolutions in literary theory have, like colonialist education systems, proved a double-edged sword. Imperial education systems effected colonial subjectification, but they also paved the way for subversive and eventually revolutionary processes. Like earlier modes of literary education, contemporary literary theories – specifically Marxist and post-structuralist – have on the one hand offered new possibilities for Anglo-canonical dis/mantling, but in their establishing of new kinds of hegemonies they have, perhaps inadvertently, often acted, as Barbara Christian notes, to reinforce the old divisions and institute a neo-colonialism in literary studies.

Education thus remains one of the most powerful discourses within the complex of colonialism and neo-colonialism. A powerful technology of social control, it also offers one of the most potentially fruitful routes to a dis/mantling of that old author/ity.

# 75

## Minute on Indian Education

### THOMAS MACAULAY*

HOW, THEN, STANDS the case? We have to educate a people who cannot at present be educated by means of their mother-tongue. We must teach them some foreign language. The claims of our own language it is hardly necessary to recapitulate. It stands pre-eminent even among the languages of the west. It abounds with works of imagination not inferior to the noblest which Greece has bequeathed to us; with models of every species of eloquence; with historical compositions, which, considered merely as narratives, have seldom been surpassed, and which, considered as vehicles of ethical and political instruction, have never been equalled; with just and lively representations of human life and human nature; with the most profound speculations on metaphysics, morals, government, jurisprudence, and trade; with full and correct information respecting every experimental science which tends to preserve the health, to increase the comfort, or to expand the intellect of man. Whoever knows that language has ready access to all the vast intellectual wealth, which all the wisest nations of the earth have created and hoarded in the course of ninety generations. It may safely be said, that the literature now extant in that language is of far greater value than all the literature which three hundred years ago was extant in all the languages of the world together. Nor is this all. In India, English is the language spoken by the ruling class. It is spoken by the higher class of natives at the seats of Government. It is likely to become the language of commerce throughout the seas of the East. It is the language of two great European communities which are rising, the one in the south of Africa, the other in Australasia; communities which are every year becoming more important, and more closely connected with our Indian Empire. Whether we look at the intrinsic value of our literature, or at the particular situation of this country, we shall see the strongest reason to

* From *Speeches of Lord Macaulay with his Minute on Indian Education* selected with an introduction and notes by G. M. Young, Oxford: Oxford University Press, 1935.

think that, of all foreign tongues, the English tongue is that which would be the most useful to our native subjects.

The question now before us is simply whether, when it is in our power to teach this language, we shall teach languages in which, by universal confession, there are no books on any subject which deserve to be compared to our own; whether, when we can teach European science, we shall teach systems which, by universal confession, whenever they differ from those of Europe, differ for the worse; and whether, when we can patronise sound Philosophy and true History, we shall countenance, at the public expense, medical doctrines, which would disgrace an English farrier, – Astronomy, which would move laughter in girls at an English boarding-school, – History, abounding with kings thirty feet high, and reigns thirty thousand years long, – and Geography, made up of seas of treacle and seas of butter.

We are not without experience to guide us. History furnishes several analogous cases, and they all teach the same lesson. There are in modern times, to go no further, two memorable instances of a great impulse given to the mind of a whole society, – of prejudices overthrown, – of knowledge diffused, – of taste purified, – of arts and sciences planted in countries which had recently been ignorant and barbarous.

The first instance to which I refer, is the great revival of letters among the Western nations at the close of the fifteenth, and the beginning of the sixteenth, century. At that time almost every thing that was worth reading was contained in the writings of the ancient Greeks and Romans. Had our ancestors acted as the Committee of Public Instruction has hitherto acted; had they neglected the language of Cicero and Tacitus; had they confined their attention to the old dialects of our own island; had they printed nothing and taught nothing at the universities, but chronicles in Anglo-Saxon, and Romances in Norman-French, would England have been what she now is? What the Greek and Latin were to the contemporaries of More and Ascham, our tongue is to the people of India. The literature of England is now more valuable than that of classical antiquity. I doubt whether the Sanscrit literature be as valuable as that of our Saxon and Norman progenitors. In some departments, – in History, for example, – I am certain that it is much less so.

Another instance may be said to be still before our eyes. Within the last hundred and twenty years, a nation which had previously been in a state as barbarous as that in which our ancestors were before the crusades, has gradually emerged from the ignorance in which it was sunk, and has taken its place among civilised communities. – I speak of Russia. There is now in that country a large educated class, abounding with persons fit to serve the state in the highest functions, and in no wise inferior to the most accomplished men who adorn the best circles of Paris and London. There is reason to hope that this vast Empire, which in the time of our grandfathers was probably behind the Punjab, may, in the time of our grandchildren, be pressing close on France and Britain in the career of improvement. And how was this change effected? Not by flattering national prejudices: not by feeding the mind of the young Muscovite with old women's stories which his rude fathers had believed: not by filling his head with lying legends about St. Nicholas: not by encouraging him to study the great question, whether the world was or was not created on the 13th of September: not by calling him 'a learned native', when he has mastered all these points of knowledge: but by teaching him those foreign languages in which the greatest mass of information had been laid up, and thus putting all that information within his reach. The languages of Western Europe civilised Russia. I cannot doubt that they will do for the Hindoo what they have done for the Tartar. . . .

It is impossible for us, with our limited means, to attempt to educate the body of the people. We must at present do our best to form a class who may be interpreters between us and the millions whom we govern; a class of persons, Indian in blood and colour, but English in taste, in opinions, in morals, and in intellect. To that class we may leave it to refine the vernacular dialects of the country, to enrich those dialects with terms of science borrowed from the Western nomenclature, and to render them by degrees fit vehicles for conveying knowledge to the great mass of the population.

# 76

# *The Beginnings of English Literary Study in British India*

## Gauri Viswanathan*

This paper is part of a larger inquiry into the construction of English literary education as a cultural ideal in British India. British parliamentary documents have provided compelling evidence for the central thesis of the investigation: that humanistic functions traditionally associated with the study of literature – for example, the shaping of character or the development of the aesthetic sense or the disciplines of ethical thinking – are also essential to the process of sociopolitical control. My argument is that literary study gained enormous cultural strength through its development in a period of territorial expansion and conquest, and that the subsequent institutionalization of the discipline in England itself took on a shape and an ideological content developed in the colonial context. . . .

English literature made its inroads in India, albeit gradually and imperceptibly, with a crucial event in Indian educational history: the passing of the Charter Act of 1813. This act, which renewed the East India Company's charter for commercial operations in India, produced two major changes in Britain's role with respect to its Indian subjects: one was the assumption of a new responsibility towards native education, and the other was a relaxation of controls over missionary work in India. . . .

In keeping with the government policy of religious neutrality, the Bible was proscribed and scriptural teaching forbidden.

The opening of India to missionaries, along with the commitment of the British to native improvement, might appear to suggest a victory for the missionaries, encouraging them perhaps to anticipate official support for their Envangelizing mission. But if they had such hopes, they were to be dismayed by the continuing checks on their activities, which grew impossibly stringent. Publicly, the English Parliament demanded a guarantee that large-scale proselytizing would not be carried out in India. Privately, though, it needed little persuasion about the distinct advantages

* From 'The Beginnings of English Literary Study in British India' *Oxford Literary Review* 9(1&2), 1987.

431

that would flow from missionary contact with the natives and their 'many immoral and disgusting habits'.

Though representing a convergence of interest, these two events – of British involvement in Indian education and the entry of missionaries – were far from being complementary or mutually supportive. On the contrary, they were entirely opposed to each other both in principle and in fact. The inherent constraints operating on British educational policy are apparent in the central contradiction of a government committed to the improvement of the people while being restrained from imparting any direct instruction in the religious principles of the English nation. The encouragement of Oriental learning, seen initially as a way of fulfilling the ruler's obligations to the subjects, seemed to accentuate rather than diminish the contradiction. For as the British swiftly learned to their dismay, it was impossible to promote Orientalism without exposing the Hindus and Muslims to the religious and moral tenets of their respective faiths – a situation that was clearly not tenable with the stated goal of 'moral and intellectual improvement'.

This tension between increasing involvement in Indian education and enforced noninterference in religion was productively resolved through the introduction of English literature. Significantly, the direction to this solution was present in the Charter Act itself, whose 43rd section empowered the Governor-General-in-Council to direct that 'a sum of not less than one lac of rupees shall be annually applied to the revival and improvement of literature, and the encouragement of the learned natives of India' (Great Britain 1831–2: 486). As subsequent debate made only too obvious, there is deliberate ambiguity in this clause regarding which literature was to be promoted, leaving it wide open for misinterpretations and conflicts to arise on the issue. While the use of the world 'revival' may weight the interpretations on the side of Oriental literature, the almost deliberate imprecision suggests a more fluid government position in conflict with the official espousal of Orientalism. Over twenty years later Macaulay was to seize on this very ambiguity to argue that the phrase clearly meant Western literature, and denounce in no uncertain terms attempts to interpret the clause as a reference to Oriental literature:

> It is argued, or rather taken for granted, that by literature, the Parliament can have meant only Arabic and Sanskrit literature, that they never would have given the honourable appellation of a learned native to a native who was familiar with the poetry of Milton, the Metaphysics of Locke, the Physics of Newton; but that they meant to designate by that name only such persons as might have studied in the sacred books of the Hindoos all the uses of cusa-grass, and all the mysteries of absorption into the Deity.
>
> (Macaulay 1835: 345)

This plea on behalf of English literature had a major influence on the passing of the English Education Act in 1835, which officially required the natives of India to submit to its study. But English was not an unknown entity in India at that time, for some natives had already begun receiving rudimentary instruction in the language more than two decades earlier. Initially, English did not supersede Oriental studies but was taught alongside it. Yet it was clear that it enjoyed a different status, for there was a scrupulous attempt to establish separate colleges for its study. Even when it was taught within the same college, the English course of studies was kept separate from the course of Oriental study, and was attended by a different set of students. The rationale was that if the English department drew students who were attached only to its department and to no other (that is, the Persian or the Arabic or the Sanskrit), the language might then be taught 'classically' in much the same way that Latin and Greek were taught in England.

It is important to emphasize that the early British Indian curriculum in English, though based on literary material, was primarily devoted to language studies. However, by the 1820s the atmosphere of secularism in which these studies were conducted became a major cause for concern to the missionaries who were permitted to enter India after 1813. Within England itself, there was a strong feeling that texts read as a form of secular knowledge were 'a sea in which the voyager has to expect shipwreck' (*Atheneum* 1839: 108) and that they could not be relied on to exert a beneficial effect upon the moral condition of society in general. This sentiment was complemented by an equally strong one that for English works to be studied even for language purposes a high degree of mental and moral cultivation was first required which the mass of people simply did not have. To a man in a state of ignorance of moral law, literature would appear indifferent to virtue. Far from cultivating moral feelings, a wide reading was more likely to cause him to question moral law more closely and perhaps even encourage him to deviate from its dictates. . . .

The uneasiness generated by a strictly secular policy in teaching English served to resurrect Charles Grant in the British consciousness. An officer of the East India Company, Grant was one of the first Englishmen to urge the promotion of both Western literature and Christianity in India. In 1792 he had written a tract entitled *Observations on the State of Society among the Asiatic Subjects of Great Britain*, which was a scathing denunciation of Indian religion and society. What interested the British in the years following the actual introduction of English in India was Grant's shrewd observation that by emphasizing the moral aspect, it would be possible to talk about introducing Western education without having to throw open the doors of English liberal thought to natives; to aim at moral improvement of the subjects without having to worry about the possible danger of inculcating radical ideas that would upset the British presence in India. Moral good and happiness, Grant had argued, 'views politics through the safe medium of morals, and subjects them to the laws of universal rectitude' (Great Britain 1832: 75). The most appealing part of his argument, from the point of view of a government now sensing the truth of the missionaries' criticism of secularism, was that historically Christianity had never been associated with bringing down governments, for its concern was with the internal rather than the external condition of man. . . .

As late as the 1860s, the 'literary curriculum' in British educational establishments remained polarized around classical studies for the upper classes and religious studies for the lower. As for what is now known as the subject of English literature, the British educational system had no firm place for it until the last quarter of the nineteenth century, when the challenge posed by the middle classes to the existing structure resulted in the creation of alternative institutions devoted to 'modern' studies.

It is quite conceivable that educational development in British India may have run the same course as it did in England, were it not for one crucial difference: the strict controls on Christianizing activities. Clearly, the texts that were standard fare for the lower classes in England could not legitimately be incorporated into the Indian curriculum without inviting violent reactions from the native population, particularly the learned classes. And yet the fear lingered in the British mind that without submission of the individual to moral law or the authority of God, the control they were able to secure over the lower classes in their own country would elude them in India. Comparisons were on occasion made between the situation at home and in India, between the 'rescue' of the lower classes in England, 'those living in the dark recesses of our great cities at home, from the state of degradation consequent on their vicious and depraved habits, the offspring of ignorance and sensual indulgence', and the elevation of the Hindus and Muslims whose 'ignorance and degradation' required a remedy not adequately supplied by their respective faiths. Such comparisons served to intensify the search for other social institutions to take over from religious instruction the function of communicating the laws of the social order.

It was at this point that British colonial administrators, provoked by missionaries on the one hand and fears of native insubordination on the other, discovered an ally in English literature to support them in maintaining control of the natives under the guise of a liberal education. With both secularism and religion appearing as political liabilities, literature appeared to represent a perfect synthesis of these two opposing positions. The idea evolved in alternating stages of affirmation and disavowal of literature's derivation from and affiliation with Christianity as a social institution. The process illuminates and substantiates what Lowenthal has called a central factor in the construction of every ideology: the self-conscious glorification of existing social contradictions. A description of that process is reconstructed below from the minutes of evidence given before the British Parliament's Select Committee, and recorded in the 1852–3 volume of the *Parliamentary Papers*. These proceedings reveal not only an open assertion of British material interests but also a mapping out of strategies for promoting those interests through representations of Western literary knowledge as objective, universal, and rational.

The first stage in the process was an assertion of structural congruence between Christianity and English literature. Missionaries had long argued on behalf of the shared history of religion and literature, of a tradition of belief and doctrine creating a common culture of values, attitudes, and norms. They had ably cleared the way for the realization that as the 'grand repository of the book of God' England had produced a literature that was immediately marked off from all non-European literatures, being 'animated, vivified, hallowed, and baptized' by a religion to which Western man owed his material and moral progress. The difference was poetically rendered as a contrast between

> the literature of a world embalmed with the Spirit of Him who died to redeem it, and that which is the growth of ages that have gloomily rolled on in the rejection of that Spirit, as between the sweet bloom of creation in the open light of heaven, and the rough, dark recesses of submarine forests of sponges.
>
> (*Madras Christian Instructor and Missionary Record* 11(4) 1844: 195)

This other literature was likened to Plato's cave, whose darkened inhabitants were 'chained men . . . counting the shadows of subterranean fires'.

The missionary description was appropriated in its entirety by government officers. But while the missionaries made such claims in order to force the government to sponsor teaching of the Bible, the administrators used the same argument to prove that English literature made such direct instruction redundant. They initiated several steps to incorporate selected English literary texts into the Indian curriculum on the claim that these works were supported in their morality by a body of evidence that also upheld the Christian faith. In their official capacity as members of the Council on Education, Macaulay and his brother-in-law Charles Trevelyan were among those engaged in a minute analysis of English texts to prove the 'diffusive benevolence of Christianity' in them. The process of curricular selection was marked by weighty pronouncements of the 'sound Protestant Bible principles' in Shakespeare, the 'strain of serious piety' in Addison's *Spectator* papers, the 'scriptural morality' of Bacon and Locke, the 'devout sentiment' of Abercrombie, the 'noble Christian sentiments' in Adam Smith's *Moral Sentiments* (hailed as the 'best authority for the true science of morals which English literature could supply') (Great Britain 1852–3). The cataloguing of shared features had the effect of convincing detractors that the government could effectively cause voluntary reading of the Bible and at the same time disclaim any intentions of proselytizing. . . .

To disperse intention, and by extension authority in related fields of knowledge and inquiry proposed itself as the best means of dissipating native resistance. As one government publication put it, 'If we lay it down as our rule to teach only what the natives are willing to make national, viz., what they will freely learn, we shall be able by degrees to teach them all we know ourselves, without any risk of offending their prejudices' (Sharpe 1920). One of the great lessons taught by Gramsci, which this quotation amply corroborates, is that cultural domination operates by consent, indeed often preceding conquest by force. 'The supremacy of a social group manifests itself in two ways', he writes in the *Prison Notebooks*, 'as "domination" and as "intellectual and moral leadership". . . . It seems clear . . . that there can, and indeed must be hegemonic activity even before the rise of power, and that one should not count only on the material force which power gives in order to exercise an effective leadership' (Gramsci 1971: 57). He argues that consent of the governed is secured primarily through the moral and intellectual suasion, a strategy clearly spelled out by the British themselves: 'The Natives must either be kept down by a sense of our power, or they must willingly submit from a conviction that we are more wise, more just, more humane, and more anxious to improve their condition than any other rulers they could have' (Farish 1838: 239).

Implicit in this strategy is a recognition of the importance of self-representation, an activity crucial to what the natives 'would freely learn'. The answer to this last question was obvious to at least one member of the Council on Education: the natives' greatest desire, averred C. E. Trevelyan, was to raise themselves to the level of moral and intellectual refinement of their masters; their most driving ambition, to acquire the intellectual skills that confirmed their rulers as lords of the earth. Already, he declared, the natives had an idea that 'we have gained everything by our superior knowledge; that it is this superiority which has enabled us to conquer India, and to keep it; and they want to put themselves as much as they can upon an equality with us' (Great Britain 1852–3: 187). If the assumption was correct that individuals willingly learned whatever they believed provided them with the means of advancement in the world, a logical method of overwhelming opposition was to demonstrate that the achieved material position of the Englishman was derived from the knowledge contained in English literary, philosophical, and scientific texts, a knowledge accessible to any who chose to seek it.

In effect, the strategy of locating authority in these texts all but effaced the sordid history of colonialist expropriation, material exploitation, and class and race oppression behind European world dominance. Making the Englishman known to the natives through the products of his mental labour served a valuable purpose in that it removed him from the plane of ongoing colonialist activity – of commercial operations, military expansion, administration of territories – and de-actualized and diffused his material presence in the process. In a crude reworking of the Cartesian axiom, production of thought defined the Englishman's true essence, overriding all other aspects of his identity – his personality, actions, behaviour. His material reality as a subjugator and alien ruler was dissolved in his mental output; the blurring of the man and his works effectively removed him from history. As the following statement suggests, the English literary text functioned as a surrogate Englishman in his highest and most perfect state: '[The Indians] daily converse with the best and wisest Englishmen through the medium of their works, and form ideas, perhaps higher ideas of our nation than if their intercourse with it were of a more personal kind' (Trevelyan 1838: 176). The split between the material and the discursive practices of colonialism is nowhere sharper than in the progressive rarefaction of the rapacious, exploitative, and ruthless actor of history into the reflective subject of literature.

How successful was the British strategy? That is clearly a topic for another paper, though it is worth noting that the problematics of colonial representations of authority have been brilliantly analysed by Homi Bhabha . . . in his essay 'Signs Taken for Wonders'. [This account] provides a compelling philosophical framework for analysing native interrogation of British authority in relation to the 'hybridization' of power and discourse, the term Bhabha uses to describe the nontransparency of the colonial presence and the problems created thereby in the recognition of its authority. Though my purpose in this paper has primarily been to describe a historical process rather than to do a microanalysis of the techniques of power, the question of effectiveness of strategy is never far removed. Indeed, the fact that English literary study had its beginnings as a strategy of containment raises a host of questions about the interrelations of culture, state, and civil society and the modes of assertion of authority within that network of relations.

# 77

# *On the Abolition of the English Department*

## NGUGI WA THIONG'O*

1. This is a comment on the paper presented by the Acting Head of the English Department at the University of Nairobi to the 42nd meeting of the Arts Faculty Board on the 20th September, 1968.
2. a) That paper was mainly concerned with possible developments within the Arts Faculty and their relationship with the English Department, particularly:
    i)   The place of modern languages, especially French;
    ii)  The place and role of the Department of English;
    iii) The emergence of a Department of Linguistics and Languages;
    iv)  The place of African languages, especially Swahili.
   b) In connection with the above, the paper specifically suggested that a department of Linguistics and Languages, to be closely related to English, be established.
   c) A remote possibility of a Department of African literature, or alternatively, that of African literature and culture, was envisaged.
3. The paper raised important problems. It should have been the subject of a more involved debate and discussion, preceding the appointment of a committee with specific tasks, because it raises questions of value, direction and orientation.
4. For instance, the suggestions, as the paper itself admits, question the role and status of an English Department in an African situation and environment. To quote from his paper:

   The English Department has had a long history at this College and has built up a strong syllabus which by its study of the *historic continuity of a single culture throughout the period of emergence of the modern west,* makes it an important companion to History and to Philosophy and Religious Studies. However, *it is bound to become less 'British', more*

* From 'On the Abolition of the English Department' *Homecoming: Essays* London: Heinemann, 1972.

*open to other writing in English (American, Caribbean, African, Commonwealth) and also to continental writing, for comparative purposes.*

5. Underlying the suggestions is a basic assumption that the English tradition and the emergence of the modern west is the central root of our consciousness and cultural heritage. Africa becomes an extension of the west, an attitude which, until a radical reassessment, used to dictate the teaching and organization of History in our University. Hence, in fact, the assumed centrality of the English Department, into which other cultures can be admitted from time to time, as fit subjects for study, or from which other satellite departments can spring as time and money allow. A small example is the current, rather apologetic attempt to smuggle African writing into an English syllabus in our three colleges.

6. Here then, is our main question: If there is need for a 'study of the historic continuity of a single culture', why can't this be African? Why can't African literature be at the centre so that we can view other cultures in relationship to it?

   This is not mere rhetoric: already African writing, with the sister connections in the Caribbean and the Afro-American literatures, has played an important role in the African renaissance, and will become even more and more important with time and pressure of events. Just because for reasons of political expediency we have kept English as our official language, there is no need to substitute a study of English culture for our own. We reject the primacy of English literature and culture.

7. The aim, in short, should be to orientate ourselves towards placing Kenya, East Africa, and then Africa in the centre. All other things are to be considered in their relevance to our situation, and their contribution towards understanding ourselves.

8. We therefore suggest:
   A. That the English Department be abolished;
   B. That a Department of African Literature and Languages be set up in its place.
   The primary duty of any literature department is to illuminate the spirit animating a people, to show how it meets new challenges, and to investigate possible areas of development and involvement.

   In suggesting this name, we are not rejecting other cultural streams, especially the western stream. We are only clearly mapping out the directions and perspectives the study of culture and literature will inevitably take in an African university.

9. We know that European literatures constitute one source of influence on modern African literatures in English, French, and Portuguese; Swahili, Arabic, and Asian literatures constitute another, an important

439

source, especially here in East Africa; and the African tradition, a tradition as active and alive as ever, constitutes the third and the most significant. This is the stuff on which we grew up, and it is the base from which we make our cultural take-off into the world.

10. Languages and linguistics should be studied in the department because in literature we see the principles of languages and linguistics in action. Conversely, through knowledge of languages and linguistics we can get more from literature. For linguistics not to become eccentric, it should be studied in the Department of African Literature and Languages.

In addition to Swahili, French, and English, whenever feasible other languages such as Arabic, Hindustani, Kikuyu, Luo, Akamba, etc., should be introduced into the syllabus as optional subjects.

11. On the literature side, the Department ought to offer roughly:
    a) The oral tradition, which is our primary root;
    b) Swahili literature (with Arabic and Asian literatures): this is another root, especially in East Africa;
    c) A selected course in European literature: yet another root;
    d) Modern African literature.

    For the purposes of the Department, a knowledge of Swahili English, and French should be compulsory. The largest body of writing by Africans is now written in the French language. Africans writing in the French language have also produced most of the best poems and novels. In fact it makes nonsense to talk of modern African literature without French.

## 12. *The Oral Tradition*

The Oral tradition is rich and many-sided. In fact 'Africa is littered with Oral Literature'. But the art did not end yesterday; it is a living tradition. Even now there are songs being sung in political rallies, in churches, in night clubs by guitarists, by accordion players, by dancers, etc. Another point to be observed is the interlinked nature of art forms in traditional practice. Verbal forms are not always distinct from dance, music, etc. For example, in music there is close correspondence between verbal and melodic tones; in 'metrical lyrics' it has been observed that poetic text is inseparable from tune; and the 'folk tale' often bears an 'operatic' form, with sung refrain as an integral part. The distinction between prose and poetry is absent or very fluid. Though tale, dance, song, myth, etc. can be performed for individual aesthetic enjoyment, they have other social purposes as well. Dance, for example, has been studied 'as symbolic expression of social reality reflecting and influencing the social, cultural and personality systems of which it is a part'. The oral tradition also comments on society because of its intimate relationship and involvement.

The study of the oral tradition at the University should therefore lead to a multi-disciplinary outlook: Literature, Music, Linguistics, Sociology,

Anthropology, History, Psychology, Religion, Philosophy. Secondly, its study can lead to fresh approaches by making it possible for the student to be familiar with art forms different in kind and historical development from Western literary forms. Spontaneity and liberty of communication inherent in oral transmission – openness to sounds, sights, rhythms, tones, in life and in the environment – are examples of traditional elements from which the student can draw. More specifically, his familiarity with oral literature could suggest new structures and techniques; and could foster attitudes of mind characterized by the willingness to experiment with new forms, so transcending 'fixed literary patterns' and what that implies – the preconceived ranking of art forms.

The study of the Oral Tradition would therefore supplement (not replace) courses in Modern African Literature. By discovering and proclaiming loyalty to indigenous values, the new literature would on the one hand be set in the stream of history to which it belongs and so be better appreciated; and on the other be better able to embrace and assimilate other thoughts without losing its roots. . . .

## CONCLUSION

One of the things which has been hindering a radical outlook in our study of literature in Africa is the question of literary excellence; that only works of undisputed literary excellence should be offered. (In this case it meant virtually the study of disputable 'peaks' of English literature.) The question of literary excellence implies a value judgement as to what is literary and what is excellence, and from whose point of view. For any group it is better to study representative works which mirror their society rather than to study a few isolated 'classics', either of their own or of a foreign culture.

To sum up, we have been trying all along to place values where they belong. We have argued the case for the abolition of the present Department of English in the College, and the establishment of a Department of African Literature and Languages. This is not a change of names only. We want to establish the centrality of Africa in the department. This, we have argued, is justifiable on various grounds, the most important one being that education is a means of knowledge about ourselves. Therefore, after we have examined ourselves, we radiate outwards and discover peoples and worlds around us. With Africa at the centre of things, not existing as an appendix or a satellite of other countries and literatures, things must be seen from the African perspective. The dominant object in that perspective is African literature, the major branch of African culture. Its roots go back to past African literatures, European literatures, and Asian literatures. These can only be studied meaningfully in a Department of African Literature and Languages in an African University.

We ask that this paper be accepted in principle; we suggest that a representative committee be appointed to work out the details and harmonize the various suggestions into an administratively workable whole.

James Ngugi
Henry Owuor-Anyumba
Taban Lo Liyong
24th October 1968

# 78

# The Neocolonial Assumption in University Teaching of English

JOHN DOCKER*

THE ARGUMENT OF this paper is that there is a ruling anglocentric assumption in university teaching of English, an assumption derived from the total experience of colonialism and neocolonialism in Australia. In colonial and neocolonial historical situations, a hierarchy of cultural importance and value is imposed by the colonising power, both on the conquered indigenous societies, and on the white agents of colonial oppression themselves. The white colonising society removes the indigenous culture to an inferior level by virtue of the superiority of the metropolitan culture it is establishing. But by that same ultimate criterion of, and rationale for, the right of invasion of other peoples' territories, the white colonial society is itself, by its own removal from the metropolitan centre, forced into a necessary inferiority in what Frantz Fanon calls the 'hierarchy of cultures' (Fanon 1970: 41). It is metropolitan-derived, but not metropolitan, both European and not European, both superior to what is displaced and threatened by the inevitable inferiority of distance from the cultural source. The neocolonial cultural matrix itself becomes subject to profound psychological disturbance, at once guilty of enforcing inferiority on others, and haunted by self-doubt and self-contempt before the metropolitan culture's necessary superiority.

In terms of university teaching, the anglocentric assumption implies that 'standards' can only be formed by studying the great tradition of English literature, from Chaucer on. This literature is the product of a matured cultural history extending for centuries and centuries of great works: so mature that it need not concern itself with the merely temporary and accidental, but rather with the eternal human condition in all its subtlety and complexity. Metropolitan literature is universal, and so can be

* From 'The Neocolonial Assumption in University Teaching of English' in Chris Tiffin (ed.) *South Pacific Images* St. Lucia, Queensland: SPACLALS, 1978.

studied in a truly literary way. The consequence of the anglocentric assumption for teaching is that English literature must remain as the 'core' of a student's courses. Australian or 'Commonwealth' literatures can be included as options, but cannot be considered as central to a critical education. When studying post-colonial literature, students are not seen to be forming their critical values, but rather to be applying values and standards learnt from studying English literature. This assumption is enforced by university hierarchy (the god–professor); by the system of recruitment of staff (appointing people, English, American, or Australian, whose primary teaching interests are expected to lie in English literature); and by the use of tenure to enforce anglocentric stability and continuity. The reverse side of the metropolitan image of universality is that the cultures of the colonised, or of white colonial cultures, are raw, young, likely to be strident and too simply concerned with the local and temporary, the political and national: they commit the Nationalist Fallacy, the confusing of literary with patriotic values, and so remain at a relatively inferior cultural level. And to deal with them criticism must unfortunately become non-literary and sociological.

The pre-World War II concern of European literature with questions of race, nationality, cultural tradition, and notions of pre-industrial community, is obscured and disregarded. . . .

Since 1945 . . . an anti-ideological attitude has developed, derived both from the experience of racism in World War II, and from the Cold War in the fifties and sixties. In this view, ideologies – fascism, nazism, communism, racism – have wreaked havoc on the world, creating disastrous divisions and conflicts. The particular consequence for criticism was that it should focus not on the relationship between literature and ideologies, but on universal human feelings and dilemmas, and how these are realised in the intricate structures of literary creation. In reconciling tensions and ambiguities into a complex, self-sufficient whole, a poem or novel is creating a sense of human wholeness, rising above the world of merely local and temporary ideas and ideologies. Literature expresses a metaphysical idea of human freedom which is superior to history, the world of division and disharmony.

But at the same time as European criticism was shedding history, post-colonial literatures were revealing an interest in questions of community, of ethnic and national identity, of the cultural effects of industrialisation and urbanisation, and of the continuity or discontinuity of traditions. Such an interest can be seen not only in literature but in the Négritude movement, or in Wole Soyinka's essays *Myth, Literature and the African World* (1976). The response of European criticism has largely been to attempt to see post-colonial literature in post-World War II European terms of what is universally human, and to chide the emergent literature for being concerned precisely with the cultural and historical questions that had previously obsessed a major part of European literary culture.

Australia is not an isolated example of 'cultural cringe', to use A. A. Phillips's superb phrase for neocolonialism. Indeed, the very feeling that one's culture is uniquely inferior vis-à-vis the metropolitan culture is itself a neocolonial mystification. In effect, the inferior culture is always relating itself directly to the metropolitan source from which it derives, rather than seeing, as has been shown by the Caribbean writers Fanon and George Lamming (1960), that neocolonialism imposes common structural features on both the colonised and the colonising everywhere. Just as Caribbean societies relate to their metropolitan sources like Britain or France rather than to each other, so in Australian intellectual life there has been a lack of interest in the experience of fellow colonising societies like New Zealand and Canada. . . .

[In Australia] a general distinction has to be made between the research interests of teachers of literature in university departments, and their actual teaching. It may be that many literature teachers have a strong interest in Australian or other post-colonial literatures and devote a great deal of their research time to them. But the actual teaching remains anglocentric, dominated by the assumption that English literature is central and necessary to a student's critical education. For the staff as well as for students Australian and other post-colonial literatures can be important and absorbing, but in terms of teaching practice are always regarded as secondary.

Neocolonialism is the imposition of the metropolitan power's dominant cultural values: it *had* to come to terms with literature in Australia, and it has done so by appearing at every stage to encourage its existence and growth. But it has never permitted Australian or other post-colonial literatures to impinge on actual university teaching. It has carefully guarded the institutional privilege of training teachers of literature, and of effecting the penetration of the educational system by anglocentric values. The institutional authority and power of neocolonialism does not come merely from the hiring of staff from England and America. The continuous core of every Australian university English department is probably composed of Australians committed to remaining in Australia. It is the strength of neocolonialism that it works through Australians who have internalised anglocentric assumptions, and who propagate them in their teaching. And they propagate them the more tenaciously and persistently because fundamentally they are always striving to become what they cannot be, metropolitans secure and confident in the knowledge of being metropolitans. This striving accounts for the distinctive style of English departments, revealing a delusive yearning for a metropolitan possession of a thousand-year history of literary culture.

The danger faced by post-colonial literary study is that, like the study of Australian literature before it, it will be fobbed off as an interesting option. The challenge of post-colonial literature is that by exposing and attacking anglocentric assumptions directly, it can replace 'English literature' with 'world literature in English'. . . .

445

It is the challenge of those interested in post-colonial literature not simply to offer empirical studies of particular authors, but to see it as questioning our received methods of literary criticism and of university teaching of literature.

# 79

# Ideology in the Classroom
## A Case Study in the Teaching of English Literature in Canadian Universities
### ARUN P. MUKHERJEE*

GENERALLY SPEAKING, WE, the Canadian university teachers of English, do not consider issues of the classroom worth critical scrutiny. Indeed, there is hardly any connection between our pedagogy and our scholarly research. A new teacher, looking for effective teaching strategies, will discover to her/his utter dismay that no amount of reading of scholarly publications will be of any help when she faces a class of undergraduates. In fact, the two discourses – those of pedagogy and scholarly research – are diametrically opposed and woe betide the novice who uses the language of current scholarly discourse in the classroom. . . .

The short fiction anthology I used for my introductory English 100 class – I deliberately chose a Canadian one – includes a short story by Margaret Laurence entitled 'The Perfume Sea.' This story, as I interpret it, underlines the economic and cultural domination of the Third World. However, even though I presented this interpretation of the story to my students in some detail, they did not even consider it when they wrote their essays. While the story had obviously appealed to them – almost 40 per cent chose to write on it – they ignored the political meaning entirely.

I was thoroughly disappointed by my students' total disregard for local realities treated in the short story. Nevertheless, their papers did give me an understanding of how their education had allowed them to neutralize the subversive meanings implicit in a piece of good literature, such as the Laurence story.

The story, from my point of view, is quite forthright in its purpose. Its locale is Ghana on the eve of independence from British rule. The colonial administrators are leaving and this has caused financial difficulties for Mr. Archipelago and Doree who operate the only beauty parlour within a

* From 'Ideology in the Classroom: A Case Study in the Teaching of English Literature in Canadian Universities' *Dalhousie Review* 66(1&2), 1986.

radius of one hundred miles around an unnamed small town. Though the equipment is antiquated, and the parlour operators not much to their liking, the ladies have put up with it for want of a better alternative.

With the white clientele gone, Mr. Archipelago and Doree have no customers left. The parlour lies empty for weeks until one day the crunch comes in the shape of their Ghanaian landlord, Mr. Tachie, demanding rent. Things, however, take an upturn when Mr. Archipelago learns that Mr. Tachie's daughter wants to look like a 'city girl' and constantly pesters her father for money to buy shoes, clothes and make-up. Mr. Archipelago, in a flash of inspiration, discovers that Mercy Tachie is the new consumer to whom he can sell his 'product': 'Mr. Tachie, you are a bringer of miracles! . . . There it was, all the time, and we did not see it. We, even Doree, will make history – you will see' (221).

The claim about making history is repeated twice in the story and is significantly linked to the history made by Columbus. For Mr. Archipelago is very proud of the fact that he was born in Genoa, Columbus's home town. The unpleasant aspect of this act of making history is unmistakably spelt out: 'He [Columbus] was once in West Africa, you know, as a young seaman, at one of the old slave-castles not far from here. And he, also, came from Genoa' (217).

The symbolic significance of the parlour is made quite apparent from the detailed attention Laurence gives to its transformation. While the pre-independence sign had said:

> ARCHIPELAGO
> English-Style Barber
> European Ladies' Hairdresser (211)

the new sign says:

> ARCHIPELAGO & DOREE
> Barbershop
> All-Beauty Salon
> African Ladies A Specialty (221)

With the help of a loan from Mr. Tachie, the proprietors install hair-straightening equipment and buy shades of make-up suitable for the African skin. However, though the African ladies show much interest from a distance, none of them enters the shop. Two weeks later, Mercy Tachie hesitantly walks into the salon 'because if you are not having customers, he [Mr. Tachie] will never be getting his money from you' (222). Mercy undergoes a complete transformation in the salon and comes out looking like a 'city girl,' the kind she has seen in the *Drum* magazine. Thus, Mr. Archipelago and Doree are 'saved' by 'an act of Mercy' (226). They have found a new role in the life of this newly independent country: to help the African bourgeoisie slavishly imitate the values of its former colonial masters.

These political overtones are reinforced by the overall poverty the story describes and the symbolic linking of the white salon operators with the only black merchant in town. The division between his daughter and other African women who go barefoot with babies on their backs further indicates the divisive nature of the European implant. Other indications of the writer's purpose are apparent from her caricature of Mr. Archipelago and Doree, a device which prevents emotional identification with them. The fact that both of them have no known national identities – both of them keep changing their stories – is also significant, for it seems to say that, like Kurtz in *Heart of Darkness*, they represent the whole white civilization. The story thus underplays the lives of individuals in order to emphasize these larger issues: the nature of colonialism as well as its after-math when the native élite takes over without really changing the colonial institutions except for their names.

This, then, was the aspect of the story in which I was most interested, no doubt because I am myself from a former colony of the Raj. During class discussions, I asked the students about the symbolic significance of the hair straightening equipment, the change of names, the identification of Mr. Archipelago with Columbus, the *Drum* magazine, and the characters of Mr. Tachie and Mercy Tachie. However, the students based their essays not on these aspects, but on how 'believable' or 'likable' the two major char-acters in the story were, and how they found happiness in the end by accepting change. That is to say, the two characters were freed entirely from the restraints of the context, i.e., the colonial situation, and evaluated solely on the basis of their emotional relationship with each other. The outer world of political turmoil, the scrupulously observed class system of the colonials, the contrasts between wealth and poverty, were non-existent in their papers. As one student put it, the conclusion of the story was 'The perfect couple walking off into the sunset, each happy that they had found what had eluded both of them all their lives, companionship and privacy all rolled into one relationship.' For another, they symbolized 'the anxiety and hope of humanity . . . the common problem of facing or not facing reality.'

I was astounded by my students' ability to close themselves off to the disturbing implications of my interpretation and devote their attention to expatiating upon 'the anxiety and hope of humanity,' and other such generalizations as change, people, values, reality, etc. I realized that these generalizations were ideological. They enabled my students to efface the differences between British bureaucrats and British traders, between colonizing whites and colonized blacks, and between rich blacks and poor blacks. They enabled them to believe that all human beings faced dilemmas similar to the ones faced by the two main characters in the story.

Though, thanks to Kenneth Burke, I knew the rhetorical subterfuges which generalizations like 'humanity' imply, the papers of my students made me painfully aware of their ideological purposes. I saw that they help

449

us to translate the world into our own idiom by erasing the ambiguities and the unpleasant truths that lie in the crevices. They make us oblivious to the fact that society is not a homogeneous grouping but an assortment of groups where we belong to one particular set called 'us,' as opposed to the other set or sets we distinguish as 'them.'

The most painful revelation came when I recognized the source of my students' vocabulary. Their analysis, I realized, was in the time-honoured tradition of that variety of criticism which presents literary works as 'universal.' The test of a great work of literature, according to this tradition, is that despite its particularity, it speaks to all times and all people. As Brent Harold notes, 'It is a rare discussion of literature that does not depend heavily on the universal "we" (meaning we human beings), on "the human condition," "the plight of modern man," "absurd man" and other convenient abstractions which obscure from their users the specific social basis of their own thought . . .' (Harold 1972: 201).

Thus, all conflict eliminated with the help of the universal 'we,' what do we have left but the 'feelings' and 'experiences' of individual characters? The questions in the anthologies reflect that. When they are not based on matters of technique – where one can short circuit such problems entirely – they ask students whether such and such character deserves our sympathy, or whether such and such a character undergoes change, or, in other words, an initiation. As Richard Ohmann comments:

> The student focuses on a character, on the poet's attitude, on the individual's struggle toward understanding – but rarely if ever, on the social forces that are revealed in every dramatic scene and almost every stretch of narration in fiction. Power, class, culture, social order and disorder – these staples of literature are quite excluded from consideration in the analytic tasks set for Advanced Placement candidates.
>
> (1976: 59–60)

Instead of facing up to the realities of 'power, class, culture, social order and disorder,' literary critics and editors of literature anthologies hide behind the universalist vocabulary that only mystifies the true nature of reality. For example, the editorial introduction to 'The Perfume Sea' considers the story in terms of categories that are supposedly universal and eternal:

> Here is a crucial moment in human history seen from inside a beauty parlour and realized in terms of the 'permanent wave.' But while feminine vanity is presented as the only changeless element in a world of change, Mrs. Laurence, for all her lightness of touch, is not 'making fun' of her Africans or Europeans. In reading the story, probe for the deeper layers of human anxiety and hope beneath the comic surfaces.
>
> (Ross and Stevens 1988: 201)

Though the importance of 'a crucial moment in history' is acknowledged here, it is only to point out the supposedly changeless: that highly elusive thing called 'feminine vanity.' The term performs the function of achieving the desired identification between all white women and all black women, regardless of the barriers of race and class. The command to probe 'the deeper layers of human anxiety and hope' – a command that my students took more seriously than their teacher's alternative interpretation – works to effectively eliminate consideration of disturbing socio-political realities.

This process results in the promotion of what Ohmann calls the 'prophylactic view of literature' (63). Even the most provocative literary work, when seen from such a perspective, is emptied of its subversive content. After such treatment, as Ohmann puts it, 'It will not cause any trouble for the people who run schools or colleges, for the military-industrial complex, for anyone who holds power. It can only perpetuate the misery of those who don't' (61).

The editor–critic thus functions as the castrator. He makes sure that the young minds will not get any understanding of how our society actually functions and how literature plays a role in it. Instead of explaining these relationships, the editor–critic feeds students on a vocabulary that pretends that human beings and their institutions have not changed a bit during the course of history, that they all face the same problems as human beings. . . .

Surely, literature is more than form? What about the questions regarding the ideology and social class of the writer, the role and ideology of the patrons and the disseminators of literature, the role of literature as a social institution and, finally, the role of the teacher–critic of literature as a transmitter of the dominant social and cultural values? Have these questions no place in our professional deliberations?

# 80

# Education and Neocolonialism

### Philip G. Altbach*

THE OLD COLONIAL era, some say, is dead. Evidence? Most formerly colonial areas are now independent nations. On the ruins of traditional colonial empire, however, has emerged a new, subtler, but perhaps equally influential, kind of colonialism. The advanced industrial nations (the United States, most of Europe, including the Soviet Union, and Japan) retain substantial influence in what are now referred to as the 'developing areas.'

Traditional colonialism involved the direct political domination of one nation over another area, thus enabling the colonial power to control any and all aspects of the internal and external life of the colony. The results of colonialism differed from country to country, depending in part on the policies of the ruling power and in part on the situation in the colony itself. Neocolonialism is more difficult to describe and hence to analyze. In this essay neocolonialism means the impact of advanced nations on developing areas, in this case with special reference to their educational systems and intellectual life. Modern neocolonialism differs from traditional colonialism in that it does not involve direct political control, leaving substantial leeway to the developing country. It is similar, nevertheless, in that some aspects of domination by the advanced nation over the developing country remain. Neocolonialism is partly a planned policy of advanced nations to maintain their influence in developing countries, but it is also simply a continuation of past practices. . . .

Neocolonialism . . . is not always a negative influence, just as colonialism itself had some positive effects in several areas. The focus here, however, is generally on the negative results of educational neocolonialism precisely because the consequences are important for the recipient countries and because they have not yet been adequately analyzed. Neocolonialism can be quite open and obvious, such as the distribution of foreign textbooks in the schools of a developing country. It is, however, generally more subtle

* From 'Education and Neocolonialism' *Teachers College Record* 72(1) (May), 1971.

and includes the use of foreign technical advisors on matters of policy and the continuation of foreign administrative models and curricular patterns for schools. Some developing countries rely, for example, on expatriate teachers for their secondary schools and colleges. These teachers, regardless of their personal orientations, cannot but inculcate Western values and views in the schools. Most developing countries have maintained the colonial pattern of school administration and many have altered the curriculum only slightly, thus retaining much of the orientation of colonial education (see Ashby 1967; Kazamias and Epstein 1968). . . .

Reliance on foreign models was dictated in part by the colonial government. Indigenous educational patterns were destroyed either by design or as the inadvertent result of policies which ignored local needs and traditions. Colonial powers seldom set up adequate educational facilities in their colonies and immediately limited educational opportunity and, in a sense, hindered modernization. In addition, existing facilities reflected the needs of the metropolitan power, and not of the indigenous population. The inadequacies of the modern educational system, outmoded trends in curriculum, and the orientation of the schools toward building up an administrative cadre rather than technically trained and socially aware individuals needed for social and economic development can be linked in many countries to the colonial experience. . . .

Most colonial powers, when they concentrated on education at all, stressed humanistic studies, fluency in the language of the metropolitan country, and the skills necessary for secondary positions in the bureaucracy. Lawyers were trained, but few scientists, agricultural experts, or qualified teachers were available when independence came. Emerging elite groups were Western-oriented, in part as a result of their education. In some instances, in fact, individuals were even unfamiliar with their own indigenous language.[1]

Colonial educational policies were generally elitist. In India, British educational elitism assumed the title of 'downward filtration' – a system by which a small group of Indians with a British style education supposedly spread enlightenment to the masses (see McCully 1943). 'French assimilationist' policies also worked in this direction. Indigenous cultures, in many cases highly developed, were virtually ignored by colonial educational policy. Trends toward modernization, in many cases spurred by European-style education, were at the same time skewed by foreign control of the educational system.

Schools were established slowly by colonial governments, and even strong local pressure for education did not create a sufficiently large system. Some colonial powers, such as the Belgians, felt that higher level training for indigenous populations was bad policy, and thus when the Congo gained independence in 1960, there were only a handful of college graduates. The French, with their reliance on a totally French educational system for a very limited number of 'assimilated' individuals, produced only a small number of graduates. While British policy allowed for some measure of freedom and local initiative and did provide more opportunities for secondary and higher education, it neglected primary education. In contrast, both the French and the Belgians devoted funds to primary education, with the Church often providing the teaching manpower. Despite these differences and some regional variations, the colonial powers administered without much regard for the educational aspirations of local populations.

Political independence changed relatively little educationally in most developing countries. Few countries, despite the militancy of nationalist movements or deep feelings of enmity toward the former colonial powers, made sharp breaks with the educational past. In most cases, for example, Indian, Pakistan, Burma, and Singapore, the educational system expanded quantitatively, but did not alter much in terms of curriculum, orientation, or administration. In a number of countries, notably in formerly British Africa, higher education remained firmly rooted to its English curriculum and orientation, and in the immediate postindependence years, expanded very slowly indeed. Even nations which had never been under colonial domination, such as Thailand, Liberia, and Ethiopia, came under Western educational influence because of increased foreign aid and technical assistance. . . .

The continued use of European languages in many developing countries is one of the most important aspects of neocolonialism and the impact of the colonial heritage on the Third World. In a few cases, such as Indonesia, the colonial language (Dutch) was discarded, and a linguistically diverse national polity shifted to an indigenous language. In a number of developing countries, such as Nigeria, Ghana, India, Pakistan, and most of French-speaking Africa where there is no single indigenous national language, there has been a tendency to use the metropolitan language in administration and sometimes in education. The trend is to slowly replace European languages with indigenous media, but the process has been slow and difficult. What is more, linguistic change in the schools has not always been accompanied by curricular change.

European languages have tended to remain influential among elite groups even after the schools have shifted to indigenous languages. In some countries, higher education is conducted in the metropolitan language even after change takes place at lower levels. In addition, elites have often sent their children to private schools conducted in a European language in an effort to maintain their privileged position. The continued importance of European languages has other repercussions as well. Strong intellectual links with the metropolitan country are generally maintained, with the result that indigenous intellectual life and cultural development may be hampered, or at least deflected. In India, for example, research on Indian languages is undeveloped, in part owing to the great stress on expression in English and the prestige of publishing in English language journals.

Indian economists have been more concerned with 'model building' and theory than with the sometimes undramatic local problems of development. Indian sociologists have been criticized in scholarly journals for their ignorance of local issues and social structures and their stress on Western-oriented sociological theory. The major advanced states, particularly the English- and French-speaking metropolitan powers, have helped to maintain the educational and linguistic status quo by subsidizing textbooks and journals. They provide scholarships for students to study in the metropolitan country and send large numbers of teachers and technical personnel to developing areas. All of these factors help to direct the intellectual energy and attention of developing areas from their own situations to the international intellectual and scholarly community. . . .

American aid to overseas universities has tried to 'depoliticize' aspects of higher education. The founding of technical universities in various Latin American countries is an indication of this orientation (see Myers 1968). Such new institutions have functioned in direct competition with the established 'national universities.' The stated reason for developing these new institutions instead of upgrading existing universities is that a technologically-oriented curriculum is impossible to implement in the older institutions. It is significant that the older universities in Latin America are often dominated by leftist elements and that the newer institutions provide a counterbalance to strong left-wing influences in Latin American intellectual and political life. The technical universities have stressed a more innovative curriculum in the sciences. They have also adopted, in many cases, an American style academic organization.

To facilitate American policy goals, particular models of higher education have been exported and specific kinds of programs supported financially. American style 'land grant colleges' have been established in a number of developing countries, including India, Nigeria, Indonesia, and several Latin American nations. These institutions are based on a close relationship between the government and the university in opposition to academic traditions of independence in some developing nations. It may be, of course, that this model is suitable for developing areas, although the fact that land grant style universities have proved successful in several countries is due at least in part to the very large infusions of money and technical aid which have poured into them. . . .

The results of American policy are rather similar to the British colonial educational policies of the nineteenth century in that existing metropolitan institutions are exported to the developing areas, often in forms somewhat below domestic standards and sometimes without much adaptation to local conditions.

Advanced nations have been active in promoting particular academic disciplines and specialties, and the emphases which have been given may provide an insight into the motivations of the donors. American assistance has established an American Studies Research Institute in India, complete with a scholarly journal in which Indian academics may write on American-related topics. Of no basic relevance to India's modernization, this institute will help to produce over the long run a group of Indian professors favorable to the American cause, and perhaps professionally tied to it.[2] . . .

It is no surprise that relations between advanced industrial nations and developing countries in many respects are unequal. The influence of the advanced industrial nations has continued beyond the period of traditional colonialism and is one of the basic facts of economic, political, and social life of the developing world. Despite the self-evident nature of these facts, much of the analysis of the social, economic, and educational development of the Third World has ignored this basic aspect of the situation.

One cannot be optimistic about an immediate end to neocolonialism in any sphere, and perhaps especially in education. If anything, the scientific and educational gap between the advanced and the developing countries is growing. . . .

Only when an adequate understanding of modern neocolonialism in its many facets is achieved will [it] be possible to change the domination of West over East to a more equitable arrangement in an increasingly interdependent world.

## NOTES

1  In Singapore, where much of the ruling elite is composed of British-educated Chinese, the post-independence Prime Minister, Lee Kwan Yew, issued an order that members of the government should learn Chinese. Lee, a graduate of a British university, taught himself Chinese in order to communicate with his constituency.

2  The Americans have not been the only ones concerned with promoting the study of their own country overseas. Soviet funds have been given to establish departments of Russian studies at the University of Delhi and other institutions in developing countries. The German and French governments subsidize professorships in the study of German and French language and culture, and provide visiting professors without cost to universities in developing countries. These programs, while not crucial in diplomacy or power politics, do build up a group of individuals in developing countries who have strong ties to the particular metropolitan country.

# 81

# *The Race for Theory*

## Barbara Christian*

I have seized this occasion to break the silence among those of us, critics, as we are now called, who have been intimidated, devalued by what I call the race for theory. I have become convinced that there has been a takeover in the literary world by Western philosophers from the old literary élite, the neutral humanists. Philosophers have been able to effect such a takeover because so much of the literature of the West has become pallid, laden with despair, self-indulgent, and disconnected. The New Philosophers, eager to understand a world that is today fast escaping their political control, have redefined literature so that the distinctions implied by that term, that is, the distinctions between everything written and those things written to evoke feeling as well as to express thought, have been blurred. They have changed literary critical language to suit their own purposes as philosophers, and they have reinvented the meaning of theory. . . .

It is difficult to ignore this new takeover, since theory has become a commodity which helps determine whether we are hired or promoted in academic institutions – worse, whether we are heard at all. . . . Perhaps because those who have effected the takeover have the power (although they deny it) first of all to be published, and thereby to determine the ideas which are deemed valuable, some of our most daring and potentially radical critics (and by *our* I mean black, women, third world) have been influenced, even coopted, into speaking a language and defining their discussion in terms alien to and opposed to our needs and orientation. At least so far, the creative writers I study have resisted this language.

For people of color have always theorized – but in forms quite different from the Western form of abstract logic. And I am inclined to say that our theorizing (and I intentionally use the verb rather than the noun) is often in narrative forms, in the stories we create, in riddles and proverbs, in the play with language, since dynamic rather than fixed ideas seem more to our liking. How else have we managed to survive with such spiritedness

* From 'The Race for Theory' *Cultural Critique* 6, 1987.

the assault on our bodies, social institutions, countries, our very humanity? And women, at least the women I grew up around, continuously speculated about the nature of life through pithy language that unmasked the power relations of their world. It is this language, and the grace and pleasure with which they played with it, that I find celebrated, refined, critiqued in the works of writers like Morrison and Walker. My folk, in other words, have always been a race for theory – though more in the form of the hieroglyph, a written figure which is both sensual and abstract, both beautiful and communicative. In my own work I try to illuminate and explain these hieroglyphs, which is, I think, an activity quite different from the creating of the hieroglyphs themselves. As the Buddhists would say, the finger pointing at the moon is not the moon.

In this discussion, however, I am more concerned with the issue raised by my first use of the term, the *race for theory*, in relation to its academic hegemony, and possibly of its inappropriateness to the energetic emerging literatures in the world today. The pervasiveness of this academic hegemony is an issue continually spoken about – but usually in hidden groups, lest we, who are disturbed by it, appear ignorant to the reigning academic élite. Among the folk who speak in muted tones are people of color, feminists, radical critics, creative writers, who have struggled for much longer than a decade to make their voices, their various voices, heard, and for whom literature is not an occasion for discourse among critics but is necessary nourishment for their people and one way by which they come to understand their lives better. Clichéd though this may be, it bears, I think, repeating here.

The race for theory, with its linguistic jargon, its emphasis on quoting its prophets, its tendency towards 'Biblical' exegesis, its refusal even to mention specific works of creative writers, far less contemporary ones, its preoccupations with mechanical analyses of language, graphs, algebraic equations, its gross generalizations about culture, has silenced many of us to the extent that some of us feel we can no longer discuss our own literature, while others have developed intense writing blocks and are puzzled by the incomprehensibility of the language set adrift in literary circles. There have been, in the last year, any number of occasions on which I had to convince literary critics who have pioneered entire new areas of critical inquiry that they did have something to say. Some of us are continually harassed to invent wholesale theories regardless of the complexity of the literature we study. I, for one, am tired of being asked to produce a black feminist literary theory as if I were a mechanical man. For I believe such theory is prescriptive – it ought to have some relationship to practice. Since I can count on one hand the number of people attempting to be black feminist literary critics in the world today, I consider it presumptuous of me to invent a theory of how we *ought* to read. Instead, I think we need to read the works of our writers in our various ways and remain open to the intricacies of the intersection of language, class, race, and gender in the literature. And it would help if we share our process, that is, our practice, as much as possible since, finally, our work *is* a collective endeavor. . . .

Let me not give the impression that by objecting to the race for theory I ally myself with or agree with the neutral humanists who see literature as pure expression and will not admit to the obvious control of its production, value, and distribution by those who have power, who deny, in other words, that literature is, of necessity, political. I am studying an entire body of literature that has been denigrated for centuries by such terms as *political*. . . .

[But] I feel that the new emphasis on literary critical theory is as hegemonic as the world which it attacks. I see the language it creates as one which mystifies rather than clarifies our condition, making it possible for a few people who know that particular language to control the critical scene – that language surfaced, interestingly enough, just when the literature of peoples of color, of black women, of Latin Americans, of Africans began to move to 'the centre.' Such words as *center* and *periphery* are themselves instructive. *Discourse*, *canon*, *texts*, words as latinate as the tradition from which they come, are quite familiar to me. Because I went to a Catholic Mission school in the West Indies I must confess that I cannot hear the word 'canon' without smelling incense, that the word 'text' immediately brings back agonizing memories of Biblical exegesis, that 'discourse' reeks for me of metaphysics forced down my throat in those courses that traced *world* philosophy from Aristotle through Thomas Aquinas to Heidegger. 'Periphery' too is a word I heard throughout my childhood, for if anything was seen as being at the periphery, it was those small Caribbean islands which had neither land mass nor military power. Still I noted how intensely important this periphery was, for US troops were continually invading one island or another if any change in political control even seemed to be occurring. As I lived among folk for whom language was an absolutely necessary way of validating our existence, I was told that the minds of the world lived only in the small continent of Europe. The metaphysical language of the New Philosophy, then, I must admit, is repulsive to me and is one reason why I raced from philosophy to literature, since the latter seemed to me to have the possibilities of rendering the world as large and as complicated as I experienced it, as sensual as I knew it was. In literature I sensed the possibility of the integration of feeling/knowledge, rather than the split between the abstract and the emotional in which Western philosophy inevitably indulged. . . .

Because I am a curious person, however, I postponed readings of black women writers I was working on and read some of the prophets of this new literary orientation. These writers did announce their dissatisfaction with some of the cornerstone ideas of their own tradition, a dissatisfaction with which I was born. But in their attempt to change the orientation of Western scholarship, they, as usual, concentrated on themselves and were not in the slightest interested in the worlds they had ignored or controlled. Again I was supposed to know *them*, while they were not at all interested in knowing *me*. Instead they sought to 'deconstruct' the tradition to which they belonged even as they used the same forms, style, language of that tradition, forms which necessarily embody its values. And increasingly as I read them and saw their substitution of their philosophical writings for literary ones, I began to have the uneasy feeling that their folk were not producing any literature worth mentioning. For they always harkened back to the masterpieces of the past, again reifying the very texts they said they were deconstructing. Increasingly, as *their* way, *their* terms, *their* approaches remained central and became the means by which one defined literary critics, many of my own peers who had previously been concentrating on dealing with the other side of the equation, the reclamation and discussion of past and *present* third world literatures, were diverted into continually discussing the new literary theory. . . .

My major objection to the race for theory, as some readers have probably guessed by now, really hinges on the question, 'for whom are we doing what we are doing when we do literary criticism?' It is, I think, the central question today especially for the few of us who have infiltrated the academy enough to be wooed by it. The answer to that question determines what orientation we take in our work, the language we use, the purposes for which it is intended. . . .

My concern, then, is a passionate one, for the literature of people who are not in power has always been in danger of extinction or of cooptation, not because we do not theorize, but because what we can even imagine, far less who we can reach, is constantly limited by societal structures. For me, literary criticism is promotion as well as understanding, a response to the writer to whom there is often no response, to folk who need the writing as much as they need anything. I know, from literary history, that writing disappears unless there is a response to it. Because I write about writers who are now writing, I hope to help ensure that their tradition has continuity and survives.

# Part XIV

## Production and Consumption

# *Introduction*

Considerable energy has been spent, as many of the pieces in this Reader testify, on theorising the possibilities for post-colonial cultures recovering or developing identities, national cultural self-sufficency and confidence, or speculating as to how destructive the representation of colonials and post-colonials within the discursive modes of colonisation have been. Again, a lot of energy has been spent in discussing issues of language choice and of the need to recover pre-colonial languages. Yet the processes of patronage and control by which the colonial and neo-colonial powers continue to exercise a dominant role in selecting, licensing, publishing and distributing the texts of the post-colonial world, and the degree to which the inscriptive practices, choice of form, subject matter, genre, etc. is also subject to such control, have received far less attention than they deserve. This wider sociological dimension of post-colonial textual studies, is, as André Lefevere argues, resident principally in 'refracted texts' such as school or university reading lists. The power of such texts has been discussed already in the section on Education. In the area addressed by this section conditions change rapidly, and many of the essays here are already outstripped by events, for example Peter Hyland's piece on Singapore writing would need now to be corrected to indicate the rapid rise in local publication there in the last ten years or so. Equally, there is a need for updating and extending the pioneer work of S. I. A. Kotei and Philip Altbach reproduced here. No area of study seems to us to be more urgently in need of address at the present time, and the pieces we reproduce here are intended as much to stimulate the production of more current assessments of the material conditions of cultural production and consumption in post-colonial societies as they are authoritative accounts of the present situation.

Who consumes and produces the texts for the 'post-colonial' world, who canonises them, who acquires them and has them available as physical objects is an important but neglected precondition for more abstract and theoretical discussions of the agency of the post-colonial subject. As well as the continuing control of these elements by neo-colonial forces, it is impor-tant to document the effect of attitudes within the post-colonial world to the very idea of publishing. As Peter Hyland notes, in some post-colonial

463

societies cultural production has been seen as a luxury that these societies cannot afford. Elsewhere, as Altbach notes, the new independence comprador class sees national literatures (including texts in the 'prestigious' ex-colonial languages) as suitable for annexation to the construction of their own power and prestige. The lesson to be drawn from this is that cultural production and its effects is important in any society and it is perilous to neglect it. Altbach also points, as does Kotei, to the complex relations between colonial and neo-colonial cultural producers and the ways in which the ex-colonies are available both as suitable markets for cultural products and as the source for exotic products for sale on the home market. As Altbach also notes, even the 'liberal' enterprises of cultural development programmes may have an adverse effect on the development of independent and self-sufficient modes of cultural production in the post-colonial world by creating a product which undersells the local entrepreneur, preventing the development of a self-sufficient and economically sustainable local industry. W. J. T. Mitchell speculates on how one of the most powerful neo-colonial powers (itself both an ex-colony and an ex-empire, as he rightly perceives) might set about addressing this problem at least at the level of the academy.

Kotei's report, now more than a decade old, points to a situation which seems to be not only continuing but worsening. The crisis of documentation in areas such as Africa to which he makes reference is simply not being addressed at a time when, ironically, Europe and America are congratulating themselves on their enlightenment in having discovered and promoted the writings of the post-colonial world. As a recent issue of the Filipino cultural magazine *Solidarity* has indicated, economic security is no guarantee of the development of local product and control. The situation in South and South-East Asia shows that even where the technical skill and infrastructure of production exists, and may be strongly utilised to produce an industry successfully serving off-shore clients, the development of the production of books aimed at and reflecting the needs and concerns of the local market does not automatically follow. Countries such as Australia and Canada, too, because their domestic market remains relatively small, find that the study of their own culture may be restricted by such factors as publishers' budgets to the famous and canonical authors, or those endorsed by the power of the absent 'centre'. Thus in Australia several critical books on a Nobel winner such as White or a Booker prize winner such as Malouf or Carey will be adjudged viable, whereas studies of important but less internationally acclaimed writers such as Judith Wright or Dorothy Hewett may be less likely to be published since they command no interest in the world market.

It is by such material practices that the fate of post-colonial literary work is often determined. It is this which allows these books to come into existence, which gives them their chance to effect their 'work in the world'. For this reason it seems to us to be one of the most important and so-far largely neglected areas of concern and a fitting topic with which to conclude this Reader.

# 82

# The Historiography of African Literature Written in English

## André Lefevere*

A LITERATURE ... CAN be described as a system, embedded in the environment of a civilization/culture/society, call it what you will. The system is not primarily demarcated by a language, or an ethnic group, or a nation, but by a poetics, a collection of devices available for use by writers at a certain moment in time.... The environment exerts control over the system, by means of patronage. Patronage combines both an ideological and an economic component. It tries to harmonize the system with other systems it has to co-exist with in the wider environment – or it simply imposes a kind of harmony. It provides the producer of literature with a livelihood, and also with some kind of status in the environment.

Traditional African literature is a perfect illustration of this state of affairs. The artist, we are told, has interiorized the implicit poetics of the community, which supports him at least in terms of status, 'he is a spokesman for the society in which he lives, sharing its prejudices and directing its dislikes (in a limited form of satire) against what is discountenanced' (Dathorne 1974: 3), and he does so by making use of certain genres. The illustration matches the model so perfectly because the patronage is totally undifferentiated, i.e. the system allows of one ideal of literature, and only one, and also because the patronage is able to exert its control directly and immediately. Since the literature is oral, not written, and since the artist is therefore a performer, the audience will immediately make its displeasure felt if the artist makes a mistake in the telling or in the reciting – an immediacy that is lost in the transition from oral to written literature. The illustration also works so well because the model sidesteps one complicating factor for the sake of clarity. This must now be corrected by redefining poetics and patronage as constraints influencing the production of literature, rather than simply as factors guiding it in what appears to be a suspiciously mechanistic

* From 'Interface: Some Thoughts on the Historiography of African Literature Written in English' in Dieter Riemenschneider (ed.) *The History and Historiography of Commonwealth Literature* Tübingen: Gunter Narr Verlag, 1983.

manner, and by adding the language in which literature is produced as another constraint. The concept of constraint(s), as used here, implies that all statements made about it are more or less double-edged, or rather, that the reader/hearer is supposed to supply the other side of the coin, so to speak. Constraints can always be honoured and subverted. Their importance lies only partially in their bare existence, the other part being the spirit in which they are taken. Producers of literature may subvert these constraints, or they may be quite happy to work with them or within them.

Literature, then, is produced in the zone of tension where the artist's creativity comes to terms with the constraints. The writer will not reject those constraints out of hand in systems with undifferentiated patronage, because he quite simply has nowhere else to go – but silence. Literary revolutions, on the other hand, tend to occur in systems with differentiated patronage, in which different ideals of literature are allowed to coexist, and in which literature produced on the basis of those different ideals is read by different groups of readers.

Interface, and that is what mainly concerns us here, is the situation which arises when two systems interact, in this case the English system and the African system, so that a kind of hybrid poetics comes into being, combining elements from the historically dominated system (the African one) with elements from the historically dominant system (the English one), and acting as a constraint on the production of literature within the dominated system, while it leaves the dominant system relatively unaffected. . . . Interface is regulated first and foremost by the power and/or prestige of the respective environments of the respective systems, by the power of their respective patronages and the policies they are willing to adopt, and by what use the different poetics have for each other. It strikes me that the concept of interface might at least be useful in developing a chronology that is capable of accommodating more complex factors than one mainly based on theme, or even on a mere succession of decades, or of events occurring outside the system. I would propose shifts in the nature of patronage as the factor that demarcates chronological periods in the development of a system. If events in the environments lead to a changed social role for a group that has exercised patronage, changes are likely to take place inside the system. If they do not, changes are much less likely, no matter how momentous the events may be in other respects.

The prestige of an environment may be less readily measurable, by an independent observer, than its power, and in the early stages of the interface there was no doubt as to where power lay. Technology figures as the prominent de facto criterion between the civilized and the primitive, and it was soon to be provided with an ideological justification. 'Primitiveness, essentially a product of political domination, received, in the second part of the nineteenth century, an almost authoritative stamp from social Darwinism' (Obiechina 1975: 15). The English system quite logically occupied the dominant position in the interface – dominant with a

vengeance since it was, at first, quite simply proclaimed that African literature did not exist, just as Du Bellay, for example, dismissed Medieval
Literature more or less out of hand. It lived on, of course, for quite some
time after its dismissal, as did traditional literature in British Africa, but
those who produced it would gradually find out that it did not confer the
same status on them as before, certainly not in the new urban communities, precisely because the African patronage, or rather, the patronage inside
the African system, had lost its status-conferring power. The African system
was forced on the defensive and the English system had no use for it. As a
result, interaction was a very one-sided affair. . . .

Refractions of original texts in the English system became the main
instrument in the institutionalization of that system as the main, or even
the only one in the interface. Probably the most influential refracted texts
in this respect were school anthologies, introducing these originals in
schools and on other levels of education, as these became gradually more
available. The ideology of the groups that acted as patrons for different
schools and, later, universities played the most important part here. Surveys
and anthologies of English literature must have read quite differently
according to the sub-ideology they were trying to propagate (a fascinating
field of study here, be it said in passing, and one very little cultivated). I say
sub-ideologies, because they were all united in the main ideology: that of
the white man's civilizing mission and of his superiority. In universities the
most influential refracted text was what it still is (it is also the shortest one
by far): the reading list that introduces the canon of a literature as modified by successive changes in taste, that seemingly elusive amalgam of
ideological, economic and poetological factors.

Environmental patterns such as these served to discredit the old
African patronage even more, but they did little to encourage the production, by Africans, of literature in English that would closely follow the
poetics of the English system, precisely because they did not replace the old
African patronage. In fact, the two patronages remained quite distinct for
some time, one producing, at best, various variants of Couriferist literature
in African writers, the other producing essentially what it had always
produced, but which was now much less honoured and sought after.

The literature produced on the basis of English poetics and under
English patronage could hardly be other than that of Couriferism, in which
interface means the total hegemony of one system over another. Hegemony
is used here in the fullest sense of the word, which means not only acceptance, which may range from the grudging to the resigned, of English
constraints, not least among them the language, but identification with
those constraints: this is the way it has to be, not just the way it is.
Patronage selects the themes that can be treated, emphasizes certain techniques and rejects others, according to the changing appreciation of
elements of the poetics, and sees to it that the language is used 'correctly.'
In short, we have here a clear-cut case of patronage by stipulation.

The same patronage by stipulation made its appearance in the only case in which European patronage tried to take the place of African patronage within the African system: in the production of literature in the vernacular. The motive was, of course, ideological: 'the missionaries who ran the printing presses' (Owomoyela 1979: 28), and it introduced a new means of literary communication into the African system: the text. Only the text really necessitates the production of other texts as a control mechanism in systems with undifferentiated patronage and as weapons in the struggle between rival poetics in systems with differentiated patronage, since the control mechanisms of oral literature are a lot more direct. This kind of patronage could again bestow status, in the writer's immediate environment and without the need for the writer to produce in a different language. He did, however, have to produce on the basis of a different, or a hybrid poetics, and certainly on the basis of a different ideology: 'The christianized vernacular writer took the decisive step of separating himself from the group' (Owomoyela 1979: 28).

Being essentially ideological in nature, this kind of patronage exerted both a destructive and a conserving influence on African poetics, or rather, it turned that poetics into a kind of 'selective poetics,' in which elements (themes mainly, characters and situations, since genres are inherently neutral and symbols can always be allegorized, witness the wholescale allegorical colonization of classical literature undertaken within the West European system, and by the same ideology, some fifteen centuries earlier) unacceptable to the ideology are rejected, whereas others are allowed. The rejected elements eventually vanish if the ideology manages to extend its hegemony over the whole system, they go underground if it does not. In doing so it saves many elements of the rejected poetics, which may emerge again later, such as the ballad after three centuries in the West European system, and a number of themes and other elements after a few decennia in the interface situation we are analyzing here.

The underground elements could only be allowed to 'hybridize' the poetics of the interface after another shift in patronage, in which a hybridized group of readers is willing to patronize the literature based on such a poetics, and in which the old dominant patronage group is willing to tolerate and, eventually, accept it. There were environmental reasons for this, of course: urbanization, the institution of cash economy, industrialization and the progress of Christianity contributed to a situation in which the African 'removed himself from a community where status and social hierarchy had determined the individual's place in society and where the individual counted in terms of the group to which he belonged, and entered a situation in which he was free to assert, if only in a limited way, his own individuality' (Obiechina 1975: 5).

This was instrumental in creating a potential patronage, which would see its sense of its own worth dramatically boosted by the obvious demonstration of the white man's vulnerability provided by World War II, while another factor was instrumental in setting up a group of potential producers: the 'popular press,' owned by Africans, which 'gave the common man his first apprenticeship at literary expression in print' (Obiechina 1975: 12). The new patronage group found itself ready and able to confer status on writers who produced on the basis of the new hybrid poetics, which, as a result, acquired enough status itself to challenge the dominant, English poetics.

This process was also helped by the fact that refracted texts had, in the meantime, begun to travel the other way. But refractions of a dominated poetics penetrate into the system organized around the dominant poetics only if they are first filtered through the dominant system. The more that system becomes familiar with texts from the dominated system, the less rigorous the filtering process is likely to be. There is a fairly continuous progression, therefore, from philological refractions, where the motive is, once again, ideological – one needs to know languages in order to be able to carry out missionary activities – to translation, without a doubt the type of refracted text that has done most to introduce African literature to other literary systems which ignored, or denied its existence, to writing in West European languages, among them of course English by Africans. At first this type of writing tends to respect English poetics in all but one element: theme, which is frankly African, and gives these writings a kind of exotic novelty value. Hence the emergence of the autobiography as one of the dominant genres in African English literature, until it is succeeded by the novel, which gradually Africanizes more and more elements from the basically English poetics, and, in doing so, reaffirms the status of the hybrid.

Poetological, as opposed to ideological interest in African poetics was not all that often expressed within the English system until after World War I, when it was found that African poetics, and the literature produced on the basis of it, could be invoked, often with little or no factual knowledge, as an example of a certain ideal of literature that would challenge the then dominant one. This poetological interest on the part of certain groups within the English system coincided with a mainly ideological interest expressed by the emerging African nationalist leaders, who needed an African literature, preferably a great one, in order to counteract the overwhelming cultural claims of the colonizers. In the independent African nations this same attitude has given rise to a most interesting type of translation, in which vernacular literature from the different languages inside a new nation is translated into English (or the other European language that functions as the nation language) not primarily for export, but for internal use: a 'foreign' language is used to reinforce a sense of 'national' cultural identity.

The hybrid poetics is also accepted for economic reasons: there is, quite simply, money in it, particularly in the recent past, when anything that came out of Africa would get published by Heinemann, Longmans,

Macmillan and a number of publishers in the United States. Finally, it would seem, the hybrid poetics has produced its hybrid patronage: the canonization of works and writers that is now going on, is not the work of Africans only: it is also carried out in London, in various centers in the United States and in Europe.

Being a hybrid system that is still developing, that is in its first stages even, African English literature, and other African literatures written in European languages, can teach us a lot about the way in which literary systems as such originate and develop. We shall only learn what we need to learn in that respect, though, if we resolutely broaden our research, away from the canon. That is, if we are not content with commenting on the works that form the canon, but if we also want to shed light on the factors that are instrumental in the canonization process. To be able to do that, we must include non-canonized works in our surveys, and show what parts they play, and we must also include refracted texts much more than has been done up to now.

Systematization on the basis of a model of this type will not only teach us something about the field we want to investigate, but also about the model we are trying to use, since new information will inevitably tend to modify the model. The danger inherent in this type of approach is that the model, the system, tends to be given some kind of ontological status, that the 'map' and the 'territory' become confused, or even interchangeable. This danger can only be counteracted by means of continuous feedback between those among us who work in the territory itself, and those who try to make maps.

# 83

## *Singapore*
### *Poet, Critic, Audience*

PETER HYLAND*

SINGAPOREAN POETS (AND I limit myself here to poetry simply because it is the most developed genre) have not found an audience. Although the actual size of the poetry-reading public is difficult to ascertain, it is indubitably very small, and confined pretty much to people educated in the English department of the University of Singapore. Poetry is consequently associated with a certain sort of elitism (the phrase 'ivory tower' is one frequently used in Singapore), though one not officially encouraged. Indeed, the official view puts poetry firmly in its place as a frivolous activity, 'a luxury we cannot afford,' as Mr Lee Kuan Yew said in 1969, suggesting the paramount importance of material development. The prime minister's view was apparently still the official one some ten years later for, responding to opinions put forward in a forum on English language and literature in Singapore, the then member of Parliament for Anson and latterly president of Singapore, Mr Devan Nair, took the extraordinary step of attacking them in a speech in Parliament on the 1980 budget. On this very unlikely occasion, Mr Nair said: 'if we throw our Government front benchers, our back benchers, our technocrats, systems engineers, entrepreneurs, skilled workers, civil servants and managers into the ocean, there will not be any Singapore. But throw the arty-crafty reality-dodgers into the ocean, and you might get a bit more literary and spiritual realism.' Now Mr Nair is himself a very literate man, and behind the rhetoric here he is not saying that there should be no literature in Singapore.

What lies behind his idea of 'literary and spiritual realism' is the view that literary activity should be firmly in support of the material aims of Singapore. This attitude, of course, creates a certain anxiety in the writers, and indeed in the very forum attacked by Mr Nair, the poet and novelist Goh Poh Seng complained: 'Living in a new country, living in an age where nationalism is the important thing, has created a great dilemma for writers,

* From 'Singapore: Poet, Critic, Audience' *World Literature Written in English* 23(1), 1984.

especially in Singapore, where we have no tradition behind us and politics and economics is such a force that we are told, very explicitly, what to write about . . .' (Goh Poh Seng 1980: 1–16). For, of course, the government reflects the ethos of the nation: for men struggling upward, poetry may very well be a luxury they think they can't afford.

Now it may be that this intense concern with materialism affects attitudes not only to poetry, but also to English as a medium for the writing of poetry. English is only one of four official languages used in Singapore, and is not the language of any of the traditional cultures of the Singaporean people. It has from its first use in colonial Singapore been the language of social and economic advancement. It is the language used for communication with the larger world, and the most urgent reason for that communication, obviously, is the material and political development of Singapore. It is difficult, therefore, to see the language as a vehicle for creative rather than pragmatic expression, and we are not surprised to learn that, even though English is the language of easiest access for Singapore as a whole, in the ten years up to 1976, there were seventy-three books of poetry published in Chinese for only twelve books published in English (Nair 1977: 1–4). So, while there can be little doubt that if there is to be a *Singaporean* literature in the future it will have to be in English, rather than Chinese, Tamil or Malay, there still seems to be a widespread wariness about using English for poetic expression.

Still, poetry is being written. In his introduction to the anthology *Seven Poets*, written in 1973, Edwin Thumboo felt able to refer to a 'respectable but not large' body of verse, but worried about the 'real danger in hasty and pretentious judgement.' In 1970 Robert Yeo, echoing Thumboo, thought that younger poets had 'though small, a body of achievement to guide them,' but felt, nevertheless, uncomfortable about using the word 'poetry': 'half of the time it may be more accurate to speak rather of verse and writers of verse' (Yeo 1970: 14). This cautious, almost apologetic, note was, perhaps, justified at the time, because the body of verse was certainly small. Even by 1976 the output was low: as we have seen, in the ten years up to that time only twelve books in English had been published. But between 1977 and 1982 twenty-seven volumes by individual poets were published, as well as eight anthologies, including four by children. In 1980 the Ministry of Culture, perhaps reflecting a change in the official attitude to literature, began the publication of *Singa*, a journal devoted to the arts and literature, and containing a substantial amount of poetry. It would seem, therefore, that there is vitality in the literary world of Singapore. The volume of publishing may be misleading, however, if it suggests either that there is now a predominance of 'poetry' over 'verse,' or that there is a much increased audience for the poetry.

Ban Kah Choon complained in 1978 that writers are too easily inclined to 'rush into print without proper respect to the muse' (Ban Kah Choon 1979: 21). It is certainly true that it is rather too easy for a writer to see his work get into print in Singapore, and there is a sad lack of crafts-manship in much of what appears. A number of books contributing to the apparent boom in publication were published privately by their authors, or by vanity presses, and while this does not mean that a book so produced will be bad, it does mean that an unnecessary amount of ill-considered verse appears in print, and it also means that to many of the writers the absence of an audience is irrelevant.

For the more serious writer, however, this absence must be a cause for worry. The poet Lee Tzu Pheng wrote in 1971: 'It is futile to expect that poetry should be widely read in Singapore,' and went on to console herself with the idea that quality rather than quantity of readership is important (Lee Tzu Pheng 1980: 25). But the final verse in her collection *Prospect of a Drowning* suggests that she feels the futility of communicating with nobody:

> words are only wind
> children of the mind
> give nothing if nothing
> is accepted.
> (Lee Tzu Pheng 1980: 25)

Or take this extract from a poem entitled 'words' from Arthur Yap's collection *down the line*:

> words need people to fill their blanks,
> quick eye-flicks across the page:
> a page of contained dimensions
> housing a pharynx
> that, from edge to edge
> is still,
> still as a minute glottal sphinx.
> > (Yap 1980: 36)

So aware is Yap of the lack of people to fill the blanks of his words that there seems at times in his poetry the danger of a retreat into a cryptic, almost private, language that defies the absent reader.

One function of criticism, at any rate in a developing literature, is to bridge the gap between poet and reader, to act as intermediary, so that there are no elitist questions of 'writing down' to the audience. In a situation like that in Singapore the function of the critic is crucial if it is to be demon-strated that poetry is not a luxury, and that no society can really afford to be without it. . . .

[Significant developments have taken place in the last decade or so in Singaporean writing, with the emergence of an increasing number of new writers. It is possible, without exaggeration, to speak of a flowering in Singaporean writing especially since the mid-1980s; nevertheless some of

Hyland's points about the ideological constraints within which the function of literature is conceived still have force for this as for other post-colonial cultures where the argument that literature and culture as a whole is a 'luxury' new societies can ill afford may still all too frequently be heard. Eds.]

# 84

# Postcolonial Culture, Postimperial Criticism

## W. J. T. MITCHELL*

The United States may well be the first nation in history to realize that it has been an empire only as it ceases to be one. Americans are less disturbed by the idea of imperial decline than with the notion that the word 'empire' could ever apply to us.

Yet we may have to acknowledge our status as an empire and achieve a clearer understanding of the process of imperial decline and its corollary, decolonization, if we are to make sense of the transferences and reconfigurations now taking place in the world's literary culture.

To begin with a massively general impression: The most important new literature is emerging from the colonies – regions and peoples that have been economically or militarily dominated in the past – while the most provocative new literary criticism is emanating from the imperial centers that once dominated them – the industrial nations of Europe and America.

Horace noted long ago that the transfer of empire from Greece to Rome (the *translatio imperii*) was accompanied by a transfer of culture and learning (a *translatio studii*). Today the cultural transfer is no longer one-way. But what is the nature of the transference going on between the declining imperial powers and their former colonies, and between contemporary literature and criticism?

It is easy to find evidence to support the idea that the former imperial centers today excel in criticism while former colonial nations are producing the most exciting literature.

Witness the recent Nobel Prizes won by writers outside the mainstream of European and American literature. Last fall, for example, the Egyptian novelist Naguib Mahfouz became the first Arab ever to win the Nobel Prize for literature. Nigerian Wole Soyinka became the first African writer to win the Nobel Prize for literature in 1986. Probably just politics, you say – a form of global affirmative action?

* From 'Postcolonial Culture, Postimperial Criticism' *Transition 55*, 1992. (First published in a shorter form in the *Chronicle of Higher Education*, 19 April 1992.)

If so, the British seem to have joined the game as well. The Booker Prize no longer seems to go routinely to an Englishman. When Keri Hulme, a Maori-Scottish feminist mystic from the remote west coast of New Zealand's south island, wins Britain's most prestigious literary prize with her first novel, we know that familiar cultural maps are being redrawn.

The literary map of the Americas is in even greater flux. A mere recitation of such familiar names as Carlos Fuentes, Maria Vargas Llosa, Gabriel García Márquez, Jorge Luis Borges, and Julio Cortázar is enough to suggest a cultural *translatio* from South to North, from Spanish to English; from the 'circumference' (as seen by citizens of the US) to the center. Afro-American writers like Toni Morrison, Zora Neale Hurston, and Alice Walker are read in and out of the classroom, translating literary energy from the internal margins of American culture to its centers.

There is also a *translatio* from East to West, from the exiles, dissidents, and colonial subjects of what we used to call the 'Evil Empire' – Milan Kundera, Joseph Brodsky, Jerzy Kozinsky. Why are those writers adopted so readily by American readers? Could it be that literature expressive of resistance to the 'other' empire, the Evil One, is especially congenial in its reinforcement of our anti-imperialist self-image, reassuring us that 'empire' is, after all, still a European problem?

If the balance of *literary* trade has shifted from the First to the Second and Third Worlds, the production of *criticism* has become a central activity of the culture industries of the imperial centers, especially those in institutions of higher education. Over 30 years ago the novelist and critic Randall Jarrell mournfully declared that Europe and the United States were entering an 'age of criticism.' One wonders how he would have greeted the literary developments of the 1980s: *Time* and *Newsweek* devote space to deconstruction; the *New York Times* covers critical movements at Yale and Duke Universities in full color; academic critics write best-selling books on 'cultural literacy' and 'the American mind' and become instant talkshow celebrities.

Even the most ordinary academic critic can now aspire to participate in a global network of what Edward Said has called 'Traveling Theory,' in which critics fly between conferences on semiotics, narratology, and paradigm change in places like Hong Kong, Canberra, and Tel Aviv.

If criticism has to some extent muscled in on the traditional cultural exports of the Western Empires – literature, history, philosophy, the fine arts – it has done so in an odd and unpredictable way. Traditionally, such exports tended to support the authority of the imperial center. English culture was transported to the 'natives' and the colonial settlers in the full confidence that it would have a civilizing influence, while serving as a continual reminder of where civilization was really located – in the imperial center.

Contemporary criticism, by contrast, tends to subvert the imperial authority. Scepticism, relativism, and 'anti-foundationalist' modes of thought such as pragmatism and deconstruction may come to the Third World from the First, but they conspicuously lack the authoritative force of traditional imperial culture. Critical movements such as feminism, black studies, and Western Marxism may offer stronger assurances of authority and purpose, but they can hardly be said to speak with the authority of the imperial center.

On the contrary, they are in the paradoxical position of bringing a rhetoric of decolonization from the imperial center. Perhaps this is why so many imaginative writers of the Third World (J. M. Coetzee in South Africa, Ian Wedde in New Zealand, Toni Morrison in 'African America') look with wary fascination on contemporary criticism – unsure whether it is a friendly collaborator in the process of decolonization, or a threatening competitor for limited resources.

The relationship between critical movements in the First World and literary developments in the Second and Third Worlds is too complex to be reduced to any simple formula. But the relationship is one we must begin to explore further. We ought to resist the notion that this relationship merely reflects the traditional economic relations of imperial centers and colonial peripheries. It is surely wrong to say that cultural 'raw materials' are coming from the colonies to be turned into 'finished products' by the critical industries of empire.

If one thing is striking about Latin-American writers like Carlos Fuentes and Gabriel García Márquez, it is the total absence of colonial provinciality in their work, and the presence of a sophisticated cosmopolitan awareness, including an awareness of contemporary criticism.

At the same time, one should not minimize the dissonance between post-imperial criticism and post-colonial culture. Criticism may find itself preaching a rhetorical de-centering and de-essentializing to cultures that are struggling to find a center and an essence for the first time. Conversely it may find itself bringing an imperial theory of culture into a situation that resists any conceptual totality.

The strategic location and historical timing of a critical idea may be as important in a period of global reconfiguration as any transcendental claims to truth that it might want to make. Instrumental rationality and Western 'problem-solving' tactics may not always be welcome or appropriate in Third-World cultures that are rediscovering their ethnic traditions. The very idea of 'rationality,' in fact, may have to be replaced by a pluralized concept of 'rationalities' in the post-colonial era. . . .

When the neo-conservative National Association of Scholars reacts to the emergence of ethnic and women's studies by declaring that 'the barbarians are in our midst,' we recognize the hysterical rhetoric of an empire in decline. Allan Bloom's characterization of Afro-American studies as 'the Little Black Empire' plays on similar buzz-words, simultaneously denigrating the value and inflating the threat of the barbarians by projecting imperial ambitions onto them.

E. D. Hirsch's *Cultural Literacy* promises a 'quick fix' for an empire whose appetite for diverse cultures has outstripped its ability to digest them into a single national identity. Hirsch offers lists of terms, names, great books, and authors as an alternative for critical method and as a substitute for cultural community. Lynne Cheney's report on the 'Humanities in America' sounds the alarm to defend the 'American = Western = Universal Human' values from the depredations of ethnic and women's studies, and her position as director of the National Endowment for the Humanities would seem to place her at the front lines, at least with regard to support for research.

The neo-conservative attack on contemporary criticism may well be a blessing in disguise for those who hope for an alliance between post-colonial culture and post-imperial criticism. For one thing, it should produce some solidarity among academic feminists by providing a clear sense of the common threat to standards of literary excellence and scholarly responsibility. Genuine conservatives in the academy should be the first to welcome the production of real literature among emerging nations and peoples, a development which fulfills (albeit in an unsuspected way) the ancient imperial dream of the *translatio studii*. Conservatives should also be the first to oppose what Barbara Herrnstein Smith has recently called the 'querulous populism' of the New Right, its attempt to impose by political coercion and appeals to an uninitiated mass audience the views which it has been unable to make convincing in the context of professional debate. The pretence of the academic New Right that it is only concerned with eternal, human values while others are reducing everything to politics, is now wearing very thin.

Even more important than the negative aspects of the neo-conservative reaction is the challenge it poses for those who work the criticism of culture to articulate a comprehensive vision of their work. We need a vision that is sensitive to the local particularities of the global decolonizing process, and yet capable of identifying common interests, opportunities for alliance and collaboration. We must have a story, if not as simple, at least as compelling as the gloomy jeremiads decrying the 'decline of the West,' the 'fall of the American empire,' and the 'destruction of the white races.'

Perhaps an outline for such a story might be found by retracing the American ideology of anti-imperialism and connecting it with the great Western models of more or less graceful imperial decline. France, England, and ancient Athens all had the advantage of knowing and acknowledging themselves as empires from very early on. For Americans, perhaps, the difficult move is the acknowledgment that we are and have been for some time an imperial power – not a uniquely 'chosen people' whose destiny is given, but a people whose destiny has yet to be chosen. The unique gift of the American empire might be to combine the sober realism of this acknowledgment with a serious commitment to the idealism – as distinct from the self-deluding ideology – of our anti-imperialist traditions.

George Washington showed us how to read the history of empire when he invoked the example of Cincinnatus, and refused the wrong kind of power at the right time. Only after Athens lost its navy did it become in fact what Pericles had, at the height of its power, hoped for it to be – 'the School of Hellas.' Perhaps American higher education can aspire to such a role in the next century – a world school for intelligent, peaceful, and productive decolonization. The idea of a 'university' might then well live up to its name.

# 85

# *The Book Today in Africa*

## S. I. A. KOTEI*

### THE AFRICAN ENTREPRENEUR PUBLISHER

Three sets of conditions determine the success or failure of private indigenous enterprise in an African country. The first comprises the general state of affairs in the country concerned, particularly the national political economy. If national policy actively favours private enterprise, then it should be expected that the necessary facilities will be provided; if there is a tendency to centralization or state monopoly of particular industries, then private enterprise is not encouraged. In any case, the extent to which the state will make foreign exchange available to an indigenous entrepreneur will depend on the importance of his industry to the national scale of priorities.

The second set of conditions is endemic to the enterprise itself: that is, availability of the requisite manpower, skills and appropriate technology.

The third and perhaps the most vital condition is the existence of consumer market forces. Two crucial questions can be asked here. First, assuming there is a demand for the services or products of the enterprise, is the market size large enough to make it economically viable? Second, is the market value of the product within the purchasing power of the consumer public?

Where the entrepreneur publisher is concerned, the book industry in Africa has been affected by all of the above conditions. The only constant factors are the second and third, conditions, that is, manpower/technology, and the market. . . . Those African nations which have had a relatively strong economy in recent years, matched by socio-political awareness of the role of the book in development, have also had a relatively healthy book industry. . . .

A remarkable example is the *Onitsha Market Literature* which burst upon the Nigerian reading public in the 1950s (Obiechina 1971, 1972, 1973).

* From *The Book Today in Africa* Paris: Unesco, 1981.

It was a phenomenon of literary profusion without comparison anywhere in Africa, before or since. In reference to the remarkable success achieved (in a financial and technical sense) it could be reported that printing and publishing had become eastern Nigeria's healthiest industry (Harris 1968: 226). Many of these 'industrialists' not only wrote their boy-meets-girl novelettes and rapid-results cram-books, but also printed, published and sold them.

How can one account for the ability of *Onitsha Market Literature* to achieve success without any of the persons involved having received much training in writing, printing, publishing or book-selling? For one, there was a ready market of buyers who were eager to learn from reading any and all accessible material.

Nevertheless, it is true that Third World publishing is full of pitfalls for the untrained, uninitiated entrepreneur. Indeed the book trade is regarded as the most risky business in the world today, after film-making (Hasan 1975: 1–8). With increasingly tough competition, the amateur publisher would be ill-advised to enter the profession without adequate training.

Publishers in Africa have in most cases ignored this admonition. Their concern to alleviate the book hunger precipitates a decision to publish on a large scale at a national level, though professional manpower is lacking. Inability to gauge accurately the size of the potential market is one other predicament faced by the beginning entrepreneur publisher. There are hardly any studies of reading habits to guide his choice of specialization or distribution targets. Therefore, he adopts a trial-and-error method, unless, of course, he goes into the assured market of textbook publishing. Even here, he has to compete with established publishers, both national and foreign. . . .

Currently, the most popular themes (from the sales point of view) are the novelettes variously described as 'popular fictions', 'boy-meets-girl', or 'market literature'. They have no serious political axes to grind but they tend to be moralistic in their social comment and portrayal of ethical stands.

If an author cannot find a local publishing house to publicize his views, he either relies on his own devices by establishing a private press or sends his manuscripts abroad (Armah 1975). The African writer's deprivation was passionately expressed by the President of the Ghana Association of Writers in 1973 as follows:

> If you [the writer] set out to print anything on your own, the printing costs will stagger you. If you manage to print, the distribution diffi-culties will blow your mind. If you give your stuff to a local publisher, you will sympathize so much with his problems that you may not write again. . . . So all our best work . . . appears first to an audience which either regards us like some glass-enclosed specimen . . . or like an exotic weed to be sampled and made a conversation piece . . . or else we become some international organization's pet.
>
> (Okai 1973: 4)

Private book production thrives on direct relations between authors and printers. The absence of publishers in Mauritius means that an author bears the entire cost of publishing (Jacob 1974). In Ethiopia, described as a 'society without publishers', a co-operative approach among authors has also been adopted. A number of authors with manuscripts to publish pay a regular monthly subscription to have their manuscripts published in turn. The effects of the above compromises are that production is small in quantity, the book itself is made small in order to make savings on paper and printing costs.

The alternative to self-reliance is for an author to submit his manuscript to an established local publisher – often thereby running the risk of it never seeing the light of day, or having to wait interminably before being published. Many manuscripts suffer this fate not because they are worthless or of lesser value than those that get published, but simply because publishers get so many unsolicited manuscripts that their backlog is always much more voluminous than production. It becomes impossible to maintain a proper balance between input and output ratios because of innumerable technical, financial and manpower constraints. In this respect, it is pertinent to observe that most of the complaints that are lodged against state publishing houses by authors concern delays in publishing their manuscripts, rather than inefficiency in design or even failure to pay royalties. None the less, there have been cases where a commissioned author refused a contract because he feared that an African publisher either could not guarantee good book design, or lacked the facilities for wide international distribution. There are now African houses who excel in book design, but who cannot promote wide enough sales at home or abroad to make it worth the writer's while to submit more manuscripts. . . .

## THE CRITIC

Probably because of these constraints, the doyen of African creative writers – Chinua Achebe – has called for a kind of collectivization in which the writers and their audience will move together in a dynamic evolving relationship, through the publisher who must operate in the same historic and social continuum. 'It stands to reason that he [the publisher] cannot play this role from London or Paris or New York' (Oluwasanmi *et al*. 1975: 44). His work must be published in Africa itself, where the local publisher, with the liveliness of local imagination, can seize upon the peculiar characteristics of a place to operate more effectively within the social milieu. The truly successful writer, for his part, must be both a mirror and an image of the values of his society.

One way of interpreting Achebe's call for the African writer to operate in a 'historic and social continuum' is for all writers to work together to reach a sizeable continental audience. To achieve this objective one must assume again that there is a historic and social continuum running across the continent backed by a common culture. The fact is that African peoples have had different historical experiences and live in multiple, heterogeneous, cultural milieu. Therefore the themes will not be quite the same.

However, from the organizational point of view, writers could come together to find common frames of reference. Accordingly, a Union of Writers of the African Peoples spearheaded by dramatists, novelists and poets in sub-Saharan Africa has been formed. . . .

## THE STATUS OF THE WRITER

The social status of writers is relative to the degree of audience-appreciation. Throughout the world, the degree of recognition or status that society accords to any group of professional persons is roughly commensurate with the degree of service which the society receives or expects from that group. The village teacher is seen by most rural dwellers as an indispensable asset to the community where education of the young is concerned; he is accordingly a highly respected citizen even though his remuneration might not be high, when compared with that of a doctor or minister of religion. Often he receives compensation in kind from grateful villagers who would make donations of foodstuffs and household equipment. Besides, the mere fact that he has acquired a certain degree of education, plus the literate skills which most members of his society do not possess, places him in a class apart from themselves. . . .

Most African writers communicate with a tiny subculture within society. Among this group, the writer enjoys considerable social standing; beyond it he gets nothing but passive recognition. Unless the writer (anywhere) is bent on making literature a solitary art he must get onto the popular bandwagon. In Kenya, David Maillu's Comb Book Series with titles such as *The Flesh: Diary of a Prostitute*, *The Komon Man*, *Dear Monica* and *My Dear Botile* are the most successful popular fiction. One reason why this kind of market literature is more widely read than the polished English novels of the Heinemann series is precisely because the latter do not fully communicate. A writer must meet with his readers in a common environment. . . . What of the African writer's economic status? In developing countries, the facilities for researching a subject are minimal; this makes the human investment truly enormous because the author neither has access to many good reference libraries nor research assistants. It can therefore be understood why some African writers find the normal 10–15 per cent royalty unattractive.

When Ethiope, an officially sponsored publishing house of the former Mid-Western State of Nigeria, offered an author £100 as advance for his manuscript, he promptly declined. Ironically the multinationals, who are in a better financial position to encourage African writers, are less prepared to pay reasonable advances. The 'African Writers' series, which supposedly exists to promote African literature, could only make an offer of £50 to an African writer (which he too declined) as advance payment. Later, Heinemann paid £500 to Houghton Mifflin of Boston, United States, for sole Commonwealth rights to publish the same title.

The situation is no better where copyright is concerned. Most countries in the Maghreb lack national copyright protection for the author; they seem moreover to have abstained from both the Berne and the Universal Copyright Conventions (UCC). They can thereby avoid paying royalties to authors outside the region whose books are published locally. Conversely their own authors do not get any protection inside or outside the region (Botros 1978: 572). When this fact is coupled with low royalties (resulting from the low price of Arabic books) and high rate of taxes, it is difficult for an author writing in Arabic to live solely on his literary earnings.

The dilemma of writers everywhere, and one which slows their productivity, is that very few can make a living from their craft. As can be expected, therefore, African publishers have difficulty in attracting local authors, who look more to the developed countries where sales figures will get them closer to subsistence levels. They can then be sure of at least a minimal but steady financial compensation for their labours.

# 86

## *Literary Colonialism: Books in the Third World*

### PHILIP G. ALTBACH*

The products of knowledge are distributed unequally. Industrialized countries using a 'world' language – notably, the United States, Britain, France, and to a lesser extent, West Germany and the Soviet Union – are at the center of scientific research and scholarly productivity. These same countries dominate the systems which distribute knowledge; they control publishing houses and produce scholarly journals, magazines, films and television programs which the rest of the world consumes. Other countries, especially those in the Third World, are at the periphery of the international intellectual system (Shils 1972).

This essay will examine the relationship between industrialized and developing countries by looking at a small but important aspect of this relationship – the world of books and publishing. The discussion is predicated on several ideas. First, the unequal distribution of intellectual products results from a complex set of factors including historical events, economic relationships, language, literacy and the nature of educational systems. Second, industrialized nations have benefited from their control of the means for distribution of knowledge and have at times used their superiority to the disadvantage of developing countries. Third, patterns of national development, the direction and rate of scientific growth, and the quality of cultural life are related to issues of intellectual productivity and independence. Third World nations have not often paid sufficient attention to these issues because of their overwhelming concern with more immediate problems of development.

There are not enough books to meet the rapidly growing needs of the developing countries. The shortage is not a problem which can be solved simply by printing vast quantities of books, but a complex issue which involves a number of national needs, from printing technology to research support. Some Third World countries lack the technical facilities for mass

* From 'Literary Colonialism: Books in the Third World' *Harvard Educational Review* 15(2) (May), 1975.

production of books, and some lack indigenous authors to write on subjects of national concern in languages that most literate citizens understand. Even where books exist to serve a national culture, they often cost more than individuals or even institutions can afford.

At present, there is a shortage of books for 70 percent of the globe. The nature of the Third World 'book hunger,' as Barker and Escarpit have recently called it, can be seen in the fact that the 34 industrialized countries with only 30 percent of the population produce 81 percent of the world's book titles (Barker and Escarpit 1973: 16). Although literacy rates in these nations are higher than in developing countries, the rates alone do not begin to account for the disparity in book production.

Figures for Asia dramatically illustrate the book gap. In 1967 the 18 developing countries of the region with 28 percent of the world's population, accounted for only 7.3 percent of the total number of book titles and 2.6 percent of the total number of copies produced per year, and half of these were textbooks (Unesco 1967). This represents only 32 book titles per million population, while in Europe the average was 417 per million. . . .

Book publishing does not function in a vacuum; it is related to other elements in a society and has international dimensions as well (Altbach 1975b). The following discussion will not analyze all elements of publishing in developing countries – a complex process in any society. Rather, it will treat those particular weaknesses of Third World publishing which perpetuate the dependent position in which most developing nations find themselves.

This is not to say that Third World publishing is totally dependent on industrial cultures or that accomplishments have not been achieved. Indeed, given the odds against creative independent publishing, a number of developing nations have made impressive gains. Nor should it be inferred that industrialized nations have manipulated Third World publishing solely for their own national interests and economic gain. Third World dependence on industrial nations for intellectual products results from a complex set of interrelated factors. . . .

Colonial languages have been used as a means of national unification in a number of Third World nations, particularly those in which no one indigenous language commands the loyalty of the entire population. In addition, ruling elites in Third World countries have often used the colonial language to protect their own privileged position. As long as only 10 percent or less of a population has access to the language of political and economic control, that language represents a source of power.

The colonial language has also been the medium for scholarship. The continued domination of the highest levels of the educational system by Western languages has resulted in a paucity of technical and scholarly books in indigenous languages. English or French continues to be a key to graduate education and to research studies in the Third World, even in countries with some commitment to indigenous languages.

Furthermore, libraries and institutions, which comprise the bulk of the market for scholarly and non-fiction books, are accustomed to buying books in European languages. Even where classes are conducted in the indigenous language, a Western language is usually necessary for library research. Thus, authors wishing to write for a national audience and to reach their intellectual peers generally write in a European language.

Even in Indonesia, one of the few former colonies which has made a concentrated and fairly successful effort to promote the use of an indigenous language, *Bahasa Indonesia*, indigenous scholarly books and advanced textbooks do not yet exist and materials in English are widely used. It is my estimate that in India, about half of the book titles are published in English, while only 2 percent of the population is literate in English. In both Anglophone and Francophone Africa, virtually all books are published in the metropolitan language. In many former colonies the 80 to 95 percent of the population who do not know English or French are effectively barred from the higher levels of education. (Latin America is an exception in this regard since either Spanish or Portuguese is the language of a great majority of the population and a large regional market for books exists. The two publishing giants of the region, Mexico and Argentina, have fairly effectively used this linguistic unity to build thriving publishing industries.)

Publishers are an integral part of this colonial tradition. Indian publishers, for example, do not follow a consciously neocolonialist policy of trying to maintain foreign influence on the subcontinent. Rather, they perceive that the largest market for books is in English and that, in fact, the only national market is for such material. Hence, a complex web of economic and intellectual relationships and traditions makes it difficult to stop publishing in European languages. . . .

Therefore, Third World intellectuals tend to look toward a Western audience. If there is a prestige in publishing, it lies in writing for such Western journals as *Encounter* or *Les Temps Modernes*, or in having a book published in London, New York, or Paris. Publication abroad may bring money and the opportunity to communicate with other Third World intellectuals, since communication seldom runs directly between one developing country and another but is mediated through advanced nations.

There is little circulation of books or journals among Third World nations, even between those with the same language. It is significant that *Jeune Afrique*, an influential African journal with a multinational circulation, is published in Paris. The enterprising Nigerian publisher, Joseph Okpaku, came to New York to start his Third Press, which specializes in African and black subjects. It is perhaps indicative of the difficulties involved in regional publishing that it is often easier to travel between Dakar or Abidjan and Paris than between various African capitals.

The economics of publishing concerns much more than the cost of producing a book in a particular country. Rates of literacy, reading habits of the population, government policy toward books, copyright regulations and the nature of libraries are all part of the economic equation (Smith 1966 and Bailey 1970). For example, low literary rates, low per capita purchasing power and a diversity of languages – all common in Third World nations – contribute to a limited market for books. Many of the smaller developing countries find it economically impossible to publish most kinds of books because the internal market is simply too small. Even in such large nations as Nigeria, India and Indonesia, only some textbooks, certain kinds of popular fiction, and religious books are profitable to publish. Although labor costs are lower than in the West, total costs are high since print runs are small and distribution is difficult.

Book distribution may be the single most serious dilemma of publishing in the Third World. Dan Lacy divides the problem into three elements: (a) the actual demand for books as distinguished from the need; (b) the network of distribution, for example, booksellers and wholesalers; (c) the means of conveying information about books, such as reviews, advertising and book-trade journals. Low reader density, great distances between settlements, and poor transportation facilities make book distribution in developing countries particularly difficult (Lacy 1973). Just as developing countries themselves are at the periphery of the world's knowledge system, regions outside of capital cities, especially rural areas, which are often completely without access to books, periodicals or newspapers, are at the periphery of knowledge systems within these nations.

An important part of the Third World's cultural dependency stems from political and trade relationships with industrialized nations (Altbach 1971: 543–58). Industrialized nations export their products, in this case, books and expertise, to the developing countries. Foreign aid programs, while seeking to provide help to developing countries, often deepen existing patterns of dependence (Mende 1973). Knowledge, then, is a part of the neocolonial relationship.

Commercial arrangements built up over years of colonialism persist in many developing countries. Branches of British and French publishers continue to operate in the Third World, and in some places dominate the publishing scene (Nottingham 1969: 139–44). The advantages of foreign firms – expertise, the backing of foreign capital and a worldwide distribution network – have made the emergence of indigenous publishers even more difficult than might otherwise have been the case. . . .

Foreign aid programs have had an impact on publishing in developing countries. While the United States has sponsored the largest aid effort, other countries have also engaged in aid programs. For example, the English Language Book Scheme (ELBS), sponsored by Britain, each year sells more than 1 million copies comprising several hundred titles, intended mainly for use as college and university textbooks. On a considerably smaller scale, West Germany and the Soviet Union have also sponsored intellectual assistance, including aid to publishing.

Foreign aid, particularly intellectual assistance, cannot be separated from the policy goals of the donor country or, for that matter, from the policies and orientation of the recipient nation's government. The American rationale for book–related aid programs has involved both the technical importance of books in the development process and the ideological elements of anti-communism (Benjamin 1969; Barnett and Piggford 1969). Between 1950 and 1964, the United States Information Agency assisted in the production of 9,000 editions and printed 80 million copies in 51 languages (Benjamin 1969: 72).

The Indo-American Textbook Program (PL480) was one of the largest American efforts. Under the PL480 program more than 1,000 different textbooks were reprinted in English for use by Indian college and university students, and more than 4 million copies were distributed at subsidized prices. Although the titles were predominantly in the natural sciences, the reprints included many topics in the social sciences and humanities. The Indian government gave full approval to the program and a joint Indo-American committee selected the textbooks. With the recent cooling in Indo-American relations and changing US foreign aid priorities, textbook aid has virtually ended in India.

Like similar programs in other countries, the Indo-American Textbook Program had certain negative results. In some fields, particularly the social sciences, American books were not relevant to the Indian situation, and the orientations of American social scientists reflected their own ideological biases. Yet the subsidized books tended to drive their more expensive unsubsidized domestic counterparts off the market. The artificially low prices for American books gave buyers a distorted sense of the real cost of books. Finally, several subsidiaries of US publishers were able to establish themselves in the Indian market through the aid programs and their growth may have retarded the development of indigenous Indian publishing. . . .

Do aid programs help Third World publishers to establish strong roots and to bring out relevant locally-written books? Or do they circulate materials which the industrialized countries think will win them influence at the cost of discouraging the development of local publishing? The answers to such questions are complicated, but certainly require more attention at the planning and implementation stages of aid programs than they have been given to date. . . .

A final problem which developing countries face in their quest for intellectual independence is that of copyright, which traditionally has worked to the advantage of the industrialized nations and only now is beginning to change (Gidwani 1968; Barker and Escarpit 1973: 88–102). Copyright regulations have made it difficult and expensive for Third World nations to translate and publish materials originally appearing in the West. Western publishers have often preferred to export their own books rather than to license reprinting in developing nations because larger profits could be realized. Recently, changes in international copyright arrangements have permitted developing countries to reprint and/or translate educational materials more freely than before and at modest cost (Unesco 1973). These changes, made when the industrialized nations began to realize that copyright agreements were being violated with increasing frequency, will no doubt help the developing countries to obtain the printed materials they need at prices they can afford. . . .

The following suggestions are intended to provide some ideas which can be easily implemented and which may help to ameliorate the existing inequalities in the world of books and publishing. . . .

As a first step, communications between Third World nations should be improved so that common problems and issues can be discussed directly without being mediated through institutions and publications in the industrialized nations. This is particularly important on a regional basis, for example, among the nations of Francophone Africa and of Southeast Asia. As a part of communications development, Third World countries must also create viable means of book distribution among themselves, and between themselves and the industrialized nations.

With the strengthening of indigenous publishing and internal distribution facilities in the Third World, intellectuals need not publish their work abroad. Such an effort should include financial and technical assistance from the public sector when necessary. Foreign scholars working in developing nations should publish their findings in the countries where they conduct their research. In this way local publishing will be strengthened and relevant research will be available to local audiences. The intellectual infrastructure in many Third World countries needs to be strengthened in other ways. Libraries, journals which review books, and bibliographical and publicity tools for publishing should be supported.

In addition, major national policy questions which relate directly to books, including the language of instruction in the educational system, levels of literacy and the ownership of the publishing apparatus, must be solved by Third World governments with an understanding of their implications for the balance of intellectual production. Part of any language reform effort should be assistance to publishing in indigenous languages. Finally, Third World leaders must carefully evaluate foreign aid programs to ensure that their nations benefit without local publishing industries or intellectual autonomy being undermined.

# Bibliography

---

Abramson, Harold J. (1973) *Ethnic Diversity in Catholic America*, New York and London: John Wiley.

Achebe, Chinua (1958) *Things Fall Apart*, London: Heinemann.

Achebe, Chinua (1971) *Beware, Soul Brother*, London: Heinemann.

Achebe, Chinua (1973) 'Named for Victoria, Queen of England' *New Letters* 40(1) (Fall): 15–22.

Achebe, Chinua (1973) 'Where Angels Fear to Tread', in G. D. Killam (ed.) *African Writers on African Writing*, London: Heinemann.

Achebe, Chinua (1974) *Arrow of God*, 2nd ed., London: Heinemann.

Achebe, Chinua (1975) *Morning Yet on Creation Day*, Garden City, NY: Doubleday.

Achebe, Chinua (1988) *Hopes and Impediments: Selected Essays 1965–1987*, London: Heinemann.

Adam, Ian and Helen Tiffin (eds) (1991) *Past the Last Post: Theorizing Post-colonialism and Post-modernism*, Hemel Hempstead: Harvester Wheatsheaf.

Agnew, Jean-Christophe (1983) 'The Consuming Vision of Henry James', in Richard Wrightman Fox and T. J. Jackson Lears (eds) *The Culture of Consumption: Critical Essays in American History*, New York: Pantheon.

Ahmad, Aijaz (1987) 'Jameson's Rhetoric of Otherness and the "National Allegory" ', *Social Text* 17: 3–25.

Akshara, K. V. (1984) 'Western Responses to Traditional Indian Theatre', *Journal of Arts and Ideas* 8 (July-September).

Aléxis, Jacques Stephen (1956) 'Of the Marvellous Realism of the Haitians', *Présence Africaine* 8–10.

Aléxis, Jacques Stephen (1960) *Romancero aux étoiles*, Paris: Gallimard.

Allen, Philip (1971) '*Bound to Violence* by Yambo Ouloguem', *Pan-African Journal* iv(4) (Fall): 518–23.

Altbach, Philip G. (1971) 'Education and Neocolonialism', *Teachers College Record* 72(1) (May): 543–58.

Altbach, Philip G. (1975a) 'Literary Colonialism: Books in the Third World', *Harvard Educational Review* 15(2) (May): 226–36.

Altbach, Philip G. (1975b) 'Publishing and the Intellectual System', in *Annals of the American Academy of Political and Social Science*.

Althusser, Louis (1972) *Montesquieu, Rousseau, Marx*, London: Verso.

Alvarez, A. (1971) *The Savage God*, London: Weidenfeld & Nicolson.

Amin, Samir (1977) *Imperialism and Unequal Development*, New York: Monthly Review Press.

Amuta, Chidi (1989) *The Theory of African Literature*, London and New Jersey: Zed Books.

Anderson, Benedict (1983) *Imagined Communities: Reflections on the Origin and Spread of Nationalism*, London and New York: Verso.

Andreski, Iris (1971) *Old Wives' Tales*, New York: Schocken.

Annamalai, E. (1978) 'The Anglicized Indian Languages: A Case of Code-Mixing', *International Journal of Dravidian Linguistics* 7(2): 239–47.

Appiah, Kwame Anthony (1991) 'Is the Post- in Postmodernism the Post- in Postcolonial?', *Critical Inquiry* 17(2) (Winter): 336–57.

Appiah, Kwame Anthony (1992) *In My Father's House: Africa in the Philosophy of Culture*, London: Methuen.

Aquin, Hubert (1968) *Trou de Mémoire*, Ottawa: Cercle du Livre de France.

Armah, Ayi Kwei (1975) 'Struggles to Find a Local Publisher', *Asemka* 4 (University of Cape Coast Press).

Arnold, David and David Hardiman (1992) 'The Colonial Prison: Power, Knowledge and Penology in Nineteenth Century India', in Ranajit Guha (ed.) *Subaltern Studies 8* Delhi: Oxford University Press.

Asad, Tolal (1973) *Anthropology and the Colonial Encounter*, London: Ithaca Press.

Ashby, Eric (1967) *Universities: British, Indian, African*, Cambridge, Mass.: Harvard University Press.

Ashcroft, Bill, Gareth Griffiths and Helen Tiffin (1989) *The Empire Writes Back: Theory and Practice in Post-colonial Literatures*, London: Routledge.

Ashcroft, W. D. (1989) 'Constitutive Graphonomy' in Stephen Slemon and Helen Tiffin (eds) *After Europe: Critical Theory and Post-colonial Writing*, Mundelstrup: Dangaroo.

Atodevi, Stanislas, S. (1972) *Négritude et négrologues*, Paris: Union Générale d'Éditions.

Atwood, Margaret (1972a) *Surfacing*, Toronto: McClelland & Stewart.

Atwood, Margaret, (1972b) *Survival*, Toronto: Anansi.

Atwood, Margaret (1985) *The Handmaid's Tale*, Toronto: McClelland & Stewart.

Austin, J. L. (1962) *How to do Things with Words*, Oxford: Clarendon Press.

Bail, Murray (1980) *Homesickness*, Melbourne: Macmillan.

Bailey, Herbert Jr. (1970) *The Art and Science of Book Publishing*, New York: Harper & Row.

Baillie, Robert (1986) *Les Voyants*, Montreal: Hexagone.

Baker, Houston A. Jr. (1986) 'Caliban's Triple Play', *Critical Inquiry* 13(1): 182–96.

Bakhtin, M. M. (1975) 'Epic and Novel: Toward a Methodology for the Study of the Novel', in *The Dialogic Imagination: Four Essays*, ed. Michael Holquist, trans. Caryl Emerson and Michael Holquist (1981), Austin, Texas: University of Texas Press.

Bakhtin, M. M. (1984) *Rabelais and His World*, Bloomington, Ind.: Indiana University Press.

Baldwin, James (1964) *Notes of A Native Son*, London: Michael Joseph.

492

Ban Kah Choon (1979) 'A Review of Creative Writing in Singapore, 1978' *Commentary* 3, (3): 18–26.

Baran, Paul A. (1962) *Political Economy of Growth*, New York: Monthly Review Press.

Barker, Francis (ed.) (1983) *The Politics of Theory*, Colchester: University of Essex.

Barker, Ronald and Robert Escarpit (1973) *The Book Hunger*, Paris: UNESCO.

Barnett, Stanley and Robert Piggford (1969) *Manual on Book and Library Activities in Developing Countries*, Washington, DC: Agency for International Development.

Barth, Frederick (1969) *Ethnic Groups and Boundaries: The Social Organisation of Culture Difference*, Boston: Little, Brown.

Barthes, Roland (1957) *Mythologies*, Paris: Seuil; trans. Annette Laneas (1972), London: Jonathan Cape.

Barthes, Roland (1970) *Empire of Signs*, Paris: Seuil; trans. Richard Howard (1983), London: Jonathan Cape.

Bebey, Francis (1979) 'Paris Interview', 20 August 1977, cited by Norman Stockle in 'Towards an Africanisation of the Novel: Francis Bebey's Narrative Technique', in Kolawole Ogunbesan (ed.) (1979) *New West African Literature*, London: Heinemann.

Benjamin, Curtis (1969) *Books as Forces in National Development and International Relations*, New York: National Foreign Trade Council.

Benjamin, Walter (1973) *Charles Baudelaire: A Lyric Poet in the Era of High Capitalism*, trans. Harry Zohn, London: New Left Books.

Berndt, Ronald M. (1954) *Arnhem Land: Its History and Its People*, Melbourne: Cheshire.

Berry, Reginald (1986) 'A Deckchair of Words: Post-colonialism, Post-modernism, and the Novel of Self-Projection in Canada and New Zealand', *Landfall* 40: 310–23.

Bhabha, Homi K. (1983a) 'Difference, Discrimination and the Discourse of Colonialism', in *The Politics of Theory*, Proceedings of the Essex Conference on the Sociology of Literature, July 1982, Colchester: University of Essex.

Bhabha, Homi K. (1983b) 'The Other Question . . . Homi Bhabha Reconsiders the Stereotype and Colonial Discourse', *Screen* 24 (November–December): 18–36 (First published in Barker 1983).

Bhabha, Homi K. (1984a) 'Representation and the Colonial Text: A Critical Exploration of Some Forms of Mimeticism', in Frank Gloversmith (ed.) *The Theory of Reading*, Brighton: Harvester.

Bhabha, Homi K. (1984b) 'Of Mimicry and Men: The Ambivalence of Colonial Discourse', *October* 28: 125–33.

Bhabha, Homi K. (1985a) 'Signs Taken for Wonders: Questions of Ambivalence and Authority Under a Tree Outside Delhi, May 1817, in Francis Barker *et al.* (eds) *Europe and Its Others* Vol.1, Proceedings of the Essex Conference on the Sociology of Literature July 1984, Colchester: University of Essex; also *Critical Inquiry* 12 (1985): 144–65.

Bhabha, Homi K. (1985b) 'Sly Civility', *October* 34: 71–8.

Bhabha, Homi K. (1988) 'The Commitment to Theory', *New Formations* 5: 5–23.

Bhabha, Homi K. (ed.) (1990) *Nation and Narration*, London: Routledge.

Bhely-Quenum, O. (1982) 'Écriture noire en question (débat)', *Notre Librairie* 65.

Bishop, Alan J. (1990) 'Western Mathematics: The Secret Weapon of Cultural Imperialism', *Race and Class* 32(2): 51–65.

Bokamba, Fyamba G. (1982) 'The Africanization of English', in Braj B. Kachru (ed.) *The Other Tongue: English Across Cultures*, Oxford and New York: Pergamon Press.

Botros, Salib (1978) 'Problems of Book Development in the Arab World with Special Reference to Egypt', *Library Trends* (Spring).

Brahms, Flemming (1982) 'Entering Our Own Ignorance: Subject–Object Relations in Commonwealth Literature', *World Literature Written in English 21(2)* (Summer): 218–40.

Brantlinger, P. (1988) *Rule of Darkness: British Literature and Imperialism 1830–1914*, Ithaca: Cornell University Press.

Brathwaite, Edward Kamau (1967) 'Caribbean Theme: A Calypso', sung by the author on *Rights of Passage* (1969), London: Argo Records.

Brathwaite, Edward Kamau (1967–8) 'Jazz and the West Indian Novel', Part I *BIM* XI(44) (1967): 275–84; Part II *BIM* XII(45) (1967): 39–51; Part III *BIM* XII(46) (1968): 115–26.

Brathwaite, Edward Kamau (1971) *The Development of Creole Society in Jamaica 1770–1820*, Oxford: Clarendon Press.

Brathwaite, Edward Kamau (1973) *The Arrivants*, London: Oxford University Press.

Brathwaite, Edward Kamau, (1975) *Other Exiles*, London: Oxford University Press.

Brathwaite, Edward Kamau (1984) *History of the Voice: The Development of Nation Language in Anglophone Caribbean Poetry*, London and Port of Spain: New Beacon.

Brennan, Timothy (1990) 'The National Longing For Form', in Homi K. Bhabha (ed.) *Nation and Narration*, London: Routledge.

Brilliant, Lawrence, with Girija Brilliant (1978) 'Death for a Killer Disease', *Quest* 3 (May/June): 1–16.

Brodber, Erna (1989) 'Sleeping's Beauty and the Prince Charming', *Kunapipi* 11(3): 1–4.

Brontë, Charlotte [1847] (1980) *Jane Eyre*, New York: Oxford University Press.

Brown, David A. Maughan (1985) *Land, Freedom and Fiction: History and Ideology in Kenya*, London: Zed Books.

Brown, Lester R. (1984) 'Putting Food on the World's Table: A Crisis of Many Dimensions', *Environment* 26(4) (May): 14–26.

Brown, Russell M. (1978) 'Critic, Culture, Text: Beyond Thematics', *Essays on Canadian Writing* 11 (Summer): 151–83.

Brydon, Diana (1987) 'The Myths that Write Us: Decolonising the Mind', *Commonwealth* 10(1): 1–14.

Brydon, Diana (1988) 'Troppo Agitato: Reading and Writing Cultures in Randolph Stow's *Visitants* and Rudy Wiebe's *The Temptations of Big Bear*', *Ariel* 19(1): 13–32.

Brydon, Diana (1991) 'The White Inuit Speaks: Contamination as Literary

Strategy', in Ian Adam and Helen Tiffin (eds) *Past the Last Post: Theorizing Post-colonialism and Post-modernism*, New York and London: Harvester Wheatsheaf.

Bulbeck, Chilla (1991) Unpublished Paper, Faculty of Humanities Research Seminar, Griffith University, Nathan, Queensland.

Cabral, Amilcar (1973) *Return to the Sources: Selected Speeches*, New York and London: Monthly Review Press.

Cairns, David and Shaun Richards (1988) 'What Ish My Nation?', in *Writing Ireland: Colonialism, Nationalism and Culture*, Cultural Politics Series, Manchester: Manchester University Press.

Carby, Hazel V. (1982) 'White Woman Listen! Black Feminism and the Boundaries of Sisterhood', in Centre for Contemporary Cultural Studies, University of Birmingham, *The Empire Strikes Back: Race and Racism in 70s Britain*, London: Hutchinson.

Carby, Hazel V. (1987) *Reconstructing Womanhood: The Emergence of the Afro-American Woman Novelist*, New York: Oxford University Press.

Carpentier, Alejo (1972) *Explosion in a Cathedral*, trans. John Sturrock, Harmondsworth: Penguin.

Carter, Paul (1987) *The Road to Botany Bay: An Essay in Spatial History*, London: Faber.

Cary, Joyce, (1949) *Aissa Saved*, London: Michael Joseph.

Cary, Joyce (1961) *Mister Johnson*, London: Longman.

Cathcart, Sarah and Andrea Lemon (1988) *The Serpent's Fall*, Sydney: Currency.

Césaire, Aimé (1946) *Et les chiens se taisaient*, in *Les Armes Miraculeuses*, Paris: Gallimard.

Chakrabarty, Dipesh (1992) 'Postcoloniality and the Artifice of History: Who Speaks for "Indian" Pasts?', *Representations* 32 (Winter): 1–26.

Chang, Jen Hu (1970) 'Potential Photosynthesis and Crop Productivity', *Annals of the Association of American Geographers* 60 (March): 92–101.

Chatterjee, Partha (1986) 'Nationalism as a Problem', in *Nationalist Thought and the Colonial World: A Derivative Discourse*, Tokyo and London: Zed Books for United Nations University.

Chernoff, John Miller [1979] (1981) *Aesthetics and Social Action in African Social Idioms*, Chicago: Chicago University Press.

Chinweizu, Onwuchekwu Jemie and Ihechukwu Madubuike (1985) *Towards the Decolonization of African Literature*, London: Routledge & Kegan Paul.

Chow, Rey (1986–7) 'Rereading the Mandarin Ducks and Butterflies: A Response to the Postmodern Condition', *Cultural Critique* 5: 69–93.

Christian, Barbara (1987) 'The Race for Theory', *Cultural Critique* 6: 51–63.

Clark, John Pepper (1972) in Dennis Duerden and Cosmo Pieterse (eds) *African Writers Talking: A Collection of Radio Interviews*, London: Heinemann; New York: Africana.

Clifford, James (1980) Review of *Orientalism*, by Edward Said, in *History and Theory* 12(2): 204–23.

Closs, M. P. (1986) *Native American Mathematics*, Austin, Texas: University of Texas Press.

Cohen, Leonard (1966) *Beautiful Losers*, New York: Viking Press.

Columbus, Christopher [1825] (1960) *The Journal of Christopher Columbus*, 'discovered' 1791, trans. Cecil Jane 1825, revised edn. Louis-André Vigneras, London: Anthony Blond.

Conrad, Joseph (1902) *Heart of Darkness*, ed. Paul O'Prey (1983), Harmondsworth: Penguin.

Conrad, Joseph [1925] (1945) *Nigger of the Narcissus*, London: Dent.

Cooley, Dennis (1987) *The Vernacular Muse: The Eye and Ear in Contemporary Literature*, Winnipeg: Turnstone.

Coombes, Orde (ed.) (1974) *Is Massa Day Dead? Black Moods in the Caribbean*, New York: Doubleday.

Crapanzano, Vincent (1985) 'A Reporter at Large', *New Yorker* March 18: 8–10.

Crosby, Alfred W. (1986) *Ecological Imperialism: The Biological Expansion of Europe 900–1900*, Cambridge: Cambridge University Press.

Curnow, Allen (1962) *A Small Room with Large Windows*, Oxford: Oxford University Press.

Dash, Michael J. (1974) 'Marvellous Realism: The Way out of Négritude', *Caribbean Studies* 13(4): 57–70.

Dash, Michael (1989) 'In Search of the Lost Body: Redefining the Subject in Caribbean Literature', *Kunapipi* 11(1): 17–26.

Dathorne, O.R. (1974) *The Black Mind*, Minneapolis: Minneapolis University Press.

Davey, Frank (1988) *Reading Canadian Reading*, Winnipeg: Turnstone.

Davies, Robertson (1972) *The Manticore*, Toronto: Macmillan.

Davis, Gregson (ed.) (1984) *Twenty Poems of Aimé Césaire*, Stanford: Stanford University Press.

Davis, Jack (1982) *Kullark/The Dreamers*, Sydney: Currency.

Davis, Jack (1986) *No Sugar*, Sydney: Currency.

Davis, Jack and Bob Hodge (eds) (1985) *Aboriginal Writing Today: Papers from the First National Conference of Aboriginal Writers Held in Perth, Western Australia 1983*, Canberra: Australian Institute of Aboriginal Studies.

Dawes, Neville (1960) *The Last Enchantment*, London: MacGibbon & Kee.

de Lauretis, Teresa (1984) *Alice Doesn't: Feminism, Semiotics, Cinema*, Bloomington, Ind.: Indiana University Press.

Deleuze, Gilles and Félix Guattari (1987) *A Thousand Plateaus: Capitalism and Schizophrenia*, trans. B. Massumi, Minneapolis: University of Minnesota Press.

Depestre, René (1977) *Rainbow for the Christian West*, trans. Joan Dayan, Amherst: University of Massachusetts Press.

Derrida, Jacques (1981) 'The Double Session', in *Dissemination*, trans. Barbara Johnson, Chicago: University of Chicago Press.

Desjardins, Thierry (1976) *Le Martyre du Liban*, Paris: Plon.

Dinesen, Isak [Karen Blixen] (1937) *Out of Africa*, London: Puttnam.

Docker, John (1978) 'The Neocolonial Assumption in University Teaching of English', in Chris Tiffin (ed.) *South Pacific Images*, St. Lucia, Queensland, SPACLALS.

Donaldson, Laura E. (1988) 'The Miranda Complex: Colonialism and the Question of Feminist Reading', *Diacritics* 18(3): 65–77.

Dorfman, Ariel (1983) *The Empire's Old Clothes*, New York: Pantheon.

Dorsinville, Max (1974) *Caliban Without Prospero: Essay on Quebec Black Literature*, Erin, Ontario: Press Porcepic.

Dorsinville, Max (1983) *Le Pays natal: essais sur les littératures du Tiers Monde et du Québec*, Dakar: Nouvelles Éditions Africaines.

Duncker, Sheila (1960) *The Free Coloured and Their Fight for Civil Rights in Jamaica 1800–1836*, Unpublished MA Thesis, University of London.

During, Simon (1985) 'Postmodernism or Postcolonialism?', *Landfall* 39(3): 366–80.

During, Simon (1987) 'Postmodernism or Post-colonialism Today', *Textual Practice* 1(1): 32–47.

Eagleton, Terry (1975) *Myths of Power: A Marxist Study of the Brontës*, London: Macmillan.

Edwards, Philip (1979) *Threshold of a Nation*, Cambridge: Cambridge University Press.

Egejuru, Phanuel Akubueze (1980) *Towards African Literary Independence: A Dialogue With Contemporary African Writers*, Westport, Conn.: Greenwood.

Elk, Black/Neilhardt, John G. (1972) *Black Elk Speaks: Being the Life Story of a Holy Man of the Oglala Sioux As Told Through John G. Neilhardt (Flaming Rainbow)*, London: Barrie & Jenkins.

Emecheta, Buchi (1976) *The Bride Price*, New York: G. Braziller.

Escobar, Arturo (1984–5) 'Discourse and Power in Development: Michel Foucault and the Relevance of his Work to the Third World', *Alternatives* 10(3) (Winter): 377–400.

Eyre, Edward John (1845) *Journals of Expeditions of Discovery into Central Australia and Overland from Adelaide to King George's Sound, 1840–1*, 2 vols, London: T. W. Boon.

Fanon, Frantz (1952) 'The Fact of Blackness' in *Black Skin, White Masks* (*Peau noire, masques blancs*, Paris: Seuil), trans. Charles Lam Markmann (1968), London: MacGibbon and Kee.

Fanon, Frantz (1961) *The Wretched of the Earth* (*Les damnés de la terre*), trans. Constance Farrington (1965), London: MacGibbon & Kee.

Fanon, Frantz (1967) *The Wretched of the Earth*, trans. Constance Farrington, Harmondsworth: Penguin.

Fanon, Frantz (1968) *The Wretched of the Earth*, trans. Constance Farrington (1963), New York: Grove Press.

Fanon, Frantz (1970a) 'Algeria Unveiled' in *A Dying Colonialism* (*L'an cinq de la révolution Algérienne*), originally trans. as *A Study in Dying Colonialism* by François Maspéro (1965), New York: Grove Press.

Fanon, Frantz (1970b) *Toward the African Revolution*, trans. Haakon Chevalier, Harmondsworth: Penguin.

Fanon, Frantz (1991) *The Wretched of the Earth*, Preface by Jean-Paul Sartre, trans. Constance Farrington (1963), 1st Evergreen Edn, New York: Grove Press.

Farah, Nuruddin (1970) *From a Crooked Rib*, London: Heinemann.

Farish, J. (1838) Minute dated August 28th 1838, Political Dept, Vol. 20/795, 1837–9 (Bombay Records); quoted in B. K. Boman-Behram (1942), *Educational Controversies of India: The Cultural Conquest of India under British Imperialism*, Bombay: Taraporevala Sons.

Fee, Margery (1989) 'Why C. K. Stead Didn't Like Keri Hulme's *the bone people*: Who can write as Other?', *Australian and New Zealand Studies in Canada* 1: 11–32.

Ferguson, Moira (1986) See Prince, Mary (1986).

Fiedler, Leslie (1971) *The Collected Essays of Leslie Fiedler*, New York: Stein & Day.

Field, Barron (ed.) (1825) *Geographical Memoirs on New South Wales: By Various Hands*, London: John Murray.

Figueroa, John (1970) 'Our Complex Language Situation', in *Caribbean Voices* Vol. 2 *The Blue Horizons*, London: Evans.

Fischer, Louis (1954) *Gandhi: His Life and Message for the World*, New York: New American Library.

Ford Smith, Honor (1985) 'Sistren: Jamaican Women's Theatre', in D. Kahn and D. Neumaier (eds) *Cultures in Contention*, Seattle: Real Correct.

Forster, E. M. (1942) *A Passage to India*, London: Dent.

Foucault, Michel (1970) *The Order of Things*, London: Tavistock .

Foucault, Michel (1980) *Power/Knowledge: Selected Interviews and Other Writings 1972–1977*, trans. Colin Gordon *et al.*, ed. Colin Gordon, New York: Pantheon.

Foucault, Michel (1988) 'The Ethic of Care of the Self as a Practice of Freedom', in *The Final Foucault*, eds J. Bernauer and D. Rasmussen, Cambridge, Mass.: MIT Press.

Fox-Genovese, Elizabeth (1982) 'Placing Women's History in History', *New Left Review* 133 (May–June).

Francis, E. K. (1947) 'The Nature of the Ethnic Group', *American Journal of Sociology*, 52: 393–400.

Gallagher, Catherine and Laqueur, Thomas (1987) *The Making of the Modern Body: Sexuality and Society in the Nineteenth Century*, Berkeley: University of California Press.

Garner, Stanton B. Jr. (1990) 'Post-Brechtian Anatomies: Weiss, Bond, and the Politics of Embodiment', *Theatre Journal* 42(2): 145–64.

Gates Jun., Henry Louis (1991) 'Critical Fanonism', *Critical Inquiry* 17: 457–70.

Geertz, Clifford (1988) 'Being There, Writing Here', *Harper's Magazine* (March).

Gellner, E. (1983) *Nations and Nationalism*, Oxford: Basil Blackwell.

Gidwani, N. N. (ed) (1968) *Copyright: Legalized Piracy?*, Bombay: Indian Committee for Cultural Freedom.

Gikandi, Simon (1991) 'Narration in the Post-colonial Moment: Merle Hodge's *Crick Crack Monkey*', in Ian Adam and Helen Tiffin (eds) *Past the Last Post: Theorizing Post-colonialism and Post-modernism*, Hemel Hempstead: Harvester Wheatsheaf.

Gilbert, Helen (1992) 'The Dance as Text in Contemporary Australian Drama: Movement and Resistance Politics', *Ariel* 23(1): 133–47.

Gilbert, Sandra M. and Susan Gubar (1979) *The Madwoman in the Attic: The Woman Writer and the Nineteenth-Century Literary Imagination*, New Haven, Conn.: Yale University Press.

Giles, Fiona (1989) 'Finding a Shiftingness: Situating the Nineteenth-century Anglo-Australian Female Subject', *New Literatures Review* 18: 10–20.

Gilman, Sander (1985) *Difference and Pathology: Stereotypes of Sexuality, Race and Madness*, Ithaca: Cornell University Press.

Godard, Barbara (1987) 'Mapmaking', in B. Godard (ed.) *Gynocritics: Feminist Approaches to writing by Canadian and Québécoise Women's Writing*, Toronto: ECW Press.

Godfrey, Dave (1972) Interviewed by Graeme Gibson in *Eleven Canadian Novelists*, Toronto: Anansi.

Goh Poh Seng (1980) 'Forum: English Language and Literature in Singapore', *Commentary* 4(2): 3–14.

Goldie, Terry (1989) *Fear and Temptation: The Image of the Indigene in Canadian, Australian and New Zealand Literatures*, Kingston: McGill-Queen's University Press.

Gramsci, Antonio (1971) *Selections from the Prison Notebooks of Antonio Gramsci*, ed. Quintin Hoare and Geoffrey Nowell Smith, London: Lawrence & Wishart.

Gray, Stephen (1984) 'A Sense of Place in New Literatures, Particularly South African English' *World Literature Written in English* 24(2) (Autumn): 224–31.

Great Britain (1831–2) *Parliamentary Papers* Vol. 9, Appendix I, Extract of Letter in the Public Department, from the Court of Directors to the Governor-General in Council, dated 6th September, 1813.

Great Britain (1832) *Parliamentary Papers* Vol. 8, 'Observations on the State of Society'.

Great Britain (1852–3a) *Parliamentary Papers* Vol. 29, Evidence of Maj. F. Rowlandson.

Great Britain (1852–3b) *Parliamentary Papers* Vol. 32, Evidence of the Rev. W. Keane.

Great Britain (1852–3c) *Parliamentary Papers* Vol. 32. Evidence of Horace Wilson.

Griffiths, Gareth (1994) 'The Myth of Authenticity' in Chris Tiffin and Alan Lawson (eds) *De-Scribing Empire: Post-colonialism and Textuality*, London: Routledge.

Guha, Ranajit (ed.) (1982) *Subaltern Studies 1: Writings on South Asian History and Society*, Delhi: Oxford University Press.

Guha, Ranajit (ed.) (1983) *Subaltern Studies 11: Writings on South Asian History and Society*, Delhi: Oxford University Press.

Gunder-Frank, Andre (1967) *Capitalism and Underdevelopment in Latin America*, New York: Monthly Review Press.

Gunew, Sneja (1987) 'Culture, Gender and Author Function', *Southern Review* 20(3): 261–70.

Gunew, Sneja (ed.) (1988) *Beyond the Echo*, St. Lucia: University of Queensland Press.

Gunnars, Kristjanna (1989) *The Prowler*, Red Deer, Alberta: Red Deer College Press.

Hadjinicolaou, Nicos (1982) 'On the Ideology of Avant-gardism', *Praxis* 6: 52–68.

Haley, Alex (1976) *Roots*, Garden City, NY: Doubleday.

Hall, Stuart (1989) 'New Ethnicities', in *Black Film, British Cinema*, ICA Documents 7, London: Institute of Contemporary Arts.

Hamilton, Cicely [1909] (1981) *Marriage as a Trade*, London: The Women's Press.

Hanna, Judith L. (1987) 'Patterns of Dominance: Men, Women and Homosexuality in Dance', *The Drama Review* 31(1): 22–47.

Hardy, Thomas [1874] (1952) *Far From the Madding Crowd*, London: Macmillan.

Harlow, Barbara (1987) *Resistance Literature*, New York and London: Methuen.

Harold, Brent (1972) 'Beyond Student-Centred Teaching: The Dialectical Materialist Form of the Literature Course', *College English* 34 (November): 200–14.

Harper, Peggy (1969) 'Dance in Nigeria', *Ethnomusicology* 13(2): 280–93.

Harris, J. R. (1968) 'Nigerian Enterprise in the Printing Industry', *Nigerian Journal of Economic and Social Studies* 10(1) (March): 221–33.

Harris, Wilson (1970a) 'History, Fable and Myth in the Caribbean and the Guianas', in *Explorations: A Selection of Talks and Articles 1966–81*, ed. Hena Maes-Jelinek (1981), Mundelstrup: Dangaroo Press.

Harris, Wilson (1970b) *Sleepers of Roraima*, London: Faber & Faber.

Harris, Wilson (1970c) *History, Fable and Myth in the Caribbean*, Georgetown: Ministry of Information and Culture.

Harris, Wilson (1973a) *Tradition, the Writer and Society*, London and Port of Spain: New Beacon.

Harris, Wilson (1973b) 'A Talk on the Subjective Imagination', *New Letters* 40, (Autumn): 37–48.

Harris, Wilson (1981) *Explorations: A Selection of Talks and Articles 1966–1981*, ed. Hena Maes-Jelinek, Mundelstrup: Dangaroo Press.

Harris, Wilson (1985) 'Adversarial Contexts and Creativity', *New Left Review* 154 (November–December): 124–8.

Harrison, Dick (1977) *Unnamed Country: The Struggle for a Canadian Prairie Fiction*, Edmonton: University of Alberta Press.

Harrison, Nancy (1988), *Jean Rhys and the Novel as Women's Text*, Chapel Hill: University of North Carolina Press.

Hasan, Abdul (1975) 'Introducing Publishing in the University Curriculum: The Delhi Experiment', Unpublished paper read at the Commonwealth African Book Development Seminar, Ibadan, 2–14 February.

Healy, J. J. (1978) *Literature and the Aborigine in Australia 1770–1975*, St. Lucia: University of Queensland Press.

Hegel, G. W. [1892] (1956) *The Philosophy of History*, New York: Dover Publications.

Heidegger, Martin [1971] (1977) 'The Origin of the Work of Art', *Poetry, Language, Thought*, trans. Albert Hofstadter, New York: Harper & Row.

Heller, Agnes (1984) 'Can Cultures be Compared?', *Dialectical Anthropology* 8 (April): 269–74.

Higham, John (1975) *Send These to Me: Jews and Other Immigrants in Urban America*, New York: Atheneum.

Hill, Samuel Charles (1927) *Catalogue: Home Miscellaneous Series*, London: India Office Library.

Hobsbawm, Eric and Terence Ranger (eds) (1983) *The Invention of Tradition*, Cambridge: Cambridge University Press.

Hodge, Bob and Vijay Mishra (1991) *The Dark Side of the Dream: Australian Literature and the Postcolonial Mind*, Sydney: Allen & Unwin.

Hodgins, Jack (1977) *The Invention of the World*, Toronto: Macmillan.

Holst Petersen, Kirsten (1984) 'First Things First: Problems of a Feminist Approach to African Literature', *Kunapipi* 6 (3): 35–47.

Holst Petersen, Kirsten and Anna Rutherford (1976) *Enigma of Values: An Introduction to Wilson Harris*, Aarhus: Dangaroo Press.

Holst Petersen, Kirsten and Anna Rutherford (eds) (1986) *A Double Colonization: Colonial and Post-Colonial Women's Writing*, Mundelstrup: Dangaroo.

hooks, bell [Gloria Watkins] (1989) 'On Self-Recovery', in *Talking Back: Thinking Feminist, Thinking Black*, Boston: South End Press.

Horton, R. (1967) 'African Traditional Thought and Western Science', *Africa* 37. Also in M. F. F. Young (1971) *Knowledge and Control*, London: Collier Macmillan.

Hovell, W. H. and H. Hume (1831) *Journal of Discovery to Port Phillip, New South Wales*, ed. W. Bland, Sydney: Hill Libraries Board.

Hudson, Joyce (1978) *The Walmatjari*, Darwin: Working Papers of the Summer Institute of Linguistics.

Huggan, Graham (1989) 'Decolonizing the Map: Post-Colonialism, Post-Structuralism and the Cartographic Connection', *Ariel*, 20(4): 115–29.

Hughes, Everett Cherrington and Helen MacGill Hughes (1952) *Where Peoples Meet: Racial and Ethnic Frontiers*, Glencoe, Illinois: Free Press.

Hulme, Keri (1985) *the bone people*, Auckland: Spiral in association with Hodder & Stoughton.

Hulme, Peter (1986) *Colonial Encounters: Europe and the Native Caribbean 1492– 1797*, London and New York: Methuen.

Hume, David (1934) *A Treatise of Human Nature* Vol. 1, ed. A. D. Lindsay, London: J. M. Dent.

Hurston, Zora Neale (1979) 'How it Feels to Be Colored Me', in Alice Walker (ed.) *I Love Myself*, Old Westbury, NY: Feminist Press.

Hutcheon, Linda (1988a) *A Poetics of Postmodernism: History, Theory, Fiction*, London and New York: Routledge.

Hutcheon, Linda (1988b) *The Canadian Postmodern: A Study of Contemporary English-Canadian Fiction*, Toronto: Oxford University Press.

Hutcheon, Linda (1989) 'Circling the Downspout of Empire: Post-colonialism and Postmodernism', *Ariel* 20(4):149–75. Rpt. in Ian Adam and Helen Tiffin (eds) *Past the Last Post:Theorizing Post-colonialism and Post-modernism*, Hemel Hempstead: Harvester Wheatsheaf.

Hyland, Peter (1984) 'Singapore: Poet, Critic, Audience', *World Literature Written in English*, 23(1).

Irele, Abiola (1981) *The African Experience in Literature and Ideology*, London and New Haven: Heinemann.

Jacob, H. (1974) *Mauritian Book Development*, Paris: UNESCO.

Jahangir, Asma and Hina Jilani, (1990) *The Hudood Ordinances: A Divine Sanction?*, Lahore, Rhotas Books.

Jahn, Janheinz (1966) 'Caliban and Prospero', in *A History of Neo-African Literature*, trans. Oliver Cobum and Ursula Lehrburger, London: Faber & Faber.

Jameson, Fredric (1984) 'Literary Innovation and Modes of Production: A Commentary', *Modern Chinese Literature* 1(1): 72–85.

Jameson, Fredric (1986) 'Third World Literature in the Era of Multinational Capitalism', *Social Text*, 15 (Fall): 65–88.

Jameson, Fredric (1988) 'Cognitive Mapping', in Cary Nelson and Laurence Grossberg (eds) *Marxism and the Interpretation of Culture*, Urbana: University of Illinois Press.

JanMohamed, Abdul R. (1983) *Manichean Aesthetics: The Politics of Literature in Colonial Africa*, Amherst: University of Massachusetts Press.

JanMohamed, Abdul R. (1985) 'The Economy of Manichean Allegory: The Function of Racial Difference in Colonialist Literature' *Critical Inquiry*, 12(1): 59–87.

Jeffares, A. Norman (1965) Introduction to *The Commonwealth Pen*, ed. John Press, London: Heinemann.

Jones, M. G. (1938) *The Charity School Movement*, Cambridge: Cambridge University Press.

Jordan, Winthrop (1969) *White Over Black*, Harmondsworth: Penguin.

Joseph, Gloria and Jill Lewis (1981) *Common Differences: Conflicts in Black and White Feminist Perspectives*, Boston: Beacon Press.

Kachru, Braj B. (1978) 'Code-Mixing as a Communicative Strategy in India', in James E. Alatis (ed.) *Report of the Twentieth Annual Round-table Meeting on Linguistics and Language Studies* (Monograph series on language and linguistics), Washington DC: Georgetown University Press.

Kachru, Braj B. (1982a) 'The Bilingual's Linguistic Repertoire', in B. Hartford, A. Valdman and C. Foster (eds) *Issues in Bilingual Education: The Role of the Vernacular*, New York: Plenum.

Kachru, Braj B. (ed.) (1982b) *The Other Tongue: English Across Cultures*, Chicago: University of Illinois Press.

Kachru, Braj B. (1986) *The Alchemy of English: The Spread Functions and Models of Non-Native Englishes*, Oxford: Pergamon Institute.

Kanneh, Kadiatu (1992) 'The Difficult Politics of Wigs and Veils: Feminism and the Colonial Body', Paper presented at the Conference on Gender and Colonialism, University College, Galway (May).

Katrak, Ketu H. (1989) 'Decolonizing Culture: Toward a Theory for Postcolonial Women's Texts', *Modern Fiction Studies* 35(1): 157–79.

Kazamias, A. M. and E. H. Epstein (eds) (1968) *School in Transition* Parts 1 and 2, Boston: Allyn & Bacon.

Keith, W. J. (1985) *Canadian Literature in English*, London and New York: Longman.

Kiernan, Victor (1969) *The Lords of Human Kind*, Boston: Little, Brown.

Kincaid, Jamaica (1988) *A Small Place*, London: Virago.

King, Phillip (1827) *Narrative of a Survey of the Intertropical and Western Coasts of Australia Performed Between the Years 1818 and 1822*. (2 vols) London: John Murray.

Kinsella, John (1993) *Full Fathom Five*, Fremantle, Western Australia: Fremantle Arts Centre Press.

Kipling, Rudyard [1901] (1963) *Kim*, London: Macmillan.

Kline, M. (1972) *Mathematics in Western Culture*, Harmondsworth: Penguin.

Knorr, Klaus (1944) *British Colonial Theories*, Toronto: University of Toronto Press.

Kotei, S. I. A. (1981) *The Book Today in Africa*, Paris: UNESCO.

Kroetsch, Robert (1974) 'Unhiding the Hidden: Recent Canadian Fiction' *Journal of Canadian Fiction* 3(3):43–5.

Kroetsch, Robert (1975) *Badlands*, Toronto: New Press.

Kröller, Eva Marie, (1985) 'The Politics of Influence: Canadian Postmodernism in an American Context' in M. J. Valdes (ed.) *InterAmerican Literary Relations*, Vol. 3, New York: Garland.

Lacy, Dan (1973) 'Practical Considerations, Including Financial, in the Creation, Production, and Distribution of Books and Other Educational Materials', in Francis Keppel (ed.) *The Mohonk Conference*, New York: National Book Committee.

Lamming, George (1960) *The Pleasures of Exile*, London: Michael Joseph.

Lancy, D. F. (1983) *Cross-cultural Studies in Cognition and Mathematics*, New York: Academic Press.

Laplanche. J. and J. B. Pontalis (1980) *The Language of Psychoanalysis*, trans. Donald Nicholson-Smith, London: Hogarth Press.

Larson, Charles (1971) *The Emergence of African Fiction*, Indianapolis: Indiana University Press.

Larson, Charles (1973) 'Heroic Ethnocentrism: The Idea of Universality in Literature', *American Scholar* 42(3): 463–75.

Laurence, Margaret (1963) 'The Perfume Sea', in *The Tomorrow-Tamer*, London: Macmillan.

Laurence, Margaret (1970) 'Ivory Tower or Grassroots?: The Novelist as Socio-Political Being', in William H. New. (ed.) *A Political Art: Essays in Honour of George Woodcock*, Vancouver: University of British Columbia Press.

Lawson, Alan (1983) 'Patterns Preferences and Preoccupations: The Discovery of Nationality in Australian and Canadian Literatures', in Peter Crabbe (ed.) *Theory and Practice in Comparative Studies: Canada Australia and New Zealand*, Sydney: ANZACS (Australia New Zealand Association for Canadian Studies).

Lawson, Alan (1986 and 1991) 'A Cultural Paradigm for the Second World', *Australian–Canadian Studies* 9(i & ii): 67–78.

Laye, Camara (1956) *L'Enfant Noir*, Paris: Plon.

Lean, Glendon A. (1991) *Counting Systems of Papua New Guinea*, Lae, PNG: Department of Mathematics and Statistics, PNG University of Technology.

Lee, Dennis (1974) 'Cadence, Country, Silence: Writing in Colonial Space', *Boundary 2* 3(1) (Fall): 151–68.

Lee, Dennis (1977) *Savage Fields: An Essay in Literature and Cosmology*, Toronto: Anansi.

Lee Tzu Pheng (1980) *Prospect of a Drowning*, Singapore: Heinemann Educational.

Lefevere, André (1983) 'Interface: Some Thoughts on the Historiography of African Literature Written in English', in Dieter Riemenschneider (ed.) *The History and Historiography of Commonwealth Literature*, Tübingen: Gunter Narr Verlag.

Lenin, V. I. [1916] (1969) *Imperialism: The Highest Stage of Capitalism*, Chicago: Chicago International.

Le Page, Robert and David DeCamp (1960) *Jamaican Creole*, London: Macmillan.

Lévi-Strauss, Claude (1972) *The Savage Mind*, London: Weidenfeld & Nicolson.

Lewis, Gordon (1978) *Slavery, Imperialism, and Freedom: Studies in English Radical Thought*, New York and London: Monthly Review Press.

Lindfors, Bernth, Ian Munro, Richard Priebe and Reinhard Sander (eds) (1972) *Palaver: Interviews with Five African Writers in Texas*, Austin, Texas: University of Texas Press.

Lorde, Audre (1981) 'The Master's Tools Will Never Dismantle the Master's House', in Cherrie Moraga and Gloria Anzaldúa (eds) (1983) *This Bridge Called My Back: Writings by Radical Women of Color*, Latham, NY: Kitchen Table Press.

Lorde, Audre, (1989) 'Age, Race, Class, and Sex: Women Redefining Difference', in Russell Ferguson *et al.* (eds) *Out There: Marginalization and Contemporary Culture*, New York: New Museum of Contemporary Art and MIT Press.

Lotman, Yu M. and B.A. Uspensky (1978) 'On the Semiotic Mechanism of Culture', *New Literary History*, IX(2): 211–32.

Lyotard, Jean-François (1986–7) 'Rules and Paradoxes and a Svelte Appendix', *Cultural Critique*, 5 (Winter): 209–19.

Macherey, Pierre (1978) *A Theory of Literary Production*, trans. Geoffrey Wall, London: Routledge & Kegan Paul.

McCarthy, Eugene (1985) 'Rhythm and Narrative Method in Achebe's *Things Fall Apart*', *Novel* 18(3) (Spring): 243–56.

Macaulay, Thomas B. (1835) 'Minute on Indian Education', in *Speeches of Lord Macaulay with his Minute on Indian Education*, selected with an introduction and notes by G. M. Young (1935), Oxford: Oxford University Press.

McCully, Bruce (1943) *English Education and the Origins of Indian Nationalism*, New York: Columbia University Press.

McDougall, Russell (1987) 'Achebe's *Arrow of God*: The Kinetic Idiom of an Unmasking', *Kunapipi* 9(2): 8–23.

McLeod, A. M. (1961) *The Commonwealth Pen*, Ithaca, NY: Cornell University Press.

Magdoff, Harry (1978) *Imperialism from the Colonial Age to the Present*, New York: Monthly Review Press.

Mais, Roger (1955) *Black Lightning*, London: Jonathan Cape.

Mais, Roger (1974) *Brother Man*, London: Heinemann.

Malouf, David (1985) *12 Edmonstone Street*, London: Chatto & Windus.

Malouf, David (1988) *Blood Relations*, Sydney: Currency Press.

Manning, Charles A. W. (1968) 'In Defense of Apartheid', in C. D. Moore and A. Dunbar (eds) *Africa Yesterday and Today*, New York: Bantam.

Mannoni, O. (1964) *Prospero and Caliban: The Psychology of Colonization*, New York: Praeger.

Marchak, Patricia (1978) 'Given a Certain Latitude: A (Hinterland) Sociologist's View of Anglo-Canadian Literature', in Paul Cappon (ed.) *In Our Own House: Social Perspectives on Canadian Literature*, Toronto: McClelland & Stewart.

Mariátegui, Carlos José (1971) *Seven Interpretive Essays on Peruvian Reality*, Austin, Texas: University of Texas Press.

Marx, Karl (1963) *The Eighteenth Brumaire of Louis Buonaparte*, New York: International Publishers.

Memmi, Albert (1965) *The Colonizer and the Colonized*, New York: Orion.

Mende, Tibor (1973) *From Aid to Recolonization: Lessons of a Failure*, New York: Pantheon.

Menninger, K. (1969) *Number Words and Number Symbols: A Cultural History of Numbers*, trans. Paul Broneer from the new German edition, Cambridge, Mass.: MIT Press.

Mercator, Hondius Janssonius (1636) *Atlas or a Geographicke Description of the World*, Facsimile edition in two volumes with an introduction by R. A. Skelton (1968), Amsterdam: Theatrum Orbis Terrarum.

Mercer, Kobena (1987) 'Black Hair/Style Politics', *New Formations* 3: 33–54.

Merleau-Ponty, Maurice (1945) *La Phénoménologie de la perception*, Paris: Gallimard.

Meyers, Jeffrey (1973) *Fiction and the Colonial Experience*, Totowa, NJ: Rowman & Littlefield.

Missionary Register (1818) Church Missionary Society, London, January 1818, pp. 18–19.

Mitchell, W. J. T. (1992) 'Postcolonial Culture, Postimperial Criticism', *Transition* 56.

Mittelholzer, Edgar (1960) *Latticed Echoes*, London: Secker & Warburg.

Mittelholzer, Edgar (1961) *Thunder Returning*, London: Secker & Warburg.

Moag, Rodney F. (1982) 'The Life-Cycle of Non-Native Englishes: A Case Study', in B. Hartford, A. Valdman and C. Foster (eds) *Issues in Bilingual Education: The Role of the Vernacular*, New York: Plenum.

Mohanty, Chandra Talpade (1984) 'Under Western Eyes: Feminist Scholarship and Colonial Discourses', *Boundary 2* 12(3), 13(1) (Spring/Fall): 333–58. Reprinted in Chandra Talpade Mohanty, Ann Russo and Lourdes Torres (eds) *Third World Women and the Politics of Feminism*, Bloomington, Ind.: Indiana University Press (1991).

Mohanty, S.P. (1989) 'Us and Them': On the Philosophical Bases of Political Criticism, *New Formations* 8 (Summer): 55–80.

Moodie, Susanna [1852] (1962) *Roughing It in the Bush*, Toronto: McClelland & Stewart.

Moraga, Cherrie (1984) *Loving in the War Years*, Boston: South End Press.

Moraga, Cherrie and Gloria Anzaldúa (eds) (1983) *This Bridge Called My Back: Writings By Radical Women of Color*, Latham, NY: Kitchen Table Press.

Morgan, Henry J. (ed.) (1882) *The Dominion Annual Register and Review*, Montreal: John Lovell.

Morris, Meaghan (1988) 'Tooth and Claw: Tales of Survival and Crocodile Dundee', in Andrew Ross (ed.) *Universal Abandon?: The Politics of Post-Modernism*, Minneapolis: University of Minnesota Press.

Mphahlele, Es'kia [Ezekiel] (1962) 'Press Report', Conference Of African Writers, *MAK/V* 2.

Mphahlele, Es'kia [Ezekiel] (1964) 'The Language of African Literature', *Harvard Educational Review* 34 (Spring) 298–306.

Mudimbe, V. Y. (1973) *Entre les Yeux* Paris: Présence Africaine.

Mudimbe, V. Y. (1976) *Le Bel Immonde*, Paris: Présence Africaine.

Mudimbe, V. Y. (1979) *L'Écart*, Paris: Présence Africaine.

Mudrooroo (1985) 'White Forms, Aboriginal Content', in Jack Davis and Bob Hodge (eds) *Aboriginal Writing Today: Papers from The First National Conference of Aboriginal Writers Held in Perth, Western Australia 1983*, Canberra: Australian Institute of Aboriginal Studies.

Mudrooroo (1991) *Master of the Ghost Dreaming*, Sydney: Collins.

Muecke, Stephen (1983) 'Ideology Re-iterated: The Uses of Aboriginal Oral Narratives', *Southern Review* 16(1).

Mukherjee, Arun P. (1986) 'Ideology in the Classroom: A Case Study in the Teaching of English Literature in Canadian Universities', *Dalhousie Review* 66(1&2): 22–30.

Mukherjee, Arun P. (1990) 'Whose Post-colonialism and Whose Post-modernism?', *World Literature Written in English* 30(2): 1–9.

Mukherjee, Meenakshi (1971) *The Twice-Born Fiction: Themes and Techniques of the Indian Novel in English*, Delhi and London: Heinemann.

Mukherjee-Blaise, Bharati (1983) 'Mimicry and Reinvention', in Uma Parameswaran (ed.) *The Commonwealth in Canada*, Calcutta: Writer's Workshop Greybird.

Murdock, George P. (1931) 'Ethnocentrism', in Edwin A. Seligman and Alvin Johnson (eds) *Encyclopedia of the Social Sciences* Vol. 5, New York: Macmillan.

Murnane, Gerald (1984) *The Plains*, Ringwood, Victoria: Penguin.

Myers, Charles N. (1968) *US University Activity Abroad: Implications of the Mexican Case*, New York: Education and World Affairs.

Naipaul,V. S. (1961) *A House for Mr. Biswas*, London: André Deutsch.

Naipaul, V. S. (1962) *The Middle Passage*, London: André Deutsch.

Naipaul, V. S. (1967) *The Mimic Men*, London: André Deutsch.

Naipaul, V. S. (1974) 'Conrad's Darkness', in *The Return of Eva Peron*, New York: Knopf.

Nair, Chandran (1977) 'The Current State of Creative Writing in Singapore', in Chandran Nair (ed.) *Developing Creative Writing in Singapore*, Singapore: Woodrose Publications.

Narasimhaiah, C. D. (ed.) (1978) *Awakened Conscience: Studies in Commonwealth Literature*, New Delhi: Sterling; London: Heinemann.

Narogin, Mudrooroo (1990) *Writing from the Fringe: A Study of Modern Aboriginal Literature*, South Yarra, Victoria: Hyland House.

Nettleford, Rex (1968) 'The Dance as an Art Form – Its Place in the West Indies', *Caribbean Quarterly* 14 (March–June): 127–35.

Neumaier, D and D. Kalin (eds) (1985) *Cultures in Contention*, Seattle: Real Comet Press.

New, W. H. (1978) 'New Language, New World' in C. D. Narasimhaiah (ed.) *Awakened Conscience: Studies in Commonwealth Literature*, New Delhi: Sterling; London: Heinemann.

New, W. H. (ed.) (1975) *Among Worlds*, Erin, Ontario: Press Porcepic.

Ngaté, Jonathan (1988) *Francophone African Fiction: Reading a Literary Tradition*, Trenton, NJ: Africa World Press.

Ngugi wa Thiong'o (1964) *Weep Not, Child*, London: Heinemann.

Ngugi wa Thiong'o (1965) *The River Between*, London: Heinemann.

Ngugi wa Thiong'o (1967) *A Grain of Wheat*, London: Heinemann.

Ngugi wa Thiong'o (1972) *Homecoming: Essays*, London: Heinemann.

Ngugi wa Thiong'o (1977) *Petals of Blood*, London: Heinemann.

Ngugi wa Thiong'o (1981a) 'The Language of African Literature', in *Decolonising the Mind: The Politics of Language in African Literature*, London: James Currey.

Ngugi wa Thiong'o (1981b) *Writers in Politics*, London: Heinemann.

Ngugi wa Thiong'o (1983) *Barrel of a Pen*, London: New Beacon Books.

Nottingham, John (1969) 'Establishing an African Publishing Industry: A Study in Decolonization', *African Affairs* 68.

Nowra, Louis (1979) *Visions*, Sydney: Currency.

Obiechina, E. N. (1971) *Literature for the Masses*, Enugu: Nwanko-Ifejika Publications.

Obiechina, E. N. (1972) *Onitsha Market Literature* (African Writers, 109), London: Heinemann Educational Books.

Obiechina, E. N. (1973) *An African Popular Literature: A Study of Onitsha Market Pamphlets*, Cambridge: Cambridge University Press.

Obiechina, E. N. (1975) *Culture, Tradition and Society in the West African Novel*, Cambridge: Cambridge University Press.

Ohmann, Richard with Wallace Douglas (1976) *English in America: A Radical View of the Profession*, New York: Oxford University Press.

Okai, Atukwe (1973) 'The Role of the Ghanaian Writers in the Revolution', *Weekly Spectator*, Accra, 14 July, p. 4.

Okara, Gabriel (1963) 'African Speech . . . English Words', *Transition* 10 (September): 15–16.

Okara, Gabriel (1970) *The Voice*, London: Heinemann.

Okot p'Bitek (1966) *Song of Lawino*, Kenya: East African Publishing House.

Oluwasanmi, E., E. McLean and H. Zell (eds) (1975) *Publishing in Africa in the Seventies: Proceedings of an International Conference on Publishing and Book Development Held at the University of Ile-Ife, Nigeria, 16–20 December 1973*, Ile-Ife: University of Ile-Ife.

Omvedt, Gail (1980) *We Will Smash this Prison*, London: Zed Press.

Ortiz, Alicia Dujovne, (1987) 'Buenos Aires (An Excerpt)', in *Discourse* 8 (Fall–Winter).

Ouologuem, Yambo (1968a) *Le Devoir de violence*, Paris: Seuil.

Ouologuem, Yambo (1968b) *Bound to Violence*, trans. Ralph Manheim, London: Heinemann Educational.

Owomoyela, O. (1979) *African Literatures: An Introduction*, Waltham, Mass.: Crossroads Press.

Pache, Walter (1985) 'The Fiction Makes Us Real: Aspects of Postmodernism in Canada', in Robert Kroetsch and Reingard H. Nischik (eds) *Gaining Ground: European Critics on Canadian Literature*, Edmonton: NeWest.

Parameswaran, Uma (1976) *A Study of Representative Indo-English Novelists*, Delhi: V. Publishers.

Parekh, Bikhu (1989) *Colonisation, Tradition and Thought: Ghandi's Political Discourse*, London: Sage Publications.

Parmar, Pratibha and Valerie Amos (1984) 'Challenging Imperial Feminism', *Feminist Review* 17 (Autumn): 3–19.

Parry, Benita (1987) 'Problems in Current Theories of Colonial Discourse', *Oxford Literary Review* 9(1&2): 27–58.

Pateman, Carol (1988) *The Sexual Contract*, Stanford, Calif.: Stanford University Press.

Patterson, Orlando (1964) *The Children of Sisyphus*, Harlow, Essex: Longman.

Patterson, Orlando (1967) *An Absence of Ruins*, London: Hutchinson.

Pearson, Bill (1982) 'Witi Ihimera and Patricia Grace', in Cherry Hankin (ed.) *Critical Essays on the New Zealand Short Story*, Auckland: Heinemann.

Pêcheux, Michel (1975) *Language, Semantics and Ideology*, trans. Harbans Nagpal (1982), London: Macmillan.

Pence, Ellen (1982) 'Racism: A White Issue' in G. T. Hull, P. B. Scott, and B. Smith (eds) *But Some of Us Are Brave*, Old Westbury, NY: Feminist Press.

Peters, Lenrie (1965) *The Second Round*, London: Heinemann.

Philp, H. (1973) 'Mathematical Education in Developing Countries', in A. G. Howson (ed.) *Developments in Mathematical Education*, Cambridge: Cambridge University Press.

Pinxten, R., I. Van Doren, and F. Harvey (1983) *The Anthropology of Space: Explorations into the Natural*, Philadelphia: University of Philadelphia Press.

Plamenatz, John (1973) 'Two Types of Nationalism', in E. Kamenka (ed.) *Nationalism: The Nature and Evolution of an Idea*, Canberra: Australian National University Press.

Powell, Joseph M. (1976) *Environmental Management in Australia 1788–1914*, Oxford: Oxford University Press.

Powers, William (1990) 'When Black Elk Speaks, Everybody Listens', *Social Text* 24: 43–56.

Press, John (ed.) (1965) *The Commonwealth Pen*, London: Heinemann.

Prince, Mary [1831] (1986) *The History of Mary Prince, a West Indian Slave, Related by Herself*, (ed.) Moira Ferguson, London: Pandora.

Quirk, Randolph, Sidney Greenbaum, Geoffrey Leech and Jan Svartvik (1972) *A Grammar of Contemporary English*, London: Longman.

Rabasa, José (1985) 'Allegories of the Atlas', in Francis Barker *et al.* (eds) *Europe and Its Others* Vol. 2, Proceedings of the Essex Conference on the Sociology of Literature July 1984, Colchester: University of Essex.

Rabasa, José (1993) *Inventing A-M-E-R-I-C-A: Spanish Historiography and the Formation of Eurocentrism*, Norman, Okla., and London: University of Oklahoma Press.

Ramchand, Kenneth (1969) 'Terrified Consciousness', *Journal of Commonwealth Literature* 7 (July): 8–19.

Ranger, T. O. (1975) *Dance and Society in Eastern Africa*, London: Heinemann.

Rao, Raja [1938] (1963) *Kanthapura*, Bombay: New Directions .

Rao, Raja (1978) 'The Caste of English' in C. D. Narasimhaiah (ed.)*Awakened Conscience: Studies in Commonwealth Literature*, New Delhi: Sterling; London: Heinemann.

Rhys, Jean (1968) *Wide Sargasso Sea*, Harmondsworth: Penguin.

Richardson, Henry Handel (1930) *The Fortunes of Richard Mahony*, Collected Edition, London: Heinemann.

Richardson, John [1832] (1967) *Wacousta or The Prophecy*, Toronto: McClelland & Stewart.

Richler, Mordecai (1989) *Solomon Gursky was Here*, Markham, Ontario: Penguin.

Riemenschneider, Dieter (ed.) (1983) *The History and Historiography of Commonwealth Literature*, Tübingen: Gunter Narr Verlag.

Robertson, W. (1928) *Coo-ee Talks*, Sydney: Angus & Robertson.

Ronan, C. A. (1983) *The Cambridge Illustrated History of the World's Science*, Cambridge: Cambridge University Press.

Rosaldo, M. Z. (1980) 'The Use and Abuse of Anthropology: Reflections on Feminism and Cross-Cultural Understanding', *Signs* 5(3): 389–417.

Ross, Andrew (ed.) (1988) *Universal Abandon?: The Politics of Post-Modernism*, Minneapolis: University of Minnesota Press.

Ross, Malcolm and John Stevens (eds) (1967) *In Search of Ourselves*, Toronto: J. M. Dent.

Roumain, Jacques (1978) *Masters of the Dew*, London: Heinemann Educational.

Rushdie, Salman (1983) *Shame*, London: Jonathan Cape.

Rushdie, Salman (1984) *Shame*, New York: Vintage.

Rushdie, Salman (1988) *Satanic Verses*, Harmondsworth: Penguin.

Saadawi, Nawal el, Fatima Mernissi and Mallica Vajarathon (1978) 'A Critical Look at The Wellesley Conference', *Quest* IV (Winter).

Said, Edward (1978) *Orientalism*, London: Routledge.

Said, Edward (1984) 'Permission to Narrate', *Journal of Palestine Studies* 13(3): 27–48.

Said, Edward (1988) 'Through Gringo Eyes: With Conrad in Latin America', *Harper's Magazine* (April).

Salkey, Andrew (1976) *A Quality of Violence*, London: New Beacon Books.

Salutin, Rick (1984) *Marginal Notes: Challenges to the Mainstream*, Toronto: Lester and Orpen Dennys.

Sangari, Kumkum (1984) 'The Changing Text', *Journal of Arts and Ideas* 8 (July–September).

Sangari, Kumkum (1986) 'Of Ladies, Gentlemen, and the Short Cut: *The Portrait of a Lady'*, in Lola Chatterjee (ed.) *Women/Image/Text*, Delhi: Trianka.

Sangari, Kumkum (1987) 'The Politics of the Possible', *Cultural Critique* 7: 157–86.

Sapir, Edward (1931) 'Conceptual Categories in Primitive Languages', *Science* 74.

Sartre, Jean-Paul (1965) *Anti-Semite and Jew*, trans. George J. Becker, New York: Shocken.

Saul, John Ralston (1988) 'We Are Not Authors of the Post-Novel Novel', *Brick* (Winter): 52–4.

Schaff, William Leonard (ed.) (1963) *Our Mathematical Heritage: Essays on the Nature and Cultural Significance of Mathematics*, New York: Collier Books.

Schwartz-Bart, André (1959) *Le Dernier des justes*, Paris: Seuil.

Schwarz-Bart, Simone (1982) *The Bridge of Beyond*, trans. Barbara Bray, London: Heinemann.

Schweinitz, Karl (1983) *The Rise and Fall of British India: Imperialism and Inequality*, London: Methuen.

Sechi, Joanne Harumi (1980) 'Being Japanese-American Doesn't Mean "Made in Japan" ', in D. Fisher (ed.) *The Third Woman: Minority Women Writers of the United States*, Boston: Houghton Mifflin.

Seton-Watson, Hugh (1977) *Nations and States: An Enquiry into the Origins of Nations and the Politics of Nationalism*, Boulder, Colo.: Westview Press.

Sharpe, Henry (ed.) (1920) *Selections from Educational Records* Part 1, 1781–1839, New Delhi: Government Printing Office.

Sharpe, Jenny (1989) 'Figures of Colonial Resistance', *Modern Fiction Studies*, 35(1) (Spring) 137–55.

Shils, Edward (1972) *The Intellectuals and the Powers and Other Essays*, Chicago: University of Chicago Press.

Shore, F. J. (1983) 'On the Language and Character Best Suited to the Education of the People', in Peter Penner and Richard Dale MacLean (eds) *The Rebel Bureaucrat: John Shore (1799–1837) as Critic of William Bentinck's India*, New Delhi: Chanakya.

Shridhar S. N. (1982) 'Non-Native English Literatures: Context and Relevance', in Braj B. Kachru (ed.) *The Other Tongue: English Across Cultures*, Chicago: University of Illinois Press.

Sinha, Narendra K. (1970) *The Economic History of Bengal 1793–1848* Vol. 3, Calcutta: Firma K. L. Mukhopadhyay.

Sirkin, Gerald and Natalie Robinson (1971) 'The Battle of Indian Education: Macaulay's Opening Salvo Newly Discovered', *Victorian Studies* 14: 407–28.

Sistren, with Honor Ford Smith (ed.) (1985) *Lionheart Gal: Life Stories of Jamaican Women*, London: The Women's Press.

Slemon, Stephen (1986) 'Revisioning Allegory: Wilson Harris's *Carnival*', *Kunapipi* 8(2): 45–55.

Slemon, Stephen (1987) 'Monuments of Empire: Allegory/Counter-Discourse/Post-Colonial Writing', *Kunapipi* 9(3): 1–16.

Slemon, Stephen (1988a) 'Magic Realism as Post-Colonial Discourse', *Canadian Literature* 116: 9–23.

Slemon, Stephen (1988b) 'Post-Colonial Allegory and the Transformation of History', *Journal of Commonwealth Literature* 23(1): 157–68.

Slemon, Stephen (1990) 'Unsettling the Empire: Resistance Theory for the Second World', *World Literature Written in English* 30(2): 30–41.

Slemon, Stephen (1991) 'Past the Last Post', in Ian Adam and Helen Tiffin (eds) *Past the Last Post: Theorizing Post-colonialism and Post-modernism*, Hemel Hempstead: Harvester Wheatsheaf.

Slemon, Stephen (1994) 'The Scramble for Post-colonialism', in Chris Tiffin and Alan Lawson (eds) *De-Scribing Empire: Post-colonialism and Textuality*, London: Routledge.

Smith, Barbara (ed.) (1983) *Home Girls: A Black Feminist Anthology*, New York: Kitchen Table Press.

Smith, Datus Jr. (1966) *A Guide to Book Publishing*, New York: Bowker.

Smith, M. G. (1982) 'Ethnicity And Ethnic Groups In America: The View From Harvard', *Ethnic and Racial Studies* 5: 1–22.

Smith, Paul (1988) 'Visiting the Banana Republic', in Andrew Ross (ed.)

*Universal Abandon?: The Politics of Post-modernism*, Minneapolis: University of Minnesota Press.

Sollors, Werner (1986) *Beyond Ethnicity: Consent and Descent in American Culture*, Oxford and New York: Oxford University Press.

Southey, Robert (1951) *Letters from England*, London: Cresset Press.

Soyinka, Wole (1976) *Myth, Literature and the African World*, Cambridge: Cambridge University Press.

Soyinka, Wole (1984) *A Play of Giants*, London: Methuen.

Sparrow, The Mighty (1963) *One Hundred and Twenty Calypsos to Remember*, Port of Spain: National Recording Company.

Spengler, Oswald [1926] (1962) *The Decline of the West*, New York: Random House 1962.

Spillers, Hortense (1990) 'Metathesis: Reading the Future, Future Reading', paper given at the Modern Language Association Convention, Chicago, December.

Spivak, Gayatri Chakravorty (1985a) 'The Rani of Simur', in Francis Barker *et al.* (eds) *Europe and Its Others* Vol. 1, Proceedings of the Essex Conference on the Sociology of Literature July 1984, Colchester: University of Essex.

Spivak, Gayatri Chakravorty (1985b) 'Can the Subaltern Speak?: Speculations on Widow Sacrifice', *Wedge* 7(8) (Winter/Spring): 120–30.

Spivak, Gayatri Chakravorty (1985c) 'Three Women's Texts and a Critique of Imperialism', *Critical Inquiry* 12(1): 43–61.

Spivak, Gayatri Chakravorty (1986) 'Imperialism and Sexual Difference', *Oxford Literary Review* 8: 1–2.

Spivak, Gayatri Chakravorty [1987] (1988) *In Other Worlds: Essays in Cultural Politics*, New York: Methuen.

Spivak, Gayatri Chakravorty (1988b) 'Can the Subaltern Speak?' in Cary Nelson and Lawrence Grossberg (eds) *Marxism and the Interpretation of Culture*, London: Macmillan.

Spivak, Gayatri Chakravorty (1989) 'Reading *The Satanic Verses*', *Public Culture* 2(1) (Fall).

Stam, Robert and Louise Spence (1983) 'Colonialism, Racism and Representation', *Screen* 24(2): 2–20.

Stavrianos, L. S. (1981) *Global Rift: The Third World Comes of Age*, New York: William Morrow.

Stead, C. K. (1985) 'Keri Hulme's *the bone people* and the Pegasus Award for Maori Literature', *Ariel* 16.

Strobel, Margaret (1991) *European Women and the Second British Empire*, Bloomington, Ind.: Indiana University Press.

Suleri, Sara (1992a) *The Rhetoric of English India*, Chicago: University of Chicago Press.

Suleri, Sara (1992b) 'Woman Skin Deep: Feminism and the Postcolonial Condition', *Critical Inquiry* 18(4) (Summer): 756–69.

Sutton, P. (1988) *Dreamings: The Art of Aboriginal Australia*, Melbourne: Viking.

Taussig, Michael (1987) *Shamanism, Colonialism and the Wild Man: A Study in Terror and Healing*, Chicago: University of Chicago Press.

Terdiman, Richard (1985) *Discourse/Counter-Discourse: The Theory and*

*Practice of Symbolic Resistance in Nineteenth-Century France*, Ithaca and London: Cornell University Press.

Thompson, Robert Farris (1979) *African Art in Motion: Icon and Act*, Los Angeles: University of California Press.

Threadgold, Terry (1986) Introduction to *Semiotics, Ideology, Language*, Sydney: Sydney Association for Studies in Society and Culture.

Thumboo, Edwin (ed.) (1973) *Seven Poets: Singapore and Malaysia*, Singapore: Singapore University Press.

Tiffin, Chris (ed.) (1978) *South Pacific Images*, St. Lucia, Queensland: SPA-CLALS.

Tiffin, Chris and Alan Lawson (eds) (1994) *De-Scribing Empire: Post-colonialism and Textuality*, London: Routledge.

Tiffin, Helen (1987) 'Post-Colonial Literatures and Counter-Discourse' *Kunapipi* 9(3): 17–34.

Tiffin, Helen (1988) 'Post-Colonialism, Post-Modernism and the Rehabilitation of Post-Colonial History', *Journal of Commonwealth Literature* 23(1): 169–81.

Todd, Loreto (1982) 'The English Language in West Africa', in R. W. Bailey and M. Görlach (eds) *English as a World Language*, Ann Arbor: University of Michigan Press.

Todorov, Tzvetan (1982) *The Conquest of America: The Question of the Other*, trans. Richard Howard, Ithaca: Cornell University Press.

Tostevin, Lola Lemire (1989) 'Contamination: A Relation of Difference', *Tessera* 6 (Spring): 1–15.

Trevelyan, C. E. (1838) *On the Education of the People of India*, London: Longman, Orme, Brown, Green and Longmans.

Trinh T. Minh-ha (1989) *Woman, Native, Other: Writing Postcoloniality and Feminism*, Bloomington, Ind.: Indiana University Press.

Trinh T. Minh-ha (1991) *When the Moon Waxes Red: Representation, Gender and Cultural Politics*, New York and London: Routledge.

Tsao-Hsueh-Chin [1792] (1958) *Dream of the Red Chamber*, London: Routledge & Kegan Paul.

UNESCO (1967) *Book Development in Asia: Report on the Production and Distribution of Books in the Region*, Paris: UNESCO.

UNESCO (1973) *Records Of the Conference for Revision of the Universal Copyright Convention*, Paris: UNESCO.

van den Berghe, Pierre L. (1967) *Race and Racism: A Contemporary Perspective*, New York: John Wiley.

Van Herk, Aritha (1986) *No Fixed Address*, Toronto: McClelland & Stewart.

Van Toorn, Penny (1990) 'Discourse/Patron Discourse: How Minority Texts Command the Attention of Majority Audiences', *Span* 30: 102–15.

Vargas Llosa, Mario (1984) *The War of the End of the World*, New York: Farrar, Strauss, Giroux.

Vaughan, Michalina and Margaret Archer (1971) *Social Conflict and Educational Change in England and France 1789–1848*, Cambridge: Cambridge University Press.

Viswanathan, Gauri (1987) 'The Beginnings of English Literary Study in British India', *Oxford Literary Review* 9(1–2): 2–26.

Viswanathan, Gauri (1989) *Masks of Conquest: Literary Study and British*

*Rule in India*, New York: Columbia University Press.

Waddington, C. H. (1977) *Tools for Thought*, London: Jonathan Cape.

Walcott, Derek (1974) 'The Muse of History', in Orde Coombes (ed.) *Is Massa Day Dead? Black Moods in the Caribbean*, New York: Doubleday.

Walley, Richard (1989) *Plays From Black Australia*, Sydney: Currency.

Waterman, Richard Alan (1952) 'African Influence in the Music of the Americas', in Sol Tax (ed.) *Acculturation in the Americas*, Chicago: Chicago University Press.

Watts, Alan W. (1970) *Nature, Man, and Woman*, New York: Vintage Books.

Weber, Samuel (1982) 'Metapsychology Set Apart', in *The Legend of Freud*, Minneapolis: University of Minneapolis Press.

*West Australian* (1991) Monday, 12 August, p. 9.

White, Hayden (1982) 'The Politics of Historical Interpretation: Discipline and De-Sublimation', *Critical Inquiry* 9: 113–37.

Whitlock, Gillian (1992) 'Outlaws of the Text: Women's Bodies and the Organisation of Gender in Imperial Space', Paper presented at 'Australia/Canada Post-colonialization and Women's Texts' Conference, Research Network, Calgary Institute for the Humanities (February 13–16).

Whorf, Benjamin Lee (1952) *Collected Papers on Metalinguistics*, Washington DC: Foreign Service Institute, Department of State.

Wiebe, Rudy (1973) *The Temptations of Big Bear*, Toronto: McClelland & Stewart.

Wilkes, G. A. (1981) *The Stockyard and the Croquet Lawn*, London and Melbourne: Edward Arnold.

Williams, Bernard (1985) *Ethics and the Limits of Philosophy*, London: Fontana.

Williams, Raymond (1984) *Writing in Society*, London: Verso.

*World Almanac and Book of Facts 1984* (1983) New York: Newspaper Enterprise Association.

Yap, Arthur (1980) *down the line*, Singapore: Heinemann Educational.

Yeo, Robert (1970) 'Poetry in English in Singapore and Malaysia', in *Singapore Book World* 1(1).

Young, Robert (1990) *White Mythologies: Writing History and the West*, London & New York: Routledge.

Zabus, Chantal (1991) *The African Palimpsest: Indigenization of Language in the West African Europhone Novel*, Cross Cultures 4, Amsterdam and Atlanta GA: Rodopi.

Zaslavsky, Claudia (1973) *Africa Counts*, Westport, Conn.: Lawrence Hill.

# Index